The
Crawford Papers

David Lindsay, 27th Earl of Crawford
and 10th Earl of Balcarres, 1871–1940

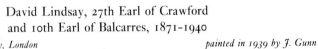

painted in 1939 by J. Gunn

The
Crawford Papers

*The journals of David Lindsay
twenty-seventh Earl of Crawford
and tenth Earl of Balcarres
1871-1940
during the years 1892 to 1940*

EDITED BY

JOHN VINCENT

Manchester University Press

The Crawford Diaries © The Earl of Crawford 1984
Annotations and editorial commentary © John Vincent 1984

First published 1984
by Manchester University Press
Oxford Road, Manchester M13 9PL
and 51 Washington Street
Dover, New Hampshire 03820, USA

British Library cataloguing in publication data
Crawford, David Lindsay, Earl of
The Crawford Papers.
1. Crawford, David Lindsay, Earl of
2. Statesmen – Great Britain – Biography
I. Title   II. Vincent, John, 1937-
941.08'092'4   DA574.C74

ISBN 0-7190-0948-0

Library of Congress cataloging in publication data
Crawford, David Lindsay, Earl of, 1871-1940.
The Crawford Papers.
Includes index.
1. Crawford, David Lindsay, Earl of, 1871-1940.
2. Great Britain – Politics and government – 1901-1936.
3. Statesmen – Great Britain – Biography. I. Vincent,
John Russell.   II. Title.
DA574.C74A33 1983 941.08'092'4 [B] 83-17492
ISBN 0-7190-0948-0

Printed in Great Britain
by Butler & Tanner Ltd, Frome and London

*In memory
of David Crawford*

Contents

Editor's note

David Lindsay, 27th Earl of Crawford and 10th Earl of Balcarres (1871-1940), often known to his contemporaries as Bal, left 54 volumes of handsomely bound diaries. In 1975 his eldest son David asked me to edit them. In 1976 he died. I am most grateful to this remarkable and much-loved man for having entrusted me with this work.

The diaries run with few gaps from 1892 to 1940. They overshadow what remains of Bal's correspondence, the chief part of which was lost in the Blitz. They were briefly cited in Lord Blake's *The Unknown Prime Minister*, but otherwise have hardly been used.

The present Lord Crawford has given much time and thought to this work, and his advice and encouragement have been invaluable.

Without generous help from the Lindsay family and from the Pilgrim Trust, publication in the present extensive form would not have been possible. I, and Manchester University Press, express our deep gratitude.

The editors at Manchester have been a pleasure to work with, and have spared no pains to do justice to a former Chancellor of their University.

The number of those who have assisted with inquiries is legion. May I offer them a general confession of indebtedness? To two scholars in particular this book owes more than I can say for their special combination of erudition and practical sagacity: Nicolas Barker of the British Library, and Alan Bell, now of Rhodes House Library. Without their devotion, this part of the heritage of the Lindsays would never have received full due.

Introduction

When the twenty-seventh Earl of Crawford died in March 1940, Baldwin, Neville Chamberlain, Churchill, Attlee, Eden and Harold Macmillan sent long handwritten letters of condolence to his family, the King sent a telegram, and Dr Lang, Archbishop of Canterbury and an old friend, was the preacher at the memorial service. In his own locality, the Wigan Examiner *gave the whole of its front page to the event. That Lord Crawford was a man of distinction was agreed by all. The editor of his diaries has to try to convey something of his quality. This is not easy. Unlike Greville or Hervey, he lacked those frailties which often assist the survival of a reputation. Although well known to the leading men of three generations, from Joseph Chamberlain to Winston Churchill, from William Morris to Lutyens and Munnings, he was happy when his achievements were unpublicised. His distinction, moreover, touched many fields, not easily brought together in one view. Speak of him as Unionist Chief Whip, and one may not at once recall that he was also the father of the Standard Loaf of world war I, the author of the Crawford Report of 1926 which recommended that the British Broadcasting Corporation should be created, the founding father of the National Art-Collections Fund, the author of scholarly books on Italian renaissance sculpture, the owner of the finest private library in the country, a leading Lancashire industrialist, and an active chancellor of two universities. He might be easily and wrongly forgotten, were it not for his diaries which show him as an anecdotist and historian of his own times, a voice of alert critical intelligence speaking from the point of view of enlightened traditionalism: a conservative moralist whose criticisms of the fundamental irresponsibility, personal and governmental, of early twentieth-century liberalism do not lack weight.*

What was he, and what did he do? He inherited family estates which were industrial rather than agricultural, and which involved a unique paternal relation with the coal and steel town of Wigan. He inherited a great library, encrusted with strange collections, but in his eyes valuable above all for the purpose it served. 'Great estates liberally administered by the possessors of beautiful things freely placed at the disposition of the public, are still entities of value, though less potent than in feudal days: but even in what are styled "democratic times" they may still perform a special function towards the community as a whole', he wrote in 1923. As a party politician he had a successful, though short and interrupted, career. He was a successful Unionist Chief Whip in the difficult years 1911–13. He saw the Parliament Act pass, Balfour resign, Bonar Law arrive – and nearly resign a year later. To the political historian, he is important because his papers, unlike those of most Chief Whips, survive in some quantity, and are remarkably informative about developments, hour by hour, in the House of Commons. Of Conservative Chief Whips between the break with Peel in 1846 and the appointment of 'Bal' in 1911, we have a significant amount of information about only

Introduction

one (Aretas Akers-Douglas, first Lord Chilston, who served with distinction under Salisbury).

Elevation to the House of Lords on his father's death in 1913 ended a promising party career. In the first war he at first served as a volunteer in the ranks (this at forty-three), as an RAMC orderly in a front-line dressing station in Flanders (the only cabinet minister involved in the war not to serve as an officer). Between 1916 and 1922 he was again a minister, though more administrator than party politician. For six months he was Minister of Agriculture in Asquith's coalition. He seems to have been the only diarist in Asquith's cabinet in its final phase. His accounts of its meetings, the most direct we possess, show its unfitness for its task. Taking office at a time when the question of serious food shortages, perhaps even of starvation leading to surrender, first became of central importance, Crawford found himself trying in vain to press drastic solutions upon a comatose cabinet and an indifferent Lloyd George. He was present at the crucial Unionist meetings which overthrew Asquith, and left a careful record of events. Crawford's great work, however, during and after the war was as chairman of the Royal Commission on Wheat Supplies, which fed first the nation and then most of the world.

In 1922 Crawford returned to the cabinet. He was therefore able to record the closing months of the Lloyd George administration from the inside, as he had done for the final period of Asquith's government. In particular, he has left a novelist's impression (though factual) of the behaviour of ministers during the final crisis of the Lloyd George government, which is worth any amount of official cabinet minutes. The Chanak episode of 1922, when Britain was on the verge of war with Kemal Ataturk's Turkey for several weeks, is now an obscure incident, but Crawford's notes show extremely well how Lloyd George handled his cabinet, and so have a much wider significance. What stands out is the Prime Minister's modesty and sense of humour when in a tight spot, rather than any attempt to play the great man.

When the Lloyd George coalition fell in 1922, Crawford, like the other coalition conservatives, went into the wilderness, in his case not to return to active politics. From 1922 to 1940 he touched the national scene in two ways. He was a pillar of the cultural establishment of Baldwin's time. He was also a close observer of some of the greatest men of his day, chiefly through devoted attendance at Grillions and other dining clubs where the eminent rubbed shoulders in an enforced and often revealing intimacy.

Crawford, who had not been a Chief Whip for nothing, invented the application of the skills of statecraft to culture. In the 1890s he guided the select committee which turned the dusty, decadent and corrupt South Kensington Museum into what became the modern-V. & A.: an undoubted success. In the 1900s he set the infant National Art-Collections Fund on its feet, with the object of keeping the new wave of American millionaire buyers at bay. This too was a success, though not without dramatic incident and undertones of intrigue. Then, in the 1920s, came office here, there and everywhere; at the National Gallery (the most ferociously quarrelsome), the National Portrait Gallery (the pleasantest by far), the British Museum (the most determinedly comatose), the Royal Fine Art Commission (the most expert, and therefore the most waywardly irresponsible) and many other bodies, down to the Glass Painters' Society

2

Introduction

and the chairmanship of a minor London hospital. From the point of view of public gain, perhaps Crawford's main achievement was to sow the seed of the idea that the British Museum should consider the art of display, rather than hiding as much as possible from laymen's gaze. The museum has indeed named one of its rooms after him, in recognition of his redoubtable advocacy of what in his early days was an unpromising cause.

Baldwin's England rested on a decency which was supposedly innate in the English character, and was best exemplified by a countryside which, if it still existed, was under threat, not least from the motor car. Crawford, who was obviously acceptable to Baldwin, was a central figure in the official world of art and culture in the broadest sense between the wars. The most obvious example was his chairmanship of the committee that recommended the setting up of the British Broadcasting Corporation in 1926. This had a political and ethical dimension for men like Crawford (and probably Baldwin): it represented the triumph of decency over irresponsibility (i.e. the press lords) in the same way that Baldwin's victory over Lloyd George had done. Crawford's second action in the 1920s was to give institutional form to vague anxieties going back to Hardy, by setting up the Council for the Preservation of Rural England. Not particularly successful in practice, it nevertheless enunciated a set of ideas and feelings about what rural England should be, which after the second war, and under the leadership of Crawford's eldest son, found institutional expression in the transformation of the National Trust into the largest voluntary mass organisation in England. The process by which the old aristocratic feeling for land became the urban middle class attachment to the countryside is not easily spelled out, but somewhere near the centre of it was Crawford (and his son). 'Landscape is the best bred thing in England', Crawford said in one of his many proselytising lectures on its saving power. Somewhere behind Crawford was Baldwin, with his belief in rural evocations as a source of national unity: and behind them Kipling and William Morris, both friends of Crawford. It is a large subject.

Crawford was almost the last of the Lindsays to live at Haigh. (His son lived there briefly in 1940–47.) The Scottish house at Balcarres, in Fife, was used in Crawford's day chiefly for summer holidays. Haigh, massive and indestructible, stands on a hillside in a great and fine park overlooking Wigan. No owner of it, however reticent and studious, could avoid being a kind of presiding deity for the town. Hostility of any sort between the Wiganers and their great house is quite absent from the diary. Even in the Labour Wigan of the post-1918 era, Crawford was made permanent chairman of the public library committee, succeeding his father in the post: which hardly suggests ill will. Indeed, Wigan library, under its remarkable scholar-librarian Hawkes, was a very fine affair. As for the local colliers, Crawford hobnobbed on easy terms with them, particularly the older ones, and certainly did not regard them as a threat to the social order or even to his own fortunes. He was horrified at the 'rationalisation' forced on his company by Montagu Norman and the banks in the 1930s, because it meant the end of paternalism. Even after closures and mergers, something of the old family tradition remained in the new Lancashire Steel of 1939, and Orwell's propagandist account of Wigan life misses this historical dimension.

The successive Earls of Crawford and Balcarres were the Medici of Britain. Many

3

Introduction

other landed families have had more wealth, and over a longer period. Some have applied their wealth for short periods, but with less skill, as at Mentmore. Many great collections founded in the eighteenth century ceased to grow in the nineteenth. Few old families were at the peak of their acquisitive instincts during the great lull between the dispersals of the Napoleonic period and the dramatic appearance of American buyers in Edwardian times. That was the time to buy, and that was when the Lindsays bought most heavily. No family has sustained its interest over four generations so fruitfully, or combined collection, scholarship, and innovation with such impact upon the development of whole subjects.[1] They showed what aristocracy might have meant, and what in nineteenth-century Britain it usually failed to mean.

To understand the craftsmanship, insight and integrity of the narrator, who by the standards of the political and cultural worlds was saved only by a bluff stubbornness from the danger of being a paragon, one requires some knowledge of the family tradition on which he drew, and which he wished to uphold. The Lindsays were Scottish, and eminent only in a Scottish way, until the end of the eighteenth century. One Earl of Crawford had jousted at Richard II's tournament of 1390, another was a prisoner of Cromwell for nine years. All were essentially Scottish, not least in one respect: money was not plentiful. An English heiress, and a move to Lancashire, proved the answer.

In 1780 Alexander, sixth Earl of Balcarres, who came from that collateral line of the Lindsay family which eventually, after a period of abeyance, inherited the title of Crawford in 1848, married Elizabeth Dalrymple, the heiress of the old Haigh estate outside Wigan, famous for its excellent coal since the days of Leland and Camden. This coal, of a type known as cannel, had rare properties: it could be turned on a lathe for ornament, and a summerhouse built of it had a polish as fine as black marble. Lord Balcarres, as he continued to call himself, made the crucial decision to sell his impoverished and overburdened Fife estate, and to become English. He founded what one might call the Lancashire Lindsays, who remained in that county until the end of the second world war, son succeeding father in direct line, each contributing to what eventually became a common family achievement. The move to England was justified; but though fortune came, it came laboriously and slowly.

When Earl Alexander succeeded to his Scottish property in 1768, he had £1,000 in gross rental, deeply encumbered and supporting ten siblings. He was a poor man. Marriage brought him, in 1780, an English estate worth perhaps less. The house, Haigh, was inhabited only by gipsies and squatters, and lay open to the winds. The estate had long lacked a resident male owner. Penury in Lancashire threatened to replace penury in Fife. But Earl Alexander, who had been educated at Göttingen, was no trifler. After fighting in the American war, becoming a general, commanding Jersey, and being Governor of Jamaica (1794–1801) he settled down, with relish, to the coal trade, to the exclusion of other interests and even of reasonable comfort. The rain continued to pour

---

[1] See Nicolas Barker, *Bibliotheca Lindesiana. The Lives and Collections of Alexander William, 25th Earl of Crawford and 8th Earl of Balcarres, and James Ludovic, 26th Earl of Crawford and 9th Earl of Balcarres* (London: Bernard Quaritch, 1977). For the Roxburghe Club.

4

Introduction

through the roof of the old Hall for the last thirty years of his life, and the question of gardens was always left until tomorrow.

Earl Alexander taught himself the whole business of mining, personally employing, promoting, rewarding and dismissing each man in his pits on the model of master and servant. 'Colliers we are, and colliers we must ever remain', he enjoined his heirs, adding 'the trade of a coalmaster is our vocation.' In one sense, his principles were anti-aristocratic. 'Nothing can be more fatal... than an inclination to buy land: the indulgence of such a wish would be destructive of our system as colliers, and keep our family in an unceasing poverty and distress.' Instead of laying acre to acre in conventional fashion, Earl Alexander bought hundreds of small plots, solely with a view to making the mining of the coal in their vicinity impossible to anyone but himself. Yet, for all his commercial statesmanship, and lack of interest in enrichment in any personal sense, he would not have acted as he did but for his conception of time and family. From his youth, he wrote, his object had been 'to break asunder the vile trammels of that intolerable bondage which had for many centuries levelled our family with the dust', and he turned to the magic of compound interest, employed upon what he called an aggrandising fund. 'Twenty years in my aristocratic way of thinking is to be reckoned as one hour.'

By 1823 Earl Alexander was drawing an income of £5,000 a year from his works, and was paying £20,000 a year in wages. His son James, twenty-fourth Earl of Crawford (1783–1869), was a practical, shrewd businessman who consolidated with great success. He had mechanical genius, a nose for markets – he would get up at 4 a.m. to catch the first train to Liverpool to haggle with coal chandlers over his goods – and an insistent belief in modernisation. It was he who built the new Haigh Hall, a great, indestructible house of which he was architect. Probably this was the first private dwelling to have a three-storey lift.

He also acquired a Scottish estate at Dun Echt (which later passed to the Cowdrays), and in moments of gloom might deny his father's creed. 'The land ought to be the inheritance of the aristocracy, and the less they meddle with trade the better.' In fact, whatever he may have said, he was a central figure in the development of the Lancashire coalfield, and of the Wigan engineering industry. He built his own steam engine for cutting the stones for building Haigh, designed an astronomical clock, and introduced the manufacture of locomotives to Wigan. He was popular enough with his colliers, so much so that they sat up all night to guard his house against Chartist rioters from Bolton; and the hospitality of his beer cellars was a memory that long outlived him. Before he died, however, Earl James, faced with the pressure of increasing competition, had merged his interests with those of others in the Wigan Coal and Iron Co., in which professional management largely ran the daily business of the firm. The new concern was one of the great businesses of late Victorian Britain. Successive Lords Crawford, including the diarist, continued as chairmen of the board; and up to the 1920s, and probably beyond, they made it their policy never to sell a share in the company, despite well-intentioned advice, the force of which they did not deny, against having all their eggs in so risky a basket. 'Colliers we are, and colliers we must ever remain!' wrote Lord Crawford in

Introduction

1923, quoting Earl Alexander, and adding with pride, 'We rank among the big coal merchants of Europe. Pay all the attention you can to the peddling of coal. Earl Alexander was a wholesaler in practice, Earl James was the same on principle. I am a retailer, heart and soul!'

The great Lindsay collections were therefore not built up, as is often the case, from capital, for no capital was ever realised. They were established by zeal, taste, discernment and originality, from income, and on a low market. The son of Earl James began the process. The twenty-fifth Earl (1812–80), known through most of life and in retrospect as Lord Lindsay, was the greatest bibliophile of his day, in point of quality and instinct for arrangement. More concerned with the inside than the outside of books, he was a writer on a strange array of topics, on Etruscan inscriptions and on German ballads, on family history and on linguistics. He was perhaps the best genealogist of his day. If this suggests an itinerant rather than a disciplined scholarship, then his Sketches of the History of Christian Art *(1847) redresses the balance, marking an important shift away from received opinion, in the direction later taken by Ruskin. As a book collector, his object was to obtain the earliest, and the best, edition of each work, and in the course of doing so he raised Quaritch, his main agent, from a stall in Covent Garden in the 1850s, to a position of European eminence, though, curiously, Lindsay probably only once visited Quaritch's shop.*

Ludovic, the twenty-sixth Earl (1847–1913), was a man whose rare attainments and studious inclinations equalled those of his father. He greatly extended the literary and historical collections of the Bibliotheca Lindesiana. His collection of Napoleonic and French Revolutionary documents was of the first importance. His own leaning was, however, to science, even to spiritualism, where his father had inclined to art and literature, but he had a very strong grasp of system. (As to the spiritualism, he held a live coal in his hand without pain, at the instance of the famous medium Home. This caused his neighbour Lord Derby to suspect him of 'latent unsoundness'.) He was an FRS, an FSA, a trustee of the British Museum, a president of the Camden Society, a president of the Royal Astronomical Society at 31, and chairman of a London hospital. He maintained his own astronomer and observatory, and achieved important results by going on an expedition to the Indian ocean, at great cost to himself, to observe the transit of Venus. Asthma, rheumatism and the extreme frugality of his wife's table made it desirable to escape the damp and pollution of Wigan in his later years, and accordingly he spent much time at sea in his yacht, usually taking a botanist or geologist with him.

When at sea, as he might be for six months at a time, Ludovic needed objects of study that took but little space; accordingly he became one of the founding fathers of philately, considered as the scientific study of the production and use of stamps. His collection in due course passed to George V. Closely related to his attitude to philately was his method of classifying and cataloguing ballads and broadsheets, by the initial line; simple enough once someone had thought of it, but the starting-point of all science in the subject.

Ludovic's interest in public affairs in the conventional sense was slight. Though a company director, and for seven years an MP, he had no wish to make a mark other than by developing new branches of study. Still, he did well as a Wigan MP (1874–80) until

6

Introduction

his father's death removed him from the Commons. He came top of the poll in two elections, ahead of his Conservative partner in what was then a two-member seat; and to stop a mining seat like Wigan from going Liberal in 1880 was an achievement. Indeed, had Wigan followed the normal pattern for such seats, it ought to have been a bastion of radicalism in the late Victorian period. The reverse was the case. Between 1874 and 1918, except for a few months in 1910, Wigan was Conservative. One can probably conclude that the horny-handed Tory Democrats of Wigan liked a lord, even if his most notable parliamentary achievement was to introduce chess to Westminster. Ludovic, a fine athlete in youth, had in any case passed into local legend by jumping across the mouth of a pit shaft.

To this tradition and inheritance the writer of these diaries succeeded in 1913. His role was of necessity a defensive one. In 1880 Earl Ludovic had to face £10,000 in duties on succession. In 1913 Lord Crawford had £107,000 to pay, on his father's net estate of £321,000. This was the point, therefore, at which the family collections ceased to expand significantly or to enter upon new fields. There had been realisations before, notably when the manuscript collection went to the infant John Rylands Library in 1900, but growth in other areas continued until 1913. The French collections, for instance, included over one thousand letters of Napoleon I. The task of the diarist was to conduct a retreat in good order: to replace completeness by selectiveness, to shed quantity rather than quality, to avoid undue dispersal of specialist material, and to maintain a fair balance of fine things in family possession. This transformation of the principle behind the collections from Victorian open-handedness to elegant economy was largely successful, although what Crawford did for the material under his own roof was but little compared to what he did by way of cultural statesmanship for the nation. As a very moderate-sized landowner, with a gross rental of £7,800 from land in the early 1920s,[2] Crawford depended entirely on the fortunes of the Wigan Coal and Iron Company, which after the war were indifferent or bad, paying no dividends after the mid-1920s. What his ancestors had done from income, Crawford managed to do, in new ways, without income.

Crawford, like his ancestors, was cut to no stock pattern. He did not smoke or drink, yet spent his happiest evenings at London dining clubs. He never fished, could not hunt, rarely shot, and had no interest in racing, yet looked the image of a burly and genial farmer. Unlike Balfour, he did not find himself drawn to the links. He liked the sombreness of Haigh, spent as much time as possible in Wigan, and deplored the way other Lancashire landowners had deserted their posts for less smoky climates, leaving no society in the vicinity. 'The flight of professional people to Southport and of the landowners to more attractive counties further afield, makes it more than ever incumbent upon us to keep loyal to Lancashire,' wrote Crawford.

His social experience was not confined to his own class. It may be suspected that his

---

[2] The properties in 1923 were Haigh, 3,307 acres: Balcarres (Fife), 2,826 acres; Leuchars (Fife), 2,615. The Dun Echt estate in Scotland, of 8,880 acres, was sold to the Cowdrays before the first war. Balcarres, alienated to a junior branch of the family in the time of Earl Alexander, was recovered in the 1880s with the help of Lady Wantage, an aunt of attractive qualities who had the Overstone banking fortune behind her.

7

Introduction

work in the East End of London in the 1890s, and his enlistment as a private in the first war (giving a false age and declaring himself a bachelor in order to be accepted) had an abiding effect on him. In the case of the East End, he saw that simply leaving the poor to do as they liked, unguided by the friendly paternalism he knew in Wigan or the frugal morality of Fife, produced disastrous results. The East End, in fact, weaned him from semi-liberal sympathies and left him a rather contemptuous opponent of optimistic New Liberalism. He had seen too many drunks and heard too many hard luck stories. 'A close and intimate acquaintance with these problems', he wrote in middle life, 'discounts one's faith in the easy solution of legislation, and how the doctrinaire idealisms break down when confronted with the living facts of the situation.' In wartime, he reached equally conservative conclusions. He shared to the full the working-class private's feeling against unworthy middle-class temporary officers. The task of conservatism was to provide worthy leaders, and to keep middle-class individualism in order. (Crawford's work in the hospital and art world, indeed, consisted largely of trying to stop petty quarrels among professional men like doctors and architects, and of keeping at bay commercial intruders like Duveen.) He also reacted against the attempt to make art into a secular ideology: 'to make art our national idol is impossible'. Though his political principles were no more worn on his sleeve than his unobtrusive churchmanship, he can fairly be described as a Christian Conservative who, like Baldwin, thought class conflict could be overcome, and the poor best guided, by a responsible and serious ruling class acting on principles of good will, duty and sacrifice. In this connection it may be noted that the author nearest to his heart was the ascetic Thomas à Kempis, with his insistence on the virtue of obedience. 'Send me a small Thomas à Kempis', he asked his wife, when at the age of forty-three he joined the RAMC as a private in 1915.

If the context of the diaries is Wigan and family and company, their broader interest is not autobiographical. The diarist writes of what he hears, be it impressions of politics, literature, society, or art, and keeps himself in the background. In political matters, he was for a period so accurate and minute an observer, that the central portions of this book relating to 1911–22 are of substantial academic importance. The sections before 1906, and after 1922, are more relaxed, and concentrate on the good anecdote, the significant impression.

Crawford's advice to his son well conveys his combination of prudence, forethought, and high principle.

You will live through difficult times. Legislation may well assume a punitive character, specially directed against those who are rich and as such liable to prejudice and rancour. That such tendencies exist cannot be denied, nor indeed is it a novel aspect of Mother Nature. But the discreet and dignified employment of wealth goes far to provide its own defence against such attacks. We do well to maintain the most friendly relations with our tenantry and with the big staff of the Wigan Coal and Iron Company – to look upon Haigh woods as the pleasure resort of a town with which we are intimately associated. We should share our artistic patrimony with all who can benefit from our possessions. Nor do I in the least think

Introduction

myself materialistic for paying close attention to business matters and to safeguarding our property, for it represents the skill, diligence, foresight, and self-sacrifice of our ancestors. On the contrary these are qualities of which we should be proud, so long as wealth is not the vehicle for ostentation or self-seeking. *Ne glorieris in divitis si adsunt.*

Haigh Hall now belongs to Wigan Corporation. The Lindsay family left Lancashire for Scotland at the end of the second war. Lord Crawford's papers were very largely destroyed in the blitz. What remains is the main series of diaries, running with hardly a break from 1892 to 1940, in over fifty volumes. There are also some war and travel diaries, which, because of difference of theme and tone, have hardly been used, though his war diaries give an unusual corporal's eye view of RAMC work in a front line dressing station in Flanders. For the period 1911–18, a significant amount of political memoranda survive, and these have been interwoven with passages from the diary. What appears to have disappeared almost entirely is his political correspondence as Whip and Minister: what remains is almost entirely in the form of notes taken at the time for his own reference. In the following selection, a considerable amount of governmental material for the period 1916–22 has been omitted, while on the other hand his papers as Chief Whip have been printed virtually in full. The reason is that there is only one Chief Whip, and his records have a unique authority, whereas in 1916–22 Crawford was only one of a large number of lesser ministers. Of material of general interest in the diaries, it has been possible to include most of what seemed to show the famous in a new light, or to catch aspects of their characters not elsewhere recorded, though much information of potentially rich interest, especially on the inner workings of the world of art, remains to be gleaned. The usual editorial liberties have been taken in rendering a casually written text suitable for publication.

I

Oxford and Bethnal Green, 1892-4

*Magdalen head of the river – Wilberforce on his diocese – a Wigan
election – working class Toryism – entry into social work – Bethnal Green
episodes – the Charity Organisation Society – Whitechapel enjoyments – Toynbee
Hall – the Salvation Army as an employer – artisans as political
thinkers – Scottish genteelism – an enterprising teetotaller – retrospect at
twenty-one – a Gladstone snub – Gladstone visits Oxford – coming of
age festivities – Lord Alfred Douglas in lilac – T. H. Huxley looks back.*

*Lord Balcarres, familiarly known as Bal, began his diaries while an undergraduate at
Magdalen, Oxford. These were successful and happy years. Office seems to have sought
him, rather than he it. He was secretary, treasurer, and (unopposed) president of the
Oxford Union, and secretary of the Canning Club, and the student press portrayed him
as an 'Isis Idol'. Such a record suggests the brilliant and pushy egotist. The opposite was
the case, the diaries showing a detached and relaxed humorist with a distaste for worldly
ambition, except in the sense of consciously seeking the best company. He was already
deeply versed in art, but sure England was not to be saved thereby. He found the
sulphurous aestheticism of the nineties objectionable. Social work impressed upon him the
immorality of the poor. He was, in matters of art and money alike, not a little moved by
Scottish puritanism. He led, and won, the fight to ban Zola's novels from the Oxford
Union library, F. E. Smith and Belloc being his principal opponents. Archbishop
Benson, meeting Balcarres in 1893, described him as 'reading for his first, and greatly in
earnest – a little disposed I should think to remodel or remove all institutions, but not
too much so for his age. A fine high-toned fellow and with a knowledge of Italy, minute as
to dates, lives, and works, which makes one ashamed.'*

*Balcarres the successful undergraduate, active in union politics, in Wigan elections, in
a boys' club in Oxford and in social work in the East End, training himself the while as a
connoisseur, touched only lightly in his diary on his own affairs, preferring to concentrate
on the idiosyncrasies of other people.*

16 MAY 1892
I am assured that a diary must deal with nothing but people. So this is to become
congealed personalities – all rasping one another.

10

Received a letter from John Burns[1] about railway accidents: he says that every man employed in shunting etc. is either killed or injured once in seven years.

26 MAY 1892
Magdalen head of the river: tremendous enthusiasm: we all swam about in the water opposite our barge and during the operation I nearly lost my signet ring: at 8.15 we had a huge 'buck supper' entertaining as guests the New College and B.N.C. eights. There was also a good sprinkling of old Magdalen men: after Hall had been made to run with champagne we proceeded to the meadows where we made three vast bonfires: many dons perambulated the walks and 'enjoyed' their cigars.

15 JUNE 1892
Ottley[2] told me a good story of Bishop Wilberforce: a layman was travelling with the Bishop and they came to Winchester: by the station they heard a humming noise like a swarm of bees. The layman asked what it was. The Bishop seemed surprised at his companion's ignorance and at length said: 'why, it is the diocese of Winchester snoring!'

16 JUNE 1892
At the boy's Institute in Oxford I said goodbye to all my friends and some of them were very sad that I have to go: they are a funny rough set of boys but some of them are delightful and lovely: I shall miss them very much.

During the general election Balcarres was in Wigan.

28 JUNE 1892
We were just sitting down this morning to begin our business in the Conservative committee room when in walked Darlington bringing with him a short stout fellow with teeth very far gone and a rubicund complexion. This worthy whom Darlington introduced as 'a new member of our committee' was greeted with loud laughter. I was surprised, and on inquiry found it to be Mr Aspinwall[3] the labour candidate. He is a very pleasant hearty fellow and we had a most friendly conversation: he is popular I think, and deservedly so, though his views are somewhat mistaken: he is in fact a real jolly jovial unthinking fellow.

30 JUNE 1892
At the club I had a good long talk with Aspinwall and his two agents . . . They appear

[1] John Burns (1858–1945), artisan, labour leader and Liberal cabinet minister, resigning office in 1914; a keen bibliophile, and an ally of the diarist from the later 1890s, first in reforming the South Kensington museums, and secondly as a source of political information. From 1902, Burns used to dine with Bal twice a week. How many secrets Burns gave away one can only guess.
[2] The Rev. Robert Laurence Ottley (1856–1933), Fellow and Dean of Divinity at Magdalen, 1890; Principal of Pusey House, 1893; Regius Professor of Theology, 1903.
[3] T. Aspinwall, unsuccessful Lib–Lab candidate for Wigan in 1892 and 1895.

to have had a noisy evening . . . Some Orangemen had made effigies of Aspinwall and Wilson: Hewlett[4] went to see them and forbade their being brought out: however they turned up amidst an ovation of brickbats when Aspinwall began his open air meeting. There was great danger of a free fight. The Irish radicals round Aspinwall kept saying, 'Give us the word, and we will go and kick them to death' – and had not Aspinwall prudently restrained them there would have been an attack, and I venture to say more than one man of either side would have been clogged to death.

1 JULY 1892

After dinner we went to a meeting of the Carters' Union – a trades union of workmen connected with wheels: Sir Francis[5] gave them a capital speech dealing with what the government has done for horses, roads, technical education, and trade . . . But the treat of the evening was to come. We went on to the King's Head Club, and there received the best welcome I have ever seen or received. This club, founded fifty years ago, is really a benefit society for Conservative churchmen. Simpson took the chair and his brilliant speech was enthusiastically received. Powell then gave an address – then I was called upon: I was graciously pleased to be facetious: whether it was the associations of the martyred King or whether it was the tropical heat of the little room crammed with 250 people I can't say: but I managed to keep them laughing thoroughly for the best part of a quarter of an hour. I think they were much pleased: and I was made an honorary member amidst great applause. A collier called Ward made the best electioneering speech I have ever heard in Wigan. It was simply marvellous. His matter was capital and his choice of words was excellent: but he is quite uneducated and pronunciation and grammar alike unknown to him. He is a little clever honest-looking fellow with beautiful teeth: I must say I was immensely impressed by him. The evening was enlivened by the broadest song I have ever heard. It began in a low minor rhythm and gave a realistic picture of all sorts of funny things: F. S. Powell didn't half like it.

The Conservatives held Wigan, and Balcarres was now free to take up social work in the East End, despite paternal fears for his political orthodoxy. Lodged in a Bethnal Green garret, he began to make himself useful, chiefly by assisting the work of the Charity Organisation Society. Balcarres was concerned mainly with interviewing applicants for relief to ensure that they had no hidden resources, with writing letters to check their bona fides, and with seeing people who wanted to send their children into the country.

13 JULY 1892

One has to follow a certain etiquette. For instance, it is wrong to call much before 3.30 – and when one reaches the house one mustn't knock too loud or else the

---

[4] General manager, Wigan Coal and Iron Co.
[5] Sir Francis Sharp Powell (1827–1911), MP (Cons.) Cambridge 1863–8, W. Riding N. 1872–4, Wigan 1885–1910; created baronet 1892; known in Wigan as 'the Buzzer': a Tory Democrat.

inmates take offence. It is easy to see that many of the applicants do their best to cheat you – but Walker who is an old hand soon detects and exposes an imposter. One man claimed help because his father was a 'real Christian man'. 'And this is why I know he was a real Christian man – because three weeks before he died he saw an electric light travel round the room: and if that doesn't prove it, I don't know what does.'

14 JULY 1892

In the morning I attended the weekly committee meeting of the C.O.S., which lasted about an hour and a half. It struck me that unnecessary objections were constantly put in the way of those who were in favour of relieving any case: in fact I thought the meeting more parsimonious than charitable. Numbers of cases were deferred or rejected though in most cases help seemed urgently needed: however I am told that what seems severity is often leniency: indeed the C.O.S. was never meant to give grants out of its own purse. It was originally intended to organise and regulate the charity of others. But I fancy that it wastes a good deal of time: what with enquiries and verification months are sometimes frittered away while the applicant may be in abject poverty. But I must withhold criticism until I have further examined their procedure.

16 JULY 1892

Whitechapel road on Saturday night is marvellous: hundreds of thousands turn out to drink in the new week: all available space on the pavement and edge of the great road is occupied with booths in which everything imaginable is sold, from oilcloth to readymade boots. And there are numberless Aunt Sallies, bowls, skittles, and punching machines, not to mention air guns, all ranged along the pathway. Everything is illuminated with flaring lamps which throw a weird chiaroscuro over the teeming populace: from the top of a tram the sight is little short of marvellous: as you pass along you can see a boy winning coconuts or being weighed: perhaps a few yards further on a fellow is shooting at a target which affords but little protection to those on the main road: poisonous refreshments are in great demand, and cheap literature and clothing abound. Then there are lots of little girls who carry about oyster shells and hold them before you in a pleading manner, asking the passers-by to 'remember the grotto'. It is a quaint habit, and as in some cases they burn an old candle end in the shells, I connect the custom with some medieval practice in days when King Multitude did not forget vigils and fast days and when a lighted taper carried an odour of sanctity: but nowadays King Multitude burns sacrifices in the gin palace which is worshipped by drunkenness and secularism.

17 JULY 1892

I went to take an evening class in St Bartholomew's school . . . A lot of boys are always too naughty to be admitted: so they used to climb over the wall into the playground and collect a number of young firebrands who threw rubbish into the doorway, broke the windows, covered their friends with ink, and their teacher with dirty water . . . The result of such conduct is that a chucker-out always attends, and when necessary, as frequently happens, two or three boys have to be escorted back to the street in the middle of a hymn or homily.

. . . All Father Jay's parish is in the condemned area. Every house has to be destroyed and the L.C.C. have voted £400,000 towards this object. The houses are closed one by one, and the families have to find other homes. Each family has one room: when they are evicted, a second family shares the place, and so on. One C.O.S. worker says that he found a room occupied by five families, one in each corner and one in the middle of a biggish room. He asked one of the inmates if he did not find it hot and stuffy. 'No' was the answer 'except when the gentleman in the middle brings in a lodger.'

21 JULY 1892

I visited Toynbee Hall today: I think I was rather disgusted with the place, though in certain ways the work is good. . . . Toynbee is a palace: art and culture take precedence of teaching the elements of morality. We were shewn into the drawing-room: I may call it a 'saloon' as no single word can better describe it. Papered with 'Morris' at five shillings a yard, it presents a smart appearance, while somewhat vulgar pictures adorn the walls. The saloon is filled with luxurious armchairs sitting in which we watched and envied the residents who were drinking choice teas and mouthing well-baked breads. The dining-room is sumptuous, the lecture-room superb. The passages are like a photography showroom and the library rivals our Bodleian. The Quadrangles are festooned with Japanese creepers and comforted with cosy seats: behind the house is a very fine tennis court, and I shuddered to think of the little back yard at home where we had just been playing squash fives. So I rejoiced in my heart that my lot had not fallen to Toynbee: our new Oxford House which I had been condemning as too luxurious, compares with Barnett's palazzo as would a pawnbroker's shop to the Papacy. The whole thing seems to be managed upon an aggressively secular basis: and what angers me more than anything is the knowledge that men go down there on purpose to teach the doctrines of anarchy and socialism. I fail to see how these drawing-room crumpets can ever influence the masses: a platinotype reproduction of Rossetti's Beatrice will not captivate the Whitechapel artisan: and if all these luscious works of art are there to captivate varsity men, I would suggest that the residents should move the hall to Kensington where I presume their aesthetic ideals of universal amelioration would be more appreciated. However, I must say that their aim is more to get at school teachers than working men. But why have all this ill-placed culture? Were they to combat the secularism rampant among school board officials, a far nobler ideal would be in view: and the amount of good done would be immeasurably greater than what they can ever hope to realise by teaching inartistic tutors the meaning of Pascal and Ghirlandaio.

. . . Perhaps I was embittered by not being asked to tea! Anyhow I will always contend that poverty-stricken districts must be improved through the heart rather than through the mind: and that pure philanthropy will never emanate from proud settlements where art is the idol... Is East London to bow down before literary cult, and Raphael and Praxiteles? To make art our national idol is impossible... I admire and respect Toynbee Hall, but I am truly alarmed at its method.

22 JULY 1892
I had to take seven children to Dunmow in Essex... Many of these children had never been into the country before and I had to tell them what a tree was, and which animals were cows. One boy saw a big flock of sheep and explained to his neighbour that they were pigs!... They will be away for a fortnight and I have no doubt they will return looking more angelic than ever. We have now sent off 700 or 800 and the emigration will go on during the whole of August... The parents nearly always do their best to help us in raising the necessary funds.

23 JULY 1892
About midnight we sallied forth to the Whitechapel road which always is seen at its best and worst on Saturday night. We were repaid for our pains. As we were passing one of the innumerable tents erected close to the pavement, a man rushed out of one of them with great yells. I immediately recognised him as a genuine Kaffir: so we paid and went inside, and two Zulus went through a marvellous performance. They stamped upon white hot pieces of metal, and passed them over their hands, feet, and tongues: as we were standing a few feet off them we could see that it was absolutely bona fide, and we could hear the hissing of the hot metal as it touched the damp flesh. Then amidst a babel of incantations one of them went through a few steps of the strange and stately Zulu war dance.

27 JULY 1892
One of the chief delights of the people is the barrel organ. Wherever the organs go, they collect enormous crowds of women and children who dance to the music: they don't go in for anything so vulgar as round dancing, but they form into groups and lines, and perform the most charming Shoreditch pavanes and Whitechapel sarabandes. Their movements are both decorous and graceful, and they excel in every variety of step and skirt dancing. Owing to the fact that they begin when three or four years old, the girls attain a proficiency which can never be excelled by the affected professionals. There are often crowds of people watching the girls 'do the kick' as it is called.

2 AUGUST 1892
I have devoted the whole day to the Children's Country Holiday Fund... In some ways I think this work is the most satisfactory. The parents are very grateful. The children are enraptured, and the organisers always get thanks. Now if we give relief to an applicant for the C.O.S. or if we send them away to a convalescent home, our

action is always looked upon as the necessary concomitant of need: and those whom we assist think that they are doing us no small favour if they accept anything from us ... Our pensioners too would be mortally offended if their allowance came late. To see a little gratitude is always a comfort and encouragement: we get so much abuse and kicks that we almost forget that this century can acknowledge kindness. Broadly speaking, the East End is intolerably selfish: exceptions are rare, and can be found more often among those who are under the sphere of our influence than elsewhere.

3 AUGUST 1892

After lunch Mitchell and I went over the First Elevator of the Salvation Army, in Hanbury St. About a hundred men are here, employed in various forms of joinery: tons of firewood are chopped, a gross of tambourines are turned out weekly, and their showrooms display a quantity of solid and tasteful furniture. The whole place is cleverly managed and judiciously organised. The joiners seemed well cared for, neatly clothed, and adequately fed. The whole place was respectable and the moral tone of the 'elevator' was good. The only fault I would urge about the management of the concern was the autocracy of Adjutant Bullen who was our cicerone. Mitchell asked him what class of men were being employed. Bullen said that among others there was a solicitor, an M.A. of Dublin. 'I have made him my secretary' calmly announced Bullen the Bully: whereat I was rather disgusted. The man whom we saw later appeared to be a quiet harmless fellow worth fifty of General Booth's myrmidons.

The other charge is against the whole system. I have constantly heard East End parsons say that the Salvation Army fails to reach the lowest classes. General Booth talks grandiloquently about his work among the submerged 'tenth'. Apart from the fact that the 'submerged' population proper of London scarcely amounts to three per cent of the inhabitants, this 'elevator' certainly does not employ a single man who could be called submerged. Class A in Mr Charles Booth's map represents the submerged people, those who are criminal and vicious, living without prospects or desire of permanent work. I saw no-one who would answer to this description. The men were with ten or twelve exceptions skilled artisans, doing work which would bring in from fifteen to fifty shillings a week. Some of these joiners may have been drunkards or thieves: but I protest against the persistent and reiterated statements of General Booth, that his elevators are carried on for the benefit of the most destitute classes. Anybody who applies for assistance will be allowed to fill a vacancy, provided that he says he possesses neither money, tools, nor friends. No inquiry is made. So the ipse dixit of any man in blindly accepted.

15 AUGUST 1892

In the Evening to the 'Clay Pipe Club' in Univ. where they held an informal political discussion. The two features of our debate (on the part of the working men members) were an absolute disregard for facts and a total ignorance of politics.

When a fallacy is hopelessly exposed they will not admit their mistake. Abuse follows argument: a political opponent cannot be allowed to have done anything whatsoever to have improved education or social life. As all the members are rabid radicals and socialists, it is not surprising to hear a man seriously assert that the only reason we have not been embroiled in continental warfare during the past six years is that Lord Salisbury was afraid of retribution at the hands of the artisan electorate. These men were brutally ungenerous. Landlords are thieves, capitalists, murderers. No moneyed man, they say, has ever conferred a beneficial law upon the working classes. Mr Gladstone is a humbug – all conservatives are liars – and when we ask these fellows what they want they cannot answer us. They mildly suggest payment of members: and we ask what is to follow that – so they reiterate 'oh we shall pay our members of Parliament.' ... These are the people who imagine that Government pays the Bishops, and that law making can remove national depravity. And the most distressing thing is that these fellows refuse to be convinced. They conceive a notion in their volatile brains – and wild horses will not tear it forth. Statistics of course are hopeless. Quotations naturally enough are scouted as worthless. Authoritative and influential statesmen are considered vain place hunters – and schemes of reform are held to be the cunning method of accumulating capital for the moneyed classes. They want labour members, and labour members they must have: but then they utterly fail to suggest any definite line of policy which these men are to adopt ... Another poor chap believed that none but labour members could deal with alien immigration and so on. Each man has his own fad, the solution of which is to be found in payment of members.

On the whole I was disgusted. I admire rational radicalism, and the intelligent Gladstonian deserves the approbation of all impartial politicians. Generosity and moderation among political opponents are a great factor in successful government. But that a body of decently educated men should degrade themselves by obstinate ignorance, makes one regret the repeated extensions of the franchise. Bigotry is too colourless a word to apply to their tenacity of false belief, false facts and false hopes. Nothing will bring them to their senses until a greengrocer manages our imperial finance, or a draper leads the House of Commons.

Balcarres returned to Scotland for a family holiday during which teas and treats were provided for the village schoolchildren, and the family dressed up and were photographed as housemaids. While there he visited Edzell, an early Lindsay castle no longer in the family, at the foot of Glenesk in Angus, remarkable for its sculptured garden wall (1604) and as fine as anything in Scotland. During 1892–4 Balcarres remained a prominent Oxford figure, but maintained his link with Bethnal Green. When he came of age, the homage paid by Wigan showed the vitality of the feudal spirit; his reactions to a church tea party among the genteel middle class of Fife suggested that it was rather at that level, than among working men, that he found it most difficult to feel at home.

Oxford and Bethnal Green

All were incapable of uttering a sentiment upon any subject other than the weather, the views, or the manse: subjects torn and tattered till all their clammy prose has actually oozed out. The dining room walls perspired the most pious society manners; and the company positively exuded good words. How can the minister live among such? The custom of these black smiling ogresses is to gather up every crumb on their plates and to butter them on to their bread. They say 'I will trouble you for just half a cup of tea' – and they say thank you to each person who successively passes the cup to the end of the table: then they say thank you when the tea is poured out and when the sugar is put in. Then they murmur it twice again when cream and milk is added, and then comes another series while the cup is being passed back to them. They stir it up in the most aggressively tedious manner, and proceed to take one carefully modulated mouthful every third minute. I felt inclined to slap them on the cheeks saying 'Don't smile and peculate crumbs. Eat and let us go away.' Life was not given us to waste with grinning gratitudes.

19 SEPTEMBER 1892
Today I have assumed the guise of Pilgrim, wandering through the land of the Lindsays.

After a long journey I reached Edzell. Mrs Dawson Rowley immediately took me out to see the goal, my shrine, namely Edzell Castle; and I venture to say that no worldly shrine could be more beautiful or touching. To describe the ruined keep – the gardens, sculpture or heraldry would be impertinent: I would not venture to attempt such a thing now. I can only say that the fact of its ever having left the family is the subject of a disappointment infinitely deeper than regret. To my mind the place itself seems hallowed – far more sacred than Balcarres can ever be to me, and I pray that my newly realised ambition may be fulfilled, namely that it should be bought back and should be reinhabited by one of my brothers... To me it seems almost a duty. When I think of restoring the Lindsays I get enthusiastic. Philanthropy I blush to confess becomes pale, and art is colourless. They do not make me burn. Possibly it is because I feel that others can do them so much better than myself: but on the other hand my inclination to work out a fame for the Lindsays is far stronger than that of any other Lindsay alive unless it is Edward. I know all the Lindsays who are closely connected with me: they do not burn. That is why I feel it my duty to get to work.

24 SEPTEMBER 1892
We made a great expedition to see the Forth Bridge... We were sitting on a bench waiting for the train when an aged gentleman with white beard, clean linen, and no tie, came up, and said gravely to Leone,[6] 'Do you not think, sir, that it will be a sign of progressing civilisation when young gentlemen do *not* smoke their pipes in the

---

[6] Leone Caetani, later Duke of Sermoneta, first cousin of the diarist; a great Arabic scholar.

railway stations?' This rather startled Leone who has never smoked a pipe in his life; and Evelyn promptly told him so, whereupon the old chap said 'Oh, I knew that, but I thought he would like to hear my opinion upon the subject.' I immediately drew closer to study the interesting case of lunacy. He then produced the inevitable tract, and said, 'I am a Teetotaller.' Nothing abashed, Leone answered, 'and are you also a vegetarian?' This was a nasty blow to the Temperance gent, but he boldly put the paper into Leo's hand and said that it cost a penny – adding that he had already sold 55,000. Leone placed a penny in his hand and murmured guilelessly 'Ah, you must have made quite a big fortune' – another nasty knock; and the Teetotaller veered off somewhat grieved, and prowled about the station like the lion seeking somebody to devour. The tract was a biography of the man's daughter, who died twenty-three years ago. It is one of those truly awful productions of the 'Protestant evangelical union' – a name to make one shudder, a history to make one yawn. Poor man, the harm he must do by propagating blasphemy is awful.

10 OCTOBER 1892

I came of age to-day. It was not a very alarming function, as so few people remembered it...

I have had the good fortune to stay in Germany and Italy, besides less important visits to Holland and France. This has given me the dilettantist knowledge of painting, heraldry, architecture and Wagner.

Eton and Oxford. Have taught me to respect 'moods' and 'motives'.

Haigh has taught me the value of books. Balcarres the fascination of Lindesiana.

Politics have come spontaneously. I cannot identify their generation. They give me the deepest reflection: so I have gone through an election, have tried to study oratory – have slummed 'rerum cognoscere causas'. Great good fortune has made me secretary of the two most important clubs in Oxford, the Union and the Canning.

I have chucked the army: by now I should have worn a red coat for fifteen months: of all tribulations I have escaped this is the greatest. My pleasures consist in building castles in the air: in looking at trees: in writing and receiving letters: in talking about the arts.

My ambition is to raise the clan name and estate to a position it has never occupied before.

I detest walking to church in batches of six or seven.

I can't stand the 'hearty man'.

'Good works' and ostentatious 'good workers' make me shudder.

I loathe Oscar Wilde.

15 OCTOBER 1892

I went to see Cottenham.[7] What can one say to a freshman who has ordered 2000

[7] Sir Kenelm Charles Edward Pepys, fourth Earl of Cottenham (1874–1919): succ. father, 1881.

cigars: who is on the point of hiring a third horse? who has decided to cut all lectures? who has a glass of brandy and water on his windowsill at four in the afternoon? Lady Cottenham wrote to me the other day begging me to visit him...

23 OCTOBER 1892

I went to tea with Cowley[8] who told me an amusing story about Mr Gladstone. Somewhere about 1875 Prof. Sayce[9] (a great friend of Cowley's) reviewed Mr Gladstone's Homeric studies somewhat unfavourably. Some eight years later Professor Sayce, who had been somewhat injudiciously rejected as Professor of Hebrew, wrote a work on the Hittites in which he mentioned one of Mr Gladstone's theories that they were connected with a Homeric tribe bearing the same name in comparative philology. A few days after, he received a curt postcard saying ' I am glad that there is *one* thing in my book which you think worth repeating.'

24 OCTOBER 1892

I went to hear Mr Gladstone lecture on medieval universities. The undergraduates, relegated to the upper gallery of the Sheldonian, were not admitted to the building until 2.15. When I reached the Broad St about 1.30 I found a crowd numbering some 500 'junior members', massed in front of the gateway. There we waited for five and forty minutes, we seethed, and swayed, and swore and sweated. Now and then a man would nearly faint, and somehow or other was got out of the tight wedge: my toes were tramped on thirteen times in one short vacillation of nine seconds: my gown was torn to shreds. Most people lost their collars: some their tempers: Schuster of New College lost his trousers, and the little Burmese noble left his clothes behind him.

But on the whole an Oxford crowd is good-natured. It spends its time in saying funny things.

'Three cheers for the flowing tide', when one oceanic lurch suddenly overwhelmed us. 'Damn the flowing tide' from somebody whose gown departed from its home with a weird shriek. But we got in after all: though many were left behind: the journey to the top was wearying and those whose wind had been bagged immediately proceeded to faint.

Then Mr Gladstone lectured, sometimes inaudibly, occasionally political, always superb.

The medieval university was a biggish thing, I find: at any rate, Canning, Shelley, and Lord Salisbury came in somehow or other.

When enumerating certain old professors with their familiar names, he mentioned Bradwardine, and added with an almost aggressively triumphant hiss, 'Doctor invincibilis'. So the radicals cheered immensely. Later on the Tories

---

[8] (Sir) Arthur Ernest Cowley, kt. (1861–1931), Fellow of Magdalen College, Oxford; Bodley's Librarian 1919–31.

[9] Rev. Archibald Henry Sayce (1845–1933), Professor of Assyriology at Oxford 1891–1919; author of numerous works on the Hittites.

cheered the name of our Chancellor. Both parties made a bad mistake. The lecture lasted an hour and a half, we applauded immensely at the end; and he looked most imposing as he bowed himself out of the south door of the Theatre, the daylight brightening the outlines of his scarlet robe. Then he drove away...

The lecture came out of Rashdall's[10] brain. His work on medieval universities is in the Press. Mr Morley, when Mr Gladstone found that he had undertaken a task utterly beyond him, wrote to Rashdall to detail his chief's dilemma. So Rashdall sent the proof sheets of the forthcoming work. Doubtless the Reverend Rashdall of Hertford College will wake up one summer morning to find himself a snug canon, or a cosy bursar.

No less than 300 people came from London alone. On Redletter lecture days those who fail to appreciate black letter professors, find to their cost, that laydom has superseded our university status. So Mr Gladstone was scarcely heard by young Oxford. But we saw him, and doubtless under the decades of social equality to come, it will be valuable to have heard and seen a great liberal statesman.

7 APRIL 1893

Coming of age celebrations have begun. At 12 today I received a deputation of the tenantry headed by old Mr Rawcliffe. There were about eight of them, and they made me a magnificent present of three silver bowls with filigree work around the edges, really extremely handsome and solid. After I had answered, I was presented with a perfectly magnificent golden watch and chain given by the Rawcliffe family, beautifully engraved with my crest and a very suitable inscription.

8 APRIL 1893

Eight deputations today:

1. School teachers under Mr James and Humphrey who gave me a very fine copy of Ruskin.
2. Employees of the Estate... from whom I received a magnificent travelling case.
3. The King's Head Club – a deputation consisting of the entire club, some 400 in all. They came up in a procession 250 yards long with blue ribands and a brass band, and gave me a capital reception and embodied their good wishes in an illuminated address. After a rush for drinks they marched off under Alderman Smith. I think they were all pleased with themselves...

9 APRIL 1893

Deputation from Aspull and Blackrod Local Boards and from Haigh Rural Sanitary Authorities. Speech. Splendid presentation of illuminated address, portraits of employees, and silver dessert service from the Wigan Coal and Iron Company... All told there are fifty-three people staying in the house.

[10] Very Rev. Hastings Rashdall (1858–1924), Dean of Carlisle from 1917; author of *The Universities of Europe in the Middle Ages* (1895).

Oxford and Bethnal Green

Additional deputations from: Mayor and Corporation; Primrose League; Wigan Wheelers Club, who turned up 40 strong; Dunecht tenantry; Volunteer officers with silver presents.

Three big luncheons: on Wednesday to gentry, magistrates, etc.: on Thursday to Wigan Coal and Iron Company, about 500 men: on Friday 400 cottagers and tenants. On Friday night, dance in the tent, 400 people there: I led off with Mrs Stewart. During the week I have made about twenty speeches, deadly work.

2 MAY 1893

What a grateful world we live in! Last holidays Father fed 1200 people, danced 650, entertained 150 others, and was only prevented by an epidemic from giving a school treat to 7000 children. And now a man writes to the Radical print in Wigan complaining that somebody or other wasn't invited, adding as a suggested reason the insinuation that his being a methodist or dissenter was the cause of our not inviting him. And the letter is signed 'Fair Play'!

3 MAY 1893

After singing on Magdalen Tower on May morning, the choir habitually go into the walks and cross over the little bridge ... There they sing again. On Sunday when they went there, they found that a lot of men ... were bathing. Ottley went forward and told them to dress and depart as soon as possible. This they did and the choir advanced. Imagine the horror of our excellent Dean of Divinity at finding Alfred Douglas lying in the middle of the road, sunning himself with very little on, but covered over like a babe in the wood, with masses of lilac. Truly aesthetic!

19 MAY 1893

Had tea with the President[11] where I met Professor and Mrs Huxley, a lady with the broadest and amplest forehead I have ever seen on a woman.

Huxley told me that he nearly broke down at the beginning of his lecture, having had a bad attack of influenza a few weeks ago. 'It is thirty years since I last spoke in Oxford – in fact though I have often been here I have never given an address or lecture since 1863 when I spoke at the meeting of the British association. We were then in the middle of the great Darwinian controversy: I was a very great friend of Darwin and those of us who were intimate with him knew what a good kindhearted and generous man he was. The acrimony displayed against us was of an extraordinary virulence: we were naturally attacked as being criminals, lunatics and atheists; but we were young strong men in those days, and I can tell you that we hit back pretty hard, because we were savage at the obloquy showered on Darwin. We knew that we were in the right, and we knew that our views would ultimately be accepted. But that the consensus of public opinion should have acquiesced in our

---

[11] Sir T. H. Warren (1853–1930), president of Magdalen College, 1885–1928.

doctrine so soon has always been a matter of great surprise to myself: and now I am actually considered by some to be a more or less respectable character. The initiative of the attack was not taken by the church. The pious layman is even a greater profligate than the average clergyman: indeed clergymen are ruled by their parishioners; and a liberal-minded presbyterian minister once told me that his views were necessarily modelled on those of his elders.'

'I am proud to say that I have never changed my name (on my visiting cards). I am now, and always have been Mr Huxley plain and simple. A German connoisseur once addressed me as "Herr Doctor Medecin Professor T. H. Huxley Esquire", which was a strange combination. I found out that he had studied the question carefully before writing to me.'

24 JUNE 1893

The school treat in honour of my coming of age took place today having been postponed at Easter time owing to epidemics. 5,100 children, about 4,000 grown-ups and three brass bands put in an appearance. I stood under the portico and the whole lot marched past me in procession . . .

II

Youth, 1894-1900

*Bayreuth – Cosmo Lang's dream – East End mob violence – the Bethnal Green
Guardians – Burne-Jones on impressionism – elected MP – William Morris – an
Irish scuffle in the House – Goschen's stories of Gladstone – Lady Diana Cooper
aged three – the O'Shea case – bicycling with Balfour – the Royal Irish
Constabulary – Chamberlain's daughter – Labouchere and the Cretan
atrocities – Salisbury in hot water over his clothes – the Jubilee – the Queen's
garden party – the Duchess of Teck – Lord Cadogan's intellect – how Rosebery
voted – Haldane at Waddesdon – Chamberlain's confidences – Walter Pater on
Burne-Jones – Balfour during the Fashoda crisis – public life in Wigan – Kate
Greenaway and Ruskin – first impressions of Winston Churchill – Balcarres's
reform of the Victoria and Albert Museum.*

*When Balcarres left Oxford in the summer of 1894, with the presidency of the union, a
third class degree in history, and some experience of social work and of electioneering
behind him, he was still every inch an undergraduate, and his mental world, except where
his precocious understanding of art was concerned, was largely limited to Oxford. It did
not, for instance, extend to London society in any of its many senses; for Balcarres,
though politically 'liberal' over such issues as payment of members and employers'
liability, was a young man of conservative tastes who preferred burrowing among the
treasures of country houses to the lights of Mayfair. He was already, though in his own
eyes no speaker, bitten by the political bug: and he was already a protectionist at heart.*

*As his coming of age celebrations showed, he was unashamedly treated as the heir to
great fortune and influence, a role he never questioned: and his bachelor years, up to his
marriage to Miss Constance Pelly in 1900, show an intelligent widening of interests and
involvements in many spheres of life – a grand tour of the foothills of art, literature and
politics.*

*His first vacation after leaving Oxford was taken with Cosmo Lang,[1] who was
induced by Balcarres to undergo a diet of art galleries and Wagner.*

6 AUGUST 1894
The regime of a Bayreuth festival is not comfortable. To begin with, the barrack
band opposite generally wakes me up at 5 a.m. Breakfast at 9 (bread and butter),
lunch at 11, first act at 4, ices during first and second pauses... Then supper
between 9.30 and 10.30; innumerable cigarettes because one is deliberately loafing
half the day.

[1] Cosmo Gordon Lang (1864–1945), Archbishop of Canterbury, 1928–42.

24

1894–1900

There was one young Dominican friar perhaps nineteen or twenty years old with so beautiful a carriage and so noble a countenance that Lang fell in love with him.

16 AUGUST 1894
A good dream of Lang's – it occurred years ago when he was thinking about the advisability of joining the Church of Rome. The scene was laid at Torquay station. Lang had bought a first class ticket to town: he got into his carriage looking forward to a journey of comfort and ease. Suddenly a little man came to the door: his face was covered with a sort of black veil. All he said was 'You had better travel third class with me'. So Lang got out rather mystified and nervous: he followed the stranger to the third class compartment and got in: the little stranger then revealed himself as Newman. Lang woke with a start and the railway train vanished into space: but the obvious moral to give up all comfort in return for the austerity of Rome was sufficient to make him unhappy for some time.

From September 1894 to May 1895, Balcarres worked at the Oxford House settlement on Charity Organisation Society cases.

23 SEPTEMBER 1894
At three the head took me to Spitalfields where Collins, 'Parson Collins' as he calls himself on the posters, had collected a remarkable congregation ... It was in the bleak and ugly parish church, and never was I more astounded at the congregation. Induced partly by the promise of some tea, partly by the nasty weather out of doors, and let us hope, largely from higher motives, some 250 of the most ill-conditioned men I have ever seen, assembled. They were in rags and tatters, some without boots and shirts, all of them in absolute destitution. As an example of this: a young fellow sitting by me was in filthy rags, he turned to his neighbour and said 'well I'm not nearly as ashamed as I thought I should be: there are lots of blokes worser dressed than I am' – and I should have unhesitatingly described the speaker as a black, or at any rate a dark blue.[2] The head gave an excellent address: the singing was hearty and genuine – and what gave me infinite satisfaction was their reverence. Now I am sure half these men had never been to church before – certainly since childhood, but they behaved with all the dignity which strange to say is not really uncommon in the East End. There were exceptions of course. One poor old soul kept dozing off to sleep, but an illkempt comrade persistently awakened him. Again – one of the best dressed of them, apparently a low class coster, turned round in his seat, with his back to the altar, and with coarse gesticulations and talk tried to distract those around him. Not a man took any notice of him, they sang more attentively than ever, and the coster turned away disgusted

---

[2] Used in Charles Booth's colour scheme to indicate the worst grades of destitution and criminality.

at the unsportsmanlike congregation. 'Another nasty one for the Devil' as I once heard said by somebody in the Salvation Army.

Few church services have made so deep an impression on me. The squalor, misery and vermin (from which alas, I still suffer) was unparalleled: and even if these congregations can only be got together by the promise of some tea and baccy after the service – what then? some of these poor souls will assuredly be helped – and who shall blame 'Parson Collins'?

. . . Coming home I met a vast crowd, seven or eight hundred of them, escorting four policemen who were taking up a couple of men. I walked close by them, and when we had got a hundred yards past the Salmon and Ball, that is to say an equal distance from the police station, one of the men by a skilful manoeuvre fell down in front of the policeman: there was a wriggling mass on the pavement: after eight or ten seconds the fighting got serious and of course the crowd doubled itself, a nasty lot of people emerged from Pitt St, throwing stones and hacking the Bobbies. I got close up to one of the latter and politely suggested that it was time to blow his whistle as the rescue party was beginning to get murderous. This was a new idea to the policeman who was a bit stunned, and he promptly gave a signal. In a moment's time a couple of herculean constables came out of the station and rushed to the scene of action: not enough to tackle two men and a big crowd. Two or three more put in an appearance a minute or two later and finally after twelve men had got together, hitting out wildly and with horrible fury at the crowd, the two prisoners were got into the station. By this time there was a crowd of nearly 2000 people of whom more than half were children on the outskirts of the mob. These children amused themselves by hissing, and guerilla warfare, throwing stones and brickbats which seldom reached the right people.

A gruesome sight: had it been anywhere but in East London I should have run in and fought – at one moment a policeman was I believe on the point of being terribly kicked. Fortunately we were so near the station that I trusted to relays of the force. Had I run in, it would have been necessary for me to have taken refuge in the police station, or else I should have required an escort home. In any case every window in Oxford House would have been broken at nightfall. We have to be careful not to prejudice our position in any way, but it is hard to carry out this prudent maxim at the expense of looking a coward.

25 SEPTEMBER 1894

At three I went to the Poor Law Guardians meeting till four thirty. As this meeting generally lasts till seven I did not really see much. However I was there long enough to find that the chairman was hopelessly incompetent: absolutely unable to rule insubordinate guardians. Sometimes three or four were on their legs at once, all trying to speak: hence much shouting and confusion. All those who did speak impressed me with the dangers attendant on elected guardians. Though there was a good deal of uproar I must say that very little ill-temper was displayed.

Secondly I noticed their treatment towards the inmates who came before the board. It is often said that the COS[3] is harsh and domineering and that we subject our applicants to brutal examination. But for harshness commend me to the Bethnal Green Guardians. I venture to say that no applicant to the COS has ever received such treatment as was meted out to the inmates of this workhouse. Though it was brutal I was to a certain extent gratified by so palpable a proof that at any rate the COS is not the institution which deals most harshly with distress and pauperism.

2 OCTOBER 1894

I took an hour's walk to get rough proportions of the public houses which only sell beer and spirits compared with those which advertise other things. I went from Bethnal Green workhouse to Limehouse basin and home by another route, walking at the ordinary rate, results as follows: 16 advertising ginger ale, 1 advertising bread and cheese, 2 advertising coffee, 6 advertising cider, 6 advertising Bovril; 31 in all which do not trust entirely to beer and spirits. 51 advertise nothing in their windows except intoxicants. 82 in all: therefore I passed a pub every 45 seconds.

12 DECEMBER 1894

I went round visiting, chiefly for my Christian school. It is most delightful work, all the children know me and follow me in crowds through the streets telling me their hopes and disappointments. The poverty round Pereira St is terrible, yet I cannot say that the people are unhappy: certainly the children are not.

26 DECEMBER 1894

Bank holiday. Drunkenness is such a commonplace nowadays that to describe it is a superfluous and stale story: people call it rant and sentimentality and a political dodge: but it exists – good God – the things I saw tonight show how ludicrous have been the efforts of church and chapel and parliament. Blatant drunken-ness – sodden drunkenness, satanic, here, there and everywhere. At the bottom of Brady St I found a man fighting with his wife, hacking her in the stomach and shins. She was fighting too, and the child in her arms must have been stunned for it never cried out when it received a hard blow – perhaps it was drunk too – who knows. I found myself fighting also, and the little drunken man went into the gutter like a log, but got up in a minute and fought again tooth and fist, boot and nail: but what can a beast about 5 ft 3 do when fighting against sobriety. However the gutter made him a bit sober or frightened and he crawled away.

26 JANUARY 1895

At 5.30 a man came to ask for clothes, required before 9.0 on Monday morning. This on a Saturday night, correspondence with his prospective employer being therefore impossible. I took the address of the man, and went off to Hackney. I

---

[3] The Charity Organisation Society, which tried the difficult task of giving relief only to those who really needed it: and hence had its critics.

interrogated policemen and telegraph boys: searched postal guides – enquired in numerous shops, aroused scores of idle housemaids – but never succeeded in finding the correct house. I got home tired and disappointed at 8.0.

Query: was it a waste of time?

28 JANUARY 1895

Visited some sanitary cases in a street redolent with scarlet fever and diphtheria: then at 3.30 to Toynbee Hall, a conference to promote university settlements in large provincial centres: the speakers included Barnett, Percy Alden, Archdeacons Browne and Wilson, Bishop of Rochester, Sir John Gorst, Professor Jebb, a man from Chicago and all sorts of other people. The speeches led one to believe that the sole problem staring us in the face was the economic problem! Fools and knaves and worse to squander an opportunity in prattling about culture and civic enthusiasm. The speeches were strangely empty – strangely shortsighted. I was deeply disappointed and came away marvelling... Old Nichol Street reminds one that in some places at least moral problems are of greater moment than economic difficulties.

After six or seven months I have seen a good deal of the E. End. One is disillusioned, and one is enlightened. But the possession of accurate knowledge derived from personal observation prevents those dreams about East London which so many persons find so fascinating. To myself this knowledge has dispelled many dreams; shattered many illusions, blighted many hopes.

4 APRIL 1895

I dined at the New Gallery... Richmond[4] and Burne-Jones chaffed one another in a pleasant homely way, but now and then their conversation was on subjects of deeper interest and importance. Talking about the modern school of impressionists, men who paint a sky which shuts in the picture and shuts out the air as the wall of a back yard would do – Richmond was bitter and pessimistic. He argued that the rising generation was tainted with French mannerisms and indecency and that years, perhaps generations would have to pass before a return to purer thought and craft can be reasonably expected. And perhaps he was right. Burne-Jones however took a brighter view. 'It will pass in ten years, and fifteen years hence there will scarcely be a relic of its abominable stench.' Richmond and Burne-Jones were agreed about the worthlessness of the modern art critic, Berenson for instance, Morelli or Richter who cannot see the beauty in a picture while they are discussing its authorship. The advice tendered by Burne-Jones was sound. 'Disregard them entirely; refuse to argue, and speak about the most flippant topic which occurs to your mind.' They were also agreed about the high appreciation of English art shewn by the best of the modern French painters.

---

[4] Sir W. B. Richmond (1842–1921), a successful painter.

14 APRIL 1895

I lunched with Burne-Jones... He took me to see William Morris where I spent a couple of hours very happily... All Morris's autograph mss of poetry etc. are handsomely bound in red morocco 'merely in order to enhance their value; a good binding turns the pennies into pounds when books find their way to the auction room, especially musty old books of manuscript poetry.'

20 APRIL 1895

To Madresfield. The Tecks there. The only human remark made by His Royal Highness to me was 'By Jove, what a deuce of a crop of hair you've got' – and in church!
   Princess Mary quite fascinating.[5]

7 JUNE 1895

I am elected member of parliament[6] and feel inclined to laugh at it. So absurd that I should be an MP... When I went to Oxford I though that I had ended boyhood. On leaving Oxford a year ago I thought I ought to consider myself a man: some months in east London has not made me feel older. I am now the youngest MP in years, and certainly in sentiment – that is why it seems absurd.

7 JULY 1895

I spent two hours with William Morris at Kelmscott, enjoying it much, only he has always got such funny guests with long hair and blue canvas shirts and red ties and he has got such delicious daughters and he drinks out of such a marvellously big tea cup.

3–6 AUGUST 1895

In camp with the Church Lads Brigade: of this I am Major. Enjoyed it immensely, though much grieved at the things creeping innumerable in my tent...

15 AUGUST 1895

Tanner,[7] while Harrington was speaking, shouted out 'that's a lie.' The Speaker was up in a moment and called on Tanner to withdraw. Dr Tanner hesitated for a few seconds and then we saw a scene was to take place. He refused to withdraw whereupon the Speaker named him with a promptness which has excited universal admiration. Tanner sat still; the Speaker called in the officers of the house to do their duty, and Gossett clasping his little sword marched towards this antiparnellite Cleon. Tanner by now had utterly lost self-control. He got into the middle of the

[5] See below, 1 November 1897.
[6] The seat, Chorley in Lancashire, was uncontested both in this by-election, and in the general election later in 1895. Balcarres was 'sad indeed, to think that I shall not live again in Bethnal Green'.
[7] Dr C. K. C. Tanner, MP (Nat.) Cork Co. (Mid-), 1885–1906: a Wykehamist who suffered illness from overeating while imprisoned by Balfour.

gangway, a few feet from the mace, and trembling with impotent passion pointed to Chamberlain and as he retreated down the house screamed at the top of his strident voice Judas Judas Judas Judas, Judas, – five times this ugly word: and was then lost to view. A scuffle took place close to the bar, with whom I do not know.

'And I am awfully, most awfully afraid he wasn't drunk' said Swift MacNeill[8] as we walked up Whitehall together when the House adjourned. Nevertheless I cannot help thinking that Tanner was drunk – was able to plead that unenviable excuse.

That Tanner should make a fool of himself is of course nothing new and nothing remarkable. The incident connected with his latest suspension of paramount importance was the admirable dignity with which Mr Gully[9] rose to the occasion, and performed an unpleasant duty.

18 AUGUST 1895

I lunched at Kelmscott with William Morris. He was in tremendous form and very reactionary. Especially angry with Bodoni whose 'sweltering brutality' was only to be equalled in typographical ugliness by Baskerville: he was also very angry with railways especially the one in his part of Oxfordshire which had completely demoralised the village of Lechlade. 'Now we have got the Tories in, I most devoutly hope we shall have a long spell of retrograde legislation.'

I had a good look at a lovely new book lately bought from Rosenthal, the one upon whose track I set him a few weeks ago. His library is certainly the most charming I have ever seen. The scholarly disposition of the books adds enormously to their beauty – and all his books have their original bindings, or else their modern coverings are executed in good taste...

From Kelmscott to the Grange. Sir Edward was busy or tired and did not come down, but I spent some time with Lady Burne-Jones who shewed me three mss illuminated and scribed by Morris, F. Murray and Wardle. Books of singular delicacy and charm – I confess that I have never seen anything like them. I thought the art of illumination was lost to modern generations. Not so. These three books are among the most lovely I have ever seen, though in justice to bygone artists I must admit that the wealth and depth of colour is not so great as that in a fourteenth or fifteenth century book. But these three volumes, gift books to Lady B.-J., are of rare beauty.

Lady Burne-Jones seemed weighed down with the responsibility of possessing such treasures – and is determined to give them to some public library on her death. I suggested the little place in South London which her genius and enthusiasm has started on a prosperous career. And I saw the Flower book: a series of watercolours by Sir Edward illustrating the ethos of Flowers... Traveller's Joy – what a fair name – and the picture represents three kings in desolate landscape finding a Child destined to be a Joy to all who read the story aright.

[8] J. G. S. MacNeill, QC, MP (Nat.) Donegal S. 1887–1918: an ascendancy figure descended from Dean Swift and from the Lairds of Barra.
[9] The Speaker.

Gradually Balcarres gravitated towards the more interesting people in politics, and especially towards the circle around the two Balfour brothers, which stood rather apart from and above an otherwise prosaic Conservative Party.

26 AUGUST 1895

To my infinite surprise Arthur Balfour spoke to me this evening. The rank and file of our party generally consider themselves to be merely voting automata regulated by the orders of their political leaders – this is an outcome of the singular rarity of any personal acquaintance between a conservative member and a conservative minister. It is a great contrast with the attitude of the Liberal leaders towards their supporters: Mr Gladstone for instance always made a point of knowing every member of of his party – this perhaps sounds pleasant and nothing more, but it is really the secret of that astounding cohesion which (in spite of many differences of opinion) has animated the whole Liberal party.

29 AUGUST 1895

A very pleasant dinner party with Goschen[10] as host... The First Lord of the Admiralty tells good story after good story with a fluency which is simply enervating: twenty or thirty during dinner I should think all first hand and first class. Those about Mr Gladstone interested me most; the late prime minister in spite of acute political differences has always kept up his friendship with Goschen and stays or dines with him whenever he can. Some years ago W.E.G. was with him in the country and received an address of congratulation from the villagers: the spokesman was the local postmaster ... and his speech began thus – 'As one public man addressing another, I beg to offer etc.' – and proceeded though a Tory and speaking before a crowd of Tory villagers to make a fulsome series of perorations. Mr G made a charming speech, and it was suggested that he should read the lessons in church. Goschen refused on behalf of Mr G. The church was nevertheless crowded next morning with sightseers, and Mrs Gladstone subsequently expressed regret that her husband had not read the lessons because 'then the people would have seen his face.' 'This wifely concern touched me,' said Goschen, 'and I have often noted it. Once in Edinburgh Mr G was hooted at the corner of a street. Mrs Gladstone boldly turned round, faced them and said "Never mind, William, they are only gentlemen" – a comforting reflection to the premier, and an unmerited compliment to his depreciators.'

'Mrs Gladstone's love and admiration for her husband has developed into a sort of idolatry: I remember during the great debates on the Egyptian question, I was announced as determined to move the adjournment of the House. In the Yard I met Mrs G who said to me, "Now Mr Goschen, I hope you won't be *too* naughty;

[10] G. J. Goschen, first Viscount Goschen (1831–1907), a right-wing Liberal until 1886, thereafter a Liberal Unionist; Chancellor of Exchequer, 1886–92, First Lord of Admiralty 1895–1900; described in diary, 4 February 1907, as 'blind, voiceless, and singularly uncouth in appearance and gesture: but a commanding intellect and most sympathetic'.

remember that my husband seeks guidance from above and does everything for the best." It went to my heart, and my speech was bald, vapid, dull: I docked it of all the ornaments of debate, to an intense personal sacrifice, having exscinded everything that would make it piquant and acid.'

17 OCTOBER 1895

The Granby children are most heavenly: the little one, Diana,[11] now three years old, recites poetry with an accuracy which is simply marvellous. It is however necessary to follow with the book as her diction is such that it is quite impossible to understand one single word she says.

30 OCTOBER 1895

To Bethnal Green . . . The East End of London terrifies me now: a few months ago I was fascinated into working all I knew: but the vastity of the problem has an awful depressing effect on me.

6 JANUARY 1896

At Hatfield. Cranborne told me that when the Prince Consort went to Hatfield he expressed his surprise that such a place should belong to a subject: and he has never been forgiven for his indiscretion.

We dined from thirty-five to forty every night. Is anybody intimate with Lord Salisbury? are his relatives ever taken into confidence? I have met him several times and now have stayed four or five days in his house – yet I have never spoken to him, neither has he done so to me. It is rather attractive this distant attitude towards those around him: it impresses one with a halo of mystery circling about the man whose words are heeded in the remotest parts of the world. Were he more talkative – in fact if he had spoken to several of his guests whom he does not know by sight – our curiosity would have been gratified but our admiration could not have been increased.

Lady S is sharply contrasted with him: you are at home with her immediately and she gives the impression of reserve, strength, and harboured wit. Of the sons, about whom it is said that their ability varies inversely with their age, I hold that Robert[12] has the future before him.

8 FEBRUARY 1896

All day in East London. I was appalled. I have lost all my nerve and tremble when I go into a house. I had to visit ten cases as S. R. D. Almoner. I felt useless, impotent – could give no advice, no help: only money. And what are cheques

---

[11] Lady Diana Manners, later Lady Diana Cooper, Viscountess Norwich. Her mother, Violet, Lady Granby, later Duchess of Rutland, was a Lindsay born at Haigh.

[12] Lord Robert Cecil (1864–1958), created Viscount Cecil of Chelwood, 1923; third son of the premier.

without charity? I am cut to the quick at my own worthlessness amid so much glorious effort.

16 FEBRUARY 1896

Spent the day with William Morris and Burne-Jones. Is Morris getting an old man? It suddenly occurred to me that his years are almost full – as he groaned when pulling out a big folio manuscript he seemed weary and only talked by fits and starts: worst sign of all he did not do justice to the new books he showed me. Now and then he flashed out into the good Saxon expletive when describing some gross American plagiarism or piracy against himself – devil – hell – blackguard – he never says damnation: his passion is eminently English even in diction.

A pathetic figure this William Morris, and to me, irresistibly attractive. He seems to feel that in some respects his life has not been the success for which he has longed. A profound poet and artist, he thinks that he has only helped his countrymen to beautify their surroundings whereas his real aim has been to beautify their lives. The result of his work has been to refine our luxury rather than to diminish our poverty: he feels this keenly. Kelmscott House and its treasures do not give him unmixed joy. Succeeding generations will give Morris the credit which he is apt to deny himself.

In February 1896 Balcarres became private secretary to Gerald Balfour, then the reforming Chief Secretary for Ireland (1895–1900) and brother of Arthur Balfour, later premier.

7 MARCH 1896

I dined with Gerald Balfour my chief, a small family party, George W. E. Russell being the only outsider – for I now count as a member of the family. Balfour a little flinty this evening, but his wife all smiles. Russell made us all laugh with his stories: without doubt a brilliant raconteur: yet half journalist, half pedant, and looks to boot, somewhat like a gouty tenor.

20 MARCH 1896

With the Custs [13] in the evening. Arthur Balfour, J. Whistler, Mrs Beerbohm Tree, Duke of Leeds, Whibley, [14] Arthur Lyttelton, and others. Enjoyed it very much.

9 MAY 1896

Lord Stanhope's water closet in Chevening house is quite one of the most admirable I know. It is decorated with perhaps a thousand square Dutch tiles, illustrating biblical scenes: set decorously in painted panelling.

[13] Harry Cust was ex-editor of the *Pall Mall Gazette*, a Soul, and friend of Arthur Balfour: the cleverest of the smart set, and the smartest of the clever set: 'de Custibus non est disputandum'.
[14] A Tory littérateur and biographer of Lord John Manners: at an earlier Cust dinner in 1896 the diarist noted that Whibley 'got very fond of me about midnight and persisted in giving me little hugs'.

Youth

Sir Edward Clarke told us many things about the O'Shea trial which brought
Parnell to his knees. It appears that long before the adultery was brought before the
court, O'Shea laid his case before Manning! Manning secretly sent information to
Rome and it was there proposed that a court of enquiry should be
held – presumably composed of worldly cardinals. O'Shea objected and the matter
rested a while until it came before the law courts: but during the interval there were
strange negotiations between O'Shea and certain legal firms as to representation at
the trial. On more than one occasion the injured captain was in imminent danger of
losing the papers upon which the ultimate conviction was based.

22 JUNE 1896
I bicycled back to London from Osterley with Arthur Balfour who told me that on
Tuesday last it was practically settled that the education bill should be entirely
dropped. This discounts the influence which the speech of Sir John Kennaway is
supposed to have had on the cabinet.

Mr Balfour had a difficult task before him this afternoon – the task of retreating
from a strong position rendered untenable by his own carelessness: whether he did
his work well or ill must be settled hereafter: but this morning coming back to
London he was free from care – he decided to banish all thought about his
humiliation: and so – prattling on architecture, bicycles, street paving, dust,
terracotta, tramways, policemen – so back to the metropolis.

19 JULY 1896
I fared to Hammersmith to see William Morris before he starts for Spitzbergen.
Though weak and weary in body, his intellect always aflash: and of course he was
picturesquely indignant *sicut suus est mos* ... This time Maunde Thompson[15] has
galvanised him to wrath by saying that there was no really English School of
illumination. Morris's fury was boundless. 'Though not much of a patriot' he said 'I
must frankly confess myself damned.' And indeed there is good ground to be angry
with Sir Edward's attitude towards his own country.

I saw his new books: the Chaucer so admirably bound by Cobden Saunderson:
the New Bestiary, nine hundred pounds worth of pictures – the adorable
Hegisippus, and psalter bought from Lord Aldenham: it lacked four leaves, the
calendar and the litany and was yet worth a thousand pounds! I would rather have it
(*c'est Morris qui parle* ...) I would rather have it than a gallery containing 29 pictures
by Reynolds, 37 by Gainsborough and 133 by Romney ... and yet some of us say
that there is no charm in intolerance.

Thence to Hammersmith Terrace to worry F. G. Stephens,[16] one of the original
Pre-Raphaelite Brotherhood: a quaint crammed cosy little place and a wan old

---

[15] Sir E. Maunde Thompson (1840–1929), principal librarian of the British Museum 1888–1909.
[16] Frederic George Stephens (1828–1907).

gentleman who tells stories about bygone friends and others whose ideals have changed: Wallis, Millais, Holman Hunt, Arthur Hughes, Alma Tadema, Rossetti, Palmer, Blake.

There are numberless drawings and pictures given him during the last fifty years – I was struck by a picture of my host when young – a portrait signed by Holman Hunt in 1847 – and upstairs was the fellow panel to that upon which Holman Hunt painted the wonderful thing of Claudio and Isabella. It was done in 1850 or thereabouts when Hunt and Stephens in direst poverty went into Longacre and bought two wooden panels from a man who bought old coaches to break up: these panels came from an ancient hackney coach ...

22 JULY 1896

I was talking with a cabinet minister today – or rather he was talking to me as he is a peer and so can only gather information with difficulty. The point which exercised him arose from his fear that the failure of Mr Balfour would bring Mr Chamberlain to the front. He failed to understand that men should prefer an unpopular but capable leader to one whose ability seems to vary inversely to his personal charm. For my part I believe that all will be forgiven to Mr Balfour if during the next session he shews himself somewhat more alive to the vast importance of his position.

6 OCTOBER 1896

At night I became a Druid: and addressed a hundred local Druids assembled at the Joiners' Arms. They use beer nowadays, instead of woad, do these Druids.

The death of William Morris is a sad loss to me: he filled a gap in my life – among my acquaintances: I know none to replace him, though this applies with an hundredfold strength to many others.

26 OCTOBER 1896

At Dublin Castle; the fortress of Saxon rule: and yet the Saxons in command all talked with a monstrously Irish brogue.

3 NOVEMBER 1896

Six hours at the depot of the Royal Irish Constabulary. I have seldom spent a more interesting day. It was the official visit of the chief secretary and every department had to be examined carefully. I do not care to recall all we saw, the stables, drill, march past, store rooms, recreation rooms, weights and measures departments; cookhouses, infirmary, physical exercises, libraries, dormitories, sitting rooms, sergeants' quarters, officers' quarters, transport departments, clothing stores, fire engines and heaven knows what else. It may be gathered that such an analysis would be somewhat tedious. Two things however are worthy of record: the school and the firearm arsenal.

We began with the first: a smallish room, arranged like an ordinary Board school room with 120 men sitting in tiers; men who are 38 inches round the chest and who average 5 ft 9 in in height. These were recruits, subjected to a viva voce examination for our benefit. They answered promptly and with unerring accuracy.

Herein lies the secret of their success. They were asked questions about law and order and general conduct. The strictest rules are enforced in their official manuals: the personal character seems to be gently crushed – some would say absolutely stifled. The answers they gave might have been the answers given by boys to the sternest instructors of a Jesuit Cosmos. The constable learns that he must not think of himself: only of the 'force'; he becomes an impersonal agent acting for a vast automaton which is to him the personification of administrative wisdom.

These men were recruits of six months' standing. In a few days they will be distributed all over Ireland believing in the doctrine of implicit unquestioning obedience to their superior officers.

And then came a curious scene. A man was called forward by Sir Andrew Reed: he was a rather ugly man, but burly and strong – a man of five and forty perhaps a sergeant-major or something corresponding to that rank. He was curtly ordered to address the recruits. 'Young fellows,' he began 'I have been ordered to address you, I'll just say to you what others said to me five and twenty years ago: I will repeat what they told me when I was a recruit before a single one of you young fellows was born.'

Then followed one of the most remarkable lay sermons to which I have ever listened – passionate though calm, ideal in its advice though practical also; he touched upon the ordinary claims of honesty, sobriety, purity: gave sound counsel on everyday subjects of wet clothes, meals, thrift, and suddenly on a sign from his superior officer he stopped short, without the glamour of peroration or applause, saluted the Chief Secretary and returned to his place... It was an interlude of a curious kind – that we should hear this man's advice on self-denial – advice begun and ended by a word, but which nevertheless moved people besides those for whom it was primarily intended.

Thence through a score of departments to the storehouse filled with arms confiscated under crimes acts: a huge place with some thousands of weapons. A pathetic sight too, though in this case one must gulp down one's pathos, for crime, generally of a brutal character, is portrayed in every weapon here.

The pathetic side lies in the character of the weapons: a gas pipe for instance, set into a log of wood and bound round and round by bits of tin, with an awkward hole bored into it whereby to ignite the powder by means of a match. Then there are swords; court swords, old rapiers which have graced the side of Irish beaux in the eighteenth century, military swords, swords taken in battle from the French; antiquated bayonets and guns sent from America: here and there an old swivel duck gun; a heap of blunderbusses, and the most motley collection of pistols which it is possible to conceive.

Note that the danger is to the assassin rather than to the man he hopes to kill: notice also that half these weapons are homemade, some of them having most curious appliances to fire them. And note also that the Irishman is not inventive so far as offensive weapons are concerned. Every gun and sword is ticketed, and has the owner's name on it together with some details of the outrage with which the weapon was or was meant to be connected. The government is now prepared to give them back and applications are constantly being made for them by those from whom they were taken, and by their relatives who consider them interesting family relics.

But a hundred pounds judiciously placed in Birmingham or Liège would work more destruction than the vast number of weapons here collected. It is wise to give them back their toys: for the moonlighter places more confidence in them than he would in foreign or 'Saxon' engines of destruction.

9 NOVEMBER 1896

Now staying at the Lodge is Miss Chamberlain whose sole topic of conversation, sole source of humour, sole standard of comparison and sole larder of anecdote are derived from her respected father. An eminent man doubtless; but not quite eminent enough to be the gold mine of social intercourse.

17 NOVEMBER 1896

In the afternoon the attorney-general to whom gruesome things are wont to appeal, took me to the ancient parish church of St Michan's, hard by the Four Courts. Here I was taken into some vaults and shown human corpses which owing to the dryness of the atmosphere have shrivelled, but never decayed. A sexton proudly displayed these sad relics: one is traditionally supposed to be the carcass of O'Connor, a descendant of the great King of that name. The corpse has lain there 200 years. He took the foot and the hand of this poor shell, and showed with pride that the thews and sinews are yet supple: the nails upon the fingers are unchanged: the hands bend as though life were still in them.

In November, Balcarres returned to Lancashire to play the part of a good constituency man: in the course of a week he held five political meetings, opened a chrysanthemum show, laid a foundation stone, patronised a Roman Catholic bazaar, and was installed as a Buffalo. All this, moreover, in a safe seat in the depths of rural Lancashire! Then he returned to Dublin.

28 NOVEMBER 1896

This gala night at the Opera quite an event of political importance . . . The piece was full of dialogue and incident calculated to arouse nationalist enthusiasm. So it did, but the enthusiasm caused by the presence of Lord Cadogan, Gerald Balfour, and Lord Roberts[17] was even greater . . . Tonight we heard the orchestra play 'God Save the Queen': and we sang it. For many years the national anthem has on these occasions been drowned by 'God Save Ireland'. Ten years ago the production of this play would have heralded riots: a few years ago a prohibitive price was asked for the vice-regal box in the border to prevent the Lord-Lieutenant's attendance.

---

[17] Lord-lieutenant, Chief Secretary, and commander-in-chief in Ireland respectively.

Youth

Tonight, in spite of groans and hisses, the reception was overwhelming. Signs of the times: and grateful is the Irish government for symptoms such as these.

Balcarres went to London for the opening of parliament.

19 JANUARY 1897

Talking with John Burns, I learned that he stuck in some of the mosaic blocks which now brighten the wings of the Archangel Michael in St Paul's Cathedral: moreover, that his forearm and wrist was the model used in the cartoon of St Luke. Burns was in the great dome: he had been watching the artist who, he said, had made the Apostle's arm too slender: so the doors of the muniment room were locked while Burns' brawny limb was copied: and there we can see it in colour and form to this day.

23 FEBRUARY 1897

Yesterday Labouchere made a passionate speech on a motion for adjournment to call attention to the Cretan affair.[18]

In the smoking room this afternoon we talked. I was sitting with a newspaper before me:

'Any more martyrs?' 'No' I said 'there seems to be a lull for the moment.'

'O damn it!' answered Labouchere, 'these martyrs are nuts for us: the damnedest set of scoundrels going. We are thriving on them. In a few weeks the British nation will think that Lord Salisbury is longing to massacre every rascal in Greece or Armenia! I shan't stop 'em.' And then after a few minutes talk about the by-election pending in Halifax he went on: 'I have just sent over a description of a cartoon which I want them to issue for Billson.[19] It's to be coloured: lots of red, and yellow ochre. A maiden is seen clinging to a cross: we'd better show a good bit of bosom. (Dress torn by some carnal fellow): she represents Crete, and perhaps it would be well to write it on the edge of her dress. Behind her is an obvious Turk preparing to cut her up. Arthur Balfour, Goschen and Lord Salisbury are callous spectators. Oh, Lord Salisbury must have a distinctly lecherous look; that would be very telling. The only thing I'm anxious about is to prevent the man from showing too much bosom. It mustn't be a cartoon which the honest women of Bradford would mind showing in their windows.'

Here is a faithful rendering of Labouchere's talk – smoking room gossip I admit; but this haunt is about the only place where Labouchere is really serious. Of course he considers politics to be a game in which much is effective and all is fair; but it

[18] The allied fleet, after due warning, had fired upon Cretan insurgents in order to protect Turkish civilians from attack (21 February 1897). Henry Labouchere (1831–1912) was a leading radical MP and journalist specialising in the exposure of scandals.
[19] Alfred Billson, the successful Liberal candidate.

seems worthwhile to chronicle such an opinion on a terrible crisis, even when the talker is utterly beneath contempt.[20]

2 JUNE 1897

Robert Cecil, Marquess of Salisbury and Knight of the Garter, is in hot water. The other day he discovered that he was wanted at a drawing-room: he posted off to Arlington St and dressed without the help of his valet.

He then arrived an hour late at the Palace. He was dressed in the tunic of an Elder Brother of Trinity House: he wore the hose of a Privy Councillor; his Garter over the wrong shoulder: an incongruous hat and curious old-fashioned shoes with strangely wrought buckles: some lace about the throat was misplaced and he had a sword. The Prince furious: literally in a passion. 'Here is our foreign minister dressed like a guy – Europe in a turmoil – twenty ministers and ambassadors looking on – what will they think' he wheezed, 'what can they think of a premier who can't put on his clothes?'[21]

21 JUNE 1897

The colonial troops had a procession[22] in East London. Their lunch was provided in Victoria Park where 300,000 people assembled to cheer them. There were 128 police and the crowd kept perfect order and seemliness. It is wonderful – indeed few things more so – this control which the police exercise over vast crowds.

The Nationalists refuse to take part in our commemoration: but many of them to whom I have spoken bitterly resent the action of Dillon and Redmond which has compelled them to hold aloof. One of them today at our Post Office in the H. of C. was protesting that he should pay a halfpenny and not a penny for the postage of sundry small parcels he was sending to Ireland. There were flags – Union Jacks, bunting, and so forth, together with a few print handkerchiefs covered with emblems of the royal family. He thought they could go as newspapers – but the official wouldn't allow it. 'In any case' said the Nationalist to us, 'if I can't enjoy the Jubilee myself there is no reason why my friends in Ireland shouldn't have something to remember it by.'

22 JUNE 1897

The Great Day.[23]

Everything seems to have gone off with brilliant success.

... I hear one of the most remarkable manifestations of loyalty not in the

[20] Another Labby story: when Sir Charles Dilke returned to Westminster after his unsavoury divorce, Labby, wishing to show friendliness, took a place next to Dilke, saying, 'Dilke, I think it is the duty of adulterers to stand shoulder to shoulder'. (Diary, 23 January 1940.)

[21] Cf. George Leveson Gower, *Mixed Grill* (1947), pp. 95–6, where Salisbury makes the retort, 'It was a dark morning and I am afraid that at the moment my mind must have been occupied by some subject of less importance'.

[22] For the Queen's diamond jubilee.

[23] The jubilee.

newspapers though more worthy of golden type than many of the touching stories with which they are daily filled.

It is from Lady Ampthill who travelled down in the royal train from Scotland to Windsor, about a week ago I should think. The train is luxurious in every way – one of those vast things which combine the maximum of speed with the minimum of noise and vibration. Anyhow she could not sleep: she happened to pull up the blind of her carriage window about four in the morning and was surprised to see a number of people lining the permanent way. From that moment until the train got home Lady Ampthill thought no more of sleep. The hedge or palings which protect the railroad marked a continuous line of people who had tramped across country to witness the passage of the train – people who knew that they could not see their beloved Queen, but who were glad to see the train which carried her along. In the remoter rural districts the people were thin in numbers – in the more populous countries sometimes thirty, forty deep – all this on a dark threatening grey morning.

As the train glides by at its own immense speed, though quietly as a serpent, the men took off their hats and the women held up a handkerchief or sometimes kissed their hands: in no single case did anybody raise a cheer for the Queen's rest is valued by her subjects. Thus did thousands upon thousands of humble folk celebrate this famous occasion not by seeing the Queen – that is granted to comparatively few – but by welcoming her royal train.

It seems to me to be the deepest manifestation of loyalty and devotion which can be conceived. They knew full well that they would receive no recognition, not even the smallest acknowledgment from the Queen – indeed but for an accidental chance the Queen would never have heard of their pilgrimage. But such things cannot be banished into oblivion. The Queen duly heard about it and was more moved by Lady Ampthill's story than by any of the numerous stirring moments which have hitherto marked the celebrations.

24 JUNE 1897
The Great Naval Review at Spithead. Without drawing upon our fleet in the Pacific, the Mediterranean, and other distant waters, the Admiralty assembled twenty-five miles of ships.

2 JULY 1897
Is it true what they tell me about the Queen? Punctilious and precise in all things, nothing vexes her more than having the 'things' moved in her sitting-rooms: and very human too. They say that her study at Buckingham Palace which is only occupied six or seven times a year illustrates this. When she leaves it there are naturally many things lying about on tables, chairs and on the floor – books for instance, shawls, and old envelopes. These are carefully picked up; numbered, catalogued, inventoried: chalkmarks are made upon the carpets, pins stuck on to

chairs. When the Queen is next expected everything is replaced with scrupulous care.

It is a passion for homeliness which has developed this curious taste: it is probably her homeliness which has contributed more than many great qualities to the immense personal love for her which is so conspicuous among our bourgeoisie.

3 JULY 1897

We scarcely expected that the Queen would entertain us so royally at Windsor: for the trouble, worry and also the expense cannot have been small. We turned up in hundreds, including two Nationalists whom the Queen asked to be presented to her. She was looking very well, very young and very happy. She stayed a long time among her faithful commons, scores of whom, including plenty of Radicals and not a few Labour members were brought up to her carriage: we had a free run of the castle, perfect weather, ample refreshments: bands, a thousand chairs and finally Imperial tobacco. It was magnificent...

I. Frank Lockwood[24] presented to the Queen: his daughter pressing him with many of us standing around as to what the Queen said to him: F.L. refused point blank: but being urged vehemently he answered: 'You may rest assured, my dear, that nothing passed between us which your mother would have blushed to hear.'

II. The Duke of Portland, dressed in the Windsor uniform and looking like a subpostmaster in semi-mufti, received a florin from an honourable member.

III. The Lord Advocate meets Jamie Caldwell[25] our paragon bore: later on the Lord Advocate meets me in the lobby: puts two fingers through two (of my) buttonholes and tells how he remarked to Jamie that it would take a week to see the treasures at Windsor Castle: and a month would be necessary to learn to know them. 'I'm not sure' says Jamie, 'my sister and I went through them all.' 'And what did you like best?' – 'Well I think the silver key with which H.M. opened the Glasgow waterworks.'

IV. Jacoby,[26] member of the kitchen committee, whip of the advanced radicals, epicure, flatfooted and Ishmaelite, found the champagne immensely to his taste. It was iced with infinite prudence and forethought; not a bit too much, not a degree too little. To a small group of enthusiastic radicals he murmured 'If the Prince of Wales wants his civil list increased I am ready to support his application tomorrow.' And then back to the iced champagne inviting me to come too.

25 JULY 1897

The forthcoming royal visit to Ireland. Prince George[27] went to A.J.B. and pointed

[24] Sir Frank Lockwood (1846–97), MP (Lib.) 1885–97; Solicitor-General, 1894–5.
[25] James Caldwell (1839–1925), MP (L.U., then H.R.) 1886–92, 1894–1910; Scottish calico printer.
[26] (Sir) James Alfred Jacoby (1852–1909), MP (Lib.) Mid-Derbs. 1885–1909.
[27] Later George V.

out that he didn't at all want to go to Ireland, that he was doing it on behalf of the ministry and so forth: finally adding that the government asked him to go – which is not the case. Then he said that it would be a severe drain upon his purse and could the government help him?

Meanwhile the Lord-Lieutenant[28] to Gerald Balfour: he is to entertain the royal party at the viceregal lodge: he didn't invite the Prince, doesn't in fact want the Prince to come at all, and – to make a long story short is only doing it on behalf of the government – having been almost asked to do so.

Could the Chief Secretary help him – is there any available secret service money? Dear! Dear!! Dear!!!

Chamberlain's speech on the South African committee[29] was a strangely impassioned affair: striking in its way. I was sitting just behind him. His nervous agitation was at times almost painful: his notes shook in his trembling hands and once or twice he could not read his manuscript extracts. I afterwards learned that farther off in the House people didn't notice his confusion.

28 JULY 1897

Of all curious things give us Lord Salisbury's speech on the compensation bill. He never (or at any rate seldom) uses a ms note. But in the middle of his speech the other day we saw him furtively fumbling in various pockets: finally he discovered his purse; a great big purse: this he unwound and turned out a lot of rubbish from which he selected a morsel of crumpled paper. This he flattened out and read to the House: it was about the coal trade of Genoa, quite irrelevant.

Quo facto he rolled up the scrap of paper, solemnly replaced it in his purse, which was then secreted in his breast pocket while we looked on with humble awe at the unusual process.

One of Nicol's[30] constituents in Argyllshire, worth £40,000 a year, begged his M.P. to support his application for a lighting buoy or something akin off one of his island fortresses. Donal Nicol tried, but Board of Trade refused. The constituent though disappointed did not despair. He asked Nicol if he would apply for a post instead – that is a stone pillar marking the dangerous spot. 'What would it cost?' asked Donal: 'Oh, not more than two or three pounds,' was the prompt and guileless reply.

29 AUGUST 1897

The reception accorded to the Duke and Duchess of York[31] has been most gratifying. It was feared at one time that there would be disturbance, and possibly outrage... Happier counsels have prevailed. Assuming that the remainder of the visit continues with unbroken success the results will be far reaching. 1898 will be a

[28] Lord Cadogan.
[29] The committee of enquiry into the Jameson Raid.
[30] D. N. Nicol, MP (Cons.), Argyll 1895–1903.
[31] Later George V and Queen Mary.

critical year in the history of Ireland: not perhaps so critical as 1798 but nevertheless a new starting point. Local government we hope may be established on a secure popular basis: the country may be opened up to the British visitor who will learn that nothing can be found east of St George's Channel which can vie with the natural charms of Ireland: while the literature and art of Ireland are still a closed book to the majority. We also look forward to an immense development of Irish industries; lace, cloth, jewellery, carving; most of which together with the crafts of furniture and plate have well nigh vanished from the island: moreover there is hope in cheese, comfort in eggs, expectation in butter.

So many times have people seen the new epoch dawning up for Ireland: how many times has the golden age been promised, and a millennium been predicted. In point of fact there has always existed a potential improvement of Ireland: and it has always eluded realisation. Thus one's hopes are tempered with caution, discounted by experience reminiscent of failure. Yet one is glad to hope again.

8 OCTOBER 1897

Busy in London, where I heard all the news; Howorth furious about Ritchie's intervention in the engineer dispute: also Carson, who says that much as he distrusts Ritchie's judgement he prefers him with all his shortcomings to Lord James who is dishonest. Bowles rampaging about the death duties which must be blotted out – or else the government must go. It is said that Walter Long, a radical at heart is proposing allotment legislation of a most drastic character: we hope this is not the case for our ministers have overstepped the patience of Toryism two sessions running. With regard to this progressive conservatism Howorth told me a strange thing – if true – namely that he had lately received a letter from Lord Salisbury begging Howorth to use his influence with Arthur Balfour in this matter as the Markiss[32] fears that we are going too far in our scheme of dishing the Whigs. Indeed it might be more properly urged that the government is dishing the Tories. It is probable that Howorth has strained an interpretation of this letter, though it is difficult to obliterate its significance. Meanwhile the old stories of resignation are afloat. The Premier is old for his years and heavy for his legs and longs to throw off the burden of office – and in favour of Lord Lansdowne: of whom it may be observed that his position in the social world rather than his personality in political circles has brought him into prominence. He is an honest staightforward and cautious man, admirably fitted to do routine work and quite incompetent to direct the foreign policy of Great Britain.

1 NOVEMBER 1897

The death of Princess Mary[33] came to me as a sad surprise. She was the only member of the royal family whom I can say that I knew well. Her kindness and

[32] Lord Salisbury.
[33] HRH Princess Mary, Duchess of Teck; daughter of the first Duke of Cambridge, son of George III; mother of Queen Mary.

courtesy to myself was unfailing, and for few persons have I entertained feelings of such profound esteem and affection. Her character was admirable and her grace and dignity were truly royal. Though in latter years it became impossible for her to pursue the active life to which she has been accustomed, I have heard men say that they still thought her the most handsome and stately woman of the day. This is no exaggeration. Indeed her carriage and address were such that it was literally a privilege to be in her company: I used to meet her often both in London and in the country, and my regard for her was increased on every occasion. We used to have prolonged talks about the distribution of the articles of clothing collected by the society of which she was the life and soul. I was always struck by the penetration and memory she showed. Seldom did I mention a parish in East London to which it was proposed to make a grant without some remark falling from her which would show that she was acquainted with the special needs and difficulties of the particular district in question. Herein lay the secret of her successful labours, and of the love which she inspired among her colleagues.

She will not soon be forgotten: and it will be impossible to find anyone to take her place.

4 NOVEMBER 1897

Gerald Balfour is working eight and ten hours a day at the local government bill. The details are vexatious and involve almost greater thought than the organic outlines. And the hardest work of all consists in the process of installing the principles of the measure into the turgid brain of His Excellency the Lord-Lieutenant of Ireland. Few man have a more decorous and dignified manner than Lord Cadogan[34] and there have been few men in his position who have entertained more generously: in fact so far as this country is concerned he is an ideal Viceroy. But that Ireland should be represented in the cabinet by him is a source of endless trouble: Lord Ashbourne is there to help him but he is not the accredited minister. Lord Cadogan does not understand the elements of government, local or imperial, and he is very slow to learn. G.W.B. spends hours and hours in coaching him: and after a morning of this wearing work Lord Cadogan will blandly ask some question which will show that all the labour has been in vain. It was bad enough last year about the Land Bill: this year a hundred times worse.

8 NOVEMBER 1897

Gerald Balfour leaves this evening for London where he must persuade the cabinet to accept the main features of the Local Government Bill for next session. So I am here alone with Lady Betty[35] and her three sweet children. But tête à tête with Lady Betty affords the best company imaginable. She is to begin with a well of humour:

[34] Lord Cadogan, Lord-Lieutenant from 1895 to 1902, sat in the cabinet throughout his period of office; while Gerald Balfour and George Wyndham, who as Chief Secretaries effectively controlled Irish policy, were not included in the cabinet during those years.

[35] Eldest daughter of the first Earl of Lytton, Viceroy of India; m. Gerald Balfour, 1887, and d. 1942.

then her reading has been extensive and prudently chosen. For years past she has lived among men who rule this country and help to rule the greater world: and this has quickened her critical faculties which gives acumen and breadth to her talk on everyday matters. There is moreover an unerring logic together with the warmest of hearts: what a combination!

17 NOVEMBER 1897

The National Conservative Union boisterously passed the motion favouring a royal residence for Ireland. So too the cabinet. They agreed unanimously to establish one. Hicks Beach in particular was enthusiastic and promised to find the necessary funds. Lord Cadogan was deputed to wait upon the Duke of York who readily engaged to carry out the desire of the Government.

But of course the Queen had to be asked and she gave an absolute *non possumus*. No cause can be alleged though she remarked that the climate was unhealthy.

This is a terrible disaster: far more serious than it may sound. An opportunity has been lost of doing a great thing – popular, and reconciliatory. Political questions would not have been involved as it was merely proposed to establish a royal residence without interfering with the lord-lieutenancy. One often wonders why Ireland has been treated with such scant courtesy by H.M. Had more trouble been taken by the royal family during the last forty years there can be no doubt that the crying evil of absenteeism would have been reduced to a minimum.

5 DECEMBER 1897

I spent the day with C. T. Redington,[36] head of Irish education. His sayings:
1) Celtic is both dead and dying. No efforts will save it: the people are too uneducated to learn it, and a knowledge of the vernacular will not benefit them in the least. I have seen the language gradually dying away in the west.
2) A middle class is growing up in the villages. There always was a bourgeoisie in the towns but the villages are now beginning to change. Twenty years ago there was one dead level throughout the villages. This birth of rural bourgeoisie is an indubitable sign of progress.
3) Some years ago there was mismanagement at Kingstown station. An enquiry was held and it transpired that there was a large trade in old disused railway tickets. The guards and porters disposed of these to persons who were anxious to obtain drink in public houses, which comfort was denied them unless they could show themselves to be bona fide travellers. Publicans did not trouble themselves about the dates. This is now all changed.

12 JANUARY 1898

Afternoon: presided at a meeting of the Wigan Temperance and Rescue Society: dreary dismal nonconformity: afterwards tea in a Baptist Chapel. They kept telling

---

[36] C. T. Redington (1847–99), resident commissioner of national education, Ireland, and vice-chancellor, Royal University, Ireland, from 1894.

Youth

me stories about 'the Lord', their homely sobriquet (as the words sound on their lips) for Almighty God.

7 FEBRUARY 1898
Cumming Macdona[37] sent 10,000 Christmas cards to his constituents, or rather to every voter and proprietor in the division. He has received two letters of thanks, one from the Rural Dean, the other from Lord Salisbury, a property owner. A charming card – specially coloured and prepared, and suitably inscribed with a Xmas greeting. I think that at least some of the Rotherhithe Tories might have said thank you.

11 FEBRUARY 1898
The Home Rule debate marks an epoch, and the little rift will gradually widen.[38] One regrets the fact for one reason alone, namely the probability of renewed outrage which may result from a knowledge that English Liberalism having laid aside lukewarmness for Home Rule, has begun to be its open foe. Still we must watch at the Irish Office.

15 FEBRUARY 1898
Let me note for future satisfaction that Engledow[39] who is a Nationalist told me sotto voce that he was dreadfully afraid the Irish Local Government Bill might be too extreme in its provisions.

16 FEBRUARY 1898
Lord Balfour of Burleigh[40] illustrating the good government of Scotland and the satisfaction of the people with their parliamentary ministers, told me that on the opening day of the session his work at the Scots Office was concluded in twenty minutes. He received no letter and only two visits from M.P.s: one Radical and one Conservative, who in each case called in order to thank the Secretary for what he had done during the recess.

27 FEBRUARY 1898
At the Carlton I watched Hicks Beach[41] reading a French novel. He began at the

[37] J. C. Macdona, MP (Cons.) Rotherhithe, 1892–1906.
[38] Redmond had failed to elicit any but the most perfunctory commitment to home rule from the English Liberals.
[39] C. J. Engledow, MP (Nat.) Kildare N. 1895–1900: after leaving Cambridge, he had entered the colonial service.
[40] Alexander Bruce, sixth Baron Balfour of Burleigh (1849–1921), Secretary of State for Scotland 1895–1903. The Scottish Office had been set up in 1885.
[41] Sir Michael Hicks Beach, first Earl St Aldwyn (1837–1916); Chancellor of the Exchequer 1895–1902; known as 'Black Michael' after *The Prisoner of Zenda* (and because he was never happier than when refusing a favour to a friend).

end and worked steadily backwards through the book. This chinoiserie must be the result of too close an attention to the far eastern problem.

2 MARCH 1898

At night I walked through low streets in Greenwich and Deptford . . . I find I lose my nerve in such places. Not long ago when they were familiar to me the impression of these horrors upon my mind acted as a motive power to individual effort. Being now removed from all useful work the things I see make me sick and afraid. The other night while walking in a low court in Soho a poor cripple was moving along when suddenly one of his crutches broke in the middle. He fell heavily to the ground and after agonising groans his body complained by convulsive twitches and contortions. I think it must have been some horrible injury of the spine.

3 MARCH 1898

Twenty four hours later, dining with Lord Rosebery: sumptuous fare and splendid house: brilliant conversation. We were twelve, but Asquith stumbled in a quarter of an hour late, making thirteen . . . We were amused to learn that Lord Rosebery having made a strong speech for the progressives, voted today at the County Council election for a moderate candidate. He explained that he did this because he thought it necessary as an ex-chairman of the Board, to be impartial: and also because Mr Antrobus is a good man. As to his second vote, the choice lay between a progressive watchmaker and a progressive journalist: 'Here too I had to be honest, so I voted for the watchmaker as the least dishonourable man.'

25 MARCH 1898

A very pleasant dinner with the Asquiths: and much good cheer: too good cheer perhaps, but never mind. Arthur Balfour in excellent humour and laughing at Zola for swearing by Nana and la Terre instead of by Almighty God . . . And our host with satisfaction glowing all over his face, now unhappily becoming somewhat big.

1 APRIL 1898

The famine trouble in Ireland is still somewhat acute: in six or eight weeks time the crisis will really begin . . . The Duke of York wants to give £50. Lord Cadogan is to see him today and will try to persuade him to give the money to the Congested Districts Board with instructions to devote it to some object of permanent utility. But the Duke can't hold his tongue and in a short time he will no doubt be telling people that he wanted to subscribe . . .

21 APRIL 1898

Dined with Admiral Maxse: also there Asquith, Warkworth, Lyttelton, Arthur Balfour. Clemenceau, worried and haggard at heart, but brimful of wit and humour, kept us laughing incessantly. A.J.B. firmly convinced not only of the illegality of Dreyfus's conviction, but of the man's innocence. Clemenceau asked outright that our military attaché should be allowed to give evidence, and he believes that if this man can be got into the box the whole trial will go in favour of Zola.

6 MAY 1898

A most pleasant luncheon party in Arlington St with the Granbys. The guests were many, but those of interest were Lord Salisbury and Cecil Rhodes ('I feel as if I were sitting in the company of the two greatest criminals of the age' remarked Harry Cust).

Both the big men in good mood; laughing and chaffing and saying good things – bludgeon versus rapier, and the rapier did not always win. There is a certain diffidence about Rhodes – one feels that he is not quite sure how to put down his fork or whether he might help himself to fruit: but not nervous enough to make other people uncomfortable: only nearly. And as to his face it is enigmatic. It would be almost as easy to urge that it is the face of a weak man as of a strong man: at any rate it has weak features – and indeed the character and achievement of the man show that in some respects he lacks penetration. For instance, he has never found strong men to help him ... Then he is vain. Albert Grey says the vainest of the vain men: as soon as we sat down to lunch he asked Violet Granby to make a picture of him, and she consented readily enough, admiring the face and the man. Then came the important question of pose: he is attached to his full face; she to profile: the only escape is for Violet G. to make two pictures; and they will both be striking.

26 MAY 1898

I went to see Mr Gladstone lying in state, several times. I stood in the reserved space and watched the crowd go surging past at the rate of 150 and at times 200 every minute. An orderly well-dressed respectful crowd; patient and submissive to the police who allowed them no delay for expressing their sentiment and regret. Scores of people passed by – hundreds I should say, without looking at the catafalque at all. They simply walked along the gangway as they might have walked down Whitehall noticing nothing. Others talked quietly with their wives and daughters just looking at the coffin as they went by but without showing signs of recognition or intelligence. This doesn't mean that a callous rabble strolled through Westminster Hall: not a bit. The people wanted to see the triumph and when they reached the death chamber they forgot to look at its central feature. They had been in the crowd, in Westminster Hall, and beside the dead statesman: they thought they had seen him lying in state, and their grandchildren will be told the history of Gladstone's last resting place above the earth; yet they could not tell one whether the coffin was covered with a pall or not, for they didn't happen to look to see.

This was so strange that many members of parliament standing by tried to analyse the feelings which would bring a man for miles to see a coffin at which on his arrival he did not cast one passing glance. We came to the conclusion that the cause must be sought in this fact: that the Briton does not enjoy doing a thing so much as in the recollection of having done it; and perhaps some secrets of our great deeds as a nation be traced to this general attitude of the British mind.

Others walked by with little children who were lifted up to gaze on the funeral pile. Some grandchildren of these little mites may be living in the year 2018... Then again others passed by with a murmured prayer and the sign of the eternal cross: for such as these the cataclysm of the world can have no terrors.

18–20 JUNE 1898

At Waddesdon. I have never stayed in a palace before and the experience has not been without interest: a huge party... Haldane for instance: 'I love luxury' he says – 'notwithstanding my ardent radicalism, and you know I am a communard at heart. But I admire my host, he does things so very well. Think of his first election. When he was declared member the rejoicing in the village was such that no less than 143 of his gardeners are reported to have embraced one another in mutual congratulation: it is true that there is a liberal element in the neighbourhood – and I am glad to learn that no less than sixty-five other gardeners refused to join the demonstration of their colleagues... Yes – I do love all seemly luxury. When lying abed in the mornings it gives me satisfaction when a lacquey softly enters the room and asks whether I will take tea, coffee, chocolate or cocoa. This privilege is accorded to me in the houses of all my distinguished friends: but it is only at Waddesdon that on saying I prefer tea, the valet further enquires whether I fancy Ceylon, Souchong, or Assam.'

... But certainly Waddesdon is a marvellous creation; a real creation – not an old mansion taken over with its gardens, park and stabling – but a vast chateau built by its present owner, surrounded by endless gardens planned by him, and towering over a big park reclaimed from agricultural meadows by our host. And Baron Ferdinand whose hands always itch with nervousness, walks about at times petulantly, while jealously caring for the pleasure of his guests. I failed to gather that his priceless pictures give him true pleasure. His clock for which he gave £25,000, his escritoire for which £30,000 was paid, his statuary, his china, and his superb collection of jewels, enamels and so forth ('gimcracks' he calls them) – all these things give him meagre satisfaction: and I felt that the only pleasure he derives from them is gained when he is showing them to his friends. Even then one sees how bitterly he resents comment which is ignorant or inept.

However it is in the gardens and shrubberies that he is happy. He is responsible for the design of the flower beds; for the arrangement of colour, for the transplanting of trees: all these things are under his personal control and I was astonished at the knowledge he displayed: I don't mean botanical lore, but about the history of the place. Every tree and shrub has been placed and planted by him for the place was bare upland when he bought it twenty years ago. Point to an oak or a maple and he will tell you precisely when it was planted, whence it was transplanted or whither it shall be moved in the autumn. It is only when among his shrubs and orchids that the nervous hands of Baron Ferdinand are at rest.

Youth

One night when our party had gone to bed I found myself alone with Mr Chamberlain in the billiard room, and we fell to talking about the monument to be erected in honour of Mr Gladstone. From that we proceeded to talk of Mr G and his work. Suddenly without warning, and certainly without provocation on my part Chamberlain poured forth invective with amazing freedom and warmth: I cannot remember all he said but he began by asking what policy Mr G had initiated. His finance was Peel's; Bright was the real father of Reform. The Test Acts did not originate with him, nor did Home Rule. Then Mr G supported measures of which it is notorious that he disapproved – local veto, and the attack upon the church in Wales . . .

'He never made a phrase that will live; he never wrote a book that has not been laughed out of print: and as for his foreign policy – well it was not mine.'

While admitting the personal charm of Mr G, Chamberlain has (doubtless) good cause for reminding me that on certain occasions, especially when Irish questions were being discussed, the 'aspect of the fiend took possession of Mr Gladstone's face': and of course it was Chamberlain who most frequently courted these angry flashes of gleaming wrath. 'It is his great age, and that alone which has called forth this mass of sentimentalism. When I was a younger man I felt that a centenarian Premier of Great Britain would be the most powerful autocrat of modern times: his influence would be twice that of Napoleon, four times that of Pitt when he first held office. It is the fullness of Mr Gladstone's years which has brought about this fatuous outburst of admiration: and your loyalty towards the Queen and my own is largely the outcome of this respect for ripe old age which I have always held to be the source of the greatest power in our land. The Duke of Wellington's influence was at its zenith when his age had become advanced and when his intellect had declined.'

Then followed a curious appreciation of Lord Beaconsfield 'whom I was brought up to hate, and whom I hated.' Chamberlain said frankly enough that his admiration of him would never be great, but that his respect for him was always increasing. He was the founder of Tory democracy; he could convey his meaning in a direct phrase, and he had a foreign policy . . . It was an interesting half hour and to some extent has changed my opinion about Joe.

22 JUNE 1898

In Westminster Abbey for the memorial service held for the friends of Burne-Jones: a terribly sad thing which made me cry very much. How great indeed is our loss! I remember Walter Pater telling me that although he was an enthusiastic admirer of Italian art he had to admit with reluctance that few of the old masters seem to have created beautiful faces for their own sake. In the Badia picture, and in the Magnificat one sees them: and I remember that as an instance of a face painted for sheer love of beauty he mentioned the head of the bishop in Romanino's big picture in our national collection. But these faces are rare in Italian art even though we grant that their standard and style of beauty differed widely from ours: indeed one may say that the bulk of these devotional pictures were first of all incentives to piety and then objects of beauty. Burne-Jones, in Walter Pater's mind, was one of the few men who painted faces solely for the joy of making them beautiful: in this he followed Rossetti whose type is displeasing to many, although it represents a consistent and sustained effort to produce something of intrinsic beauty. There was often something crude in Walter Pater's generalisations; but in this matter I am sure he was right – seven years ago he told me this – in 1891 – and I have never shown that the claim is unsound. No artist during the next fifteen, or perhaps twenty years will, on his death, carry with him such poignant regret as this blow has wrought among us: not Watts, not Verdi, not Puvis de Chavannes.

23 JUNE 1898

A dinner party in the H of C with Arthur Balfour; a dozen all told, quiet, orderly and decorous. I had the good fortune to sit by Frau Wagner now in London to hear the Ring. This is the second time I have seen her during this cycle – and I am more surprised than I can say at the difference between the Frau Meister at Baireuth, and plain Madame Wagner in London. There, she is queen, fearful lest the most slender display of human weakness should imperil her dynasty: so she is haughty, reticent, imperious. But in London where she has many friends and more admirers, one can see the woman: she laughs with vivacity, talks without ceasing; flies to a picture gallery in Knightsbridge, and speeds to Hampstead to take tea with an opera singer ... Enjoys herself, in a word is young again, very young. I am sure it must do her good to play with a race perhaps somewhat less phlegmatic than her own.

She is impressed with the performance of the Ring. Naturally enough the rendering does not satisfy her aspirations: but she is astonished at the intense enthusiasm of an audience, hot, uncomfortable, and ignorant of German: yet sitting through a long performance with patient zeal, and clamouring against the artist who ventures to omit scraps of his part. She anticipates an *immense* future for British music; holding that the emphatic protests against 'cutting' show a growing appreciation of perfect symmetrical art.

2–4 JULY 1898

At Highbury with the Chamberlains: orchids, marble, and unmarried daughters.

Chamberlain has refused to join the general committee of the national memorial to Gladstone: 'not without much thought, though without misgivings now that I have made up my mind. I shall doubtless be attacked, though that is immaterial: I should not escape adverse criticism if I had done otherwise.'

28 SEPTEMBER 1898

P. Landon[42] arrives ... Of news it is interesting to learn that Lord Rosebery is most anxious to marry Lady Egremont, widow of Lord E. who died quite recently: they are cousins to Landon and according to his judgment she is somewhat vulgar and would ruin a Foreign Office party.

[42] Perceval Landon (1869–1927) was a *Times* journalist.

Youth

To Whittingehame.

26 OCTOBER 1898
I imagine that tomorrow's Cabinet Council[43] will be the most critical held for some years: so an account of Arthur Balfour's preparation for it may be interesting. In bed till midday: then two hours golfing on the lawn. Biggish luncheon, and two hours walk with the 'squire's knife', an implement used for marking the doomed limbs of trees: tea and long talk: earlyish dinner and soon after nine we drove together to Dunbar.

Here we arrived with time on our hands and so we strolled down to the sea shore and watched greasy oily-looking little waves playing about in the moonlight.

We had berths opposite one another in the comfortable express and we slept well. But the First Lord talked freely about the prospects of the ritual controversy next session. His mind naturally tends towards mysticism and though opposed to aggravated ceremony he is equally disgusted at inaesthetic Protestantism. The small old-fashioned cathedral service is his ideal, tempered with the wide tolerance of a man who partakes of the sacrament both in the Anglican and Presbyterian Churches. Up till this moment he has avoided the literature of the controversy. 'I have one faculty of statesmanship, namely the power of taking a perfect holiday. I shall postpone the study of this question until the speeches are reprinted in pamphlet form. The Fashoda blue book I have not yet read: indeed it has not reached me. Rosebery can't sleep or eat in moderation owing to his impotence for holidaymaking. In this matter I am quite perfect! It is the first requirement of the public man.'

17 NOVEMBER 1898
Wigan worries me: as a family we have not done our duty by Wigan. We represent it in parliament now and then but that is not enough: indeed in some ways that scarcely counts as duty. The town is in a rotten condition. The police is proven corrupt: the sanitation is bad, the streets ill-lighted and muddy. Internecine fights on the Town Council; consequent jealousies and a total lack of co-operation. The Poor Law is disgracefully administered, there being almost as many outdoor paupers in this union as there are in Manchester.

Result that people won't live in Wigan: they go to Southport, Parbold, Gathurst, even Staffordshire. The grammar school is falling to bits. The streets are infested with beggars, who take up this occupation because the Guardians only dole out inadequate relief. So we have a decadent town – a decadent town! – whereas it should be prosperous, being situated on the highway to the North – and between Liverpool and Manchester: the centre moreover of coal and iron industries. I am

---

[43] On the Fashoda crisis, which brought Britain and France to the brink of war over an obscure African issue.

beginning to wonder whether it would not be well for me to give up my seat in parliament in order to join the Town Council and the Guardians. There is no doubt that the experience would be of much value and I believe that after a few years of energetic work great improvement could be effected. I think they would readily make me mayor and if I could keep the office for three or four years I could stifle the discreditable bickerings which generally end in a scene – or as the papers call it 'a breeze'. I should come to the work without ulterior motives: with no axe to grind, with no political aspirations; and by an impartial exercise of order it should be possible to purify the whole tone of the council. That done one might hope to begin purifying the tone of the borough and its general administration.

I can think of no work more profitable, and at the same time less gratifying. To be alternately patronised and objurgated by the average councillor of Wigan – illiterate and spiteful – heavens! what a prospect of bliss!

18 DECEMBER 1898

At Rome I met the advocate of the saints: it was in the crypt of St Peter's. The advocatus Diaboli belongs to Fame; but the man who argues on behalf of the saint (or proposed saint) is not so much heard of. His position is most lucrative for the congregation or diocese which aspires to a new beatification or sainthood is ready to incur large costs for the privilege of a fresh saint; that is a fresh source of income.

4 FEBRUARY 1899

At Peckforton, Lord Tollemache's[44] Cheshire seat. A most curious example of the British Peer: without brain capacity but not lacking a very distinct personality of his own. Our conversations on nonconformists and Eternity were interesting. Also our views on geography, 'I can't make out where Samoa is: I have been looking in the map but it must be an old edition – Samoa isn't marked. However I am now pretty sure that it is the capital of Siam.' Oh no, I said, it is an island in the Pacific ... 'But the Germans are there?' 'Yes,' I answered: and the reply was 'how the dooce did *they* get there?'

1 MARCH 1899

Lecky talked about the new life[45] of Parnell at dinner: not with much appreciation of its historical accuracy, but pleased that the work should have been printed as an instalment: though the man's cryptic nature and his hatred of committing what he thought to paper may render it useless for future biographers to try to add to the life. Lecky thinks superstition was the most notable feature in his character.

9 MARCH 1899

I met Miss Kate Greenaway, strange little rather winsome creature with an odd way

[44] The second Baron Tollemache (1832–1904), MP (Cons.) W. Cheshire 1872–85; succeeded his father 1890

[45] R. Barry O'Brien, *Life of Charles Stewart Parnell.*

of pronouncing her words. She writes once a week to Ruskin – has done so for years: and never gets an answer: though she well knows how sadly her correspondence would be missed were she to discontinue the practice. I liked this loyal affection which does not claim acknowledgment.

27 MARCH 1899

I told Lord Halifax[46] that it would be dangerous for him to speak in Lancashire. He proposed meetings at Stockport, Liverpool, and Manchester. I assured him that private meetings would cause misrepresentation and that he would undoubtedly get his head broken at a public gathering. No popery men are grand at storming a platform. After we had walked up and down Pall Mall six times he became so confidential that I had to tell him how deeply I regretted his precipitate and ill-considered action during the crisis.

22–4 APRIL 1899

Fowler[47] talked, exuded Radical history of the past ten years. Perhaps he guessed that my memory could not retain his pronounced opinions on Radical colleagues and their policy... then as to Mr Gladstone. Fowler said that nobody was more interested in the speech made by Fowler in proposing the Parish Councils Bill than Mr Gladstone himself. Mr G's mind was still full of Ireland and he had not had time or perhaps inclination to study the measure when under consideration by the Cabinet. 'Gladstone was as ignorant of my proposals as any member of the front opposition bench.'

And as to the House of Lords. Fowler says that if the Peers would dine in the gilded chamber one night a week their position would be enormously strengthened. There is much wisdom in the remark. If the country could be persuaded that the Peers really mean business and are ready to sacrifice their home comforts for public matters they would rise in popular estimation. But as things now are they seldom sit longer than an hour or two, making people think them distinguished dilettanti whose sole object is to hurry through their work.

5 MAY 1899

Ian Malcolm gave us lunch, Linkie, I, and Warkworth to meet Winston Churchill. Here is a coming man: pugnacious, obstinate and nervous – he cannot sit still. A curious halting shuffle in his voice which must make it difficult for an audience to hear him. Hugh Cecil's defence of slavery was disconcerting to Churchill who is not yet skilled in (or accustomed to) such forms of dialectics. There is a bumptiousness about him which will soon wear off – he isn't more than three and twenty. After that, if he will consent to be humble and obscure for a few years there is no reason

---

[46] Sir Charles Lindley Wood, second Viscount Halifax (1839–1934), leader of the extreme Anglo-Catholics. Militant 'Protestant' feeling was running high in the north, with outbreaks of violence.

[47] H. H. Fowler, first Viscount Wolverhampton (1830–1911), Liberal politician; president of the Board of Trade 1892–5, and the first Methodist to sit in the cabinet.

why he should not become a power in the land. In some ways he resembles his father closely. Altogether a bright and pleasant déjeuner.

17 MAY 1899

Edward Carson told me that the first time he ever saw the Queen was at the celebrations two years ago – He broke down – could not help crying: and what a tribute from the man who is the most pitiless prosecutor in the kingdom.

While still a parliamentary infant, Balcarres successfully undertook a measure of reform which both demonstrated his sureness of touch as a politician, and gave him a standing in the world of art administration which he was never to lose. His war against the South Kensington Museum of Science and Art (as it then was) was perhaps the bitterest conflict of his career. There were good reasons for this. The museum, part science, part art, was scattered around various temporary buildings, mostly far from fireproof, and was administered by 'certain engineers' whose main concern was not museum work at all, let alone art in particular, but the use of the Science and Art Department of the Privy Council, which ran South Kensington, to organise a national framework for secondary education in these fields. To some extent, therefore, the question as to what the great collections in the museum were for, had simply not been asked; but there were questions of maladministration which went well beyond mere apathy. Nepotism, sinecures, the purchase of forgeries, absence of cataloguing, employment of untrained staff – in these and other areas South Kensington made no attempt to maintain the standards of the day.

Balcarres could not count on much official support. Arthur Balfour was perhaps sympathetic. (When thanking him warmly for granting the inquiry, Balcarres went so far as to claim that 'I have been agitating for it incessantly during the past twelve months'.) With a young man's zeal, Balcarres even advocated a second inquiry to set up a central plan for all the great national collections. The responsible ministers, the Duke of Devonshire and his normally active vice-president, Sir John Gorst, were not helpful. The diarist reported a long private interview with the Duke, commenting 'Poor man, how he yawned!' Gorst, a natural reformer, was said by Balcarres to acknowledge the case against the museum but to be too indolent to take effective steps. This was somewhat unfair, as Gorst was immersed in major legislation in 1896, and from some time in 1897 had begun to devote his energies to plans, ultimately successful, for reorganising the whole school system under the local authorities.

When the committee began to meet, in March 1897, these differences of preoccupation soon became open antagonism, and in July Gorst resigned from its chairmanship. The committee did its work with great thoroughness, its meetings continuing into 1898, and its final report[48] *furnished a definitive account of an era in the life of the museum. The most*

---

[48] Science and Art, Select Committee: *Report from the Select Committee on the Museums of the Science and Art Department* ...; 1897 (H.C. 223), XII and (H.C. 341), XII; 1898 (H.C. 175), XI, and (H.C. 327), XI.

notable practical recommendation was that the science and art museums should be rehoused in different buildings on opposite sides of Exhibition Road, but the exposure of abuses was in itself a major achievement. Balcarres, with help from other members of the committee, from Arthur Balfour, and from the working-man radical John Burns, had laid the foundations for the modern Victoria and Albert Museum. The science museum developed as a separate entity, while the new art museum, rechristened by the Queen, was begun in 1899 and opened in 1909.

28 JULY 1898

Carried the report of the select committee on the museums of the Science and Art department. It has given me hard work during two whole sessions: my next objective must be to carry into effect some of the reforms we have suggested.

III

The downfall
of the Unionists,
1900–05

*Marriage – John Burns on Jews – Lord Roberts's weakness – Joseph
Chamberlain's table talk – impressions of Salisbury at home – the Duke of
Devonshire's failings – the King's unpopularity – becomes a Whip – Lord
Dudley's extravagance – cost of Bibliotheca Lindesiana – Joseph Chamberlain in
poor health – Lord Crewe's finances – the party goes to pieces – but partially
recovers – Balfour and the Dogger Bank incident – Balfour's neglect of
backbenchers – redistribution fiasco – Redmond woos Labour – Alec Hood's
popularity – personal plans – the Glamis ghosts.*

*In 1899 Balcarres set out on a tour of the far east, travelling across Siberia. His
departure was connected with his rejection by Miss Constance Pelly, a granddaughter of
old Lord Wemyss (1818–1914) who as Lord Elcho had led the Adullamites in 1866.
The obstacle in his path was unusual, and his despair profound. A rival kinswoman had
succeeded in persuading each of the pair that the other was acting only to oblige their own
relatives, and that each secretly wished to be released from their apparent intentions. It
took time and the determined intervention of aunts to bring about marriage on his return
in 1900.*

*Meanwhile the world of politics was passing through one of those periodic changes
which separate one political generation from another. The Conservative regime of Lord
Salisbury ceased to look inevitable and began to look merely old. The Boer war dragged
on from 1899 to 1902 without credit to the ministry. The 'khaki' election of 1900
produced a huge government majority but did not gain for ministers the confidence of
their supporters. In 1903, Chamberlain made a break for tariff reform from which the
Conservatives did not recover for a generation. From early 1904 the government was
living on its nerves. The balance of prejudice, of restiveness, of talent, was tilting towards
'democracy' – that vague word summarising the mixture of irresponsible politics and
economic spoliation which Conservatives had always feared in their picture of the future.
Balcarres was, with reservations, a Balfour man, and Balfour in turn marked him out for
office; but the diary describes, without illusions, the failure of a party that deserved to
fail.*

The downfall of the Unionists

After Balcarres became a Whip late in 1903, the diary assumed a more political tone. The hairbreadth escapes of 1904 and 1905, the apparent imminence of defeat and a general election throughout those two sessions, featured prominently. 1904 was the year when hope failed for the Conservatives.[1] Yet even in the apparent heyday of 1900–02, Balcarres was conscious of Unionist weakness, above all in people, and of the declining position of the United Kingdom.

Balcarres also began to figure as a statesman in the world of art. In 1900 he passed an Ancient Monuments Protection Act, in 1901 he became a Fellow of the Society of Antiquaries, in 1903 he became a founding father of the National Art-Collections Fund. As a trustee of the National Portrait Gallery, he obtained experience which later made him a formidable guardian of the British Museum and the National Gallery, and his comment, 'how well our Board works compared with that of the National Gallery' was to prove amply justified. His two books on renaissance sculpture showed him as scholar as well as connoisseur, and as a true Lindsay rather than a conventional party whip.

David Lindsay, the late Lord Crawford, and the first of eight children, was born in Edinburgh on 20 November 1900, commencing a family life of modest and uneventful happiness. By happy coincidence, the child was christened in the episcopal cathedral on the day the second marriage of his great-grandfather Lord Wemyss was announced; and at a family gathering the infant had the unusual pleasure of meeting his great-grandfather's mother-in-law. Queen Victoria was much pleased to learn of David's birth.

'Diaries and married life disagree' noted the writer in 1901, and certainly the Balcarres of the Edwardian period was not the inveterate diner-out that he became in the 1920s. In any case, from 1903 to 1913 his duties as a Whip required him to spend every evening of the session in the House, a practice that decidedly sharpened his natural awareness of human frailty. It should perhaps be noted that the fastidious Balcarres had chosen an even more fastidious wife, religious, even mystical, in a way that he was not, somewhat hypochondriacal, and definitely not of common clay. The African explorer Sir Harry Johnston was seen as 'such a common little man' and Seddon, the New Zealand premier, as 'rather common-place and noisy'. Even Rodin, who rather improbably was found at lunch with Mr Justice Darling, appeared 'just like a good middle class Free Kirk elder'. (Middle class is one of the diarist's most pejorative terms; a ministerial dinner given by Austen Chamberlain was condemned as 'a most foul and greasy meal – expensive, ostentatious, middle class, and uneatable'.) Folly may be recorded unwittingly, as when Albert Grey, just back from Rhodesia, proclaimed in March 1900 that the Boers were too sensible to go on fighting with no prospect of gain. Others who figured without credit were Maurice Baring, 'the worst-mannered man I know', Lord Portsmouth, on account of his 'foul and offensive conversation', Eustace Balfour who habitually overdrank, and Curzon, 'worn out with fatigue, and inexpressibly common' whose return to parliament after India was regarded without

---

[1] The loss of the Ayr Burghs (30 January 1904) first made the probable date of dissolution the dominant topic of speculation. Setbacks in 1903 could still be explained by local factors, e.g. in Woolwich by publicans' annoyance, and in Rye by a tactless choice of candidate.

pleasure in the Whips' room. ('Lord, how we will bore him, and he, us!') In contrast, the future George V was 'absolutely bent down with grief' in the Lords on the death of Queen Victoria.

Three small pieces of inside information may also be mentioned here. One MP[2] claimed to have spent £50,000 on his constituency; while at a Chamberlain dinner party,[3] twenty-five men subscribed £22,500 to the Tariff Reform League. An early case of censorship is mentioned: the author of a book on the far east submitted his proofs to the Foreign Office, who excised all references to recent massacres there by a friendly power.[4]

None of these comments arose from Balcarres' experience as Whip, about which he gave away few secrets. We do however learn that the new Conservative agent, Captain Wells, was 'singularly haphazard' and that his offhand and unbusinesslike methods' led to many complaints – and this with an election looming.[5] Party renegades like Seely[6] and Churchill were liable to invidious comment. In Seely's case, the diarist recalled that his vanity, his ruling vice, had led him to commit an action during the Boer war which caused him to be put under arrest – a curious entrée into the limelight for a future war minister. The hostility of another malcontent, Spenser Wilkinson, the military theorist and a leader-writer on the Morning Post *from 1895 to 1914, was explained in terms of his disappointment at not being made secretary to the Committee of Imperial Defence.[7]*

About three very personal objects of dislike, Esher, Rosebery and Winston Churchill, the diarist was irrational, but probably representative of average Conservative opinion. Hating Rosebery's 'moody grandiloquence', the diarist deplored his retirement to a Neapolitan villa and pronounced that 'such an unreliable personage' had neither the physical nor the mental stability to lead a great party. The diaries testify that it was Rosebery the man, and not his policies, that prevented ordinary Conservatives from wanting anything to do with his fishing in troubled waters.

Esher was disliked as a 'whisperer', and perhaps as a decadent. He was not seen as an energetic moderniser; Esher, the diarist was told by the two senior men on the Public Accounts Committee, was the most incompetent official who ever had to explain his departmental finance.[8] If suspicion about Esher arose from the very quietness of his modus operandi, *the opposite was true of Churchill, whose inability to fade into the background socially compounded his political delinquencies. In addition, the Edwardian Churchill 'spouting as usual in his vain and priggish manner'[9] was apt to present his*

[2] J. Bigwood, MP (Cons.) Brentford, Middlesex 1886–1906; diary, 14 July 1904, when Bigwood had been returned unopposed since 1892.

[3] Diary, 28 July 1904.

[4] Charles Clive Bigham, later second Viscount Mersey, *A Year in China, 1899–1900* (London, Macmillan, 1901).

[5] Diary, 16 February 1904.

[6] J. E. B. Seely, first Baron Mottistone (1868–1947); served in S. Africa, winning DSO, 1900–01; MP, Isle of Wight 1900–06; resigned his seat and was re-elected unopposed as a dissident Unionist, April 1904; Secretary of State for War, 1912–14, resigning after Curragh mutiny.

[7] Diary, 31 October 1904.

[8] 26 April 1904.

[9] 7 March 1902.

differences with Tory orthodoxy as a moral issue, an approach rather ill-matched with his naked appetite for power.

The prime minister's health and spirits were a subject of repeated discussion. When Chamberlain ran amok in 1903 over tariff reform, Balfour 'looked ten years older than he did a month ago' and was 'evidently much depressed'.[10] *In 1904, after a gruelling session, he was simply 'very tired',*[11] *despite illness early in the year; but in 1905, something more than fatigue entered into comments. Early in the session Miss Balfour thought her brother was very well, but Evan Charteris thought another twelve months in office would kill him.*[12] *In the spring Balfour 'was very seedy and appears to be in pain'.*[13]

If Balfour's spirits drooped, Asquith, the life and soul of any select Unionist dinner table, was often at hand to provide affable stimulation.[14] *Whether the host was Harry Cust, or Lord Robert Cecil or the Cowpers, and whatever the strains of current controversy, Asquith was to be found 'filling his skin with champagne' or 'quite drunk on several occasions',*[15] *quite at ease in a Unionist country house in the company of Austen Chamberlain, even at the peak of his campaign against Austen's father. The private Asquith of 1904, as glimpsed by Balcarres, is not very different from the Asquith of 1924. No other figure of the period was linked by the diarist with undue indulgence in drink; the trait was distinctive even in 1904.*

During the early 1900s the patriarchal position of the Crawford family in their part of Lancashire had hardly begun to change. Without seeking to be, they were naturally cast in the role of a local royal family. Old Lord Crawford lived in a scholar's world of books, astronomy and philately, but the tradition went on regardless. The Haigh estate was a poachers' paradise for Wigan working-men. The park was used for manoeuvres by the Church Lads' Brigade. Even the prospective decline of the Wigan pits, and the successful opening up of a new coalfield in Nottinghamshire to see the family company through the twentieth century, had little effect on the family part in local junketings. The sheer numbers involved in local ritual are now something of a surprise. When Lady Crawford opened the technical college in Wigan, five thousand assembled for the occasion; when Balcarres gave away prizes at Bolton technical school, there were two thousand present. Beneath these grand gatherings there was a lower level of more miscellaneous functions where the presence of a Lindsay was indispensable: smoking concerts in working-men's clubs, meetings on church reform, presiding over a lecture on Ruskin, lecturing (by Balcarres) on 'Old and new fiction' to Chorley Literary Society. If there was an element of potential dissidence in Balcarres' constituency, it would have come from popular protestantism. When in 1900 Balcarres was elected unopposed for the third

[10] 11 and 16 June 1903.
[11] 4 August 1904.
[12] 10 February 1905.
[13] 27 May 1905.
[14] E.g. 9 March 1900, 26 June 1900, 16 June 1903.
[15] Diary, 20 November 1904.

time running, he noted 'they would make a formidable contest by running a no-popery man'.

HAIGH. 3 MARCH 1900

Since the last entry in my journal I have crossed two oceans and three continents: and my beloved has become my wife.

And while I am thus ten years older I have grown twenty years younger.

7 MARCH 1900

I got the second reading of my Ancient Monuments Protection Bill, being warmly congratulated by all parties in the House.[16]

30 MARCH 1900

I was today moved to make a speech in the House of Commons – my first attempt. Sixteen minutes, a thin House just before dinner time, and people were good enough to say that I interested them.

6 APRIL 1900

T. W. Russell,[17] in order to convince me of the material benefits arising out of the Queen's visit to Dublin, tells me that the present week alone will cause an increase in the net profits of his hotel of no less than £250.

At Easter, Balcarres took his bride home to Haigh, where she liked the books but was dismayed by the haunting blackness of the Wigan landscape, with its 'bituminous trees, Cimmerian grass, ebony leaves'. His constituents, irrespective of politics, subscribed to present a massive silver gift. In the hope of ensuring beauty in 'this dark smoky place' at least during the spring, thirty thousand wood hyacinths were planted in surrounding woods.

3 MAY 1900

A very interesting talk with St John Brodrick[18] about the Congo Free State and the action of the Belgian officials (according to St John, and he ought to know). Atrocities which are without parallel abound throughout this region particularly in connexion with the India rubber trade and the blame for all this rests ultimately with the King of the Belgians.

[16] Steered through the Lords by Lord Avebury (formerly Lubbock), the genial inventor of bank holidays, who also appears in the diaries as a notorious last minute absentee from meetings of the Society of Antiquaries at which he was due to preside.

[17] Thomas W. Russell, MP Tyrone South 1886–January 1910, Tyrone North October 1911–18; at this time a Liberal Unionist, later a Liberal; an insurance agent and temperance hotel proprietor in Dublin; son of a Fife stonemason.

[18] St John Brodrick, first Earl of Midleton (1856–1942), Under-Secretary for Foreign Affairs, 1898–1900; Secretary of State for War 1900–03; held junior posts at War Office 1886–92, 1895–8.

The downfall of the Unionists

A Nationalist member tells me that a million is estimated to have been spent in Dublin alone during the Royal visit – a sum, that is to say, of a million in excess of the ordinary expenditure of the period.

22 JUNE 1900

In the afternoon Connie and I went to Hertford House, where a large party invited by Alfred Rothschild and Rosebery assembled to meet the Prince of Wales. The number of Jews in this palace was past belief. I have studied the anti-semite question with some attention, always hoping to stem an ignoble movement: but when confronted by the herd of Ickleheimers and Puppenbergs, Raphaels, Sassoons, and the rest of the breed, my emotions gain the better of logic and justice, while I feel some sympathy for Lüger and Drumont – John Burns, by the way, says the Jew is the tapeworm of civilization.

26 JUNE 1900

The Duke of Westminster has been sent to the Base by Lord Roberts for disobedience. The Duke of Marlborough has been warned that he is in danger of being sent home. It is curious that a man like Lord Roberts should allow his wife to nominate all his aides-de-camp. Kerry, Stanley, Downe, Gerard, two dukes, a Bruce and I don't know how many more – peers or peers to be all of them. In India Roberts and Her Ladyship were known as 'Bobs and Jobs' a very apt term. The misfortune of course is that these men are not going to make the army their career; so that the immense educational value of these positions is lost to those men who in time to come will be our generals.

19 OCTOBER 1900

...St John Brodrick spent the morning with us [*in Edinburgh*] and lunched; we talked about reconstruction of the government and he seems to think there will be uncommonly little – not that he or anybody else denies its urgent necessity; but that Lord Salisbury shrinks from doing something unpleasant. No doubt it must be a distasteful function to tell a hulk like Chaplin or an ass like George Hamilton, or an old woman like Jesse Collings, that their offices should be vacated; but if Lord Salisbury is afraid to incur the unpleasant process of sacking his subordinates – well he should scarcely take upon himself the responsibility of forming a government. His business is to form a strong government and to hold it together. If he fails in the first duty the catastrophe of discontent will swiftly bring the government to an end. For my part I believe Lord Salisbury is still strong enough to insist upon reconstruction: I hope so. If he is as weak as our opponents claim, we shall muddle along in our old groove and the country will grow tired of us very soon.

2 NOVEMBER 1900

St John Brodrick and Selborne[19] to the War Office and Admiralty; Lansdowne to

[19] William Waldegrave Palmer, second Earl of Selborne (1859–1942); MP 1885–95; succeeded father, Gladstone's Lord Chancellor, 1895; Under-Secretary for colonies 1895–1900, first lord of Admiralty

the Foreign Office. The latter is said to be well-suited to his post as he can talk French and is good-mannered; as if these two squirmy qualities are needed in a diplomatist who has also force... St John and Selborne will do their work well enough, but they are scarcely first class men for positions of such first rate importance. St John in particular is faced at the outset by the fact that for ten years he has defended the existing staff and system. Selborne, whose business capacity I have often admired at the Church Defence Committee, will not have so difficult a task, though I think the admiralty also needs the stern hand of a bold reformer.

I have been deluged by hysterical telegrams and letters from Miss Marie Corelli whose wrath, righteous in this case, has been aroused by the proposal of Sir Theodore Martin[20] to erect as a pendant to Shakespeare's monument at Stratford-on-Avon, a bas-relief of Lady Martin, his deceased wife, who was an actress of some note. It would indeed be a disfigurement if the idea were carried out, for Helen Faucit is far from deserving of so high an honour.

8 NOVEMBER 1900

The new ministerial appointments are announced this morning... Arnold-Forster[21] I suppose has earned promotion, and he has studied naval problems: but the man's nature is acidulous and he is not popular in the house... George Wyndham[22] will not find a bed of roses at Dublin, and he will scarcely have the force of his predecessor: but he will follow in those lines, and at the end of his term of office will be as unpopular among the Unionist fry of the calibre of Saunderson, Abercorn, Ardilaun etc., as G.W.B. is at the present moment: and if the government lasts five years, George Wyndham will be white-haired at the time of the dissolution.

14 DECEMBER 1900

Travelled to London with Sir George Kekewich[23] with whom I had a long and interesting talk on educational matters. He told me that he never saw Gorst or the Duke of Devonshire more often than twice a month, the latter seldom so often. There is danger of complete stagnation.

29 DECEMBER 1900

We had two days covert shooting[24]... St John Brodrick shot both days, and the

---

1900-05; High Commissioner for South Africa 1905-10; president, Board of Agriculture, 1915-16, resigning over Ireland, and did not again hold office. For further descriptions, see below, 3 March 1905, 4 March 1911.

[20] Martin (1816-1909), the biographer of the Prince Consort, was a trustee of Shakespeare's birthplace, 1889-1909. Helen Faucit became Mrs Martin in 1851, and died in 1898.

[21] H. O. Arnold-Forster (1855-1909), Secretary of the Admiralty 1901-3, Secretary for War 1903-5.

[22] George Wyndham (1863-1913), Chief Secretary for Ireland 1900-05; forced to resign, 1905, by resentment at his attempts to conciliate Irish Catholic opinion.

[23] Sir G. W. Kekewich (1841-1921), secretary of Board of Education, 1900-03.

[24] At Gosford, seat of Lord Wemyss.

rest will do him good. The meeting of parliament naturally meant hard work – he has averaged seventeen hours a day and looked worn out. Arthur Balfour's opinion of his capabilities is growing much, and his view is that if any man can reform the army it is St John . . . He has a heavy hand: no lightness of touch, few gleams of humour, and he is growing deaf: but he has courage . . .[25]

For my own part the position in which I find myself, and the prospects of further work of a parliamentary nature must involve controversy and bitterness: perhaps also obloquy and recrimination. That is the essential basis of our system, and it is a state of things which none but the giant or the genius can hope to modify. I therefore accept it in full measure, trusting that here and there some good may supervene, or that some catastrophe may be averted. For we face catastrophe: we may be on the eve of changes in our imperial status of which it is impossible to guess the ultimate results. Our commercial supremacy is doomed; our commercial pre-eminence will be irrevocably lost before our boy goes to school. Yet we have enjoyed a great and in many ways a most glorious century.

1 AUGUST 1901
Father tells me he is going to sell the manuscripts: under rather curious conditions. The price he is to receive is undoubtedly high, but the real fact is that he has become tired of his books and takes neither pride nor pleasure in them.[26]

9 AUGUST 1901
The First Lord [27] looks fagged out. The session has of course been trying but the unchanging burden of anxiety caused by the war has contributed most of all to his care. Chamberlain on the other hand seems to grow fresher and more youthful every day:[28] truly a wonderful man.

. . . The Nationalists are dead beat. I went through the 'no' Lobby and found them lying about on the benches, absolutely exhausted. Last night they were drinking very hard and had not the courage to begin again this evening. Unhappily we cannot profit by their lassitude, as the Blenheim garden party makes it impossible to hold a really late sitting.

29 OCTOBER 1901
To Whittingehame. Arthur Balfour, Gerald Balfour, William Holdsworth, Findlay owner of the *Scotsman*, J. Chamberlain. Wives, daughters, a party of twenty all told.
Some of Chamberlain's conversation and aphorisms.
l) No working man is really the better for being able to read and write.

[25] Within a year his wife, Lady Hilda Brodrick, died. Connie, her first cousin, said that nobody fully realised how great was the assistance she gave her husband.
[26] Balcarres considered this a disastrous decision.
[27] Arthur Balfour
[28] The diarist soon afterwards wrote (22 January 1902) 'the opinion grows that Chamberlain's speech on Monday represents the highest level in debate and statesmanship to which he has hitherto attained'.

2) Talking of the quotation from Dryden or Pope (nobody knows its source) which he made in his recent speech at Edinburgh: 'A quotation is most valuable, I often invent them and nobody is a bit the wiser'.

3) A.J.B. talking of the financial troubles of foreign countries. 'I wish all foreign nations to be prosperous and every foreign government to be in financial straits'. J.C. 'I quite agree with you, but I don't know with which foreign nation to begin'.

4) 'I believe our commercial position to be good, for we are doing more business and making more money than at any period of our history. I however consider it more patriotic when making speeches on the subject to take a humbler line, and to say that things will not always go so well with us – unless you subscribe to the Birmingham University'.

5) 'A man came to see me about this University. He had attended a meeting at Devonshire House called by the Duke to raise funds for Cambridge. My visitor said the Duke made a very sensible speech but the professors were deplorably stupid and dull. He left without subscribing the £50,000 he thereupon gave me for Birmingham. The gift is anonymous, and if I am not mistaken there is still more to come. So far as I know the man had never spent an hour in Birmingham'.

21 DECEMBER 1901

[*At Hatfield*] . . . Lord Salisbury at meals is delightful. He eats largely and between whiles fires off amusing comments and questions. At breakfast, having come home from his daily tricycle ride he was most entertaining about the bones of St Edmund and said that if his advice had been asked he would have suggested sending the relics to the Royal College of Surgeons in order to ensure that they were of human origin 'which would have saved them all the ugly scandals which resulted from the damaging attacks made by a gentleman who is an expert on cattle and pigs'.

All over the park are footpaths covered with asphalt along which the premier takes his rides. These paths have been made at enormous labour and expense, deep cuttings having been made in order to reduce the smallest hills to tolerably level tracks. There is one cutting nearly a hundred yards long and ten foot deep, contrived to remove a little hill – which was only ten foot high! – four or five hundred tons of gravel had to be disposed of! He thoroughly enjoys his exercise and is always in terror lest he be ambushed by some of the numerous grandchildren who all think him fair game. Recently at Beaulieu two of them were found by their mother on a wall above his Lordship's favourite walk, where they were awaiting his arrival with two huge jugs of water.

22 MARCH 1902

A *bon mot* of Lord Salisbury's: 'I must really learn to play bridge because I want to get to know the Duke of Devonshire'.

10 APRIL 1902

A lot of our men are getting restive about these new procedure rules holding that the

The downfall of the Unionists

Conservative party is forging fetters by which we shall be mercilessly bound when the Radicals come into office. After all we have more to fear from legislation than we have to gain by it. Our programme is of necessity of moderate, even of scanty proportions and we need not or should not hasten unduly to carry into effect our good schemes. On the other hand our opponents on regaining power will harry and harass us at every turn and we shall groan beneath the rules which give the Executive such an increased power.

19 APRIL 1902

Three stories of the Duke of Devonshire:

1) At a Cabinet Council, the question of Manchuria was discussed – having been considered by the Cabinet for weeks previously as the problem was really acute. G. W. Balfour got up and went to a map of China, and was joined by the Duke, who asked innocently 'where *is* Manchuria?'

2) The late Queen first imparted her idea of visiting Ireland to the Duke, and directed him to tell Lord Salisbury and to enlist his sympathy. A few days later the premier became minister-in-waiting at Osborne and the Queen said to him, 'What do you think of my little plan?' Completely mystified, Lord S. told her that he had heard nothing about it, and it then transpired that the whole question had eluded the memory of the Noble Duke.

3) A few days ago Dudley[29] drove up Pall Mall to dine at Devonshire House. His carriage had to stop opposite St James's Palace, and he noticed that the King passed him. Following the Royal Carriage up St James's Street and into Piccadilly he was horrified (being dressed in a sort of smoking jacket) to see it precede him into Devonshire House. He and the King met in the hall where the servants received them with surprise – for the Duke of Devonshire was not at home. After 35 minutes' delay, he was rooted out of the Turf Club hard by, and confessed that he had completely forgotten having invited His Majesty to dinner. The King was much annoyed, and retaliated upon Dudley whom he rebuked for dining out a week after his *grrr*eat-aunt had died – a fact which in his turn Dudley had quite overlooked.

In a few years time we shall have a solemn and pompous biography of the Duke of Devonshire, portraying him as the ideal landlord, minister and host!

5 JUNE 1902

This afternoon in the Lords, the Prime Minister moved the vote of thanks to our soldiers. He is a failing even a passed man. I was astounded, and greatly shocked.

15 JUNE 1902

A growing anxiety about the private life of the King becomes manifest. The other

[29] William Ward, second Earl of Dudley (1867–1932), Lord-Lieutenant of Ireland, 1902–5, Governor-General of Australia, 1908–11; declared in November 1902 that Ireland should be governed in accordance with Irish ideas; pardoned the Maamtrasna murderers of the 1880s; see also under 7 December 1903.

66

night when going to the Opera there were cries of 'where's Alice?'[30]: the box at the Abbey to be filled by his friends is called the 'Loose Box' and preachers are beginning to inveigh against his racing proclivities. It is the saddest pity, for already much has been forgiven him.

16 JUNE 1902
It is told that the King presented his most recent photograph to Lord Salisbury; who took it in his hand and murmured foggily 'Poor old Buller'.

21 JUNE 1902
... On all sides one hears that he [the King] is growing less popular. At Aldershot they called out 'King of the Jews' – and if his patronage is meted out so much to the Hebrews his action will be bitterly resented. There is much dormant anti-semitism, specially against its prevalence in Park Lane and Grosvenor Square.

24 JUNE 1902
The King was operated on this morning. All is postponed.

25 JUNE 1902
... A singular incident between 5 and 6 this morning, the flag above Buckingham Palace slipped downwards and for some time remained at half mast. The public seems scarcely to realise that the King's condition is critical.

16 OCTOBER 1902
... Harcourt seems much stronger than during the summer; I had a word with him and was pleased to find him in better voice and spirits than previously. A fine blustering humbug of an English gentleman: his defects ensure unstinted popularity – on our side of the House.

28 DECEMBER 1902
... I continue to be occupied by my projected essay on Donatello[31]: a most fascinating theme, rendered all the more interesting from the fact that no book, excepting a popular handbook which quotes no authorities, has been published in English on the subject. At the same time the problems are difficult as much controversy as to ascriptions seems to have been raised by foreign critics.

5 APRIL 1903
Shaw-Lefevre[32] told me that he composed the inscription for Lord Beaconsfield's statue, and having done so asked the opinion of Lord Wemyss who suggested that after the words 'twice Prime Minister' he should add 'and once a lawyer's clerk'.

[30] Mrs Keppel
[31] *Donatello* (London, Duckworth, 1903).
[32] G. J. Shaw-Lefevre (1831–1928), first Baron Eversley of the second creation: Chief Commissioner of Works, 1880–04, 1892–4.

The downfall of the Unionists

The political situation is still nebulous. Chamberlain however is still hard at work proselytising. I am still on the fence, with strong inclination to come down on Joe's side; not on the ground of popularity for that is more than doubtful – but because I don't see how we can continue to lie down.

7 JULY 1903
Presided at the inaugural meeting of what is to be a great museum league.[33]

24 JULY 1903
Dinner with Lady Elcho. Prime Minister there: we all went on to the Palace Theatre and saw biograph pictures of the Irish motor race: also a wonderful conjuror.

9 OCTOBER 1903
Received a telegram from Arthur Balfour offering me a Junior Lordship of the Treasury with the responsibility of representing H.M. Office of Works in the H. of C. Assuming the telegram to be genuine I accepted the offer. I was tempted by the Office of Works bait: without it, I should have declined.[34]

Balcarres resigned his seat on taking office, as was then obligatory, and stood for re-election. After three unopposed returns, this was his first contest, and his majority of 1,428 was better than expected. He made thirty-three speeches, three at collieries and one at a Wesleyan bazaar.

5 NOVEMBER 1903
Let me record by the way that a girl of 12 or 13, Polly something – very ill-kempt and dishevelled, hoarse with cheering, followed me wherever I went in Chorley – she managed to keep close to my motor car, and rode for miles on the step – in the middle of sometimes three and even four thousand people. She never lost her place – and finally after the result was declared, I again found her at my coat tails, and she whispered in a harsh and raucous voice 'We've got you in': – a dear child – the most pleasing episode of the contest.

7 DECEMBER 1903
Lady Cowper half in amusement, half indignant tells us that Dudley[35] came to stay

---

[33] See *Twenty-Five Years of The National Art-Collections Fund 1903–1928* (Glasgow, 1928) for an account of this body, which was formed chiefly to resist the great US collectors. At this initial private meeting Balcarres accepted the chairmanship, which he held until 1921, although he was not the originator of the project. The first open meeting 'went very well, but mean jealousies and spites were apparent' (diary, 11 November 1903). The NACF was a success, membership rising from 550 in 1904 to 7,000 in 1928; its first great purchase was the Rokeby Venus by Velazquez (1906). The first painting purchased by the fund, a Watteau, went with fine disinterestedness to the National Gallery of Ireland.

[34] Having been the youngest MP, Balcarres now became the youngest minister in the Commons.

[35] See above, 19 April 1902. By 1905 Dudley sought to resign because of his financial straits, having been twice writted by Irish tradesmen. Dudley was perhaps as much sinned against as sinning; when

at Panshanger a short time ago (without his wife). He brought one valet, one footman, one loader, one chauffeur, one hairdresser, one chiropodist – six in total. It is infamous conceit and vanity. I suppose the Viceregal household in Ireland is equipped on this scale of magnificence.

17 JANUARY 1904

After some labour, I today concluded an elaborate calculation as to the cost of the Bibiliotheca Lindesiana. The estimate is of course approximate only but probably gives a fair statement of the financial position of the Library. The years are from 1851 to 1900 inclusive. During this period, cash has been spent to the amount of:

	£135,000
Interest (simple at 3%)	£85,000
	£220,000

It is quite fair to include interest in the outlay, as expenditure on books represents the only investment made by my family during the last half century.

Against this cost we have received, by sale in 1887 (with interest at same rate):

	£28,000
by sale of MSS and interest	£159,000
	£187,000

20 JANUARY 1904

The death of Arthur Strong[36] is a sad and serious loss to me. I grieve for his wife, but the blow is so personal to myself that I look at the matter from my own point of view. I owed him much; he certainly was responsible for the invitation I received to write on Donatello: and he was anxious for me to begin research for a work of more ambitious character. I now lose the one and only friend to whom I would instinctively turn for profound criticism and farseeing advice. I have lots of other 'friends' but I would not even care to ask their advice on any but commercial or political problems. Poor Strong: for years he nearly starved, and now that he is courted, the retribution of past privations comes home to him, and he succumbed to weakness engendered long ago.

Lady Dudley had an operation for appendicitis in autumn 1902, the fees came to £1,700, including 500 guineas to a London surgeon who came over too late to operate, and 100 guineas to the Court doctor for holding Lady Dudley's hand while going off under the anaesthetic. For Dudley's naive lavishness in Ireland, see the account by his private secretary, Sir Lionel Earle, *Turn Over the Page*, pp. 49–57.

[36] Strong was librarian at Chatsworth. An ardent appreciation of him by the diarist appears in Sandford A. Strong, *Critical Studies and Fragments. With a memoir by Lord Balcarres* (1905).

The downfall of the Unionists

2 FEBRUARY 1904

Consternation at Balfour's illness; it is assumed he will be absent for eight to ten days. If he returns to work prematurely he is bound to break down again later on . . . As for Austen Chamberlain's reply,[37] I confess I was alarmed at his manifest weakness and vacillation. He was perilously near a breakdown. Many indeed will actually say that he failed. Akers-Douglas[38] is nominally leading the House, but is incapable of replying to a general debate.

3 FEBRUARY 1904

. . . Austen's speech last night was a marked and notable failure. We have made an ill-omened debut. People discuss an Easter dissolution.

The following are those who can be counted on to vote against us on all occasions: T. Gibson Bowles, J. Dickson Poynder, W. Churchill, T. W. Russell, Wood (Down), Mitchell (Tyrone), Wilson (Falkirk), Wilson (Worcester). The following will soon do likewise: E. Beckett, Hugh Cecil, Ivor Guest, Sir J. Gorst, Seely, Crawford Smith, George Kemp (?), Lambton (?)

5 FEBRUARY 1904

Chamberlain's speech[39] last night was a remarkable performance in many ways. He had been subjected to acrimonious personal attack throughout the debate, and finally replied in a highly controversial spirit. He made good points, and turned the flank of his opponents with customary skill . . . Our men cheered C. a good deal, and certainly gave him a magnificent reception.

On the other hand it is obvious that he has aged. Anxiety or overwork is beginning to tell upon his physique: his colour, a luminous sallow hue, does not connote good health, while a certain hesitation in the selection of words, and an occasional lack of grammatical construction, showed that preoccupation or excitement were disconnecting the structure of his remarks. Finally I heard it said that 'Joe has lost his parliamentary manner' – that is to say his speech was more (than ever) suited to the platform than to the green benches. This criticism is not altogether just: yet it is so far accurate that some of the old stagers say a thorough holiday is imperative, or else he may lose the ear of the House.

6 FEBRUARY 1904

Asquith is dismayed at the brilliancy of Campbell-Bannerman's speeches. He says that if this standard is maintained, it will be impossible to send CB to the Lords.[40]

---

[37] A defensive and uncertain speech, much interrupted, in the debate on the Address.

[38] Aretas Akers-Douglas, first Viscount Chilston (1851–1926), Conservative Chief Whip 1885–95; First Commissioner of Works 1895–1902; Home Secretary, 1902–5; Viscount, 1911; see Lord Chilston, *Chief Whip: the political life and times of Aretas Akers-Douglas, first Viscount Chilston* (1961), which made him the only chief whip to be the subject of a modern historical study based on private papers, the present work apart.

[39] An aggressive justification of government policy over the South African war.

[40] The standard was perhaps not maintained: 'C.B. seems to have lost his memory or his nerve' (diary, 29 March 1904).

11 FEBRUARY 1904

We estimate our majority on Monday at 46.[41] Many Nationalists would like to support the government being fair traders, but their wirepullers are too strong.

13 FEBRUARY 1904

There is no doubt that Chamberlain is in much less vigorous health than most people imagine. He suffers much from neuritis in the head; and I question if his holiday will make him well again.

...Went to Osborne to see how the House looks after being filled up as a convalescent home for naval and military officers. The statuary and paintings are simply grotesque: fancy if the Prince Consort had been a man of taste! Vast sums have been squandered – thousands of pounds spent yearly I should imagine – up to his death. A connoisseur would have easily made the finest collection in Europe with such an outlay at his command.

22 FEBRUARY 1904

Alfred Lyttelton made another speech on Chinese labour:[42] able in its way but marred by a certain asperity of voice which is not borne out by his smiling countenance. The result is that the newspaper men think his remarks virulent and acrimonious, whereas members in the house itself (to whom he addresses himself exclusively), see by his face that he does not mean to be disagreeable. Hence the divergence of criticism between M.P.s and journalists.

25 FEBRUARY 1904

A snap division immediately after the dinner adjournment nearly ended the career of the Government. We had anticipated the coup – Robert Spencer[43] had been urging his men to attend at 9 p.m. sharp: (he told Herbert Gladstone nothing about the scheme). But our boys disregarded the warning and we were nearly beaten...
Acland-Hood[44] furious; but also rather amused at the disappointment of the

[41] John Morley's free trade amendment to the Address was defeated 327–276, majority 51, on Monday 15 February. Akers-Douglas, winding up for the government, pledged it to oppose any duty on raw material or food, thus making a fairly successful bid for Unionist free trader support. Balfour was absent ill, and Chamberlain stayed away following the death of his friend Powell Williams. The outbreak of the Russo–Japanese war, known on 7 February, may have helped the government.

[42] Alfred Lyttelton (1857–1913), Colonial Secretary 1903–5, who sanctioned the use of Chinese coolies in the Rand gold mines, 1904.

[43] Charles Robert, sixth Earl Spencer (1857–1922), Liberal MP and junior Whip; half-brother of the fifth Earl, the Liberal statesman, whom he succeeded in 1910; created Viscount Althorp, 1905.

[44] Sir Alexander Fuller-Acland-Hood, fourth Baronet and first Baron St. Audries (1853–1917); educ. Eton and Balliol; m. daughter of fourth Lord Ventry (owned 93,000 acres in Kerry); army officer 1875–92, Capt. Grenadier Guards 1885–92; succ. father, 1892; MP (Cons.) Somerset W. 1892–1911; junior Whip 1900–02, Chief Whip 1902–11; created peer, 22 June 1911, not in *DNB*. The family estate in Somerset consisted of 11,000 acres producing £17,000 gross rental in 1873. Hood's papers in Somerset Record Office do not include any significant material relating to his career as Whip.

The downfall of the Unionists

opposition: 'If I were Radical whip I would put this damned government out of office in a fortnight'.

3 MARCH 1904
Acland-Hood is furious at the desire of country constituencies to have semitic candidates – Van Raalte, Marks, Ashley, Van Laun, and so forth, in preference to good old-fashioned Tory country gentlemen. There is an idea that two general elections will occur during the next three years, which in itself is enough to alarm the average man with modest income. But our party will suffer severely through this cosmopolitan type of candidate, not to mention the prospects of corruption which are involved. Thus Van Raalte, now standing for Dorsetshire speaks English as broken and foreign as is that of Strauss or Gustav Wolff. The number of Jews in Parliament is considerable, but as a rule they represent towns which does not signify so much.

6 MARCH 1904
After a month of the session I can perhaps generalise to the extent of saying that the work is less arduous or at least more interesting than I anticipated. A whip's duties are manifold, including much that is of necessity tedious, such as guarding the door, and the need of being on the spot during the whole parliamentary day. But whipping is not so monotonous or colourless as most people think: certainly during these critical times much depends on the skill with which the whips (to whom much is told in confidence) can influence the hesitating or recalcitrant member. The strain is, however, great, and I am tired out every night. It is not a job for an excitable or passionate temperament. Coolness and perhaps also something akin to nonchalance are required. Harry Forster[45] is I think the best of the crew, though he is handicapped by an unfortunate deafness.

22 MARCH 1904
Akers-Douglas told me that he invented the system of 'marking in' by which we are able to calculate our numerical strength in the House of Commons. He is a most skilful wirepuller, and his methods of organisation are wonderful: but as a speaker and debater his abilities are nil.

29 MARCH 1904
We adjourned for the Easter Recess. We have survived eight weeks; not without great effort. For my part I think that genuine accidents excluded, we shall go on

[45]Henry William Forster (1866–1936), first and only Baron Forster (cr. 1919) of Exbury House, Hants., and Southend Hall, Kent (in earlier life); Deputy Lieutenant Kent and MP Sevenoaks 1892–1918 and Bromley 1918–19; junior Lord of the Treasury 1902–05, continuing as opposition Whip thereafter; financial secretary to War Office 1915–19; both sons killed in war; Governor-General of Australia 1920–25.

until one fine day we shall be beaten in committee on the Licensing Bill.[46] A few months ago people were afraid of the Budget: now they are much more nervous about the Liquor problem. And they have good cause. Meanwhile we have suffered enormously from the Yellow Labour agitation, and a dissolution of parliament at this juncture would mean absolute annihilation. The general impression is that we ought to hang on for the rest of the year by which time some of the lies and misrepresentations will have spent their force and potency. We could then go to the country and our position would no doubt cause us much alarm and give great joy to the Radicals: but at least our numbers would be greater than they would be now.

12 APRIL 1904

Octavius Leigh Clare K.C., M.P.[47] wants to be made a Judge: and asked me to pave the way for his application. I will do what I can. He is able, has worked hard, and drafted my marriage settlement.

18 APRIL 1904

Wimborne[48] has practically declared against the Conservative party: a contingency which would have been avoided had we acceded to his application for an Earldom. It is on much the same plane as the source of much animosity shown to Balfour, which arose from his detection of the Duchess of Devonshire in her customary cardsharping.

22 APRIL 1904

I estimate that the last week has improved our prospects fifteen per cent. Alexander Hood puts it as high as twenty-five per cent, and I hope he may be correct, though I feel his estimate is unduly sanguine. That there has been a marked slump in radical elation is however perfectly obvious.

At the same time one must observe that our position is so precarious that we do not receive the credit due to us. Thus the Anglo-French agreement[49] has practically had no effect on the party outlook, although its importance is inestimable. It would have been adequate to add six months to the life of any ordinary government in any ordinary time. It is a real triumph for Lord Lansdowne, who has bargained better than many people fully realize: and it has done two other things. It has had a profound influence on the tone of the Russian press and it has sobered the bouncing Pan-Germanists. There is an uneasy feeling in Berlin that German isolation, despite the *Dreibund*, is on the verge of accomplishment. I am delighted; we have

[46] The Licensing Act enabled compensation to be paid to publicans whose licences were withdrawn on grounds of general policy, the money coming from a fund levied on the trade. The measure enraged publicans and temperance fanatics equally.

[47] O. L. Clare (1841–1912), MP (Cons.) Eccles 1895–1906: appointed Vice-chancellor of the County Palatine of Lancashire, 1905.

[48] Sir Ivor Guest, first Baron Wimborne (1835–1914): created peer, 1880.

[49] Published 12 April 1904.

The downfall of the Unionists

one inveterate and unrelenting foe, and that is the German Empire, beginning with the Kaiser himself.

5 MAY 1904

We understand that Lord Crewe is now on the brink of bankruptcy – gambling and racing. Hamilton tells me that the Dublin tradesmen are still unpaid for goods they supplied while Crewe was Lord-Lieutenant ten years ago.[50]

8 JUNE 1904

The sheep shearing in Hyde Park is just finishing. It is a source of great interest to the Londoner whose knowledge of the sheep is very slender. I heard a man talking to his small daughter who wanted to know if the sheep were savage. The man didn't think so – but he said they can 'bite and kick dreadfully'.

23 JUNE 1904

Parliament. We have passed through awful days: three more such days and we shall break down under the strain. We have been trying to make progress with a contentious Budget while our available majority in the House has been sinking almost to the vanishing point. Our men will not attend. They are bored, tired, apathetic; many of them intensely selfish and stupid. What course should be adopted I fail to see. A party meeting is suggested: but that would merely give a chance to the Wreckers to injure the cause: others suggest that Balfour should write to the idle and recalcitrant: that would of course offend the industrious and loyal members who would like equally to receive a letter from the chief.

The remedy for this disease which has been long growing, and which has now reached an acute stage, should have been provided months ago by Balfour himself. A little personal effort on his part would have done it: a little social intercourse with his supporters who have deep feelings of affection towards him, but who from one cause or another go through entire sessions without exchanging one word with the Prime Minister. I wanted months ago to suggest that A.J.B. should make a point of entertaining at informal dinner parties twenty to thirty members every week – not those who meet him in society, but the vast majority of those hardworking provincial members to whom a *dîner sans façon* with the Premier would be an event of great importance. It would be an unconscious stimulus to their party loyalty: and would provide a personal string upon which in time of stress the leader could effectively play. I never made the suggestion – for I never speak to Balfour or rarely. Incidentally I may say that an unconscious source of grievance is that during divisions Balfour is nearly always buttonholed by an officious minister or some toadying busybody. The most easily approached of men but in some ways the most difficult of access.

I think we shall go to pieces.

[50] Robert, first Marquess of Crewe (1858–1945), Liberal statesman, who, as Lord Houghton, had served as Lord-Lieutenant of Ireland, 1892–5. Crewe was Rosebery's son-in-law.

74

... Churchill meanwhile has been acting as leader of the Opposition on the Aliens Bill.[51] Asquith, as an ex-minister and ex-home secretary was disgusted to find himself ousted by this whipper snapper. I confess I find Churchill's manners and record most distasteful.

30 JUNE 1904

Surely an impossible rumour – *videlicet* that Willy Grenfell[52] is to be made a peer and succeed Minto in Canada. On all grounds such an appointment would be indefensible; for he is a man of no power or personality: still more because his wife has been in love with the Prime Minister (or vice versa) for ten years. Yet the story reaches me from a quarter which could scarcely be called ill-informed.

10 JULY 1904

How ill-advised of Arthur Balfour to allow Ailwyn Fellowes[53] to become director of the Great Eastern Railway, at a moment when there is conflict between railways and agriculture in respect of railway rates; Fellowes representing the Board of Agriculture in his parliamentary capacity, and at the same time defending a railway company attacked by his own department.

19 JULY 1904

We hear of St John Brodrick's latest bon mot. J. Chamberlain was inveighing against the ever-growing luxury of modern times compared with his recollections of a generation ago. 'The increase is purely relative' said St John, 'and depends wholly upon the kind of society one frequents'.

20 JULY 1904

The House sat from 2 p.m. yesterday till 4 p.m. this afternoon – very tiring. Spencer Charrington,[54] aged 86, gallantly led us throughout this prolonged session. No incident of note, except that Churchill's physical stamina broke down.

[51] Dropped by the government, 7 July 1904, but reintroduced and passed in 1905, becoming the first immigration act. Churchill had been adopted for a Manchester seat with an influential Jewish vote in April 1904; the bill was chiefly about keeping out Russian Jews.

[52] William Henry Grenfell (1855–1945), created Baron Desborough in 1905. Although Grenfell twice swam Niagara and shot in the Rockies, he never held a major office in Canada or elsewhere. A Gladstonian Liberal MP (1880–82, 1885–6, 1892–3) who had once been Harcourt's private secretary, he was now MP (Cons.) Wycombe, 1900–05. His remarkable wife inherited Panshanger from Lady Cowper when that family became extinct in 1913.

[53] Hon. Ailwyn Fellowes (1855–1924), farmer, company director, and agricultural statesman; second son of first Lord De Ramsey; MP (Cons.) Hunts. N. or Ramsey, 1887–1906; junior office, 1895–1905; president of the Board of Agriculture, 1905; a casualty of the 1906 election, not re-entering parliament; chairman, Agricultural Wages Board, and Deputy Director of Food Production, 1917–19; chairman of Norfolk County Council, 1920–24; created Baron Ailwyn, 1921.

[54] Spencer Charrington (1818–11 December 1904), brewer and MP (Cons.) Mile End 1885–1904.

The downfall of the Unionists

Spencer Charrington is to be presented with a silver trophy, to commemorate his staying powers. By the way, the breakfast of the gallant old man consisted of a large steak and a pint of beer.

29 JULY 1904

... The Oswestry election[55] is a serious blow for us all, not only for Chamberlain. We are very much in doubt as to the result of the vote of censure on Monday: we don't yet know how many men will be available, or indeed how a certain section will vote. If we survive Monday handsomely we ought to survive the session. On the whole the complications in the Near East tend to strengthen the government in the House of Commons.

1 AUGUST 1904

The vote of censure – Balfour's speech was certainly somewhat obfuscated – but we came well out of the division,[56] to the manifest anger of the Radicals whose last chance is now gone. At one time they expected to beat us, and the most cautious among them made certain that our majority would be insignificant.

3 AUGUST 1904

... Rosebery's letter in *The Times*[57] seems to foreshadow a definite attempt to form a central conservative party comprising the Free Trade element. We are going to have trouble this autumn at the annual gathering at Southampton. A section of the party wants Balfour to hasten the pace. One noticeable feature of the session has been the effacement of seceders like George Hamilton, Ritchie, and Hicks Beach. Their attendance has been extremely bad, and they perhaps realise (especially a placeman-pensioner like George Hamilton) how great a sacrifice is entailed by the private member who votes regularly in order to keep his government in power.

16 AUGUST 1904

Prorogation of parliament – what a bitter disappointment to the Radicals who confidently reckoned upon the spoils of office and the pleasures of power, six

---

[55] A Liberal gain in a seat which otherwise, even in 1906, has always been Conservative. Bridgeman, the future minister, stood as a supporter of Chamberlain's full programme, the first Conservative by-election candidate to do so since the Gateshead by-election (21 January 1904); hence the significance of the defeat.

[56] The government won 288–210, with 52 Unionist abstentions, against a motion attacking Lansdowne, Selborne, and Victor Cavendish for having taken prominent positions in the now protectionist Liberal Unionist party organisation. The Oswestry result, by encouraging anti-Chamberlain Unionists, actually helped the government, while Chamberlain's call for a colonial conference (1 August) could be read as backing down.

[57] *The Times*, 3 August 1904, p. 6. Rosebery assented to Chamberlain's proposed imperial conference, provided (1) there were no food taxes (2) prior agreement was reached by British politicians on imperial policy, and (3) British representatives were 'not merely partisan or official, but men of national weight'.

months ago! They determined to eject us from the government, and indeed fully expected to do so: they were all at loggerheads as to the filling of the posts in the new ministry – and after all we survive. The whips deserve some credit for incessant labour throughout a trying and laborious session. Balfour has done much to keep us together; while a resolute group of stalwarts has attended so regularly as to form a bodyguard all through the session: to them are due the best thanks of the country. Meanwhile the Radicals are distracted on questions of principle and policy, Home Rule being still their chief stumbling-block: their attitude will not be dictated by anything except the precise numerical majority obtained at the next election. I may add that there are some members who firmly refuse to admit that we shall be seriously beaten at the next election.

As matters stand, and testing the situation from a whip's point of view, I question if we shall last much beyond Easter. During the past session we secured the attendance of men who mean to retire, but whom we persuaded to retain their seats almost on the understanding that a dissolution could not be long delayed. When parliament reassembles, these men will be more than ever fatigued and it is probable that a certain number will absent themselves altogether. We shall lose more byelections, and the Free Food element will become more restive, and will gradually fall into the way of voting against us on non-fiscal questions: all this must weaken the government and we shall have to make special precaution against snap divisions – the chief danger during the past session.

3 OCTOBER 1904

To Gosford ... Had a talk with Arthur Balfour, and urged him to mention in his speech tonight that Redmond expects to hold the balance of power in the next parliament. Balfour was not aware of the controversy now raging in Ireland about Dunraven's devolution scheme. He was much interested, also pleased that George Wyndham should have issued a manifesto. Seeing however that he was wholly ignorant of the problem, I begged him to say nothing – he had suggested a passing reference – for I felt that he would perhaps make a faux pas and betray his bad coaching. Sandars wired Balfour to remind him that Sir W. Harcourt died on Saturday.

4 OCTOBER 1904

By the way Balfour told me that the two Chamberlains were much opposed to his scheme of a conference to be followed by a general election throughout the empire: they desire a conference to be followed by immediate legislation without consulting the electorate; a wholly impracticable scheme.

24 OCTOBER 1904

We reached Whittingehame at teatime, and found that Arthur Balfour was of course leaving by the night train for London. He told us that the earliest intimation of the

The downfall of the Unionists

North Sea outrage[58] reached him by telegram from Hull before the morning papers arrived. He thought it a hoax, and actually delayed taking action until the *Scotsman* arrived showing the dire truth of the report. Balfour then wired to concentrate the Fleets: the Scottish squadron is to move south and the other squadrons will rally at Gibraltar: he further ordered that public notification was to be made: but at dinner time a telegram from Lansdowne came saying that the Fleets had received orders but that no announcement was being made pending the First Lord's return to town.

Whereat Balfour seemed very angry, and hurried off to wire again.

25 OCTOBER 1904

Arthur Balfour looked very grey and worried: almost old: Gerald bears up wonderfully well considering that some of these poor trawlers have been decapitated. Lady Frances[59] insists upon reading aloud long extracts from the newspapers, which is an infernal bore.

9 NOVEMBER 1904

Working hard preparing notes for my book on the evolution of Italian sculpture.[60] The subject sounds so obvious, and is so virginal, that I fear others must be engaged on the same theme. Unless we are beaten early next year I really don't see when and how I shall find leisure to make the book.

24 NOVEMBER 1904

To London. Dined with Arthur Lee,[61] who told me that the Board meeting of the Admiralty, when the disposition of our fleets for war with Russia was determined, only lasted 45 minutes: so carefully and so completely had the organisation been matured during times of peace.

15 JANUARY 1905

This time last year people promised an Easter dissolution, then Whitsuntide, then August: and the predictions never came true. Their prophecies are more likely to be realised during the forthcoming session. In the first place we meet so late that it is unlikely the government means to introduce a redistribution bill:[62] hence a certain

---

[58] The Russian Baltic fleet, passing the Dogger Bank on its way to attack Japan, attacked a group of British trawlers in the night, maintaining fire for about half an hour. The incident occurred on 21 October, but news did not reach Hull till Sunday, 23 October. The British fleet mobilised to detain or intercept the Russian vessels should it prove necessary; and on 28 October Balfour was able to announce a peaceful settlement based on ample Russian amends.

[59] Lady Frances Balfour (1858–1931), wife of Eustace Balfour (d. 1911), the premier's brother; daughter of the eighth Duke of Argyll (1823–1900); see below, 12 October 1911.

[60] *The Evolution of Italian Sculpture* (London, John Murray, 1909).

[61] Arthur Lee, first Viscount Lee of Fareham (1868–1947), MP (Cons.) Fareham 1900–18; civil Lord of Admiralty, 1903–5; successful ministerial career, 1915–22; Baron, 1918, and Viscount, 1922; presented Chequers to nation, 1917; a vigorous collector and instrumental in establishing the Courtauld and Warburg Institutes.

[62] See below, 14 July 1905.

number of our friends will be alienated... The outlook is therefore gloomy, especially for the whips, and if a disastrous session is followed by a disastrous defeat (of myself) I shall be galled and furious.

16 FEBRUARY 1905

Arthur Stanley[63] tells me that he is prepared to get enough men to abstain on any division, to ensure our defeat, and without the tactics becoming known. He is keen for an early dissolution, and prepared to compass it in a friendly and avowed manner. But though many agree with his object, I doubt if it would be easy to get men deliberately to act in beating the government: we shall probably incur defeat without this careful organisation.

24 FEBRUARY 1905

St John Brodrick and Gerald Balfour met a man called Keswick[64] at a country house. After dinner they were much interested in his conversation and his great knowledge of Far Eastern affairs: and finally told him how valuable his experience would be if placed at the disposal of the country in the House of Commons.

Well, said Mr Keswick, I may as well state at once that I have been a loyal supporter of yours in the House for the last five years! – an illustration of the attitude of our leaders towards the rank and file: a constant source of weakness and complaint.[65]

Rutherford,[66] one of the Liverpool members, surprised us by saying that during the Everton contest, the name of the prime minister not only failed to excite interest or enthusiasm among his supporters, but that in certain cases our speakers had to be warned against introducing his name for fear of hostile demonstrations from our own friends: perhaps an exaggerated story, but symptomatic.

Speaker's dinner... George Wyndham absent – they say he has broken down. Walter Long is bubbling with wrath at the tactics of his colleague, and says that the McDonnell incident produced the one and only serious row in the cabinet during the past ten years.[67]

3 MARCH 1905

Selborne's appointment[68] is all right – but the praise which is being lavished upon him is very foolish. He is a good sound hardworking stupid fellow, without a gleam

[63] Hon. Arthur Stanley, MP (Cons.) Ormskirk 1898–1918, son of the sixteenth Earl of Derby.

[64] W. Keswick, MP (Cons.) Mid-Surrey 1899–1912.

[65] W. E. Brymer, MP (Cons.) Dorset S. 1891–1906, told the diarist in July 1905 that he had never exchanged one word with Arthur Balfour, not even a good morning.

[66] W. W. Rutherford, MP (Cons.) Liverpool West Derby 1903–18, and Edge Hill, 1918–23. The Everton by-election was on 22 February 1905.

[67] 'I do not hear a murmur of regret at Wyndham's resignation' (diary, 6 March 1905).

[68] As High Commissioner for South Africa, 1905–10, *vice* Milner. For Selborne see above, 2 November 1900, and below, 4 March 1911.

of humour, or an ounce of charm: all his success (and it has been great) is attributable to splendid perseverance and invincible good humour. He will get on well with everybody, Boer, Bond, and Jewboys – and when they show signs of turbulence will show them that he means to retain the upper hand. Much common sense, and no false ideas; plenty of assurance, and no vainglory – with such qualities he ought to succeed, though it is now obvious that the danger of losing a reputation in S. Africa is greater than the chance of making one.

6 APRIL 1905

This Brighton election[69] is a fair knockout blow, the full importance of which will not be realised for several days. Arthur Balfour's exclamation was 'how very funny'. What is so cynical about the whole thing is that Lady Wimborne and the earnest Protestants of Brighton polled a unanimous vote in favour of an atheistic unfrocked parson... Fred Smith[70] came to ask me if he should offer to retire from the candidature of the Abercromby division in order to find a seat for Loder: Stock the sitting member would gladly bring about a vacancy. I pointed out one good reason to make his generous suggestion untenable.

29 MAY 1905

To London... Dined with Cowpers, meeting an offensively decadent little beast called Max Beerbohm. I knew the creature at Oxford: in those days there was a marked absence of virility: nowadays he is merely disgusting.

6 JULY 1905

Walter Long told me that Austen Chamberlain is without exception the best Chancellor of the Exchequer he has ever worked with,[71] and that Victor Cavendish is the most painstaking financial secretary.

7 JULY 1905

After dinner with the Wenlocks, I sat next A.J.B.... While we were talking over dessert, Chamberlain *père* was making what proved to be rather a savage, though covert, attack on Balfour. It is possible that Joe is pleased at the Kingswinford result:[72] annoyed at Balfour's determination to proceed with Redistribution, involving the prolongation of this parliament for 12 or 14 months: and vexed into the bargain, that if the redistribution proposals are carried, he will lose the potential

---

[69] The Liberals won by nearly a thousand in a seat which they had not even contested in 1900 (5 April 1905). Loder, the defeated Conservative, was seeking re-election on taking office.

[70] Frederick Edwin Smith, first Earl of Birkenhead (1872–1930); MP (Cons.) Liverpool Walton 1906–18, Lord Chancellor 1919–22.

[71] The diarist earlier noted the 'unequivocal success' of Chamberlain's budget speech in 1904, and the good reception given to his budget in 1905.

[72] In this W. Midlands by-election the Conservatives won easily.

assistance, and the radicals will lose the inevitable opposition of 20 or 25 nationalist members.

Hence perhaps a certain acerbity which is moreover more or less excusable in a man of seventy who feels that time is slipping away. For my part I am weary of this stage of the fight: so is Acland-Hood – tired to death, but fighting on with dogged resistance, beating the Radicals at every manoeuvre, anticipating every variety of attack: and in short creating a record in skill and strategy, so far as the whips' activity is concerned. His colleagues support him with ceaseless energy – Hamilton, Valentia, Edmund Talbot, Harry Forster, myself, and Hayes Fisher who replaces Savile Crossley for the moment. Each of us contributes something to what has hitherto proved a formidable bulwark.

And after all it is not a mean job – no mean hankering after emolument and power, as ill-informed critics assert. We are playing a very big game. The Aliens Bill must be passed, for a week's real revolution in Russia might well cause the emigration of half a million poor wretches, and whither would they go if not to London? There are also other questions of paramount importance – Morocco, Manchuria, the Transvaal; the terms of peace, the renewal and extension of our alliance, the development of the Anglo-French accord. And on these things, on all topics of international gravity I have no confidence in a Radical cabinet collectively, and little if any in Edward Grey.

None the less I sigh for release.

9 JULY 1905
I watched the procession of demonstrators march down Pall Mall to their rendez-vous in Hyde Park – to support the unemployed bill.[73] They cheered while passing the Reform Club, and hooted while passing the Carlton, though we are responsible for this measure – responsible also for letting it expire. There were apparently no unemployed in the procession: but lots of flags, and well-dressed people actually in top hats: also bicycles and smartish young women with red rosettes. An orderly and prosperous assembly, which by the way must have got drenched later on in the rain. On the whole I imagine the unemployed bill is the most unpopular measure among our men which has been introduced during the last ten years.

Since the last redistribution of constituencies in 1885, population changes had led to great anomalies in the size of seats. Romford had 217,000 electors, Newry only 13,000. Ireland was over-represented by about thirty seats, a fact against which Chamberlain had started an outcry in 1901. Politically, it made sense for the government to introduce

---

[73] An act, passed in August 1905, to turn voluntary committees set up by the government in 1904, into permanent machinery to promote labour exchanges, farm colonies, and emigration – but not to pay relief, create public works, or interfere with Poor Law principles. The future Lord Parmoor, the Labour minister, was one of those who opposed this bill as going too far.

The downfall of the Unionists

a scheme which would unite the party, which would make the Liberals exhibit themselves as an ally of Irish nationalism, and which would remove suspicions roused by the Wyndham affair earlier in 1905 that the premier had leanings towards home rule. A government resolution announced on 11 July, for discussion a week later, would have led to the disappearance of twenty two mainly Catholic seats in Ireland. Before any vote was taken, however, the Speaker ruled that the resolution was really a series of resolutions, which would have to be discussed separately. For this there was no time. The premier at once withdrew the motion, but said he would proceed by bill next session instead. At a party meeting ('unemotional and on the whole a success' noted Balcarres) on 18 July, Balfour urged the party not to relax their efforts in the lobbies. Two days later Redmond defeated ministers 200–196 on a minor Irish vote. On 24 July, Balfour announced the decision of the cabinet not to resign.

14 JULY 1905

This redistribution scheme has fallen like a bombshell in our midst. Nobody wants it, nobody. The strongest advocates of the principle feel that our scheme is half-hearted, and preserves anomalies which are little short of ridiculous. The nationalists are of course furious, and will resort to every form of political and physical violence to defeat us. Ten days ago we were getting along pretty well, for nobody anticipated 'business' – and now at the fag end of a moribund session we are asked to deal with a problem which would require six weeks during the fresh and vitalised period of our sittings.

What will happen? I suspect that the Speaker will rule that the resolution must be split up into sections. We must accept his judgment.

... The difficulty of maintaining our numbers during the last week has been great.

17 JULY 1905

The Speaker's ruling is against us: his decision had been anticipated, and was discounted. Redistribution is off.

20 JULY 1905

Midnight. Snapped! – or rather we knew there was a big scheme on hand, we were fully prepared, we duly warned the boys, and none the less, within 48 hours of our party meeting we were beaten in a fair and square fight. There is no more to be said, and no explanation, still less extenuation, is possible. On Tuesday we learned that Thursday would be important. Yesterday further indication came to hand. Hood issued an extremely urgent whip, couched in a language which could not possibly be misunderstood.

I was at the door between 11 and 12. At 11.0 we had a majority of 40 on paper. At 11.30 several radicals had come in and I intercepted Eddy Stanley in the lobby, and told him to telephone to the clubs etc. At 11.45 half a dozen radicals entered in a bunch: at 11.50 half a dozen more. We were then beaten by 3 or 4 votes.

The scene was quite interesting. Channing simply went crazy. Redmond shouted himself hoarse. Balfour was icy.

21 JULY 1905

Analysing the division took us all morning. We find 60 odd of our men were absent unpaired. Tariff Reformers and Free Fooders both voted and were absent unpaired: there is no fiscal moral at any rate to be drawn. The Ulster Unionists however were badly represented, 5 or 6 being away unpaired, and on Irish estimates too, which is bad.

24 JULY 1905

Balfour's speech anouncing the government's determination to continue in office was long and somewhat too technical: we didn't expect to hear so much about Lord Melbourne and the Bedchamber crisis. I fancy however that its very length and the multitude of constitutional problems touched upon (always in an icy voice) served to quiet the House and lead them towards a dispassionate consideration of the position.

...Of course the cabinet contains men who have no idea of the ordinary workaday difficulties of holding a party together when it has become demoralised. Arnold-Forster, for instance, or Lansdowne or Alfred Lyttelton are absolutely inexperienced in the wiles and dangers of Parliamentary life. They perhaps contributed to the decision of the government – who knows?

26 JULY 1905

The King is excessively angry at Winston Churchill's attack on A.J.B., and makes no secret of his opinion that Churchill is a born cad.

4 AUGUST 1905

A month ago nobody would have predicted that the unemployed bill even in its emasculated form, would have passed through the committee stage on a Friday afternoon. This however has happened, much as some of our men dislike the bill. I fear that it may raise up hopes which cannot be realized, and therefore do as much harm as good. Redmond has made a bargain with a certain group of Labour members – they support Home Rule in return for his advocacy of their measure. There has undoubtedly been an estrangement between various sections of the opposition. The Labour members who have always been weak appendages of the Liberal party foresee a great enlargement of numbers and power after a general election. They begin to feel restive and desire to assert their independence. Redmond on the other hand begins to fear that the Liberals may be correct in estimating their majority over Nationalists and Conservatives at 60 to 90. Hence Redmond's efforts to capture the Labour party which Dilke will in all probability direct. The situation is piquant and points to a curious confusion of parties.

The downfall of the Unionists

6 AUGUST 1905

A long talk with Harry Chaplin[74] at the Carlton – he is strongly against dissolving in the autumn and wants to call parliament together in January and to arrange a suitable defeat, early enough to prevent the Radicals from carrying any legislation of importance. There is much to be said for these tactics. I myself want to arrange our fall in such a manner as to force C.B. to meet the House before a general election – for instance at a date when even in a minority he would be compelled to pass the Mutiny Act. 48 hours of government would enable us to bully and cross-examine C-B to our hearts content: and would give us a strategic position of attack which we do not now possess.

Meanwhile however we have to survive another week. We have received from an unimpeachable source – a Liberal member – who has before now stood us in good stead – that a desperate attack will be made tomorrow, and possibly renewed at subsequent sittings. Our members have been fully warned both by whips and articles in the press – the latter somewhat too sensational for my taste. I think the boys will turn up in sufficient force to stave off defeat – otherwise Heaven help us!

10 AUGUST 1905

The problem of the recess – its duration and its policy, is extremely delicate. Chamberlain wants an autumn dissolution, so does A.J.B. in his heart. Hood on the other hand is all for deferring it. He wishes to take a fall early next session, to resign rather than dissolve, to give C.B. the privilege of forming a ministry prior to consulting the electorate. We will then fight the radical programme on a new register.

It must not however be supposed that the Tariff Reformers are unanimous in favouring an autumn appeal. Harry Chaplin and Jesse Collings are dead against it, also Sir Fortescue Flannery[75] if he counts! Free-fooders such as Edgar Vincent[76] equally deprecate a dissolution in the autumn, and the party as a whole would be intensely annoyed. I predict therefore that Hood will have his way: for on the whole I imagine him to be the most powerful man in the government.

Nobody inspires more affection than Alec Hood. The radicals have cheered him loudly three times during the last month. His purple countenance and bristling moustaches seem to appeal to all the anaemic and whiskered nonconformists: this ex-adjutant of the Grenadiers with all the sternness of a drill sergeant on parade, has a singular personal charm in conversation. Hood and Valentia are the only two men I know to whom the radical is physically incapable of showing discourtesy. Hood's success also accounts for much of his popularity: our opponents pay an unconscious tribute to his foresight and determination. Next to the prime minister he is by far

[74]Henry Chaplin, first Viscount Chaplin (1841–1923), MP (Cons.) Mid-Lincs. 1868–1906, Wimbledon 1907–16; created peer, 1916; won Derby, 1867.

[75]MP (Lib. Unionist) Shipley 1895–1906.

[76]Sir Edgar Vincent, first Viscount D'Abernon (1857–1941), MP (Cons.) Exeter 1899–1906; financial expert and ambassador.

the most popular man in the Commons and many members would even place him first.

Then there is the other side to his character, known only to those in the 'Room', to his colleagues – and to the luckless individual who has words with the chief whip. On occasions when a recalcitrant minister, say Pretyman[77] or Brodrick does not agree with some ukase issued by us, an interview takes place. The threats, and the picturesque langauge in which they are clothed seldom fail – never fail. The culprit vanishes silently and obeys, while we note the conversation for precedents we may one day have to follow. Nobody could be more loyal to his subordinates. Hood has a good team – between us we are capable of directing the whole party: and no chief whip has ever taken his colleagues more fully into his confidence: our discussions on the course of public business have been invaluable, the rareness of our mistakes being a sufficient justification.

14 SEPTEMBER 1905
Pondering over the possibility – at this stage I will not say probability – of my being defeated at the next election, I note down occupations which in the event of disaster must replace my political occupations. Here is a list of things to which attention can suitably be turned.

Study   book on Italian sculpture – equestrian statues.[78]
             „   on Art and the State.[79]

Business   Huntingdon estates (Connie Balcarres)[80]
             Wigan Coal and Iron Co. (Notts. coalfield)[81]

Haigh   Rehang pictures – naive labels.
             Catalogue and arrange miniature collections.
             Amplify catalogue of Bibliotheca Lindesiana.
             Family letters at Haigh. Arrange and bind.[82]
             Index Library letters.
             Bind my private correspondence.[83]
             ? build rooms over boudoir and Long Room.
             Clean and revarnish pictures – arrange china.
             Index Lady Anne's memoirs – get copies of Lindsay etc. descent
             portraits elsewhere: genealogies.

[77] Ernest George Pretyman (1860–1931), MP (Cons.) Woodbridge 1895–1906, Chelmsford 1908–23; held junior office 1900–05, 1915–19.

[78] Published 1909.

[79] No such book published, but a theme for many lectures.

[80] Connie's inherited property, eventually sold.

[81] Virtually the sole source of family income.

[82] Now largely bound.

[83] Mostly destroyed in second war.

The downfall of the Unionists

Balcarres   Planting on estate.
                Catalogue and number pictures.
                Collect engravings of Lindsay houses.
                ? Enlarge Dower House accommodation.

General   Visit Spain, Greece, Constantinople and as much elsewhere as feasible.
                Family history of last 70 years – say since 1800.
                Family genealogy, complete record of all descents.
                Portraits of all descent ancestors – engravings.
                Attention to Society of Antiquaries, National Art Collections Fund, Society for the Protection of Ancient Buildings, National Trust, National Portrait Gallery.
                Continue political collections dealing with art matters.
                Make occasional speeches so as to keep in practice.

21 SEPTEMBER 1905

I hear that Edward Grey is trying to learn French: the deduction is obvious: what is less easy to understand is how he managed to serve for three years at the Foreign Office without learning one single word of the language of diplomacy. I have a poor opinion of him.

2 OCTOBER 1905

Connie and I motored from Balcarres to Glamis Castle... I am amazed at the phenomenal ignorance of the castle and its contents, displayed by Lord and Lady Strathmore,[84] and the two eldest sons. The second son asked his mother about the identity of a portrait which turned out to be a portrait of his own grandmother. They are nice boys, and Strathmore is a delightful man: by the way he put two pellets into my wrist while we were driving some grouse this afternoon.

As to the Glamis ghosts, let me say at once that there certainly is a ghost, though the family never sees it. The last witness was the butler, who was confronted by the apparition among some rhododendrons, after a copious supper.

The Lyons talk freely about ghosts and invent stories to suit the idiosyncrasies of each guest. They were careful however not to tell us too spicy stories, as they felt we might be offended if the Tiger Earl was maltreated. The late Lord Strathmore was far more discreet – indeed he took steps to stop certain weird noises which occurred at night: and among other things he removed a thick wall (close to the crypt) because the door in that wall could not be kept shut. One might lock the door, or push a wardrobe against it but the door always clicked itself open. So the late man laid this ghost by removing it bodily.

[84] Claude George Bowes-Lyon, twelfth Earl of Strathmore (1855–1944), succeeded 1904; father of the Queen Mother.

As to the alleged secret, I soon fathomed the mystery. There *is* a secret: the secret is 'that there is *no* secret'.

Seldom were electoral prospects so clear as in the autumn of 1905. A by-election at Barkston Ash (14 October) brought a Liberal gain in a seat not contested since 1892. Thereafter the question was whether Chamberlain would use the coming election defeat to topple Balfour and become leader himself. In mid-November Chamberlain completely captured the party conference; and, answering an appeal by Balfour for unity, he threw caution to the winds (21 November) with the challenge, 'No army was ever led successfully to battle on the principle that the lamest man should govern the march of the army'. On 4 December Balfour resigned, the Liberals under Campbell-Bannerman took office, and the preliminaries of the general election of January 1906 began.

1 JANUARY 1906
For New Year's Day read Thomas à Kempis beginning *caveas tumultum hominum quantum potes.*

IV

In the wilderness, 1906-10

Chamberlain's 'devil of a row' – Lord Randolph's blackmailing of the Princess of Wales foiled by Hartington – the education question – rumours of Campbell-Bannerman's remarriage – list of worthless specimens among Unionist backbenchers – skill of C.-B. in deceiving his party – a Rothschild saved from bankruptcy – John Burns's bibliomania – how the whips cultivated the press – the Tweedmouth episode – Lloyd George depressed about pensions – curious epistolary habits of late Lord Derby – character of a Fife stationmaster – Westminster attacked by women – Victor Grayson's secret life – the education bill of 1908 – Asquith's attentions to a dancer – Tory lack of ministerial timber – Balfour the victim of government confidences – Lloyd George at sea over the budget – Goodwood and Petworth contrasted – Lloyd George relaxes with 'bits of muslin' – a suffragette justifies assassination – corruption in Lancashire elections.

The Liberal landslide in the general election of January 1906 reduced the Unionists to 157 seats. This completely altered Bal's standing, though not his job, in their ranks. Previously merely a promising young man, he now joined the pathetically small band of full-time Conservative politicians left in an overwhelmingly hostile House of Commons. He did not become important overnight, but he became very necessary.

After a tough Chorley election campaign (fifty speeches, 450 questions answered) Bal went to Scotland to help Balfour with the split in the Conservative Party over protection (which Bal supported) and over Chamberlain (whose methods he disliked).

25 JANUARY 1906
At night to Whittingehame. Both the defeated Balfours at home. I confess that they scarcely seem to realise that many people place some responsibility for our rout upon their shoulders. A.J.B. has been dreadfully low about his defeat but has now recovered equanimity.

26 JANUARY 1906
Balfour showed me a long letter just arrived from Chamberlain – twelve large pages. It is in many ways a remarkable document, and not easily construed.

88

He admits that outside Birmingham, the Liberal Unionists have ceased to exist. He was asked to lead the House until Balfour's return, but declines to do so unless invited by a party meeting. This of course we cannot allow, at any rate until the first part of the session is past.

Is the letter a threat? He actually had the impertinence to invite Balfour to Highbury – what a tactless and improper thing to do! Balfour said no, and they will now meet in London instead, which is more in accordance with fitness and propriety. The letter indicates that a further period of dual leadership is impossible, that the majority of our members subscribe to the Birmingham policy, and that at his age Chamberlain must soon make up his mind whether to take his place on a back bench or not. Well, we don't want him to do that, though Bob Cecil who hasn't yet taken his seat, threatens to make a public protest if Chamberlain occupies the leadership even for a week.

Is Bob Cecil as rash as his brother Hugh? and as Balfour says, is Chamberlain living in a fool's paradise or a fool's purgatory?

Anyhow the two protagonists will meet a week hence, and I trust will accept the solution I suggested, by which the technical difficulty of leadership can be overcome.

Let Akers-Douglas, incompetent as he is, be our leader: his position entitles him to the post: and as leader let him speak on the election of the Speaker. He can then retire for the moment, and Joe, without being our leader, can make his fighting speech, the first from our side on the address. The situation is extremely delicate: I trust to Balfour to devise a fair solution.

In afternoon to Gosford. Lord Wemyss told me 1) that the Madonna and child by Botticelli (£200 ex Northwick sale) was refused by the National Gallery because the roses were badly painted, 2) that the Madonna and child by Mantegna was lent to Burne-Jones who copied the drapery in his King Cophetua picture, 3) the Lady by Paris Bordone used according to tradition to be a full length.

3 FEBRUARY 1906
Received this letter from Salisbury[1] – Jim Cranborne as was – a lithographed thing:

---

[1] James, fourth Marquess of Salisbury, 1861–1947; eldest son of the Prime Minister, succeeding his father in August 1903; MP (Cons.) NE Lancs. 1885–92, Rochester 1893–1903; chairman of Church Parliamentary Committee, 1893–1900; fought in Boer War: Under-Secretary for Foreign Affairs 1900–03, Lord Privy Seal 1903–5, president of the board of trade 1905: Lord President of the Council 1922–4, chancellor of the Duchy of Lancaster 1922–3: Lord Privy Seal 1924–9, leader of the House of Lords 1925–29; resigned as party leader in the Lords, June 1931; important in overthrowing Lloyd George in 1922 and Chamberlain in 1940. Balcarres had already noted (diary, 13 March 1905) 'a universal belief in Jim Cranborne's complete and invincible incompetence' and that while under-secretary for foreign affairs he had allegedly 'to be forbidden to give answers to supplementary questions'.

In the wilderness

Dear Balcarres,

It is so important at the present time to obtain a clear idea of the opinion of the Unionist party in those constituencies which have returned Unionist members to parliament, that I venture to hope you will excuse me, if I ask what line was taken by the party in the course of the recent contest in your constituency on the subject of the taxation of food. I need not say that your reply will be treated as private...

I am bound to say that I resent this catechism from one whose incompetence has been a contributory cause to our disaster. Good fellow as Cranborne is, his tact is not generally visible: and it would not be unfair to reply that the taxation of food has doubtless injured the party – though we have also suffered largely from nepotism, sacerdotalism, and inefficiency.

5 FEBRUARY 1906

To London. At four had conference with Hood and Harry Forster. There is a devil of a row on. Chamberlain has advanced far beyond the position as outlined in his letter to Balfour. He says A.J.B. must either follow the full Tariff Reform policy or else (failing a nonentity as leader) Chamberlain will secede, sit on a back bench, refuse the opposition whips, and create a new party by fighting every seat.

Balfour is firm. They discussed the question on Friday night from 8.45 till 12.45, but could devise no settlement. Chamberlain is also firm and has left London.

The party meeting will have to be called, dangerous as such a gathering is at a stage when we don't know one another by sight, and before we have been able to compare notes. It seems to me that Chamberlain, drunk with his personal success at Birmingham, and surrounded by a group of defeated sycophants, rather confuses the situation. His policy is clearly more acceptable than Balfour's to the party: hence he argues that a majority of members would follow him into the wilderness to form a new group. This is an error. The majority of Tariff Reformers would prefer A.J.B. as leader: and Chamberlain's refusal to lead in the event of Arthur's deposition indicates a knowledge that the Conservative party, to use Walter Long's words 'will not be led by a bloody Radical'. Walter Long as usual has been loyal throughout, though a thorough-going protectionist.

The article in today's *Times* is an accurate statement of the position, and the leader in the *Telegraph* is a fair exposition of the official view we take.

6 FEBRUARY 1906

Today opinion in the Carlton is hardening in our favour: perhaps owing to the activity of the whips. My talk with Matthew Ridley[2] yesterday did good. But

[2] Sir Matthew White Ridley, second Viscount Ridley (1874–1916), MP (Cons.) Stalybridge 1900–04; succeeded father, 1904; assistant private secretary to Austen Chamberlain from 1904.

nothing we can do will obviate a split if Chamberlain is determined to secede. The whole crisis springs from Chamberlain's age: were he ten years younger, he would perhaps let matters rest for six weeks – let things mature and solve their own problems.

Austen Chamberlain and Arnold-Forster would retire with Joe. Arnold-Forster won't help them much! Haldane is an immense success at the War Office: yet he has literally done nothing except keep a civil tongue in his head. We have our doubts about Gilbert Parker[3] whom we can't get hold of. But it is difficult to determine the sources of the strength of the movement against Balfour: anyhow so far as members and ex-members are concerned, Balfour is more formidable to the government than Chamberlain. They accuse Balfour of compromise on the fiscal question: the charge may be just: but Joe will compromise on every other subject imaginable in order to gain his paramount object.

7 FEBRUARY 1906

Again progress in a satisfactory direction may be reported: though we shall have to hold the party meeting, which I think a dangerous resort. However Matt Ridley assures me that a letter he has received from Chamberlain will make it clear that the Tariff Reform group will be content, while taking our official Whips, to organise a special group of their own as was the case in the last parliament with the military and agricultural members.

If this be so our difficulties are largely solved, and the chief outstanding problem is the amendment Chamberlain proposes to move to the Address. But I must wait to see Chamberlain's letter in print before saying that the crisis is past.

Long talk with Hood. Drafted some notes for him to give to A.J.B. as to points for the Chief to allude to in his speech. The question of procedure at the meeting and the selection of persons to be invited remain unsettled and require much thought.

I hear a good account of Sandars'[4] health. His absence during these weeks has not been a source of weakness to the party. He is far from popular.

9 FEBRUARY 1906

The situation is much improved. There remain difficulties about the party meeting – a large number of ex-members who were beaten at the election being most anxious to attend. If they were invited, the time of the meeting would be occupied by lectures from Bowles,[5] Hugh Cecil, and Arthur Elliot on the one hand, and from Parker, Smith, Goulding, and Chaplin on the other. We should have an all night sitting. Moreover it seems to me that we should also be obliged to invite our unsuccessful candidates who did not sit in the last parliament. I am suggesting that we should hold a representative conference of the whole party later on.

[3] Sir Gilbert Parker (1862–1932), Canadian thriller writer; MP (Cons.) Gravesend 1900–18.
[4] John Satterfield Sandars, PC (1853–1934), private secretary to A. J. Balfour, 1892–1911.
[5] Thomas Gibson Bowles (1844–1922), MP (Cons.) King's Lynn 1892–1906; joined Liberals, 1906; MP (Lib.) King's Lynn January–December 1910; founded *Vanity Fair*, 1868.

In the wilderness

Venning[6] says Balfour ought to have two months complete rest: for my part, if A.J.B. can successfully stand the worry of the next two or three weeks, his mind will be relieved so much that his mortal frame will recover without effort.

12 FEBRUARY 1906

Chamberlain wants to move a long argumentative resolution, pledging the party to all sorts of detailed policy on Tariff Reform: a perfectly fatal error. Balfour is to meet him tomorrow, and will try to dissuade from so disastrous a course. Chamberlain's frenzied haste is suicidal – and I fear he is being encouraged by a lot of members who for present purposes have ceased to be Conservatives.

15 FEBRUARY 1906

Party meeting at Lansdowne House. Few people expected the publication, prior to the meeting, of what amounts to a concordat between A.J.B. and Chamberlain. It is possible that had our party meeting not been announced this 'definition rather than compromise' as Chamberlain calls it, would never have been made. The immediate result was of course to let the enemy know at the same moment as ourselves, the basis of agreement, while it deprived the party gathering of its dramatic interest.

The Duke of Devonshire was angry and I imagine that he will have now to organise a little somnolent caucus of his own: my fear is that he may draw towards himself a number of people – Victor Cavendish for instance, or Edgar Vincent, whose loyalty to the party has hitherto been maintained by strict adherence to Balfour's views. They may feel that the official programme goes too far and may consequently decide that their election pledges – succinct and specific – prevent their adherence to what has I suppose become our recognised policy. For my part I think that these good people who are wandering in the wilderness of opposition, take too serious a view of the situation. There is ample time and opportunity to restrict or extend our proposals before we shall be called upon to formulate any precise scheme.

Balfour's reception was apathetic: Devonshire's hostile, Chamberlain's enthusiastic. Hugh Cecil was heard with impatience.

Lord Curzon, though unqualified, attended the meeting. I lunched with him at the Carlton, but as yet do not know if he will take any definite action, though he is opposed to Chamberlain. I think he is wise enough to bide his time.

17 FEBRUARY 1906

Dined with the Bensons.[7] Rob quotes Lord Rothschild as the authority for the following.

[6] Sir Edgcombe Venning (1837–1920), consultant, St George's Hospital.

[7] Robert Henry Benson, merchant banker and connoisseur (1850–1929) m. 1887 Evelyn, daughter of Robert Holford of Dorchester House, perhaps the greatest collector of his day. Rob and Evie Benson were distant relatives and close friends of Balcarres and his wife. Benson was a trustee of the National Gallery from 1912.

Some 20 or 25 years ago when Lord Blandford[8] was engaged in divorce proceedings, his case was vehemently argued and defended by Lord Randolph Churchill: in fact Randolph took charge of the defence. One day he appeared at Marlborough House, and in an interview with the Princess of Wales, told her that he possessed thirteen letters by the Prince, in which both the Prince and Lady Aylesford (?) were seriously compromised. Randolph did not mince matters, and told the Princess frankly that unless she contrived to stop the case then proceeding, the scandal would extend to the most exalted quarters.

The Princess at the time said nothing about this brutal attempt to blackmail. But a few days later, the Marquess of Hartington asked Randolph to meet him at the Turf Club, to give an explanation of his conduct. Several other members were in attendance. Hartington then said that an ugly rumour had reached himself and his friends: and that he believed the letters did not in point of fact exist. Whereupon Randolph produced them all from his pocket, and placed them beside him on the table.

The Duke's hand fell heavily on the letters – grasped them, and in a moment they were burning in the fire: 'I think no more need be said about this story' muttered the Duke, and left the room.

I believe every word of the tale.

1 MARCH 1906
Poor Curzon, walking with the help of a stick, seems far from well. I think he would like to be in parliament again, but feels that he would be treated much as an ordinary mortal: a prospect from which he shrinks. He is moreover opposed to Chamberlain, and doesn't yet wish to be too much involved in private polemics.

5 MARCH 1906
Balfour and Chamberlain are both too ill to come this week and the fiscal debate is again perforce postponed. Chamberlain is making great difficulties about the amendment to be moved with the result that our party will assuredly be split. For the moment this is immaterial, but the subsequent effects will be serious.

18 MARCH 1906
The party must pull itself together. This week we missed a great opportunity – failed for lack of organisation and courage. Herbert Gladstone's[9] new regulations have virtually wrecked the administration of the Aliens Act. We were dormant, comatose; and have practically let the whole thing go by default. We had a splendid case, and three or four men both anxious and competent to defeat

[8] George Charles, Lord Blandford, eighth Duke of Marlborough (1844–92); succeeded father, 1883; divorced, 1883.
[9] Herbert John Gladstone, first Viscount Gladstone (1854–1930), youngest son of the premier; Home Secretary 1905–10.

In the wilderness

Gladstone in debate: and yet nothing was done. The discussion only lasted an hour and a half – Carson gave his party away; and Gladstone who is a pudding, and ill-mannered to boot, was justified in treating the matter as a mere detail upon which he had not been seriously criticised. I begged Balfour to take the matter up, but he is still tired and unable to assume an active role. We ought unquestionably to have attacked the Home Secretary hotly. His offensive and overbearing attitude has made him fair game; and though we were outmanoeuvred today we shall get home again before long. Gladstone is the weakling of the cabinet: pompous, sententious, and wholly lacking those human qualities which often make a most successful parliamentarian, out of indifferent materials. His insolence in replying to civil questions has already bred enemies on his own side of the House: yes, with luck we will make his position uncomfortable.

1 APRIL 1906

A visit to Lady Wemyss, and thence lunch ... Began at 2.0. These late luncheons are *démodés* and tiresome. Few people nowadays lunch later than 1.30, and our organisation does not provide for the vexatious interval between 1.30 and 2.0.

Lady Rayleigh[10] gives a good account of A.J.B. and says he is thoroughly enjoying his rest cure and the total absence of responsibility.

24 APRIL 1906

It ought to be possible to defeat Birrell's[11] odious Education Bill. The Roman Catholics as a church will oppose it, though whether the Nationalists are persuaded or coerced into fighting the measure is problematical. They have been bought by C-B and of all people they are the most reluctant to break even a corrupt parliamentary bargain. But the harmony between the Irish and English R.C. hierarchy is fairly close; and I doubt not that Dr. Bourne and his colleagues will have considerable influence over Redmond via O'Dwyer and Logue.[12] Healy will fight the bill: that seems certain: and his attitude may tend to keep up the jealous rivalry between himself and Dillon. So much the better for us, and so much the worse for Birrell. As regards the Anglican Church, we show a remarkable solidarity of opinion. James Hereford[13] wants to be a Radical archbishop and Henson[14] wants a Liberal-episcopal throne. Their influence is virtually nil: but there are rocks ahead. The report of the Ritual enquiry will be issued before long, and I fear it will divide and

[10] Evelyn, daughter of J. M. Balfour of Whittingehame by Blanche, daughter of James, second Marquess of Salisbury; sister of Arthur Balfour.

[11] Augustine Birrell (1850–1933), MP (Lib.) Fife W. 1889–1900, N. Bristol 1906–18; president of Board of Education 1905–7, Chief Secretary for Ireland 1907–16.

[12] Francis Alphonsus Bourne (1861–1935), Archbishop of Westminster 1903–35, Cardinal from 1911; Edward Thomas O'Dwyer (1842–1947), Bishop of Limerick; Michael Logue (1840–1924), Archbishop of Armagh 1888, Cardinal from 1893.

[13] John Percival (1834–1918), headmaster of Clifton College, 1862–79; of Rugby, 1887–95; Bishop of Hereford, 1895–1918.

[14] Herbert Hensley Henson (1863–1947), Bishop of Durham 1920–39.

94

dishearten our people. It will alienate Ulster members and also Scottish unionists from fighting the government and it will throw an apple of discord into our midst. It will probably be impossible to mention our trust deeds entitling the schools to teach the doctrines of the Church of England without being met by hostile queries of 'what are the doctrines?' and so forth.

We don't fight a losing battle well; but I am not without hope.

22 MAY 1906

Lunched with C-B in Downing St to discuss various art matters.

9 JUNE 1906

The garden party at Haigh has been a marked success. The flowers, the children, and above all the refreshments, proved irresistible attractions. 2,300 people came expectant and left satisfied.[15]

16 JUNE 1906

The political situation is puzzling. In the first place we cannot detect the source of Birrell's so-called 'concession' on clause two of the Education Bill: and we are therefore ignorant of the nature or extent of the pressure which induced him to make so far-reaching a change. Our party is clearly innocent, for the government tries to ignore our arguments, indeed does so with ostentation. I don't think the Roman Catholics brought it about either, while if the motive power came from the Liberal Churchmen, we should probably have collected some information about it in the lobby: at any rate I am sure that Birrell has not done it of his own volition.

... Birrell is not a successful strategist. He is of course without experience: but many skilled men are beside him from whom he might learn that curt and caustic replies are inadequate weapons with which reasoned arguments can be met. Our position though absurdly weak from the point of view of numbers, is in other respects strong. We know our case – Anson, Wyndham, A.J.B., Bob Cecil, Butcher, Craik – together with Cave, Salter, Evelyn Cecil,[16] and two or three others, form a combination of parliamentary and educational knowledge far outweighing the powers of Lough[17] and Birrell – for on them alone the burden of the battle rests. Their colleagues on the front bench, and their expert supporters

---

[15] The cost was £280, paid by Bal, whose bank balance was then reduced to £300.

[16] Sir William Reynell Anson, third Bt. (1843–1914), Warden of All Souls from 1881; Vice-chancellor of Oxford 1898–9, MP (Cons.) Oxford University 1899–1914; George Wyndham (1863–1913), Chief Secretary for Ireland 1900–05; Sir Henry Craik, Bt., (1846–1927), MP (Cons.) Glasgow and Aberdeen universities 1906–18, secretary of Scottish education department 1885–1904; Sir Arthur Clavell Salter (1859–1928), MP (Cons.) Basingstoke 1906–17, barrister and judge; (Sir) Evelyn Cecil, first Baron Rockley (1865–1941), MP (Cons.) E. Herts. 1898–1900, Aston Manor 1900–29, private secretary to premier, his uncle, 1891–2, 1895–1902.

[17] Thomas Lough (1850–1922), MP (Lib.) Islington W. 1892–1918; tea merchant; secretary to the Board of Education, 1905–8; once employed Ramsay MacDonald as secretary.

behind, such as Macnamara, Yoxall, Kekewich, Dilke,[18] (and many more), hold their peace for parliamentary reasons. Hence the contest is between argument and numbers: and victory lies with the crowded division lobby.

Birrell will improve. He has relied too much upon his faculty to make the House laugh, and to condense into half a dozen witty phrases some treatise upon a knotty educational problem. Hence his failure ... He trusts to Lough, a common vulgar mind, and Lough I am bound to say has thrown over his chief on every possible occasion ...

But we must not trust to the Lords. I tell the popular audience to pin its faith to the parent, and I imagine I am right. Some people seem to think the Lords will, or ought to, evict the Bill on second reading. The Lords will do nothing of the sort: indeed they will show circumspection in amending the Bill in committee. I had a talk with Lansdowne the other day on some questions of procedure, and he confirmed my opinion that the Lords (as represented at any rate by our leaders) are in a nervous, not to say jumpy, condition. They feel a marked disinclination to be ended, or mended either. Much amusement is evinced by the prevalent gossip that C-B is unwilling to fulfil his pledges to make certain peerages. The constituencies have felt their pulse since January, and there is an appreciable slump in Liberalism: enough in any case to endanger one or two seats which rumour says are to be vacated.

5 JULY 1906
The last month has marked a distinct advance in Balfour's position in the House. Not only do the Radicals listen, but they crowd in to hear him speak.

20 JULY 1906
Dined with Arthur Balfour. The old Duchess of Devonshire[19] playing bridge – hence her sobriquet of Ponte Vecchio ...

24 OCTOBER 1906[20]
The Radicals count upon a conflict with the House of Lords. If society scandals be true, they will find that the morals of those in the upper chamber (and their wives) will provide them with good arguments, concrete and abstract.

[18] Thomas James Macnamara (1861–1931), MP (Lib.) N.W. Camberwell 1900–24, Minister of Labour 1920–22; a teacher, and president of the National Union of School-Teachers from 1896; (Sir) James Henry Yoxall (1857–1925) MP (Lib.) Nottingham W. 1895–1918, general secretary of above union 1892–1924; Sir George William Kekewich (1841–1921), MP (Lib.) Exeter 1906–10, secretary of Board of Education 1900–03; Sir Charles Wentworth Dilke (1843–1911), statesman, remaining in the Commons until 1911.

[19] Countess Louise d'Alten, of Hanover, m. (1) Duke of Manchester, 1852, (2) eighth Duke of Devonshire, 1892; she d. 1911. See above, 18 April 1904. 'Eddie' Stanley, seventeenth Earl of Derby, was married to her youngest daughter, born during the period of her first marriage.

[20] After the adjournment of parliament on 4 August, Bal went on holiday to Germany, seeing a good deal of Arthur Balfour at Bayreuth, and being 'amazed and astounded by the material progress of

The Duke of W- is having a domestic *crise*, so they say: I repeat the allegations. So is the Duke of M- but he won't try for a divorce, because of his affection for the Marquess of L-whose son Lord C- is a guilty party. Mr A- is mixed up with the Countess of W- who cannot be sued by her husband, who was recently caught with (I fancy) his sister-in-law. G. L-brother of the Earl of D-, had a horse-whipping from B-, the brother of Lord G-: consequently the former has been dismissed by the Countess of D-: he looked after the racing interests of Lord D-. The K- was most anxious to take sides in this imbroglio, being prevented with the greatest difficulty. As for the poor Duke of Portland, a most honourable ménage, he is trembling as to the outcome of the Druce case; they say the Duke will find it difficult to retain his estates.

3 NOVEMBER 1906

The borough council elections in which we have swept London, are encouraging: but there are great dangers. It will not be easy to maintain the high pressure needful to strike home our blow when the County Council elections come on in March.

18 NOVEMBER 1906

The government is not happy: otherwise we should have less hysterics from Lloyd George and Birrell. They don't want to dissolve; and they don't see how to continue twelve months without doing so; but they make such a fuss that I should not be surprised if the Lords were to take fright.

However this particular Education Bill can't pass and that very fact may well bring about an election in June. Nothing would bore me more profoundly. We should win 100 seats I dare say, but the government would come back stronger than ever. Its huge unwieldy majority is a perpetual source of danger; and the wirepullers would gladly be rid of the earnest and progressive type of supporter, who develops a conscience at the least convenient moment.

The House of Lords has not strengthened its position. At a conference in the summer where there were many peers and bishops as well as members of our House, I pointed out boldly that any attempt to reform the Education Bill, and make it into a fair and workable measure would fail: the reason being that the peers have neither the knowledge nor the diligence to grapple with the problem. I therefore urged them to confine their energies to six or eight strong commonsense amendments, leaving the remainder of the bill with all its blemishes and imperfections.

This course, naturally, has not been pursued. Results: the Lords have been in chaos: they have not improved the Bill: they refuse to comply with Lansdowne's

Western Germany'. During the autumn there are several entries about Bal's ultimately successful attempt to stop a restoration of Holyrood Chapel as a place of public worship. The second Duke of Abercorn (1838–1913) makes an appearance as 'quite a typical Duke: with so little power of concentration that he can scarcely concentrate his mind long enough to read a little article in the *Daily Mail*'.

advice, and their mismanagement has been sufficiently marked to produce a reaction against the tradition that the House of Lords are a businesslike assembly. Meanwhile they ramble along without method or policy, and the public has lost all interest in their debates. When the Bill returns to us, the government will be able to reply with scorn and contumely: the Lords will have sent us a ridiculous Bill, maimed and mangled, but useless for our own purposes. Their failure makes it imperative that they should pass the Trade Disputes Bill, otherwise their fate would be sealed.

8 DECEMBER 1906

In our House the boys are becoming less and less influenced by the mannerless interruptions of the Labour and socialist members. Their interjections are symptoms of disapproval, stupid and vulgar. The Nationalists are more serious for their interruptions are ceaseless and often sadly to the point. However, it is satisfactory to note the progress which is undeniable.

15 DECEMBER 1906

Victor Cavendish[21] was quite shaking yesterday when we went home together. He had a stormy interview with his uncle who ended (oddly enough) by kicking over the fender. Victor couldn't explain exactly what happened but the poor old Duke[22] was in an ungovernable temper. He will try to spike our guns over this education business.

21 DECEMBER 1906

Bryce[23] to go to Washington, why I can't say. This ambassador requires at least one of three qualifications: (a) he should be a gentleman or (b) his wife should be a lady, or (c) one of them should have money. Bryce fails on all counts.

But he is a marvellously clever man and the appointment will doubtless appeal to

---

[21] Victor Cavendish, ninth Duke of Devonshire (1868–1938); succeeded his uncle, the former Lord Hartington, 1908; MP (Lib. Unionist) W. Derbs. 1891–1908; Whip, 1900–03; financial secretary to the Treasury, 1903–5; Governor-General of Canada, 1916–21; Colonial Secretary, 1922–4.

[22] Spencer Compton Cavendish, eighth Duke of Devonshire (1833–1908).

[23] James Bryce, first Viscount Bryce (1838–1922), Chief Secretary for Ireland, 1905–6, ambassador at Washington, 1907–13. Cf. diary, 8 March 1907, complaining of Bryce's gaucherie in writing to a Washington friend complaining of the cost of footmen, and hinting he would like to employ negroes ('one can well imagine the horror and disgust which such a suggestion evoked in Washington'.) The diarist's brother Ronald had 'never served under a man who pays less attention or shows fewer civilities towards his subordinate staff' retaining as he did 'the attitude of a pedagogue towards schoolboys' (8 July 1907). Hardinge was offered Washington by Grey but refused, having so recently returned from St Petersburg. Grey and the King pressed him, the latter summoning him to Sandringham. Hardinge suggested Bryce as an alternative, at which the King was delighted and undertook to persuade Campbell-Bannerman. Then came rather a long pause, and Hardinge was surprised to learn that Rosebery had been approached by ministers. Rosebery refused, and Bryce, entering diplomacy at nearly seventy, 'chattered incessantly till the day of his return to Britain' (diary, 12 July 1939).

the Irish Americans – perhaps that is why Roosevelt is said to have asked for him. Churchill won't go to the Irish Office – says his health is too delicate, which may be true. . . . The session has made C-B indispensable . . . Lloyd George has done well in his bills though his weakness and instability about the Welsh clause of the Education Bill has of course reduced his success. He is civil in the House but too blatant on the platform. Burns has done admirably – firm, courteous, consistent. Crewe has also done very well. Birrell has made a great mark and should be a good leader of the House. Yesterday he had a fit of hysterics. His speech on the Education Bill was the vapouring of a lunatic – he screamed at us, battered the table and vomited threats – the symptoms of an overwrought and heated mind. Poor devil I suppose he has had a fearful strain on his mind for the last ten days. He can have a rest now, unless they are cruel enough to send him to Dublin.

One feature of the session is that Dilke is now a complete nonentity without following or influence. Redmond is becoming turgid. With his growing stomach he has lost all that incisive analysis which ten years ago marked his speeches. Bob Cecil, Butcher,[24] Fred Smith, and Cave[25] are our best men: how short we are, outsiders fail to realise.

4 FEBRUARY 1907

People seem to be attacking A.J.B. in the press on the plea of inactivity . . . They little realise how profound would be our chaos and how overwhelming our impotence would become were A.J.B. to retire from the leadership of the opposition for a single month.

14 FEBRUARY 1907

Luncheon of Conservative agents to meet Hughes[26] our new head agent. He made a good impression: seems a shrewd man and is certainly an expert on registration and election law which is a vast improvement on his two predecessors.

3 MARCH 1907

Spent afternoon at Carlton. The members are amazed at our success in the County Council elections. To have won these 46 seats is a veritable triumph: it will check the rampant extravagance of the past few years and will serve to limit further commitments. Moreover the blow to ministerial prestige is serious . . . The outlook for the moment is bright, though a small clique of tariff reformers of extreme stupidity are making mischief hard.

[24] Samuel Henry Butcher (1850–1910), MP (Cons.) Cambridge University 1906–10; married a daughter of Archbishop Trench of Dublin; classical scholar; died just after winning December 1910 election.

[25] George Cave, first Viscount Cave (1856–1928, MP (Cons.) Kingston 1906–18; Home Secretary 1916–19; created peer, 1918; Lord Chancellor 1922–4, 1924–8.

[26] J. Percival Hughes, principal agent of the Conservative party from 1907; formerly private secretary to Col. Burnaby; called to bar 1896.

In the wilderness

4 MARCH 1907

Curzon tells me that he means to decline the chairmanship of the L.C.C. – reasons of health actuate him in part: also the knowledge that this post lasting for three years would probably prevent his entering parliament. We have a safe and soft seat in London waiting for him if A.J.B. can make up his mind to offer it. But Balfour is rather nervous. Hornsey is available at any moment.

9 MARCH 1907

Oddly enough the radicals are profoundly convinced that their defeat at the L.C.C. was owing to the women's vote. This I doubt: but they must have good ground for their belief which is almost universal. It certainly had considerable effect on the female suffrage question.

10 MARCH 1907

The latest scandal is that C-B proposes to re-enter the holy state of wedlock: the young thing to be honoured is a Scandinavian matron who was companion to the late Lady C-B.

29 APRIL 1907

Harry Chaplin has behaved badly about the Wimbledon seat. Ronaldshay[27] was brought home from abroad in order to stand: the local people were not only agreeable but were flattered and delighted. Then somebody intervened, presumably Austen Chamberlain, and the pressure brought to bear upon the association made them revise their verdict, and Ronaldshay was dismissed. Harry Chaplin won't be much use at Westminster: his florid speech and rotund person will do no more than provoke laughter – while he is thoroughly lazy, and can't be guaranteed to play the game.

17 MAY 1907

The two metropolitan byelections have made the government nervous... Two baronets, Pearson[28] and Christopher Furness[29] to wit, must await the dissolution before receiving the long promised rewards of peerages. Meanwhile they boycott the House of Commons.

John Redmond told a friend the other day that during his long parliamentary experience he could recall no opposition which so readily seized its chance. On our

---

[27] Laurence John Lumley Dundas, Earl of Ronaldshay (1876–1961), eldest surviving son of the first Marquess of Zetland; MP (Cons.) Hornsey 1907–16; succeeded 1929; Secretary for India, 1935–40; a leading freemason, and chairman of the National Trust 1931–45. Chaplin was elected for Wimbledon in May 1907, his Liberal opponent being Bertrand Russell.

[28] Sir Weetman Dickinson Pearson Bt., first Viscount Cowdray (1856–1927); MP (Lib.) Colchester 1895–January 1910; created baron 1910, viscount 1916.

[29] Sir Christopher Furness, first Baron Furness of Grantley (1852–1912); created peer, 1910; MP (Lib.) Hartlepool 1900–January 1910; shipowner, shipbuilder and industrialist.

skill he made no comment – that indeed is exiguous: but we are determined, and on the whole singularly free from the internecine strife which we might expect after the débâcle – and we act far more harmoniously than the radicals did during the last ten years. Our working members number about 40 to 45 at the very outside. The remainder are ill, idle, or incompetent. The strain upon the fighting group is consequently terrific, and our new procedure rules aggravate our difficulties. How much stronger we should be if only it were possible to secure active men to replace politicians of the type of Kimber,[30] Stone,[31] Henniker Heaton[32] – the fainéant members: or utterly useless people like Haddock,[33] Harrison-Broadley,[34] or Colonel Walker.[35] But the most worthless place high value upon themselves. Batty Tuke[36] I am told thinks himself indispensable, while John Talbot[37] imagines that were he to retire Hugh Cecil might lose the seat. All this is discouraging. Still we are beginning to make progress and the radicals know it.

20 MAY 1907

Churchill's attack on Austen Chamberlain is unpardonable. Austen may have his weak points – not that Churchill can know them: but to make party capital out of his eyeglass and buttonhole, thus making a vicarious stab at Joe Chamberlain who is probably on his deathbed, will assure the outer public that Churchill like his father, is a born cad.

9 JUNE 1907

It is rather significant that the Oxford Union should have voted for Home Rule by such a decisive majority. It is true that John Redmond spoke, and I doubt not that his influence went far to convince the waverer: he is a good speaker, and well able to adapt his tone to his audience. None the less the vote is disquieting. They say the undergraduate is very socialistic just now, while at Cambridge they are even more radical. Much of this *outré* view of politics is evanescent. In my day at Oxford I

[30] Sir Henry Kimber, first Baronet (1834–1923), MP (Cons.) Wandsworth 1885–1913, solicitor and company director.
[31] Sir John Benjamin Stone (1838–1914), MP (Cons.) Birmingham E. 1895–January 1910; formerly a Birmingham manufacturer, but latterly inclined to photography and world travel; official photographer to the 1911 coronation.
[32] John Henniker Heaton (1848–1914), MP (Cons.) Canterbury 1885–December 1910; created baronet, 1912; postal reformer with Australian business interests; wrote book on aborigines.
[33] George Bahr Haddock (1863–1930), MP (Cons.) N. Lonsdale 1906–18; recreations hunting, shooting.
[34] Col. Henry Broadley Harrison-Broadley (1853–1914), MP (Cons.) Howdenshire 1906–14.
[35] Col. William Hall Walker, first Baron Wavertree of Delamere (1856–1933), MP (Cons.) Widnes 1900–19; created peer, 1919; a breeder, rider, and owner of fine racehorses; gave his stud to the nation, 1916, to found a national stud.
[36] Sir John Batty Tuke (1835–1913), MP (Cons.) Edinburgh and St. Andrews universities 1900–January 1910; leading specialist in mental disease, particularly hysteria; director of asylum.
[37] John Gilbert Talbot (1835–1910), MP (Cons.) W. Kent 1868–78, Oxford University 1878–January 1910.

remember rather similar episodes, where even Conservative clubs showed themselves highly advanced, for the sake of some passing pose or paradox. I fear however that the movement at Oxford today is based upon a more serious basis.

... Joe Chamberlain seems to be hopelessly incurable: and yet optimistic reports are issued by the family, deceiving nobody, and scarcely compatible with what the public knows having seen the poor man carried from the railway compartment to his private carriage. The theory is that the stroke arose from nicotine poisoning, caused by excessive tobacco, which regular exercise might well have averted: but few people led a more sedentary life than Joe, and he now has to pay a cruel penalty. Why these mysterious statements about his progress are published every other day cannot be explained, unless indeed Joe himself requires assurance that he is getting on well.

24 JUNE 1907

C-B certainly keeps his party together in a wonderful way. They are stupid and inexperienced men who greedily accept drafts upon futurity, believing that they will all be honoured in the fulness of time. Group after group seek interviews, and after presenting some ultimatum, withdraw it upon nebulous assurances about next session. How long these parties can be played is a nice problem: the skill with which C-B has procrastinated up to now is unquestionably brilliant.

29 JUNE 1907

The advanced Tariff Reformers do not dare let things take their course: they are positively frightened of letting well alone, and feel that they are bound to create opportunities of airing their policy. Whatever the country may feel, they always come off second best in the Commons. Austen Chamberlain had to be warned the other day that he must not push matters too far, and he was frankly told that the older section of Conservatives look upon him with suspicion, alleging that in order to achieve his fiscal ideal he would sacrifice the Church, Constitution, the land and the Union. There is some exaggeration in this view, but the substratum of truth is there, and Austen had to be warned. He has taken it to heart. Meanwhile it looks as though another section of the Tariff Reform League were trying to put Bonar Law[38] forward as leader. He is an able man, and a good speaker: but all his speeches are prepared with immense care, and I question if his extempore utterances would be out of the common. In any case I doubt if his manner and prestige could lead a party for a month with success. I like him, and we have always been good friends: but he has the bourgeois fear of being overlooked, believes in fact that he is boycotted: he was affronted at not being made a cabinet minister in 1903, he who only entered parliament in 1900!

[38] Andrew Bonar Law (1858–1923), premier 1922–3.

8 JULY 1907

I don't know why the Duke of Sutherland[39] should have invited me to become a
vice-president of the Tariff Reform League, to be sandwiched between Pearson[40]
and the two Chamberlains. The League is not conducted upon lines which inspire
much confidence in our whips' room; and were I to take a prominent post in its
hierarchy, I should doubtless be expected to do some of their intriguing for them.
The really keen tariff reformer often profoundly distrusts the methods of the Tariff
Reform League. I of course declined the invitation.

10 JULY 1907

Rumours abroad that C-B was secretly married a fortnight ago. Surely we ought to
be able to ascertain the truth.

31 JULY 1907

I dine with John Burns about twice a week – and have done so for the last five years.
I first got to know him ten years ago when he and I were on the South Kensington
committee of enquiry. We were then known as the 'Busy Bees', a nickname invented
by the Department before they realised how formidable we were. Burns is now
communicative; more so than ever in fact, and he tells me many curious things
about his work. On the whole I imagine that he has a profound abhorrence of the
Board of Guardians type of person. He has ordered so many enquiries and the
results have been so remarkable that I have sometimes wondered if he is laying the
foundation for some great reform which will sweep them away altogether. Such a
scheme would receive a good deal of support from our side. Burns's opinion of the
Labour party is entertaining. I really think he dislikes them as much as they hate
him.

Meanwhile the accession of wealth ('£2000 a year because I am doing four men's
work' as he remarked) has developed latent tastes which he has hitherto been unable
to gratify. Burns is a bibliophile, and he often shows me some new
acquisition – works dealing chiefly with public affairs: he is fond of early pamphlets
about the poor law and local government, and he has made quite a choice collection.
A few days ago he bought a third folio of Shakespeare for £12 – a good bargain if
the volume is perfect. What a pity that Burns loses self-control when on the
platform. Excitement and verbosity carry him much further than his considered
judgment justifies, and he says things which are not only inconsistent with his
personal views but which also conflict with his departmental and administrative
action.

[39] Cromartie Sutherland-Leveson-Gower, fourth Duke of Sutherland (1851–1913); succeeded
father, 1892; MP (Lib.) Sutherland 1874–86, as Lord Stafford.
[40] Sir Cyril Arthur Pearson, first Baronet, newspaper owner (1866–1921); Wykehamist founder of
Daily Express; purchased *Standard*, 1904, and tried to buy *The Times*, 1907; a protectionist before
Chamberlain, he founded Tariff Reform League, 1903; described by Chamberlain as 'the greatest
hustler I have ever known'.

In the wilderness

A Band!

I hate being serenaded by bands, though the children quite enjoy it. Happily the plethora of brass bands which visit Haigh have been greatly reduced, and only two are now tolerated. In old days, I mean in the time of my great-grandfather,[41] as many as thirty or forty bands used to turn up between Xmas and the New Year. Each band used to receive half a sovereign and as much beer as their paunches could control; they also received many kind words from the old gentleman who must have been an odd mixture of geniality and the other thing.

LORD BALCARRES TO LORD MIDLETON,[42] 1 JANUARY 1908

Some twelve months ago I was deputed to attend a small private conference at which certain lobby correspondents and editors of three or four newspapers attended. They said that they thought they were rather neglected, and I naturally asked them what remedy they proposed. In accordance with their wishes I undertook to be available whenever any accredited representative desired advice from the whips; and accordingly we have maintained a constant touch with certain prominent organs of public opinion. The results I must confess have been discouraging. We have constantly given them hints and advice and we have even gone further and prepared paragraphs and short articles for their use; but to our disappointment we have frequently found that the hints are disregarded and that the paragraphs remain unpublished! The fact is that much information is given, and freely given, but the editorial departments of the papers, which must of necessity depend on their lobby correspondents (who are in hourly communication with ourselves) have shown very little desire to avail themselves of opportunities which they have asked us to create. The lack of cohesion is more prominent between the editors and their staffs than between the newspapers and our party whips.

24 JANUARY 1908

At Chorley ... Tonight I learned that the Radical agent has been sacked: also that the Radical paper is going to turn definitely socialist. All this is bad news. I wish the local ministerialists had been able to keep their party organisation on its legs a little longer. They now abandon the field to the Labour party: although not organised in any way as yet, they know their strength, they can improvise electoral machinery at a few days' notice: and in short they form a combination infinitely more threatening

---

[41] James, twenty-fourth Earl of Crawford (1783–1869); succeeded 1825.

[42] In reply to a proposal by Midleton, seen by Balcarres as a deaf, boring, elderly and ineffectual intriguer of a harmless kind, that Balfour needed 'a sort of chief of staff' to keep him in touch with the party, and suggesting Balcarres for the post. Midleton claimed support from Hood, Balfour and Lansdowne for this intrigue, which was partly aimed at Balfour's existing factotum Sandars, who, Midleton said, 'has been ruled out by everyone for this'. Balcarres firmly rejected the idea, adding that Sandars was 'at the same time shrewd and broad-minded, able to humour the foibles of Arthur Balfour and also to control in certain matters where guidance is necessary'.

than anything I ever fear from the Liberals. The outlook is unfavourable. Even in the Conservative Club there are oldish members who would vote for a socialist without hesitation or secrecy. My strength lies chiefly in the education question: to some extent in fiscal reform, and perhaps most largely of all upon my old associations with the constituency. But I can't say that I like the prospect of fighting a good class of labour candidate.

29 JANUARY 1908

Walter Rothschild[43] is on the verge of bankruptcy. Papa has already paid his debts once or twice: now, he has speculated, he has expended huge sums upon a rather indifferent book about extinct birds, and they say that a lady friend has absorbed many shekels.

Anyhow poor fat Walter has raised money on the post-obits of papa and mamma. The former is furious: most of all that for the first time in history a Rothschild has speculated unsuccessfully. It is a great blow to the acumen of the family. They say that a meeting of the Tribe will be summoned at Frankfort or Vienna, or wherever the financial headquarters are, so that Walter may be tied up more severely in the future. We don't want him to resign his seat, though I fancy it is pretty safe. Personally I rather like him. He has certainly this much which is interesting – namely a clumsiness of person, voice, and gesture which is quite unique.

30 JANUARY 1908

Alick Hood tells me that Pearson asked him to buy the *Times* on behalf of the Conservative party or at any rate to invest a large sum of money in it.[44] Alick would have refused even if there had been a million at his disposal.

31 JANUARY 1908

There is a grave difficulty in the immediate future, the Church Discipline Bill. Last year its promoters had no luck in the ballot – now they are first. The act would probably be a dead letter in most cases, but it would create all kinds of opportunities of persecution: the immediate effect of its introduction will be to split the Church party, especially in Lancashire, and thus prejudice in a really serious manner the united fight we were prepared to make about education. It will ease the heavy burden on the shoulders of McKenna,[45] and will add to the load we have to carry.

---

[43] Lionel Walter, second Baron Rothschild, FRS, Ph.D., (1868–1937), MP (Lib. Unionist) Mid-Bucks. 1899–January 1910; authority on zoology. His debts were said to be 'between £750,000 and £1,000,000'.

[44] See above, 8 July 1907.

[45] Reginald McKenna (1863–1943), Liberal statesman and financial authority; financial sec. to Treasury, 1905–7, president of the Board of Education 1907–8, First Lord of the Admiralty 1908–11, Home Office 1911–15, Chancellor of the Exchequer May 1915–December 1916.

In the wilderness

I fancy that the bolder spirits in the government may be tempted to rush an early dissolution, soon after Easter when the old age pension scheme has been outlined. But I don't think that bait would really be very tempting. We should certainly be strengthened in arguing for tariff reform to meet that liability. The government knows that we are unprepared for an election – I don't know how many constituencies there are in which we have not yet secured candidates. To that extent they would take us at a disadvantage. We should however win many seats, though not enough to give us a majority.

The government would then be reconstructed on a more radical basis, their majority would be more compact and loyal (most of the cranks having been *ex hypothesi* defeated). They would claim the electoral sanction for a hundred wildcat schemes and in one sense would be more powerful than before. At the same time the substantial increase in our own numbers would greatly relieve us of the killing strain to which we are now subjected.

. . . All the same I hope they won't collapse: we cannot be ready for the fight until January 1909 at the earliest. Personally the sooner the election comes the better would be my chances in Chorley, for the Labour party has not yet managed to supersede the Liberal organisation which is now on its deathbed . . .

27 FEBRUARY 1908
Licensing Bill introduced. The government is growing old: and its members are getting nervous . . . If the old age pension scheme is unsatisfactory and if the budget demands a continuance of the duties on tea, sugar, etc., an early election is quite possible: and it is improbable that a dissolution can be postponed for twelve months. In one way the sooner it comes the better: the longer it is deferred the greater the probability of our being returned by a small margin which would be perfectly fatal. What we should like would be this government sent back with five and twenty or thirty votes to the good. We could then smash them up in a session, and return to power with a working majority would be secured. Our troubles would then begin. I notice a reluctance upon the part of the extreme Tariff Reformers to argue their case in the House of Commons with anything like the zeal which they display in the constituencies. All the same the party as a whole is far more united and solid than was the case a year ago. The number of surviving Free-fooders is small.

6 MARCH 1908
The Tweedmouth episode absorbs all attention . . . We dined at Lansdowne House. The German ambassador was there. As we left the dining room Lord Lansdowne said to me 'Thank heavens he hasn't tried to talk about poor Tweedmouth'[46] but as

---

[46] Edward Marjoribanks, second Baron Tweedmouth (1849–1909), First Lord of the Admiralty, 1905–8, President of the Council, 1908; incurred censure for alleged naval disclosures to Wilhelm II, 1908; became insane.

the evening wore on, the ambassador became more and more restive. Connie and I were among the last to leave the house, but everybody was outstayed by the distinguished foreigner who as the last guest was leaving the room, went over to our host and drew him apart into the small saloon. I should have liked to hear that conversation.

Lansdowne however must have been prepared for the debate. In the afternoon both before and after the hurried cabinet which met in Asquith's room, Tweedmouth was lobbying and trying to put his case before anybody he met. Actually he asked to see Hood. Alec was away so he closeted himself with Jack Sandars for nearly half an hour: and offered to show him the letters. Sandars like a wise man refused to see them, not wishing to make himself *particeps criminis*. Then Tweedmouth left Westminster to go to Lansdowne House. Sandars leapt to the telephone to put Lansdowne *au courant* with the most recent developments.

... Tweedmouth we all know. He is a pauper, and were he to retire he would be absolutely bankrupt: so he does not mean to relinquish his comfortable income. He will not hesitate to stoop down to retain his position. His record is not bright: we have not forgotten a singular episode connected with the Nationalist party fund, and from 1892-5 he was recognised as the most shrewd and least scrupulous asset of the Liberal party.

But he has gone too far. A weak man, specially subject to female cajolery, Lord Tweedmouth, immensely flattered with the Emperor's civilities, has been gossiping: his friends re-gossiped the whole thing and now the public is demanding explanations. Hence the fuss.

7 MARCH 1908

All the papers are wrong. Of that I am convinced. It is assumed that the Emperor wanted to influence Tweedmouth. Not a bit. Tweedmouth's statements about the two-power standard have been too precise. The Kaiser wanted to do to Tweedmouth what he had already done to Goluchowski and to Delcassé. He wanted to get rid of him.

The methods have been perilously near success. The Kaiser had taken his measure of the First Lord, had 'sized him up' and realised that only one poisoned weapon was efficacious, namely flattery. We may punish Tweedmouth but we must not let him resign.

8 MARCH 1908

Castlereagh[47] writes to say that from private information he is pretty sure that Wilhelm has been carrying on a clandestine correspondence with Haldane. Nothing would surprise me less: but whether it would be wise for us to pillory the arch-humbug is a different matter. The radicals raised the Tweedmouth episode in the House, and they will gladly do the same for Haldane. Why should we interfere?

[47] Charles, Viscount Castlereagh, later seventh Marquess of Londonderry (1878–1949); MP (Cons.) Maidstone 1906–15; succeeded father, 1915; Air Minister, 1931–5.

In the wilderness

22 MARCH 1908

If only our men would wake up and do some work in the House! If only we could exchange our comatose baronets for some active and loyal party men – we should then have a terrific effect upon the ministerialists who are cowed and dejected beyond belief. In the country good work is being done: in the House of Commons activity is limited to about 30 to 40 Unionists. It is really a disgraceful state of things and I am surprised how seldom the newspapers draw attention to our apathy.

28 MARCH 1908

Burns talks about three more years of office: it can't be done!

3 APRIL 1908

I have always allowed myself to doubt the depth of this Irish demand for higher education. A country cannot really want university teaching until it has shown some keenness in relation to elementary education. Ireland is the only scrap of the British Empire in which the white population does not insist upon elementary teaching being obligatory.

10 MAY 1908

Victor Cavendish came to the House of Commons the other afternoon and loafed about for four hours to his great happiness. Poor Victor is sadly lost in the Lords though I doubt not he will find compensations. The Duchess says that he can't think what to do in the evenings and that he writes all sorts of needless letters to kill time. London in fact is so wearisome to him that he is to be sent to Chatsworth and Hardwick to supervise their obsolete systems of drainage – at any rate while in the country he is less liable to fret over forced absence from Westminster. Victor tells me that Dick[48] is greatly incensed at having to pay death duties at the rate of 18 per cent upon Holker and this is producing some reaction against his radicalism. Dick thinks he will be a pauper on £20,000 a year or so. Well well – some people are hard to please. I am sorry for Lady Evelyn[49] who was really devoted to Holker where *d'ailleurs* she has spent most of her married life and where her numerous offspring have been brought up. I wonder what the future of Chatsworth will be. It must be nearly three-quarters of a century since there was a nursery in that massive pile and a good deal of reconstruction will be needed before the family can be fitted in. The gossips say that Victor will take up all the old Duchess's sporting and gambling friends in order to fill the house as their own circle of acquaintance has always been kept most restricted – probably from reaction against the lavish and rather unsavoury standards of the *ancien regime*. Anyhow the late Duke saved enough money to make it relatively easy for his successor to enter into possession.

[48] Lord Richard Cavendish (1871–1946) of Holker Hall, Lancs; nephew of the eighth Duke, and brother of the ninth Duke of Devonshire; MP (Lib. Unionist) N. Lonsdale Division (Lancs.) 1895–1906, which he contested unsuccessfully as a Liberal in 1906. The eighth Duke, better known as Lord Hartington, had just died, on 24 March 1908.

[49] Lady Evelyn Fitzmaurice m. 1892 Victor Cavendish, ninth Duke of Devonshire.

24 MAY 1908

Mother has received an extraordinary pamphlet about Violet Granby now Duchess of Rutland. It is most scurrilous. It is written by a German governess who appears to have been in charge of the children for two or three years. She does not sign her name, but this is added in MS together with her address, and an invitation to all and sundry to examine the original documents upon which the allegations are based. Her real grievance seems to be that she was cheated out of a few pounds of her salary which considering the haphazard ways of the Granby family is more than probable. The gravamen of the charges is however much more serious, for it makes specific accusations of immorality... It is however most difficult to follow, as the composition is much involved, the English very faulty, and the woman's habit of putting initials to replace names makes any study of the document a real fatigue. Nevertheless the upshot is pretty clear and in more than one place it is directly stated that Harry Cust is the father of the girl Diana.[50] I haven't seen the latter for years but I have always heard that her likeness to her reputed father is quite striking.

30 MAY 1908

Poor Muriel Marjoribanks has been telling us sad stories of Tweedmouth her father-in-law. He seems to be hopelessly insane. For the last few weeks his speeches have contained wandering passages. Some remarks he made in the House of Lords when addressing himself to a panegyric of Campbell-Bannerman, were mercifully suppressed by the newspaper reporters, but there must have been three or four hundred people who actually heard his perfectly cruel reference to the personal charms of Lady Campbell-Bannerman... Now we learn that he is quite off his head and his mania seems to have assumed a disagreeable complexion.

I am sorry for Dudley[51] and his wife. They are just home after a trying time in South Africa – looking forward to some amusement during the season, prior to his taking up a military post in Lancashire. They arrive in time to see Lord Tweedmouth resign a lucrative portfolio carrying much patronage, to receive a sinecure of small emoluments: he is absolutely ruined in fortune, and now he is obliged to resign everything else and lead a life of enforced retirement.

31 MAY 1908

The Duchess of Norfolk presents her spouse with a son and heir. This reflects immense credit on both parties. I wonder what Ned Talbot[52] will think, since he

[50] Lady Diana Cooper

[51] Sir Dudley Marjoribanks, third Baron Tweedmouth (1874–1935), who succeeded his father in 1909. His wife Muriel was the daughter of St John Brodrick, the Unionist minister. In his salad days, Bal noted, young Tweedmouth was as extravagant as his father.

[52] Edmund Bernard Fitzalan-Howard, first Viscount Fitzalan of Derwent (1855–1947), known as Lord Edmund Talbot from 1876 to 1921; created peer 1921, KG, 1925; MP (Cons.) Chichester 1894–1921; junior Lord of the Treasury, 1905; joint parliamentary secretary, 1915–21; chief Conservative Whip, 1913–21, succeeding Balcarres; Lord-Lieutenant of Ireland, 1921–2; an R.C.

has been the heir apparent for fifteen or twenty years, but he is one of the very best fellows in the world, and nobody could ask a more ready and willing colleague in the House of Commons: nonetheless it must be hard to change expectations in so sudden a manner.

12 JUNE 1908

An invasion of librarians – a hundred altogether I dare say. We had a pleasant exhibition for them in the drawing room: they walked about the libraries, drank tea, listened to speeches with deference, and I fancy left with a pleasant impression of Father's very genial hospitality.

15 JUNE 1908

Lord Derby's[53] death was sudden, though his family knew that his heart was weak. He was one of the most delightful of men, and at the same time the most indolent. With him it was almost a monomania to refrain from answering letters. His correspondence on public questions was scandalously neglected, and he actually refused to allow his willing sons and competent secretaries to reply on his behalf.[54] I must have written dozens, even scores of letters, on business subjects – appointments to the magistracy, public engagements and so forth, but never an acknowledgment! I remember however that in 1903 I wrote to thank him for lending me a motor car for a byelection, and to my amusement received a long reply commenting on my letter. I had told him that his car had carried to the poll some of the electors who had helped to win his historic election in 1868 when he defeated Lord Hartington: and this aroused such pleasant memories that he took up his pen and wrote! His personal charm of manner was so great that all these oversights and lazinesses were forgotten, and I know of nobody whose influence was so great throughout Lancashire. Eddie Stanley will scarcely replace him: too fussy – but a real good fellow at heart.

18 JUNE 1908

I took a visitor over the House... We went down to the terrace, and were there harangued by a stout suffragette who had brought a steam launch close up to the balustrade. She made a capital speech, and at one moment nearly lost her balance (physical) for the tide was running high. I wonder when these good ladies will begin to break up my meetings.

19 JUNE 1908

Lloyd George scarcely conceals his unhappiness about the Old Age Pensions Bill.

[53] Frederick Arthur Stanley, sixteenth Earl of Derby (1841–1908), Conservative minister, and Governor-General of Canada 1888–93; succeeded his brother 1893.

[54] Derby's family recalled (diary, 10 May 1937) that on his death they found in his writing table a number of letters from Queen Victoria, in their envelopes, unopened. Also, according to his son, the Queen once had to write to him three times when he was in Canada before she could extract a reply.

The prospect of putting 3d. on the income tax next year must be rather disheartening.

Connie and I dined at Devonshire House – alone. I fear that the possession of much wealth and the care of many great houses, may go far to upset the happiness (or at any rate the repose of mind) of my old friend Lady Evelyn[55] as I still call her. She is literally overwhelmed with projects, wants to do everything at once, regrets everything done during the last twenty years, and altogether is in a frame of mind almost *entêtée* and quite alien to her usual coolness and decision. Everything is to be reorganised, reformed: and indeed in some ways I fancy the new broom is required. The under-butler has for the last 35 years had sole charge of the key of the strong room containing the priceless collection of gems, the miniatures, and the family jewels. He is honest as the day, and boasts that during his tenure of office nothing has ever been lost except a silver spoon which disappeared after a garden party at Lismore. Nonetheless I should be inclined to let this functionary retire on a comfortable pension – in no other way will it be possible to regain control of that key.

It is a magnificient heritage and dear old Victor remains calm and unimpassioned amidst all the perturbations of the Duchess: but he is sadly out of the world – out of his own world I mean, the House of Commons, where he has laid the foundations of a life which has now undergone a cruel *déracinage*. It will be some years before he can re-create his atmosphere – but I think he would gladly take office under a Conservative, even under a protectionist government.

20 JUNE 1908

To Windsor for the garden party. It is really good of the King to entertain with such freedom and bonhomie.

Every peer and every member of Parliament seemed to be there, but outside that circle I seemed to know few people. Ten years ago I should have been acquainted with one out of every five of those invited. This parliamentary grind is indeed crushing. I scarcely ever 'go out', rarely dine at home, and I might almost say I have altogether stopped visiting my friends. Nowadays I never make a new acquaintance except by chance. I regret it, and very deeply. I want to know people, to enlarge the scope of acquaintance if not of friendship, but the House of Commons is a hard task master, continuous and unrelenting – my function is to be there week in and week out, trying to persuade our colleagues that work has got to be done, and that it is they who must do it. But how wearisome, how dispiriting it all is. How coldly do they respond, how unwillingly will the average member share the burden whether at Westminster or in the constituencies! I am often worn out with fatigue, and disheartened in morale, wondering whether I also could not abandon public obligations in order to gratify personal tastes and private avocations. I would not like to retire: were I to do so the many occupations which would spring up would fail

[55] The new Duchess of Devonshire

to fill the void – and I should not like to turn my back on the enemy after facing him for so many years. Nevertheless it is hard to be absorbed to the exclusion of all other interests, to see that self-sacrifice does not bring any material benefit to the party – most of all to realize how many of our idle and ignorant members say that this, that or the other can well be done by 'one of the whips'. The poor whips are indeed patient beasts of burden . . . This concentration of work upon the shoulders of a few men – about forty all told in the House of Commons – is of course bad for those men who accept the responsibility for they have no time to think or to rest. It is equally demoralising for the shirker and fainéant while the party at large is becoming effete intellectually – and if the election took place tomorrow and if we were returned with a majority of a hundred it would be almost impossible to form a government! There is a confession – but true. We have not got the men who are capable of manning the public offices.

27 JUNE 1908

Altogether the political situation is so confused, and the future so obscure that any piece of bad luck might produce a cabinet crisis of formidable dimensions. Bonar Law tells me that after a careful examination of electoral prospects he has come to the reluctant conclusion that we should have a substantial majority at an immediate dissolution. Heaven forbid!

2 JULY 1908

Lord Cadogan[56] must be a pretty rich man. By Chelsea's death he saves well over £20,000 a year which he was paying in insurance premiums and so forth, while I imagine that the capitals to be paid to him in pursuance of this demise must be enormous. Poor man, I am sorry for him, and wonder again and again why two such people as Cadogan and his good wife should have suffered such affliction from their offspring. I hope the boy may be well cared for, but his blood is against him. I don't detect much character or stability in the Sturt stirps. At Eton Chelsea was spoiled, at College petted, in Parliament fêted at first and subsequently overlooked. Then he fell into the hands of the gamesters and went to the Devil.

12 JULY 1908

We have now parted from the Old Age Pensions Bill, the most corrupting bit of legislation passed in my time. It will put temptations in our way – one side will outbid the other; promises to reduce the age, to remove disqualifications, and perhaps even to enlarge the dole will be exacted from our candidates as much as from the radicals, with serious effects upon our national finance, and entailing far more grave results upon our legislative integrity.

[56]George Henry, fifth Earl Cadogan (1840–1915), succ. 1873; Lord-Lieutenant of Ireland, 1895–1902. His first son died young; his second son, Viscount Chelsea (1868–1908) married a Sturt and left one boy who died in 1910. Chelsea was a former private secretary to the First Lord of the Treasury.

18 JULY 1908

A series of articles in the *Standard*, directed against the apathy of Unionist members of parliament, has attracted a good deal of attention. Some of our men are annoyed: others including myself, hold that the criticism though based on very insufficient knowledge, is much more likely to improve matters than the reverse ... Where the articles have been unfair is in their criticism of Balfour. The writer has no conception how hard the Chief works, and how lamentable would be the substitution of any alternative leader. The rank and file of the party is not idle because their leaders fail to encourage them, although they allege that excuse. The explanation is simply that they prefer idling and fiddling about in their clubs. To suggest that they are busy in their own constituencies is fatuous: to assume that they would gladly take up work in the House of Commons is equally absurd. To my mind the saddest aspect of the outlook is not the hopeless apathy of people like McIver, Kimber, Burdett Coutts, Benjamin Stone, Fardell,[57] and many others (mostly knights and baronets) – as they are and always must be drones – but the otiose callousness of men like Percy, Alfred Lyttelton, Bonar Law is really distressing, especially where we have to deal with ex-ministers who mean to be in the next government, and some of whom have had seats found for them after their defeats at the general election. Indolence on their part is triply indefensible.

By the way, people have not noticed the tendency of our ex-ministers to gravitate to London in quest of safe seats. We have now got Chaplin, Balfour, Percy,[58] Bonar Law, W. Long, Alfred Lyttelton – too large a proportion of metropolitan members for any future cabinet. The London member is seldom in touch with provincial movements, and a cabinet would be amply advised on all London questions by one or at most two members representing metropolitan constituencies.

11 AUGUST 1908

Our clansman Thomas Lindsay has recently retired from the honourable post he has long held under the North British Railway Company, *videlicet* that of stationmaster at Kilconquhar. Having worked faithfully for many years he was about to have become entitled to no mean pension – but rather than be beholden to his employers, this queer dour character retired a few weeks before his qualification for this pension was mature! He now lives in the village, works hard in his cottage garden, and assures his visitors that the strain of digging potatoes has reduced his weight by 28 pounds ... None the less, there he is, and shortly to receive as a testimonial from ten local landlords who have all by turns shuddered under

[57] Sir Lewis McIver, first Baronet (1846–1920), MP (Lib. Un.) Edinburgh W. 1895–1909; William Burdett-Coutts, formerly Ashmead-Bartlett, (1851–1921), husband of Baroness Burdett-Coutts, but himself an American, MP (Cons.) Westminster 1885–1921; (Sir) Thomas George Fardell (1833–1917), MP (Cons.) S. Paddington 1895–1910.
[58] Henry Algernon George, Earl Percy, (1871–1909) MP (Cons.) Kensington S. 1895–1909, eldest son of the seventh Duke of Northumberland; Under-Secretary for India 1902–3, for Foreign Affairs 1903–5.

In the wilderness

Lindsay's tyranny about excess weight of luggage, an armchair of luxury and comfort wherein his portly frame may ease its lofty independence.

Lindsay, I should say, can perhaps afford to dispense with a pension since he has long since conducted with success the avocation of coal merchant. The skeleton in his cupboard is connected with Mrs Lindsay, who is not Mrs Lindsay. Long ago he became engaged to a young woman of the neighbourhood, for some while a housemaid of Prentice's; this match however did not take place and Lindsay took to his bosom the damsel who still reposes in his confidence; whom the world calls and believes to be his duly appointed wife, but with whom no legal ceremony has ever taken place, for the other party (still believed to be unmarried) pronounced that she would bring an action for breach of promise the moment Lindsay proclaimed his wedlock with the rival. Hence a domestic arrangement which has subsisted successfully for many years without the sanction of the Mother Kirk.

25 AUGUST 1908

The Bluchers[59] are here. He is more anti-semitic than ever, and more than ever convinced that the future of Europe can only be secured by re-establishing a complete system of forced labour.

8 SEPTEMBER 1908

The Duchess of Connaught and Princess Patricia came to tea. The former (probably also the latter) distressed at the hostile reception afforded to Prince Arthur[60] when he visited Glasgow two or three days ago. The local socialists seized the opportunity of inflaming the unemployed workmen – a solid mass of these wretched men stood outside the Town Hall and were well drilled into hooting the Prince on each occasion of his appearance. I doubt if any personal note could be detected – the object being demonstration and a form of self-advertisement which could not fail to become notoriety. Nonetheless the aspect is displeasing and I doubt whether a Royal Prince has been thus persistently attacked for a hundred years.

13 OCTOBER 1908

In view of an expected riot this evening, caused by a nefarious combination of suffragettes, unemployed, and hooligans, an emissary of the government came to the Speaker, and suggested that with our connivance, we should collapse discussion on the Children's Bill at 7.15 – go home, and abandon an empty and dark Palace of Westminster.

The Speaker was not unwilling – but Alec Hood was adamant. In the first place, he said that this would unduly curtail our discussion on the Children's Bill: that we

[59] HSH Gebhard, Prince Blucher von Wahlstatt (b. 1836, the third prince, descended from the hero of Waterloo) and his wife Wanda. Blucher's 'plea for the re-establishment of torture was little short of masterful'. (diary, 31 August 1908.)

[60] HRH Prince Arthur (1883–1938), son of Prince Arthur, Duke of Connaught (1850–1942), seventh child of Queen Victoria; the Connaughts were related to the Bluchers.

should be made to share the charge of cowardice, and that he was not inclined to make things easy for the most incompetent and bombastic government we have ever had. Alec neither believes in running away nor in easing the path of Gladstone and Asquith. So we sat on; made a fool of Herbert Samuel – while thousands of police kept the crowd at a distance from Westminster. It was a disagreeable night: for though cowed by superior forces, the demeanour of the demonstrators was sullen and fierce.

16 OCTOBER 1908

Sir Bindon Blood[61] has been to the whips' room to talk about Indian politics, his desire being as Alec gathered to persuade us to use our influence to prevent discussions in the House. Well – I don't think we ever contemplated anything of the kind; and indeed it was at the instance of John Morley acting through myself that our men put blocking motions on the paper months ago, which have effectually stopped motions for adjournment. Sir Bindon doesn't seem to be an alarmist, but his views on the situation are grave. He says that the Sikhs can no longer be trusted!

... Grayson[62] was again suspended this afternoon, this time for an indefinite period. He is a horrid fellow with a most vicious countenance. For some reason or other he has made a dead set against me in my constituency, having attended four or five meetings I should think in the last three years. As I have never come into collision with the creature I was at a loss to explain the matter: but on making local enquiries I discovered that the chairman of the Independent Labour Party at Adlington (one Roberts I think) has a 'housekeeper' for whom Grayson has a marked taste: so he goes to my part of Lancashire whenever he can, and the socialists en revanche insist on his repaying them and the *bonne amie* by a speech full of scurrility and excess.

21 OCTOBER 1908

Burns came to talk while I was having my food in the tea room, which is deserted between 8 and 9. He talked as usual with great freedom. The right to raise a penny rate to help the unemployed has been the bone of contention in the cabinet – and he tells me that the opposition to his views emanated from Lloyd George and Churchill. As regards the speech made by the former at Swansea, Burns is of opinion that it contributed greatly to the prevalent unrest of the unemployed, and that the flippant manner in which Lloyd George talks of transferring money from one class of the community to another, has fomented acrimony. Burns feels deeply on the subject and his speech next Monday may cause heart burning as well as surprise.

22 OCTOBER 1908

Burns has been telling Bob Cecil exactly what I had just noted – in fact John

---

[61] Gen. Sir Bindon Blood (1842–1940); commander in Punjab 1901–7.
[62] Victor Grayson (1882–?), MP (Soc.) Colne Valley 1907–January 1910; disappeared.

In the wilderness

('Honest John Burns' they no longer call him) seems to be acting imprudently. He is in a condition bordering upon the hysterical – overworked, overwrought – and wounded by the hostility of his colleagues, who should back him up in view of the bitter animosity of avowed foes... Lloyd George with his lightweight humour calmly says he thinks Asquith has fathered the financial crisis on him in order to save his own reputation, and with the *arrière-pensée* of destroying that of his successor. This however is not so. Asquith whom I dislike and cannot admire (far from sober this evening) does at least possess the cabinet tradition and his parliamentary experience is wide. He was brought out and brought up by Mr G and he is one of the few members of the cabinet who are imbued with the time-honoured attitude which should be preserved between colleagues. His eulogy of Burns on Wednesday last was proper and suitable – he is the only cabinet minister in the House of Commons with the possible exception of Grey, who is capable of acting in the old style: when we come to the McKennas, Georges, Runcimans, and to such boobies as the Gladstones and the Sinclairs, we meet a type of mind which may be astute and aggressive, or which may be slow and tolerably safe – but all alike are divorced from every tradition which animated the old school. It is a pity: and to be frank I question if our side are much better.

23 OCTOBER 1908

Altogether there is none of that blessed uneventful calm which predicates public content and ministerial loyalty. The Nationalists are in a state of civil war. The radicals are cold and distrustful – the Labour men in as great a fright as anybody. The government cannot live another 18 months.

Meanwhile the Conservative party is wholly unprepared – not to say unfitted, for assuming the reins of government.

26 OCTOBER 1908

Burns on the unemployed – he made the hair of the Labour members stand upon end. He made his colleagues wince and his supporters groan with ill-concealed discomfort. Burns on the unemployed means a rigorous onslaught upon the unemployable with whom he is too apt to confuse the innocent and helpless victim of economic disturbance. This afternoon he carried his attack too far, and is making needless enemies among people who cannot help admiring his courage, and desiring to give him help.

13 NOVEMBER 1908

A bitter radical called Hugh Lea[63] who sits for St Pancras or thereabouts says that there are only six or eight safe radical seats in the metropolis. At this rate we should be strong enough to carry a tariff reform bill – though my desire would be to be beaten at the next election by a handful of votes: to remarshal our forces and then form a strong government backed by a convinced party.

[63] Hugh Cecil Lea (d. 1926), MP (Lib.) St Pancras E. 1906–January 1910; newspaper proprietor.

1906-10

22 NOVEMBER 1908

A new education bill arrived this morning – number four! What a miserable record for three years of Liberal education ministers. And I doubt if this bill can hope to pass in its present form... The broad observation is that it purports to be a compromise – but it accepts all from us and gives nothing in return – or to be more accurate the bill devises elaborate and crushing methods of denying to us in substance those rights of which we shall only secure the shadow.

... It is obvious that the Archbishop has been duped. He is no lawyer, no draftsman; he is unaccustomed to deal with astute and unscrupulous ministers; he does not quite realize that his negotiations are conducted with terror-stricken ministers who are shivering on the abyss of an electoral débâcle – men who are not oversensitive to the claims of equity and fair play. Why should we expect the government to be just? Their career was begun in fraud and misrepresentation and it has been marked throughout by harshness. However they have completely bamboozled our good Archbishop. His motives are good. He received certain verbal promises, and in return made verbal concessions. These concessions are embodied with unmistakeable clearness and precision in the first clause of the new bill: but the compensations which he was led to expect are framed in such a manner as to be practically worthless – so much hedged about and involved in conditional restrictions that they may actually do more harm than good. If only he had taken some competent and worldly layman into his confidence! Instead of doing this he has been guided by prelates as pious and as unsophisticated as himself – and when at a late stage he seems to have felt some measure of hesitation he called in Chancellor Dibdin[64] – and of all people in the world Sadler![65] Too late!!

I fear that he will now acquiesce in all this elaborate make belief. Hitherto I had some confidence in his Scottish shrewdness, believing that if the government acted in a dishonest fashion he would boldly repudiate the compromise and throw the whole responsibility for failure upon Runciman.[66] I gather that this is not likely to occur. I deplore the situation. If only the government had been decently honest we might have agreed to terminate a controversy which has lasted too long; the only pleasing feature of the situation is that education itself is not suffering now, nor seriously threatened by a continuance of the dispute. There has been greater actual progress in the last five years than in the previous twenty.

24 NOVEMBER 1908

Conference in Balfour's room about the Education Bill. *Sederunt* A.J.B., George Wyndham, Akers-Douglas, Austen Chamberlain, Walter Long, Lord Lansdowne.

[64] Sir Lewis Tonna Dibdin (1852–1918), ecclesiastical lawyer, judge and administrator; chancellor of various dioceses; first Church Estates Commissioner, 1905–30.

[65] Sir Michael Ernest Sadler (1861–1943), educational authority, formerly a civil servant; at this time (1903–11) Professor of Education at Manchester.

[66] Walter Runciman, first Viscount Runciman of Doxford (1870–1949), president of the Board of Education 1908–11.

In the wilderness

How we are divided! Balfour himself has not finally decided how he will vote on the second reading.

25 NOVEMBER 1908

Busy day ... I got an urgent message to go to the Lords to see the Bishop of London, my dear old friend Ingram.[67] I should say that yesterday I sent him a memo showing the illusory character of the so-called right of entry. This had opened his eyes somewhat and I found him in a state of great anxiety: he assured me that he had been dragged on by his loyalty to the Archbishop, that he was now hesitating what line to take in view of the structure of the bill. He gave me a scrap of paper which he had intended to send me in case a meeting were impossible ... Dr Ingram had shown my memorandum to the Archbishop who in his turn has felt obliged to revise his opinion or rather to state that the bill does not embody the undertakings he received. The document is written in pencil and I copy it here for future reference, exactly as it reached me.

Dear Balcarres,

The Archbishop writes this.

'I wholly agree with this, and it is *quite* clear that we are *in no way* committed to the clause *as it stands* any more than we are committed to the financial terms, which *as they stand* seem to me quite impossible.'

I certainly myself should vote against the Bill as it stands. You must not *quote* the Archbishop.   A. F. London.

This document, containing a holograph repudiation by the Archbishop, and a precise statement by the Bishop of London, showed me that doubts were beginning to harass the prelates. I showed it to A.J.B. who was immensely interested in this psychological study of episcopal meaning: and at his request returned to see A. F. London, who authorised Balfour to state tomorrow that the undertakings with regard to transfer, contracting out, and right of entry as embodied in the Bill, were so illusory that in its present form, the Bishop would have to vote against the Bill as a whole.

And London is chairman of the settlement committee!

29 NOVEMBER 1908

Pike Pease[68] lunched with Chamberlain yesterday, and came back rather depressed:

[67] Arthur Foley Winnington-Ingram (1858–1946), Bishop of London 1901–39; head of Oxford House, Bethnal Green, 1888–97, i.e. during the diarist's residence there.

[68] Herbert Pike Pease, first Baron Daryngton of Witley (1867–1949), MP (Lib. Un.) Darlington 1898–January 1910, December 1910–23, latterly as a Conservative; cr. peer, 1923; Liberal Unionist Whip, 1906–10, Unionist Whip, 1911–15, Assistant Postmaster-General 1915–22; ecclesiastical commissioner 1923, president of Church Army, vice-chairman, house of laity, church assembly; married a dean's daughter; member, executive of Liberal Unionist Council and of Tariff Reform League.

not that he expected to find Joe anything but a broken man, but because the incurable optimism of his family is so insistent as to be really painful. It would be a misfortune for Joe himself were he to return to public life – for his power is gone.

9 DECEMBER 1908

Balfour made an altogether admirable speech on procedure. It is he who now guides the House on points of parliamentary government, and the radicals listen with solemn attention to his lectures upon faulty management and leadership. What he said about autumn sessions and their influence upon the succeeding legislation was received with subdued enthusiasm – and his warnings in 1906 have been so well justified by subsequent events that nothing short of dire emergency will ever induce Asquith to hold another autumn session.

19 DECEMBER 1908

Robert Cecil and young Bowles[69] are probably the most useful men in the rank and file of our party – and in fact with the exception of Arthur Balfour himself are probably the most regular and painstaking of us all. Nobody attends with greater punctuality than these two, and few are more able and determined. I cannot help feeling that under the present conditions of finance, a little tact and forbearance on the part of Tariff Reformers, would make it easy for Bob Cecil and his friends to join us to the extent of supporting a general tariff. That is all we need ask at the present juncture. The idea of losing their support – and not only that but the prospect of having them outflanking us when in office, is really serious.

This has been rather a slack week politically ... There is a palpable reaction after Asquith's grandiloquence, and a reluctance to enter upon any decisive campaign. The majority is so large that regular attendance is quite unnecessary, and consequently the Radical party has a very easy time. Why precipitate matters? Why sacrifice emolument and distinction? Above all why throw away scores and scores of seats which can be retained at any rate up till the hour of dissolution. Our impression is that the wiser men who want a general election before an internal crisis arrives have been overruled in the cabinet. There is an idea that fifteen months hence trade may have materially improved – not an extravagant prediction – and that with this partial solution of the unemployed problem one source of recent disaster will vanish. There is some truth in this view; but ... even if this trouble be removed fresh problems will crop up. Finance is not going to be easy. It is to be predatory to an unparalleled extent – but very little gratitude will be shown by those who are ostentatiously allowed to escape from their share of responsibility. I doubt not that owing to the threats of George and Asquith people are already

[69] Geoffrey Frederic Stewart Bowles (b. 1877) MP (Cons.) Lambeth, Norwood division 1906–January 1910; son of Thomas Gibson Bowles (1842–1922), a renegade Conservative MP. 'Young Bowles' and Lord Robert Cecil unsuccessfully contested Blackburn as Unionist free traders in January 1910.

beginning to revise their finances and family dispositions. One is justified in resisting methods which are both unequal in incidence and vindictive in intention.

6–8 JANUARY 1909

Motored over to Chatsworth to shoot. The gamekeeper very confidential, and assured me that things will look up under the new Duke. The Duchess settles down slowly, and is still much perturbed about enormities committed by her predecessors. Certainly it is difficult to justify dear Lady Louisa[70] for having destroyed many autograph letters because they were alleged to compromise Georgiana,[71] Duchess of Devonshire! And doubtless many foolish things have been done with tapestry, furniture and so forth. But what a wealth of original decoration remains in this house which assuredly must be quite unique! I doubt if anybody could take more scrupulous and loving care of such treasures than does Lady Evelyn, and I fancy that a few years hence she will have organised her possessions in an admirable fashion. Perhaps it is not unnatural that she should feel sadly pressed for time and that some problems are not quite fully considered. She has many doubts about the efficacy of Mrs Strong who occupies herself with the higher criticism and is said to disdain the more necessary requirements of methodical arrangement.

The Chatsworth Library is certainly one of the richest I have ever seen, but I confess that it is arranged in an unbusinesslike manner. There appears to be no adequate system of press-marking, and no proper shelf catalogue: as the greak bulk of these treasures are on open shelves there is real danger of loss and peculation, especially as the number of people who go to Chatsworth is so enormous... The Duchess tells me that a suspicious number of Chatsworth bookplates are on the market... Twelve months could profitably be spent in making the great suite of State Rooms inhabitable. The number of fine things in these two houses is astonishing – and then one must remember also that Lismore, Bolton, Devonshire House and even the Eastbourne chalet have priceless pictures and furniture. Victor makes no secret of his dislike of Ireland and would gladly dispose of Lismore though it would be difficult to find a purchaser.

3 FEBRUARY 1909

There is occupation for many years in the Muniment Room at Haigh, and I sometimes think it may be our only resource in time to come. Death duties are nowadays so high, and family obligations so severe and in our case of such long standing, that one is obliged to look upon our incomparable library as the only realisable asset with which to meet our debts. Heaven forbid that we should ever be driven to sell our paintings and family portraits, still more that we should for the

---

[70] Lady Louisa Cavendish (1835–1907), daughter of the seventh Duke, and sister of the eighth Duke of Devonshire; m. 1865 Admiral the Hon. Francis Egerton, second son of Francis, first Earl of Ellesmere.
[71] Georgiana, daughter of John, first Earl Spencer, m. 1774 William, fifth Duke of Devonshire. She d. 1806.

second or third time be obliged to part with our ancestral home! But it is no use living in a fool's paradise, no use blinding oneself to the concrete facts of the situation. A desperate struggle in the event of my father's death will be necessary in order to maintain these precious memorials. And if such a struggle should be accompanied by a serious depression of trade, then farewell to much if not everything which has for several generations past conferred a distinction upon our family.

11 FEBRUARY 1909
What a house![72] Water'ouse!! I never saw anything quite so loud, so vulgar, so inept: neither charm nor magnificence, neither modesty nor opulence, neither comfort nor scale. It is a deplorable specimen of what one expects some nouveau riche municipality to erect as its town hall. Cast-iron Gothic, ugly pavements, bad mosaic which makes one expect hotel lavatories at every turn, all combined with a perfect avalanche of tawdry decoration and mesquinerie, seem to make Eaton something wholly unique. I was really quite nonplussed by this strange medley, and slept badly in bedroom no. 98.

15 FEBRUARY 1909
A lot of rumours which have been prevalent for several months are now renewed in connection with Asquith and Lloyd George, with respect to their morals, that is to say. Mrs Asquith abroad at the opening of the session has coloured the tale which I am disinclined to believe, of her frank annoyance with dear Henry[73] for his marked attentions to Miss Maud Allan.[74]

17 FEBRUARY 1909
Of political news there really is a dearth, so we are contented to learn in the lobby that an old lady in the West of Ireland who is duly in receipt of an old age pension, has just been safely delivered of a strapping son.

21 FEBRUARY 1909
The only political reflection which occurs to my mind is that the fiscal debate of Thursday and Friday marks a turning point in the history of this controversy. For the first time since 1903 we have had the best of the argument! Hitherto our speeches and arguments however telling they may have proved in the country, have so far as the House of Commons is concerned, been ineffective against the attacks of the Free-traders. Their forces are unquestionably better equipped than our own:

[72] Eaton, the Duke of Westminster's seat in Cheshire.
[73] The premier
[74] Miss Maud Allan (1879–1956), dancer, actress, pianist, writer, b. Toronto; 'revived the lost art of the classical dance'; performed privately before Edward VII at Marienbad, 1907 (Sir F. Ponsonby, *Recollection of Three Reigns*, p. 242); invited to Asquith garden party in Downing St, to disquiet of nonconformist conscience; took London by storm in *The Vision of Salome*, 1908; the subject of malicious rumours in the Pemberton Billing case, June 1918.

their speeches have shown a fluency of conviction and a wealth of resource and analogy which have on certain occasions absolutely paralysed our men, and have even driven zealous tariff reformers to refrain from provoking debate. Now we meet upon more equal terms: our opponents still rely upon the prestige of political victory and commercial success: but they seem less confident and they are certainly far more attentive to our proposals. Financial pressure is beginning to reconcile a small section to fiscal heresy. The Nationalists are frankly in the market.

We are receiving overtures from Radical members who wish to come over to our side: but we are in a delicate position, having already candidates adopted to fight those very seats, and with good prospects of winning; but we don't wish to be churlish towards the wavering ministerialists, though wavering Unionists like Bob Cecil and Bowles have deliberately defied us during the last few days.

26 FEBRUARY 1909

Had a long talk with Sandars about A.J.B.'s views on the situation. Jack Sandars tells me that for the first time for just twenty years the Chief is frankly alarmed at the political situation, or rather at the general outlook of this country. He is nervous about the state of the army, really frightened about the actual disposition and organisation of the fleet, still more about its prospects in the immediate future, while the financial chaos and imbroglio checks the progress of desirable reforms and renders precarious our hopes of a real two-power standard navy.

7 MARCH 1909

I have no faith in Asquith who is really a weak man, and whose flabbiness would long since have been detected had it not been for his full-blooded and sonorous phraseology. Nothing deceives people more than this kind of flatulence.

... Well, all I can say is that I should be terror-stricken if Asquith were to resign tomorrow. We are not ready: we would win seats by the score, but probably too few to ensure a really powerful majority ... In another sense we are ill-prepared to stock the Treasury bench. I do not see where ministers are to be drawn: only a small proportion of our front bench can receive office again, while the backbench population notwithstanding its immense opportunities has seldom risen to the occasion, and could ill provide us with the needful quota of under-secretaries.

Our essential ministers are: Balfour, Walter Long, Austen Chamberlain, Percy, Bonar Law. Those who are too ill to hold office again are: Arnold-Forster, Joe Chamberlain, perhaps Arthur Lee (but we never know whether he is malingering or not), Harry Chaplin. Those who are entitled to hold office, but who will forfeit their claims unless they do a little work for the party, are: George Wyndham, Alfred Lyttelton, Anson, Pretyman, (and Percy might perhaps be included). Too old: Jesse Collings, Valentia. Too effete: Stuart-Wortley, Tom Cochrane, Hamilton. Too ornamental: J. G. Talbot, Sir H. Fletcher, Mark Lockwood, Sir J. Kennaway (privy councillors who sit on the front bench by virtue of their dignity).

Of Akers-Douglas, I say nothing except that his advice is essential to a cabinet, but fatal to a department. Who remains? – one must exclude Bob Cecil and Bowles, excellent men, both of them. Gilbert Parker – means to be secretary of state. Cave – excellent attorney-general. F. E. Smith – insufficient standing to act as a law officer, and would not say thank you for a subordinate post. Goulding, Remnant, Leverton Harris, Hills, Winterton: vanguard of the Tariff Reform pushers, all mixed up in confederacy, and not too reliable.

Helmsley,[75] Lane Fox, Hicks Beach: competent and calm: but Charlie Helmsley will in the course of nature receive a summons to the peers. Butcher might take the Education office. Salter could do any departmental work well. Jim Mason would be an excellent secretary to the Board of Trade. Then we come to a battery of light artillery: Morpeth, James Hope, Bridgeman, Ashley, Joynson-Hicks – all good men in their way but no fundamental force in any one of them. Younger and Mitchell Thomson rather bigger calibre.

... The outlook from the point of view of ministerialisation is full of discouragement.

10 MARCH 1909

Churchill is now credited with a desire to withdraw from the sphere of avowed party politics. His growing unpopularity among Radicals, and his failure to outstrip Lloyd George and Harcourt, have led him to review his prospects with some care: accordingly he is credited with a determination to succeed either Albert Grey or Selborne.[76] Both these appointments fall vacant within the normal term of his office, and one or the other would naturally fall to his share were he to enter his claim. But what about Sinclair, the excellent and decorous Baron Pentland?[77] We always assumed that he was to go there on the double qualification of having been a failure both as cabinet minister, and as aide-de-camp in Canada to Lord Aberdeen. I imagine the Canadians would not relish Churchill as Governor-General.

We dined at Lansdowne House ... The Spanish ambassador and his wife did not have a public altercation as is sometimes the case. Bobby Spencer assured Connie that he has witnessed encounters between the two, across the dinner table, scenes so violent as to make one's blood run cold: and the ambassador always concludes by a parthian shot, by murmuring 'Ah, you should have seen my first wife: she *was* a lady and she really was good-looking.'

Lord St Aldwyn, formerly Hicks Beach, was at the dinner, but kept taciturn until Tariff Reform was mentioned.

... After flashing his eyes a bit, Beach said, 'Well, perhaps Tariff Reform may produce certain benefits: we are a rich country, and we are disgracefully wasteful: if Tariff Reform makes us less rich, it will at least make us more thrifty.'

[75] Charles Duncombe, Viscount Helmsley, second Earl of Feversham (1879–1916), MP (Cons.) Thirsk 1906–15; an MFH; succeeded grandfather 1915, killed in action 1916.
[76] In Canada and South Africa respectively.
[77] Scottish Secretary 1905–12, governor of Madras 1912–19.

In the wilderness

After dinner Bob Reid[78] buttonholed me, as he didn't know more than two or three people in the room, and felt shy . . . It is singular how readily members of the government confide their grievances and aspirations to ourselves. Balfour is the safe home of many confidences, and Sandars has more than once impressed upon him the danger of accepting private assurances which may prejudice his freedom in debate. But so genial, so kind-hearted is our leader that he will generally listen to these representations from men like Seely for instance or Churchill who have climbed the ladder by unscrupulous obloquy and misrepresentation of the very man whose assent they now wish to secure. The fact is they see in Mr Balfour the most formidable of destructive agencies. The other night John Morley came to him and said he was very anxious about naval affairs. Balfour however foresaw the trap, and said, 'You may tell me what you like, though my sources of information are nearly as good as your own: but I warn you in any case that nothing you may say is likely to prevent me from following McKenna in the debate next week, and denouncing him as having departed from the policy publicly accepted by the cabinet.' Morley was dumbfounded and said little.

Haldane is more canny and less scrupulous. After making a speech which contained some sensational proposition duly veiled in obscure language, he went next morning to Carlton Gardens, asked to see A.J.B. – was ushered upstairs, and in his saponaceous way smothered Mr Balfour with a lather of vague generalities and precise prayers, and did so with so much effect upon Balfour's heart that his speech in the House of Commons that afternoon puzzled a good many of our members as to the explanation of the unexpected tenderness towards Haldane.

How I hate them all! Insincere, canting, timorous, sycophantic.

12 MARCH 1909

Arnold-Forster[79] was certainly unpopular. His acrid tones, his didactic manner, and a hostility of style alienated supporters and annoyed his enemies. But he was a remarkable man, one who was profoundly convinced of the justice of his own policy, a man who always shrank from compromise, and who advanced argument with a sincerity of purpose which nobody could refuse to acknowledge. His health has long been precarious, and his death was accordingly no matter for surprise. Much regret was expressed in the lobby this afternoon and many people were glad to attribute to his prolonged suffering much of the asperity which prevented his career from being pronounced successful. Personally I was always on the most friendly terms with him, and we have cooperated from the beginning of this parliament in exposing the

---

[78] Robert Threshie Reid, first Earl Loreburn (1846–1923), Lord Chancellor 1905–12; created Baron, 1906 and Earl, 1911.

[79] An unusual number of deaths depleted the Unionist leadership at this period, many of them untimely. The party lost Arnold-Forster (12 March 1909) in his early fifties; Earl Percy (22 December 1909) in his late thirties; Lord Cawdor (8 February 1911) at sixty-three; George Wyndham (8 June 1913) at nearly fifty; Alfred Lyttelton (4 July 1913), killed by a cricket ball in his late fifties; and Sir William Anson (4 June 1914) in his early seventies.

fundamental dangers of the policy of naval and military reduction. Arnold-Forster was always ready to give time and trouble to anybody who was anxious to master the intricacies of Haldane's venture. Alas that his offhand and supercilious manner should have made acquaintances instead of friends, enemies in the place of critics.

Soon after our defeat, Haldane in top hat and frock coat went down to Aldershot to inspect the troops and to talk to the officers. His beaming countenance, his profession of complete ignorance, and three or four capital stories soon softened the hearts of the soldiers who had begun by being very suspicious and taciturn. After spending most of the day with them, and incidentally having done full justice to some excellent hock, he bade farewell: turning to the officers present, eight or ten of them, he expressed his fervent desire to strengthen the army, to hear grievances and wherever possible to provide remedies, in short to be the *beau idéal* of War Ministers. 'Of course' he said 'I know nothing: I make no profession of military experience. But I may be useful. I feel like a newly married bride. In a year's time you may hear of an interesting event. On the other hand, you may hear of nothing. The future alone can show, but somehow I feel confident that after a suitable number of months have elapsed, there may be an episode of an interesting nature.'

Bully Oliphant[80] had worked himself up to a point of enthusiasm. 'Well Sir' he exclaimed, 'I don't know what is going to happen either: but of this much I'm sure, that whatever you may produce will be more satisfactory than Arnold-Forster's bantlings, for he has had an immaculate conception every month!'

4 APRIL 1909
London is strangely dull just now. There seems to be a lack of animation in society, a want of enterprise in business, and an absence of big men in literature and art.

7 APRIL 1909
Even today Asquith can't fix the date of the budget; it really is unparalleled, the indefinite protraction of discord or flabbiness in the cabinet.

22 APRIL 1909
Parliament is frankly bored just now. There will be some interest in the budget next week, but the House as such is tired out; scores of Radicals have already declined to submit themselves to reelection, many others will follow their good example, while the remainder are nervously cultivating their constituencies to the detriment of parliamentary attendance. Ministers however mean to stick on through thick and thin. There will be no more dissolution for four more years if the decision is left to the cabinet.

[80] Gen. Sir Laurence James Oliphant (1843–1914), commanded Home District 1903–6, GOC Northern Command 1907–11.

In the wilderness

As to the Budget, our opinions will be less fluid tomorrow; but as to its delivery there can be no doubt that Lloyd George's failure was absolute and definitive. Had it not been for Balfour's intervention in which he suggested an adjournment, there must have been a vulgar collapse, for Lloyd George who could readily speak six or eight hours at a stretch about disestablishment, was so totally ignorant of the technical matters on which he tried to read us a long ill-constructed essay, that his fatigue became overwhelming, his words were inaudible, and to obviate a painful farce his purgatory had to be checked. After the interval somebody wisely gave him milk which was tinged with a pleasant straw-coloured ingredient, and he stumbled through the latter half of his discourse with more regard for the full stops, and without treating the Treasury commas like semi-colons. But what a deplorable exhibition! It was an intellectual atrophy which produced the physical weariness. The poor soul was reading phrases which conveyed nothing to his mind, and the effort was too great. It really was distressing to watch his fumbling, stammering progress through a maze of meaningless facts and figures. To some extent it was his own fault, since he fatigued himself and the House too by starting off with ninety minutes of meandering rhapsody about what the Liberal party may some day achieve.

30 APRIL 1909
Whittaker says it is a pantomime budget . . . Burns apologised for the affair by saying that 'George isn't class for that sort of job.' We asked the clerks at the table, and Nicolson with true professional feeling announced that the Chancellor of the Exchequer is even a worse reader than Sir Francis Palgrave, who was notorious for clumsy and hesitating pronunciation.

We shall however soon forget the absurdities of the speech when we realise the vindictiveness of its policy. A good many people will find themselves threatened: they will no doubt exaggerate the evils they expect to incur, will encourage others to do the same, and an agitation against the aggregate will spring up which will probably damage the government. But the Finance Bill must pass, and we shall appreciate the extent of hardships involved by the number of economies effected . . .

2 MAY 1909
This afternoon at the Carlton Club much grumbling about the budget. I think our men mean to work: if they take a really strong and persistent attitude it will be possible to drive the government into a corner, perhaps making it difficult for them to pass any other contentious measure. It is obvious that the Treasury has under-estimated the yield of the new taxation: so universal is this low assessment as to suggest that we are now laying the foundation for a dissolution budget in 1911. If our theory is correct and the government finds itself with a surplus of five or six millions twelve months hence, they could remit much indirect taxation, rush

through a redistribution bill and then have an election between the hay and the corn harvests.

I fancy that the underestimate of yield from the new taxes has been deliberately framed on a gigantic scale, in order that the government may make frequent and perhaps far-reaching concessions without impairing this certainty of a tremendous surplus. With this money they will have an asset twelve months hence with which much taxation can be remitted, the balance being devoted to development schemes by which many votes can be bought ... If old age pensions have not saved them, is it likely that they will find mercy from a disgusted electorate to whom afforestation and foreshore reclamation are offered as a palliative to deep-seated industrial diseases?

Lloyd George is adroit, unscrupulous, and as a rule equable in conducting debate. He well knows how to surrender a small point with outward reluctance while maintaining the essentials of his policy. Several times during this parliament his conciliatory manners, and his openly avowed desire to avoid injustice have smoothed away real difficulties, leaving his opponents mollified and keeping himself secure. And let me say that his treatment of these negotiations has been admirable and has reflected much credit on himself. This policy will no doubt continue and various parties will imagine themselves to have been fairly met and may consequently abandon open hostilities while grumbling in a quiet way. The whole thing turns on Lloyd George's ability or rather upon the cabinet's consent to effect compromises of this nature.

A visit to Sussex showed the two sides of Edwardian country house splendour.

As to Petworth, the contrast of the splendid pictures with the dirt and squalor of the House moved me to pity. I have never seen such neglect. The great show apartments containing this superb collection are carpeted with tattered linoleum, the windows grubby, the fireplaces almost rusting. As for the chapel, which is apparently used as the electrician's workshop, I have seldom seen a more melancholy vista. The big gallery with mud-coloured walls is a kind of lumber room: with a little care, intelligence, and expenditure what a splendid achievement this gallery would be.

After a perfectly enchanting drive we found ourselves at Goodwood. The Duke of Richmond (a peppery little Duke I should say) and a handsome daughter, Lady Helen, gave us tea and showed off the pictures. Here is care and affection well bestowed and amply repaid. Without taste they have disposed their possessions to great advantage, while the fact that this is a family accretion of pictures rather than the collection of an astute amateur, gives merits to the Goodwood *pinacoteca* which the Petworth pictures can never acquire.

In the wilderness

18 MAY 1909

Lloyd George passed a most uncomfortable day wondering what the deuce is meant by contango or arbitrage.

21 MAY 1909

We have had four days this week of Budgeting, and the poor Chancellor has excited pity among the most heartless of his opponents by the lamentable flounderings and confusions. His only chance is to seize hold of some extraneous matter, and to evade the real issue by raising clouds of oratorical dust ... He does not try to rebut our arguments, neither can he look to his colleagues for efficient help. It is noteworthy how seldom Asquith attends.

He is perhaps annoyed, perhaps amused by Mrs Asquith's gaffe. Her exhibition of French dresses has roused the ire of provincial modistes who have passed resolutions of angry protest. Mrs Asquith's explanation is weak, for it is notorious that her guests were pressed to buy dresses only suitable for demi-mondaines: ... and the dresses in question were of the most *outré* character, daring to a degree which even alarmed Mrs Asquith herself. Sir John Fisher[81] was there, so they say, and remarked that never in his life had he witnessed such a naval exhibition.

12 JUNE 1909

I wonder what is the real forecast of the session as contemplated by the cabinet ... Rumour has it that immense concessions will be made, though I doubt whether the government can afford to drop any of the new land taxes. They are in the forefront of the bill, and though their financial merit is for the moment nugatory, it would be a lamentable confession of weakness to abandon the really crucial features of the bill ... The government can't explain their scheme – all sorts of contradictory explanations are vouchsafed, which are not only destructive in themselves, but which are inconclusive when separately considered. Lloyd George hasn't the faintest notion of his much vaunted plan.

18 JUNE 1909

This has been a week of secret negotiations in parliament: the licensed trade have been pressing Lloyd George, Liberals who disapprove of the land taxes have been trying to steel themselves into doing a little more than make lamentations in secret. Then the Welsh members have been cajoled or intimidated into an acquiescence in the abandonment till next year of Welsh disestablishment.

3 JULY 1909

As for politics the week has been dull – a kind of interlude, during which the Radicals are organising a campaign in the country while we have been content to maintain a pressure in the House of Commons. The peers are getting restive and it is

---

[81] Admiral Sir John Fisher, first Baron Fisher (1841–1920), First Sea Lord 1904–10, 1914–15.

with difficulty that we restrain them from announcing their intention to throw out the Bill on second reading. Such an announcement would be premature and as such bad tactics: moreover, the country at large does not seem as yet to be profoundly moved . . .

8 JULY 1909

The 'Cave' which talked profusely about the land taxes a month ago has caved in after some savage intimidation. I find a reaction against the opinion recently held that the Lords should reject the budget, but the radicals are still nervous.

10 JULY 1909

In afternoon I went to the V. and A. Museum – I haven't been there for some time, and I was amazed at the wealth of things which I cannot recollect having seen before. The storerooms have been ransacked and wonderful objects have been discovered . . .

What a triumph for – old Sir Charles Robinson.[82] He it is whose unerring flair, thirty years in advance of his generation, made this inimitable collection: a great gathering of European art which I fancy must always remain unrivalled. Poor old fellow – during the last few years his eyesight has failed and unscrupulous dealers have persuaded him to buy forgeries – but if only he had not been driven out of South Kensington Museum thirty or forty years ago by jealous men who could not pretend to his knowledge and experience, the nation would have secured his services for another fifteen or twenty years, in which circumstances all the errors and absurdities of Robinson's successors would have been avoided, and the museum would be half as rich again as it is today. However one cannot complain. It is and always must remain a triumphant testimony to the genius of one man – the greatest museum expert of the nineteenth century: beside whom the much vaunted and greatly feared director of Berlin is almost insignificant. Robinson's catholicity of taste was as remarkable as his courage and conviction.[83]

15 JULY 1909

The House sat eighteen hours last night . . . Our men are really worn out by these constant sessions of twelve and fourteen hours, and it is now clear for the first time that instead of the guillotine, we are to be subjected to a system of exhaustion. The government is wise, for this policy will injure them less and the opposition more. Lloyd George however must be tired, and though his temper stands the strain well,

---

[82] Sir John Charles Robinson, Kt. (1824–1913), first superintendent of art collections of the South Kensington Museum 1852–69; HM Surveyor of Pictures 1882–1901.

[83] Cf. diary, 28 February 1903: 'If only they had not quarrelled with their only genuine expert in the sixties, the collections would now have been unsurpassed and unsurpassable in the whole world; but during these last thirty years we have fallen behind and the collections, certainly of sculpture, have almost ceased to grow. Berlin has taken the lead and the London staff can hardly compete in point of cash, and cannot approach Berlin for expertise, nerve, and courage.'

his intellect is going to bits. Hugh Cecil told me that he attended a deputation to the Chancellor this afternoon and came away with the feeling that he had been arguing with a stupid and somewhat peevish child, who failed to appreciate the tenor or bearing of serious and considered argument... It is true that we have dragged concessions from them, so much so that much of the increment value clauses will be inoperative: nonetheless we are setting up machinery which can be speeded up and perfected whenever the next government is short of money. If we continue to weaken the land clauses we shall in a way strengthen the government for the Lords will become more and more hesitating to take action.

23 JULY 1909

We hoped to win the High Peak.[84] I feel that our failure may mark the beginning of a reaction in favour of the Budget... I fancy ministers think they have now proved the popularity of the land clauses...

24–5 JULY 1909

To Hackwood, the fine place Lord Curzon has taken from Lord Bolton... I can't bring myself to be more than civil to Harcourt.[85] His easy opulence, his jewelry, his perfumes, all the appurtenances of petit maître and sycophant combined – these things jar upon my nerves and I long to tell him he is a hypocrite and impostor.

Birrell at all events is no toadie! He talks very loud – raps the table, and generally conducts himself as though he were on the Treasury bench: how worn and weary his face becomes.

Mrs C. Vanderbilt came this afternoon. This is the millionairess now known as the 'Kingfisher', but Alice[86] I believe has foiled this ambition to get hold of the King.

6 AUGUST 1909

Tomorrow if all is well I depart for Bayreuth. I am sorry to miss the most interesting week of the budget... but I have earned repose. I don't think I have had one day off the whole session.

11 AUGUST 1909

... In one respect however, the Bayreuth audience is better fitted to cope with the intellectual effort of the tetralogy: for the foreign element his virtually disappeared,

---

[84] The Liberals held the seat (22 July) with a reduced majority but an increased Liberal vote, suggesting that the government had ceased to be unpopular with its own supporters as had recently been the case.

[85] Lewis Harcourt, first Viscount Harcourt (1863–1922), Liberal politician and son of Sir William Harcourt; first Commissioner of Works, 1905–10, 1915–16; Secretary of State for Colonies 1910–15; Viscount, 1917; described in diary, 2 April 1908, as an 'adroit parliamentarian' and 'jewelled radical' whose colleagues envied his 'well-groomed and supercilious demeanour'.

[86] Mrs Keppel.

and is replaced by Germans who at any rate can master the text and follow the recitative. It is no exaggeration to say that a dozen years ago the bulk of the audience was French and English... and the Germans occupied a wholly subordinate sphere. Nowadays they amount to ninety per cent of the audience. In a way I am sorry, and with it vanishes the catholicity of tribute to a man of outstanding genius.

Moreover the entity of the crowd has deteriorated in consequence... It used to be well-dressed... Now all is changed. The crowd is German and the crowd is dowdy... Then again the crowd behaves in a middle class way, mobbing all those in whom it is interested.

23 AUGUST 1909

Much has happened in my absence. Fred Smith began to promote a memorial to A.J.B. asking him to use his influence to prevent the Lords from throwing out the Finance Bill. No adequate explanation of the scheme, unless Fred is doubtful about his seat. Alick Hood sent for him, and he gave an undertaking not to pursue the idea – but to Alick's annoyance went straight off to Churchill's room, where the result of the interview was doubtless wheedled out of him by flattery and chaff. Opinion is hardening that the Lords should take drastic action on the second reading.

25 AUGUST 1909

There is a widespread idea that a dissolution is imminent whether the Lords pass the bill or not. If they reject it the election would come forthwith, and the government would probably introduce a bill to antedate the register which comes into force in England on 1 January... If on the other hand the Lords accept the bill, the government if they have courage, would do well to dissolve in the new year while our men are depressed, and while many will be accusing the House of Lords of being a cowardly appendage to the constitution. Surely we may as well be hanged for a sheep as for a lamb.

... If only three or four hundred more men had supported us at High Peak! Had that contest been won by our party the Finance Bill would be dead today. On what small issues depend the determination of vital problems. Let me add that our men are recovering from the slump.

26 AUGUST 1909

I see Ribblesdale[87] is appointed trustee of the National Gallery and Edgar Vincent as well, the number being increased accordingly. Both are good fellows however, and neither of them could pass an elementary examination as to the authorship of a dozen masterpieces in the collection. There is humour in the selection of Ribblesdale. He is Mrs Asquith's brother-in-law – and thinking he would like the trusteeship, made an application to the premier. Asquith, always ready to honour

---

[87] Thomas, fourth and last Baron Ribblesdale (1854–1925); succeeded 1876.

his relations ... gladly consented and gave the necessary instructions. The Treasury as usual blundered and appointed instead of Lord Ribblesdale an equally good fellow, equally incompetent, called Lord Redesdale. Tableau. However Asquith solemnly increases the number of trustees and Ribblesdale's ambition is realised.

In September the government suddenly changed to delaying tactics over the Finance Bill.

... Probably the Government has just begun to realise that after all the peers are not intimidated, that they may throw out the bill, and that if we hastened unduly in our House the crisis might arise in October whereas they prefer January with its new register. The electoral effect of postponing a dissolution till the new register comes into force, is by way of adding votes to the Radical Party, though I fancy it is just as likely to help the socialists.

7 SEPTEMBER 1909
This is the first day of the constitutional crisis. Nothing, it is true, has happened – but for the first time there are indications of a slump in commonsense. Rumours of all stages of extravagance are being canvassed seriously. For instance Lloyd George at dinner tonight dropped a casual remark about Rosebery indicating that if he made a violent speech the government might dissolve before the bill went to the Lords. This obiter dictum reached us within an hour ... For today, it is sufficient to note the fluid and jumpy state of Lobby opinion, the prevalence of gossip, the avidity for news, and the readiness with which ridiculous ideas are seriously promulgated.

9 SEPTEMBER 1909
A long talk with Alfred Lyttelton and Percy: both of whom are opposed to drastic action (that is, to any action except quiescence) by the peers. Percy surprised me by saying that Bonar Law took his view. If Bonar Law is wobbling, can it be that the illustrious recluse of Highbury is changing his mind? A few weeks ago he was all for rejection. He probably detects the electoral weakness of passive resistance. Bonar Law, Percy, Alfred, comfortable in rich metropolitan seats, do not realise that if the Lords pass the bill there would be a tremendous outcry among our supporters ... We should be split; we should be charged with accepting the alternative to Tariff Reform, we should look upon ourselves as a dejected, indeed as a defeated party. What would the government do? – why dissolve in January, press home their tremendous advantage and probably win by a majority of 300 thereby gaining a definite mandate for a dozen predatory schemes.

10 SEPTEMBER 1909
Hughes[88] is optimistic and thinks we might obtain a working majority – but heaven

[88] The Conservative chief agent

help us if we were returned by thirty votes! I fancy that today a general election would return the radicals by a majority fairly dependent on the Nationalist vote.

11 SEPTEMBER 1909

Our expectation of wearing out Lloyd George has equally failed, because he doesn't stay to be worn out! He has hardly been in attendance during the licensing clauses, and next week we understand that Haldane will take his place. George's slack attendance is of course without precedent.

16 SEPTEMBER 1909

The efforts made by Alick Hood to reconcile constituencies and members where the Free Trade Unionists have caused difficulty are not likely to prove successful. Bob Cecil it is true has come to a provisional understanding with his association which may save his seat; but even so there is much heartburning in Marylebone. Abel Smith[89] will be beaten: likewise Bowles in Norwood. The fact is that Bob has inspired the other two to revolt against the official policy of the party – Bob escapes, and his admirers are doomed. Bob as Alick says in his broad way has seduced a young housemaid and an elderly cook: he effects a respectable marriage himself, late in life, and then is the cause of his two old friends being turned on to the street.

17 SEPTEMBER 1909

Lloyd George keeps wonderfully fresh. He takes life very easily, but I should think casts doubled burdens upon his staff who are worked to death, and often enough thrown over for their pains.

Today there was another painful affair which has not yet become public. Walter Long and George Wyndham have been fighting the Irish Land Bill successfully. On the third reading today they both came down to the House, and each expected to wind up the debate. Walter then found that George had been asked to conclude the case. He was perfectly furious. He is the ex-chief secretary, he is chairman of the Irish Unionists and he is an Irish member. On the other hand G.W. is author of the settlement which Birrell wishes to destroy. George I believe offered to withdraw, but that would not have removed the gravamen – namely that Walter Long had not been consulted. He therefore sat there in the sulks, wrote furious letters to Alick Hood and Arthur Balfour, and has actually retired to Rood Ashton until he receives ample apology.

Really this touchiness partakes of the grotesque. All this session Walter Long has been overworked, his nerves are most irritable, and outbursts of temper have not been infrequent. He should however recollect that others also are working at high pressure, and that an oversight of this kind should not be taken *au grand sérieux*: neither is this the moment when the attention of the party should be dissipated on

[89] Abel Henry Smith (1862–1930), MP (Cons.) Christchurch 1892–1900, Herts. E. 1900–January 1910.

problems of etiquette. This crisis has of course arisen before, since nobody is more apt to take umbrage than Walter. He is jealous of Wyndham and I think it possible that the Budget Protest League would not have been founded unless on returning from South Africa he had found that Austen Chamberlain was achieving a marked success. I wonder how the two great parties in the state compare in this matter of jealousy. On the whole Balfour's leadership has kept us aloof from personal problems, which will I hope never be resurrected – unless he has the misfortune to give Jim Cranborne[90] a place in a future government.

19 SEPTEMBER 1909
Talking of manoeuvres here is a true story showing the caddish tactlessness of Churchill. He is on his way to be the guest of the Emperor William at the German manoeuvres. Bertie[91] in Paris received instructions from the F.O. to find a French officer to show C. over the battlefield of – Sedan! – Sedan: think of it that in order to provide Churchill with a topic of grateful conversation with the Kaiser, a French officer should be detailed to explain and illustrate a great outstanding humiliation of the Republic. Bertie (not oversensitive himself) was aghast at the idea – but a man was found – though whether Churchill actually went or not, I cannot yet say.

20 SEPTEMBER 1909

The Whips were making preparations for Balfour's speech at Birmingham.

...Alick Hood received the proof sheets of the programme, containing the resolution to be moved the day after tomorrow. To our horror we found that it contained a direct invitation, or rather direction, to the House of Lords to throw out the budget! Such a course would have been fatal. The resolution was actually drafted by Joe, who is not quite in touch with recent developments, and therefore fails to realise that what the Radicals are longing for, is a 'storm signal' from Balfour to the peers. We called in Austen Chamberlain who realised the danger forthwith. A new formula was devised and sent down to the Midlands by special messenger. I only hope Austen wrote to pacify Papa! We have had a narrow escape.

21 SEPTEMBER 1909
Mark Lockwood[92] is trying to corrupt the Chancellor.[93] The other night, Thursday I think, he took him to the Gaiety Theatre, thence to the apartments behind the curtain, thence in company with two or three 'bits of muslin' to the Savoy Hotel where they all supped and amused one another till the small hours in

[90] Lord Salisbury
[91] Francis, first Viscount Bertie of Thame (1844–1919); created Baron, 1915, Viscount, 1918; ambassador at Paris 1905–18.
[92] Lt.-Col. Amelius Richard Mark Lockwood, first Baron Lambourne (1847–1928); MP (Cons.) Epping 1892–1917; created peer 1917.
[93] Lloyd George

the morning when Mark shot the Chancellor into Downing St at 2.30 a.m. Next day Lloyd George's temper was execrable. I don't think he is overfond of parliamentary work though he loves the prestige and flattery. Sam Evans[94] therefore has to do much of the Chancellor's work. As Bowles said to me today, Sam Evans looks exactly like a dishonest butler. No description could be more terse and accurate.

24 SEPTEMBER 1909

What the electoral possibilities are, puzzles me. The accounts we hear are conflicting. The Budget League meetings are good, while our protest meetings are usually indifferent and often bad. It is an effort for our people to get up a successful gathering unless we have a prominent speaker, while the Radicals experience no such difficulty.

26 SEPTEMBER 1909

Fred Smith has been making awkward revelations about the breakup gangs hired by the Radical party. Their tactics were so successful in 1906 that one cannot be surprised at renewed intimidation and violence in 1909. It is well that we should be prepared, and we must warn the public in advance that these interruptions are carefully organised from headquarters despite all denials. Pease and Birrell know nothing about it – that I admit: but the actual phrases which are shouted out, and the actual methods of interruption, are identical in Newcastle and Truro: there is a common origin, and a well-equipped source of inspiration somewhere, not yet located.

28 SEPTEMBER 1909

Here are two items of interest. Sir George Murray[95] told Tom Cochrane[96] that if instead of discussing the money resolutions of the finance bill, we had taken a series of divisions and reserved ourselves for the measure itself, the government could not have introduced the bill! – that is to say the bill wasn't drafted – wasn't ready for presentation.

    The second significant observation was made to John Gretton[97] by Chalmers,[98] the ultra-radical chief of the Board of Customs. He stated, without any qualifications, that so much of the land clauses as are workable owe that quality to

[94] Sir Samuel Thomas Evans (1859–1918), MP (Lib.) Mid-Glamorgan 1890–1910; Solicitor-General 1908–10; President, Probate, Divorce and Admiralty Court, 1910–18, an appointment described (diary, 7 March 1910) as 'a capital jest – for we long foresaw he would end there, expecting however that he would figure as co-respondent rather than as supreme judge'.

[95] Sir George Herbert Murray (1849–1936), permanent secretary, Treasury, 1903–11.

[96] Hon. Thomas Cochrane, first Baron Cochrane of Cults (1861–1951); p.p.s. to Chamberlain 1895–1901, Under-Secretary, Home Office, 1902–05; created peer, 1919.

[97] John Gretton, first Baron Gretton (1867–1947), MP (Cons.) Derbs. S. 1895–1906, Rutland 1907–18, Burton-on-Trent 1918–1943; brewer; led Diehards in 1921–22; cr. peer 1944.

[98] Robert, first Baron Chalmers (1858–1938), chairman, Board of Inland Revenue 1907–11 and master of Peterhouse, 1924–31.

our criticism and attack: without them the measure would have been grotesque.

Leverton Harris[99] had a conference with the Rothschild tribe. They are nervous, and mean to work up East London.

It is clear that the Radicals want an election in January – I mean that they prefer it to a December election. I cannot fathom the causes of such a preference. Unemployment will be so serious three months hence that it will exclude many other topics: it may help us, it may help the Socialists but it can't help the government.

29 SEPTEMBER 1909
A story is percolating the Lobbies and doubtless a few days hence will echo in the press that Rosebery foresees a close fight, and that he may be called upon to lead a coalition government. I see no grounds for such an assumption even if parties be equally divided...

This afternoon John Burns volunteered this aphorism 'apart from myself there isn't one member of the cabinet whose backbone ain't made of tripe'.

30 SEPTEMBER 1909
For some days past there have been indications that the King is getting nervous. As he properly observes a constitutional crisis at his time of life is no laughing matter. He has long foreseen the conflict, and while at Marienbad wrote a letter to the Prince of Wales dealing with the problem, evidently wishing the latter to make known the royal desire that the affair should be honourably adjusted. His view is that both sides should give way: that the government after third reading in the Commons should submit the Finance Bill to a general election, and that the Lords on their part should consent to pass the Bill without further ado, in the event of a Radical majority. So prevalent is the belief that this policy may be accepted, that we are warning our agents to be prepared for an early dissolution.

4 OCTOBER 1909
To London. Travelled with Henry Granby,[100] to whom I told home truths about the tactless intervention of peers: alas they and especially the Dukes have queered the pitch for us. Their threats and peevishnesses have wrought incalculable damage to the party.

5 OCTOBER 1909
Dined at Derby House: went with A.J.B. who looks tired and returned to H of C with St Aldwyn who will clearly speak out against tampering with the Finance Bill.

[99]Frederick Leverton Harris (1864–1926), MP (Cons.) Tynemouth 1900–06, Stepney 1907–11, Worcs, E. 1914–18.

[100]Henry, eighth Duke of Rutland (1852–1925); succeeded his father, the former Lord John Manners, in 1906; previously known as Lord Granby: MP (Cons.) Melton 1888–95.

Nobody has ever been able to understand why Hicks Beach, so strong and self-reliant, is always cautious to a dangerous extent. I dare say he may be right in expecting a defeat – but would not that defeat be more severe if, and after, we had abandoned a bold and courageous policy?

Rosebery writes to withdraw from the contest: people are already betting that he will vote in favour of the Bill. What a rotter the man is when character comes to be tested ...

Peers are slumpy: that is I notice a tendency to say that perhaps after all the Bill might well pass. This tendency will increase for ten days, then there will be the reaction, and finally the Lords will do something drastic. At present they are very apt to wobble.

7 OCTOBER 1909

Masterman[101] is to become president of the local government board. Tiresome little person, with the aspect of a seedy biblewoman, and with a cockney accent which throbs on the drum of the ear.

22 OCTOBER 1909

The bulk of our people would prefer a January dissolution as the universal belief is that time is in our favour.

5 NOVEMBER 1909

Debate on Lords amendments to Irish Land Bill – a ridiculous situation, for Birrell is longing to treat, but is in a fright. A conference is to be held: he besought Walter Long not to let McDonnell be a member of the conference, since he, Birrell, can't abide the man, and indeed is not on speaking terms with him. Birrell is sick to death of the whole job, but doesn't want his obstinacy to involve a state of seething disorder throughout Ireland. Walter Long treats him like a spoilt child.

7 NOVEMBER 1909

Our party wirepullers maintain a confident optimism as to the outcome of a general election. I wish I could share it... To my mind the whole outlook is damnable.

9 NOVEMBER 1909

In evening talk and walk with St John Brodrick who always views political matters with big spectacles. Most of our people distrust his judgment because they cordially dislike his personality. It is true that he makes a *faux pas* now and then, and on certain occasions he gives cause for offence: but I have never understood why he should have incurred real unpopularity among our supporters. Personally I have a

---

[101] Charles Masterman (1873–1927), politician, author, and journalist; MP (Lib.) W. Ham N. 1906–11, SW Bethnal Green 1911–14, Rusholme 1923–4; Under-Secretary, Home Office, 1909–12; financial secretary to Treasury, 1912–14; chancellor of Duchy of Lancaster, in cabinet, 1914–15; director of propaganda department 1914–18.

great regard for him, affection also, and he has always shown a keen desire to be helpful to me. Loyalty to his party is also one of his unswerving principles. At the present moment he is in one of his pessimistic moods, and herein all good Tories must share his apprehensions: but unlike so many of them, having once realised the course decided by the party leaders, he means to fight his best, and to encourage the laggard... I wish all our men were equally loyal! The other day Henry Bentinck[102] fell upon me in wrath (as if the crisis were bred by me) saying that if the Lords laid hands on the Finance Bill he would withdraw his candidature...

11 NOVEMBER 1909

Lord Lansdowne showed me over his house...He is very anxious about the political outlook, and tells me that the situation of the Town Planning Bill is critical. He seems to think that Burns is ready to compromise but that the cabinet wishes the measure to be wrecked.

25 NOVEMBER 1909

Jack Pease[103] won't move Portsmouth writ, so I won't move Uxbridge: I promised him both elections or neither. Meanwhile he tells me that we shall prorogue on Friday,[104] not adjourn... this is sabotage on a mean and petty scale – one of Churchill's small and ignoble triumphs.

The object is clear. If we win the election, our ministers would have to be re-elected, and then we would have to proceed with indemnity bills forthwith. The delay would be so great, that it might be impossible to squeeze in the 1909–10 budget before 31 March. If they win, there will be no delay about re-election and the indemnity bills could not be opposed.

26 NOVEMBER 1909

At Club talked over the situation with many peers. Cawdor[105] decidedly hopeful, but annoyed (like many of us) at the rash manner in which George Curzon has tried to arrange a peers' campaign without cooperating with our central office. Tom Legh[106] not hopeful: he never is! Humphrey Sturt[107] confident that in six

---

[102] Lord Henry Cavendish Bentinck (1863–1931), half-brother of sixth Duke of Portland; MP (Cons.) Norfolk NW 1886–92, Notts. S. 1895–1906, January 1910–29; of notably independent views.

[103] Joseph Albert Pease (1860–1943), second son of Sir Joseph Whitwell Pease, Bt., the first Quaker baronet; created Baron Gainford, 1917; MP (Lib.) Tyneside 1892–1900, Saffron Walden 1901–10, Rotherham 1910–17; Chief Whip 1908–10, chancellor of Duchy of Lancaster, 1910–11, president of Board of Education 1911–15, postmaster-general 1916; chairman of BBC, 1922–6, and vice-chairman, 1926–32.

[104] Parliament was prorogued, preparatory to dissolution, on 28 November.

[105] Frederick Archibald Vaughan, third Earl Cawdor (1847–1911), chairman of GWR 1895–1905, First Lord of Admiralty 1905; MP (Cons.) Carmarthenshire 1874–85; succeeded father, 1898.

[106] Thomas Legh, second Baron Newton (1857–1942), diplomatist and politician; MP (Cons.) Newton division of Lancs. 1886–98; succ. father, 1898; paymaster-general, 1915; Controller, Prisoner of War Department, Foreign Office 1916–19.

[107] Sir Humphrey Napier Sturt, second Baron Alington (1859–1919); succeeded father 1904; MP (Cons.) Dorset E. 1891–1904.

months time the cry will be 'Monarchy or Republic', but he failed to explain the sequence of events.

5 DECEMBER 1909

How I loathe and abominate this forthcoming election, with its waste of time trouble and money, with all the virulence and vulgarity from which there can be no escape... These election interludes are indeed but little to my taste. I detect nothing amusing, or sporting in such contests... During the normal sessions of this parliament the work has been too protracted and absorbing to permit the daily attention to family matters which a parent of my standing and with so many pledges to posterity should never forego without a serious misgiving – and now when one would in the ordinary way be contemplating a Christmas of pleasure, with lots of amusement for the children, it is disheartening to be preoccupied with external affairs and so largely to throw the children back upon governesses and nurserymaids.

6 DECEMBER 1909

I began campaigning today, quite a big meeting in Wigan with an audience of 2500... There were a lot of socialists present who behaved extremely well.

8 DECEMBER 1909

The Radicals have led the field almost unchallenged for ten days, and the *Times* gives Churchill three or four columns, while condensing Austen Chamberlain into one and a half. A.J.B. is in bed – Bonar Law ill, Alfred rather ineffective – Harry Chaplin for whatever he is worth abroad, and so on. Thus we have made no headway. I am inclined to think this doesn't matter. Sentiment moves in waves, and we are at the lowest point of depression prior to the polling. During Xmas we shall not materially improve our morale: we shall guzzle while the socialists will preach: but immediately after the new year I think our position will improve, and if we have good fortune (for these cycles of favour and disfavour seem somewhat fortuitous) we should be in fighting form and full-hearted enthusiasm by the date of the earliest urban pollings. If these go well there will not be any serious reaction – if they go badly the débâcle will extend to all the rural constituencies particularly those remote from London.

15 DECEMBER 1909

Spoke at Coppull Moor to a lot of colliers, a hopeless audience, not personally hostile in any sense, but restricted in political outlook, probably as apathetic towards Liberalism as towards Conservatism, and only anxious to hear the views and share the politics of a Labour member.

24 DECEMBER 1909

I don't know what to make of the political situation. Our meetings continue to be the subject of disorder by Radicals, theirs never suffering from interruption – Lloyd George pursues his policy of scurrility, venomous in its fervour, poisonous in its effects upon one class of mind: but the Liberal party has so far lost its self-respect that protest against this blackguardism can no longer be expected. It is still possible that a section of moderate thinkers may resent it sufficiently to transfer their votes to us: but their numbers must be small, and George has doubtless estimated his profit and loss account, hoping to gain a dozen votes for every one lost through his violence and unfairness. His attacks upon Curzon, Milner, and St. John Brodrick have been marked by exceptional virulence. What a thoroughgoing little cad the man is and how significant is the contrast between the Chancellor on the Treasury Bench and the mean attorney on the tub. In the House of Commons he poses as the moderate and reasonable man, tempered by a meed of sycophancy. When he rants elsewhere all the worst faults of the demagogue – *suppressio veri*, lack of generosity, and bullying bluster, seem to take mastery: alas! how I hate this unreasoning aspect of politics.

30 DECEMBER 1909
To London ... To Central Conservative Office, to Tariff Reform League, to Jack Sandars – all seem to be hopeful of the political outlook. Walter Long a little less optimistic than usual: he was much amused by the circumstances of his first meeting in the Strand – last night. He is accustomed to audiences of thousands, but of his prospective electors only 150 put in an appearance.

31 DECEMBER 1909
Percy's death has been a great shock to all. He was an old friend, contemporary at Eton, Oxford and now for fifteen years in the H of C. As a politician he was indolent, requiring great effort to persuade him to take an active or prominent part – in fact we never succeeded in persuading him to do so, although his isolated efforts were brilliantly successful. There were few men on our side who felt less obligation or who showed less loyalty to the party as such, but when he was driven to make one of his rare speeches, everybody was impressed by the masterly treatment of the controversy at issue. His tastes were really alien to politics. Assyriology and day dreaming occupied all his leisure time; and a passion for travelling, especially among the Turks whom he dearly loved, made him anxious to shake off the responsibilities of political life: so firmly rooted was this love of archaeology on the one hand, and his reluctance to be seen at Westminster on the other hand that he often discussed retirement from the turmoil, greatly to the disgust of his father – had the latter died first Percy would have gradually disappeared from the public eye.

1 JANUARY 1910
As to politics, today the outlook seems very black. The persistence of interruption and disorderliness at our meetings, even in places where we are strong, is an ominous sign ...

None the less Tariff Reform is bound to win: perhaps we may wait five years – ten years, but the artisan will insist upon it, though his idea will be narrow protectionism with no aspiration for unity or imperial consolidation...

The prospect is indeed vague and threatening: and it seems that whatever may happen in January we are doomed to a further period of turmoil, to at least one more election in the immediate future, an election which will be really savage.

They tell me Joe Chamberlain is confident of an effective victory.

5 JANUARY 1910
Good meetings in Chorley. But I hear from canvassers that there is a sort of sullenness among the canvassees – no abrupt or hostile refusal to discuss matters, but at the same time a reluctance to express any opinion. I don't know how far this is prevalent: it is certainly absent among the women, but among the actual voters connotes a frame of mind tending towards socialism. For the first time, the crop of anonymous letters always produced by a general election is openly atheistic in tone.

7 JANUARY 1910
In afternoon had an interview with a suffragette called Farquharson. She belongs to the militant section, but disapproves of extreme methods. I asked what these were, and she frankly told me that the most advanced advocates of female suffrage are prepared to assassinate the leaders of any party which does not grant the franchise. Personally this young woman (with a twinkle, or rather a glitter in her eye which suggests hysteria, if not lunacy) thinks such a course justifiable in itself, but bad policy, as it would in her opinion retard the movement.

8 JANUARY 1910
I got a letter from Percival Hughes our head agent, not only hopeful in tone, but quite optimistic. He is a reticent man, shrewd, and well informed; and though I know him well I question whether he would have committed such a sentiment to paper without pretty strong ground in justification. It is evident that the first canvassing returns are favourable. Bravo! Let us hope he may be right; but we have to keep up the pressure for a week longer. If we continue our utmost there is scarcely time for a reaction to set in before the earliest pollings – and if they go right their influence upon the remaining constituencies will be immense.

But But But – the accounts of our meetings continue to be dispiriting. It is difficult to say if the rowdiness is caused by small peripatetic gangs, or whether it really does represent a fundamental hostility; whether in short there is still a silent and thoughtful voter who is going to turn the scale in our favour. So far as my constituency is concerned, although I shall have held fifty meetings of all sorts before the end of the contest if all goes well, there are none the less hundreds and hundreds of voters who will never have heard me speak during this fight. What are they going to do? The issue lies in their hands.

In the wilderness

22 JANUARY 1910

My majority is 2212 – a substantial increase over previous figures. My people have worked with zeal and loyalty quite unsurpassable.[108] . . . Our election has come six weeks too soon – for the argument was all on our side and we were doing well – but longer tillage of the soil was required for a fruitful harvest.

22 JANUARY 1910

Spoke in Southport division. The bribery by Baron De Forest[109] the mongrel Radical candidate is literally indecent. He is spending something like £1000 per week according to all calculations. A cabman or railway porter gets a sovereign for any service however nominal, and the good people who keep lodging houses are being debauched into believing that if 'the Baron' is returned, Southport will become a smart and fashionable watering place: what a grotesque idea, yet these silly people believe it and many it is said will cast their votes accordingly. For my own part I think the whole of Lancashire will be disgraced by returning such a corrupter of political life.

LORD BALCARRES TO LADY WANTAGE,[110] 22 JANUARY 1910

Connie is the cynosure and centre of attraction. At an ordinary meeting in Chorley a crowd varying from 500 to 5000 people will congregate outside the hall to see her depart, and if possible to shake hands. That is the ideal of the girl who works in a cotton mill or weaving shed, and next morning she tells her friend, 'I shook hands with her' – no more need be said, for they all have tried, and all understand what it means.

---

[108] Balcarres's campaign centred on the need for imperial federation to help unemployment and meet the threat from German and American competition. He claimed that this prevented his opponent fighting on anti-landlord and financial issues. 'Not 1 in 40 questions related to the budget!' The 'R.C. vote was pretty solid in my favour, and for the first time the Church bestirred itself and had an excellent Church Defence Association.' His chairman said that if the voters had been quietly assured that everyone who supported him would be entertained to a hotpot supper, his majority would have increased by a thousand. On one evening in this campaign the diarist attended four such suppers.

[109] Baron Maurice Arnold De Forest, Count Bendern (b. 1879), defeated at Southport, January 1910, but MP (Lib.) W. Ham N. 1911–18; naturalised in Liechtenstein, 1932, thereafter residing at Biarritz until his death c. 1955.

[110] The diarist's aunt.

V

The constitutional crisis of 1910

State of parties – Asquith nonplussed by Queen Alexandra's wit – unseemly incident at Portsmouth – Asquith's masseur protests against whisky before breakfast – the government surrenders to the Irish – Lord Chilston's papers – death of the King – Churchill blamed for the demise – 'They have killed him' – the funeral – Lady Wimborne a 'paying Guest' – Lord Beauchamp – the constitutional conference – Kitchener as a collector – superior flair of the radicals – the second general election.

The election of January 1910 returned 274 Liberals to 272 Unionists, with the Irish Nationalists holding the balance. The parliamentary Labour Party, under its new chairman Barnes, provided a fairly reliable government ally. Immediately after the election, the question arose as to what price the Liberals would pay for Irish support. For some time the issue was unclear, though ministers initially would have preferred a reconstruction of the membership of the House of Lords to the abolition of its veto which the Irish demanded, with a view to obtaining Home Rule. Pressure from all quarters, however, forced ministers to change course, and a revived Liberal – Irish compact and a Veto Bill emerged as the main events of the first part of the year.

Parliament was opened on 16 February, with the King's speech on the 21st. The 'People's Budget' of 1909, still not passed, prevented any other new departures being attempted, and with the views of the Irish uncertain until early April, the spring was a period of 'wait and see'. However, on 14 April Asquith committed the government to a Veto Bill, passed if necessary by a creation of peers, and thus, having met Redmond's terms was able to pass the budget with little further opposition. It left the lower house on 27 April, went through the Lords the next day, and became law on 29 April, the day parliament adjourned for the spring recess.

Had all gone according to plan, the summer of 1910 would have been occupied by a constitutional crisis over the attempt to restrict the powers of the House of Lords by the Veto (or Parliament) Bill. Instead, the sudden death of Edward VII on 6 May altered the political timetable, and at times between then and November seemed likely to lead to a notable suspension of normal party conflict. Though Asquith had introduced the Veto Bill in April, it was allowed to drop, and during the summer sittings (8 June – 3 August), Parliament confined itself to largely non-contentious and unimportant legislation.

The constitutional crisis

In response to a strong public feeling, the government allowed The Times *of 8 June to indicate its wish for a private conference. The constitutional conference, of four leaders each from the two main parties, first met on 17 June. It was, said Balfour, 'exactly like a cabinet, but much more united'. The last of its twenty-one meetings was on 10 November, when it broke up without agreement and without disclosure of its proceedings. It was also stated that a dissolution would take place in December, after a short intervening session (15–28 November) for routine business.*

The election of December 1910 was a stalemate, with 272 Liberals and 271 Unionists returned. The minor parties, also little changed, continued to maintain the Liberals in power. The Liberals, as before, fought on the issues of free trade and the curtailing of the powers of the upper house. Home rule was sedulously avoided by ministers. Apart from one hint dropped by Asquith in his Albert Hall speech of December 1910, no minister said anything of consequence on home rule until polling was well advanced. The Unionists however, changed their approach, Balfour undertaking in a speech on 29 November not to carry out tariff reform without putting the issue to a referendum.

23 JANUARY 1910

It now looks as though the socialist coalition will be dependent for its existence on the goodwill of the nationalists: a parlous situation which must end in a further election. People are rather apt to think that the Nationalists owing to their desire for Tariff Reform are predisposed to support our party. Nothing could be more erroneous. For Home Rule they have been prepared to sacrifice the R.C. schools, and for Home Rule they are perfectly willing for the time being at any rate, to forego the advantages which Ireland would derive from Tariff Reform: and as a certain section of the Nationalists, particularly those under Dillon's influence are Radical in sympathies, it is quite probable that a *modus vivendi* will enable Asquith to hold office for some little time to come. The idea of another general election within the next few months makes me vomit! But I fear it cannot be long delayed. What the summer will bring forth nobody can predict. I fancy however that where strategy is required, our party will shew itself better versed in parliamentary tactics than Asquith and Co. – nothing is more noteworthy than the clumsy fashion with which the P.M. has handled problems requiring a delicate touch, and whenever he has been able to put himself in the wrong he has done so.

28 JANUARY 1910

I am afraid our situation is parlous. Our newspapers treat the election as a triumph for Tariff Reform – which of course it is up to a certain point – but the cohesive power of the different sections of our opponents is greater than our people imagine They are not nearly so centrifugal as we should wish; were it not for a probable crisis with the Lords their majority is adequate to keep them in office for three years. I suppose however that George and Co. will force poor weak and washy Asquith to fly high, to undertake ambitious schemes, and thus to provide an early conflict with the other House. On the other hand if the Lords announced that they would pass the

Finance Bill, as Lansdowne could manage to do prior to the opening of parliament, it would be difficult for Asquith to extract the 'assurances' he demands – for my own part I can never make out from whom these pledges are to emanate: presumably from the King, who must be anxious as to the issue.

On one point Asquith has been adroit, for he has got through the election without giving the smallest indication of his policy about Home Rule and the second chamber. It is true this may prejudice him later on when he comes to claim a mandate – but the country at large is in complete ignorance as to the scheme: to that extent he can claim a free hand. When in Fife the other day I heard extraordinary stories about the brusque and abrupt manner with which he treated civil questions anent his policy. As time goes on he becomes less and less mellow – one would have expected otherwise from more causes – (more sources) than one.

2 FEBRUARY 1910
At Carlton talked with many people...

Every speculation is directed to the date of the dissolution: but the unexpected may occur and the government may live longer than one would anticipate. Longevity is however dependent upon their abandonment of many vaunted pledges and principles. What we have to guard against is a dissolution for which we could be held responsible. It would go hard with our party if we plunged the country into the turmoil of a further election without good cause. The dislocation of business, the check to enterprise, and the resultant loss and confusion would cause a serious reaction, especially in those commercial centres where it is more than ever necessary for us to improve our representation.

13 FEBRUARY 1910
Of one thing we may be certain, that nervousness will make the cabinet postpone the crisis as long as possible. Our men, who are just paying their election bills look forward with dismay to the repetition of these huge expenses, and the Radicals must feel the same anxiety, though I am told their party chest is well equipped. Harry Samuel[1] tells me that our contract for posting mural cartoons and literature amounted to something like £15,000, and he assures me that in Lancashire *alone* the central Radical office spent over £20,000 – our figure was for the whole of England. Undoubtedly in the north the Radicals fairly outposted us. I wonder in what form and in what guise Carnegie's contribution reached the National Liberal Federation.

15 FEBRUARY 1910
Speculation – that is the theme of every conversation. Here is my view – that Redmond will come to heel, that the Finance bill will pass rapidly, that a Veto bill will be pressed through quickly and that a dissolution following upon drastic amendment by the Lords will occur between the hay and corn harvests.

[1] Sir Harry Simon Samuel (1853–1934), MP (Cons.) Limehouse 1895–1906, Norwood January 1910–22.

The constitutional crisis

It is however clear that one section of the cabinet is so needy that the loss of emolument becomes a serious consideration. Asquith for instance, Lloyd George, Churchill and McKenna are all living in riotous luxury and cannot wish to return to humdrum lager beer and lemonade. The Prime Minister in particular is almost a pauper and the extravagance of Mrs Asquith, together with his inability to earn much more than a couple of thousand a year on returning to private life, are potent agencies against surrendering office unless driven to do so. Grey on the other hand lives gently, but is trying to save money. It is notable that in spite of his large salary his name is always absent from subscription lists raised to mitigate foreign disasters.

24 FEBRUARY 1910

Oh the temperament of the new House of Commons! For the last four years we have worked under disadvantages of unique extent – and our fight was courageous in the extreme, for we were throughout disheartened by the terrible paucity of numbers, by the overweening bearing of our opponents, and by the galling sense of our own defeat. Now all is changed. We attack a glum and dejected government. Cheers now greet our speakers from the furthermost benches on the Speaker's left: even a bad argument now receives greater applause than would have been granted twelve months ago to a brilliant repartee. And the more I survey our new men the more confident do I become that among our recruits there are many who are not only keen and zealous, but active and competent allies.

...John Redmond came to me this evening, very anxious about Monday's debate when we are to deal with Asquith's motion taking away private members' time. He was very frank: wanted to know our idea, and observed that our position was in many respects identical with his – neither party wants a) to support the government b) to oppose the government in such a way to produce an early crisis c) or to be accused of weakness by abstention.

I was unable to help him – but he could not conceal his anxiety. The fact is that the little group of ten independent nationalists is able to sway the whole Redmondite faction, which in turn by combining with us can evict the government tomorrow. My Irish colleagues tell me that the feeling there against the Finance bill really becomes acute as its clauses are better understood – in fact that the bill arouses infinitely greater hostility than three months ago – if this be the case, or at least if Redmond finds himself driven to vote against the Budget, then the government is finally defeated. But we must ensure that there shall be no preliminary defeat on a minor or domestic issue, allowing them an opportunity of resigning prior to a big catastrophe.

25 FEBRUARY 1910

Today we discussed hops – a small debate. During the division we had a panic, fancying that we might beat the government and I held back twenty men whom we directed to refrain if necessary from voting: however we ascertained that the government had a good majority so self-effacement was unnecessary.

1910

26 FEBRUARY 1910

Now I am on election stories, an Irish example is worth quoting. John Redmond fully expected to defeat Tim Healy, and actually sanctioned the outlay of twenty-seven shillings for an effigy of the latter to be publicly burned to celebrate the defeat. However Tim Healy won, and Redmond allowed the effigy to be sold to some Unionists, who paid sixteen or seventeen shillings for it, and despatched it to Tyrone, where it masqueraded as T. W. Russell, and was offered up as burnt sacrifice on our victory. There is at any rate this resemblance between Tim and T.W. – both wear beards. But somebody asked Tim Healy how anybody could have mistaken the two images – ah said Tim, I suppose they turned the coat and shewed the Nationalist seams.

At the Carlton this afternoon many rumours consequent upon the visit of Asquith to the King followed by a prolonged cabinet. That the government will modify its policy, or rather its procedure in response to the shameless pressure of disloyal supporters, is generally accepted as inevitable. But up to Easter they must adhere to their programme, which leaves no time for anything but imperative financial business... I attach little credence to the view that Churchill or Lloyd George, or both, are intriguing against Asquith in order to supplant him. Times are too hard: and the crisis too acute to permit either of them any reasonable expectation of being supported by this House of Commons. Rosebery I imagine is hugging himself in the expectation of forming an interim government – a caretaker's ministry, but I hope we shan't be mixed up with him.

I MARCH 1910

Complete calm at Westminster, and expectation of its continuance for some time to come... A.J.B. was happy: but he isn't well, and the immediate crisis having collapsed, will go abroad in two or three days – so much the better. A thorough rest, with plenty of golf and some sunshine will do him all the good in the world.

LORD BALCARRES TO LADY WANTAGE, 4 MARCH 1910

There was an amusing scene the other night at the Austrian Embassy – the Queen was there, and eating rye bread of which she is fond – and she kept pushing bits to Asquith begging him to try 'the offal'.[2] I don't think it was very discreet on her part, as there were dozens of people at the dinner and scores of footmen, but Asquith lost his temper and got very rude – then the King could not help laughing, and altogether people wished they were dining elsewhere.

8 MARCH 1910

In afternoon took a class of new members who bombarded me with questions about procedure. I must have another later on, as the task of mastering our occult parliamentary methods needs much assistance from those who know.

[2] A theme of Liberal propaganda was that protection had reduced the Germans to eating rye bread and offal.

The constitutional crisis

LORD BALCARRES TO LADY WANTAGE, 11 MARCH 1910

The object of this manoeuvre is quite freely admitted. If the government resigns say about 15 May, then there will no money in the till, or rather no authority to spend it. Were Balfour to assume office he could not dissolve parliament before pressing a vote on account and a consolidated fund bill, the two processes needful to make expenditure legal. He could form a government, but he would of course ask to dissolve. Money for the public services during the interim being indispensable he would have to ask parliament to grant it. Without a majority he could not force his bill through; everything would have to be done by agreement. So Lloyd George would be able to make the business last a month or six weeks during which he would bombard the powerless government with questions, censures, and so forth, queering the pitch prior to an election.

It is very artful. People think that probably Harcourt is the contriver of the scheme, as it is a brilliant combination of cunning, adroitness, and malignity.

.. We asked Tim Healy his opinion. First he gave us his estimate of the effect, that it would ensure us a majority after the election. Then he gave us his view of the cause, the explanation of this much cogitated strategy. 'It is,' he said, 'a government of upstarts – a group of men lacking cabinet tradition. Their irresponsibility is shewn in their recklessness. It is un-English, that is to say doesn't conform to the English tradition of the solid and solemn treatment of governing the country. We might do that sort of thing in Ireland, but we would do it a d—d sight better'.

17 MARCH 1910

Arthur Lee (whose speeches on naval matters are quite excellent) told me of a droll circumstance which happened at Portsmouth shortly before Xmas. Charlie Beresford was abusing the government for having refused to move the Portsmouth writ, whereupon somebody called out, 'What about Uxbridge; why don't the Tories move the Uxbridge writ?' Beresford without a moment's hesitation cried out – 'because we don't want to be caught with our breeches down.' This vastly amused an enormous woman sitting in the middle of the room. She continued to split her sides with laughter long after the general merriment had subsided – then the public began to laugh again, at her this time, and finally when the second pause arrived, when the rest of the people were tired of laughing so much, the stout lady, still in fits of mirth emitted a report which was like the boom of a twelve inch gun. Of course this upset everybody – there was a perfect pandemonium in the midst of which she fired a second shot, and for fear of hysterics and perhaps fearing more explosions, she was conducted out of the room.

Five minutes later when calm was re-established Charlie, with a face of judicial solemnity remarked 'I will now resume my speech after that unseemly interruption' – but none the less his speech was never ended: he started the audience off again: cheers were drowned by laughter and no business was possible.

1910

LORD BALCARRES TO LADY WANTAGE, 25 MARCH 1910
Asquith is all the time touting for invitations to country house parties – many of his colleagues do the same – for they thoroughly enjoy the good things of life. I never saw a lot of men who so thoroughly appreciate a good dinner party and a good vintage. There are some strange stories about Asquith who so far as outward appearance goes, has again taken to over-indulgence. Lack of exercise has led him to be periodically massaged. The other day he nearly dismissed the masseur who protested against his taking whisky and soda before breakfast.

4 APRIL 1910
Asquith invented a nickname for his government which we will tie tightly round their necks! To half a dozen questions he replied 'Wait and see' – he did not mean it to be humorous, but I fancy absolute poverty of idea, possible mental coma caused by excessive alcohol, suggested this rapid iteration.

LORD BALCARRES TO LADY WANTAGE, 5 APRIL 1910
Asquith is a mass of nerves and . . . contradicts himself every hour. He sits fidgetting away, rubbing greasy palms together and looking the picture of distress, for nobody is less able to show an impassive countenance during the stress of criticism. I really believe that he lost his head yesterday when in answer to question after question he repeated the formula, 'Wait and see'.

10 APRIL 1910
The political crisis really does seem imminent. I am coaxing my supporters to look upon a dissolution as a public scandal. So it would be, for this fumbling government has no mandate to introduce revolutionary changes into our constitution. Meanwhile I record an odd symptom of our political kaleidoscope. Our unionist friends in the South of Ireland do not yet seem to have grasped what is ominously clear to Redmond: namely that under a Home Rule system a combination between O'Brien and our Ulstermen would submerge the official Nationalists. O'Brien is already near to our standpoint, land purchase being his primary objective. Redmond on the other hand, enjoying a comfortable seat at Westminster, and drawing £1000 a year as chairman of the Nationalist party, may prefer to avoid a crisis which might really produce a Home Rule Act, and with it his own downfall. This is an aspect of party politics on which we do not at present publicly descant!

13 APRIL 1910
Here at least is a substantial bit of news. Haldane told Croal,[3] the responsible editor of the *Scotsman*, that the government cannot escape defeat on Monday next. Croal tells Balfour. We believe him in so far as the present situation goes, but none the less we have always held that Redmond will brandish the sword until the last minute and

[3] John P. Croal (1852–1932), editor of *Scotsman* 1905–24.

then that one party or the other will give way to secure harmony. However Haldane was so emphatic that the differences about dragging the King into the fight may have become irreconcilable.

In conversation with Jack Sandars, I was asked if in the event of our securing a majority I would become Chief Whip. Nothing in the world would distract and bore me more than continuing in the whips department – moreover as I told him I am not only unversed in but totally unfitted for that part of the work which involves control of our party funds and organisation. Hitherto my activity has been confined to parliamentary work. Jack said that the two spheres should be separated and it seems that a scheme has been discussed by which the patronage secretary would be relieved from all those obligations connected with the constituencies, thus freeing him for business in the House of Commons.

Even so I should hate the post. And I am almost certain that apart from the fact that the head whip would inevitably become the referee in doubtful or disputed cases, members would not know the outside chairman of the organisation well enough to make them ready or anxious to take his advice. Much of the work would gradually fall back upon the shoulders of the patronage secretary. In any case I went into the Whips' room in 1903 since when I have had no leisure during the parliamentary session, and for the last four or five years I have done all the dirty work of the party. Others dine out because it is known I am too loyal to abandon my responsibilities (or theirs). I am anxious for a period of repose, anxious also for some little freedom to pursue my own avocations. Still I feel the force of Jack Sandars' plea that assuming Alick Hood and Harry Forster receive departmental posts there is no alternative to myself in 'the room' as we call it. Our situation is unsatisfactory for during these critical times he is engaged half the day at the central offices interviewing candidates, agents and chairmen, and thus unable to watch the trend of parliamentary opinion and debate.

14 APRIL 1910
A busy and momentous day. After a series of cabinets the government has decided to surrender. Redmond triumphs, but looks somewhat embarrassed by the palms of victory – indeed he may suffer from having forced the hand of the government. The decision to capitulate was only reached today, and Redmond's interview with Asquith did not take place till 6.30. The P.M. hurried into the House, but he was unable to make his announcement prior to the division. Consequently by 10.0 a second suite of divisions again foiled him.

The house was excited and petulant when he began. Balfour roused some animosities, and when Lowther adjourned the House tempers were roused, cries echoed, and members did not leave the chamber. For two or three minutes one expected a fiendish explosion, the effect of which would have been far more widespread than the scuffle of 1893. I caught sight of Walter Erskine,[4] and he

[4] Walter Hugh Erskine, b. 1870, assistant Serjeant-at-Arms in the House of Commons 1900–29; third son of Sir Henry David Erskine, Serjeant-at-Arms from 1885.

promptly acted on my suggestion of lowering the lights. This cooled ardour and the chamber rapidly emptied itself – but the lobby continued a scene of splutter for many minutes.

18 APRIL 1910

What the King thinks we shall shortly know: for the moment people are wondering why Churchill (not the most filial of people) has hurried to Paris to meet Mrs Cornwallis-West,[5] who in turn had hurried northward from Biarritz. Why this haste? It looks as though it was necessary to warn Churchill of something which might arise in the course of yesterday's debate.

21 APRIL 1910

Tonight the Nationalists made a beastly row. The whole business had been carefully pre-arranged, partly in order to collect money in the USA, partly also to provide some counter-irritant in Ireland where the Nationalist acceptance of an obnoxious finance bill is but little appreciated.

22 APRIL 1910

Our party at the moment is somewhat depressed, somewhat lethargic, and apt also to 'grouse'. Dillon the other day with gloomy lightness railed at us for being glum, and not without cause. We cannot see any hopeful issue to this controversy in which time is all on the enemy's side – a few weeks or months may make the impasse so acute that guarantees will be sought and obtained to the permanent detriment of our political stability. This being so some of our men – how many of them it is impossible to determine, begin to think that we have played our cards badly, though for the life of me I cannot see any action in which even with knowledge or prevision of subsequent events we could have adopted a different course. On the other hand zealous members think that the government will have to resign rather than dissolve, in which case A.J.B. would form a stopgap administration pending the general election. If members of the old gang find their way back into office under A.J.B. there would be an open revolt. It is felt that people like St John Brodrick, Salisbury, Eddie Stanley, Bromley-Davenport[6] and one or two others of this kidney are hanging on to A.J.B.'s coat-tails and may bore him into giving them posts. I hope not: but one cannot tell, and the Chief may really be in danger of committing a disastrous mistake.

25 APRIL 1910

Bob Douglas today told me that he has been recently overhauling his old correspondence and has just lately destroyed fifty-three letters addressed to him by

---

[5] Formerly Lady Randolph Churchill; mother of Winston.
[6] Sir William Bromley-Davenport (1862–1949), MP (Cons.) Macclesfield 1886–1906, financial secretary to the War Office 1903–5.

The constitutional crisis

Queen Victoria, and over sixty from Lord Salisbury.[7] He is a curious secretive person – and obliterates all record of his past official career. One of the documents he means to keep is the original compact between our party and the Liberal Unionists – annotated by Joe Chamberlain.

7 MAY 1910

The King died late last night.

... I wonder if London shares a sentiment which has invaded me – a feeling of resentment and shame that this precious life should have been needlessly thrown away by the ignorance and inexperience of physicians. It is true they called in a specialist yesterday when his advice must have proved unavailing: but it is surely unpardonable that all these days when the trouble must have been visibly brewing, his own medical men should have allowed the King to pursue his ordinary avocations with more than his ordinary zeal. After all they must have clearly detected this breathless asphyxiating cough – and yet allowed themselves to prescribe the ordinary remedies for a chill or for bronchitis. There is some resemblance to the crisis ten years ago when the King was brought to the point of death by the utter incapacity of his doctors to diagnose a dangerous symptom. Then, by the mercy of providence the surgeons were able to save his life – now precautions have been taken too late.

The extent of the national loss cannot for the moment be assessed ... Here in England during the brief reign of the King we have come to look upon the monarch as the source of inspiration in moments of disquiet and complexity: and I will engage that nine out of ten ordinary 'men in the street' viewed our political difficulties with calm if not with apathy, from an unspoken conviction that the King would extricate us somehow or other from 'the mess'.

Now a month before the constitutional difficulty becomes acute we lose the most shrewd and farsighted of monarchs. Such a situation apart from its personal aspect to us all may well produce a condition of alarm. It does not follow that the crisis could have been overcome even by the force, tact, and diplomacy of King Edward; none the less we cannot but feel disquiet, profound and deepseated, at being thus forced to grapple with a political situation more dangerous than any we have experienced in living memory, deprived as we are of the controlling influence and personality of the sovereign.

8 MAY 1910

In church today prayers were offered up for King George, for Alexandra Queen Dowager, for the Prince of Wales and other members of the royal family. Queen Mary seems to have been forgotten. Hitherto her personality has been overclouded, and she has tended to withdraw herself from observation, at any rate when in

[7] The present Lord Chilston, biographer of the above, is unable to confirm the accuracy of the statement. However, the Chilston papers contain only one letter from the Queen. Akers-Douglas was nicknamed 'Bob Akers' at Oxford, after Sheridan's 'Bob Acres' in *The Rivals*.

England. Those who know her predict that she will take no inconsiderable share of public applause: the late King froze her up – frightened her, and now that her survey will be free much can be expected of her. Both she and her husband have always been looked upon as hostile to what was known as the 'King's set': they have from time to time shewn antipathy to the rich and semitic entourage which was encouraged at Buckingham Palace. Latterly this reserve may have been somewhat mitigated but the Sassoons and Rothschilds, together with a rather fast type of racing magnate will find their status less prominent than formerly. I don't think King George is overfond of horse racing: for the moment he devotes all his energies to shooting, and this will insensibly tend to alter the hosts of royalty.

But the old country families with great sporting estates are no longer able, from many causes, to entertain upon the requisite scale. A few of them, Knowsley and Chatsworth for instance, enjoy secular powers of entertainment on a gigantic basis: but the ordinary peer who thirty or forty years ago was well able to encompass the outlay may well shrink nowadays from a week which may cost anything from five to ten thousand pounds. Moreover I doubt if anything can well reduce this killing standard. Society in short has to prepare for many changes, both of manner and of personnel. I think the change will be for the good.

9 MAY 1910.

There is certainly a feeling widely prevalent in lower middle class circles in London, that the King's death was accelerated by anxiety caused by Asquith's announcement that the cabinet intend to bring pressure on the Throne. That the King was upset we all know: he was for instance furious when Churchill indicated an alliance between the Throne and the Commons, and I fancy that Asquith's eleventh hour surrender to the Nationalists, blurted out in parliament before it was possible to communicate the memo to Biarritz, carried with it an uncomfortable flavour of disrespect. At the same time, galled as the King was by this lack of courtesy (to place it no higher), it is difficult to believe that a man of his spirit and self-reliance could have really taken the slight so much to heart as to prejudice his general health. However he did feel the affront deeply: so much so that the new King can hardly conceal his sentiments on the matter. Cecil Manners[8] tells me that when Churchill, as home secretary, was summoned to the Palace when a demise seemed imminent, he was left *downstairs*: not even admitted to an antechamber of the royal apartments. I wonder if this is true . . . That Churchill is without conscience or scruple, without a glimmer of the comities of public reserve and deference, we all know, and all, even his closest friends, admit.

King George, without the great knowledge and immense patience of his father, is not so well able to control his emotions, and where Edward could have maintained silence, George is apt to make a pronouncement. I fear that during the last few months he has given opinions which he should have kept for himself, and there may

[8] Lord Cecil Manners (1868–1945), MP (Cons.) Melton 1900–06, third son of the seventh Duke of Rutland.

be a feeling already of antagonism between him and the government. This of course would be regrettable from every point of view: but he is entitled to take a firm attitude – indeed has he not already sworn to *maintain the constitution*? How is its preservation compatible with advice dictated by Churchill?

... Anyhow I pray that his conduct will be marked by personality and decision. The instructions issued this afternoon to theatre managers that places of entertainment are to be reopened at once strikes the true note of solicitude and affection. There will be a gratified response from the public during what should be its holiday season. I wish that he had a larger circle of friends who would influence him in worldly matters. I feel for instance that many people unconnected with narrow Nonconformity would rejoice at the dispersal of the racing stud. Jack Sandars tells me I am wrong in thinking that he is not interested in racing – that he has taken little share in these things because it was ordained that father and son should not at the same time own racehorses. Let him attend race meetings – as many as he chooses – but I can't help feeling that the smart racing women, the Marcus Beresfords,[9] the Newmarket sycophants and the semitic sportsmen form a circle from which he would do well to withdraw, and in which he cannot fail to continue if he is the actual possessor of racehorses. For the moment all racing is suspended – for twelve months I think the embargo runs, and a fitting opportunity presents itself of quietly escaping from these dangerous meshes. For danger there must always be – one stupid or vicious jockey might produce a scandal of real intensity.

... By the way the late King won a race, his first this season, on the very day of his death. Early in the morning they wired to know if the horse should be withdrawn; the horse was ordered to run – he won – and thinking that the news might bring about a cheering reaction the King was awakened from a stupor to be told the news. He was delighted – took a telegraph form and wrote a message of congratulations which was illegible.

10 MAY 1910

Hamilton[10] tells me of a conversation with his mother, [*the Duchess of Abercorn.*] She is a very good personal friend of Queen Alexandra – and he himself the late King's godson. Well – the Duchess was telegraphed for – and the Queen immediately burst out 'They have killed him, they have killed him.' The Duchess with her calm wellbred manner expressed her sorrow, indicating at the same time that she regretted that the crisis had at any rate begun in the House of Lords. Thereupon the Queen assured her that the crisis proper had nothing to do with it – that the constitutional difficulty was one the King was fully prepared to face. She then went

[9] Lord Marcus de la Poer Beresford (1848–1922), son of fourth Marquess of Waterford; starter for Jockey Club 1885–90; manager of Sandringham stud.

[10] James Albert Edward, Marquess of Hamilton (1869–1953) treasurer of HM Household 1903–5, MP (Cons.) Londonderry City 1900–13; succeeded as third Duke of Abercorn, 1913; godson of Edward VII; first Governor-General of N. Ireland 1922–45.

on to say that what really produced the fatal anxiety was Asquith's speech to the Nationalists, the King having left for Biarritz with an understanding almost amounting to a positive pledge that during his absence Asquith would never mention the sovereign's name in connection with public policy. This must be true – the authority is so good. Perhaps there is some collateral illustration in the significant baldness of a paragraph in this evening's papers: that the Prime Minister had an audience of the King; that the Prime Minister did not see Queen Alexandra.

11 MAY 1910

As for Asquith's speech[11]–it was of course turgid – but none the less a well-phrased and decorous panegyric. How I wish A.J.B. would condescend to read his orations as Asquith does – I mean those which depend so largely upon the adjustment of balanced phraseology. Nothing will induce him to take this precaution. He refuses to prepare more guidance than can be jotted on to the face of a long envelope – I have kept lots of them as examples of note taking – while Asquith, like a wise man thinks more of the external than of the internal effect of the speech. He directs it to the public and to posterity, and consequently does not object to that which A.J.B. abominates – namely reading an essay instead of making a speech.

For a time all thoughts of politics ceased as the country gave itself up to the funeral of Edward VII.

19 MAY 1910

A day or two after his death I kept noticing bright patches of colour. Today people in the streets turn round with a shocked impression at any gaudy or noticeable costume. Mourning is followed by supermourning more noticeable every hour[12] ... People really are profoundly stricken, do firmly feel a personal as well as a State loss, and look upon the late King as a friend and protector.

20 MAY 1910

This is the funeral day ... I have been very low – what affects me most is the humbler sources of pathos. Not the dead marches and the tolling bell, not these tremendous movements of crowned monarchs or the thousands of troops: what really goes to my heart and makes me gulp down the tears are infinitely more precious demonstrations. As I went down to Windsor, it was the black rags hanging on the little mastheads of the brick barges: in Windsor cloisters it was not the superb wreaths ... I was far more touched by the tribute sent by the sandwichmen, a wreath from 'some embroideresses of Bethnal Green' – and a handful of faded lilies

[11] The party leaders moved an address of condolence.
[12] The mourning in London, Balcarres noted, was far more than anything which followed the death of Queen Victoria.

The constitutional crisis

of the valley in an old cardboard box... At Windsor, it is true, costliness is still to many people an essential. In London on the other hand there are hundreds or rather thousands of plain wreaths formed of laurel, cypress and ilex, decorating the streets and frontages, each authenticated with the name of some school or society, club or individual...

As a spectacle the service in St George's was noble. We did not have long to wait – and when the choir and Archbishops moved down to the western door the ante-chapel was flooded with sunlight. Then came the procession – the catafalque borne with unerring skill by guardsmen – then the King and Queen Alexandra – plaintively acknowledging the inclined heads to right and left. The Kaiser followed looking sternly determined to check external emotion. Then came the strangest motley of mankind... Never again can I expect to see so diverse a throng. The variety of uniforms from the Chinese Prince to the Armenian patriarch, from the Greek and Servian to the plain persons from the United States: mayors of French towns, burgomasters of German health resorts – sailors, soldiers, diplomatists – men of science and art – the actor, the theologian, the physician – never I say can one again hope to witness so palpable and so diverse a testimony of respect.

... The crowd in the first place was stupendous. In Hyde Park it was in some places a hundred yards deep. Everybody who walked in the procession tells me that what was most impressive was the positive silence of the crowds – their awed demeanour, and the fact that nobody was smoking. This surely is a rare sign of respect.

Then again the handling of these masses was carried out with judgement. It is no easy matter to control a million people, crushed within a narrow compass – hot tired dusty – many of whom had been waiting twelve hours – 1600 of whom required medical assistance during the day, for the temperature was stifling. But the police and ambulance were admirable. What a relief to the former that all is safely concluded... The more responsible officials have been watching anxiously for the foreign anarchist. Eight or nine monarchs and as many heirs apparent – all gathered within the space of a dozen yards – must have presented a tempting bait to the mad bombthrower. Pretty nearly every secret service force in Europe has been well represented in London during these few days, and last night the Russian official effected a bag of suspicious characters who are locked up safely until the royal envoys have departed. Scotland Yard had a plain clothes detective posted in the crowd at twenty-two yards distance – a cricket pitch – on either side of the roadway. This man arrived among the first and throughout the morning moved about unobtrusively within his beat watching and noting his neighbours. But the Commissioner was not really afraid of an outrage among the standing spectators. The crowd is so dense that it is almost impossible for a man to raise his arm to throw the bomb: his neighbours would prevent it – the real danger lies from the occupants of the windows. Thence it would be easy to drop an explosive into the very heart of sovereignty – and Henry has had a good deal of difficulty with owners of these

156

houses who have not given him the assistance he expected – in letting him visit the rooms in question, where necessary examine the letters and contracts of those who hire the apartments, and in certain cases have a quiet peep at the tenants themselves. All however has passed off without any attempt or suggestion of assassination.

21 MAY 1910

To Haigh in the afternoon.

Now I am away from London I see the central features emerging from these days of national mourning. The grief in the first place has been genuine and sincere, deep-seated and expressed with dignity and reserve.

King George has begun to establish a reputation for which he would not have been credited a few months ago, for calm and dignified correctness.

Queen Alexandra who has gradually been escaping the public eye by withdrawing herself more and more from State functions, and indeed from this country as well, has suddenly found herself again in the centre of canvas – has occupied her station with great persistence, has re-rivetted many hearts, and perhaps will in consequence spend more of her widowhood in this country than we ever expected.

. . . But on one condition, namely that she does not unduly trespass upon the sphere of her daughter-in-law. The Queen has behaved with touching self-restraint towards the Queen Dowager: she has pressed the latter to occupy the forefront, to be chief mourner, to enforce upon the public how great her status has been and how fully she appreciates their sense of loss, as well as their condolence with herself. The Queen, or Queen Mary as she is improperly called, has shewn a complete self-effacement which I think is right royal on her part.

26 MAY 1910

The general impression is that our business being settled and that of the Lords resting in Rosebery's discretion, the government will have a week's breathing space after our assemblage in which to negotiate with Redmond, who in his turn is still watching events.

9 JUNE 1910

Still hot and House rose very early. What a ridiculous situation it is. Vague uninformed talk of compromise – the only thing I can say with some confidence is that while the party is ready enough to enter into a conference, few are prepared to effect any large compromise. . . There is a general impression that after Walter Long's statement – whether authorised or not I can't say – the government will take the initiative towards a round table discussion. We could not refuse to agree to such a procedure though we might well insist that the basis of negotiation shall be an unconditional acceptance of the bicameral system. There will be much manoeuvring about this business – how to enter and above all how to withdraw! . . . For the moment little but speculation is recordable. Arthur Lee tells me that Roosevelt had full, and indeed cordial assent from Edward Grey for his speech about Egypt. He told Grey what he intended to say, Grey approved, and has since expressed his personal satisfaction. This is pretty clear – for Arthur Lee has been Roosevelt's host and has been familiar with the whole situation as it has gradually developed. But how much does this lower Grey in one's estimation! Though it cannot be justly alleged that he inspired Roosevelt, he has cordially – almost gratefully – endorsed a root and branch condemnation of his own vacillating policy.

...By the way, Arthur Lee tells me an interesting thing, namely that letters are now beginning to pour in from the valley of the Nile thanking Roosevelt – begging, imploring him to maintain his robust criticism ... They have indeed suffered, these hard-worked officials who have built up Egypt: and during the last year or two they have been discouraged by the thought that their own future is prejudiced by the passion for shelving them for natives who after 1500 years of oppression are unable to do more than act as subordinates.

10 JUNE 1910

I perused Asquith's letter to Balfour suggesting a preliminary conversation, informal, prior to discussing a more serious conference. The letter was dated yesterday, not marked private, indicating that it reflects a cabinet decision, but the middle class sentiment and wordiness show the composition to be Asquith's own. Balfour's assent to the proposal struck me as wondrous frigid: civil but terse to a point bordering on curtness. I find that Walter Long's announcement was quite unauthorised and that in certain quarters it aroused a good deal of vexation.

...Of course the danger of the conference lies in the fact that A.J.B. will probably commit the fatal error of treating George, Churchill and Co. as gentlemen, whereas they will descend to any meanness to score a point after negotiations are broken off, which I look upon as inevitable.

11 JUNE 1910

In the Carlton it is generally assumed that a conference will take place, but doubt is freely cast upon newspaper statements that negotiations have already been begun. The prospect on the whole is looked upon with indulgent favour, though I find my own apprehensions are shared by many who think that A.J.B. will be too softhearted...

13 JUNE 1910

Most entertained by a debate about the Dorset byelection, two Radical members having tried to stop the issue of the writ to mark public displeasure at Lady Wimborne's ostentatious bribery. Her action was certainly disgraceful. She is now called the 'Paying Guest'.[13]

---

[13] Sister of Lord Randolph Churchill; she married Sir Ivor Guest, created Lord Wimborne 1880.

16 JUNE 1910

A.J.B. tells me the conference is to meet tomorrow. This is about the first bit of information I have received on the subject. I fancy he is rather nervous – but many of the Radicals seem really angry that any such conference should take place. It would have been suicidal for us to decline the government's overtures . . . House d—d dull.

17 JUNE 1910

We had arranged to take Irish estimates on Thursday. Elibank this afternoon comes to us begging that Post Office votes shall be substituted: because he doesn't want the Nationalist members over here during the early stage of the conference! He is frightened of them, not only of their direct intervention, but because they will corrupt his docile lambs. Under the circumstances Alick Hood consented to postpone the Irish votes – not wishing to do anything liable to lay him open to the charge of being hostile to the attempted concordat.

. . . Beauchamp[14] a cabinet minister! I don't know why, but this strikes me as inexpressibly funny. One of my oldest friends, I fancy I know few people whose natural sentiments are more reactionary. In this respect he is like his uncle Philip Stanhope. But in old days independence was in vogue, and moreover it had to be displayed to impress Papa, the most straitlaced and pompous old prig I ever saw. Hence certain divergencies in the family, followed soon after Beauchamp's succession to the title by his governorship of New South Wales. It wasn't quite a success, and I fancy that on returning home he felt neglect and oversight, much as is the case with so many repatriated proconsuls. I remember at Hatfield old Lord Salisbury saying to him as we left the dining room, 'I suppose you feel quite strange when your rising from a chair is not accompanied by the National Anthem'. Anyhow he left our party and has been a staunch adherent of the New Radicalism.

18 JUNE 1910

In constituency all afternoon. I don't know how many processions of schoolchildren I witnessed.

I went to see one Bentham, a collier in Standish whom I sent on a tour in January to be a witness against George's[15] lies about black bread and offal. Bentham is a huge muscular fellow, Radical or rather Labour in proclivities, and to that extent biassed against my policies. His views on the German industrial system were decided and interesting and although he has not been converted to Tariff Reform, like so many of those who accompany these parties, he will give chapter and verse to

[14] Sir William Lygon, seventh Earl Beauchamp; succeeded his father in 1891; formerly, as Viscount Elmley, a close undergraduate friend of Balcarres, and president of the Oxford union: governor of New South Wales, 1899–1902: changed parties and took minor office in 1905–7 with Liberals: appointed Lord President of the Council, 1910.
[15] Lloyd George

rebut all those ridiculous fables about the starving semi-barbarism of Germany, tales which are still spread about by ignorant or unscrupulous radicals.

28 JUNE 1910

While the Radicals are full of apprehensions of betrayal our party which has behaved admirably throughout the conference is beginning to feel that apart from the constitutional question we show too little fight. I understand and I sympathise. Since our return to Westminster after the King's funeral, we opposition whips haven't 'held the door'. The work is continuous and fatiguing, but essential to the maintenance of discipline and for the information of enquiring members. The moment the door is released, disorganisation sets in with the excusable feeling that men are not wanted, and that nobody cares or enquires whether they are present or not. This kind of rot spreads rapidly and has a reflex if not a direct action upon the spirits of the party organisations all over the country. Moreover there is a deepseated feeling that too many of our leading men while away an otiose existence too far off the scene of battle. George Wyndham, Arthur Lee, Bonar Law, and above all Alfred Lyttelton are seldom seen except when some topic of personal interest arises, and the fellowship which should thrive between the officers and rank and file is becoming atrophied.

30 JUNE 1910

Asquith announced an autumn session which made us groan in our hearts, for we had hoped for a respite: indeed a few days ago Asquith himself forecast a prorogation about the middle of August: and there is no reason why such a course should not be easily accomplished. However the dissidents and conference wreckers won't have it, and the last stages of the Finance Bill are to be gaily suspended till midwinter... Last year delay was to paralyse our public life: this year the government proposes much the same thing for tactical reasons.

1 JULY 1910

A.J.B. is nervous about the conference, and to my surprise told me he did not want it to be concluded soon. The fact is that he is anxious about its termination, being unwilling to incur the responsibility of breaking off negotiations.

6 JULY 1910

I talked to Austen Chamberlain about the conference which is being continued in Balfour's absence, and a further meeting is to be held this week. Austen said he could be trusted not to give the party away – and that the sitting was to elucidate certain points upon which no decision could or would be taken. I suppose Lloyd George who isn't educated is making researches into Stubbs.

But what can they be doing? are they preparing a written constitution, are they investigating the origin of the Privy Council or the Writ of Summons, or are they merely marking time – is it a conspiracy of obstruction? For the life of me I cannot hazard an opinion, for the whole thing is so paradoxical, and one might say so absurd that none of us can guess why this talk of compromise is so seriously accepted.

8 JULY 1910

Dined at Carlton Gardens, where I find that A.J.B. was well enough to take part in the conference this afternoon. I thought him looking well. We discussed what is now much talked of, namely the physical coarsening of the Prime Minister... Perrier Jouet,[16] the popular sobriquet of the P.M., tells its own tale, though Balfour says that at the conference Asquith shows all his old quickness and dexterity: but he cannot last ten years longer, even if his surrenders to noisy men in his own cabinet fighting for appointments, do not render his position intolerable long before then.

9 JULY 1910

The Speaker suffers from a collision with a Bishop: a real Bishop not a suffragan: therein his only consolation. It appears that the Speaker was bicycling, and he says a Bishop knocked him down. The Bishop says he was walking, and that the Speaker ran over him. It is a grievous conflict between Church and State. The Bishop is sore, the Speaker's knees are excoriated, and we have seen the effects in one or two sharp rulings.

14 JULY 1910

Dined with Austen Chamberlain: a pleasant party consisting of Lord Lansdowne, Oliver[17] and Milner. We talked about political abstractions, and descending to political affairs, discussed the effect of eyesight upon public speaking. Milner can't hold his glasses on his nose, and therefore speaks without reference to his audience. A.J.B. also is so short-sighted that he can scarcely recognise a man on the front bench opposite, and likewise does not attempt to make any compromise between his subject matter and his hearers: and he claims this as a distinct advantage, as giving a collective nexus between himself and his audience whom he vaguely perceives: whereas Austen (and I) trust constantly to the fugitive signs of appreciation or the reverse for guidance or encouragement during the progress of a speech. Milner says this is all wrong, as casual indications at a public meeting should not be allowed to influence the pronouncement one way or the other: but he does not quite recognise that his own meetings are demonstrations, not the rough and ready assemblages addressed by ordinary people...

Lord Salisbury who constructed his sentences with impeccable skill was always leisurely in delivering a speech. In early life he realised that his notes would get hopelessly mixed up – his eyesight never being strong, and his handling of papers being decidedly clumsy: so he used to ruminate for an hour or two before speaking,

---

[16] A brand of champagne
[17] Frederick Scott Oliver (1864–1934), barrister and political writer.

and then made an oration faultless in its polished perfection: but he only determined the outline and never learned a phrase; and he was never misunderstood.

20 JULY 1910

Trouble is brewing about the Declaration Bill. Scotland is apparently up in arms. Nonconformists in the H. of C. who don't care a fig about the Roman Catholics are furious at the proposal that the sovereign shall pronounce himself a member of the C. of E. Ulster of course is rampaging. All the Protestant societies are preparing for the fray and doubtless members are getting anxious about the future. Tullibardine[18] had nearly 500 letters and postcards in the course of one day. This is the kind of problem which is far-reaching in results and I notice that a lot of our new men fail to realise how serious the matter is from an ordinary electoral aspect. People fancy we are no longer animated by the No Popery cry, and that our old-fashioned bigotry is dead. No greater mistake: it is merely dormant. Meanwhile though I support the Bill, I feel a sort of professional regret that the opposition is being so mishandled. The government made the initial mistake of delaying a measure which ought to have been pressed forward without the least delay: but the Protestant party went to sleep. They only began effective organisation two or three weeks ago. Had they had parliamentary experience at their command they would have shown activity long ago . . . in short I firmly believe the measure might have been killed. Now the prospects are the Bill will get through all right though I expect a couple of critical divisions. The Liverpool election is unfortunate as a symptom of what still survives in this controversy . . . I hear it said that Scotland which was angry with the Lords for throwing out the budget, will be still more furious if they don't throw out the Declaration Bill!

Burns told me that the decision to extend the period of repayment for school building loans to fifty years was made by Asquith, and that he, Burns, disapproving so strongly, had to consider whether he ought to send in his resignation. Like a sensible man he has settled to remain in office in order to fight far more serious proposals in the near future.

21 JULY 1910

It is rumoured that Haldane has assured the cabinet that Scotland being practically agnostic, the wave of indignation about the declaration oath will prove evanescent . . . Haldane is greatly mistaken if he assumes that because a Scotsman is an atheist, he is therefore likely to tolerate the Pope.

There is real danger to the government in this Bill. The more the situation develops the graver it becomes. It presents precisely that sentimental note which might work havoc – and were it not for the fact that our party is about as strongly pledged as theirs to alter the phraseology, the destiny of the government would be

[18] John George Stewart Murray, Marquess of Tullibardine (1871–1942); MP W. Perthshire January 1910–17; succeeded father as Duke of Atholl, 1917.

doomed. As a party bill they could not carry it: indeed they would incur a disastrous defeat. As a party we badly want a sentimental cry: here it is, but we can't use it.

22 JULY 1910

A leakage in the *Times* this morning about the conference: an obvious and inspired leakage. We generally attribute it to Runciman whom we know has frequently given tips to Nicholson, the zealous lobby correspondent . . . The feeling grows apace that there may be some feasible scheme as an outcome of these deliberations. I find it hard to believe in such a possibility – yet . . . .

23 JULY 1910

Had a talk with George Curzon who is collecting money for the anti-suffrage movement. He has got £15,000, but wants £100,000 or more. He says that he is working very hard and is somewhat discouraged. The other day for instance he argued forty minutes with a man, wrote him two letters into the bargain, and was only rewarded by a cheque for three guineas! Still he has taken up the task with great zeal and I doubt not will make things hum.

I was amused the other day by a story of Admiral Moore's. He was at Christie's (or some other saleroom) looking at a lot of china which Kitchener was selling, as being below the standard of his collection . . . 'But isn't it good or valuable?' queried Moore. 'Oh no, it is quite common stuff.' Then a voice behind them said 'Lord Kitchener seems to know about as much about china as on any and every other subject.'

'Who was that gentleman?' said Sparkes as the man passed away. 'Lord Curzon' replied Moore.

In point of fact Kitchener possesses some good things, though he had his disappointments. On coming home the other day he opened some cases full of pottery and curiosities which he had bought years and years ago in Egypt – never having had leisure since then to examine his treasures. But alas, he found that the scoundrels who had packed the boxes at Cairo had substituted bricks and rubbish for the precious things! Having thus been robbed, Kitchener presumably doesn't mind what he does. It is alleged that when recently in China and Japan, he kept the handsome gifts which were sent, according to the custom of those countries, on the honourable understanding that they would be returned to their owners! It is an odd sort of compliment, to send a bronze or enamel with the expectation of having your present sent back – but that is the universal system as K. must well know: and if he has really committed this grave breach of etiquette he deserves censure. He is a greedy man. Much ill will was caused by the frank manner in which he used to bargain with City Corporations and Companies who offered him their freedom, as to the nature of the gift accompanying the charter of citizenship; and he has been known to hint with unblushing insistence that he would like this, that or the other object which he has coveted in the private residences of our consuls, diplomatists and soldiers stationed abroad.

The constitutional crisis

There has been a terrific crisis at the conference, and Lloyd George's attitude was so threatening, at times so nearly bordering on insolence, that Balfour thought it was intended to break off negotiations. Our quartet kept their heads and tempers. Asquith was involved to some extent but left the impression that he wasn't chiefly responsible. So serious has the situation become that Akers-Douglas made arrangements at one of the Clubs for holding a party meeting.

Meanwhile A.J.B. held a consultation with his old colleagues, and his instructions not being very clear, an invitation to attend reached all members of our last cabinet. So to Balfour's surprise he found himself expounding the business to Ailwyn Fellowes,[19] Eddie Stanley,[20] and I suppose to Salisbury also, though I'm not sure that he was there. There is danger in accepting advice from those who have long since dropped out of the front political battleline. Eddie's advice was precipitate, Jim Cranborne's[21] generally ill-judged, while Ailwyn, one of the best whips we have had, cannot assess broad problems. A.J.B. gave a masterly exposition of the situation.

28 SEPTEMBER 1910

I see I have endowed my diary with six or seven weeks of repose. It reflects the blank and unemotional period I have spent at Balcarres ... There seems to be a good chance of a fresh outbreak of labour electioneering, analogous to that which followed the Taff Vale decision. This prospect has led some of our newspapers and M.P.s to an outburst of enthusiasm for payment of members – a policy more likely to produce cleavage among us than among the Radicals. Then there are naval problems – and above them all in the view of another class of middle class opinion, Form IV of the new Land Tax. I fancy we are squeaking too loudly about the hardships of Form IV. Then the licensed victualler is in a condition of distress though he seems likely to shift a portion of his new burdens on to the rates.

Altogether there is a juicy hotch-potch for the autumn sittings, and if we succeed in fighting the budget sturdily, and making no time-concessions, the government will find some difficulty in dealing with all those matters demanding attention. The result of the conference which may presumably be expected quite early in our sittings cannot fail to give rise to pretty long debates.

5 OCTOBER 1910

Austen Chamberlain writes hoping that A.J.B. won't give way about payment of members – a subject on which many of our men are coming to a hasty conclusion. I suppose he will refer to the topic in his Edinburgh speech today: but it is a risky

---

[19] Hon. Ailwyn Fellowes (1855–1924), created Lord Ailwyn, 1921: junior Whip, 1900–05: president, Board of Agriculture, 1905.
[20] Seventeenth Earl of Derby (1865–1948), who had succeeded his father in 1908.
[21] i.e. fourth Marquess of Salisbury (1861–1947).

business, and moreover unfortunate for him that he has to speak before any cabinet minister has made a pronouncement. It is after all their responsibility, and I think Fred Smith and others are unwise in inferring that the initiative must spring from us.

7 OCTOBER 1910

Balfour's soliloquy at Edinburgh is a curious example of his strength and weakness. His criticism of the existing situation in labour politics is penetrating and suggestive, must command attention, and will influence liberal opinion. On the other hand the serenity with which he disregarded the urgent demands for a 'fighting lead' will disconcert many, and perhaps disappoint others... As to the 'revolt' in the Unionist party (the evidence of which is chiefly drawn from Radical sources) at a distance from London it is difficult to say what actually transpires: but I much doubt if serious or influential people desire Balfour to commit the party at this stage, while the cabinet and Labour party are in a viscous condition.

19 OCTOBER 1910

Lunched with Fred Smith at the Carlton. He is very low about our prospects – that I understand: but also nervous and irritable with those who differ from him. Thus talking about the conference, he strongly argued that we ought to surrender whatever the government may demand about Irish Home Rule, on the ground that there must be give and take, and that we owe less to the Irish Unionists than to larger interests at home. The doctrine is dangerous. Our men, and I have talked to dozens, have volunteered free opinions about F.E.'s loyalty to the party. They cannot understand why he should hobnob so much with Churchill, still more how he can submit to the sycophancy of M. De Forest. I personally believe in Fred's anxiety to support the party through thick and thin, and moreover he is a convinced Tariff Reformer, and would therefore find it difficult to abandon us. None the less there is a general distrust in his bona fides: and as usual we take less trouble about nursing the wayward child than our opponents, whose finesse in such matters is both more adroit and persevering than *chez nous*.

7 NOVEMBER 1910

Austen Chamberlain came[22], and made two admirable speeches in Wigan. I heard the first, to a big audience of 4000 or so, and afterwards he addressed 2000 more as an overflow.

He tells me that I must be prepared for a January election. The conference from time to time has afforded good ground for optimism, but something or other, Home Rule I imagine, has brought about an impasse, and all the Santi Otto[23] are depressed, because they have sincerely striven to compass an agreement. Lloyd

[22] At Haigh
[23] The eight negotiators from the two parties.

The constitutional crisis

George he says has behaved well – has expressed his views with complete freedom, and has apparently done his best to be accommodating. Circumstances however are too strong, convictions too deep-seated for compromise and we must therefore *fear the worst*. I gather that the whole thing has been intensely interesting – the absence of reserve on either side making the conference as A.J.B. said 'exactly like a cabinet, but much more united'... Meanwhile even if conference fails at its next meeting, certain outstanding questions will remain to be determined – e.g. whether the public should be told that the conference has failed to agree – and nothing more: or on the other hand whether a précis of its proceedings should be issued ... Austen however says that as far as he and the other three heroes are concerned, there is no objection to the most complete publicity. That would show that our representatives haven't surrendered as much as the Irish Unionists seem to fear.

By the way the Ulster members are firing blank cartridges about Devolution, banging the Orange drum, and denouncing in future those of us who may concede something to Nationalism. In point of fact these friends of ours do not occupy the secure foothold they held ten or twenty years ago. England is bored about Home Rule, but in view of recent legislation less hostile than ever. The passage of the R.C. University Bill and of the Accession Declaration Bill show that the Orange mob is less sensitive than before, and William O'Brien is a fitful guarantee that the northern spirit will not be without sympathy in the South. All these symptoms tend to reconcile England to Home Rule. Moreover one of these days we shall awaken to find that Labour has swept Belfast, while Liberalism may again find a place in rural Ulster.

14 NOVEMBER 1910

A good deal at the Carlton talking with all and sundry. Few can rebut the unanimity of the Radical press in predicting an early election. Opinion however on our prospects is still vague, and few are the optimists who anticipate more than a fractional gain of seats to the opposition. Others it must be admitted fear we may lose some especially in the Home Counties.

At three, a letter was communicated to me from Elibank saying that Asquith will be unable to make his statement tomorrow. It is natural to assume that this postponement is due to the necessity of consulting Redmond who won't reach London until late tonight or early tomorrow morning ... Our men talk much of the nefarious influence of American dollars, but I don't think the electorate will be alarmed on this score.

At four to A.J.B. where a conference met: Austen Chamberlain, Pretyman[24], Fred Smith, Alick Hood, Bob Douglas, Bonar Law and self. The object of our discussion was to elicit views on what the Chief should say next Thursday in his Nottingham speech on the budget. Pretyman anxious for a definite pledge to repeal

[24] Ernest George Pretyman (1860–1931), MP (Cons.) Woodbridge 1895–1906, Chelmsford 1908–23; held junior office 1900–05, 1915–19.

the land taxes: after discussion it transpired that he only referred to taxes based on valuation: that excludes the reversion duty. And he has alternative proposals of a drastic character. A.J.B. would not pledge himself to repeal, though in favour of revision, and ready to allocate proceeds to local authorities. Everybody took the same view except Pretyman. Austen C. strongly urged that notwithstanding the complaints of those affected, the land taxes are popular: he said that in March 1909 we had smashed the government which owing to its land policy was re-established by the autumn. This is too true! and I fancy we should be unwise to reopen the land question more than we can help: before long the unpopularity of these new burdens will grow....

16 NOVEMBER 1910

Discomfort of the situation grows. Yesterday Harry Chaplin told us in consternation that Balfour was meditating the announcement at Nottingham that he will drop the food taxes. Eddie Stanley at the Carlton enthusiastic for him to do so. Jack Sandars also strongly in favour of such a course, and says that the Chief is being pressed from Tariff Reform quarters to execute this volte face. The food taxes of course are unpopular, and even without taxes the cost of living has alarmingly increased, and I do not doubt that the food taxes will figure largely during the election. But should we gain by dropping them? ... That it would split the party is undeniable. That Austen Chamberlain, Bonar Law, and other staunch men would be unable to join any government A.J.B. might be called upon to form is obvious, and divided counsels would again distract us....

I don't think the Chief will indicate a change of front though Salisbury who has largely monopolised him during the last few days advocates it. Many of our men are terror-struck that if Asquith resigns, we shall again find Jim Salisbury, Eddie Stanley, Londonderry and Co. in the ministry. This would produce something akin to revolt. There is a good deal of hostility to George Wyndham, and much to St John Brodrick, in each case quite undeserved. By the way if P.J.[25] resigns I think I have secured that Kitchener shall be offered the War Office. There are one or two tremendous difficulties in the way, but the stroke would be justified.

... John Burns says the government cannot fail to win 25 seats, and may win 50. George Faber[26] says we shall lose 30. Fred Smith says that we shall win 20, and that if A.J.B. forms a government on Asquith's resignation we might win 50. Alick Hood is not optimistic, neither is Bob Douglas, the most astute man in the party: but he is a cautious person and secretive.

17 NOVEMBER 1910

The Radicals work better than we do: not necessarily harder, but with greater effect. They control their press with ingenuity: they bleed their plutocrats, they distribute

[25] Asquith was nicknamed Perrier Jouet, after the brand of champagne.
[26] George Denison Faber, b. 1852, MP (Cons.) York 1900–10, Clapham 1910–18.

their honours, and they silence their malcontents with a skill which we cannot emulate. And there is of course a bond of union between all those who are invited to dip their hands in other people's pockets. Elibank deserves much credit for the zeal he has shown during the past six months. From a parliamentary point of view he is ignorant and hasn't handled his party well, nor has his arrangement of H. of C. business been good. But his work in the constituencies has been admirable. He has spent his holiday travelling about, rousing enthusiasm among local magnates, forcing them to adopt candidates, distributing cash with judgement, and generally rehabilitating an organisation which was going to bits under the clumsy handling of Jack Pease. Whatever be the outcome of the fight, Elibank stands out as one who has done much for his party: and he starts with the advantage of being a gentleman. The Radicals have had no gentleman as chief whip since Tweedmouth (not himself a *grand seigneur*!) unless one counts Herbert Gladstone who was negligible.

Meanwhile at the Carlton our men seem to be making something in the nature of a concerted attack on Jack Sandars: blaming him for the inaccessibility of A.J.B., for his aloofness from certain political movements, and also for what is not probably attributable to Jack's influence, namely the ready access to the Chief secured by some of the least efficient or least popular members of the party – friends or relatives. I think much of this criticism is due to the persistence with which Jack Sandars performs the duties of a faithful secretary, in shielding Balfour against the stranger, a duty which he may unduly extend against those who being colleagues feel they have some claims to consideration. But I look upon Sandars as one of the most astute and well-informed men in the political world, brimful of fight and enthusiasms, though I admit I was rather shocked yesterday by his readiness to drop half the Tariff Reform case because it lacks popularity. It is ungenerous to look upon him as the evil genius of the Conservative party, but that is a persistent impression.

18 NOVEMBER 1910

The confidence of our party increases, though very experienced men are sceptical of success. Two of them, good examples of men versed in electioneering, to wit Hayes Fisher[27] and Hermon Hodge,[28] agreed that so far as London is concerned, at least 50 per cent of the electorate is not swayed by pure political motives. A sentimental issue appeals to them, a predatory policy may produce momentary zeal: but politics as such are outside their ken, and beyond their intellectual grasp. As Hayes said, how can you expect a drayman who goes to work at seven, returns twelve or thirteen hours later, and goes to bed at nine p.m., to find time to read the papers or to study politics, especially as he spends his Saturday afternoon (sensible man) in watching a

---

[27] William Hayes Fisher, first and only Baron Downham (1853–1920), MP (Cons.) Fulham 1885–1906, 1910–19; president of Local Government Board, 1917–18; created peer, 1919.

[28] Sir Robert Trotter Hermon-Hodge, first Baron Wyfold (1851–1937), MP (Cons.) Croydon 1909–10; created peer, 1919.

football match, and his Sunday (wise fellow) in bed! It is to these that we are to make an appeal on a complex and easily misrepresented constitutional issue. We understand that food taxes are to form the staple weapon of our opponents and that a few days before the polling, constituencies are to be flooded with leaflets, and plastered with cartoons, in order to concentrate attention on this particular aspect of Tariff Reform.

19 NOVEMBER 1910

John Gretton[29] who has extraordinary means of securing subterranean information which has seldom proved wrong gives me this memorandum. 'There is a widespread movement on foot among the Celtic elements in the U.K. to assert predominance over the Anglo-Saxon. An understanding exists between the principal Irish, Welsh and Scotch parties to cooperate at the right time. They are careful to sow discontent in the army so as to alienate the Celt from discipline, and at least persuade him to refuse to turn on his kinsman.'

We are all familiar with the anti-military movement in Ireland, and it exists in a sporadic fashion in Wales. Hitherto Scotland has been immune, and I doubt whether this propaganda would ever gain much popularity there. The danger however exists, and the best method to combat this tendency should be carefully thought out, though there is great difficulty in meeting what is in effect the hidden working of a secret society.

One word about my informant, John Gretton, M.P. for Rutland: Colonel Gretton as he is locally called. One of the best-hearted fellows one ever met, kind, generous, self-effacing: ugly as possible, blinking at one through gold-rimmed spectacles: inarticulate, for it is almost impossible to hear a word he says, and his handwriting is simply deplorable. He has all the noble qualities of the mole, and as I said before is the man to whom I can confidently turn for advice on all sorts of subjects about which you could expect nobody to know anything.

20 NOVEMBER 1910

There may none the less be a sullen vindictiveness against the Lords, Tories, and constitution combined, equally dangerous and far more difficult to meet. I am sure that the prevailing sentiment among our men is a keen loyalty and devotion to the cause, and absolute conviction in its justice, all tempered with an aching belief that the electorate doesn't want to be persuaded.

22 NOVEMBER 1910

Lloyd George's utterance in Mile End leaves one with a feeling of nauseous impotence. His scurrility[30] is beyond competition, and admits of no reply but the appeal to sober reason – and we know that the dissolution is rushed in order to have

---

[29] See above, 28 September 1909, n. His wife's father had owned 90,000 acres in Kerry.

[30] 'An aristocracy is like cheese; the older it is, the higher it becomes.'

no time for serious and considered argument. It is upon this that he counts. He knows that he must disgust a fraction of his supporters into abandoning the Liberal party, but he has calculated the loss, and assesses the votes he expects to gain at a higher figure. What really distresses me is not his virulence or hypocrisy as such, but the fact that it all emanates from one of the most responsibly placed men in the British Empire: in short that all the high tradition attaching to the office held by great men from Pitt down to Gladstone and even Asquith should be dragged through the mire to serve a momentary party object.

24 NOVEMBER 1910

I think the spirit of our party is rising – partly because of the atrocious affronts showered upon us by Lloyd George, partly from the admirable tone of Balfour's leadership, and also owing to our belief that sobriety will prevail. I am still very low.... Fred Smith hopes for a net gain of thirty seats, and would not be surprised by thirty-five: but he is swayed by the tremendous reception which greets him wherever he goes. Alick Hood is happier than he was. Hughes[31] is immured in the Central Office and I haven't seen him for days. I am afraid the peers are not being adequately organised for the contest: moreover I see numbers of ex-M.P.s in the Carlton, capital speakers who have not been invited to help. Great efforts are being made to get things into shape, but we are late in the field. Elibank[32] made all his arrangements in September and October. Here is December on us, and in many respects we are still unprepared. Over-confidence in constituencies we won by big majorities last January is going to be one of our greatest dangers.

4 DECEMBER 1910

This last week I have addressed twenty-three meetings, and have not yet covered the ground. My opponent is equally busy, but I don't think has such good attendances. The feature of my meetings has been their attention – and an odd thing, that the number of questions sent up is insignificant compared with what was the case twelve months ago, when they tried to smother me with them.

19 DECEMBER 1910

Talked at the Carlton. Few people of consequence there. Gerald Arbuthnot[33] described his defeat at Burnley, which was owing to an extraneous colliery dispute. He afterwards called me mysteriously aside and said, 'I prophesy that in two to three months time you will be chief unionist whip. If this prove to be the case, will you make me your private secretary?' Well, I see no reason why Alick Hood should dream of resigning. He knows his work admirably: moreover I am wholly without

[31] The Conservative chief agent
[32] The Liberal Chief Whip.
[33] Gerald Archibald Arbuthnot (1872–1916), MP (Cons.) Burnley January–December 1910; private secretary to Walter Long 1894–1905, contested Burnley 1906, vice-chairman Budget Protest League 1909, vice-chancellor Primrose League 1912.

experience in electoral organisation. I have had nothing to do with candidatures, I am blissfully ignorant of everything connected with party funds and honours, I only know one election agent in Great Britain, namely my own: and into the bargain the constituency work is that which bores me most and is a sphere wherein I should not excel. Hitherto my whole energies have been devoted to making the parliamentary machine work, a task far easier than any connected with electoral responsibility outside: and I have no ambition to chain myself to work for which I am unsuited (being far too easy-going), to the exclusion of activities of greater moment on which I have a chance of doing good service.

... I confess I feel somewhat indignant at George Hamilton's[34] attitude. He talks freely about the worthlessness of our organisation, our failure to trace removals, and the ineptitude of our literature. In no respect do we deserve such censure: but that he should condemn us with such emphasis provokes one to ask what he has done to help the party. For five years he has done nothing but draw his pension, and produce a report on the Poor Laws which has been affected by a noisy minority of his colleagues. For his party at large he has done nothing except criticise our efforts and crab our aims. Now at the Carlton he is talking freely about running the party on fresh lines, as though he were among those whose influence still counts. Happily he shows no bitterness, and indeed I hope our men realise that acrimony will be of service to nobody.

21 DECEMBER 1910

The last of the elections is announced ... I never expected to lose so many seats, and I also hoped to win half a dozen more.[35] We have perhaps achieved a moral though sterile victory ... To me the outlook is black: but I will work all the harder, and stimulate my lambs to do the same.

---

[34] Lord George Hamilton (1845–1927), Conservative cabinet minister in successive administrations 1885–1903.

[35] The Unionists gained 28 seats, but lost 29, compared ith the position at the dissolution.

VI

The Parliament Act, 1911

Balfour's inactivity – family investments in industry – the parliamentary programme – the King's Speech – no successor to Balfour in sight – Northcliffe's financial interest in reciprocity – politicians and the press – Welsh patronage – Unionist schemes for reforming the House of Lords – the unattractiveness of Selborne – illness of Lloyd George – reshuffle of Unionist Whips – Walter Long's irritability   Lansdowne's bill for House of Lords reform coldly received   Lloyd George's insurance scheme and Unionist reactions – social promiscuity between political opponents – the Princes' fight at the coronation – roving eye of the Crown Prince of Germany – diarist becomes Chief Whip – personnel of the shadow cabinet – Asquith at Cliveden – Asquith's faux pas – fears of dissolution – Asquith reveals his hand – shadow cabinet on creation of peers – true position of Balfour and Lansdowne – Asquith howled down – Balfour and Lansdowne absent from London during crisis – the Unionists demoralised.

The two general election victories of 1910 put the Liberals in an extremely strong position which lasted until the closing months of 1911. Their programme was a simple one. Apart from the Parliament Bill, their only major measure was the insurance scheme of Lloyd George; and the Parliament Bill was itself as simple as possible, making no attempt to reform the composition of the House of Lords. In the spring and early summer of 1911, the Unionists had little strategy beyond slowing down the progress of the two main government measures, which they did rather effectively. In July, however, the Unionists learned for the first time that Asquith had permission to make a creation of peers in order to pass the Parliament Bill. This had not been allowed for, and created an exceptionally difficult tactical problem for the Unionists to resolve at short notice.

The party either had to connive at measures it hated, or to oppose them to the bitter end, even if it meant a radical House of Lords for years to come. These alternatives tore the party in two, and those who, like Balfour and Lansdowne, were for acquiescence, incurred deep resentment. Other difficulties, like food taxes, remained beneath the surface. When Balcarres became Chief Whip in July 1911, replacing Alick Hood, he found the party in a sad state; and between then and November, when Balfour decided to retire, things got worse rather than better.

Balcarres was a good Chief Whip. He was also, because of party reorganisation, a new kind of Chief Whip. He always took the line that agreement however crude was *better than disagreement however subtle. His period in office saw a succession of important episodes: the Parliament Bill crisis of July and August 1911, the gradual decision by Balfour to retire, the election of a new leader in unusual circumstances in November 1911, the launching of Bonar Law in 1911 and the Unionist recovery of 1912, the attack on Asquith's home rule bill in 1912, and the sudden, nearly disastrous party crisis which led to the dropping of food taxes in January 1913. Balcarres found the party in tatters. He left it with an effective leader who looked likely to win the forthcoming general election.*

When the sudden death of his father (31 January 1913) removed him to the House of Lords, Balcarres became a political ghost, unemployed until 1916, and his services as a parliamentary manager were quickly forgotten. A successful Chief Whip should never appear more than inconspicuously competent. In terms of such arcane criteria of the trade, Balcarres was unusually good at his job.

As for reorganisation, it made Balcarres the first Conservative Chief Whip of the modern type. The Liberal Unionists, who had had a distinct organisation since 1886, merged with the Conservatives in 1912; and the work of the Chief Whip, hitherto responsible for party management in both parliament and the constituencies, was divided into two parts, with a party chairman taking over work outside the House of Commons.

Parliament was opened by the King on 6 February.

I FEBRUARY 1911

The party is low-spirited, but anxious to fight. None the less there is a feeling that whatever we do must result in signal defeat. Perhaps ten days hence we shall have less cause for dejection. We are handicapped by the absence of A.J.B. who has no secretary by him on the Riviera and is more than ever reluctant to answer letters. Alick Hood[1] seemed much annoyed, as two or three things of urgency are suspended until the Chief expresses his opinion. The proposed enquiry into our organisation, the amendments to be pressed to the Address, the provision of a seat for Bonar Law[2] involving as it may a promissory note of title to the vacating member – on such matters our activity and promptitude are sadly checked. It is a sad pity that the Chief won't take a shorthand clerk with him, for his impotence to write letters ought to be compensated for by the simple agency of dictation.

The Wigan Coal and Iron Company, the ancestral business, was going through a difficult period.

We certainly want a good year or two to make good the heavy deficiencies we have recently incurred, and also to provide much-needed resources for future developments of the concern. We are even now practically pledged to spend on extensions

---

[1] Chief Whip 1902–11

[2] Bonar Law had been defeated at Manchester NW in the December 1910 general election. He was returned for Bootle, 27 March 1911.

The Parliament Act

and equipment something like £350,000 during the next ten years: and during the past decade we have replaced in the business an equivalent sum. I once asked Alfred Hewlett[3] to write a history of the Company, or rather of our share in it. Alexander VI[4] would represent the foundation;

James XXIV – consolidation;
Alexander William XXV – flotation;
James XXVI – rehabilitation;[5]

his successor – fruition, or rejuvenation. But who knows?

Notwithstanding the huge sums invested by Father in the business, sums that is to say which with his assent were charged prior to the payment of dividend, it is most improbable that any satisfactory return will be received. The increased cost of production, which will never be reduced, will absorb most of the profit which would naturally accrue to this self-sacrifice. In many ways we should be far better off had we never reinvested a penny in British industrial securities. Let us hope I may be wrong. In any case whatever be the outcome, during this double decade the Company will have undergone a process of complete rejuvenation.

3 FEBRUARY 1911

At the Central Office, a long conference with Alick Hood and Walter Long, examining the programme of business submitted to us by Elibank.[6] Briefly it amounts to this: that the parliament bill, the old finance bill, the navy and army votes, and all supplementaries are to be concluded by 12 April, before Easter. This leaves two months including recess before the Coronation.[7] ... My impression is that no subtle motives underlie these tactics... The King will be far more amenable to squeezing before the ceremonies than after them: and during the autumn he will be away, and it might therefore be difficult to get his assent to drastic action by telegraph. Hence a necessity for despatch.

I was much more interested in a conversation with Bob Douglas[8] about our own internal difficulties. He told me the whole story of the recent Lansdowne House meeting (with all that meticulous accuracy of detail which he can command: for instance he could recall where each of the seventeen participants at the conference sat at the big table!) Well, it transpires that Alick Hood was not bidden to the

[3] The manager of the company
[4] Alexander, sixth Earl of Balcarres and twenty-third Earl of Crawford (1752–1825). The earldom of Crawford had passed out of the main branch of the Lindsay family during the seventeenth century, the title being held by distant cousins until that branch died out in 1808 and the two titles were reunited. Through his wife, 'Alexander VI' inherited lands in Lancashire which were the foundation of the family fortunes in the nineteenth century.
[5] James, twenty-fourth Earl of Crawford (1783–1869); Alexander William, twenty-fifth Earl (1812–80); James Ludovic, twenty-sixth Earl (1847–1913), the diarist's father.
[6] Liberal Chief Whip 1910–12
[7] Coronation day was 22 June.
[8] Aretas Akers-Douglas, created Lord Chilston later in 1911.

gathering. It has been our invariable practice that the chief whip should attend these functions, but he was not summoned: wrote to A.J.B. to ask if he was wanted, and received rather a curt reply from Short[9] that as organisation was not to be discussed, his assistance wasn't wanted. Of course, organisation could not be excluded, and ultimately a committee was informally determined. Of course Alick should have been there. I don't know if Balfour is angry with Alick, but he could have laid no greater slight upon him than to exclude him. Bob seems to think that Jack Sandars is chiefly responsible, which I should sincerely regret. However the whole upshot of a long and uninterrupted conversation with Bob Douglas makes me realise for the first time that there is serious understatement among our leaders, and moreover that the situation is being aggravated by such circumstances as I have described which may force our leaders to take sides, ranging themselves behind one or another policy . . . Unless we can check these centrifugal tendencies we shall be in perilous danger of a collapse.

Alick is as hardworking and as loyal to the Chief as any man in the party. It would be sad if owing to tactlessness or animosity we were to lose his services. This is the moment for us to begin such reorganisation as we all admit to be desirable, though my view is that reform is much more needed in the constituencies than at our Central Office. I think that a tour should be made of local and representative centres, where an accredited member should discuss matters with the local chairmen. They say that Elibank's peregrinations have enormously helped the local people. They can't all be brought to London, and should be visited at their own centres.

4 FEBRUARY 1911
Dined with A.J.B., who entertained ex-ministers at the Ritz Hotel, the first time I have fed there. Thought it much overrated, and they gave us no fruit. Neither did the King's Speech offer attractive fare. It is the baldest and most jejune document I ever read, all important legislation in addition to the Veto and insurance being massed into a short noncommittal phrase about further matters being submitted to parliament if time permits.

As yesterday, I am still more concerned with our own situation. For the moment I cannot determine if there is serious disaffection among the rank and file, but that one or two of our ex-cabinet ministers are in a state of febrile irritability is alas only too obvious. Walter Long is sore unto hysteria. George Wyndham more touchy than ever. Austen Chamberlain (absent this evening) is notoriously hostile to the referendum though he is personally devoted to A.J.B. The Chief himself is blandly serene amidst all difficulties which he confidently assumes will be dissipated by a winning personality, reinforced by the absence of possible rivals or successors.

LORD BALCARRES TO LADY WANTAGE, 6 FEBRUARY 1911
When somebody complains of Arthur Balfour's attitude a simple query as to his

---

[9] Wilfrid Maurice Short (1870–1947), Balfour's private secretary 1894–1920.

possible successor brings the conversation to an abrupt close. There is no available heir to the throne. Austen Chamberlain who is as loyal to A.J.B. as anybody I know would not raise a finger to weaken the status of his chief. Bonar Law is out of parliament, Walter Long is not of the necessary calibre, Wyndham is distrusted by the Irish Unionists, Harry Chaplin is a hundred and one, Alfred Lyttelton is a good fellow, but generally wrong! The rest are mostly lawyers – and to talk of a change of leadership is futile when no potential substitute can be named.

6 FEBRUARY 1911

I seldom attend public dinners but tonight I went to the Constitutional Club where festivity was offered to the new members. A large muster of guests. A.J.B. rather tired I thought, but his speech was well received. Afterwards I walked back to Carlton Gardens with him and had a long talk on the general situation, and told him various things which I imagine he is not in a position to hear very often.

9 FEBRUARY 1911

Lord Cawdor[10] has been ill for three or four years and consequently his interventions in party politics have been few. We have suffered a good deal by his absence from the fighting line for he was a man of great courage and staunch convictions; endowed moreover with felicity in addressing large audiences. I fancy Lansdowne relied a good deal upon his advice.

10 FEBRUARY 1911

A note in the *Times*, in a position to suggest definite inspiration, says that the leaders in the House of Lords have decided not to introduce a bill,[11] and that the rank and file support that course. We are all puzzled, and I think all are alarmed, while several of our men are positively aghast at the proposed inaction. The idea of letting matters slide, of ignoring two adverse elections, of treating last year's resolutions as mere catchpenny verbiage! Moreover this retreat would deprive us of all bargaining power later on should the government care to entertain the idea of compromise: and it would deprive the King of such support as the concrete bona fides of the Lords could confer.

Akers-Douglas knew nothing about it – Alick Hood equally ignorant – in fact not a whip in our room but was dumbfounded, and yet they say that the rank and file concur. Later in the afternoon Jack Sandars gave us the explanation. It appears that yesterday Nicholson the lobby correspondent of the *Times* called on Lord Lansdowne, who warned him not to assume without qualification that legislation would be proposed in the Lords. Nicholson treated this as a smart journalistic

---

[10] Frederick, third Earl Cawdor (1847–1911), First Lord of the Admiralty, 1905, and one of the four Unionist negotiators at the inter-party conference of 1910.

[11] i.e. a Unionist bill for the reform of the membership of the upper house, intended to steal the thunder of the more limited government Parliament Bill which Asquith introduced on 21 February.

scoop, and published *sans phrase* what was intended as a hint to the leader-writers. Lord Lansdowne is furious and proposes to chasten Nicholson...

... It is now admitted Asquith would have no difficulty in finding his 500 peers, and that notwithstanding a hoot or two their reception would generally speaking be far from hostile.... Bristol, they say, has already forwarded to headquarters the names of fifty eligible candidates from whom Asquith is invited to make a selection.

12 FEBRUARY 1911

Perceval Landon[12] says that the enthusiasm of the *Daily Mail* for the reciprocity agreement between Canada and the USA is not caused by its satisfaction in affording an excuse to drop the unpopular food taxes, but because Lord Northcliffe who has cornered the Newfoundland supply of paper pulp, expects to net two or three millions by the tariff bargain. I should not be surprised if this be true. There is no reason apart from his peerage to make him much attached to our party, and during the last year or two he has wobbled in such a way as to suggest tergiversation. Kennedy Jones[13] moreover who exercises considerable influence upon him, is notoriously hostile to our party leaders, and at one time, in conjunction with Lord Esher (save the mark) thought of collaring the organisation of the party and hoped to run us on the lines of Tammany Hall. This petty intrigue was spoiled, and they bear us no goodwill in consequence. Meanwhile the Radical plutocrats are trying to secure control of Conservative newspapers. Mond[14] they say doesn't mind what he spends in S. Wales for press propaganda: and the *Daily Express* is not altogether in the hands of sympathetic owners. Blumenfeld's[15] cleverness however is so attractive that he has worked up a lucrative personnel who would give up the paper were its politics changed. We complain bitterly of our press – and to do it justice our press complains that the party gives it little help. My experience leads me to think that Conservative editors might receive greater encouragement, but on the other hand this desire to maintain freedom and independence precludes that close sympathy existing between the *Daily News* for instance and the Treasury. None the less we have tried to give help to newspapers. I have constantly given them news matter – often I have dictated paragraphs to the lobby correspondents – but next morning's issue shows it is ignored or ill-appreciated. I don't want our papers to adopt the slobbering sycophancy of the *Daily News*, but I heartily wish there were closer cooperation.

17 FEBRUARY 1911

A lot of our new members were much impressed by John Redmond's sonorities. I dare say that at heart he is loyal to the reigning dynasty, but he has vicious enemies

[12] Leading journalist
[13] Director of Northcliffe companies
[14] Alfred Mond, first Baron Melchett (1868–1930), Liberal industrialist and minister.
[15] R. D. Blumenfeld (1864–1948), editor of *Daily Express* 1904–32.

in Ireland, and must be discreet. I shall be greatly surprised if he and his party prove their professions of good-will by attending the Coronation. Meanwhile as an example of the sleepiness of our press, not one in ten of them referred to the superb error of judgment shown by Redmond *fils*,[16] when he said that Ireland wanted tariffs on British goods! One cannot help feeling that what young Redmond blurted out in public had been discussed over the cigars of papa!

26 FEBRUARY 1911

At Carlton, long talk with George Younger[17] and Bob Cecil. The latter – how like him – wants the peers to organise a sustained attack upon the personnel, composition, caucus, venality and so forth of the House of Commons. There is much in the idea, for our House isn't impeccable ... I fancy that if only a byelection or two would indicate discontent with the government, there would be a noticeable movement in favour of a conciliatory policy. But the very reverse is going on. Yesterday's announcement of the polling in the Forest of Dean[18] cannot fail to encourage the extremists. What an outlook it is!

LORD BALCARRES TO LADY WANTAGE, 26 FEBRUARY 1911

... Moreover those who behave well during the process[19] will be rewarded. In the parliament of 1906 no less than 28 out of 30 Welsh Liberal members received consideration of some sort or another, varying from a peerage down to a recordership ... I never saw a party so intent on the loaves and fishes of reward, and the Labour party though unable to accept knighthoods are on the watch for confortable government posts, permanent in character, which almost seem to have been created to provide patronage to deserving and subservient supporters.

LORD BALCARRES TO LADY WANTAGE, 28 FEBRUARY 1911

Today the 'Progressive' section of our party held a meeting here, attended by about 180 members many of whom frankly advocate a wholly elected second chamber – a sort of duplicated House of Commons. They seem to think they have only to ask Lord Lansdowne to introduce such a bill and that his acquiescence would secure its passage through the other House. The idea is of course absurd, for whatever Lord L. might think, he would be defeated by his supporters. The danger of our proposing the structure of a bill is that our opinion would be recorded, that it would conflict with the decision of the House of Lords, and that under those conditions a split in our party being made manifest, Asquith would be on strong ground in

[16] William Archer Redmond (1886–1932), MP (Nat.) Tyrone E. December 1910–18, Waterford City 1918–22.
[17] George Younger, first Viscount Younger of Leckie (1851–1929), Unionist Party chairman 1916–23.
[18] The Liberal majority was 344 higher than at the general election.
[19] Balcarres was arguing that any revolt against home rule from within the Liberal party was unlikely.

refusing to give facilities for discussion. The outcome of the meeting this afternoon was that two or three wise and experienced men (whom we ordered to attend) persuaded our enthusiasts to hold their hand. The meeting was adjourned, no mischief was done, and when the bill is produced by Lord Lansdowne we shall hope to persuade our party to act harmoniously in its support.

The general idea is that the reconstructed H. of Lords should consist of 300 members, divided into three sections, each numbering 100. One third would be selected by the peers from their own ranks, the second third would be nominated by the prime minister, and the third would be elected – not on the ordinary suffrage, but by delegated powers exercised by the elected members of this House.

Of course the scheme bristles with difficulties . . . but the proposal is essentially fair . . . Moreover I think it essential that we should convert our resolutions into clauses as evidence of bona fide intentions to deal seriously with the whole situation.

Need I say that one of the chief stumbling blocks is George Curzon? He has fanciful ideas about making county councils into electoral units, the immediate result of which would be introduce party politics where they are now absent. Moreover he insists upon the ex-officio element – the retired field-marshal and ambassador. These proconsuls are excellent men, but inexorable Tories, and if they wish to serve we feel that they should secure their posts according to the three roads open to them . . .

4 MARCH 1911

Selborne is the least attractive great man I ever met. I think he really is a great man, but his natural genius for organisation based upon sturdy common sense, has obliterated any vestige of imagination, if such ever existed. The result is that every comment he makes is directed to the dullest aspect of every problem one may discuss: and while the comment is often shrewd and well-founded, one is left with a disappointed feeling that if big issues can provoke such colourless and *borné* criticism, it is scarcely worth while to pursue the subject. Lady Selborne is more masculine every time I see her, and her fidgeting drives me crazy.

10 MARCH 1911

A long sitting during which Churchill succeeded in disgusting his friends and foes indiscriminately. What a cad he is.

12 MARCH 1911

I think the late sitting did our party good, and it will make the government realise what they have never yet appreciated, namely that our party is so much stronger than in the 1906 parliament that we cannot be browbeaten or ignored.

. . . Crewe's illness is serious. Lloyd George too, according to information which sounds reliable, is far more ill than the communiqué from his doctors leads one to believe. He has been absent for a fortnight or so, and is only in London a day or two at a time. Tubercular complaint rather than a cancerous growth is what seems most

The Parliament Act

feared. Asquith has had to leave England owing to the illness of his daughter, but accounts are favourable and the girl is on the road to recovery.

LORD BALCARRES TO LADY WANTAGE, 12 MARCH 1911

The cabinet is becoming alarmed at the outbreak of illness in their numbers. Harcourt and McKenna have both been seriously ill. Morley and Wolverhampton have both left the House because they found the strain overpowering. Crewe and Lloyd George are both *hors de combat*. The latter I fancy is causing much more anxiety to his friends than the public knows. There was a suspiciously reassuring bulletin about him two or three days ago, but his prolonged absence from Westminster has made his party most uncomfortable, the probability being that the trouble is tubercular in origin. I hope he may recover. From a selfish or party point of view his death would do us immense harm! for a kind of myth would become associated with his name, whereas if he returns to the fray there must ensue a lamentable exposure of the folly of some of his much boasted taxes. . . . A general impression is beginning to take root that except in cases of exceptional vitality four or five years of cabinet responsibility is sufficient to break the health of the normal citizen.

The party is working together much better: in fact the improvement in our harmony is most marked. There may be a recrudescence of trouble when Lord Lansdowne introduces his reform bill, but not I hope in any way serious.

17 MARCH 1911

Elibank came to see me to arrange a deal about the revenue bill. He is getting nervous, and says he will not allow Churchill to have any more 'bloody rows'. So he means to bring Lloyd George up to London to interview Austen Chamberlain.

Not if I know it!

19 MARCH 1911

I had a letter from Austen who says he will see Elibank d——d first! It is not for him or us to lay down the weapons in our hands. The government foresees much difficulty in getting the Revenue Bill through during the financial year, and there is no reason why we should help them to enter upon the Parliament Bill a day earlier than we can avoid. Elibank rings me up on the telephone at all hours of the day and night. Now, 10.30 p.m., he has done so again, and Connie (bless her) has just told him I have gone to bed.

. . . Uncomfortable talk with Sandars. He says Alick Hood will retire from the position of Chief Whip, but will retain control of the Central Office:[20] in fact will give his whole energies to that work. Harry Forster will likewise leave the Room – I shall then be in command so far as parliamentary work is concerned, my duties

[20] Acland-Hood was created Baron St Audries in the coronation honours list, 20 June 1911, but did not continue to retain control of Central Office, which went to the new party chairman, Steel-Maitland.

180

beginning and ending with the session. I should require further assistance. Hamilton has resigned, Valentia is seventy: Ned Talbot seedy – youthful energy and enthusiasm are more than ever needful.

I hate it. The other day I calculated that there are only six or eight and twenty men in the party with more service behind them than I have contributed. I was in office for two years or so, which has carried forward duties I have honestly performed for these five years in the wilderness. One gets no thanks, and much blame, and one is treated as a hewer of wood, a drawer of water by men who haven't a tenth of our experience but who think that the whip has always to be in attendance, that he is a kind of fag to all and sundry, and that if anything goes wrong the unpaid and overworked slave must bear the blame.

Seven years of this is enough to ruin any man, for parliamentary skill is atrophied by this restless incessant work. One has no time to attend to the debates, no leisure to practise speaking. All one's work is done in the lobbies. Two or three more years of it and I shall have to abandon all hope of successful office. Gladstone,[21] Pembroke, Hart Dyke, Pease, Tweedmouth, Walrond, Akers-Douglas, (and probably Alick Hood himself) have all been destroyed as real parliamentarians. I regret that my name should be appended to so melancholy a list.

LORD BALCARRES TO LADY WANTAGE, 20 MARCH 1911
It is anticipated that A.J.B. will be asked to separate the two branches of our work. At present they are inextricably combined, the head whip with his subordinates being responsible for the conduct of parliamentary business, as well as for the selection of candidates, control of party funds and indeed the broad organisation of our cause in the constituencies.

In future if the recommendations be accepted the outside work will be allotted to one man, while the House of Commons work would be exclusively retained by the other. Hood would take the constituency side, and I should have to do the parliamentary work, the six other whips being under my control.

I look forward to this with but little zest. It is of course vital for the efficiency of the opposition that our work should be guided with greater foresight and decision than has previously been the case. Acland-Hood has had far too much to do, and it is marvellous how well he has combined the dual obligations. None the less there seems to be widespread agreement both that he should be more free to deal with external organisation, and that we on the other hand should be more free to deal with parliamentary business.

LORD BALCARRES TO LADY WANTAGE, 23 MARCH 1911
It was said on unimpeachable authority that after Campbell-Bannerman's death McKenna was actually offered the chancellorship, but that Lloyd George made

[21] Herbert, Viscount Gladstone, the premier's son.

such a beastly row that the appointment had to be cancelled. This I believe to be true.[22]

...We are going to strengthen the whips' room by two new men, Wilfrid Ashley[23] and a Somersetshire foxhunting squire with maroon countenance, and incredible astuteness, one Sanders,[24] a pleasant fellow: loyal, keen, witty, and a worker. This will relieve me a good deal. Edmund Talbot I fear is in danger of a renewed attack of phlebitis, and cannot take an active part this summer. Valentia, the 'dear old Viscount', as he has been called for forty years is just on 70. It isn't the ideal age for a brisk and busy whip.

Our difficulty remains, Walter Long. He is the most paradoxical and ill-balanced person I know. One day he makes a speech of sturdy and uncompromising Toryism, and the next day larks off to York to deliver, without a word of consultation with his colleagues, an address in which he tries to go one better than the Socialists by advocating putting hospitals on the rates, and similar reforms which make people rub their eyes. He is a source of much embarrassment on the committee which is inquiring into our organisation. His jealousy of George Wyndham and Austen Chamberlain make him an unbearable nuisance from time to time, and within a few minutes he embraces us all with the most fulsome assurances of affection, admiration, and respect. All this I imagine springs from the terrific nerve strain dating from 1906 when the smallest opposition on record had to fight the strongest government in our history...

26 MARCH 1911

If Rufus Isaacs[25] is to be trusted, Lloyd George is enjoying magnificent health except for a passing fatigue of the voice. I doubt it – Isaacs protesteth too much, and there are many who question if Lloyd George will spend a month of this year at Westminster.

I can detect no weakening of ministerial opinion about the Parliament Bill.

Sanders and Wilfrid Ashley are our new recruits in the whips' room. Both are men of substance and acuteness. I don't quite understand why they are engaged at this moment without disclosing the whole plan of reorganisation, and the result is that my own position becomes more difficult than ever. The sooner my responsibilities are defined, the better for all concerned. Much remains to be done. Our organisation in the House of Commons must be strengthened and developed in every particular. Ex-ministers must attend better: whips must be better informed, conferences more frequent – discussion invited rather than deprecated. Then the connection between our parties in the two Houses must be made a reality, and I

---

[22] Not impossible, but not confirmed by other sources.

[23] W.W. Ashley, Baron Mount Temple (1867–1938), MP (Cons.) 1906–32; Minister of Transport 1924–9 and father of the traffic roundabout.

[24] Sir R. A. ('Peter') Sanders, Minister of Agriculture 1922–4.

[25] Rufus Isaacs, first Marquess of Reading (1860–1935), Attorney-General 1910–13.

foresee that in three months time I shall be engaged upon the delicate task of reforming the whips and speaking departments in the Lords.

My only hope is that I shall be able within one, two, or three years to train a good successor in our House. Ten years of one's life spent in whipping is terrific: more than ten would be overwhelming.

LORD BALCARRES TO LADY WANTAGE, 21 APRIL 1911

Balfour who seldom permits his comments to rise above a sotto voce level, amused our men very much (while we were discussing the exclusion of the protestant succession from the scope of the parliament bill) by turning round and observing in a decidedly audible tone, 'Fancy all this being settled by two Jews and one intoxicated Christian', his reference being to Samuel and Rufus Isaacs.

. . . Lord Lansdowne is low about himself, can't shake off his cold, feels weak and discouraged, and doubts if he will be able to return by the 26th when the Lords meet again.[26]

11 MAY 1911

A long talk with Alick Hood. He is going to take a peerage at the Coronation – so to my intense surprise is Bob Douglas. I take charge of parliamentary work, and the organisation and office work will fall upon somebody else. Steel-Maitland[27] is Alick's preference. The decentralisation will cause certain difficulties and perhaps friction (notably in the matter of parliamentary honours) and there may be some danger of the House of Commons losing touch with the politics of the constituencies. However division of the work is absolutely essential. Alick doesn't look forward to a peerage with much satisfaction – his means in the first place are not opulent: but he is simply taking preferment for the good of the Party. Somebody, he says, must retire after three defeats...

In point of fact though our organisation can be improved it is by no means so bad as the critics allege. No blame was attached to it a couple of years ago when we won strikingly significant byelections. It is Radical policy, not Conservative organisation which produced the débâcle. An inferior organisation will secure victory for a popular policy – but no organisation however excellent can combat a popular policy. The Budget won back the ground lost by the Radicals – and the new Insurance Bill is designed to recover whatever they have subsequently lost.

Asquith introduced the Parliament Bill on 21 February 1911. Its main provision was the limitation of the House of Lords power of veto. It did not attempt to reform the composition of the upper house. The bill finished its committee stage on 3 May, and

---

[26] Lansdowne had also had two teeth extracted on 30 March, just before a major speech 'in his frigid Whig style'.

[27] (Sir) Arthur Steel-Maitland (1876–1935), first chairman of the Unionist Party, 1911; MP (Cons.) 1910–35, Minister of Labour 1924–9.

The Parliament Act

passed its third reading on the 15th. On the 23rd it reached the House of Lords, where it was not rejected outright, but amended out of recognition in a way quite unacceptable to the Liberals. It was not until the approach of its third reading in the House of Lords on 20 July that political fever really mounted.

14 MAY 1911

The week after next the Parliament Bill comes before the Lords and however wry their countenances the second reading must be accepted. I foresee no exit from the difficulty and the bill must pass into law.

If we choose we can postpone our bow to the inevitable by precipitating another general election! What a ghastly idea, especially as we might well lose fifty seats in the process.

By the way Alick Hood and Akers-Douglas mean to retain trusteeship of the party funds. That our cash assets should be retained by two peers is apt to cause difficulties: but I will have nothing to do with this.

The House of Lords Reconstitution Bill, an opposition attempt to present themselves as constitutional reformers, was introduced into the upper house by Lansdowne on 8 May. It proposed an upper chamber partly hereditary, partly nominated, and partly elective. The government, though itself committed to a reform of membership of the upper house, found fault with Lansdowne's details and made it clear that his scheme was no substitute for the Parliament Bill. The debates, which closed on 22 May without a division on the second reading, showed that Unionist opinion was far from happy about the plan, and no more was heard of what had been essentially a clumsy exercise in public relations.

22 MAY 1911

In Lords the reception given to Lord Lansdowne's Reconstitution Bill was frigid, even hostile, many members announcing their intention of voting against the second reading. However by dint of much persuasion we kept the recalcitrants quiet, and the stage passed through unopposed. A division would have cast doubts upon our bona fides in the matter of House of Lords Reform. Lord Lansdowne's speech was very patchy, and delivered in unconvincing tones.

We had a conference – sixty or eighty Unionist members, about Lloyd George's Insurance Bill. The impression that the measure will be far less popular than was anticipated, grows apace. Our men have been gushing – and by blessing the bill before examining its content have taken upon themselves an undue share of its failure without securing any credit for its success. I implored our men not to commit themselves on the first reading, but the temptation to chatter was invincible.

Lloyd George's National Insurance Bill, brought in on 4 May, was well received at first by the opposition. In a speech at Newcastle on 18 May, for instance, Balfour commended the scheme. Later, attitudes changed sharply as the opposition realised that the measure was electorally unpopular.

24 MAY 1911

We began our debate on the Insurance Bill. The revulsion of feeling has been swift. Our men who started by blessing the bill now realise that the scheme may be most unpopular.

25 MAY 1911

Debate continued. By the end of the evening the whole scheme had been badly bruised and it is realised that without fundamental alteration it cannot pass into law.

26 MAY 1911

In this morning's *Times* there is a letter from 'A Peer' protesting at the apparent insincerity of politicians who denounce one another as revolutionists, but none the less meet in amity in social relations. The occasion of this letter is the fancy dress ball given by Fred Smith and Eddy Turnour.[28] I read the epistle and dismissed it as the growl of some old prude, but to my surprise I find at the Carlton that nine out of ten of our men warmly approve of its implied rebuke. Well, I have never junketed with Radicals. They neither entertain me nor do they break my bread. I have throughout protested against the friendliness towards men who are trying to smash us, and who moreover are succeeding in their nefarious efforts. In old days when there existed a gentlemanly understanding between the two parties which prevented the exploitation of class hatred upon which modern Radicalism depends, political differences never destroyed personal friendships. Moreover I have often been annoyed by the way ministers trade upon Balfour's old-fashioned good humour towards the Radical party. Time after time during the last five years ministers have gone secretly to A.J.B. to enlist his help. Morley, Tweedmouth, Haldane, Grey and Asquith have all made use of him. I have often protested. Suddenly this afternoon an ill-constructed letter about an obscure episode has fanned dormant sparks into flame. People suddenly worry why these private amenities should flourish which cast a questionable commentary over our published statements.

31 MAY 1911

We had a long and well-attended conference about the Insurance Bill: we came to the conclusion that unpopular as the measure may well prove to be, we ought to show no overt hostility: and we also settled that the collaboration offered – invited – by Lloyd George cannot be declined, though our emissaries must beware of making themselves jointly responsible for the scheme.

1 JUNE 1911

It is said that Fred Smith is to be made a Privy Councillor... Gilbert Parker[29] will be annoyed: he wanted that particular recognition for no assignable cause. Other

[28] Lord Winterton (1883–1962). The ball at Claridge's, a light-hearted occasion attended by politicians of both parties, belied the supposed constitutional crisis.
[29] MP (Cons.), Gravesend 1900–18.

men too will have their misgivings, for the selection of this honour emanates from Asquith, and it will be supposed that Fred has pressed his claims through his friendship with Churchill – so that it is not to our party that Fred's thanks will be due.

... Mrs Churchill by the way created no little stir by going to the fancy dress ball the other night disguised as a nun, and obviously about to enrich the world with offspring. Increase duly arrived within forty-eight hours. Her profile caused disagreeable comments. Churchill also, as a cardinal, did not inspire much respect.

2 JUNE 1911

Interview with A.J.B. about whips – accordingly invited Bridgeman and Eyres Monsell[30] to act as colleagues in place of Alick Hood and Harry Forster, due to retire.

'I wish you would find me a successor' said A.J.B. wearily after a longish conversation. I wish we could find two or three men who could approach him in wisdom, judgment, and tact. We can't: and notwithstanding all the intrigues which he seems to resent more than I expected, he cannot see that any of his colleagues are capable of his successorship. Walter Long it appears has been more intolerable than ever. I fancy his nervous and protean excitability must arise from some latent affection of the nerves.

LORD BALCARRES TO LADY WANTAGE, 9 JUNE 1911

Steel-Maitland, one of the new Birmingham members, a young fellow of great promise, much zeal, plenty of cash, and above all with a seat of comfortable safety, will in all probability be asked to take charge of what we call the 'Central Office' work. He is a competent organiser, and is ready to take over this responsible and perilous sphere.

10 JUNE 1911

Garden party to my constituents. Thousands came. It really was a great success – splendid weather, no incident, and they enjoyed themselves thoroughly.

13 JUNE 1911

Awful shindy in progress about Privy Councillorships – Hayes Fisher recommended by A.J.B., and F. E. Smith[31] claimed by Asquith, influenced as one assumes by Churchill.

Because of the coronation on 22 June, politics were quiet, but it was clear that the crisis over the Parliament Bill was only postponed. What was uncertain was the form which

---

[30] William Clive Bridgeman, first Viscount Bridgeman (1864–1935) and Sir Bolton Meredith Eyres-Monsell, first Viscount Monsell (1881–1969), both members of Conservative cabinets between the wars.

[31] Smith's claim to sit on the front bench remained an issue during summer 1911, Balfour thinking the idea ill-advised but giving no decision and leaving it for Bonar Law to settle (mem. by Sandars, 22 November 1911).

the crisis would take. Would the government seek a creation of peers? The opposition did not know. If they did, would the King grant it? The opposition hoped not (being unaware that he had already agreed to do so). If the government could not readily create peers, Unionists argued, would they not look to a dissolution and a third general election as their weapon? The Unionist Party chairman, speaking on 1 July, even predicted an election in July or August.

Parliament reassembled on 26 June. The House of Lords finished committee stage on 6 July and report stage on 13 July. The Parliament Bill passed its third reading in the House of Lords on 20 July, but with significant opposition amendments, the most important of which was in effect to exclude home rule from its provisions. The Unionist aim was to make it as difficult as possible for the King to agree to a creation of peers. Asquith's letter to Balfour (dated 20 July), indicating the King's agreement to a creation of peers in order to defeat the Lords' amendments, was published on 21 July, though this had been conveyed gradually and informally to the opposition leaders earlier in the month. This left the decision about whether to provoke a creation of peers to the opposition and produced immediate crisis in their ranks.

15 JUNE 1911

Dissolution in the air – not the distracted apathy which should normally precede a Coronation holiday, but rather that disquieting apprehension which one notices just before a general election. Opinion hardens that the crisis a few weeks hence must be solved by an appeal to the constituencies. The idea is nauseous. Asquith presumably is no longer confident that the solvent can be found in creation of peers.

. . . Sir G. Armstrong came to see me about a scandalous Admiralty job – a Capt. Ryan, H. M. S. Mars, compelled to revise an adverse report made about Churchill's brother-in-law, an incompetent young officer.

NOTES, 15 JUNE 1911

Conversation with F. E. Smith, 5.0 p.m. Yesterday Lloyd George asked to see F. E. Smith. After general conversation suggested a deal about Insurance Bill. F.E. asked for particulars. After an absence of half an hour(? at the cabinet) Lloyd George returned: proposed six weeks for all stages of Insurance Bill, and that no plural voting bill be introduced.

This day's *Morning Leader* (Spender) says that Plural Voting Bill must be used as lever to make Tories behave about insurance. N.B. this morning no less than 220 new amendments by Radicals and socialists appeared on the notice paper.

Conversation with Elibank, 5.30 p.m. There has been unfortunate difficulty about honours. He, Elibank, told Alick Hood that P.M. reserved to himself selection of privy councillorships. A.J.B. submitted three names of proposed P.C.s (Bonar Law, Curzon, Hayes Fisher). No protest was made at the time by Asquith.

Meanwhile Asquith (who had himself intended to choose B. Law and Anson) had approached F. E. Smith.

Subsequently A.J.B. wrote to P.M. saying he had learned that F.E. was to be chosen: asked explanation. (What explanation Asquith gave is not clear: but Alick is blamed for having misunderstood about list of P.C.s. Elibank says Hayes Fisher is not persona grata to London Radicals, hence preference for F.E.)

Meanwhile Elibank says he learned that A.J.B. had written to F.E. saying that he, A.J.B., was pressing for Hayes Fisher to be appointed in his place. 'A very fine thing to do,' says Elibank.

Asquith felt the situation keenly, did not want to place upon Balfour responsibility for ousting F.E. Smith; and did not want to offend his radicals by appointing Hayes Fisher.

... Anyhow Asquith has now submitted to the King four names of Conservatives whom he recommends for privy councillorships: Anson, Bonar Law, Hayes Fisher, and F. E. Smith.

NOTES, 16 JUNE 1911

Conversation with George Wyndham. An illustration of the general belief that the govt is either unwilling or unable to create peers to solve the forthcoming crisis. A rich man whose money bags Harcourt and Co. are anxious to squeeze, has been virtually promised a peerage in return for £120,000 or more which he is prepared to pay for an extension of scientific work at S. Kensington.

He has however withdrawn the gift as he says that he does not wish to be one of several hundred peers. He has however received a definite assurance that for the time being there is no intention of asking H.M. to create peers in any abnormal numbers.

18 JUNE 1911

It is said that John Redmond is accompanied by secret police when in Ireland. Can this be true? he is certainly a most unpopular personage on his own estates.

22 JUNE 1911

One of the great successes of the Coronation was a standup fight between the two kilted princes after the service in Westminster Abbey. By some imprudence the Prince of Wales and his sister were sent in a state coach with the younger brothers, but without a controlling prelate or pedagogue. When fairly started from the Abbey a free fight began to the huge delight of the spectators in Whitehall. The efforts of Princess Mary to mollify the combatants were sincere but ineffectual, and during the strife she nearly had her sweet little coronet knocked off! Peace was ultimately restored after about fifty yards of hullaballoo.

Another type of Prince is less entertaining, to whit the Crown Prince of Germany, to whom Court circles have just just bidden a cordial farewell. He is afflicted with enthusiasm towards everything that is youthful and piquante – and runs after every bit of muslin that catches his eye. The other day when playing golf he noticed a maiden who took his fancy – dismissed his equerry and insisted on playing around with the young party who was much amused. This was trivial, though apt to prove awkward: what however really might have been serious was his disappearance during the Indian trip, with a dusky damsel. He literally bolted and for thirty-six hours was lost. His staff wired to the Indian authorities who did their utmost to restore the missing lamb, and who moreover telegraphed to Berlin (presumably through the India Office) declining to incur any responsibility for the young man's conduct or personal safety. Eventually the Crown Prince turned up after having spent a 'jolly' with his acquaintance, a Burmese lady I understand of high rank and connections.

28 JUNE 1911

Conversation with Elibank. He says he appointed Soares to the govt post in order to test the feeling in the West of England.[32]

Two men whom he had agreed to invite to become peers, assuming them to be supporters of the govt, declined on political grounds to be honoured – owing to Finance Bill and Home Rule.

'Why do your men expect an election? Nothing is further from our mind.'

I replied, 'owing to activity among your men in the constituencies: to uncertainty as to the eventualities, and the wish being father of the thought among our men that we should win 50 seats. Insurance, payment of members, the home rule deficit and the Declaration of London will not win you votes, and may lose you thousands.'

Elibank repeated that he had made no preparations: and that he is anxious for an exit honourable to the peerage.

I replied that no allegation by Asquith that he was empowered to create peers would convince us ...

30 JUNE 1911

The Duchess of Devonshire will not again agree to drive in procession with Churchill: for she says she is sure she shared the hooting directed against the Home Secretary.

1 JULY 1911

I am now chief whip. During the last week I have got into harness – I have spent most of every day interviewing our men who are naturally most anxious about the situation and who cannot dissociate their views on political expediency from the results of a dissolution personal to themselves. The bulk of our men are frankly opposed to any action on our part which might involve a further appeal to the electors – but opinion fluctuates so quickly as the situation changes almost from day to day that it is impossible to predict our attitude a week hence. Steel-Maitland has begun his new work and will do it well. A.J.B. I have had great difficulty in seeing, likewise Austen and Walter Long. Lord Lansdowne more accessible.

---

[32] In the Barnstaple by-election of 11 May 1911 the Liberal majority was appreciably reduced.

The Parliament Act

I am convinced that if we go on in the old happy-go-lucky fashion nothing but disaster can follow . . . Profound feeling of dissatisfaction exists to my knowledge at the hopeless way in which the work of the opposition is carried on in the House of Commons . . . There really is a limit to human patience! I have done my best now for four years to carry out what I regard as an impossible system and a most disagreeable one, but I really cannot go on now that you are starting a new reign as chief whip without letting you know what is my view[33] . . .

6 JULY 1911

Talking of food, Lord and Lady Salisbury refused the invitation of the Asquiths to dine at the party given to the King and Queen. I fully sympathise with them. Asquith and his colleagues are out for blood. He has poured insult and contumely on the peers – why break bread or uncork champagne at his table? . . . Balfour likewise was bidden to the Downing St party. He also was incensed, but sent to Buck Palace to ask if the King would dispense with his assistance. Lord Knollys[34] consulted the King who expressed a wish that the invitation should be accepted. Accordingly Mr Balfour went, feeling that as the entertainment of an opulent dinner followed by indifferent acting was wholly unofficial, he might well have been excused. I find that this weekend we are to meet the Asquiths at Cliveden. I shall have an opportunity of noting his sobriety.

A curious and instructive conversation with A.J.B.

MEMORANDUM, 6 JULY 1911

Conversation with Mr Balfour. He has just had a conference with Lord Esher. It transpires that on the break-up of the Conference Asquith got certain guarantees, but the King insisted on a dissolution first. Hence the December election instead of awaiting the new register.

The King now wishes us to know the situation. He dislikes it, but there is no avenue of escape. (It actually transpires that a letter exists!) The King must have been badly or partially advised. The pledge was for six months in advance, and it was intended to meet such a crisis for instance as would have arisen from rejection on second reading: the King never contemplated the issue being refined down to a single point, e.g. referendum on Home Rule.

A.J.B. asked Lord Esher for his credentials. Answer: 'I was with the King two hours (? yesterday) and at end said I would talk to A.J.B., and paused for a reply. None was given.'

(I expressed regret that Lord Esher should have been the medium of communication. He is a Radical and his son a Radical candidate. A.J.B. however

[33] An explosion caused by Long being asked to speak as substitute for Austen Chamberlain at short notice.

[34] Francis Knollys, first Viscount Knollys (1837–1924), private secretary to successive Kings 1901–13.

said that Esher stands betwixt and between – that his interview would not make a commitment as would a formal conversation with Lord Knollys: that Lord Esher has no particular axe to grind, though fond of power and intrigue; and that on the whole he, A.J.B., gets much more information out of Esher than Esher out of A.J.B.)

The position is difficult. A.J.B. who has never hitherto had a communication or a word of warning from the King is surprised at the history and nature of the promise.

The shuttlecock process of sending Lords amendments to and fro is complicated. Will Asquith on receipt of amended bill move to reject them en bloc, and *simultaneously*, ask for creation of peers?

On the other hand he might accept some or all of the amendments with the single exception of the Home Rule amendment: return the bill to the Lords and on their holding out create peers, or announce his power to do so, otherwise the bill would lapse, there would have to be prorogation, new session, King's speech, delays, etc.

I observed that Asquith's announcement of the prospective creation of peers, even if precise, would not carry so much weight in saving amour propre of the peers, as if accompanied by their actual creation. Therefore I should like demonstration of proved force majeure by the creation of 20 peers – call them 'token peers'.

A.J.B. replied that prima facie he agreed: but Asquith (who he expects will ask to see him and Lord Lansdowne shortly) would probably ask for guarantees from Lord Lansdowne that under those circs the bill should pass. Supposing the Irish Unionists forced a division against it would Lord Lansdowne have to vote for the bill? and could Lord Lansdowne give guarantees?

I replied perhaps not: but having appointed 20 token peers, and thus showing his power to appoint 200, it is incredible that backwoodsmen would force their creation, thus prostituting their order, and at the same time making a potential majority for Home Rule. This argument however is not quite sound.

7 JULY 1911

Meeting of what is called the Shadow Cabinet at Carlton Gardens, Balfour presiding. I don't know whether the 'Shadow' is retrospective, or projecting – whether it is meant to indicate our next government or to pay compliments to those who have previously served. Anyhow, the room was half filled with the Ashbournes,[35] Londonderrys,[36] Chaplins,[37] Salisburys, and

[35] Edward Gibson, first Baron Ashbourne (1837–1913), Lord Chancellor of Ireland in Unionist cabinets 1885–1905.

[36] Charles Vane-Tempest-Stewart, sixth Marquess of Londonderry (1852–1915), Lord Lieutenant of Ireland 1886–9, president of the Board of Education 1902–5.

[37] Henry Chaplin, first Viscount Chaplin (1840–1923), who was refused a peerage by Asquith in 1911 when his own party wished to disembarrass itself of his presence. Cf. memorandum by Sandars, 11 November 1911: 'Henry Chaplin. It is really cruel to feed him with false hopes. He has no conception of his own uselessness. On more than one occasion I have – by order – left him out of the Shadow; but he has invariably written to say that there has been a mistake and he has appeared with the others. And A.J.B. has only laughed!'

The Parliament Act

Derbys – excellent though discredited politicians whose inclusion in a future Conservative government would create dismay, and perhaps revolt among the rank and file. Our object was of course to survey the approaching crisis, but our information as to its nature was too conflicting to permit an accurate forecast of events. Further meetings will be necessary, and it is assumed that the King would not proceed to the creation of peers without following the precedent of warning the Leader of the Opposition. There is a general belief that the King has committed himself to drastic action, and that dissolution will take place. A fortnight ago there was a contrary opinion, to the horror of our men who have thin majorities.

SHADOW CABINET, CARLTON GARDENS, 7 JULY 1911

Present among others Salisbury, Chaplin, Londonderry, Derby. Absent F. E. Smith, Akers Douglas, Carson.

Mr Balfour gave outline of previous conversation: mentioned no name as to his informant.

Lord Curzon then said he was authorised to make a communication from an eminent person in the Lords who was anxious for peace. (We concluded it to be the Archbishop of Canterbury.) Curzon's information differed essentially from that of A.J.B., notably in that his high personage denied point blank that any guarantees had been given.

Much discussion ensued.

It was generally agreed that King George had been duped and jockeyed by his ministers.

Opinion much divided.

Selborne and Salisbury announced that amended or unamended, with new peers or without them, they were determined to vote against bill at each and every stage. Lord Halsbury also said that he was most unwilling to facilitate passage of bill by abstaining.

G. Wyndham and Austen Chamberlain though not going quite so far were anxious to fight to the uttermost. Steel-Maitland and I on being asked to give impressions of members of H. of Commons agreed that 5 out of 7 considered that an election late in August would be most detrimental to our strength in parliament.

Lord Midleton argued that after Asquith has communicated with Lord Lansdowne (which is assumed to be likely) a party meeting of peers should be held, and a course of action settled. In his opinion the creation of token peers might further exacerbate existing peers, and drive them to force the creation of 200 or 300. (Is this credible?)

Lord Lansdowne naturally doesn't like party meetings as it all appears in the newspapers: but will consent to calling one when necessary.

A.J.B. was much disturbed about the position of Lord Lansdowne from whom he seems convinced that Asquith will ask for guarantees. No clear understanding was arrived at – indeed nobody offered any definite views as to meeting the difficulty – though Lord Lansdowne expressed repugnance at the idea of being expected to vote for the Parliament Bill.

I should add that St John Brodrick indicated his view that during the last two or three days something most embarrassing to the govt had occurred. He mentioned no authority, and did not define his view. A.J.B. seemed also to think that something unaccountable had happened. Is the King beginning to realise that guarantees were given under a misapprehension?

9 JULY 1911

Cliveden. Mrs Astor our hostess is the most rowdy and one of the most amusing people in evidence just now. I never saw such exuberant spirits ... Matt Ridley[38] says this is his first weekend this year and he is annoyed at its being spoiled by having to break meat with Asquith. The latter however is keeping sober and only drank five glasses of champagne last night. By the way Prince Arthur of Connaught was much offended by one of the Prime Minister's gaucheries. They were talking of the investiture at Carnarvon where P.J.[39] volunteered the remark that he did not favour the idea originally, and that Lloyd George was responsible. 'All the Princes who were invested at Carnarvon died young', and he gave a catalogue, three or four I think. It was an unhappy remark leaving rather an uncomfortable feeling round the circle which heard the conversation.

10 JULY 1911

Conversation with F. E. Smith who implored me to warn him of any errors he may commit which make him appear of doubtful loyalty.

NOTE, 10 JULY 1911

Conversation with F. E. Smith. After discussing situation of parliament bill (during which he expressed strong opinion that 'token peers' would mean connivance on our part, and therefore would injure our prestige) he continued to deal with his personal position.

He said that he was conscious of uneasiness among our men as to his relation with Churchill. On that point he is not prepared to yield, being a close friend, brother officer, etc.: but he is heart and soul with the party, though he thinks it requires alteration of perspective. His father was disinherited of his small fortune by F.E.'s grandfather for leaving the Liberal party. During and throughout our acquaintance of 17 years he has shown unbroken zeal and activity in fighting Liberalism and all its ways. He knows of doubts and possibly vexation among our men who may think his attitude ambiguous, and he only asks that whenever complaint is made he shall be informed so that an explanation may be given if necessary.

This statement that butter would not melt in his mouth was to contrast with behaviour by F.E. in coming weeks which could be read all too easily as an attempt to topple Balfour,

[38] The second Viscount Ridley (1874–1916)
[39] Asquith. The investiture of the Prince of Wales at Carnarvon castle took place on 13 July 1911.

perhaps even seize his job. Meanwhile, to add to its cares, the party was confronted by a low squabble about the office of party treasurer. The press had announced that Hood, the retired Chief Whip, was to have the post, when suddenly Long launched an intrigue on behalf of Lord Farquhar, aged sixty-seven. Involved in the cabal were Goulding, Salvidge, Blumenfeld and Aitken; and Blumenfeld explicitly threatened Balcarres with publicity and a party split unless Balfour consented to withdraw his nomination of Hood. Farquhar, the successful candidate, was a man of every possible sinister quality, and his hustling into office by crude methods by men in Bonar Law's entourage did nothing to remove the doubts felt about the company kept by the latter.

12 JULY 1911

Had twenty minutes at Paddington with A.J.B. about to start for his Welsh visit. Yesterday Elibank offered to jettison his whole cargo if we will help him pass the Insurance Bill. Our inclination is to assent, bad as the Bill is in many particulars.

15 JULY 1911

At 1.45 lunched with A.J.B. who talked with the utmost freedom before his servants. There was nothing fresh to discuss, and we chiefly talked about Elibank's proposal. A.J.B. who cordially dislikes the Insurance Bill fears that its passage with our consent would involve us in responsibility for its failure and unpopularity when a statute.

17 JULY 1911

At midday to Downing St to see Elibank. We sat in the garden, and Mrs Asquith from her drawing room window, and in view of a dozen Treasury clerks, kissed her hand at me. The woman is intolerable.

Our conference led to little. Elibank has come to the conclusion, from which I do not dissent, that pending the row about the Lords it is not much use coming to an understanding about House of Commons business.

18 JULY 1911

The crisis begins.

Last week in Wales Lloyd George remarked to A.J.B. that for want of some accommodation the country was in danger of drifting on to the rocks, or meeting a catastrophe – the exact words A.J.B. can't recall. George then hinted that a conference might prove useful, and Balfour gave a noncommittal reply. Today they met.

George showed his hand, and completely bore out the accuracy of the information previously given to A.J.B. by Lord Esher.[40]

---

[40] The point at issue was whether the King would in the last resort create peers to pass the Parliament Bill. He had in fact promised to do so before the December 1910 election, but the Unionist leaders had not been informed of his promise. Esher saw Balfour on 5 July 1911 and, finding him in doubt, impressed upon him that a creation of peers was a reality. It was not until 20 July that Asquith officially informed Balfour of the royal promise.

19 JULY 1911

Lord Knollys saw the Chief today and repeated the story, but as emanating from the King. Balfour expressed great surprise that the message should have reached him rather than Lord Lansdowne as Leader of the Opposition in the Upper House: and moreover Lord Knollys was in turn shocked that owing to his own gossip and maladroit handling, the message should have received priority from the government by George.

Lord Knollys nervous and distressed. He is a regular jackal of the government and has throughout acted as a politician rather than as courtier. He deserves to be sacked.

Balfour asked him the cause of his communication: and Knollys somewhat tactlessly conveyed what George had already adumbrated, namely that as the government does not wish to proceed to extremities, Lord Lansdowne or rather the Conservative party should be allowed to show their hand: and Lord Lansdowne should practically be asked to give guarantees that the Bill shall pass without creation of peers.

But, said A.J.B., these promises of the Sovereign are eight months old. How comes it that we have been so long kept in ignorance of the situation?

I urged most strongly that our party could not be invited to settle its attitude on the strength of verbal statements from a maundering old courtier and an unscrupulous minister. I urged that the prime minister who is responsible for the advice to the Throne must himself be the official agency of communications to ourselves. This is a matter where form is as important as substance. Knollys could be thrown over, George might lie.

My view was accepted.

MEMORANDUM, 19 JULY 1911

Conversation with A.J.B. He saw Lloyd George last night before dinner alone, and afterwards with Lord Lansdowne.

This morning Lord Knollys came to see him. Their statements coincide fully with Esher's. The King has given pledges which are unconditional as regards the number of peers to be created, though it seems the pledge was limited to the passage of the parliament bill.

Procedure – to move that Lords' amendments be now considered, and then to defer decision, so that Lord Lansdowne may confer with his friends.

Presumably Lord Lansdowne is to tell govt if it will be necessary to appoint peers at all: and if he can give no guarantee, to estimate the quantum required.

So Lansdowne is to be asked for guarantees, analogous to those Asquith has jockeyed out of the King...

20 JULY 1911

Asquith appreciates the point and has written to A.J.B.: rather an odd letter[41] in

---

[41] The text is printed in the *Annual Register*, p. 175.

The Parliament Act

which the King refers to his 'duty'. A copy of this letter was sent to Lord Lansdowne. Frequent conferences all day, prior to meeting of the Shadow Cabinet tomorrow, and the gathering of peers to discuss the situation.

21 JULY 1911

Friday: Shadow Cabinet, twenty-two present.[42] The letter was read to us. Much division of opinion, but the tone throughout was friendly except for occasional sputters from Carson. I make out the following classification of our views.

a) for acquiescence without forcing creation of peers:

A.J.B	Londonderry	Brodrick
Lansdowne	Walter Long	Alfred Lyttelton
Curzon	Bob Douglas	
Chaplin	Steel-Maitland	

b) for driving government to create peers:

Selborne	F. E. Smith	Carson
G. Wyndham	Austen Chamberlain	and (I suppose) myself
Salisbury	Lord Halsbury	

c) uncommitted either way, but tendency to support Lord Lansdowne:

Lord Lansdowne	Derby	Ashbourne (quite
Bonar Law	Finlay	unintelligible)

George Wyndham calls his supporters 'Ditchers', those who would die in the last ditch, and the remainder Hedgers, as he thinks their view liable to trimming. Curzon is the leader of the Hedgers, and very active. Selborne on the other side is the most determined, while Austen put the case admirably. Fancy our party still calling to its counsels such people as Londonderry, Ashbourne, and dear old Harry Chaplin.

I summarise the conflict in one word – *quantum*. A.J.B. would not mind 150 peers – but he is desperately afraid of 400. 150 would equalise conditions in the Lords: would show that the peers do not insist upon preserving their social status, and we should none the less retain the sole asset of the Parliament Bill, namely the two years' delay.

On the other hand, Asquith may say that 150 will not suffice. By appointing 400 he would secure immediate passage of all his bills, and we should lose our one advantage in the measure as it now stands.

21 JULY 1911

On the whole I gather that the peers' meeting[43] passed off with decorum though one man went rather far. About one-third appear to have been 'ditchers'.[44] In my

---

[42] At Balfour's house in Carlton Gardens.
[43] About two hundred Unionist peers had met the previous day at Lansdowne House.
[44] Those wishing to force a creation of peers at whatever injury to Unionist interests.

opinion, as I told the Shadow Cabinet, the publication of Asquith's letter will tend to strengthen those who advocate resistance.

By the way the letter is misleading – unintentionally perhaps: but it does convey that the guarantees have been secured in consequence of the Lords' amendments. This of course is contrary to the facts – indeed guarantees were granted before the bill was ever discussed in the Lords.

Another item worth recording is that the letter as I saw it, began 'My dear Balfour'. This was prudently replaced by 'Dear Mr Balfour'. I wonder if P.J. gave his consent to this mutilation.

The news that the dinner[45] is to be given to Lord Halsbury to thank him for his stand gives rise to questionings. Why not wait upon him at his house instead of belly gorging at a restaurant? The move is astute, and I suppose F.E.[46] is responsible. On the whole it will help the Ditcher movement. The more I consider the situation the more certain I am that resistance although accompanied by terrific risks, is our correct course. The demoralisation following acquiescence would lead to resignations among our workers, to apathy among M.P.s, and their abstention as well: while it might lead also to an organised attack upon the leadership of A.J.B. This afternoon there has been much talk among City folk about the Chief's speech on Tuesday. If he counsels surrender there might be a revolt, and if he gives no lead, someone in the audience will move a fiery resolution: if on the other hand he takes a strong line he would have an enthusiastic reception: that he is prepared to 'ditch' is open to doubt, hence these perturbations coupled with a suggestion that the gathering should be postponed.

Who knows? perhaps eighteen months hence, people will be cursing themselves for having refused to act with Lansdowne's caution.

SANDARS TO LORD BALCARRES, 21 JULY 1911

A.J.B. begged me to tell you that it would be quite an error to suppose that he – or for that matter Lansdowne – is opposed to peer creation, *say of 100 or 150*. Quite the contrary. He said that the whole burden of his song was and is against *swamping* the House of Lords, so that the whole legislative machine is handed over to the government. It is not the statics but the dynamics of the situation which weigh with him. Those, he says, who are begging to be allowed to die in the last ditch will be the first to blame their leaders if as a result of their policy every measure of the government programme could be passed through both Houses.

At the same time so long as men do not realise that danger will arise from *swamping* there is no doubt grave risk attending our immediate party interests – the consequences of which may bring disaster on our political connection and especially on the leaders.[47]

[45] The dinner to Lord Halsbury arranged for 26 July was the first overt sign that those peers who had opposed surrender on 20 July at the Lansdowne House meeting were organising a separate caucus.

[46] F. E. Smith had attacked the policy of surrender violently in the *Morning Post* of 20 July.

[47] Sandars was reporting a long talk with Balfour that afternoon, following a shadow cabinet at 11.30 that morning.

The Parliament Act

Sunday. F.E. writes a warm epistle to back up Carson.[48]F.E. is on dangerous ground – not that he differs from men of influence, but it looks as though he were playing for the reversion of a leadership – and trying at the same time to get in advance of Austen Chamberlain, who, knowing that opinion is still unformed in the party, has scrupled to lay down the law.

Carlton very empty: from what I could gather Ditchers are increasing.

The House of Commons met on 24 July to deal with the Lord's amendments, giving the first opportunity since the coronation for MPs to express their emotions.

24 JULY 1911

Shortly before meeting of the House I learned that F. E. Smith and Hugh Cecil[49] had determined to howl Asquith down. I had hurried interviews with the ringleaders, but without avail. A scene followed which did our party no credit notwithstanding the recollection that they did it to us in old days.

Moreover as I warned the malcontents, our rowdyism was unsuccessful, for although Asquith could only utter disjointed sentences, the noise issued not from a party, but from a small fraction, and Elibank turned the tables on us by letting Balfour have a quiet hearing.

The House adjourned in great disorder, A.J.B., as he told me, furious at having been accorded a hearing from Radicals after Tories had refused it to Asquith.

As to the actual hooligans, I think they are very limited in number. I really doubt if there were more than thirty who kept up an organised outcry...I note F. E. Smith; Harold Smith; Goulding, very violent; Remnant, truculent; Cooper, witty once or twice; Harry Samuel, merely vocal; R. Hunt, Sandys, Ketley Fletcher; Haddock, made his maiden speech in the process; Page Croft, it made him perspire; Kinloch Cooke, kept asking supplementaries; Willie Peel, Banbury; Archer Shee, almost named by Speaker; Hugh Cecil, Dixon, very acrimonious; Arnold Ward, Capt. Craig, Charle Craig, Peto – these men more or less.

Our behaviour was inexcusable. It was stupid, will create reaction against us, and will further split our party. Mark Lockwood, Cripps, Hardy,[50] and other respectable old fellows are arranging a meeting of protest which frankly cannot exonerate the party, but which may further embitter the situation.

Meanwhile Blumenfeld[51] says that it has a much deeper significance – the idea having been that by preventing Asquith from speaking, Radical retaliation against A.J.B. would prevent the Chief from making a speech advocating surrender...

Tomorrow's meeting is a source of the gravest apprehension to myself. If he goes

---

[48] Carson, Abercorn, and the Irish Unionists supported Halsbury and the ditchers.

[49] Provost of Eton 1936–44. Opposition taunts included, 'Who killed the King?'

[50] Charles Alfred Cripps, first Lord Parmoor (1852–1941), MP (Cons.) Wycombe 1910–14; subsequently in two Labour cabinets; and Laurence Hardy (1854–1933), MP (Cons.) Kent S. 1892–1918. Both held high positions in the Church.

[51] Editor, *Daily Express*

as far as he would wish in support of Lansdowne, our party may really be split asunder. The fighters are of course unanimous for resistance but they are not cool or calculating people, and the Chief is wisely looking ahead to the dangers of an immediate working majority in the Lords which he fears we are likely to provoke. I discussed a party meeting with him. He loathes the idea, so does Alfred Lyttelton who was there at our conversation. On the other hand I think a meeting of peers where heads could be counted would be serviceable. We may as well know where we are.

NOTES, 24 JULY 1911

Rowdiness in H. of C. There were three ringleaders, F.E., Hugh Cecil, and Goulding: not more than 30 men who consistently supported them.

On 26th Elibank told me that Asquith who he says is most sensitive, feels terribly hurt and affronted: and rather feels also that the attention we paid to Edward Grey indicates that the latter commands our respect more than the prime minister.

I told Elibank he was wrong. The reason why Grey received so quiet a hearing was because the poor man was obviously suffering from a really bad sore throat. His voice was painfully hoarse, and the odd ethics of the H. of C. prevented their taking advantage of a speaker who was so clearly ill-equipped for the fray.

* * *

Conversation with Lord Harris. He, Arthur Elliot, and Asquith dined together at Grillions. Asquith moody, upset, and nervous, but not angry. Lamented such an attack upon parliamentary institutions as our rowdiness connotes. Expressed no surprise at F. E. Smith taking a leading part in disorder, but is genuinely grieved at Hugh Cecil – great family, university member, independent in means and intellect, etc.

* * *

Conversation with F. E. Smith. Says the rowdiness was deliberately organised by him, Carson, Hugh Cecil, and Bob Cecil.

I protested. (I had warned them before the debate on the ground that they were few in numbers, and that they would do it badly: and that it would injure us more than the Radicals in the long run. In point of fact, although their row was utterly inartistic and ill-equipped they did succeed in paralysing the debate.)

F. E. Smith says that he means to repeat the row after debate is resumed – that he will sit with Linkie and be suspended if necessary: that nothing but vulgarity and unseemliness can make the necessary impression on the outsiders – and that no appeal from us will prevent a serious recurrence of disorder.

* * *

July 24, conversation with J. S. Sandars. I asked if Lord Lansdowne concurred with A.J.B. in not minding the creation of 150–200 peers. Answer yes. Lord Lansdowne does not object, his only fear being swamping.

Then why has not Lord Lansdowne said so?

J.S.S. says Curzon got hold of him, and influenced his speech to the peers on

Friday last – so Lord L. burnt his boats – treated the matter as though there were no tertium quid, no ascertainment of a quantum: in short no peers or all.

This is of course a false position, for 200 peers would secure parliament bill and would remove our troubles.

It therefore becomes to some extent a case of preserving Lord Lansdowne's consistency (and perhaps his amour propre).

A few days ago, writing to Sandars, I expressed a surprise on learning that A.J.B. did not object (at this juncture and under stress of *force majeure*) to creation of 200, in order to save party unity.

A.J.B. saw my letter – said he could not understand why I failed to understand that his whole objection was to *swamping*: and on Saturday afternoon at White Lodge A.J.B. drafted a memo to his Shadow Cabinet to make this clear.

This morning Lord Curzon saw him and persuaded the Chief to withdraw the memo. Lord Curzon has therefore prevented Lansdowne expressing his whole mind to the peers, and has subsequently prevented A.J.B. from sending written advice to his colleagues.

25 JULY 1911

Balfour's City meeting postponed, and I am glad of it. At 8.15 I had to see him, and kept him half an hour from dressing, discussing a communication to Lord Newton which seemed needlessly acrid in tone.[52]

NOTES, 25 JULY 1911

8.15 p.m., conversation with A.J.B. I had hurriedly glanced over draft of his letter which will appear tomorrow morning. I felt it might be constructed as a definite blow against the Halsbury group: that it would cause dismay and that moreover it will do him injustice as failing to convey his complete view of the situation.

He said he had been pressed so much to give a lead that silence is no longer possible. That so far as he is concerned he can only support Lansdowne. No alternative is possible – none indeed is conceivable. Those who expected him to abandon Lord Lansdowne must be singularly short-sighted or lacking experience: and so forth.

I said this is very true – but when all is said and done your view is that the creation of say 100 or 150 peers would not be an irreparable disaster: this letter indicates that creation as such – even half a dozen would not only be a constitutional outrage etc. but that its consequences would be terrific.

A.J.B.; You know my view that the end of the world will not come if *x* number of peers are created: that also, though perhaps in a modified sense, is Lansdowne's view also.

---

[52] Balfour's letter to Lord Newton (like Lansdowne's letter to the Unionist peers) counselled acceptance of the unamended bill, and warned against party divisions. Balfour's letter was rejected by a meeting of diehard peers at Grosvenor House the following day, before the Halsbury dinner.

Balcarres: Then can I tell our men? Their position is substantially your own.

A.J.B: You must not tell our men that I can compromise. There can be no collusion between ourselves and the govt, no manipulation of the division lobby. That would mean complicity and I will have none of it.

Balcarres: At the same time our men are entitled to know the innermost facts, and they as I repeat do not really conflict with your views.

A.J.B.: In a sense we may be nearer agreement than surface study of my letter will indicate.

You can tell them what you think fit, but I dislike whispering in the lobby.

Balcarres: But if you say nothing in public, whisperings are inevitable. I have to safeguard your position. It may prove untenable. Why cannot I do my utmost in this direction?

A.J.B.: I quite understand that both Lansdowne and I may have to resign in consequence of this. I am not certain if such a solution would not be a happy issue. I don't know who for the moment could replace us, but I am ready to contemplate this as a distinct possibility.

I had somewhere asked what I should say to members who ask me if it is an act of disloyalty to attend the Halsbury dinner tomorrow. He gave me no reply.

9.30 p.m., conversation with Austen C. I told him of A.J.B.'s letter... I asked him what he would do about the Halsbury dinner. He said that he did not feel he could withdraw having gone so far, that he would feel a sneak to retreat at this juncture. No disloyalty to A.J.B.

5 p.m., meeting of protest against our misbehaviour yesterday. 100 attended. Cripps in chair. Lockwood moved a resolution expressing regret. Magnus seconded.

It soon became obvious that 9 out of 10 members were averse from apologising. Radicals never expressed sorrow for howling down Lyttelton.

Conversation became general – subject before the meeting was ignored. Friendly tone maintained. Finally Cripps was empowered to convey to A.J.B. the sense of personal loyalty expressed by his followers.

No vote was taken... F. E. Smith this week has sacrificed briefs marked up to 600 guineas, in order 'to take a hand at politics.'

* * *

George Curzon has been the dominent influence both on Lord Lansdowne and on A.J.B. He never leaves the latter alone, and has prevailed on both his leaders to exclude all consideration of the Quantum or Tertium Quid.

As a parliamentarian his judgment was seldom sound: but he is so determined and persevering that he makes his wishes prevail – for he neither lacks self-confidence, and feels no scruples in forcing himself upon those he wishes to influence.

This afternoon he actually admitted to me that he had contemplated voting *for* the Parliament Bill, rather than be a party to creation of peers.

The Parliament Act

I told him in this matter he was a free agent, but for an ex-cabinet minister to follow such a course was suicide.

26 JULY 1911

The letter appears this morning. It is less polemical than I thought: but it is embarrassing that it should appear a few hours before the Halsbury dinner. It will make them think A.J.B. is trying to queer their pitch. I asked him to tell me specifically if he objects to our men attending. He said in the clearest possible manner that he holds no such objection, and added that I myself was free to go if so minded.

He persists in looking upon the creation of a quota of peers as a side issue, not as a question of principle. Under those circs one wonders why he was so emphatic about standing or falling with Lord Lansdowne.

... A new danger appears on the horizon, namely the possibility of some of our peers going so far as to support the government. This is far more serious than the Halsbury movement.

NOTES, 26 JULY 1911

Lord Lansdowne's computations up to date.

Supporters of parliament bill at final stage:

Government	70
Bishops and Unionists	30
	100

Opponents of bill, pledged: 160 (meant between 150–170)

Neutral, will walk out	140
total	300

Balance consists of 300 or so minors, peers abroad, on service, in bed, unaccountable, nonagenarian.

Cromer, Ancaster, H. Sturt, Ridley, Galway, Shaftesbury, St Aldwyn, will vote for bill if necessary.

How can Asquith run risks with this possible balance against him? I warned him that his figures are too incomplete to offer any basis.

When, how, and where are negotiations to be resumed? with whom does the next move lie? Lansdowne and the King? Self and Elibank? An indiscretion in the press? We should determine our scheme before long.

It takes 8 or 10 minutes to swear in a peer. 300 new peers would require 3000 minutes or 50 hours: say a week, and it would destroy the vocal chords of the reading clerk.

Conversation with Bonar Law. If a substantial number of peers vote against parliament bill (before or after creation of peers) it will probably involve resignation of Lord Lansdowne – and presumably also A.J.B. must fall with him. 'The worst of our situation, already far more grave than our fiscal trouble of 1903–5, in that we have so many men who think themselves as good and clever as anybody else in the party.'

During the fiscal crisis we had control of the machine, to a large extent we could guide our own policy, we were in a position to offer douceurs, and moreover the power of dissolution was in our hands. In existing circumstances we have none of the advantages of a govt and we run more than the ordinary risks of an opposition.

25 July the day of Curzon's triumph when he had got A.J.B. to write an uncompromising letter; 26th, A.J.B. rallies the malcontents without changing their opinions, while the malcontents will profess whole-hearted loyalty to the Chief.

MEMORANDUM, 26 JULY 1911

Conversation with Elibank. Asquith has written to Balfour warning him that Grey has a serious announcement to make about Morocco, at tomorrow's sitting. I promised him general support though I consider Grey a weak foreign secretary.

The position is that Germany has offered us a deliberate affront by leaving our note unacknowledged for twenty days. The situation is critical. Admiral Bridgeman is about to undergo an operation for appendicitis. The cabinet however is satisfied that Jellicoe is an admiral of experience and judgment.

I pointed out that the Russian unfriendliness synchronising with German aggression is sinister: that the release of the ex-Shah, and his entrance to Persia must be accompanied by disorder and will be followed by incursion of Cossacks. (Elibank had not noticed this.)

Lloyd George's speech was not only authorised, but was actually framed by F.O. – the statement was entrusted to him as he was a pro-Boer and is a pacifist.

Snowden M.P. will attack his speech as provocative. In doing so he will be able to attack Ramsay MacDonald, alleged by 'comrades' and 'Labor' men to be in the Kaiser's pay.

Meanwhile Germany is making an effort to Delcassé Lloyd George.

Baird M.P. on potentialities. If we abandon France, she will turn to Germany – come to terms with her – agree to revise status quo in Egypt – bring pressure to bear on us there; and with Kitchener in charge there may be a serious imbroglio. We should be isolated.

11.45 p.m. Conversation with St John Brodrick. He had heard that foreign affairs had assumed a critical position – is strongly of opinion that govt cannot carry on a dual conflict at home and abroad; and that therefore A.J.B. in announcing his support tomorrow should suggest a quid pro quo!

Conversation with A.J.B. midnight till 12.30 in the street. Nothing would be worse policy than to bargain for national advantages in face of an international problem.

I told him all I had learned about foreign affairs. He had heard a good deal tonight at dinner from Sir A. Nicolson and Tyrrell.

He says I must make a schedule of the occasions upon which the Radical govts since 1906 have crawled on their bellies to us soliciting support.

He has not received Asquith's letter.

27 JULY 1911

Conference about Insurance: A.J.B., W. Long, Austen C., Alfred Lyttelton, Bonar Law, Harry Forster.

A conversation with Elibank who told me that the foreign outlook is critical.

At midnight I caught A.J.B. and walked up and down Carlton House Terrace for half an hour: he said he would show solidarity when speaking tomorrow on the F.O. vote.

MEMORANDUM, 27 JULY 1911

Austen writes rather a disagreeable letter to A.J.B. complaining of the communication to Lord Newton: says that it was delayed so long as to make his position difficult – that there are passages in it painful, etc.

Asquith's statement in H. of C. on foreign affairs tends to obscure the domestic issue.

Newspaper editors are receiving many letters complaining of the King's action. It is said that certain resolutions of a similar nature have been passed by Cons. associations and clubs but I haven't seen any.

28 JULY 1911

The new danger I referred to is becoming acute. A large number of our peers are actually prepared to support the government. St Aldwyn[53] is working the idea: Curzon also, though he is too shrewd to admit it, but I tackled him on the subject and he became very costive.

I had an interview with Elibank who made it clear that the government is counting upon our active support. I let A.J.B. know by a memorandum, and Sandars tells me a message was sent to Lord Lansdowne. It would be constructive disloyalty to vote for the government, infinitely worse than voting against them. I think Lord Lansdowne will have to repudiate this proposal.

MEMORANDUM, 28 JULY 1911

5 p.m. Conversation with Elibank, Treasury.

Showed me letters from Lord Loreburn to Asquith, and Lord St Davids.

Latter says that 100 Conservative peers will support govt.

5.45. Dictated summary of conversation to the incomparable Mr Short. I made an error in saying that the govt can put 40 peers into the lobby. It should have been 60.

---

[53] Sir Michael Hicks Beach (1837–1916), created Viscount St Aldwyn, 1906: senior Conservative politician, 1874–1903, when he resigned over tariff reform.

7.15 p.m. Saw Sandars. A.J.B. having read my memorandum is much exercised by danger of our peers supporting govt: accordingly telephoned to Bowood to tell Lord Lansdowne.

Lord Lansdowne and A.J.B. (extremely bad hands at telephoning) agreed that such action would be most serious. (It would involve the King directly, as his court influences following on St Aldwyn's interview would be held responsible.)

29 JULY 1911

In Carlton found that the rot has spread more than I conceived possible. Here is my provisional list of our men who are actually prepared to vote for the Revolution.[54]

Camperdown, sensible and robust; Shaftesbury, always thought him so too; Harris; Sturt, snob; Beaulieu, snob; Ridley, brother-in-law of R; Galway, weak; St Aldwyn, always a funk; Desborough, incredible, but courtier I suppose; Cromer, a Radical; Donoughmore, inexplicable; Suffolk (USA); Richmond, can't understand; Roxburghe (USA); Ilchester, can't understand; Barrington, gaga; Dunmore (USA behind); Farquhar, toady;? Rutland – inconceivable; Revelstoke, courtier; Winchelsea, never heard of him;? Bishop of St Davids;? Curzon (USA).

30 JULY 1911

Sunday. Quiet all day.

Tomorrow I have to see Elibank. Is it not rather hard that A.J.B. who has my views and knows I am to talk over the matter, should leave me without guidance? Lord Lansdowne I have not seen and I suppose I must go into the conference without a word of direction.

I confess a great temptation comes over me. Were I to assume a particular tone in our conversation tomorrow Elibank would report accordingly to his cabinet and in twelve hours orders would be issued for the creation of peers. How far am I for instance entitled to assume that Lord Lansdowne will stop the rot among our own men who propose to support administration? If I am correct in thinking he must do so, and I make that point clear to Elibank, then again the government loses the support on which it is confidently counting, and must secure its own position by its own agents.

Of course I can temporise, say I am unprepared and so forth, but Elibank and Asquith want our lead, and are bringing the King up from Cowes on Wednesday (or possibly earlier) to conclude this sordid transaction.

31 JULY 1911

My interview with Elibank this morning passed off without mutual accommodation. I had at least three more with him during the day, but can give him no further information. Saw Lansdowne, A.J.B., F.E., and others.

---

[54] i.e., to vote with the government on the Parliament Bill in order to prevent a large creation of peers. 'U.S.A.' indicates the diarist's suspicion that American wives preferred anything to the diminution of the social value of their titles.

The Parliament Act

4.30 p.m. Renewal of conversation of this morning. Has seen Asquith and Lord Stamfordham. The latter frankly says that the King is averse from having to create peers; that he is anxious for Cons. peers to vote with govt.

Asquith agrees with this view. (Elibank thinks I do as well.)

I therefore told him that I could not personally countenance such action; and that I would rather 200 peers were created than that our men should vote with Administration. Moreover I pointed out that Lord Lansdowne had neither in his speech nor his circular advocated this course, and that he may entertain strong objection to it.

Asquith seems to agree that Lord Lansdowne cannot be asked to indicate more fully than his published list conveys, the tenor of his supporters, and he therefore suggests, in view of the fact that Lord Colebrooke's information is usually defective, that Elibank and I should do the arithmetic (both of us can be thrown over if necessary, neither of us can cause the King's action to be introduced, etc.).

5.30 p.m. Elibank read me an extract from a letter of Lord Knollys to Asquith (presumably just received) in which Knollys says he is desired by the King to say that he thinks it would be fair for the govt to tell the Conservatives how many Liberal peers will vote (Elibank says 65) and that per contra a similar statement should be made by the Conservatives. (This can only refer to our men who mean to vote with the govt).

MEMORANDUM, 31 JULY 1911

It seems to become a contest between Selborne and Curzon – a personal embittered fight between two determined and somewhat jealous statesmen. Both proconsuls, both of convinced Toryism, Selborne senior qua cabinet minister and Knight of the Garter, Curzon more pre-eminent as an ex-viceroy and popular figure.

Selborne is persistent, obstinate, and full of common sense; Curzon brilliant, witty, paradoxical, and not wholly devoid of cunning.

Each is out for blood, each is determined to win: but while Selborne will be content to secure his object by the creation of Peers, Curzon will seldom forget and never forgive the smallest triumph of his adversary, even though it be limited to the ennoblement of one single solitary Radical snob.

MEMORANDUM, 31 JULY 1911

6 p.m. till 7.45. Conversation with A.J.B., Lord Lansdowne and part of the time Alfred Lyttelton. J. S. Sandars present.

I told Lord Lansdowne that our men are grievously dismayed by the attitude of St Aldwyn and those who are prepared to support govt; that this action means puppet peers being drawn from the Conservative party; that this movement cannot fail to be ascribed to the Court, with subsequent embroilment of the King. That no Cons. candidate for parliament could advocate such a course, and that it would very probably fail in preventing the creation of peers – as from inductions I have made it is likely that the passage of the parliament bill under such circumstances might well be followed by the creation of fifty (non-puppet!) peers before Xmas.

F. E. Smith tells me that fifteen of Lansdowne's peers have written to say that if St Aldywn and Co. do not abstain (as they are pledged), an equivalent no. of the remainder must be set free to vote against govt. This had some effect on Lord Lansdowne's mind.

I also told him of Bigge and Knollys, and that so many men being already pledged, the idea of swamping seems to be out of the question.

A.J.B. strongly argued that as the whole weight of their joint influence had been cast against the Halsbury group for defection, it was only fair to dissuade (if not to criticise) the other group which likewise declines to follow its leaders: both groups disobey their leaders, both should be treated in the same way.

Lord Lansdowne seemed scarcely to appreciate the argument.

A. Lyttelton strongly supported A.J.B.

After long disputation in which Lord Lansdowne kept falling back upon his view that he had indicated a policy and that that should suffice, [he] finally took away with him the draft of a letter hastily prepared by A.J.B.

This letter said in effect, 'If I were a peer, I should certainly not vote in favour of govt and I think Lord Lansdowne holds the same opinion.'

Lord Lansdowne said he thought such a document should bear his signature and appear under his responsibility. A.J.B. concurred.

Lord Lansdowne pocketed it and said he would show it to Lord Curzon. Alfred Lyttelton said in private he would be prepared to bet the letter would never see light.

A.J.B. said, 'What funny people I have to deal with: I wonder why people are quarrelsome and so jealous of each other – I love them all, but at times they vex me with their naughtiness.'

CONVERSATION WITH SIR GILBERT PARKER, 31 JULY 1911

A week ago Greenwood, M.P. (Radical) talked mysteriously about serious doings in our party. Gilbert chaffed him.

Today talk was resumed. Greenwood told him about F. E. Smith's privy councillorship – told him the story wrong. I gave a correct version.

He went on to say that during the row last last Monday F. E. Smith sent a message to Elibank to say that if the govt men would allow him to speak, he would make an attack on A.J.B. – or rather that as he had a criticism on A.J.B. he hoped ministerialists would let him speak. Greenwood says he saw Smith's letter in Elibank's room.

I think this highly improbable. Such a course would be foolish as publicity was ultimately inevitable, and moreover I have no reason for thinking F.E. meant to make any such statement. Yet what does Greenwood mean?

Tomorrow I will settle if I am to talk to F.E.

The Parliament Act

I rated Austen Chamberlain for using the word 'disgrace' in his recent letter. He showed contrition, and said it was ill-chosen to convey his view.

Lloyd George asked him if he would like an autumn session. Austen would – but didn't say so. George is tired; but Morocco news is more serious again today and an adjournment might be necessary.

1 AUGUST 1911

7 p.m. A.J.B. writes to Lord Stamfordham saying that he has heard today that Lord S. is saying that the King does not in any case mean to appoint more than 120 peers. As this conflicts materially with statements of Lord Knollys, Lord S. is requested to reply forthwith on a point which must govern Mr Balfour's public policy in the immediate future. (W. Long got the statement in conversation today with Lord S.)

7.30 p.m. Further letter sent by hand to Stamfordham, saying that it is reported in court circles that A.J.B. was not sent for in November because it was generally known he could not form a govt.

A.J.B. says he was never asked: and indicates conditions under which if he had been so invited he would not only have formed a govt but would have done so with good hopes of success.

(Both letters somewhat tart in tone.)

NOTES, 1 AUGUST 1911

Walter Long is so much affronted by Austen C.'s use of the word 'Disgrace', that he 'declines to sit on the front bench with such a scoundrel.'

Yesterday I blamed Austen for the use of the term, which he admitted to be ill-chosen, and the employment of which he frankly regretted. He did not attach the obvious interpretation to it.

Alick Hood's complimentary dinner. A great success, lion and lamb, disgraced and scoundrel sat side by side. Halsbury ate and drank everything put before him. A.J.B.'s speech admirable, Alick's scriptural quotation apposite, room crowded out. Balfour's reception most friendly.

The function may bring many of us together, and in any case should check fissiparous tendencies.

General impression that govt will make a *large* creation, that is 150 or more, but few believe that having invited statement from Lord Lansdowne, and having received his list, the 330 promises to abstain can be ignored by govt.

Loreburn's memorandum of 1 August contemplates that Unionist peers who have promised to abstain may vote against govt when peers are created. This would defeat bill, prorogation would ensure, and a *very* large creation would be necessary to prevent 'a second fiasco'.

St John Brodrick said to me that if peers are created, and so 'vulgarise our order' he might do this (as Lord Loreburn thinks possible) so that Selborne and Co. should not be the 'only heroes'. Yes, said A.J.B.: you object to your tailor being made a peer, so you mean to vote in such a way that your hatter and barber shall be ennobled into the bargain!

2 AUGUST 1911

Austen C. and Hugh Cecil both agree that meetings in addition to those fixed for Friday next are undesirable. Austen C. will attend committee tomorrow and press this point *very* strongly. (Point is that if constituencies are moved by Halsburyites, i.e. bringing influence to bear upon M.P.s, the official organisation cannot leave the matter alone – must reply – and then counter-meetings must be held.

GOSSIP, 2 AUGUST 1911

Last night at Alick Hood's dinner, F. E. Smith is said to have left the room pointedly, at the moment A.J.B. rose to speak. I did not notice it.

Lord Elibank took his seat in the Lords yesterday . . . accompanied by Harcourt (and I think Asquith) . . . It was noticed that they timed the proceedings with great nicety: it is even alleged that Harcourt was consulting a stop watch.

If 300 peers are wanted, at ten minutes apiece (Elibank *père* required $9\frac{1}{2}$ minutes) how many days of ten hours each must the Lords sit?

During the disorder in the H. of C. on Monday the 24th occupants of the Ladies' Gallery were also moved to emotion. Mrs Asquith was naturally much incensed at the cruel treatment accorded to P.J. – she expressed her feelings with much resentment, and a good deal of noise into the bargain. Finally Mrs Asquith cried out, 'What is the Speaker doing, why doesn't he stop this scandalous behaviour – why does he not clear the House?'

Mrs Lowther replied, ' I don't know if the Speaker means to clear the House, but if you make any more noise, Mrs Asquith, I shall give orders for *this* gallery to be cleared forthwith.'

*　　*　　*

Asquith's troubles are only just beginning. Action has to replace bluff, and the prospect of making 200 or 300 peers is not alluring.

To add to his difficulties, he yesterday committed the folly of changing his diet: he substituted Amontillado for Marsala – with the result that he is now absolutely speechless.

*　　*　　*

Elibank says that the only compliment he can pay us is to offer to the opposition whips an electric fan to cool our heated brows. His own installation is complete and comforting. We accept his offer.

*　　*　　*

I watched Lord Lansdowne at one of our conference the other day – he had a pencil in his hand and kept drawing his initial – a florid capital L – surmounted by every variety of coronet.

He has creation of peers on the brain, and unconsciously at his finger tips.

*　　*　　*

The Parliament Act

At Carlton Gardens A.J.B. read draft of vote of censure. It occurred to him last night, partly arising out of Stamfordham's correspondence. Lord Lansdowne concurred.

At Carlton Club Carson and F. E. Smith told me that this morning they had been discussing a similar motion for Lord Halsbury to move in the Lords. All parties on our benches in H. of C. are delighted and A.J.B. got a most prolonged greeting on making his announcement.

I saw Lord Lansdowne at 4.30 in Lords and suggested that a similar motion should be made in Lords. He suggested that a Ditcher should move it, and then mentioned Lord Halsbury.

This would be wise, as showing homogeneity, and moreover Lord Lansdowne could then conclude the debate and give it his chosen complexion: necessary as peers' debates are apt to be discursive and irrelevant.

CONVERSATION AT 4 CARLTON GARDENS, 2 AUGUST 1911, 12–1 p.m.
A.J.B. and Lord Lansdowne.

Since 7 p.m. last night A.J.B. has written three times to Bigge and has received four letters from him. These letters are somewhat contradictory, but they deny stoutly that Bigge ever said to Walter Long that the King had stated he would create no more than 120 peers.

(Salisbury also had alleged that the King on July 22 had said that no more than 120 would be created.)

Bigge indicates that the King will create as many as may be necessary in order to pass the Bill. They may have thought that 120 would suffice, hence this idea that that figure represented the maximum.

Lord Lansdowne was not much interested in this, as it conflicted with Lord Crewe's statement to Lord Cromer yesterday. Lord Crewe thinks that such a course of flooding has never been contemplated.

(Crewe of course though Leader of the Lords is probably not kept completely informed.)

St John Brodrick's letter saying that he also may break away from Lord Lansdowne causes A.J.B. real annoyance. 'For the first time I am inclined to feel angry.' 'I, on the other hand,' said Lord Lansdowne, 'have been angry now for many days past.'

Lord Halsbury has never said he would support Lord Lansdowne: on the contrary his opposition has been consistent and unbroken. That Midleton, Curzon, and Co. should after pledging themselves to support Lord Lansdowne now break away, is a form of disloyalty never urgable against Halsbury.

2 AUGUST 1911
A.J.B. is about to leave for Gastein – Walter Long (senior privy councillor) and Austen C. (ex-chancellor of the exchequer) remain. Which shall be leader in Balfour's absence?

Alfred Lyttelton suggests that on departure the Chief should publish a statement that Walter Long should act as deputy during absence.

Such a course is not exactly what would suggest itself to A.J.B. It would be an oblique blow at Austen, who has occupied the higher rank, and who has led the opposition in times gone by.

It would have an air of vindictiveness, vexation or snub, according to the temperament of the reader.

As regards the respective claims of the two disputants to lead the house, there can be no doubt that on merits Austen is incomparably the stronger man.

Austen's use of the word disgrace has done him much injury, and the lapse from good judgment will haunt him for many a month to come.

3 AUGUST 1911

I can't write politics much in this diary, as that would involve rewriting the careful notes of conversations which I record within a few minutes of their taking place. The record of this political crisis will therefore be found elsewhere.

MEMORANDUM, 3 AUGUST 1911

Announcement of autumn session. On Monday next, the 7th, vote of censure. On Tuesday 8th the Lords amendments. Adjourn ten days later.

The creation of peers takes so long that it is obvious the govt means to send the bill to the Lords for a trial trip.

If the bill be passed, well and good.

If not, parliament will be prorogued, bill reintroduced in our house under guillotine, and it will be returned to the Lords with a large number of peers.

Lord Morley would warn the peers of this – blackmail them if possible into passing the bill.

How will this announcement affect the voting?

Some peers who don't in the least mind creation of 100 or 150 peers will then be face to face with swamping.

Beach & Co. will no doubt be strengthened in their determination to vote for the govt, while the Duke of Norfolk and others who say that such an action must release them to vote against the Bill, would be weakened in this attitude, which might result in an overwhelming creation.

What is the strength of the Halsbury group? At one time F. E. Smith told me it was 110. The *Daily Mail* today says it is 70. The govt think it is smaller still, and doubtless Morley's speech would cause defections.

Of course the Lords on receiving back the bill from us, could acquiesce in five-sixths of our exclusions, could alter the referendum amendment in such a way as to return the bill to our house, and thus precipitate the crisis, or else make the govt drop their own bill.

To send the bill for a trial trip is courageous at first sight: but it means vacillation – looks as though Asquith's letter only meant bluff.

The Parliament Act

Much may happen before the autumn if the bill is now defeated – war, demise, death, hostile by-elections, etc. Redmond must be confident that immediately or ultimately his powers will be exercised to the full: otherwise he would not consent to run this risk.

4 AUGUST 1911

The post of a chief whip is always difficult but still more so when his Chief spends so much time in the country.

This afternoon, Thursday, both A.J.B. and Lord Lansdowne depart from London, till next week. Their absence from the 3rd till the 7th is most embarrassing. These are the days preceding the crisis during which their presence here is more than ever imperative. Though not a valetudinarian A.J.B. thinks much about his health. His mother did the same and nearly died by drugging herself. The Chief fancies that his internal organisation differs from that of everybody else, and he likes going from doctor to doctor discussing symptoms. His bedroom is like a chemist's dispensary. He is longing for Gastein, with its peaceful detachment together with the healing baths which have already done him much good. All this is a source of trouble during these stirring times. I do not doubt that our attitude towards public policy might well have been modified were today in the month of April instead of August.

MEMORANDUM, 4 AUGUST 1911

It occurs to me that if the Lords accepted all the decisions of the Commons, except those dealing with Home Rule/Referendum, our party would be united – and the govt would on receiving back the Parliament Bill in the H. of C. find itself obliged to ask for guarantees for the sole object of preventing a special ballot on home rule.

Such a situation could not fail to cause serious embarrassment to the govt, indeed no dilemma could present less simple means of escape.

Such a course would involve Lord Lansdowne's abandonment of his declared policy of extension – and it would also involve Lord Halsbury's acceptance of the Parliament Bill except in one particular.

Can both parties meet in view of such difficulties?

In the end of course it must mean creation of peers – but anything is preferable to the bill passing by means of Conservative votes.

5 AUGUST 1911

Govt now places its voting strength at 75, a marked advance beyond the figure of 60–65 given me a week ago by Elibank.

25 unattached bishops may increase this vote considerably.

The Forwards on the other hand are publicly credited with 65 or 70 votes – but in private they assure us that their strength is underestimated. I put it down at at least 100 nominal.

However there must be some detrition among those who joined on the assumption that resistance would only produce a limited creation, say 150.

If and when it is realised that swamping must follow defeat of the Bill, a number of the weaker vessels will crack – and abstain.

Nothing of moment was said at the two public meetings last night. Argument on one side or the other is exhausted; however the speeches seem to have been couched in terms of tolerable reason, the orators having promised me to be cautious – I saw them all except Selborne and Halsbury.

Capt. Craig, M.P., 'Asquith has sacrificed the King to his Party: while Balfour has sacrificed his Party to the King.'

Some hints of a hitch in the proceedings. It is thought that apart from reluctance bordering on panic there must have been a special reason why this govt has settled to risk the Bill in the Lords next Wednesday.

Has the King indicated that the guarantees are not exactly what the public understands – or that there is real difficulty in the actual selection of Peers? – or that the King learned for the first time from Balfour's letter to Bigge, that our party would have assumed office if such a request had been made?

That there is a pause – unexplained – is undoubted.

7 AUGUST 1911

Conversation with Lord Curzon, Lord Lansdowne, and A.J.B.

The Chief is becoming a Ditcher!

He pressed Lansdowne to support the Duke of Norfolk.

He pressed him to concentrate on Home Rule/Referendum.

He advocated creation of peers up to 150!

Lord Lansdowne would not budge. George Curzon won't let him: won't leave him.

The fact is, said A.J.B. after Lord L. and Lord C. had left the room, 'His nerve has reached such a state that he can neither look to right or left. He feels that having determined on a certain course he must adhere to it, as the effort of encompassing a fresh line is beyond human endurance.'

The effort in short is too great, and he means to let things slide, trusting that the policy originally outlined may see him through. But whither? The whole tendency of the last few days has been to strengthen the Halsbury party. Here in the H. of C. I look upon 7 out of 10 of our men as Ditchers, a much larger proportion than a week ago. Elibank indicates that tomorrow the Lords amendments will be dealt with seriatim, not en bloc. This contemplates acceptance of certain amendments.

LORD BALCARRES TO LADY WANTAGE, 7 AUGUST 1911

Asquith's speech, or that part of it relating to the precedent of 1832, was drawn from Lord Althorp's memoirs. The book is scarce . . . and Elibank charged with securing a copy ransacked the second-hand booksellers' shops, finally located a copy, bought it, and finds when it is delivered that the binding is stamped 'A. J. Balfour, 1876.'

The Parliament Act

... I cannot understand the position of those who like the Archbishop of York to whom I talked this afternoon, claim support for the government as being an act of loyalty to Lansdowne. Lord L.'s letter to Camperdown was not so explicit a repudiation of this course as I should have wished – very different indeed from the definite and decided draft on the subject which was submitted for his consideration by A.J.B.

8 AUGUST 1911

Hugh Cecil made a remarkable speech this afternoon. The general impression of these two days debate is that he has gone far to reestablish his position, while F. E. Smith has achieved a contrary result.

Apart from merits, and apart from the dexterity of their speeches, Hugh Cecil did impress one with a sense of conviction whereas F.E. created a contrary sentiment in everybody's mind.

My last word with A.J.B., having told him that our men are really desperately afraid of the Parliament Bill being carried by Conservative votes. He replied, 'all I can say is that I hope and confidently believe that Lansdowne will make his position clear tomorrow.' I doubt it.

Squiff has a cold, and has left for the country. Is this right? A.J.B. who leaves tomorrow holds no post of responsibility.

J. S. Sandars tells me that in January last after the election, he and Balfour dined at the Marlborough Club with Lord Knollys. Esher was there. After A.J.B. had talked with the utmost freedom and frankness about the situation, had given his views as to what the King should do, etc., – when the party was breaking up at midnight, Knollys said casually, 'I should say that I have the permission of the King, and it is with the knowledge of the prime minister, that I have dined with you tonight.'

A.J.B., furious, told the man that he had been entrapped. J. Sandars fortunately kept a most careful note of the conversation.

The idea that this private talk was retailed for Asquith's benefit, makes A.J.B. specially angry in view of subsequent facts.

It really is a very scandalous affair.

Walter Long entering the H. of C. yesterday afternoon, bent down to Carson who was sitting beside me. Walter has been yachting. His face is carmine bordering on vermilion. With menacing voice and threatening countenance he whispered, Carson almost trembling at what was apparently imminent, 'Carson, whatever be the outcome of this, one thing I consider it necessary to make perfectly clear to you – one point on which my mind is irrevocably made up, and I wish it put with emphasis: nothing shall ever induce me to *quarrel with you over this business*!'

He passed down the bench; Carson murmured to me, 'and what in the name of heaven did he really mean by that remark?'

Carson says politics agree with him. In ten days he has added three pounds to his avoirdupois.

Hicks Beach in Lords: good speech but providing the govt with far graver weapons to turn against the opposition than ministers have ever been able to forge for themselves.

He announced that he would not vote for the govt, but not one word did he say to discourage his group from doing so.

Lord Lansdowne on this point was decidedly weak – turned all his argument against Halsbury and none against the former group.

Steel-Maitland was asked by Lord Galway if voting with the govt would injure the chances of S. Smith, Galway's son, who is a candidate. Steel-Maitland said yes emphatically. How will this affect Papa's vote?

CONVERSATION WITH A.J.B.
'I can never forget the attacks made upon me by those who have charged me with cowardice and disgrace. Had they merely disregarded my advice about voting, I should have neglected the matter, but their publicity, the press campaign, and the speeches render their action unforgettable *and unforgivable*.' I dissented.

'I hate discipline. I support freedom of action and intellect. Hence my refusal to try to dragoon Lansdowne – who moreover is more directly concerned than I.'

'Lord Lansdowne is supersensitive in these matters. I am not.'

'Providence put me in charge of the Party at the outbreak of the fiscal crisis. By retaining office and keeping a free hand I prevented a most serious and permanent split.' (A.J.B. does not look on the secession of Churchill and co. as directly caused by the Fiscal Reform movement.)

10 AUGUST 1911
Bade farewell to A.J.B. at Victoria, on his road to Gastein.

At night the Parliament Bill carried by Conservative votes.

11 AUGUST 1911
At Baireuth they give *Parsifal* today – and I am here galled to death by the surrender of our Conservative peers.

At Lansdowne House, Curzon brimful of smug satisfaction over the victory to which he contributed a very ignoble share. John Redmond however is the real hero, and he has consummated his end without opening his lips.

CONVERSATION, 11 AUGUST 1911, LANSDOWNE HOUSE
Conversation, Lord Lansdowne, Lord Curzon, Duke of Devonshire, Lord St Aldwyn, Lord Midleton.

1. Very strong feelings expressed against probable attacks on those who supported govt last night. Beach says such a thing would break the party. Perhaps. Why did he not vote?

The Parliament Act

Lord Lansdowne evidently pleased at the outcome of the debate – only exercised about the Camperdowns. Says their number was increased by the violence of Selborne's histrionic attacks.

2. Talked about whips in the H. of Lords. We want a stronger connexion between the two houses, and of course more efficient men. Waldegrave and Churchill both voted with Halsbury last night and Lord Lansdowne says that makes their position in relation to his difficult. It is however impossible I should hope for Lord Lansdowne to suggest their resignation unless he is equally disciplinarian against the Camperdowns. To attack Waldegrave and Churchill at this juncture would provoke reprisals.

MEMORANDUM, 11 AUGUST 1911

Lovat says there is a hostile feeling towards Lansdowne, and also against A.J.B., but especially in case of former.

This is because it is believed that A.J.B. would have taken a stronger line had Lord Lansdowne permitted it. Lansdowne also might have done so, but Curzon stood in the way.

Lovat complains that 'the lead' came too late. Many had irrevocably committed themselves.

I pointed out that immediately the first communication was made to us, the meeting of peers was held.

Lovat replied that as it was assumed for months past that guarantees had been given, the conditions were not materially changed by Asquith's letter: and that the amendments should never have been moved, nor been pressed with such emphasis if their ultimate abandonment were contemplated.

He says that the 'forward' group only refrained from dividing on the second and third readings in the belief that the amendments represented the minimum and that they would receive the adherence of Lord Lansdowne.

He does not allege a breach of faith.

Being whip and teller of the Forwards his remarks doubtless reflect opinions held by many of that group.

BALCARRES TO BALFOUR,
11 AUGUST 1911

People are *very* sore that so many of our men voted for the Parliament Bill. There were at least 25 not counting bishops, as against the 'small handful of uncontrollables' to whom Lord Lansdowne referred.

My immediate function is to check this feeling of soreness from developing into something far more vindictive. Mercifully the weather keeps stifling and the prospect of London being occupied by 25,000 troops has distracted attention.

I beg all parties to go paddling at Margate rather than take 'action' now, with our nerves upset and our tempers much fatigued.

F. E. Smith writes to me in this strain. Austen this morning publishes a letter to

Walter Long, much in a similar sense. He feels that his language ten days ago was not duly weighed.

None the less there will be a movement of proscription – they may try to fire men out of clubs and similar foolish procedure.

I talked to St Aldwyn this morning – told him he was right in assuming something of the kind might happen. I then found he thought the attitude meant hostility to himself. I said No, I am only referring to those who voted with the govt. He then made a sturdy defence of those peers for their patriotism etc.: entered fully into their justification: but I may add that he did not vote in their lobby. How like him!

Equally, Rosebery spoke rotundly for abstention in the afternoon, and at night announced he would support the government, again true to nature.

St John Brodrick however was not consistent as he usually speaks much above his ability, whereas last night he never rose above his own inherent standards.

We are uncomfortable, irritable, and apprehensive of the immediate future. Lord Lansdowne gave me the impression this morning of being much relieved, and only anxious to safeguard Lord Camperdown etc. He entered with vivacity into a point relating to the expiring laws continuance bill. I rejoice in good spirits wherever I encounter them.

Lord Knollys came to the H. of C. to see Sandars last night. A new messenger showed him into my room which was empty, opened the door into my colleagues' room and said, 'Lord Knollys wishes to see Mr Sandars.' Willie Bridgeman, little knowing Knollys was standing a yard off, observed 'Let's go and kill him.'

Jack Sandars says he thinks he can trace this episode in their subsequent conversation. Really some people are too touchy for the workaday world of politics.

Lloyd George successfully translated the motion for payment of members into terms of comic opera.

LORD BALCARRES TO LADY WANTAGE,
13 AUGUST 1911

It is no good disguising the fact that intense and deep-rooted animus exists against those Conservative peers who supported the government on Thursday night. Lord Lansdowne says he attributes it to the violence of Lord Selborne and his friends: but what must that violence have been to have driven our men into the radical lobby! I am afraid that so hostile is the feeling against these men that all sorts of vindictive action may be taken against them – not indeed that much advantage could ensue; but there are many men who were prepared to acquiesce, though reluctantly, in abstaining with Lansdowne – who look upon supporting the government as an act of treachery. Garvin in this morning's *Observer* is as usual in a strain of hysteria, but his view is none the less that of a vast proportion of our party. There were dozens of men on Lansdowne's list, who would willingly have joined Halsbury but for their affection and regard for their leader.

Many of these men I fear consider they have been treated badly. They have stuck to Lansdowne and are charged with pusillanimity. Camperdown and his friends who broke away from Lansdowne are lauded in *The Times* as patriotic heroes; Halsbury and Co. with whom their sympathies really lay are denounced as hot-headed intriguers.

And now this morning, though in a guarded fashion, Garvin seems to indicate that there was complicity between Lansdowne and Lord Morley. This idea is objective and subjective. In the first place Lansdowne has made no apparent effort to check the movement to support the bill – while in the second place he, Curzon, and St John Brodrick got up in turns, and pressed Morley to issue threats of ever increasing stringency about the creation of peers. The fact is that Lord Lansdowne differed from Balfour in that he really hated the creation of peers – even if there had only been a dozen ennoblements. Balfour on the other hand abominated the idea of voting with the government – and actually drafted a letter of the most incisive style, which he suggested should be issued by Lansdowne to check this objectionable movement.

Curzon re-edited that letter (addressed to Camperdown), and *The Times* alleged without contradiction that its real intention was to support those conservatives who meant to vote in the government lobby!

If it once gets out that the 25 Conservatives voted with the assent or encouragement of Lansdowne, there may be difficulties in our party far more acute than those encountered by Gladstone in 1886. It would be impossible to check the fissiparous tendencies resulting from such a belief. For the moment 'the forwards' are fairly quiescent, and I am trying to make them slumber awhile in the hope that personal recriminations shall be postponed until after the recess – and by that time I hope we may be too busy with other things to re-open the matter.

None the less the outlook is bad. The sentimental case against resisting was unanswerable, but the party as a whole, not only in our House, but in the House of Lords too, would have enthusiastically followed our leaders in forcing the creation of peers.

Lord Lansdowne has made the mistake of believing that those who promised to abstain were actuated by merits and argument, rather than by loyalty. Nothing could be further from the truth. Among his list were men who were more keen and anxious to vote against the government than Halsbury himself – notably men who had previously served in the Commons.

So far as I can make out, on Thursday last the government had only 150 men on their lists who were possible peers.

14 AUGUST 1911

List of peers who did not support government but who from time to time indicated their intention of doing so.

Lord Harris, Alington (2nd Baron), M. of Beaulieu (2nd Baron), Hicks Beach (1st Baron), Desborough (1st Baron), Cromer (1st Earl), Donoughmore, Suffolk (m. American), Richmond, Roxburghe (m. American), Ilchester, Barrington, Bath,

Redesdale, Powis, Montrose, Ancaster (m. American), Northcliffe (1st Baron), Revelstoke (2nd Baron), and? Dunmore, Farquhar, Rutland, Clinton.

15 AUGUST 1911

The victory is the victory of Curzon, and in a secondary degree of St John Brodrick.

Halsbury was beaten, the government was in reality beaten, Lord Lansdowne was effaced: and the real power lay with the unseen influences which magnified the 'handful of uncontrollables' into a body of 30 or 35 peers in the government lobby.

In the H. of C. today conversation is naturally enough monopolised by the strikes. This serves to obscure our own difficulties and we hope against hope that the recess may act as a specific.

The Radicals however will never allow the matter to slumber. A few short questions will reopen the wound – and force us to answer as to the repeal of the parliament bill, or the reform of the H. of Lords, on both of which a reply must connote comment upon the final division in the Lords.

16 AUGUST 1911

The departure of A.J.B. for Gastein before the division on the Parliament Bill is seized upon as a sign of apathy – and makes the hostile critic allege complicity in its most naked form. J. S. Sandars is blamed for having allowed it though he was powerless in the matter: it is no good pointing out that A.J.B. booked his tickets for Thursday last (after repeated postponement) in the belief that the division would have taken place the previous night.

Meanwhile he has written to say that no letters are to be forwarded to him, as he can't be bored to read them.

This morning *The Times* publishes a statement, presumably based on Lord Curzon's inspiration, to the effect that a Halsbury victory would have been succeeded by a Lansdowne resignation.

This all tends to magnify the 'heroism' of the Camperdowns, and is a direct blow at the Halsbury group. So far as I am aware no such intimation was conveyed to them before the division. The publication of this note at this stage is evidently intended to convey a further rebuke to Halsbury and Co., hinting so far as possible that they were concerned in an anti-Lansdowne intrigue.

John Gretton, though of a normally gloomy temperament says that a re-crudescence of attack on the Balfour – Lansdowne leadership is inevitable – not in the H. of C. but among the stalwarts in the constituencies. Sustained leadership is the only thing the country can understand.

The great strike continues to divert attention from our own introspection.

It is rumoured in certain exalted circles that Lord Esher's operation for appendicitis was largely imaginary; and that an aching appendix was an internal excuse for absence during a dangerous episode.

VII

'Balfour must go':
the leadership crisis,
August–November 1911

*The strains inflicted upon the Unionists by the manner in which the Parliament Act was
passed, were slow to reveal themselves, because almost at once labour unrest became the
dominant topic. This affected much of industry during the late summer and autumn, most
dramatically in the first national railway strike (16–19 August) which produced the
first petrol shortage. The government handled matters quite well, and did not lose ground
at by-elections until November 1911. Sober opinion had however been given a shock, and
electorally the episode marked the end of the class politics of 1909–11 on which the
Liberals had ridden high.*

*Parliament rose belatedly on 22 August, adjourning until 24 October. An autumn
session, given over almost entirely to unfinished government legislation, was needed to
make up for time lost over the Parliament Act. Nineteen days were set aside for the
completion of the National Insurance Bill. The autumn session, however, was the least of
Unionist preoccupations between August and November, although their dislike of the
Insurance Bill hardened as they discovered its unpopularity at by-elections. The
question which gradually emerged during these months was that of the Unionist
leadership.*

*Balfour left London for Gastein on 10 August, brooding over wrongs which he felt
more deeply than any in his public life, but determined to come to no decision until after
his holiday. He returned to London on the night of Saturday, 2 September, and went
almost at once to Whittingehame, his house in Scotland. Apart from a visit to Balmoral
(12–15 September) he left home only to make occasional speeches in Scotland, not*

returning to London until 3 November, by which time his retirement was irrevocable. During this period of two months, Balcarres was one of relatively few figures from the political world who had more than casual contact with 'the Chief'.

Balcarres kept valuable notes of his discussions with Balfour. These, though somewhat repetitive, help to clarify how Balfour presented the issue of retirement to a chief whip whom he certainly trusted. It was Balfour, and not pressure from outside, who decided that 'Balfour must go.' His overriding reason was that he had nothing to stay on for, a reason which would have applied equally had there been no galling rebellion over the Parliament Act. His decision antedated such particular external incidents as the founding of the Halsbury Club on 7 October. Indeed, the only incident which rankled deeply was a brutal letter from Walter Long.

The notes kept by Balcarres at this period were partly used, sometimes without attribution, by Mrs Dugdale in her biography of Balfour, whence they became an element in Lord Blake's masterly synthesis of the evidence relating to the election of Bonar Law. The object of the passages below is to give the same story through the eyes of the Chief Whip, using his ipsissima verba *to convey something of the tone of Balfour's conversation and the subsequent intrigues, rather than to modify the received version given by Lord Blake.*

On 17 August Balcarres and his family reached their house in Fife on a train stoked by a booking clerk. Then an outbreak of diphtheria caused by the great heat made it necessary to send the children by boat to stay with Lord Wemyss at Gosford on the southern shore of the Firth of Forth. Balcarres was left behind for a while by himself, but soon settled down with his family in the resort town of North Berwick, noted for its choice of fifteeen golf courses. The house cost £200 for two months, but it brought him within easy reach of Balfour at Whittingehame. (Balfour used to come over to North Berwick for the golf.) The Asquiths, too, were on holiday in the vicinity.

22 AUGUST 1911

The railway strike has undoubtedly helped our party to forget recriminations during the last ten days: but I none the less look forward to the future with deep concern. How our party will be split when the Radicals propose an elective Senate! How difficult to reply to the Radical heckler who asks if we object to the Parliament Bill – why we voted for it – if we mean to repeal it, and so forth.

Many of our keenest men are disheartened, dismayed, even disgusted. Our only chance is to enrol the malcontents into a band of fighters who will oppose the government more strenuously than before, and let us hope that in attacking the enemy they may refrain from criticising each other. This however is a counsel of perfection. Much will no doubt be done in this direction, but it is impossible that they should forget the flaccid leadership of Lord Lansdowne who will gradually come to be held responsible for the Camperdown movement – that is for those who supported the Parliament Bill in the government lobby.

Much animus is felt against the Bishops. I am not surprised. Their legislative days, at any rate, are numbered.

'Balfour must go'

By rights I should be in London today for the extra sitting of the House of Commons: but Elibank telegraphed that the settlement of the railway strike made the sitting unimportant, so I remain in Fife, in comfort, but alas alone.

24 AUGUST 1911

I confess I should regret any publicity being given to Lord Wemyss's recollections.[1] Their style is too colloquial, the anecdotes though capital much too frequent, while there is a strain of personalities running through all the volumes which would not give pleasure. Moreover these pages – and there must be 300 or more – fail to represent the character, the dignity, the independence, and above all the great courage of the old gentleman. Moreover there is no attempt at systematic record of his considerable activities, for instance his long and honourable connexion with the Volunteer movement. His tremendous parliamentary career is only touched upon incidentally, likewise his remarkable experiences as connoisseur.

7 SEPTEMBER 1911

A.J.B. very prominent on the links pursued by bevies of nieces from Whittingehame. As he comes here in order to escape from his family, it is a pity they won't leave him alone. He looks extremely well, and is doubtless living in a fool's paradise.

9 SEPTEMBER 1911

Drove to Whittingehame to stay with A.J.B. Lady Frances Balfour,[2] looking well in widow's weeds, is just back from Archerfield. She says that Asquith has already settled that he will not come to London for the first fortnight of the autumn sitting. The slackness of ministers, their unconcealed indolence causes me endless surprise.

A.J.B. came to my bedroom and we had a long talk – about party meeting, party policy – future speeches and so forth. Our talk was on the whole indecisive for I cannot get him to understand the intellectual requirements of those who require a lead, not once, but frequently on the same subject. He says he cannot repeat his speeches, for unless spontaneous they bore him. None the less those who fight for us in the country, and who have won us elections in the past, do require their political stimulants in repeated draughts, and they must be humoured.

He is rather alarmed lest Steel-Maitland should progress too fast.

10 SEPTEMBER 1911

A.J.B. showed me three letters, the sequence of his earlier correspondence with Stamfordham.

The first is from A.J.B. in reply to a telegram from Sandars saying that Knollys has received no answer to the conversation between Knollys and Sandars after A.J.B. had gone abroad. The Chief writes rather a handsome letter.

[1] *Memories, 1818–1912*, by the Earl of Wemyss and March (David Douglas, Edinburgh, 1912), printed privately for the reasons noted by Crawford: available on microfilm at the Scottish Record Office.
[2] Widow of Arthur Balfour's brother Eustace.

Knollys replies in a mock heroic vein, expressing almost in so many words his regret that the days of duelling are past, and attacking the Chief all round, to which A.J.B. replies in a quiet strain: sorry that Lord Knollys should think it necessary to break off friendly relations of old standing etc., and as the Chief is to go to Balmoral tomorrow, he asks Knollys to have a letter awaiting his arrival to say whether or not they shall cut one another openly.

A.J.B.'s letter not quite so frigid or clear-cut as I should have wished.

... Mrs Asquith came over to tea from Archerfield, bringing Edwin Montagu.[3] I think the Chief really felt affronted by this intrusion – for she has been only a few days in this neighbourhood, and forcing herself here so soon creates resentment. Miss Balfour[4] is certainly much galled by it. A.J.B. pretty cool in demeanour. He feels that the face of politics has been changed by recent events, that he and his party have been maltreated, that the King of both Conservatives and Liberals has been outraged, and that it is consequently quixotic to expect that the old amicable relations between politicians in private life can continue on their former footing. I quite agree with him.

Mrs Asquith very *outré* in costume, in manners, and in conversation, and for the first time in my recollection not quite sure of her ground.

A.J.B. reading family prayers to his enormous household on Sunday evenings gives me the greatest pleasure.

11 SEPTEMBER 1911

Back to Kaimend.[5] A.J.B. to Balmoral where I trust he may enjoy himself with Lord Knollys!

23 SEPTEMBER 1911

To Whittingehame. A mass of nephews and nieces, together with other relations from whom it is most difficult to isolate the Chief. George Younger and I insisted on a good long talk with him, and impressed upon him the necessity of his adopting a strong critical line. I am certain that aggression is the chief asset of a leader at this moment – attack in all directions and the government is more vulnerable every day.

This Chief himself is in good health, well recuperated by Gastein, but feeling as most of us must do that an autumn session is an unmitigated nuisance. His interest in the striking defeat of Laurier's government is thin and vacuous. He is to stay with Alfred Lyttelton at St Andrews and they will confabulate on a subject which requires an early pronouncement.

Gerald Balfour greatly amused to find that A.J.B. thought the heading Johnson v. Wells[6] referred to a cause célèbre in the Divorce Courts.

[3] Edwin Montagu (1879–1924), Asquith's private secretary 1906–10; Under-Secretary for India 1910–14.

[4] Alice Balfour, A.J.B.'s sister, who kept house for him at Whittingehame.

[5] The house Balcarres had taken in North Berwick.

[6] A proposed boxing match between a white man and a negro. The event was cancelled because race riots were feared if the negro won.

'Balfour must go'

In afternoon to Whittingehame. The usual huge family party, together with Lady Desborough and daughter ... Mrs Drew and the notorious Dorothy,[7] much spoiled by that early fame, Hewins,[8] Steel-Maitland. Had a very long talk with the Chief – recorded it among my conversations.

MEMORANDUM, 30 SEPTEMBER 1911

Conversation with A.J.B. and Steel-Maitland. After talking over general policy, A.J.B. said rather apropos of nothing – I am coming to the conclusion that it would not be at all a bad thing for the party if I were to resign my leadership.

He spoke uninterruptedly in this strain for fifteen minutes – argued out the case, put forward the pros and cons, discussed the appropriate moment of his departure, the attitude he would thenceforward adopt in the H. of C., etc.

At the end I asked him if he was telling us his decision on the matter and he said no.

At the same time he had summoned us both to his room, there was a certain formality in his conversation, a certain logical sequence in his remarks, which made me think the matter was not unpremeditated.

I asked him in fact if his conversation were extemporary, and he said 'to the extent of repeating views which have been constantly in my own mind – but I have mentioned it to nobody else, except perhaps in a sporadic way to my sister, and I have no doubt threatened a resignation in moments of annoyance to Sandars or Short.'

His case was briefly as follows. He has led H. of C. and opposition for 20 years, probably the longest sequence for many a generation. He is getting on in years. He is 63 (he wasn't sure), his health from time to time causes anxiety. Suppose we come into office three years hence – he will be then 66 – too old to survive a long ministry.

A change sooner or later is inevitable. This is the best moment.

The party is in low water, but the autumn session must be occupied with lesser topics, in which great party strife cannot arise.

Next year will be Home Rule, Disestablishment, etc. It is only fair to his successor that he should enjoy a few months of relative calm prior to a controversial and critical session. The new man would then to able to settle down, to mature his plans, in short be enabled to formulate his policy without extraneous pressure.

Asked as to the cause of this view (which he denied to be a decision) he said that there were many symptoms of disquiet.

The diehard agitation was one, but that in itself was symptomatic of previous discontent.

The Dartford association has passed a veiled vote of censure – Dorsetshire has

---

[7] W. E. Gladstone's daughter and granddaughter.
[8] W. A. S. Hewins (1865–1931), first director of the London School of Economics, 1895–1903: MP (Cons.) 1912–18.

repeated it. Others would doubtless do the same unless handled by friendly chairmen. Wherever he looks he can detect similar views, and the press as a whole is not sympathetic.

This part of the question he put strongly and with skill. Moreover he analysed his own shortcomings in a paradoxical way. Steel-Maitland said – but which possible successor can take the points so quickly, can reply as you do to any debate on any subject?

'That faculty is one which the country does not necessarily demand in a leader. W. H. Smith lacked it. I think a slower brain would often be welcome to the party as a whole. I see all the factors of a situation, every potentiality of an argument. Perhaps this entails lack of decision. Some people blame the qualification in my speeches. They are not expressed to save myself, but to protect my party in the future, when the statements of leaders are recalled to injure the party, though the pronouncements of the lieutenant are forgotten. F. E. Smith contradicts himself once a month.'

'There would be a great thunderstorm, followed by torrents of rain: but the atmosphere would be cleared in the process and the party would ultimately come to its own.'

He thinks a political reaction of a violent type is inevitable: wishes his successor to be securely installed long before the formation of his ministry.

But who is the successor to be? A.J.B. says Austen in H. of C. and Curzon in Lords. Austen is Liberal Unionist, Curzon a Conservative. This reverses the wings as at present displayed. Thinks W. Long too discursive, too quick-tempered and above all too complimentary: 'the compliments are the only features of his speeches I can recall.'

A.J.B. would retain his seat, would sit on Front Bench, would co-operate zealously with his party, and in a limited way would take public meetings. As a Free, or Freer Lance, he thinks his criticism would in some ways be more formidable.

He also said that he wished to act soon. When we put in a plea against his rushing into resignation, he said that if he decided so to act, and deferred the actual dénouement, he would feel himself a mere warming pan for his successor.

The whole conversation was marked by force, and at times by conviction. Every objection was met by cold analysis: no argument against his view seemed to him to be influential.

1 OCTOBER 1911

Again with the Chief for an hour before proceeding to Kirk where Robertson discoursed on Pompey. A.J.B. delighted at the panegyric of Pompey which sounded strange to our ears. In afternoon most of us walked round the policies where A.J.B. during the last few years has effected many improvements, some of them costly so I hope his financial status improves: but he tells me that the value of his farm property does not increase.

'Balfour must go'

Evan Charteris[9] came. The Chief talked with great brilliance and much wit. Extraordinary knowledge of la Vendée and defence of Pitt against strictures by Fortescue.

MEMORANDUM, 1 OCTOBER 1911
Conversation with A.J.B. alone. He showed me a very long letter just received from Walter Long. W. Long says he has grave matters to write about, mentions universal disquiet, blames Chief's attitude about reorganisation, criticises Steel-Maitland, criticises adversely a phrase used by A.J.B. about Gladstonian Home Rule.

He further says that unless there is a radical change in policy and methods, A.J.B.'s leadership will be a disaster to himself and to the party as a whole.

He then talks of being relieved from cooperation on the front opposition bench.

A hostile letter, bitter, here and there confused, more often than not unjust.

'But,' says the Chief, 'this comes from my oldest colleague, my professed friend and upholder: nothing of the Diehards could be compared with this for what is called disloyalty.

'The letter in fact is a bald and brutal invitation for me to retire, but I do not think Walter can have thoughts of stepping into my shoes, otherwise he could not have proceeded by such direct methods.'

The Chief, though realising to the full Walter Long's confusions of thought, attaches importance to the letter, for it is most symptomatic of disquiet – which if it produces such epistles from 'the most loyal of the loyal' cannot fail to be deep-rooted.

Mr Balfour went on to talk with perfect calm of arrangements connected with resignation. He will speak on Saturday the 7th in ordinary strains, and on 28th inst. at Edinburgh will make the announcement. Meanwhile he must write to Lord Lansdowne, to Alfred Lyttelton and he thinks also to Bonar Law, perhaps to one or two others. A list must be made. Walter Long's letter shall be answered in the speech.

'I have no personal feelings in the matter. Whatever ambitions I may ever have had have been satiated years ago. If I wished I could make it absolutely impossible for anyone to evict me from the leadership: moreover if I resigned I could make it absolutely impossible for anybody else to assume effective leadership of the opposition. Walter asks me to change. I cannot change.'

I then asked him if his mind was really made up, and he said *no*. But I saw that to withdraw from the position he had outlined was at the moment impossible. So I temporised – and said that the scheme was unjust to the party, to himself, and to his own reputation.

I told him that he proposed to retire in such a manner as to make his exit into a retreat. He would be charged by the Maxse group of having feared to face the music

---

[9] Evan Charteris, a barrister and friend of A.J.B.

of Leeds,[10] and that if he made his announcement on the 21st, a Saturday, the bulk of our members would only hear of it on Monday the 23rd, while parliament would meet next day. We should have no leader, intrigue would distract us to the advantage of Administration, etc.

I insisted on the fact that resignation under such circumstances would colour the verdict upon a long career which has been marked by consistent high spirit and courage – that he owed it to himself to retain and cherish this valued tradition beginning with his earliest ministerial experiences in Scotland and Ireland.

This view had some effect on his mind.

He then said that if a better opportunity than the 22nd was available he would consider it. I replied that any opportunity was preferable, Leeds for instance. By that date, the middle of November, he would have made two or three strong speeches in the country, half a dozen excellent speeches in parliament, his colleagues the same, and fresh heart would be infused into our midst. By Leeds, his position strengthened, he would be able to announce his own resignation and promise cordial help to his successor, and effect his object in a cloud of glory.

'I do not know about the cloud of glory, and in real life such a thing might be embarrassing.' As an objection he observed that he would have occupied half a session as leader while his successor ought to have been preparing for home rule.

The conversation was abruptly ended at midday by our having to depart to the Kirk, where we arrived late to singing 'more discordant than usual.'

CONVERSATION WITH HEWINS, 1 OCTOBER
Said he had been talking to A.J.B., found him low and depressed. I asked about what, and Hewins said chiefly about the future of the country as exemplified in the recent strikes, and about the future of Europe as exemplified in Italy's recent attack upon Turkey.

CONVERSATION WITH MISS BALFOUR
Said that her brother was depressed about his own position, that he is tired of his responsibilities, and that at no time during the last twelve months would she have been in the least surprised to hear of his resignation.

2 OCTOBER 1911
Again in conference with the Chief, and my notes will be found elsewhere. He is really on the verge of resignation.... By the way, A.J.B. was perfectly furious at Mrs Asquith who has not only been over to pass a few hours at Whittingehame, but has been angling for invitations to stay at Whittingehame. He was vexed by her unsolicited intrusions, but is determined she shall not stay the night there.

Lady Wemyss, on the other hand, is constantly pressed to stay at Archerfield – has refused often, and after excuses had broken down under cross-

---

[10] The impending party conference.

examination, frankly told Mrs Asquith that Lord Wemyss didn't wish her to stay there, and moreover that she concurred in his desires. Thereupon Mrs Asquith triumphantly said, 'I see no reason for you to pretend to be so grand, considering that A.J.B. is constantly pressing me to go to his house.' I found that A.J.B. is becoming more and more intolerant of this pseudo-friendship, and ever more impressed by the iniquity of the government in its dealing with the King.

It appears that immediately on his arrival at Balmoral he was closeted with the King, who practically apologised for not having told him of events as they occurred. 'I hope you will not think very badly of me.' The fact is that after extracting pledges from the King, Asquith went one step further, and secured a promise that nobody at all should be told, clearly determining that our party should be kept in ignorance. At one moment the King very nearly withdrew his pledge, and he arranged to meet A.J.B. at Revelstoke's house, but when it came to the point confined himself to the ordinary topics of society. He repents what has passed, and feels that in justice to our party he should have insisted upon Asquith giving us information weeks and months earlier. All this shows that Asquith has organised a conspiracy, not against us indeed, but against the freedom of his sovereign. Such a man cannot be trusted, and can look for no countenance from those who uphold traditions of loyalty and respect towards the throne. Mrs Asquith, therefore, inveterate gossip and backbiter, must be held at arms' length, for apart from her penchant for displaying her exuberant humour, she has a more practical wish to prove that recent events have made no breach in the continuity of her social friendships.

MEMORANDUM, 2 OCTOBER 1911
Conversation with A.J.B. alone, 11.0 a.m. till 12.0.

I asked him at once if in his conversation yesterday he had allowed himself to be much influenced either by what Steel-Maitland had written, or by what George Younger and I had said to him.

He said no – he had however noted that Steel-Maitland's memoranda confirmed impressions gathered elsewhere, but that his view was formed long ago and that Walter Long's letter, received yesterday, confirmed and amplified his deductions more than everything else put together.

I then found that he had definitely settled to resign forthwith, that is, to make the announcement at Edinburgh on the 21st: he proceeded to recapitulate his position.
a) *Physical*: his age; his prospects; necessity of two foreign trips a year; increasing strain of parliamentary work, still more of cabinet responsibility.
b) *Temperamental*: begins to feel stale: many indications that in fact he is stale: has played two rounds of parliamentary golf every day for twenty years. Mental fatigue inevitable. Mental activity and interest in many other directions, and would like more time to cultivate these tastes.
c) *Political*: Change good for the party. He is tired – felt the Ditcher movement more than anything else in his whole political career – resented it more. (This surprised me). Finds that those who called loudly for a lead were prominent in

disregarding his last lead. Hence a fresh leader is imperative who can begin by securing closer discipline, etc. This part of the argument not so convincing to A.J.B. as (a) and (b).

He then said that in August he determined to come to no conclusion until he was cool, and until the perspective was more clearly defined.

Those conditions are now realised – he feels no animus, subsequent events have confirmed his earlier decision, and he proposes therefore to write to Lord Lansdowne this afternoon.

I reverted to the objection I advanced yesterday – told him that the first duty of life was to part from it handsomely – that to retire 48 hours before the House met would involve us in confusion, and would shroud his own position with ambiguity, besides laying him open to the charge of cowardice. I urged that if his decision to retire was final he could well postpone it awhile without inconveniencing himself and with great advantage to the party, and I retained full freedom to repeat all my arguments dissuading him from retiring at all.

Finally he said he would not write to Lord Lansdowne today (presumably therefore won't mention the subject on the 21st) – he will talk to Lord L. – says that in any case it would be impossible to concentrate in a letter arguments which he has taken three hours to expound in conversation.

Impressions from my three conversations with A.J.B.:

1. That he means to retire: that the occasion alone remains undecided.
2. That he means to do so on account primarily of the Ditcher Row, which was caused by his nearest relatives and oldest friends.
3. That he is genuinely convinced that a withdrawal from the leadership is essential to progress of the party.
4. That he is politically speaking a tired man, though still anxious to remain an active politician.

Jack Sandars, Balfour's factotum, had some idea that resignation was in the wind, and of course wished to prevent an event which would terminate his career as a man of secrets. On 30 September he wrote from Torquay to Balcarres, blaming Steel-Maitland, the new party chairman, for having disheartened Balfour, and made him sick of politics. Steel-Maitland, a young and zealous new broom, had alarmed his chief with gloomy reports of party morale, and demands for action. 'Now I know my dear man,' Sandars claimed, suggesting that the only way to make Balfour perform well was to make him happy and not nag him. 'Now do what you can to make A.J.B. happy,' urged Sandars, who had not seen or written to Balfour since the day the Parliament Bill was passed, and thus greatly exaggerated the part played by Steel-Maitland as Balfour's new 'confessor'. Balcarres replied to Sandars that Balfour was 'quite explicit in denying that he attached any undue weight to what S.-M. had written'.

SANDARS TO LORD BALCARRES, 5 OCTOBER 1911
A violent and almost insolent letter from Walter Long will seriously contribute to

the Chief's depression. How the letter was written and why it was written passes my comprehension: but the writer – I suppose – must not on certain occasions be taken seriously.[11]

7 OCTOBER 1911

In a letter from Miss Balfour is this sentence. 'Arthur continues well and cheerful, partly I believe because he is more definitely inclining to the course we discussed.' In other words he is making up his mind to retire from the leadership.[12]

9 OCTOBER 1911

A.J.B.'s speech at Haddington seems admirable, and the vigorous criticism of our nefarious government will add heart to our party. He has to speak again twice before the meeting of parliament and if on each occasion he strikes with decision, the clamour of malcontents will be greatly diminished.

10 OCTOBER 1911

Birthday. I am now forty, abandoning the pleasant thirties and henceforward openly addicted to middle age. In myself I feel the change but little: at the same time I am obsessed with regrets that few if any of the trees I hope to plant can grow to comfortable dimensions even if I live to the allotted span. If only opportunity had given me the inclination to begin planting twenty years ago!

LORD BALCARRES TO LADY WANTAGE, 12 OCTOBER 1911

I have spent three or four weekends at Whittingehame but the place is so much crowded by the family that A.J.B. finds it impossible to entertain more than three or four friends at a time. Last time I was there the main house party consisted of four nephews, six nieces, and five brothers and sisters-in-law!

I often wish that a wider circle could find its home at Whittingehame, because the summer and autumn weeks present almost the only chance of talking to A.J.B. when he is not overburdened with business or correspondence. He is an excellent host and I rather fancy likes entertaining in a quiet way – but the conditions are almost impossible for any consistent cultivation of his old friends, many of whom indeed prefer not to go there, for it must be admitted that cross-examination at breakfast time by Lady Frances[13] is rather a burden, and at times a great bore. I gather that she now definitely classes herself with the supporters of the government.

---

[11] Note by Lord Balcarres, 9 October: 'I saw W. Long's letter, in fact the Chief showed it me a few minutes after it arrived – it made a considerable and I fancy a lasting impression on his mind.' Sandars later (11 November) described Long's letter as 'brutal'. But cf. Long's outburst above, 6 July 1911.

[12] Cf. Balfour to Lady Elcho, 8 October 1911: 'I am thinking *most seriously* of resigning my leadership. No one knows this but Alice, Bal, Steel-Maitland and Sandars . . . Bal has persuaded me not to do it *before* the Autumn Session, but I hope to do it soon after.' (Dugdale, *Balfour*, II, 83)

[13] Lady Frances Balfour (1858–1931), fifth daughter of the argumentative and irascible eighth Duke of Argyll (1823–1900), who served in Gladstone's cabinets. She m. 1879 Eustace Balfour (d. 1911),

14 OCTOBER 1911

To Whittingehame – my fourth visit this autumn! I like the place, but I confess that I groan under the feminist propaganda with which the unfortunate guest is bombarded. Lady Frances, and dear Lady Betty,[14] both with big neglected families, are engrossed in aggressive feminism, and don't spare those who after all have some right to be ignored on such matters. A.J.B. it is true ignores them, but Lady Frances in particular, rejoicing in a good voice and an irrepressible bumptiousness constantly drowns him – and instead of A.J.B.'s charming wit and conversation we are afflicted by – well, by quite another style and substance. Lady Frances' daughter by the way, Miss Alison I think, has a pet parrot which has been taught to reiterate the words 'Votes for women? No Never, No Never.' Lady Battersea who is interested in good works gradually got worked up to a state of mental intoxication all about the progress of the sex – until she talked sorry nonsense.

15 OCTOBER 1911

Kirk and regulation walk in the afternoon. Later long and important talk with A.J.B.

Conversation with A.J.B. who says he has further considered matter – has told nobody of his ideas except Miss Balfour – would have told Gerald, but he has been absent from Scotland. Neither does he propose to speak to Alfred Lyttelton (who is in the house).

After further prolonged consideration he sees no cause to modify his desire to be relieved of the leadership.

Evidence multiplies that such a course would be as welcome to others as to himself. A ridiculous vote of censure has just reached him from Junior Imperialists in S. London.

The formation of the Halsbury Club[15] to record and consecrate the defiance of his leadership is one episode which cannot be ignored. Members of this Club differ on all constructive questions, e.g. tariff reform, second chamber, etc. They are united in disapproval of their leader's advice.

A.J.B. recapitulated the reasons for retirement, and added that he had recently consulted his Edinburgh doctor, who though not advising retirement from parliament, says that modifications of its heaviest burdens would improve the Chief's health.

---

brother of the premier. Her daughter was Balfour's biographer. Cf. diary, 30 October 1933: 'Mrs Dugdale whom I used to know as Baffy Balfour asked me to help her in her life of A.J.B. – so I gave her a mass of memoranda and notes of conversations made during the crisis of 1911 – when I failed to keep A.J.B. as our leader.... She was very frank about her mother Lady Frances, and fully realises that A.J.B. was paralysed in her presence, always fearing and not without justice, that Lady F. would give him away to the Asquiths.'

[14] Wife of A.J.B.'s brother Gerald, second Earl of Balfour (1853–1945).

[15] Formed on 7 October 1911.

He says that on these general grounds he is entitled to make a valedictory speech at Leeds: he would not find it necessary to add further reasons – 'but if my old colleagues make it impossible for me to remain leader, I should of course state in my speech that I regret to find I am no longer wanted.'

I said that as soon as the average member discovers his impending retirement, there will be a cohort of politicians crawling on their bellies and imploring him to retain his post.

That may be so, he replied: but my speech will contain no hints and still less any threats. It will simply be a definite announcement of my intention.

He then proceeded to deal with procedure, and in such a manner as to make it clear that he is seriously contemplating retirement... [16]

Who should successor be? Austen Chamberlain and Walter Long are the only possible men. Against Austen it will be said that he comes from Birmingham, that he is Liberal Unionist, that he is neither allied by family tradition or landed estates with the traditional Conservative party – that we are still weighted by the dead hand of Joe.

Walter Long has none of these disqualifications but he possesses every other conceivable one, and on the other hand few effective claims except squiredom and seniority. (Is he older than A.J.B.?)

POSITION OF LORD LANSDOWNE

Lord L. when told, will say he means to retire as well. This would be serious, as marking emphatically a split or a defeat, whereas A.J.B. retiring alone and Lord L. remaining, would dissociate the affair from the Ditcher movement.

A.J.B. is sure Lord L. would consent to retain leadership in the Lords for six months or a year. There would therefore be no occasion for peers to be invited to our meeting. This would simplify matters a good deal, and moreover would confine our selection to the leadership of the opposition in the H. of C., without involving the party as a whole.

A.J.B. by the way fancies that the 1903 chapter in the Duke of Devonshire's life, just about to be published, will revive old controversies to his own detriment – especially if, as he surmises, the volume contains correspondence and memoranda published without his assent. There is certainly one document printed which should never have appeared without consent of Gerald Balfour, who is much annoyed.

The whole conversation was calm and unemotional. I told him that in three weeks time I should be pressing him to reconsider his view, and he replied that by that time a good many others might be doing the same.

...In conversation with Miss Balfour, to whom Mr Balfour seems to have outlined his whole mind, she said that Sir Robert Finlay who was staying at

---

[16] A passage on procedure for electing a successor is omitted.

Whittingehame last week, came away from conversation with Balfour with a distinct idea that a retirement was 'in the air.'

Austen Chamberlain had opposed Balfour over the Parliament Bill, had used strong language about 'disgrace', was a leading light in the Halsbury dinner in July and in the Halsbury Club in October, and knew of F.E. Smith's anti-Balfour intrigues. He also confessed that Balfour's leadership sometimes made him nearly despair, his leader having no comprehension of the way things struck his countrymen. Despite this, he wanted to be reckoned as loyal, and was in fact so reckoned by both Balfour and the Chief Whip. What Austen did not want was either an early retirement, or an open breach; every year that passed made Walter Long, ten years older, less of a possible rival. In August Austen was at pains to impress on Sandars 'the cogency of the Chief staying on', and thought it would be wrong and unfair to leave the party. On 16 October, Austen wrote, offering friendly support in the coming session, especially over the Insurance Bill ('Personally the more I consider the Bill, the less I like it.') If Austen's object was to emerge, as he did, not only with clean hands, but as the successor expected and desired by Balfour, he managed his business well. (His distance from Balfour and his circle emerges in the account of how the resignation was gradually disclosed.) Long, on the other hand, Balfour's apparent supporter in July and August, was rocking the boat in a way designed to act strongly on a man of Balfour's temperament.

A. J. Balfour to Lord Balcarres, 18 October 1911

I send you a characteristic letter from Walter Long.[17] I have not answered it for the fact is I do not quite know how it is to be answered! I certainly do not mean to give him the denial he wants: since in all probability, the invention of the clubs will turn out to be an anticipation of the truth. I can avoid answering him till I get to London, but when he puts a direct question to me (as he certainly will) my course is not so plain.

18 OCTOBER 1911

A letter from Austen Chamberlain who like the rest of us is incensed by Lloyd George's vituperation and is anxious to adopt a far more critical attitude towards the Insurance Bill.

20 OCTOBER 1911

A.J.B. forwards me a rambling tirade from Walter Long, interesting as he says that the London clubs are gossiping about the Chief's retirement which rumour places six weeks hence.

[17] Long's letter said that speculation about Balfour's resignation within six weeks was rife in the clubs, 'and that you are only waiting until you have secured Austen's succession... Of course this is supremely ridiculous'.

233

'Balfour must go'

Reached London early in the morning... lunched with Austen Chamberlain and had a long interview with A.J.B. I shall have to keep a diary of the next month to record all the kaleidoscopic changes I foresee in our domestic political circle. We shall pass through some damnable political situations, but the party as a whole will extricate itself.

He seems in good health and is certainly in excellent spirits – told me by the way that he had said *nothing* to Finlay to excite his apprehensions.

I foresee that in the course of the next few days rumours will become more concrete and multifarious pressure will be brought to bear to make him take a more happy view of the situation. He will find these influences much more potent than any I have been able to exercise.

CONVERSATION WITH AUSTEN CHAMBERLAIN, 22 OCTOBER 1911

Has written to A.J.B. disclaiming all personal motives, says he regrets use of particular phraseology, that he is wholly loyal to the Chief, that he hopes in effect to be forgiven.

I asked about the Halsbury Club. Austen says W. Selborne is the moving spirit, that he, Austen, was not consulted, that there is no leadership question in the Club any more than in the party. That those who control it are really heart and soul with the Chief.

Object of foundation of the Club, which it is intended shall be kept small like the Eighty Club, is to develop the fighting spirit and nothing else. Moreover Selborne was actuated by a desire to control the forward element, which but for this rallying point might have ended in an organised movement against the Chief.

He says that no leader of the Club or movement has been talking about the chief's resignation or replacement. Only one prominent man is responsible for the gossip and intrigue, namely Walter Long.

(There is much truth in this. W. Long has made two or three speeches, partly patronising, partly tutelary, indicating the attitude the Chief should adopt – he has said things about A.J.B. no Diehard has ever expressed, at any rate in public.)

Says that A.J.B.'s resignation would be deplorable – in any case – but assuming that he means to go no worse moment than the present could be chosen. We are still at loggerheads. He should lead us at any rate for a couple of years, fight Home Rule for us, and if he then feels he must retire he would leave the fighting line in a blaze of glory.

(I made no observations, but recalled the Chief's opinion on this very point.)

Austen says that Walter Long has abandoned claims for the leadership, and has settled to put forward Bonar Law as his nominee when a vacancy occurs.

MEMORANDUM, 22 OCTOBER 1911

Conversation with A.J.B. 6 to 7 p.m. Says he has decided to resign. Has now told Alfred Lyttelton, but nobody in addition to those I know.

All the gossip about his resignation is based on *a priori* reasoning which will turn out to be correct.

Alternative to resignation is a party meeting. This connotes an appeal to discipline, or the employment of Harcourtian bludgeoning. He is no friend of party pressure, looks upon his party as free and independent items – will not press them either ad misericordiam or by means of threats.

He still holds that Leeds is the fitting occasion for announcement. But meanwhile – says he won't say he is not going to resign – neither will he tell them yet awhile that he is determined to go. 'It puts me in a most awkward position, stimulates gossip and tempts me to lie. Nothing however will induce me to yield to this temptation. All I shall say is that I am going to make no party statement before Leeds. Perhaps this reticence will make my intention more clear – so be it.'

I told him about the Halsbury Club. He says the explanation of its foundation is deplorably unconvincing.

He has written to Lord Lansdowne but latter is not very well and won't come to town till Thursday.

I told him about the forthcoming meeting at Devonshire House and he told me to attend it.

DIARY, 23 OCTOBER 1911
Important interview with A.J.B.

DIARY, 24 OCTOBER 1911
At one to A.J.B. It is now palpable that he has definitely settled to resign.

MEETING AT DEVONSHIRE HOUSE, 24 OCTOBER 1911, 11.30 AM[18]
St Aldwyn in chair. Curzon, Londonderry, St John Brodrick, Duke of Devonshire, W. Long, Steel-Maitland, self, Alfred Lyttelton, Bonar Law, Chaplin, Lord Derby, Akers Douglas.

Curzon took lead, said it was necessary to make a move to support leaders: that ostracism was in progress, that Halsbury Club though not ostensibly disloyal had enlisted all malcontents, etc. Proposals a) party meeting b) meetings of either house c) private deputation to A.J.B.

At the conversation it was clear that assuming Halsburyite leaders to be loyal, some of them should be approached with a view to joint representation to A.J.B.

Evidently a strong belief in party meeting.

Derby said after conversation with A.J.B. last night, he came to conclusion that the Chief meant to resign.

Alfred Lyttelton (who knows situation) said he did not believe the chief would attend a party meeting about his own leadership, as he would either have to appeal ad misericordiam, or else employ threats, neither of which would suit his

---

[18] A meeting of leaders other than the leading Diehards.

temperament. I said, no party meeting can be called except by myself, and I can only act on instruction of my leader.

Bob Douglas concurred. Then proposed to have an unofficial party meeting in A.J.B.'s absence. I said this would lead to recrimination (so it would – there would be a beastly row).

At 1.0 I left to go to Carlton Gardens. Nothing concrete occurred afterwards except that gathering is to be resumed on 24th – after conversation with Carson etc.

Conversation with A.J.B. (Sandars present.)
Told him roughly what had passed. He said that he had made no observation to Derby to justify his induction, but that none the less the induction was correct.

I repeated what F. E. Smith told me yesterday, namely that as a concrete test of his fidelity to Mr Balfour's leadership, he, F.E., would give up a £200 brief on Nov. 15–16 to go down to Leeds to oppose hostile motion of Maxse against A.J.B.

2 p.m. Met Derby at Carlton. Told him I had told the Chief what he said at Devonshire House. Eddy said that the Chief had forgotten his conversation in which the phrase occurred (relating to the Home Rule campaign next year), 'I shall not be leader then.'

CONVERSATION WITH J.S. SANDARS, 24 OCTOBER 1911
Says the Chief has definitely settled to retire, and the only outstanding point is date and circumstance.

J.S.S. has strongly objected to the Leeds meeting: a) a leader does not announce resignation to a party gathering. He can do it to his constituents, to the City which elected him at a moment of severe depression. Leeds is a moment of outlook and encouragement, not a proper occasion for a political funeral. The new leader not the old one should rally the party at this annual assembly.

b) Moreover Leeds (16 November) is too late. There will be three weeks of intrigue. Promptitude is imperative. c) He could either do it to a party meeting, which is open to many objections – or in a letter to Lord Lansdowne which would be published in the press. This would give finality – would prevent speeches which are either hostile or flattering – would allow him all the necessary freedom of argument without any of the other disadvantages.

d) Lord Lansdowne comes to town Thursday. A.J.B. has been advised by J.S.S. to go to Bowood for Sunday, and thereafter to publish his decision at the earliest possible moment. J.S.S. says the Chief is impressed by the argument, and indeed I myself think it is sound.

CONVERSATION WITH HARRY CHAPLIN, 9 P.M.
Says that A.J.B.'s three speeches in Scotland, together with those delivered here yesterday and today, show him to be not only the best living parliamentarian, but also the only conceivable leader of the party.

His resignation is unthinkable, would be disastrous to the party, and must therefore be prevented. (At the same time Chaplin does not believe it to be imminent.)

The general lobby impression is that A.J.B. is so superior to possible rivals that talk about resignation is mere speculation. None the less the Chief has told at least a dozen people, several of them gossips. Hence danger of a newspaper scoop – and importance of promptitude. This is what J.S.S. urges with great skill and pertinacity.

DIARY, 25 OCTOBER 1911

With A.J.B. at twelve. Yesterday he made a good speech. This afternoon his criticism of the government proposals for dealing with their programme was overwhelming. I heard many members say that no more formidable indictment was conceivable.

So I pride myself on having persuaded him to adopt a strong line in the three speeches delivered in Scotland since the prorogation – followed up by two admirable attacks in parliament. He seems so indispensable to the party, and his merits are so fully acknowledged that even if he abandoned the leadership tomorrow nobody could allege that an alteration was demanded by the party in consequence of defective power or intellect. He stands supreme in our ranks. He has made this more obvious than ever during the last fortnight and though these recent speeches will make us all the more dismayed at his departure, I shall at least have served him well by forcing him to invest his own exit with the display of his irreplaceable qualities. It is true that events of these last few days will not make the task of his successor more easy. But I do not want the new leader to think (as he would have done in August) that he can easily equal even if he does not surpass the achievements of A.J.B. It is well that the successor should have to win his spurs and realise the power of his predecessor. This will stimulate the activity of our new leader.

Who shall he be? For my part I can only look to Austen Chamberlain. Walter Long is hopeless, impossible. He is stale and turgid: his temper is peppery and twelve months hence will be uncontrollable. Bonar Law won't do. He seems almost to be retiring from politics so sporadic is his attendance, and so reluctant is he to take an active part in our work. Moreover he is more reserved and unapproachable every day. Wyndham is too flighty, Alfred Lyttelton too sentimental, F.E. Smith too inexperienced, Harry Chaplin fifty years too old – and so forth.

NOTES, 27 OCTOBER 1911

Conversation with Alfred Lyttelton, 5 p.m. Says that Bonar Law approached Carson at request of Devonshire House group, that Carson did not acquiesce in the proposal to make a joint representation to A.J.B. to retain leadership. That at a subsequent conference Carson repeated his unwillingness to take this responsibility upon himself. Hence A.L. feels for the first time some doubt as to Carson's courage, for his loyalty is unimpeachable.

A. Lyttelton was going to see Austen C. who he thinks does not know the whole position. If Austen would join in a representation to A.J.B., good would ensue. In the first place the Chief would be gratified, even if as seems inevitable he declined to accede to their request: and secondly Austen would be relieved from the charge (highly probable in the event of a crisis) of having been actuated by personal motives – a charge which would damage his candidature for the leadership. A. Lyttelton looks upon him as the only possible successor to A.J.B.

Walter Long is really out of the question.

Bonar Law is interested in subjects, not in politics. Whole branches of public life are a closed book to him, whereas Austen, approachable, interestable, and wedded to the whole field of political thought, has the further advantage of varied experience: whip, treasury, postmaster-general, admiralty, exchequer – quite a large range.

Memorandum from Sandars, 27 October: 'Lord Lansdowne seems to have been complacent – no simultaneous action to be anticipated.' So much the better. It makes it feasible for Mr Balfour to retire on personal grounds, whereas a joint resignation would mean a huge upheaval. Lyttelton says Lord L. has the Whig mind and is still ambitious – though his health is not robust.

MEMORANDUM, 30 OCTOBER 1911

Conversation with Alfred Lyttelton – says that on Friday evening last Austen C. was more than friendly – and proposes at meeting of the Halsbury Club to make it perfectly clear that no movement against the Chief is on foot.

Conversation with Akers Douglas and Sandars. They have both seen the Chief. A.J.B. is more disinclined to make an epistolary announcement. Present idea to address constituents ending with a note of coming triumph: but leaving his leadership intestate.

Dates to be arranged. Leeds meeting is on 16th. Time must therefore be given to new leader to make his preparations for meeting the party there.

Suppose speech is made on Friday afternoon, the 10th, the H. of C. party meeting could take place on Monday 13th. The house would not be sitting during interval, which in many ways would be a help.

Mr Balfour goes to Lord Londonderry tomorrow. Says he must tell Lady Londonderry: Sandars has already lied to her, and the Chief says he has already had to do the same thing elsewhere.

Lord Lansdowne at Hackwood this weekend with Austen and others – a mélange of diehard and live-long. Says there was a distinct sniff in the air of resignation – though nothing definite was known or stated.

On Friday or Saturday (3–4 November) the Chief would go to Tring – houseful of gossips who can retain no secret other than financial. Monday 6th: nonconformist dinner, Wednesday 8th: dinner to Hayes Fisher, Friday 10th? constituents.

I am afraid it will be most difficult to maintain reserve. The press (naturally enough) has rediscovered that the Chief is indispensable – but a week hence too many people will know the dispositions to make the preservation of secrecy possible.

MEMORANDUM, I NOVEMBER 1911

J. S. Sandars had long conversation today with Lord Lansdowne, and found him much more inclined to insist upon simultaneous resignation. Sandars strongly urged the undesirability of this, on the obvious ground that such a course would make a political crisis, and remove the whole basis of personal argument on which A.J.B. is inclined to rest his case.

Lord Lansdowne however was very sniffy. The Chief had assured him that an avoidance of simultaneity was alone necessary, and that if he really means to resign also Lord L. would lose little by deferring action until the spring.

Lord L. opines that Austen C. would succeed A.J.B. in the Commons, and apparently that Curzon would lead the opposition in the Lords. (Yesterday Selborne was elected to the Carlton which rather surprised Lord Lansdowne. Pike Pease is to be elected also. I asked Austen C. if he would do the same – and he said on general grounds he would like to, but wanted to think it over.)

MEMORANDUM, 2 NOVEMBER 1911

Conversation with J. S. Sandars. He saw Lord Revelstoke, who in turn saw Lord Lansdowne: and Lord Revelstoke impressed Lord L. with the purely party aspect of the case, namely the grave danger of simultaneous resignation, and also the advantage of Mr Balfour's resignation now, in preference to the spring. (This on the familiar ground of giving the successor a fair chance of establishing his position during a quiet time.)

Lord Lansdowne seemed to some extent impressed – but evidently has not assented to A.J.B.'s proposition.

I saw him on other matters, and found him exceedingly cross.

Austen C. tells me that on hearing of Selborne's election to the Carlton Club, he told Lord L. and suggested that they should both become candidates together. Lord L. again sniffy, and declined to be nominated himself, though not objecting to Austen's selection.

Selborne on the other hand says he wanted all the Liberal Unionists to join him, or at any rate a considerable number, but that Walter Long said he objected and that the committee 'would not stand it', i.e. would blackball freely. (This before the Parliament Bill row.)

NOTES, FRIDAY 3 NOVEMBER 1911

Mr Balfour returns from Wynyard[19] tonight. Lady Elcho, Hugh Cecil, Lady Ilchester, and Lady Londonderry between them must have gathered a good deal. None of them would refrain from asking him point blank as to the truth of the

[19] Londonderry's seat in co. Durham.

rumours which must have reached them. Gossip will therefore spread. Moreover the visit to Tring will not help to maintain reserve.

Wilfrid Ashley told me tonight that Sir Ernest Cassel wired for him to go to Newmarket on some urgent affair. Wilfrid could not go owing to his shooting party at Broadlands – I suspect Cassel has scented trouble.

NOTES, SATURDAY 4 NOVEMBER 1911

J. S. Sandars wires at 10.30 a.m., 'Events are moving fast'.

Meanwhile it is extraordinary how little the H. of C. knows, and how few seem to expect any crisis. Austen C. seems to be quite in the dark, likewise Selborne. None the less many, especially people outside parliamentary circles, are acquainted with the situation: I am agreeably surprised at their reticence, but I look forward with apprehension to a newspaper coup.

NOTES, MONDAY 6 NOVEMBER 1911

Conversation with J. S. Sandars, 1.30 p.m. Mr Balfour will not come to H. of C. today (is now with Lord Lansdowne). He is more severe on the Ditchers than before.

Those who know situation are roughly as follows: Lord Lansdowne, Lady Lansdowne, Lord Londonderry, Lady Londonderry, Lady Elcho (she is to tell George Wyndham), Akers Douglas, J. S. Sandars, Short, myself, Miss Balfour (partly), Alfred Lyttelton, Lord Rothschild, G. Curzon, Austen Chamberlain (was warned by J.S.S.),[20] Steel-Maitland (partly – not quite up to date), Lord Midleton, Lord Derby, Walter Long to be told this afternoon, Finlay (in all probability – must have guessed much), Bonar Law, Selborne (I think so, but not quite certain).

Conversation with J. S. Sandars, 5 p.m. At Halsbury Club meeting at noon today, a resolution was passed, and Lord Halsbury has communicated it to the Chief, expressing confidence in the leadership of Lord Lansdowne and Mr Balfour.

This resolution took two hours, which shows the troubled conditions of their minds. Doubtless they kept saying cui bono, and asked what impression such an announcement would make upon their supporters.

Austen C. and Lord Halsbury threatened to resign unless it was passed – and it appears that the situation is now known to Lord Halsbury, George Wyndham, and F. E. Smith – to five leading Ditchers. (Carson also must know).

They therefore will begin to make their combination.

Bonar Law it is opined would like to compete for the leadership.

As things are now so near publicity perhaps it would be advisable to hurry forward the resignation.

9 p.m. Wilfrid Ashley tells me that Sir Ernest Cassel knows, and had told him. How Cassel found out is not revealed, but his information was good, as he said our

---

[20] But cf. Lansdowne to Balfour, 2 November 1911: 'Austen . . . was dismayed when I told him that you had been seriously considering the question of retirement.' Newton, *Lansdowne*, 433.

party meeting was to be held on Tuesday. (It will probably be Monday, but his informant must have been close to headquarters.)

NOTES, TUESDAY 7 NOVEMBER 1911

1.30 p.m. Sandars has seen Long who wants delay.

3.45 p.m. Told my colleagues situation.

4.00 p.m. Interviews with W. Long and Chaplin. Lasted $1\frac{1}{2}$ hours. They are aghast – say long delay must ensue. Must postpone mass meeting at Leeds. I urged need for promptitude – delay means lobbying and intrigue. Lords to be eaten up with it. Great press campaign.

They suggested say Tuesday week for party meeting. I demurred.

At the end Chaplin saw my view clearly. W. Long shaken in his view – but not by any means convinced. Admitted that chief whip would have to summon meeting. Say they both advocated resignation by letter. Chief refused point blank.

5 p.m. Sandars sent in to say that Chief has fixed tomorrow at 4 p.m. for City meeting.

7.45 p.m. Interview with W. Long and A. Lyttelton. Both admit that immediate announcement is preferable to delay. But both – and they say A.J.B. agrees (? also Akers Douglas) claim that whip has no status. Privy councillors must meet. I said who? there are over 20. They said ex-cabinet, or rather shadow cabinet. That includes me, Steel-Maitland, Bonar Law, and F.E. Intolerable. They say this is in accordance to precedent of Harcourt's replacement by Campbell-Bannerman. I said it is difficult for me to take orders from Harry Chaplin.

It would be a caucus meeting at which each candidate would be required to urge his own claims and vote on his own merits. They said Radicals encountered and overcame same difficulty.

I again urged dangers of delay – reopening of old wounds, intrigue at Leeds, abandonment of mass meeting, etc. Both refused to see any merit in my argument.

Walter Long threatened: said if meeting were called for Tuesday (a fortiori Monday 13th) he would consider it his duty to propose adjournment or to leave meeting as a protest and to take many with him.

I had told him there were four possible men: himself, Carson, Austen, Bonar Law. I don't assume F. E. Smith is so unwise as to compete.

9 p.m. Conversation with my colleagues (Pike Pease, Ned Talbot, Bridgeman, Wilfrid Ashley, Eyres Monsell, Henderson – Peter Sanders is in Somerset). They have considered my observations this afternoon. Each agrees that despatch is advisable. Each unmistakably holds that Austen C. should succeed to leadership.

J. S. Sandars at 9.15 p.m.: Carson was told by J.S.S. this evening. King knows. All nieces know. Lady Frances will be told tomorrow at lunch. Desboroughs were told two days ago.

11.30 p.m.: see letter to Sandars. Impasse – drift – danger. Walter Long means to delay indefinitely. He must beware or else the party will take the matter out of the hands of the mandarins!

'Balfour must go'

On 7 November Asquith, speaking not in the House but to a deputation, announced his intention of simplifying the existing franchise laws, creating universal suffrage based on automatic registration of voters. This 'democratic' move was quite unexpected. A cabinet minister, Buxton, said that it came to him as a tremendous surprise, and that neither he nor his colleagues in the cabinet were aware of the decision; while the next day the King told Balfour that the announcement had not been communicated to him by the government, showing, as Balfour observed, that the decision was not that of the cabinet.

BALCARRES TO SANDARS, 11.30 P.M., 7 NOVEMBER 1911 (TUESDAY)

I telephoned to W. Long suggesting that the nine Shadow Cabinet M.P.s should meet tomorrow evening at 5, to consider procedure and issue instructions. I was met by a resolute non possumus.

Harry Chaplin came here late – much upset and could give no indication of what he thought best.

DIARY, 8 NOVEMBER 1911 (WEDNESDAY)

Arthur Balfour this afternoon announced his resignation of the leadership. The news descended upon the party as a bombshell. Stupefaction ensued. My record of what occurred will be found in the notes and impressions I jotted down from hour to hour.

NOTES, 8 NOVEMBER 1911 (WEDNESDAY)

...Conversation with Austen C., Walter Long, and Chaplin.

By 4.15 p.m. a vast preponderance of members had urged me to hold party meeting before Leeds: at least 60 men, many of them prominent and old stagers expressed this view with great decision.[21] Only one took a different view, namely Henry Bentinck who said go and be damned.

This manifestation was so spontaneous and so widespread that Chaplin and Co. readily abandoned their idea of delay: especially as it was feared that the disorganisation of our party, as displayed by inability to select a leader, would gravely imperil the acceptance of the reorganisation scheme.

I was accordingly authorised, so far as they were concerned, to issue invitations for Monday or Tuesday. After consultation with my colleagues we settled Monday.

W. Long and Austen both agreed to take no active or personal steps in canvassing. Alike they both agreed to abide loyally by any verdict given by M.P.s.

* * *

Austen – favoured by Goulding.

5.30 p.m. Helmsley – says voting must be by ballot. I agreed – but he says that there must be a vote, i.e. everybody must be compelled to signify his view, without

[21] List of names given in MS.

anybody being proposed. This involves handwriting – Helmsley probably favours W. Long.

6.0 p.m. issued telegram to members to attend at midday Monday.

Meysey-Thomson also wants ballot – indeed a second ballot. Favours Chamberlain.

6.30 p.m. A memorial being signed to ask the Chief to reconsider his decision.

7.0 p.m. Helmsley produced a list of 33 names of members who support ballot. They are not clear if they require a second ballot. The objections of delay in the latter case are serious, and involve the publication of the name of the defeated candidate.

Irish Unionists favour second ballot probably because they want to vote for Carson, but consider that he has no direct chance, and wish therefore their votes to be automatically transferred to Walter Long, their ex-chairman.

7.15 p.m. Clement Hill says each man must vote for one name, and that the man who gets the largest number must act as leader.

7.30 p.m. Elibank says that a few years ago CB predicted that Walter Long would succeed A.J.B. Willie Bridgeman says that parties are pretty evenly divided between Walter Long and Austen C. Harry Forster favours Chamberlain.

9.0 p.m. Ormsby-Gore wants second ballot. Hasn't made up his mind about leader.

9.15 p.m. Col. Williams favours Long. Says he wants the party to be led by a gentleman.

9.30 p.m. Meysey-Thompson wants a ballot because he is Liberal Unionist and would therefore have to support Austen – but really desires to vote for Walter Long.

Helmsley also frankly admits that he wants a ballot because Walter Long's partisans are not organised; hence that candidature suffers and the ballot might redress the difficulty.

Claud Hamilton thinks that Lord Robert Cecil should be leader. Unfortunately Bob won't be an M.P. by Monday next.

DIARY, 9 NOVEMBER 1911 (THURSDAY)
At the 1900 Club Claude Hay told me about yesterday's meeting – twenty or thirty people present in a grubby little city office at the end of a squalid passage – no convenience for the reporters, a telephone bell which refused to be silenced – a good deal of emotion in the Chief's speech with those occasional hesitations which mar the effect of his public speeches. It seems to have been a curious environment for the most impressive and far-reaching of his great efforts. Jack Sandars says he was away from Carlton Gardens only about seventy minutes – so the disagreeable circumstance of the resignation was reduced to the minimum.

And how the Rod of Aaron has swallowed up all the other budding staves! The great Tariff Reform meeting at the White City last night, a function of remarkable dimensions, is this morning dismissed by forty or fifty lines in the newspapers. In his exit the Chief has imposed his magnetic power upon press and public alike.

For days he has been telling his friends of his determination to resign. The secret was on many tongues, and it could not have been much longer kept: that it has been preserved inviolate so long is a tribute to the affectionate fidelity of all concerned. As for the public at large, the news came with dramatic suddenness – a profound surprise, for no newspaper achieved a scoop in this connection. Very angry were the editors in consequence.

For this I take some credit to myself. I pressed very strongly when he told me of his determination two months ago, that resignation was out of the question until he had delivered further speeches. He has made six since that date, and the two in the House of Commons were so admirable that nobody dreamt they could be his last. Moreover he has revitalised a reputation much diminished in certain quarters by his alleged weakness in August.[22]

NOTES, THURSDAY 9 NOVEMBER 1911

Conversation with Austen C. Told him proposal as to ballot. Said he did not care to intervene on a matter of procedure. Said that if parties were closely divided he would be prepared to withdraw in favour of a neutral candidate, assuming W. Long did the same.

1 p.m. Conversation with W. Long. Agreed provisionally to foregoing. Said he was willing to retire altogether – and not to stand for leadership – but his friends say it would be a betrayal. Is so worried that he means to go to the country tomorrow.

1.45–2.30 At Carlton betting is 6 to 4 in W. Long's favour.

4.0 p.m. My colleagues agree to idea of ballot – object strongly to transferable vote – say we should reduce candidates to two, and then settle offhand without speeches.

4.30 p.m. Astor says that Garvin has seen Bonar Law who means to stand. Thinks he has been persuaded by Benn (? which) and by Sir Max Aitken. Garvin and Astor prefer Chamberlain. Latter withdraws his name from the ballot memorial as he finds it is simply being used as an engine on behalf of Walter.

A. Lyttelton seems to prefer Bonar Law – as he doesn't much like Austen, but cannot believe Walter Long's temperament can stand the nerve strain after his long illness.

5.0 p.m. Rutherford of Darwen says leader must be a Churchman. I replied that that disqualifies three out of four of our candidates: and moreover that my beloved Chief was a nonconformist.

5.45 p.m. Chaplin concurs in ballot if desired by our men, but says he hates it for parliamentary purposes, a fortiori for use at a private club gathering. Thinks that

[22] Cf. Crawford's diary, 23 March 1933: 'The chief item remaining clear in my mind was my insistence that if A.J.B. really determined to resign, he should do so immediately after making a good fighting speech. He demurred – I would not yield; he consented and played up; and my manoeuvre revived a waning reputation.'

both Austen and Walter Long would withdraw if Bonar Law could unite the party.

6.30 p.m. Carson says he has definitely refused nomination; is devoted to Ireland; is at the command of Ulster – health bad. Says he prevented his Unionists (Irish) from expressing any opinion on leadership.

Says that W. Long is quixotic, chivalrous. That if Austen offered to withdraw in his favour, W. Long might in turn withdraw himself in favour of Austen! Carson says that the idea should not be dismissed, though there is a risk that Austen would be bilked.

6.45 p.m. G. Younger says the essential thing is to avoid speechmaking at the meeting. Duke agrees.

6.50 p.m. Goulding tells me officially that much against his wishes and advice, Bonar Law is determined to stand. (B. Law is acute, on certain subjects excellent, but lacks breadth of view – has never sat in a cabinet – has little departmental experience, and so far as I gather, about the most indolent member of the Front Bench – bar George Wyndham).

6.55 p.m. F. E. Smith says that some people have asked him if he would like a nomination. Says he isn't such a damned fool.

7.10 Davison Dalyell on dilemmas which can arise from transferable votes – amusing.

7.30 Steel-Maitland says W. Long's appointment would make work at Central Office most difficult.

. . . 9.30 Ned Talbot says that he would vote for W. Long in preference to Bonar Law. I am not at all sure he is right.

NOTES, FRIDAY 10 NOVEMBER 1911
11.0 am Conversation with Garvin.

12.15 p.m. Austen C. says he has considered question fully – cannot withdraw in favour of W. Long. But is willing to do so for Bonar Law – and suggests that if W. Long agrees, Bonar Law should be proposed by W. Long, seconded by himself, Austen, and thus unanimity would be secured.

Austen C. added that although he would like to be leader, such a responsibility, involving as it would the abandonment of certain earnings, while increasing his personal expenditure, would entail serious financial sacrifice.

12.30 p.m. Conversation at Eaton Square with W. Long. I told him what had passed. He said he would cordially agree, and would let Chamberlain know. He also said that many of his friends would regret the decision not to stand, but that the unity of the party made this course necessary. He has the highest regard for Bonar Law's capacity, notwithstanding his short experience as minister. Told me to announce the fact.

2.30 p.m. Audley Square (could not catch Bonar Law before.) B.L. said that the proposal took him rather by surprise, and that he could not answer offhand.

He was very frank. Said that he had definitely determined to stand, even though it would involve his defeat. He almost indicated that refusal to stand at this juncture when being pressed to do so by his friends would remove him from the list of potential candidates when a subsequent vacancy might occur.

Said that he did not really feel himself fitted for the post from inexperience. I replied that as he had entered on a candidature, ex hypothesi, he had considered his claims of some weight. He agreed, but repeated that his shortcomings were numerous – that as a widower and humble in means he could not entertain etc.

At one moment I wondered if he lacked courage for the immediate crisis – which brought my mind back to an earlier impression that his candidature was to establish a qualification for the future.

He was to go to see Austen C. who will doubtless press him to accept.

3.15 p.m. Returned to the lobby – the news has percolated – as an unofficial item. Many men look upon the solution as good, others as v. bad, notably W. Long's friends. I gathered some into my room and talked it over with them. Their argument was that a) we are choosing third best man (inevitable in face of conflict – has repeatedly occurred, but unity adds enormously to his qualifications), b) we want a county gentleman, as we are strong in the shires (W. H. Smith again – we want a town man as we are weak in the burghs), c) B. Law can't entertain – occupies no great social position – well, well, d) lack of experience (ten years only in parliament, but his value was measured by the fact that after two years he secured office). No allegation of indolence was made against him.

e) Last and chief objection: that B. Law would not be the free selection of the party, that his choice is 'arranged', undemocratic, etc....[23]

5.45 p.m. Oxford and Cambridge Club. J. S. Sandars says that if needful I could state on my own responsibility that A.J.B. would not return to our leadership. Says that the influence of Max Aitken on Bonar Law is not good, and that the way in which the *Daily Express* is promoting that candidature is American – and sinister...

6.15 p.m. Carlton. Col. Challoner says that no prominent Unionist would have supported Austen! I dare say some people believe it, but how can such a singular view be held?

8.45 p.m. B. Law says he has seen both W. Long and Austen, that both were as nice as possible, and that he feels he cannot refuse to accept their proposal, and he hopes that all will pass off quietly. I told him that the most advanced protagonists on either side would be disappointed, but that the party will see that unity is really the crucial thing.[24]

One problem which confronted the Chief Whip in managing the election was how to scotch suggestions that Balfour should reconsider, an idea which might have led to complications and delay even if there was no question of its succeeding. Sandars, who had a long talk with Balfour before he left for the country on Wednesday, said afterwards, 'To ask him to reconsider is futile. He resigned with inflexible determination which no

---

[23] A passage rebutting this idea on predictable lines is omitted.

[24] Some concluding notes on press releases, etc., are omitted.

argument could shake.' Sandars was particularly bitter about Long, of all people, appealing to Balfour to remain. To clinch matters, Sandars telephoned Balfour and at midday on the 11th received the desired telegram in reply saying, 'Reconsideration impossible'. Sandars also urged Balcarres to oppose Hugh Cecil's suggestion of Lansdowne as leader of the whole party, not just of the peers. His reasons were Lansdowne's bad health, his Whig refusal to join the Carlton, the offence he would give to the diehards, his violent opposition to an elective second chamber which would probably lead to his resignation if that became party policy, his view that he was a stopgap for Curzon, his mediocre platform abilities, and the fact that the choice would appear undemocratic. Balcarres wrote (10 November) to Hugh Cecil firmly opposing any idea of promoting Lansdowne to the leadership of the whole party.

NOTES, SATURDAY 11 NOVEMBER 1911

J.S.S. says Lady Londonderry is fulminating because B. Law isn't a country magnate.

J.S.S. doesn't think the Chief will ever again take part in H. of C. unless on an occasion of exceptional importance. He is not a newspaper reader, and will soon get out of touch – and once having lost the hang of things, will hesitate before reappearing on a stage which he once knew so well. New tastes and occupations – the completion of his dry economic researches, some philosophic speculations, golf, Whittingehame, etc., will absorb him and make his re-entry into politics impossible.

My recollection of conversations in the autumn differs from this – for he then looked forward with pleasure to excursions into the Commons, though he forswore any platform speeches.

Circumstances however will probably justify J.S.S.'s prediction, and in any case they spring from the most recent conversation. If things go well with us, the Chief will keep away lest embarrassment should attend his re-entry. If things go ill, his loyalty to his successor may well make him feel that his adventitious support will do more ill than good.

NOTES, SUNDAY 12 NOVEMBER 1911

Conversation with Bonar Law, 12–1. Among those who asked him to stand were the two Benns, Remnant, Worthington-Evans, Gilbert Parker, Baird, Griffith-Boscawen, and oddly enough, W. Peel.

I told him the full situation. Said there was undoubted discontent among those who think they are baulked of their prey! At first he had thought of attending the meeting, but I told him that was impossible, for it would curtail freedom of debate. He proposes however to be at the Club, so that if need be he could attend the gathering, either to withdraw a candidature, to agree in postponement, or to return thanks and ask for assistance.

Says that he increasingly feels the sense of responsibility, especially on such matters as India, Defence, Foreign Affairs and those problems which never having sat in a cabinet he has never heard properly discussed. This no doubt is his one source of weakness, but he has time to learn, and I fancy will receive the help of very willing colleagues. (He would have been in the cabinet had it not been for the extraordinary appointment of the present Lord Salisbury to the Board of Trade.[25])

Says he wants a whip to help while looking out for a confidential secretary – suggests Eyres Monsell for the former post and Baird for the latter. Both would do well.

He will not really regret a hostile decision, for he has received a magnificent advertisement in the press, hasn't made enemies in the process, and is young enough to bide his time. He thinks F. E. Smith has most to fear from him.

A widower with half a dozen children and a big rambling house, with an immense garden, he views with apprehension the necessity for a removal to a more central place. Certainly he lives a longish way beyond Cromwell Road.

He said that if elected the Leeds meeting would cause him difficulties, as he would have no time for proper consultation with his colleagues, and would be expected to make a great declaration of policy.

I replied that he would throw himself on the indulgence of his audience at the start, by saying that he could not offer considered pronouncements on a variety of subjects (which he would not specify. They are referendum, second chamber, manhood suffrage, payment of members, food taxes).

His audience would understand and sympathise, and I fully believe that on normal politics and dealing with subjects about which our opinions do not conflict, he would make a magnificent speech and receive a tremendous reception.

He looks forward with great interest, and with growing confidence, but is still apprehensive. Garvin said the other day to me that during the last few months Bonar Law after a long period of depression during which he has been comparing himself with himself, is rapidly emerging a greater man from despondency. Certainly the atmosphere of Pembroke Lodge, the widower's home, is wan, cheerless, dejected. Perhaps Garvin is right and that this interval had made a statesman: and if his grasp of Weltpolitik develops as his treatment of commercial matters has done, we need not face the future with alarm.

But is his temperament, apart from his capacities, thoroughly solid? Harry Forster says 'he would prefer W. Long with all his absurdities to any whisperer.' Bonar Law does whisper, and whispers into the ear of Sir Max Aitken whose judgment in the future must not weigh unduly with a House of Commons leader – if such he prove to be.

... Harry Chaplin who came to see me at 5.0, having been absent, is going to see Lady Londonderry with whom he is much annoyed, for her chatter has been both merciless and ill-conceived. (Harry, by the way, says the referendum must go, and B. Law is inclined to agree.)

Talked to George Cave who will pour oil on troubled waters if necessary. Pollock

[25] In 1905

seems friendly. The Viscount who is absorbed by the problem of placing 250 chairs in the Carlton smoking room, says that B. Law is a slacker – well I have often thought the same, but his domestic affliction must explain much of his indolence.

Lonsdale, yesterday afternoon quite furious at the tertium quid, wrote me a pleasant letter volunteering his help, and I have found that other minds have been modified in the same direction. Ronaldshay, however, very obstinate, and Helmsley too. Billy Gore always ready for a shindy.

Helmsley has great ability and much self-confidence. I have talked to him a hundred times – he is the only unionist member who has never asked my advice, though his is always placed at my disposal.

I make no forecast of tomorrow's meeting: but there is always a danger that an important person will change his mind.

NOTES, MONDAY 13 NOVEMBER 1911

Many solutions of the problem had been suggested. Some thought the Speaker[26] should resign and take our leadership. Such a course is impossible on more counts than one – for the Speaker during the last six years has been in the confidence of the govt and could not lead our party without a serious breach of honourable obligations.

George Cave's[27] name was suggested as an off-chance; others thought Robert Cecil[28] would do. The latter however happens to be a free-trader and is disqualified not being (as yet) an MP.

Col. Williams[29] supported Walter Long on various grounds – and was much influenced by the fact that though Walter is a strong tariff reformer, tariff reform would not be unduly pressed. A poor compliment alike to Walter's conviction and capacity.

MEETING AT CARLTON CLUB, 13 NOVEMBER 1911

Well attended, I think 231 present.

Chaplin began in a happy vein. Received a good reception, which at one or two phrases suggested enthusiasm.

W. Long. Good start – warmed to his subject – good sense, and fine sentiment. His reception was tremendous.

Austen C. equally warm reception, but not quite so good a speech. There was a reference to respective merits which was not apt. Moreover too much was put on record. None the less a good speech, and favourably received.

[26] Mr Lowther was the *Spectator*'s choice.

[27] George Cave, first Viscount Cave (1856–1928); entered parliament, 1906; Home Secretary 1916–19, Lord Chancellor 1922–8.

[28] Lord R. Cecil had lost his seat at the December 1910 election. He returned to parliament at the Hitchin by-election, 23 November 1911.

[29] Col. R. Williams, MP (Cons.) Dorset W. since 1895.

'Balfour must go'

Chaplin put the closure by consent, the most masterly touch of our whole proceedings.

By a nice stroke it was Carson who withdrew and introduced Bonar Law to the meeting.

By this time all doubts and hesitations had vanished. On entering Bonar Law had an ovation – all stood and cheered, with one exception, namely Banbury who remained seated in the front row. This caused comment afterwards.

B. Law made quite a good speech – it must be remembered that his difficulty was great, not being attuned to the tone of the meeting, for he had heard no speeches.

H. Chaplin – his message to A.J.B. was a great gesture.

Beresford moved a vote of thanks – made us laugh. Frank Mildmay about the senior unofficial unionist seconded. Meeting lasted 55 minutes.

On breaking up many men consented to sink their differences and to work harmoniously under the new leader.

At night the Oldham victory was announced.

... At times there was an emotional throb in the voice, but the speakers retained much self-control. There was never anything in the nature of excitement.

Up till the last moment there was a real risk that one indiscreet comment, or one pointed question might have given rise to debate which, once started, could not readily have been controlled. The result of any discussion whatever would have been wounding.

W. Long made the best speech in his life. Harry Chaplin never excelled himself in deportment.

Too many compliments were paid to me. This in a sense was tactless as it depreciated the personal responsibility of the two protagonists. I have learnt much during this week of stress. Never once have I lost my temper or displayed annoyance.

I put every man on his honour, whatever may have been his motives or desires.

I have used oblique flattery in the process: and I have throughout kept my nerve.

On the other hand many people now probably look upon me as an intriguer and wirepuller – not justly – but that is the penalty of a whip who carries instructions to their conclusion.

VIII

The impact of Bonar Law

Bonar Law's entourage – weakness of the opposition in foreign
affairs – Lansdowne on party management in the Lords – the party conference at
Leeds – Bonar Law prompted to speak on agriculture – Balfour's future – Balfour
on Anglo-French relations – dramatic change of political atmosphere – Bonar
Law's secretarial arrangements – Bonar Law on Max Aitken – Bonar Law
shrinks from difficulties – impressions of Bonar Law's first session – retrospect of
the year 1911 – a Bonar Law dinner – Law's gaffe on the Insurance
Act – discussion on food taxes – Balfour and Bonar Law compared – massive
destruction of Balfour's papers – shadow cabinet on food taxes – the coal
strike – fusion with Liberal Unionists – Balfour's return – the decline of
patriarchal relations in Wigan – shadow cabinet on food taxes – the coal
strike – the Duchess of Buccleuch's strictness – female suffrage and the
Irish – Balfour on Bonar Law – upheaval at the Carlton Club – Wigan strikers go
into business – Elibank's retirement – Ulster 'no mere matter of bluff' – Asquith's
extravagance – corrupt ministers – Bonar Law's resentment of Asquith – Asquith's
escapade in Venice – politicians ruined by drugs – analysis of Bonar Law's
success – nature of the Whips' work – Liberal financial jobbery.

*The aftermath of Bonar Law's election left few immediate difficulties. There followed
indeed a short period with a distinct character of its own, a period of Unionist revival in
which the constitutional and leadership crisis was a thing of the past, while Home Rule
still lay in the future. There was a buoyancy in the air such as Unionists had not known
since 1903. For the Chief Whip, there were some minor tasks, opposing the publication of
the recent proceedings, for instance, in order to retain a 'vagueness of recollection' which
would in future invest the meeting with greater force than any text could give. Also, there
was a danger, against which the Chief Whip warned Bonar Law, that by-election
successes would produce a strong movement to oppose the Insurance Bill on the third
reading. However, despite the popular cry against insurance, all was well, and the House of
Lords when its turn came passed the bill with exceptional rapidity and without a division
(second reading, 11 December; committee, 15 December), Lansdowne disclaiming
hostility to the bill.*

*Ruffled feelings had of course been caused, and they duly reached Balcarres. Word
came via Sandars that Lansdowne wished to retire as soon as an elective upper chamber
became Unionist policy, a statement that was not easy to interpret. The same source
reported that Austen Chamberlain would not join any government which accepted the
referendum. As Austen had thrown over Balfour's idea of a referendum and come out for*

The impact of Bonar Law

*statutory tariff reform, including food taxes, on the very night that Balfour retired, this
issue hung over Bonar Law's leadership from its very first day, though at first it seemed
less pressing than practicalities like the choice of secretaries. Austen, Sandars reported,
was also holding himself free to stand for the leadership of the party in future, possibly
when Lansdowne retired.*

*Nevertheless, it was not these grave matters, but something that quite soon turned out
to be unreal, that weighed most on the Chief Whip as he considered his new leader:*

Bonar Law's intimate friends – this is a source of anxiety to me. Some of them like
Sir Joseph Lawrence shout, they may lack prudence, but do not encompass secrecy.
Goulding is a wirepuller – but we are on good terms, and I can combat any ill-
chosen advice he offers – and the man is under some obligations to myself. Sir Max
Aitken however is far more serious. He at any rate is a whisperer. He may be a
dangerous element – I don't know.[1] I have scarcely ever spoken to him – his
attendance here is to say the least desultory; his interest in our domestic politics is
nil. Few even know him by sight. His manner is clumsy to a rare degree – his
gesture uncouth, his conversation a series of grunts, his face too old for his years.
He may be a source of strength to B.L., or he may not. If he tries to influence him
too far, or takes opportunities to undermine my influence, I shall have to fight him.
My machine is strong, and it can grind pretty close. It would be a long battle
extending over twelve months – and I am by no means certain who would emerge
victorious. But if he beats me, he will not long survive his victory.

*In summer 1911 there was a crisis in European diplomacy over competing French and
German claims in Morocco. The sending of the German warship, The Panther, to
Agadir in July, had produced an Anglo-German confrontation which took place in
public view. The diplomatic settlement of the Moroccan question took several months
longer, however, and in September a major crisis took place about which little leaked out
at the time. By November, France and Germany had reached public agreement, and the
British government was therefore anxious to place upon the opposition responsibility for
a foreign affairs debate which could no longer be avoided. Balcarres told Elibank (16
November) that he wished to avoid such collusion, the conduct of foreign affairs since
1906 having been the subject of bitter if suppressed criticism by the Unionists. Moreover,
an opposition request for a debate would force Bonar Law to make a major statement on
foreign affairs. 'To omit any feature would be a distinct error. To deal with all, an
impossibility.'*

Balcarres added an important note.

[1] In the summer of 1911, Balcarres had been shown, by Elibank, an official letter of complaint by the
Governor-General of Canada, Lord Grey, alleging that Aitken's 'financial agility' made him no fit
subject for the knighthood he had received.

'After the death of Lord Percy Mr Balfour deputed no colleague to deal with foreign affairs. Our front bench in Mr Balfour's absence is wholly unprepared for such an emergency. For the time being it might be safer to leave decisive speeches on this subject to Lord Lansdowne.'

It was not only in foreign affairs that Balfour's very pre-eminence in debate had weakened the party. Balfour bequeathed a front opposition bench in full decay. The Home Office, foreign affairs, and India, all lacked front bench spokesmen. In Balfour's absence, Balcarres predicted in a memorandum written for Bonar Law on 26 November 1911, great difficulty would be felt with these subjects, as well as with army, navy, and defence topics. Local government questions were another area of weakness. As the members of the front bench of 1905 had died, become peers, or lost their seats, they had not been replaced; their work had simply fallen, in most cases, into Balfour's hands. A new broom was badly needed to reinvigorate the front bench, and one of Bonar Law's first acts as leader was to recruit F. E. Smith, whom Balfour had kept waiting at the door.

14 NOVEMBER 1911

Bonar Law is now in the saddle, and we must all help him to take the fence. He has great ability, more self-confidence than I expected, and certainly far more ambition than A.J.B. ever displayed. We have won a by-election[2] – no glorious feat, but a vote none the less.

15 NOVEMBER 1911

Many conversations with Bonar Law about his speech at Leeds tomorrow and a dozen matters of importance demanding early thought.

16 NOVEMBER 1911

Conversation with Lord Lansdowne. Says he has been considering organisation in House of Lords in light of recommendations of the committee of enquiry. Says he proposes to call a meeting of his H. of L. colleagues – Curzon, Midleton, Selborne, Salisbury, Derby. Doesn't think he will invite Beach, and certainly won't invite Halsbury. His whips are most inadequate. Victor Churchill is too busy, Waldegrave too stupid. Moreover they did not treat him well in August.

I said that reprisals for what occurred about the Parliament Act will involve counter-reprisals, and having just emerged from a domestic crisis in the H. of C., we should not enter on a situation of equal danger in the H. of L.

He replied that he had no wish to provoke this difficulty, but that he could not ignore the report of the committee, an opportunity presented itself of strengthening the position generally.

---

[2] The Conservatives won Oldham from the Liberals on 13 November, the night of Bonar Law's election, but only because of the intervention of a Labour candidate.

The impact of Bonar Law

The report indicated that the head whip should exercise important functions in relation to social and political matters: and that in his opinion the Duke of Devonshire (with whom he has not discussed the matter) is the most suitable appointment.

I thought that this might prejudice his future in the H. of L. – if as is the case in the H. of C. the head whip is ruined intellectually (and as a rule physically as well) by the strain.

Lord Lansdowne did not agree.

MEMORANDUM, 17 NOVEMBER 1911

From all accounts the Leeds Conference was an exceptional success, delegates having apparently determined to lay aside old sources of friction and to combine in welcoming a better spirit.

Bonar Law had a better reception – Harry Chaplin and Walter Long likewise. The latter seems to have established much popularity.

Maxse came in for an outburst of hostility – I don't blame him, but the chairman who ought never to have allowed him to speak. It is not a bad sign this objection to reopening old controversies aroused such acute resentment.

Bonar Law though much tired is obviously pleased – and is gaining confidence, judging from his determination to speak on foreign affairs (which I think imprudent).

... I have still to talk about Press, reorganisation of front bench, and also another subject of moment, viz. the need of a central office or apartment where B.L. can interview people. It is too far to get to the distant villa he now occupies.

DIARY, 17 NOVEMBER 1911

The speech last night[3] is notable because B. Law refrained from a not unnatural temptation to make it sensational by a 'pronouncement'. Poor man – I worry him sadly. On my instructions he spent most of the journey back to town in a rapid study of the contagious diseases of animals, and made a capital speech in the House this afternoon.[4] My object was that he should send a spontaneous message to the farmers of Great Britain who are much exercised on the problem. The topic is one which could not conceivably have been made at any of our great mass meetings he will address – and had he not seized the opportunity afforded by this afternoon's debate, months would probably have elapsed before he showed himself conscious of the existence of agriculture.

Tomorrow he will be glad he took my advice.

[3] Speaking to the National Union of Conservative Associations (the party conference) at Leeds on 16 November, Bonar Law said he had no new programme.
[4] This speech, on cattle disease in Scotland, was Bonar Law's first speech in the House as leader.

18 NOVEMBER 1911

Slept eleven hours last night ... I have had the most fatiguing, as well as the most responsible ten days of my life.

Balfour is absolved from the duties he performed badly, and more than ever free to shine wherever he has excelled: but shall we ever see him again at Westminster?

21 NOVEMBER 1911

Lunched with A.J.B. at the Carlton Hotel – Lady Castlereagh there looking her worst.

Conversation in these beastly public places impossible so I went to his house at half past six and had a full hour's talk. He seems rather forlorn – hasn't yet felt his feet, and is naturally *désoeuvré*: talked with great freedom about foreign politics, and gave the most careful and precise instructions as to warning him of parliamentary business early next session. He evidently does mean to return to business.

CONVERSATION WITH A.J.B., 21 NOVEMBER 1911

The Anglo-French entente was embodied in a treaty (? 1904). There were no secret articles.

All we guaranteed was to give diplomatic support – and we dealt with Egypt, Morocco, Newfoundland.

Morocco has dropped out under Algeciras and so far as our Treaty is concerned that obligation is now concluded.

How does it come about that during the autumn [*of 1911*] we were apparently under obligations which amount to an offensive and defensive alliance? Has there been a further treaty?

At Balmoral Sir Edward Grey told A.J.B. what had occurred.

In January 1906 after Grey had been several weeks in office, Cambon asked for an extension of the Treaty. Grey said that all his colleagues were electioneering, that no cabinet was possible, and that in consequence the proposal could not be entertained at that juncture.

Cambon then pressed Grey to allow our general staff to meet the French general staff (? on the frontier) and to talk over strategic questions. Grey concurred in many ways more concrete than what any secret clause might have involved. In short he took covert steps towards participation in overt hostilities.

A.J.B. made no comment beyond saying that he questioned if at the time Grey realised what a tremendous step he had taken.

Gradually acting upon this initial concession, France has worked us to the point which we reached in September last, when we very nearly had to place 100,000 men on the French frontier. What have we gained? Newfoundland, Hebrides, Egypt are settled. Morocco is a country where our interests have been whittled away. Half Persia has gone to Russia. Next week half Manchuria will likely enough go to Russia, the other half to Japan, we being ousted.

A.J.B. says that on the old theory, discredited since the Crimean War, that our duty is to maintain the balance of power, Grey may be justified: and that right or wrong he acted with firmness during the crisis.

But how can he justify such an action to pacifist supporters?

I am clear that if the projected movement of troops is ascribed to our treaty, we should explain in a general fashion that our attitude never contemplated any such course.

22 NOVEMBER 1911

Conversation with Lord Lansdowne and Bonar Law on foreign affairs. Lord L. cautious and more nervous than usual.

He sees the acuteness of the fresh outburst of venom which Kiderlen-Waechter's statement will arouse.

Grey will meet them both tomorrow – he suggested seeing Bonar Law as his conversation with A.J.B. in the past has been 'useful'.[5]

The Somerset victory may well cause opinion against the Insurance Bill to harden.

Bull says there is undoubtedly truth in the rumour that difficulties have recently been encountered about Home Rule. On what point they have arisen he cannot ascertain. Dalziel referred to this probability in a recent number of Reynolds' newspaper.

I hear people questioning the skill and wisdom of Bonar Law's speech on the Railway Commission. It was an occasion on which criticism was easy. Asquith made rather an ass of himself, George shone in throwing over his leader, R. MacDonald showed himself a casuist.

Nobody that night was an unqualified success.

Anyhow we saved the government from defeat. This afternoon likewise we did the same. We won S. Somerset. Hitchin majority is increased. Surely the week has not been inauspicious.

On 21 November Balcarres discussed the question of parliamentary private secretaries with Bonar Law, who said that while he proposed to 'keep his friends', he did not intend them to govern his policy. He did not mean to offer a position to his crony Goulding, whom he thought unsuited to a post. As if to confirm Balcarres's fears, Aitken had lent Bonar Law temporary secretaries to deal with letters of congratulation, and had offered to recruit a private secretary, nominally as one of Aitken's own staff, who would be seconded to Bonar Law on approval. By way of justification, Bonar Law told Balcarres that 'Aitken is a very remarkable man, that he is very influential in political circles in Lancashire, that his "drive" and "force" are amazing. This may be so: but he takes no interest that I can see in normal politics. He is a mere wirepuller, I should say'. (Balcarres was fortunately unaware that Aitken had been pulling strings in order to

---

[5] This was in preparation for the major foreign policy debate opened by Sir Edward Grey (27 November) on the Moroccan crisis of summer 1911.

become Bonar Law's private secretary, and that Bonar Law would 'have preferred him as my secretary to anyone else'.[6] In the end the Chief Whip's ideas prevailed.

24 NOVEMBER 1911

George Stanley[7] and Baird[8] become the [*parliamentary*] private secretaries of B. Law: between them they will supply all his deficiencies: both are zealous and I think he will find them a great help. It is so necessary at this juncture to make sure that gentlemen shall be in his entourage. His private friends, or two of them, leave much to be desired.

28 NOVEMBER 1911

Bonar Law's speech on foreign affairs[9] created a good impression, his references to Germany being most welcome to the Radicals! Albert Grey was delighted with it.

Clifford Cory, Radical M.P., resigns his presidency of the Cardiff association owing to the projected Home Rule Bill.

Tonight the three naval Lords are dismissed. Following upon McKenna's promotion, this spreads a feeling of disquiet.[10]

B. Law tells me he has surrendered all his directorships at a sacrifice of £2000 a year. This shows that he means business.

Gave him memoranda on the organisation of Front Bench and on the desirability of a West End office for his interviews. On latter said he would prefer to wait.

... Today I had interviews with the following among others: Col. Sykes, Bonar Law, Banbury, Elibank, Almeric Paget, Lord Milner, Lord Churchill, Lord Lansdowne, H. Chaplin, Duke of Devonshire, P. Cambray, Frank Mildmay, Courthope, Boscawen, Nield, H. W. Forster, Page Croft, Bull, Bridgeman, Steel-Maitland, W. Younger, Pike Pease, etc.

3 DECEMBER 1911

An interesting political week. We are strengthening ourselves. Meanwhile I am rather disturbed to find that B. Law shrinks from facing the difficult problems ahead on which difficult pronouncements will ere long be demanded – referendum, food taxes, etc. He says that as the Radicals refuse to formulate their policy in advance we should equally be absolved. This may pass muster as a *tu quoque*, but the

---

[6] Blake, *op. cit.*, 110; A. J. P. Taylor, *Beaverbrook*, 71.

[7] George Frederick Stanley (1872–1938), MP (Cons.) 1910–22, 1924–9; junior office 1919–22, 1922–3; parl. sec. to Ministry of Pensions 1924–9; governor of Madras 1929–34; brother of Lord Derby.

[8] John Baird, first Viscount Stonehaven (1874–1941), MP (Cons.) 1910–25; p.p.s. to Bonar Law 1911–16, First Commissioner of Works 1922–4, Governor-General of Australia 1925–30, chairman of the Conservative Party 1931–6.

[9] Speaking in the House of Commons on 28 November, Bonar Law made a bipartisan contribution to the major foreign policy debate of the autumn session, but went out of his way to indicate his friendship for Germany, and to pour oil on troubled waters in the aftermath of the Agadir crisis.

[10] The First, Second, and Third Sea Lords were retired by Churchill somewhat prematurely.

argument is vitiated by the fact that on these and other points we have already announced policies which many members of the party greatly wish to modify.

Both Walter Long and Austen C. are indisposed – a reaction I suppose after their nervous and temperamental introspection a fortnight ago. I retain good spirits, but groan under weariness of the flesh.

LORD BALCARRES TO LADY WANTAGE, 4 DECEMBER 1911

There has been a curious and almost dramatic change of atmosphere during the last ten days. Two or three successful by-elections,[11] odd unexpected rebuffs in parliament and in the law courts,[12] a serious crisis at the Admiralty, and a general feeling of unrest in ministerial circles, have coincided with a genuine uprising against the guillotine – and we are for the first time since 1906 attacking with the conviction of impending success.

... I believe the wisest course for the government would be to dissolve before the full iniquities of home rule and disestablishment are brought home to the public. If as is probable we were returned by a smallish majority, our situation would be precarious, and at a further appeal to the electorate our opponents might regain the upper hand after a short and innocuous spell in opposition.

14 DECEMBER 1911

Conference about amalgamation of the two wings of our party. Notice short and attendance meagre. There is a strong desire for fusion.

16 DECEMBER 1911

The session ended today. So far as Bonar Law's leadership is concerned, all or nearly all look upon it as an unqualified success.

Two speeches on the platform, and half a dozen in the House: all good, some excellent: occasional interventions on informal occasions have also been well received.

He is *not* idle, as many of us thought; though there is a tendency to go home to dinner every night – 'need I stay?' is a question put to me twenty times in thirty days!

But he *is* reluctant to face certain problems of magnitude. He refuses as yet to consider the question of the Shadow Cabinet, and a fortiori to settle outstanding points, five or six of them, upon which silence cannot be permanently maintained. He is losing time in this respect. He will not make up his mind to appoint a private secretary – he delays making the acquaintance of people whom he ought to know.

[11] The first Unionist gains of the new parliament were at Oldham and Somerset S. on 13 and 23 November 1911 respectively. Another gain followed on 22 December at Ayr N., with five more in 1912. The Unionists lost one seat, Londonderry, in by-elections between 1906 and 1915.

[12] Forms used for assessment of property under the 1909–10 Finance Act had been declared invalid by the courts, to Unionist delight.

He is an odd mixture of diffidence and determination.

He is learning that his old method of committing every speech to memory is cumbersome and not necessarily successful. The admirable speech on Home Rule at Bootle received far less preparation than was customary. He will have to speak so often and on such varied topics that ample preparation will no longer be feasible.

He has hit hard. He economises time, and spares words. Our men like this.

The confidence of the party has greatly risen during the last month. Men who distrusted B.L. have revised their views. They like his demeanour, and find him far more attractive as a speaker than was anticipated. And yet, as B.L. said the other day, 'Asquith drunk can make a better speech than any one of us, sober'.

Meanwhile one records with regret that A.J.B.'s absence passes unnoticed. When we return to the topics of defence, procedure, and foreign affairs his loss will be felt – but hitherto the opposition seems reconciled to his absence.

I do not note (what at one time I feared) namely the influence on B.L. of people like Aitken, at any rate so far as political matters are concerned.

The spirits of the party are excellent.

31 DECEMBER 1911

End of a year of political significance deeper than any within my personal recollection. On taking office of chief whip, which is regularly growing in importance, I had to face the crisis of the Parliament Bill – and then later on in the autumn came the resignation of A.J.B. and the delicate tasks involved in the choice of a successor. On the whole I got through my difficulties without any serious error, and during the process learned how to use many agencies which I have hitherto neglected: in fact my quiver is now well equipped with goodly shafts. It must be remembered that the duties of an opposition whip are all the more onerous from the fact that he has no patronage or recognition to bestow. I have committed my party to nothing in the future.

The year 1912 saw a major reversal of the political tide. Many unrelated elements combined to discomfort the Liberals and hearten the Unionists. Bonar Law, though inexperienced, held his own in parliament and won the acclaim of the party out of doors. His leadership was not in question, and Balfour's conduct was irreproachable. The home rule issue suited Bonar Law, and gave no joy to the Liberals. Moreover it drew Unionist attention away from tariff reform, which divided the party and won few votes, and rallied them round a popular cry. The Liberals had no great compensating measure to inspire their supporters.

Part cause, part effect, the by-elections began to show a strong swing to the right. Manchester South, not even contested at the general election, fell to the Unionists easily in March 1912, giving them their first seat in the city. A second Manchester seat fell to them in August, again easily, and again in a straight fight. In Crewe and Midlothian, Unionist gains were caused by Labour interventions, showing that alliance was under

strain, and in a straight fight Lansbury lost his Bow and Bromley seat in November. The
Conservatives – who in 1912 at last amalgamated with the Liberal Unionists in a useful
piece of political tidying up – were already beginning to feel solid ground under their
feet, when the Liberals raised their hopes by cases of financial corruption, of which the
Marconi scandal was only one.

With the issues, the events, the news, and the by-elections stacked in their favour, the
Unionists had only one thing to fear, and fear it they did: the unresolved question of
where the party stood on food taxes. This issue, which was in fact dealt with by
procrastination until almost the end of 1912, was becoming even more sensitive, for two
reasons. One was a general rise in the cost of living. The other was a growing belief that it
was home rule which really mattered. Bonar Law had risen as a keen tariff reformer and
had been a lieutenant of Austen Chamberlain in that cause, but his emphasis on the
impossibility of treating Protestant Ulster as a conquered community, combined with the
fact that electoral victory was now apparently within reach, were gradually during 1912
weaning the party from one of its dearest beliefs.

12 FEBRUARY 1912

Long conference at B.L.'s house about fusion with the Liberal Unionist party.[13]
We sat there discussing the matter for two and a half hours – both sides being
represented, and we agreed upon a good workable scheme.

12 FEBRUARY 1912

Opposition dinner at B.L.'s house: too far off for convenience, and dinner too large
for normal appetites. I keep the menu as a souvenir of discomfort. I was rather sorry
that B.L. did not read the King's Speech with that impartiality of tone and voice
befitting so grave a document: I had warned him that no nuance of scorn was
suitable on such an occasion.[14]

14 FEBRUARY 1912

Meeting of parliament. We made a *bad* start. Asquith challenged B.L. rather heavily
about our charges of jobbery: and then extracted what amounted to a pledge on our
part to repeal the Insurance Act. We had a conversation in B.L.'s room – F. E.
Smith, Harry, Walter Long, Austen C., Alfred Lyttelton etc. and the outcome was
that B.L. was to write to the press tonight to explain his misunderstanding. He
admitted that he had made a faux pas, though he was unconscious of its crucial
extent and is anxious to retrieve the situation. The result will be that he will be
thoroughly chaffed and attacked also, though I hope that he will not seriously
prejudice the party as a whole but he committed a grave error of judgement.
    ... Our party is in good spirits ... and we mean to fight the government harder

[13] Cf. also below, 12 February, 7 March, 15 March, 18 April, and 8 May 1912.
[14] Balcarres had written asking him to read the speech in 'colourless and impartial' accents (Blake, *The*
Unknown Prime Minister, 102).

than ever but what puzzles me is how we are to beat them .... None the less the difficulties of the government must be far greater than the public know and there may well be a split or some unforeseen difficulty which will bring them low. I believe that Harcourt feels so strongly about female suffrage that he is prepared to go any length rather than acquiesce in its passage. From Labour I anticipate few obstacles, from Nationalists none: the latter will accept any bill which the government may offer.

15 FEBRUARY 1912
Bonar Law's letter appears in all the newspapers this morning ... All the latter part of the document was drafted by Fred Smith after Austen, Walter and the rest had left the room.

MEMORANDUM, 20 FEBRUARY 1912
Conversation between Lord Curzon, Lord Lansdowne, B. Law, Walter Long, as to referendum and food taxes in relation to fiscal debate on Thursday.[15]

W. Long strongly in favour of abandoning food taxes, but most anxious that B. Law should not announce their retention without consultation with colleagues ...

Austen Chamberlain (not present) is strongly opposed to abandonment, and it is alleged that this is partly in deference to his Father's wishes ...

On referendum Lord L. said that the conditions under which the original offer[16] was made have become obsolete, new circumstances created by the parliament act have superseded A.J.B.'s offer – and A.J.B. himself does not consider that as a party we are bound by the Albert Hall declaration. Walter Long however holds that the referendum eases the situation in regard to food taxes ...

B. Law nervous and low; says he won't hedge. If pressed to hedge he would prefer to resign, etc. Uncomfortable conference.

Writers of Liberal sympathies have often waxed priggish on the theme of the increasing crudity of Conservative politics under Bonar Law, as if their side had played no part in bringing about this loss of amenity. Civilised Unionists apportioned the responsibility otherwise.

LORD BALCARRES TO LADY WANTAGE, 22 FEBRUARY 1912
You lament that the grand old race of statesmen is passing away, and your remark is based on the polemical character of Bonar Law's speeches: – Well, I share your

[15] Bonar Law settled not to speak in this debate in order not to be prematurely drawn, putting Lyttelton up instead to make non-committal remarks. Long was pressing very strongly for an early decision (23 February).

[16] At the Albert Hall on 29 November 1910 Balfour had said, 'I have not the least objection to submitting the principle of Tariff Reform to a Referendum'. Cf. shadow cabinet reported below, 29 February 1911.

regret, and oddly enough Bonar Law shares it as well. Let me explain how and why the transition has occurred.

Much as I love A.J.B. and deeply as I admire his great intellectual gifts, it has long been apparent both among his supporters here and our stalwarts in the country, that people doubted the firmness of his convictions. Quite apart from an excusable hesitation about tariffs, he never showed the firmness needful to cashier an undesirable colleague, he hated discipline and thus frittered away our resources, and time after time he left people under the uncomfortable impression that they did not grasp his real meaning. Moreover his friendliness with ministers, and the knowledge that he was always accessible to their appeals, while somewhat inaccessible to many of his own followers, led to a belief, unfounded or at least exaggerated, that his philosphical mind allowed him to see good in all things, even in modern Radicalism. He did *not* 'hate the thing that is evil'.

All this was unjust, and based on misapprehension. He is one of the finest conservatives I know, and his readiness to collogue with Haldane or Edward Grey, his constant kindness to Churchill, and his studious courtesy to Radicals in parliament who did their utmost to cause him offence, did not arise from apathy about conservatism, but from his belief that such an attitude best contributed toward patriotic and efficient government.

Meanwhile notwithstanding his adherence to the old standards of parliamentary amenity, our opponents have openly abandoned the tone of courtesy and reverence which they inherited from Gladstone and Rosebery. Not only have they assumed truculent and frequently insolent airs (I myself heard Campbell-Bannerman call A.J.B. a fool, across the table of the House) – but they likewise treat the House of Commons itself with studied contempt. Quite latterly Balfour began to open his eyes to the changed conditions, and once or twice he used language which a few years ago he would have never deigned to employ. Moreover (and again quite recently) he came to realise that since 1906 the government has been out for blood, has determined to smash the class to which he belongs, and in order to encompass their object would shrink from no device likely to assist them. His revulsion against them was singularly bitter, against opponents as such, I mean. He decided never to meet in private life persons who in their public capacities were ready to break the constitution which he admired, to flout the House of Commons which he loved, and to jockey the Crown which he respected. So far did he go in this respect that last autumn he refused again and again to accede to Mrs Asquith's appeals to visit Whittingehame. His fundamental belief in the good qualities of opponents has been reluctantly dispelled.

Then came the change of leadership. The events of last summer which he took to heart (to a surprising degree) involved his abandonment of the charge of the opposition. Had he retained that post I fancy that so keenly does he feel the dangerous outlook, that he himself would have translated his resentment into speeches far more violent than any to which he has been accustomed.

The Party, in its subconscious way, likes Bonar Law's attitude precisely because it lacks those very qualities which in a Gladstone or a Balfour would conform to high parliamentary tradition. Our opponents, notably Asquith, George, and Churchill have deliberately cast aside all decency, and they like A.J.B. because he never repaid them in their own coin: they fear and they dislike Bonar Law because he is unsparing in scathing denunciation. Our friends in the country like B.L. because his attitude is uncompromising and because it conforms to their belief in his genuine distrust of the Radical Policy. His speeches help them to understand what they firmly believe, namely the utter lack of true public spirit which animates the Radical party.

And Bonar Law himself? I said just now that he also regretted what he looks upon as necessity, namely an exacerbation of public life. We cannot fight with one arm tied behind the back! We tried to argue with reason and moderation, they replied by virulence and obloquy. While we need never stoop to their methods, our supporters in the constituencies fretted under our meekness. I don't know anybody who naturally is more addicted to pure debate than B.L. with the sole exception of A.J.B. His mind is strict and precise in logic, the construction of his argument seems based on a geometrical thesis, his whole style is that of a keen logician who desires the issue settled upon the merits of argument. It is in this sense that his parliamentary career began, with a quiet deferential voice, and a retiring manner. Now, with real reluctance he feels that the world is not governed by the reasonable marshalling of fact and figure before an impartial jury – and he is driven to employ the bludgeon as well as the rapier.

Whether these weapons will increase or even retain his parliamentary reputation remains to be seen. He is still relatively speaking unversed in the House of Commons – and it is dangerous to acquire experience while leading a great party: but I think he is going to succeed. His difficulties all lie before him.

He is charming to deal with – most thoughtful and kind, melancholy in disposition, witty when moments of relaxation occur, devoted to his family, profoundly convinced of the justice of his case. With an unerring memory, much courage, great resources and industry he ought to go far.

He is still uncertain of his ground. His knowledge of men is small, and I am not satisfied that in these matters his judgment is wholly reliable. He is still self-conscious and to that extent not quite impartial in determining the line of policy. He succeeds a leader who had unrivalled qualities – and his caution leads him when coming to a decision to cast his mind twelve months forward in order to picture to himself the probable retrospect.

MEMORANDUM, 23 FEBRUARY 1912
The announcement that Asquith is to take charge of the home rule bill dispels rumours about his impending resignation.

24 FEBRUARY 1912
Jack Sandars[17] has been occupied in sorting and classifying the contents of

---

[17] Balfour's private secretary. Cf. below, 1 March 1912.

innumerable boxes in Carlton Gardens – thirty-six I fancy he said, large tin boxes which are six or eight times the size of the ordinary despatch box! What a collection of state papers! A.J.B. has given him a free hand, and he has destroyed hundreds if not thousands of letters which in the hands of careless or malicious executors would destroy or impair the reputation of colleagues. This sounds very charitable, but I should have thought their preservation might have been necessary in order under certain circumstances to explain or possibly to vindicate the attitude of A.J.B. himself. However Jack says this is not the case, as many of them are volunteered expressions of opinion and advice, but none the less damaging to the writers. I have often wondered if Sandars will be asked to go beyond this task of arranging the correspondence: probably ten of fifteen years hence Gerald Balfour will be invited to compile the materials for a biography, and I fear his treatment of a magnificent theme would be thin and ineffective. It is rumoured that A.J.B. is now pining for the pure breeze of Biarritz as an antidote to the enervating atmosphere of Cannes. From all accounts he continues to enjoy himself tremendously, and has spent an awful lot of money. He will be wanted home in three weeks or so when the Home Rule Bill is presented.

Politics – we have had a fair week, recovering lost ground, but our position is not so strong as I had expected. B.L.'s slip has caused much trouble, of which we have not heard the last.

MEMORANDUM, 29 FEBRUARY 1912

Shadow cabinet at Lansdowne House. Present: Lord Lansdowne, Bonar Law, W. Long, G. Wyndham, Halsbury, Lord Midleton, Alfred Lyttelton, Steel-Maitland and self, Londonderry, Akers-Douglas, Derby, Ashbourne, Austen C., Selborne, Finlay, H. Chaplin, Duke of Devonshire, F. E. Smith.

Lord Lansdowne began immediately with a discussion about food taxes; he said that though not partial to the scheme, he realised the advantage from a preference point of view – but he felt that whatever electoral disadvantages attached to the policy, it would do us more harm than good to abandon our attitude. We should be charged with poltroonery and the misrepresentations about dear food would continue unabated. As regards referendum he is friendly, but thinks we should say that our offer was made as an integral part of a constitutional reform, and that having been rejected by the government no longer need bind us, though we are at liberty to deal with the subject in any future reform of the second chamber. No retreat being possible in food taxes, we must be specific in restrictions (e.g. limitation of amount). A.J.B. is himself quite ready to drop referendum.

G. Wyndham first to speak after long pause, B. Law having expressed agreement, likewise Chaplin. Londonderry objected altogether to food taxes, and said that so long as we advocate them we cannot win. Derby said he would do anything in the world to see them dropped, but none the less agreed with Lansdowne that their abandonment would do more harm than good. W. Long agreed; to run away is a practical impossibility; but what is to be done now? What are candidates to say about referendum?

This question proved difficult to answer; are we to throw over A.J.B?

B. Law does not wish to do so publicly – it would appear discourteous, neither does he wish to ask A.J.B. to do it himself, which would look cowardly and unreasonable. We must carry our handicap honourably and boldly.

Selborne agreed. Alfred Lyttelton suggested asking if Canada could help us by withdrawing the claims our party has conceded. B. Law said he had reason to know that Canada would resent our change of policy, especially after the defeat of Reciprocity. Lyttelton then said that he would like to allocate the food tax product to artisan needs. Austen C. said no such pledge could be given without qualification.

Finlay said imp. [*ossible*] to drop food taxes. The subject ended, complete agreement F. E. Smith made no remark. Carson and Curzon absent.

Lord Lansdowne said he thought shadow cabinets rather cumbrous for emergencies, and proposed from time to time to ask 'sub-committees' to meet him.

This is the first Shadow held since A.J.B.'s retirement. All the obsolete mandarins were present, Ashbourne, Chaplin, Lord Halsbury, etc.[18] It would have been better to have begun the sub-committee system forthwith. The unanimity at this gathering was *most remarkable*.

DIARY, 29 FEBRUARY 1912

A very important Shadow Cabinet at Lansdowne House. To my amazement we *all* agreed to stick to the Food Taxes.

1 MARCH 1912

Short tells me that according to his calculations, since Christmas last he and Sandars have burned no less than 120,000 documents – one hundred and twenty thousand documents, from A.J.B.'s tin boxes! I protested warmly, but he assures me that the papers were either of no importance or so important that destruction was a necessity. There remain many thousands, all well arranged, but stacked in an attic in Carlton Gardens, where damp, fire or burglary might enter. I shall press A.J.B. to contrive a proper muniment room at Whittingehame.

2 MARCH 1912

Coming out of Burlington House yesterday afternoon I came across the latest sample of suffragette folly – windows smashed all along Piccadilly and Bond Street, harmless tradesmen being punished for the supposed shortcomings of the government. This monstrous and heartless outrage at a moment when all England is throbbing with anxiety about this terrific industrial trouble,[19] will further alienate

---

[18] Cf. Blake, *op. cit.*, 103. Bonar Law had wished to exclude at least Londonderry and Halsbury, but Lansdowne, who summoned the peer members, did not see how he could leave them out. Devonshire, on the other hand, a newcomer to the shadow cabinet, was there on Lansdowne's request.

[19] The coal strike

sympathy from the franchise movement, and at the same time show how little the sex is suited to gauge the trend of political philosophy. I only hope the termagants may receive exemplary sentences at the police court.

But the Coal Strike? Indeed Great Britain is reaping the whirlwind, Lloyd George having succeeded in stirring up strife where relative contentment existed a few short years ago. I hear from Haigh that the older colliers, those who know what trouble is involved by these disastrous conflicts, are aghast at the necessity of following the lead of their socialist agitators: and I doubt not elsewhere too, where men have been earning good wages, the same feeling exists. But they act like a flock of sheep ... I suppose at the back of the agitation there is some master mind, some great spider lying *perdu* at the corner of his web, but controlling every thread and foreseeing each wriggle of the captured prey. Who is this master intellect – Hartshorn or Stanton,[20] or some nameless engineer.

... At the Carlton people are moody and depressed, unable to see a gleam of sunshine in our horrible situation: one or two men think the government may be driven to resign. This I doubt.

3 MARCH 1912

Evie Benson tells me she has laid in a large stock of provisions – perhaps she is right. We have acted thus by coal: but I don't quite like giving way to panic in the matter of food. Lord Savile has armed all his servants with revolvers, but as the bullet carries a mile he has had no chance of teaching them how to shoot. Many people expect a real revolution, with arson, riot and loot – murder too.

7 MARCH 1912

Further discussion about Liberal Unionist fusion. Progress is being made, but five important people on our side, namely the chairmen of our big committees, are all less or more hostile, viz. Harry Samuel, Worthington-Evans, Crump, Sir Joseph Dimsdale, and Imbert Terry. The first two will fall into line for the good of the party, likewise in all probability will Sir William Crump: Imbert Terry however threatens a fierce agitation. Dimsdale (or cock-eyed Joe as James Hamilton nicknamed him) will follow the line of least resistance.

9 MARCH 1912

Connie and I went to see pictures, among others the exhibition of the Futurists, a bold group of Italian youths, who being unable to draw take refuge in a pompous theory which provides an excuse for ignorance and muddleheadedness.

... Asquith's speech on Friday when full of sherry was the dirge of a beaten man. But how are we to get them out? We may win by-elections, and we can worst them in argument, but so long as they sit at Westminster and draw their salaries the Coalition is safe. The reaction against Lloyd George is just beginning, but I much question if it will last long enough to influence public opinion.

[20] Harmless Labour trade unionists

10 MARCH 1912

With Evie Benson to tea. George Peel there. He has been talking to two interesting personages in the coal crisis, namely Sir George Askwith[21] and Davies, the Welsh colliery proprietor. Both agree that the prime minister has been the only one of the four ministers taking part in the discussions to show strength or resource. Grey intervenes now and then: Buxton[22] is too vapid to count, Lloyd George too sly to commit himself. As for Asquith, he is showing the effects of strain and anxiety – he looks dead-beat poor man.

Davies said that the questions put by these negotiators to the coalowners (and taken down in shorthand by their clerk) were so ludicrous, and based on so profound an ignorance of the whole situation, that when their text was read to the general assembly of employers, there were bursts of hilarity from every corner of the room.

14 MARCH 1912

I had a long talk with A.J.B. who returned to the House for the first time since his resignation of the leadership. Four months holiday and freedom from care has worked wonders. He has enjoyed every day of his absence and begins to think the time has come when he should resume public life. I see the papers say that his reappearance at this juncture is most significant, and the Radicals entertain hopes that he means to reassert his authority and thus to weaken Bonar Law. The precise reason for his return must be sought in more prosaic causes. He has come back because the Riviera has begun to fatigue his palate, and also because Lady Elcho would not allow delays in the christening of her grandson to whom A.J.B. stands godfather.

His entry was so demure (and to the House at large so unexpected) that his wish to avoid fuss and ceremony was respected: but the news spread like wildfire and everybody was frankly delighted to hear he was back. When he will take part in debate is another matter.

15 MARCH 1912

The executive committee of the National Union sanctioned the first essential step towards the fusion of the Conservative and Liberal Unionist parties. This is a great achievement, and if carried through should strengthen the morale as well as the organisation of our party.

'...Haigh is like a house preparing for a siege. In the back passage I noted hams and sides of bacon suspended from the ceilings... the lower muniment room has the appearance of the store rooms of some opulent picture dealer. It is sad, almost humiliating. During the Chartist troubles it was rumoured that the men of Bolton were preparing a raid upon our neighbourhood. Scores of colliers volunteered to

[21] Sir George Askwith, first Baron Askwith (1861–1942), chief industrial commissioner of the Board of Trade 1911–19.
[22] Sydney Buxton (1853–1934), president of Board of Trade 1910–14.

protect Haigh, and actually night after night there were these faithful watchmen who paraded round the House, in order to 'let th'Lord drink his port wine in peace'.

And today? We are animated by no less generous motives towards our men than Lord Bal was – but notwithstanding the success of our policy that those employed by the Company shall occupy positions and receive pay as good and indeed better than what others can afford – none the less the personal tie has gradually disappeared, and our men are the servants of a huge joint stock company which to them represents but little more than a machine. It is true that there is much more loyalty towards the Company as such, and affection towards it than other similar concerns can command. We have men still working, or else drawing pensions who actually worked for my great-grandfather, but notwithstanding all our efforts sentiment has changed and with it the whole face of modern industrialism. Perhaps some of the blame must rest with ourselves. My grandfather was of so retiring a disposition that he instinctively shrank from seeing strange faces. My father for years past has not had the physique to be regularly in our cold Lancashire climate: while I have devoted myself so completely to politics that my own financial and industrial concerns received inadequate attention. Even if I were more free it would be in many ways difficult, simply as a director of a company, to occupy the position we previously held where responsibility was personal, direct, and undivided: moreover, where in spite of the organisation of modern enterprise, the personal link has been maintained, precisely the same trouble exists, and the strikers are just as fully opposed to their present system of wages. The unrest which pervades Great Britain is universally distributed, and if one could only penetrate the mind of the agricultural labourer it would probably transpire that he is equally dissatisfied with his lot.

As to remedies, it seems hopeless to suggest anything. Were wages doubled, contentment would not ensue. Were industries nationalised, strikes and disorder would follow. Education will work wonders but it cannot engender peace.

18 MARCH 1912

The Duchess of Buccleuch,[23] though something of a tyrant, was one of the greatest great ladies of our generation: bitterly opposed to all the vulgarism and ostentations of the smart set, and notable for her insuperable objections to the publicity of illustrated papers and society gossip. Claude Hamilton tells me that once and once only did she bend to entertain a Jew – whom she did not know, as a specially marked compliment to the late King Edward. I have often found that people admire the manner in which she withdrew her domestic circle from public gaze – the late Lord Salisbury did the same – but few have been able to resist what is presumably a temptation of being made the subject of tittle tattle in the press ... The publication of the details of feasts, balls and so forth which is now a marked feature of the

[23] Lady Louisa Jane Hamilton (1836–1912), daughter of the first Duke of Abercorn, married the sixth Duke of Buccleuch in 1859. He died in 1914.

halfpenny press is deplorable, especially as in nine cases out of ten the pushful hosts who glory in this luxurious waste are foreigners and nouveaux riches . . . There is no doubt that these descriptions of banquets have done much to produce discontent.

24 MARCH 1912

A.J.B.'s reappearance in parliament is the subject of endless suggestion and innuendo. The Radical press universally ascribes it to a growing desire on our part to dispense with Bonar Law, who is quite calm under these attacks, and says that whatever had been the occasion of Balfour's rentrée they would have been inevitable. B.L. is making himself feared on the other side of the House.

Whereas A.J.B. was adored in parliament, he failed to strike the imagination or to fire the zeal of our supporters outside and in the constituencies. With B.L. the exact reverse will hold good.

LORD BALCARRES TO LADY WANTAGE, 26 MARCH 1912

Arthur Balfour (odd person) seriously considers the propriety of his volunteering to spend a day coal portering, if the dock people refuse to handle the stuff themselves.

29 MARCH 1912

When coming home the other night, Wednesday I think, I happened across A.J.B. and returned to Carlton Gardens where I gossiped for an hour. He certainly is in a most elastic and juvenated frame of mind, keenly interested in our proceedings and apparently enjoying his freedom to the utmost – greatly intrigued by the Futurists, so much so that words fail to describe his emotions. He is exercised about B.L.: thinks that he takes matters rather too much to heart, broods unduly upon the outcome of the future and the results of the past – in short A.J.B. says that I must watch B.L. with great care, discarding all needless engagements, or else he may get so fatigued as to produce that vile nervousness which has wrecked so many political careers. I quite appreciate the danger and have often warned George Stanley against overworking the machine. B.L. is a paradoxical combination of diffidence and decision – and in certain cases the decision he has shown has sprung from the fear of being charged with diffidence or indecision.

But I am much pleased with him. During the last fortnight the party has gone through a serious trial on the Minimum Wage Bill. We have emerged with credit and success to ourselves, and the courage shown by our men at an early stage when they ran the risk of cruel misrepresentation, is a tribute to the vitality of B.L.'s leadership.

LORD BALCARRES TO LADY WANTAGE, 29 MARCH 1912

Irish opinion is not friendly towards the measure.[24] The priests are staunchly

---

[24] Only a handful of Irish nationalists had voted for the Women's Suffrage Bill, which had just been defeated by fourteen votes.

opposed to it; but the general political situation at Westminster influenced their decision most of all. Lord Loreburn is the best friend of Irish nationalism in the cabinet, and his firm declaration at the Albert Hall that the passage of this bill would amount to a 'constitutional outrage', brought home to their minds that his resignation would under certain circumstances become inevitable. Moreover had the bill passed its second reading the government had promised a week or ten days (which means perhaps two calendar weeks) for the consideration of its further stages. This time would be abstracted from the slender time available for the huge project of home rule. The nationalists consequently took a strong line, harmonising with Irish opinion, and conforming to their own parliamentary strategy. Harcourt[25] paid the journey money of at least four who were too hard up to travel on their own purses!

1 APRIL 1912

Long conference in my room about the revivification of the Carlton Club as a force in Conservative politics. Almeric Paget is the prime advocate of reform backed up this afternoon by Walter Long, Claude Hamilton, and Johnnie Baird. It is high time something was done: for the club is rapidly falling from its high state. Not only is the food bad, the waiting atrocious and the normal comforts of club life quite deficient, but with the steady deterioration of its social qualities the Carlton which in old days was the very centre of political activity now almost ceases to count. The demand for membership decreases. The waiting period which used to be twenty-five years has now fallen to seventeen or eighteen. The candidate is of a different and less desirable type. The management and control have fallen into weak hands with deplorable results.

Much responsibility rests with Streatfield the weak and lymphatic secretary – or rather with Lord Abergavenny who jobbed him into the post. Reform of our political work must assuredly be followed promptly by pensioning off this stick-in-the-mud. So far as the committee is concerned I fancy that we all realise the desirability of drastic action though we shall doubtless encounter the violent opposition of the mandarins.

LORD BALCARRES TO LADY WANTAGE, 2 APRIL 1912

The nationalists likewise are dejected. Home rule, however satisfactory the bill may be, stands a very poor chance of outliving the two years of the parliament act. Redmond committed a fatal blunder in allowing his colleague Devlin to persuade the nationalists to let the Insurance Bill of last year have precedence over home rule.

3 APRIL 1912

These six weeks have produced many unexpected things – the defeat of the

---

[25] A Liberal cabinet minister violently opposed to female suffrage.

suffragists, the Minimum Wage Bill, the treatment of the surplus of six and a half millions, the eclipse of Lloyd George. London is full of rumours that the little man is again in trouble, again with a Jewess!

5 APRIL 1912

Meanwhile Arthur Fair[26] has been telling me the ethics of coal-poaching during the strike. The company has allowed all and sundry to collect the coal which lies about on the pitbrows: and hundreds of tons of small stuff have been gathered by armies of people working day and night. After raking the surface for a few days, and indeed burrowing pretty deep into the banks, the available supply was exhausted and fresh fields had to be found. Accordingly the surfaces where coal crops out were attacked, at Redrock and at Brock Mill. It is amazing what quantities of coal have been secured – small and poor in quality, but none the less saleable ... It is estimated that no less than 400 tons have been extracted. This is taken away in carts and peddled about the town from seven to eighteen shillings a ton. Even the big mills have been buying it ... Claims are pegged out, gangs of workmen organised, and heaps of coal awaiting removal are jealously guarded all night to prevent invasion. The work goes on at night by the glimmering light of oil lanterns.

It has now reached the degree of being a public nuisance. Not only is the roadway covered up with debris and heaps of small coal, but in one case just at the top of Leyland Mill Hill, the actual road itself is being undermined. Arthur went down to interview the raiders, and to move them on – he says they were quite reasonable. At Redrock ... the colliers appear to have had the impertinence (it is nothing less) to load four railway trucks with their spoils, to sell the cargo, and to persuade the North Western railway to remove this little train! Whither it went I know not: anyhow it is the first consignment of coal ever despatched from this station, and until the next strike occurs will be the last.

As every day passes I marvel more and more at the power of resistance shown by the community: not only owing to the calm and resolute determination to avoid rowdiness or disorder, but also at the astonishing reserve of material which the crisis has brought to light. Those who will be most blamed for the miscalculations, will be the Labour leaders who predicted that two or three weeks of strike would bring the government and the nation to its knees.

11 APRIL 1912

Perrier Jouet introduced the Home Rule Bill. Last time he addressed us (on the Minimum Wage Bill) he blubbed tears of sherry wine. Today he was both sober and unemotional: but the silly man spoilt his speech by attacking us in his concluding sentences, and as we are not in a mood to be browbeaten ... we interrupted the sequence of his sentences, ruffled his temper and spoilt the whole effect of his

---

[26] Arthur Fair (died September 1934), agent at Haigh for over thirty years, whose ability relieved the diarist 'from all the tedium of the dull Lancashire estate'.

peroration. We behaved badly no doubt, but he is responsible for the wreckage of his most carefully calculated effects. Every word by the way had been committed to type which he read to the House ... Carson made a good speech. Poor man he is ill – caught bad neuralgia in Ireland the other night – drugged himself with phenacetin and antipyrin all today – and actually was bearing mustard plasters all over his back. Notwithstanding his hardships he spoke well.

13 APRIL 1912

At Belvoir Castle – an amusing nondescript party such as my cousin Violet Granby[27] (as one still calls her) likes to collect. Lots of vague people who flitted about the background – a Master of Hounds, a young man in the City, an American actress, a pianoforte maker, an old and distinguished Jew, a young and smart Jew, together with some odds and ends whom I could not define ... Violet in her family circle pleases me though rumour says that there are moments when warfare splits the whole establishment. At any rate one must ascribe to her the credit of having restored chins to the Manners clan: another generation of the old model would have obliterated that feature from the race. ... There are few grandmothers who so well rival the attractions of their own daughters. Marjorie[28] is a fascinating little person, a real artist – actor, singer, painter – and as years go on, for she is no longer quite young, her character seems to strengthen and develop. Diana[29] with the broad calm brow is all the rage in London society but less human in tastes or conversation.

Henry[30] much occupied and in the leisure moments chaffs his family and his guests with irrepressible bonhomie. John, the boy, is I fear something of a disappointment to his father. Henry is a sportsman, John a scholar. John has no bloodthirsty tastes, and immures himself day and night in the muniment room. He is a born brocanteur, knows every stick and stone of Haddon – and although I am the last to suggest that he is under any obligation to take up politics or public life it is none the less a pity that he shows so little interest in the estates. They are vast and the responsibility of their owner must always be great, and it seems an error of judgment on his part that he should so studiously withdraw from so palpable a duty.

18 APRIL 1912

Council meeting of the National Union. We agreed to fuse with the Liberal Unionists. This will strengthen our organisation. Of course there is a good deal of jealousy but that is inevitable.

19 APRIL 1912

Primrose Day: and whether from climatic or political reasons I know not but never do I remember seeing so few floral tributes to the memory of Lord Beaconsfield. I

[27] From 1906 the eighth Duchess of Rutland.
[28] Later Lady Anglesey
[29] Later Lady Diana Cooper
[30] The eighth Duke of Rutland

fancy it must be the cold weather and yet the last few days have been like summer. Is it that people are becoming nervous about showing their politics in their buttonhole? For my part I never have worn primroses on Primrose Day – I carry them next to my heart.

22 APRIL 1912

Henry Granby came to see me at the H. of C. asking advice about Bonar Law: he has an idea that our new leader feels himself neglected and that the great political hostesses are not doing their duty by him. I wonder if this is so. Lady Londonderry it is true started in a hostile sense but Harry Chaplin talked her round and I believe she is now friendly. Lady Lansdowne, like her husband, seems to be grasping at every pretext to escape the fatigues both of politics and society. I doubt if B.L. wishes much to be entertained, though it is always gratifying to give oneself the pleasure of refusing invitations. Violet Granby I should add has done her utmost for B.L.

26 APRIL 1912

Almeric Paget with his glass eye and his stupendous neckcloth, set off by a thousand guinea pearl, is apt to be misunderstood. Appearances are certainly against him but he is one of the staunchest and most painstaking of our men, and having once evolved some idea for strengthening the party takes no repose until he has started his proposals towards success. For years past we have been grumbling about the vegetation of the Carlton Club. Almeric P. is determined to galvanise it into activity, invited every member of the committee, and eighteen or twenty of us sat down to a feast in Berkeley Square and did ample justice to the fare.

We then adjourned upstairs, and sat in a blood-red drawing room. Speeches, suggestions, keenness, and finally unanimity, Lord Londonderry our senior trustee hesitating at first. An essential is the supersession of our lymphatic secretary, Streatfield. This task would fall to Londonderry, hence his reluctance, but I suggested that Londonderry should tell him that reorganisation is in the air and that Streatfield if wise would easily be induced to ease matters by tendering his resignation. Even this made Londonderry nervous: so we clinched matters by suggesting a remark to the Duke of Abercorn[31] to the effect that if Londonderry did not sack the secretary in private before the committee meeting, he would have the still more unpleasant task of sacking him in public at the meeting. Abercorn fired his arrow, and Londonderry assured us that he would not shrink from his duty.

How valuable at times is a Duke in second childhood. Whenever in doubt we whispered something to Abercorn who promptly distributed it *coram populo*...

3 MAY 1912

Long interview with Bishop of St Davids[32] who tells me he has now addressed 105

---

[31] James Hamilton, second Duke of Abercorn (1838–1913); succeeded to title, 1885.
[32] Dr John Owen (1854–1926), Bishop of St Davids 1897–1926.

The impact of Bonar Law

meetings in England against the Welsh Disestablishment Bill. All have been keen, and only four or five of the total number have not been crowded and enthusiastic.

I often have to see the little man, and I am always interested as his conversation shows me the thoroughness and the professionalism of Welsh politics. Every statement, every movement of his opponents is studied and canvassed from each point of view, in order to effect a damaging counter-statement and counter-move. He watches Lloyd George as a cat watches a mouse, and I doubt not that the Bishop is just as closely observed by the nonconformists. The Bishop however is riding the winning horse, though he realises the tremendous peril of the Parliament Act. None the less Disestablishment grows less popular every day and Lloyd George's decision to have a series of meetings in Wales bears eloquent testimony to the growing anxiety of the cabinet.

As for politics, we hammer the Home Rule Bill, but we must admit that the electors are apathetic, though they are beginning to take more interest now that the novelty of the *Titanic* enquiry begins to wane. The newspapers which ten days ago were obliged to refuse advertisements owing to the demand of their readers for news, now devote fewer columns to the subject...

Meanwhile our Ulstermen, who resemble the Welsh in the care with which they study every pawn on the chessboard, are maturing further action of a sensational kind. I predict no issue, so paradoxical and so kaleidoscopic are the changing situations. I do however foresee two possible situations which may cause us grave difficulty: the government may offer to exclude Ulster from the Home Rule Bill, or else we may be asked to consent to disestablishment if the disendowment clauses are omitted. Either proposition would cause us grave troubles which might develop into a serious split: at the same time the government would suffer a tremendous loss of prestige.

7 MAY 1912

A large meeting of the Carlton Club committee where we unanimously accepted the resignation of the secretary, and determined to reform the Club and vitalise it as a centre of political activity.

Cyril Potter[33] came to see me about George Kemp,[34] who means to speak against the Home Rule Bill, and would also like some assurance on our part that his claims on our party will be recognised. He has long felt out of the world of society for people are no longer anxious to entertain those whom they look upon as traitors to the King and Country: moreover George Kemp has never been a Radical. He hates Home Rule, is ashamed of Disestablishment, and like many of his colleagues has no opinion of Lloyd Georgian finance. He equally dislikes Tariff Reform. Poor man, he is hard to please.

[33] A Conservative candidate active in south-east Lancashire.
[34] Sir George Kemp (b. 1866), a Rochdale flannel baron who was also a member of White's and had married a daughter of Lord Ellesmere; a Liberal Unionist MP 1895–1906, he was elected for NW Manchester in January 1910. He retired later in the summer.

I refused to authorise any promises. There are many who better deserve recognition, although they do not ask it, in return for deserting a party they can no longer conscientiously support.

8 MAY 1912
Final conference about the fusion of the two wings. B.L., Austen, Chilston,[35] and Walter Long, at whose instance we recommended a change in our title which will retain the word 'Conservative', at any rate upon our notepaper. I think this course is wise, for there is undoubtedly regret which might well develop into hostility at the idea of abandoning our historic name. I fancy W. Long has missed nearly all our committee meetings, and it is thus at the last moment that we are obliged to reopen questions which have been settled for months past. He is too busy, Walter Long I mean, to keep abreast with his numerous responsibilities: too peppery also to preserve equanimity and calm.

9 MAY 1912
The conference at the Queen's Hall was a great success, and most expeditious. We passed our resolution long before the synchronous conference of the Liberal Unionist party had fairly got to business. This fusion is excellent, and greatly to the credit of Steel-Maitland as a manager.

Division on second reading of Home Rule. I put into the lobby every able-bodied Unionist, with one single exception, Sir John Jackson,[36] the great contractor, who has no sense of political duty. George Kemp spoke, but didn't vote: we fancy he means to resign his seat. Yesterday he said he intended to make a public announcement to that effect, but I suppose somebody got at him.

21 MAY 1912
Elibank says there ought to be a third law officer . . . Rufus Isaacs certainly has had a terrific responsibility . . . He habitually rises at 4.30 a.m. – actually on the day the Titanic enquiry opened, he only began to read the depositions at five in the morning. Only a most abstemious man could survive.

23 MAY 1912
Bonar Law seems to have made a capital speech at Glasgow. He shows great staying power. What pleased me most about his recent speech at the Albert Hall, was that he had only prepared it in a very general sense, committing nothing to memory, and trusting to the sequence and intuition of the moment. This speech followed his attack on the H.R. Bill in the H. of C.: and he was thus limited in time for thought and preparation. The result will add to his self-confidence which will greatly assist him.

[35] Formerly Akers-Douglas
[36] Sir John Jackson (1851–1919), MP (Cons.) Devonport January 1910–18.

The impact of Bonar Law

I do not like the Norfolk byelection.[37] It is true we have reduced the Radical majority by fifty per cent, but the Radical victory will be treated as a triumph, not for Home Rule, Disestablishment, or Insurance, but as a proof that Lloyd George's recent excursion into bucolic problems, is the only method of retaining the shires. A minimum wage of twenty shillings a week for agricultural labourers, and the further promise that the towns shall pay for the country – these are the implied results of the recent policy – to be embodied no doubt in a budget of 1913 contrived to reestablish falling Radical credit as was the case with the Finance bill of 1909.

But can this be successfully accomplished twice in five years?

2 JULY 1912

General meeting at the Carlton, to consider the new rules put forward by the committee – increasing our membership by 200, reducing the unwieldy numbers of the committee, appointing a chairman of the Club. All these reforms are desirable, and they carry with them the appointment of a political subcommittee which if well handled may be of real service.

Londonderry in the chair. He allowed members who were elected in the fifties to prose their reminiscences – he put all the questions wrong – some of them he omitted altogether until challenged: he forgot to count the votes and so on – he is not a brilliant M.C.! Father raised his voice in protest against our proposals, but Londonderry effectually queered his pitch (likewise that of other malcontents) by confusing the issues on points of order. Ultimately we settled to make the changes, Father and his friends taking their defeat in excellent good part – he being still rather timorous that some of the new members will rob him of his favourite sofa.

3 JULY 1912

One of those visits from St John Brodrick, when he feels the statesman all over, talks in mysterious ellipses, swears one to secrecy on topics which are the talk of the town, and finally after half an hour's confidential whisperings leaves one hopelessly bewildered.

4 JULY 1912

There is a battle royal in progress between the Liberals and their socialist allies. We watch with interest – *tertius gaudens*! – but it all connotes a growing consciousness of strength among the Labour party which must end in the death of historic Liberalism.

LORD BALCARRES TO LADY WANTAGE, 6 JULY 1912

The bulk of the Labour members in parliament are in reality no more than

---

[37] The Liberal majority fell from 1143 to 648 in the Norfolk NW by-election, 21 May 1912.

advanced Liberals; and there are many orthodox radicals who go a great deal further than the so-called socialists. The Labour party is small, compact, pretty well-disciplined, and by no means anxious to see its numbers materially increased. They number 42 – sufficient to allow their numbers to tell, and too small to saddle them with constructive responsibility. Whenever they have had to do more than act as critics, their failure has been manifest. Nobody knows this better than their chairman, Ramsay MacDonald, who is the biggest failure of the parliament.

8 JULY 1912

I met the whole Canadian government again tonight at dinner. B.L. entertained between sixty and seventy people at the Carlton Hotel to do honour to Borden and his colleagues – a costly and rather congested function, but as things go, well done for a hotel, under the discreet guidance of George Stanley and Johnnie Baird ... Borden sat between the two stupidest men in Britain, viz. Lords Bathurst and Londonderry, but Borden I fancy was hypnotised by Londonderry's brilliant display of ribands and orders galore ... It is very good of B.L. to have entertained us so hospitably, for he is not accustomed to these lavish outlays.

9 JULY 1912

Claude Wilbraham tells me that he has sold my car for £395 which isn't bad considering that it has borne us nine or ten thousand miles.

12 JULY 1912

Long talks with Elibank who wants us to collapse business and wind up the session. His men are dead beat and he says the same applies to us, and we should therefore agree to take an early holiday. It is quite true that my own weary Willies are anxious for repose – that is their permanent and abiding ambition. None the less I have many active and combative members who have no intention of being unexpectedly silent, and they are determined to criticise the government as though the summer were yet young and the temperature still low. Of this I am confident – that if I could keep 220 men at Westminster until 7 August, the government would infallibly be defeated, so slack has their attendance become.

28 JULY 1912

I had a long talk with St John Brodrick about politics, particularly about the future of Lords Curzon and Selborne. I gather that if we come into office tomorrow St John (who is under no illusion about his own status) would try to get A.J.B. selected as Secretary of State for Foreign Affairs.

6 AUGUST 1912

Elibank tells me that he proposes to resign his office immediately, and to retire into private life. He will take a peerage and is anxious that the Duke of Atholl should authorise him to be styled Lord Murray of Elibank.

I am surprised: and I expressed regret that he should not have been a secretary of

The impact of Bonar Law

state. However the case he put before me is based wholly on personal reasons – and has nothing to do with dissatisfaction at the recent laxity of ministerialists, nor is it connected with the forthcoming campaign against landlords.

Some time ago his father handed over the paternal estates which are penniless and in bad order. Elibank himself with his two brothers who depend upon him must make every effort to retrieve the financial position, and at one time he thought of going to Bombay or New Zealand where as governor he could still take a share in public affairs while letting the estate and effecting the economies of absence. A more lucrative office has however presented itself, giving him also greater freedom, and he hopes in the course of a few years to return to public life. I wonder if he will succeed. He will soon get out of touch with living politics. New interests will assert themselves with him and new men will step into the posts he has abandoned.

7 AUGUST 1912

I had a melting, almost tearful interview of farewell. I think Elibank is sorry to surrender his trust especially at a moment when the outlook is none too rosy. But he is making the most of his *démission* and the papers are full of him. One would think that a prime minister were retiring. More fuss is being made about it than when C.B.'s turn came to an end.

Of course Elibank has wielded great power. Asquith is lymphatic and indolent – much of his functions is now vested in the chief whip. Moreover the honours list has been substantially what Elibank chose. He gave his own father peerage last year (as a measure of precaution). Now he invests himself with a similar honour and enters into partnership with a man he ennobled a very few years ago. Lord Pearson[38] will find Lord Elibank a cool and determined negotiator well-fitted to deal with the astute Mexican financier or the emissary of the Standard Oil Trust. It is not for nothing that one goes through the experiences of a party whip.

How will the exchange of duties affect my colleagues and myself? Illingworth,[39] the successor of Elibank, has been hitherto occupied in constituency work and is unversed in the niceties of parliamentary affairs. This would at first sight appear to help us, but I doubt if we must necessarily benefit by the change of personnel. He will be suspicious, always on his guard, and when outmanoeuvred will consider he has been tricked. The conversations between Elibank and myself have always been frank and cordial. Not only did we understand each other, but each of us realised that the other knew the machine. Now in dealing with Illingworth the allusive and elliptical discussion will be impossible: he doesn't know all the practices of departments. He has never sat in opposition. Gulland[40] will doubtless see him through, but the prospect of daily intercourse with the new patronage secretary is somewhat embarrassing.

[38] Weetman Pearson, first Viscount Cowdray (1856–1927), contractor and oil magnate.
[39] Percy Illingworth (1869–1915), Liberal Chief Whip 1912–15.
[40] A Liberal junior Whip since 1909.

9 AUGUST 1912

The Manchester election is a tremendous blow to the government... The good news will invigorate our party and if only we have the good fortune to secure three or four more such contests before Xmas, we will have the government out.

12 AUGUST 1912

A flatulent and rather vulgar letter from Churchill fills a column and a half of the newspapers, attacking B.L. for his attitude towards Ulster. Had B.L. confined himself to polite expressions of sympathy and regret, the responsibility resting on his shoulders would be increased tenfold by the ultimate catastrophe.

24 AUGUST 1912

Events in Ulster are beginning to move rapidly. The announcement that a solemn covenant will be subscribed to before parliament reassembles, will perhaps bring home to the scoffing and sceptical Radicals that opposition to Home Rule is no mere matter of bluff.

8 OCTOBER 1912

Long talks with Carson, Austen C., B.L. and others about the debate of next Thursday when Asquith will propose a drastic motion of guillotine to stifle debate on Home Rule. I am most anxious that our men should not create disorder. Many of them especially Irish Unionists are anxious to do so on the ground that nothing short of suspension following turbulent scenes will impress England with the depth of their convictions. This is an error of judgment. I claim to settle such a point of discretion and I am certain that from every point of view a scene of rowdiness would be most prejudicial. Carson himself is ready to acquiesce in our view, but I can see that were we to encourage disorder he would readily lead the tumult.

LORD BALCARRES TO LADY WANTAGE, 8 OCTOBER 1912

What is worrying me is the avowed intention of Ulster members, backed up by English sympathisers, to provoke a serious row and get suspended when the home rule guillotine is proposed on Thursday next.

But a far more grave outcome would be the inevitable reprisals in Ulster iself. The Belfast people would consider their representatives had been unfairly treated and nobody can predict the issue of a violent riot in Belfast.

...That the Belfast artisans are both ready and willing to 'fire out' the nationalists – to drive them and their families outside the boundaries of the city, is admitted by all acquainted with the situation. Carson tells me that he has impressed the absolute necessity for reserve: I have been trying to convince him that to provoke demonstrations in parliament cannot fail to produce bloodshed in Belfast. In one way the government would be relieved by such a revolution. What terrifies the government is the latent strength of Ulster – the knowledge that a terrific explosion may take place any day. Once there has been an outbreak the government will know where they are – they will lay the blame on the loyalists, they will appeal to traditions of orderly government – and prosecute the ringleaders. Ulster will have been the first to lose her nerve. The imperative necessity is that she should retain self-control.

10 OCTOBER 1912

The debate went off well from first to last. We had the best of the case throughout – and although there were angry passages, no serious disorder occurred. Asquith as usual was perfunctory and turgid. Jack Tennant[41] has been explaining his absence during the last few days by saying that he (Perrier Jouet I mean) has been suffering from a carbuncle on his neck. There was no symptom of any such disorder today, and so general is the belief in Asquith's indolence that everybody calmly assumed he has been malingering. I wonder what Asquith really wants. He takes little pleasure in the patronage of his office, and he neither shares the enthusiasm of his colleagues for Home Rule, Disestablishment, etc., nor does he seem to believe in their desirability. Of course he is lazy and greedy too; and will never again be able to earn even a competence at the Bar. £5,000 a year together with free lodging, immunity from rates, and many a comfortable picking, must be of material value to him – for the extravagance of his living would of necessity be curtailed on retirement. Yet notwithstanding all this I never can quite make out why he retains office when every day that passes makes his personal position less tenable and his personal honour more elastic. It used to be believed that old Tennant[42] left secret instructions that his executors were to pay an increased allowance to Mrs Asquith so long as her husband was in power. The will says nothing on the subject but the expensive rate of their living – far in excess of the six or seven thousand a year they enjoy, certainly gives colour to the rumour.

14 OCTOBER 1912

The common talk of the lobby and the City is government corruption – personal corruption. The radicals seem to vie with one another in payment for honours and in recoupment via public contracts. Never before have such rumours been so prevalent, nor has there been so much ground for their foundation. These penniless ministers are not living at their extravagant rate upon their official salaries. Lloyd George is not building his new house out of his salary. Somebody must be financing him. Who, and above all, why?

18 OCTOBER 1912

After dinner I talked to Lady Minto,[43] who like other dethroned empresses feels the world is flat and profitless. She hates having to tell a cook that the bacon is nasty,

---

[41] H. J. Tennant (1865–1935), Liberal minister and Asquith's brother-in-law.
[42] Sir Charles Tennant (1823–1906), father of Mrs Asquith.
[43] Vicereine of India 1905–10

after so many years of greatness when such details were left to aides-de-camp. She is a woman of great charm and commendable reserve. I wish there were more who shared her dislike of notoriety and advertisement. She says that she is sadly shocked by the increasing standard of extravagance and still more by the odd and undesirable types whom she meets in good houses. This she attributes to pushful and ambitious Americans: I doubt if she is right, for the wealthy semites (Cassel[44] was sitting opposite us) are far more irresistible – they at least are clever.

21 OCTOBER 1912

Conference with B.L. – a shadow cabinet of MPs. Personally I believe them to be useful, but it is clear that B.L. dislikes them. He is always afraid of an explosion between Austen and Walter Long. Whatever the former says is immediately pronounced ridiculous and 'I never heard such a proposal' – Walter is *très difficile*, and B.L. suffers during these recurrent crises.

The effect of this reluctance to discuss all and every topic with his colleagues is to defer decisions which are overdue. We have never collectively faced amendment of the Insurance Act, Food Taxes, referendum, constitution of the House of Lords – all these outstanding questions more than ever demand a concerted lead, and were a crisis to occur unexpectedly we should have to extemporise a policy.

B.L. feels that the crisis may be deferred and that decisions taken today might therefore prove premature: moreover that our destructive criticism of the government is useful, and that we should imperil it by accentuating our internal differences. All this is true enough, yet I think it would be worthwhile to arrive at a concordat, even if only to make our colleagues act more in unison. At the same time let me make it clear that our party is working admirably, without jealousies or intrigues, and that B.L. strengthens his leadership every day. He is always gaining fresh self-confidence, his speeches become more telling and incisive, and in six months time he will overwhelm Asquith every time that personage gives battle. B.L. has never forgiven Asquith for the persistent belittlement and *dénigrement* he displayed twelve months ago – when B.L., the unknown, untried and inexperienced under-secretary, was suddenly called upon to succeed A.J.B. Asquith then behaved with studied lack of generosity. His scorn about the 'new style', his patronising airs, and a provocative attitude of supercilious superiority – all these things were small and mean: and by now he must be bitterly regretting the results of his own vanity.

22 OCTOBER 1912

Long talk with A.J.B. I can't quite make out what he wants. Either he wants to be quit of the Commons, or to take a more active part – I think the latter. Anyhow I arranged that he should have stated days and hours of attendance, two afternoons a week when he will stand by and be expected to speak. Home Rule interests him

---

[44] Sir Ernest Cassel (1852–1921), financier and philanthropist; friend of Edward VII.

tremendously and his knowledge of the subject is greater than that of any other member, Carson included.

30 OCTOBER 1912

To St Margaret's for the Benson–Wake wedding . . . A huge congregation including Asquith well primed with old sherry. He went on to the reception at Dorchester House and it was announced in the H. of C. (when he was absent from answering his questions) that he wasn't well. Old humbug! It is amusing that during these latter years of his life when most fogies of his age calm down, his amorous proclivities are taking a fresh lease of life. I can't make out the truth about the stories of his recent Venetian episode. That something perilously close to a scandal occurred is however certain: also that when the trouble arose he was masquerading in the costume of a Doge. Some people say that there was trouble in the street, but I fancy it can only have been ribald shouts directed against him when taking the air on a loggia.[45]

31 OCTOBER 1912

I met Lord Stamfordham[46] in B.L.'s room, by chance, I had never met him before . I don't recall the exact manoeuvres he pursued during the veto crisis, but I well remember that A.J.B. thought he had not behaved well . . . The substance of our conversation was about the attitude of our party towards the King if he were to assent to the H. R. Bill prior to a general election. I was so much taken aback by being questioned on such a topic, for which I was wholly unprepared, that I did not marshal my views with decision.

7 NOVEMBER 1912

Ordered a new car from Claude Wilbraham: a 25 h.p. Clement Talbot, cost to be about £850.

9 NOVEMBER 1912

Went to see B.L. this morning. He spoke twice in Lancashire yesterday and travelled up in the night train. I thought he looked weary – I told him so and expostulated at these night journeys: he said he had slept with the aid of a drug. I protested vigorously, and he said that he never used such a thing except in the train: but as he travels so much the temptation will grow and on Monday I shall find an

---

[45] 'I have now learned the facts of Asquith's escapade at Venice, from the description written by an eye-witness. It appears that he was dressed up in the costume of a Doge. Whether the incident occurred on a balcony or on the Piazza is not clear, but it is certain that after dinner, when feeling very self-confident, he cast his eyes downward, saw the red robes, forgot his role, fancied himself to be a cardinal and proceeded to raise two fingers of the right hand, with which he blessed the congregation *Pontifically*'. Whereupon somebody began to pelt him with parsnips.' (Lord Balcarres to Lady Wantage, 18 November 1912). Cf. the Venetian episodes of 1912–13 in Diana Cooper, *The Rainbow Comes and Goes* (1959) pp. 94, 105.

[46] Private secretary to George V, 1901–31

opportunity of telling him to be more cautious. B.L. is practically teetotal, but an inveterate smoker: not a good combination and one which invites the solace of sedative drugs. Churchill, Rosebery and so many others have been wrecked by drugs that it is my duty to use a word of warning.

11 NOVEMBER 1912

We beat the government at 4.15 this afternoon. There was a large muster of members, and both sides whipped their men early: but our attendance was twenty-two above theirs . . . The government whips issued a stupid statement to the effect that the mishap would involve no change in the government programme. We shall see. Apparently it is not realised that a defeat on the report stage of a money resolution is not a matter which can easily be rectified.

12 NOVEMBER 1912

Asquith gave notice that he will rescind Banbury's[47] amendment. Such a course is contrary to all precedent and practice.

13 NOVEMBER 1912

We began our proceedings by a long speech from Asquith. With the greatest difficulty my colleagues in the whips' room and I, restrained our members from howling Asquith down. He may have suspected something of the sort, for he was nervous at the beginning, but noticing our quiet demeanour he warmed to his task and at the end of his speech enjoyed himself thoroughly. Bonar Law then replied by a stinging speech, moving the adjournment of the debate; we were beaten, and sporadic disorder immediately began among our men who were furious at the levity with which Asquith determined to flout the H. of C. Disorder continued, there was a row with William Bull who was told to withdraw, and finally when Rufus Isaacs was speaking the tumult became so continuous that the House was adjourned. We resumed an hour later, and Isaacs was again prevented from speaking. Helmsley then got up – the noise continued – and the House was adjourned for the rest of the sitting.

This is the beginning of civil war. Ulster if subjected to the Hibernians will consummate civil war: but the opposition at Westminster is not going to allow the cabinet to disregard every tradition of parliament, every privilege of a minority. Our protest, which in its latter stages was conducted in a quiet and restrained fashion, was a protest against the degradation of parliament: it was directed against those who mean to rule despite parliament and who are determined to avoid the sanction of an electoral verdict. Though we were disorderly and in one sense worthy of severe censure, it will be found that our conduct, whatever its ultimate development may produce, will have saved the House of Commons from being prostituted to the cabinet of the day.

[47] Sir F. G. Banbury, first Baron Banbury (1850–1936), MP (Cons.) 1892–1924.

The impact of Bonar Law

Tomorrow we shall resume our ordered and orderly protest unless the government consents to treat us with common decency.

14 NOVEMBER 1912

On coming to the H. of C. we found that many of our men wished to begin the turmoil during question time, and to force an immediate adjournment of the House. This I prevented – and at 2.30 the Speaker told me that he had a statement to make at the end of questions, namely an adjournment to give the government and the House some leisure to reconsider the situation. This accordingly took place. The Speaker indicated that alternative (and we presume more regular) proposals might be devised to extricate the government from its difficulty and Asquith concurred. Bonar Law agreed, and House was up soon after four.

... We have gained our point. We may have damaged ourselves in the eyes of strait-laced and ill-informed purists, but we have *saved* parliament from the disaster of becoming the mere appanage of a cabinet. Had Asquith's proposal to rescind been tamely accepted as an ordinary proceeding, we should have surrendered our independence: and once lost, that independence would never have been regained. From single chamber government we should have lapsed into bossing by a corrupt oligarchy. Our protest was not the angry disappointment of thwarted success – it was something more fundamental and more far-reaching – the passionate anger at trickery and deception, at the fraudulent breaches of faith, at the broken pledges of Asquith.

15 NOVEMBER 1912

Conference with B.L. The outline of the alternative procedure was submitted to us. It is very different from the high-handed method by which the government meant to dismiss the episode. I think we shall accept the proposal as a constitutional way of dealing with the subject. A.J.B. said that Wednesday last offered the only case on which he had ever considered a parliamentary row to be justified: he did not like it at all, but would not condemn.

The momentary elation, the sense of well-being experienced by the Conservatives over their parliamentary prowess, did not last very long. The happy belief of November 1912, that the Unionists were winning on the home rule issue, was succeeded within a month by a panic about food taxes which nearly destroyed the party from within. Nevertheless, November 1912 is a good point at which to take stock of the first phase of the Bonar Law revival.

LORD BALCARRES TO LADY WANTAGE, 15 NOVEMBER 1912

Last night's meeting at the Albert Hall was very striking. They cheered Bonar Law for five minutes without interruption. This morning when talking it over, he said in his naive way, 'I think it must have been owing to the row in the Commons.' Possibly that was an element in the welcome, but the real reason was the growing feeling that Bonar Law is a straight simple and direct person, transparently honest and sincere, and one behind whom the whole party can rally.

His progress has indeed been remarkable. Wednesday was the first anniversary of his election at the Carlton Club, and since then he has worked hard, and is quickly establishing a strong position in the hearts and intellects of his party. As a debater he is decisive and uncompromising – as a leader he creates real enthusiasm, and he has a modest bearing which has silenced jealousies and prejudice.

He has still a good deal to learn. My chief anxiety is his marked disinclination to master the methods and procedure of the House of Commons. He is like a general who does not understand his artillery or a naval officer who ignores navigation. The leader of a party may find himself in a serious position if he always relies upon his whip – and though I am always beside him, occasions occur when there is no leisure for consultation . . . However I am trying to persuade him to study our complex and intricate machine.

One great improvement during the last twelve months, arising out of his growing confidence both in himself and in the allegiance of his followers, is his increased command of language, or rather the form in which it is clothed. He follows A.J.B. who was a master of dexterous phraseology – who never went further than he meant, and who could veil his utterance with singular discretion. B.L. cannot yet be certain of moulding the phrase to secure the exact complexion and form he may desire – and consequently in delicate circumstances I always feel some latent fears. Here again his progress is striking – and as he has an infallible memory there will I hope be an ever-decreasing danger of a right thing said in a wrong way.

. . . B.L. has learned another lesson – how to disregard opponents who wish to 'draw' him into a premature or unconsidered statement; at least I think he has realised what a real danger this is. I was very much amused the other day to find that John Baird, his private secretary, brought him into the H. of C. to watch Austen Chamberlain and Carson, who were sitting together, and talking, while somebody was trying to 'draw' them about the Provisional Government of Ulster. Instead of replying they sat there laughing and talking to one another . . .

16 NOVEMBER 1912

One further observation on this dramatic, scandalous, and paradoxical week. The opposition whips have shown how strong is their control over Unionist members – not in driving them into one lobby or the other which is the only thing the government whips think about – but strong in a far more essential matter. We can now convey information to every member of the party in incredibly short spaces of time – and our men recognise so fully that whatever we suggest is based upon careful thought, that they accept our advice like lambs. It was difficult for them to hear Asquith in silence, but they did it, and events justified our counsel. Then again as regards ourselves we preserve anonymity – we don't figure in the press. My name has only appeared once or twice in the newspapers while that of Pike Pease who does all the technical work of whipping, has never once been mentioned. This is good. Banbury is the hero in the eyes of the public, though he was the mere vehicle of the government defeat. Our influence is all the stronger from the fact that we move in the shadows: and our men know that whatever credit is earned is ascribed directly to themselves.

Elibank committed a great error of judgment by frequent paragraphs and communiqués. His men thought their services received poor acknowledgement, moreover these press notices were often inaccurate and were often proved to be misleading. That was another of Elibank's mistakes, which Illingworth has not yet realised. Coolness and self-effacement are the most potent agencies of successful whipping. We know it – the Radicals don't. Constant conversation and conference, avidity in listening to bores, frequent requests for advice – here are more weapons in our armoury, and to continue our success we must continue these methods, and thus retain the confidence we have earned.

17 NOVEMBER 1912

Tommy Bowles told me that the Rothschilds are prepared to finance him if he will bring an action against a member of parliament for drawing a salary without statutory authority.

22 NOVEMBER 1912

This affair of the Whitechapel seat is a small incident in the much bigger silver scandal. A little knot of Radical Jews has secured the manipulation of millions of Indian money, and the case against this hateful jobbery is developing with a rapidity which causes deep alarm among ministerialists. The circumstances are being probed with sagacity and daring by Rupert Gwynne – 'Rupee Gwynne' as a breezy Nationalist has nicknamed him. Already I detect movements in influential quarters to try to stop the revelations. Revelstoke[48] called me up on the telephone last night to say that he thought the subject had been pushed far enough, and asked me to check its further development. He gave no reasons – but if rumour be true, that the Bank of England (of which Revelstoke is a governor) has recovered its lost contract, it may well be that they are anxious, now that *their* honour and competence have been vindicated, to leave well alone. I hardly know Lord R.: and he certainly does not know me well enough to issue such a fiat. I always look upon him as a money-maker *pur sang*, and he has scrupulously refrained from identifying himself with our party. He must not be squeamish if his hints are disregarded.

30 NOVEMBER 1912

We have been wondering what line Lloyd George would take at Aberdeen. The meeting had been boomed a good deal and something sensational was expected ... Apart from a few vulgarisms and occasional appeals to rapacity, he has concluded that the time is not yet ripe for developing a comprehensive attack on property. What is the inner significance of this restraint? We know that he does not want to

---

[48] John Baring, second Baron Revelstoke (1863–1929), merchant banker. An excellent character of him, though not of wide enough interest to print, appears in the MS diary, XLIV, pp. 88, 95.

legislate *now*: the scheme is a bait for the next general election. We know also that after 11 November[49] there was a strong section in the cabinet which wished to resign. (Mrs Asquith is credited with the determination of the government to hang on). It would therefore appear that the government still hopes to outlive the next eighteen months, so that a disclosure of the new policy would be premature, or in other words would have lost its freshness before the election.

Meanwhile ministerialists are in a jumpy mood. They constantly expect snap divisions, and make elaborate plans to ward off attacks which we have never thought of making. On Thursday night the lobbies were full of rumours that Illingworth had warned the Radical agents to be ready for a dissolution in January. I don't believe it, though the information reached me from a variety of sources. If it be true, it means that the government is prepared to incur a defeat at the polls, hopes us to secure a bad majority, and then to beat us sufficiently to give them a strong majority for the next few years.

4 DECEMBER 1912
Long talk on defence with A.J.B. He is not quite so certain of his ground as in 1905: but he still ridicules the possibility of effective invasion while anything like a fleet exists.

[49] i.e. the government defeat mentioned above.

The food taxes crisis,
December 1912-January 1913

Bonar Law threatens immediate resignation – shadow cabinet of 4 December on food taxes – Gilbert Parker's earnings from novels – Churchill sacks the First Sea Lord – the King's visit to Lancashire dreaded – Asquith's 'mellow bonhomie' pleases Unionists – Curzon's asperity to Bonar Law – why the decision to drop the referendum was held back – the King 'saves Churchill's political life' – a five foot Christmas cracker – Lord Derby's life at Knowsley – internecine battles in the Unionist press – Austen Chamberlain suggests total abandonment of food taxes – Bonar Law's coolness and popularity – the late Duke of Abercorn – Carson declines Bonar Law's offer of the leadership – other leaders found wanting – Joseph Chamberlain admits food taxes to be impossible – memorial to Bonar Law universally supported – press reactions – Balfour's view – Nijinsky loses his pearl necklace – reactions to Bonar Law's announcement – Balfour's pledge on female suffrage – possible candidates for new chief whip.

During 1912 Bonar Law had consolidated his position and endeared himself to his party by concentrating on an issue for which he was ideally suited, namely the defence of Ulster against home rule. What he had not done was to make clear where his party stood on the intricacies of the fiscal question. Not surprisingly, confusion abounded, and when Bonar Law belatedly tried to lay down a doctrine, there was an explosion.

Just before the December 1910 election, Balfour had offered a referendum on tariff reform. This pledge was conditional on home rule also being put before the people, which it manifestly was not, and Balfour's pledge had in spirit if not in name lapsed by the end of his leadership, but without anything taking its place. Moreover, Balfour's pledge applied to tariff reform generally, not to food taxes as the most objectionable part of that scheme.

On 8 November 1911 Austen Chamberlain repudiated the referendum on his own behalf. Nothing happened, however, until next spring, when the shadow cabinet agreed almost without demur to a repudiation of the referendum and a commitment to food taxes. This was a private decision, not known to the party at the time. Then another delay occurred, until on 14 November 1912 Lansdowne announced, on behalf of Bonar Law and himself, an unqualified commitment to the policy agreed by the shadow cabinet in the spring. Lansdowne's speech at the Albert Hall left open no avenue of retreat. It was followed on 23 November by a poor by-election result from Bolton, which suggested that the 'overwhelming loss of public favour', the only faint hope that Unionists still had of stopping home rule, was unlikely with the millstone of food taxes around their necks. A second speech, by Bonar Law at Ashton on 16 December, though more moderate in presentation, failed to stop the rot, which took the outward form of a campaign by the Northcliffe press and an impending revolt by the Lancashire Conservatives under Derby. The latter group, due to meet on 21 December, deferred their meeting for three weeks, thus creating a timetable within which the party had to solve its problems, or face disaster.

The shadow cabinet in the spring, and Lansdowne and Bonar Law in the autumn, had acted in all innocence, unable to foresee an unexpected upsurge of feeling throughout the party which only really occurred after they had committed themselves. Bonar Law himself recognised quickly that it was no mere provincial intrigue by Lancashire free traders. 'The strongest Tariff Reformers are all coming to me saying it is impossible to fight with food taxes', he wrote on 31 December. '...I am not going to depart in the least from the policy we have laid down, though (between ourselves) I am convinced that it must in the end be modified.'[1] Bonar Law was not acting on grounds of honour alone; he had to consider whether abandonment of food taxes would unite the party any better than their retention. Uncertain on this point, he chose resignation, leaving the onus on the party of defining its position. This method of securing unity behind a drastic change of policy, without the leader being involved, reminds one how a chess-player's skill may avert the fate of Peel. Balcarres's memoranda on the shadow cabinet of 4 December (only the second held that calendar year) and on the week of crisis early in the new year, give in unprecedented detail the daily conversation at Westminster.

MEMORANDUM, 30 NOVEMBER 1912

Conference with B. Law, also present Carson, F. E. Smith,[2] and Austen Chamberlain. B. Law seemed to indicate clearly that he entertains no insuperable objection to what I will call the *Daily Telegraph* policy – i.e. no food taxes till after a second election, but that it is essential that were he to modify his attitude, that he should not do so in response to active and open pressure. Furthermore that if the Lancs. Union on the 11th presses a resolution against his Ashton policy he can see no alternative to an immediate meeting of the party, at which he would tender his resignation.[3] Accordingly he wishes the N.U. meeting to pass something in the nature of a dilatory motion. Austen C. said that he thought a party meeting should be called prior to the 11th, and assuming that MPs would rally round B. Law, then the Lancs. gathering would hesitate to take a hostile attitude...[4]

... Austen very frank: said he did not see how we could even postpone the food

---

[1] Blake, *op. cit.*, 114

[2] Smith told Balcarres that he would drop the whole of tariff reform to save church and union, especially with rumours current of a snap election in February 1913.

[3] Balcarres contemplated this with dismay. 'A.J.B., Carson, Walter, Austen, all out of the question.' Chaos would supervene, 'an election would infallibly follow – defeat by 200!'

[4] Smith offered to attend the Lancs. meeting to keep it quiet. He did not repeat his private remarks hostile to tariff reform (see n. 1 above).

taxes, which he considers inseparable from the rest of T. Reform and moreover that the counties would go against us if all T.R. benefits were to be for the urban artisan. So far as he was concerned he could not join a government which dealt only with domestic side and jettisoned that relating to Empire.

...Carson said retreat quite impossible – hauling down the flag would be dishonourable, we should be discredited, etc.

Later. Conversation with Austen. I told him the evidence – candidates ready to retire, Press more and more hostile, Birmingham itself vacillating – cost of living making food taxes more and more hated: nine out of ten[5] of our MPs anxious for an exit from the difficulty – however he is quite immovable.

Our difficulty is to some extent personal. Austen is intensely loyal to Joe. B. Law feels himself under some special obligations to Austen, and will do nothing (at any rate *now*) without Austen's consent. The postponement until November [1912] of the decision to drop the referendum – a decision arrived at in March – was chiefly owing to B.L.'s anxiety not to appear as throwing A.J.B. overboard. Here are three personal qualifications within which half our difficulties lie concealed.

MEMORANDUM, 4 DECEMBER 1912

Shadow cabinet, Lansdowne House.[6]

Present Lord L., Curzon, Ashbourne, Alfred Lyttelton, Selborne, Halsbury, Akers-Douglas, Lord Derby, Walter Long, Austen Chamberlain, Bal,[7] S.-Maitland,[8] Cave, Londonderry, Carson, B. Law, St John Brodrick, Chaplin, A.J.B., Robert Cecil, Salisbury.

1. Lord Curzon, 15 minute speech, complained that no shadow cabinets had been held since March, dealt with 5 or 6 items of policy – said we should have sub-committees to deal with each, and formulate exact proposals to submit to country.
2. Selborne spoke about Navy and Land Policy.
3. A.J.B. said he disapproved of Curzon's idea of formulating half a dozen colossal bills while we are in opposition...
4. B. Law cordially supported A.J.B.
5. Eddie Stanley[9] groused a little about tariffs, but said he would support the party.
6. Salisbury said that Albert Hall speeches were wrong; attacked them, and then said that if the Church and the Union were sacrificed, the blame would rest with Lord L. and B. Law.
7. General dissent and some vexation – immediate apology from Jim C.[10]

[5] Cf. Lord R. Cecil to B. Law, 6 November 1912, quoting a whip as having said that only 'about 20' MPs now wanted food taxes.

[6] Lord Ashbourne left a three-page account of this meeting: cf. *The Ashbourne Papers 1869–1913*, compiled by A. B. Cooke and A. P. W. Malcomson (Belfast, HMSO, 1974), 32.

[7] As Chief Whip.

[8] As chairman of the party organisation.

[9] Derby

[10] Salisbury. 'Jim Cranborne made a real fool of himself. Much discontent (and alarm) in the party about food taxes' noted Balcarres in his diary about this incident.

8. Austen C. said the Albert Hall policy was settled in March[11] at the Shadow Cabinet, which Salisbury did not attend.

9. General conversation followed. My lips remained closed.

10. Halsbury, speaking of treatment of the H. R. Bill in Lords, said that in his experience the H. of Lords had never been 'out of order'.

5 DECEMBER 1912

Gilbert Parker [12] asked if he might dedicate his forthcoming novel to me! I consented readily. He tells me that a novel brings him in £20,000 of which £5,000–£10,000 is to be paid in advance of publication. His sale is enormous.

Jack Sandars came to see me – it seems years since we met. As he grows older (and balder) his head looks more comical than ever. He now owns a racehorse and pursues its unsuccessful career all over the country. The burden of his conversation was that Churchill has sacked Bridgeman the First Sea Lord[13] – a scandalous act of tyranny recalling the most sinister features of the Fisher régime. Louis of Battenberg is clearly marked out as the new First Lord – an excellent officer, according to general testimony, but not only a German, but a German *who employs German servants*: that I do not like.

6 DECEMBER 1912

I gave some advice to Sandars which I doubt not he passed on to Bridgeman: in the evening I got a telegram 'please contradict absurd rumours about my health'. It is clear from Bridgeman's letter that his alleged ill-health is made the excuse for his dismissal.

Eddie Derby came to see me and suggested that the King should lunch at Haigh between his visits to Wigan and Blackburn ... I suppose this will have to be done, but it is a great bore and I suppose will be a costly meal – probably we shall have to renew everything from the roads to the chintzes and water-closets. I have an invincible dislike of royal chauffeurs and footmen, the most insolent class of the community ... It appears that Eddie Stanley[14] who will be the King's host during the Lancashire tour has been told that H.M. *will* not eat with Mayors, and country houses have to be requisitioned.

By the way A.J.B. told me that he is going to dine with Churchill and Battenberg next Tuesday. He seems rather embarrassed about it, as he feels that Bridgeman is being so badly treated that the engagement ought to be cancelled.

---

[11] Cf. above, 29 February 1912.

[12] MP (Cons.) Gravesend, 1900–18: Canadian author of adventure yarns.

[13] Bridgeman was succeeded by Prince Louis on 7 December 1912. He had been in poor health, but Churchill was thought to have other reasons for the change, which became a party question. For the letters, see R. S. Churchill, *Winston S. Churchill: Companion Volume Two, Part Three: 1911–14*, pp. 1675–95.

[14] Lord Derby

The food taxes crisis

Lloyd George made a ridiculous irrelevant speech – he is only effective when not obliged to deal with a concrete subject. Asquith remains the master hand, and the only gentleman of the lot: 'he can speak better drunk than any of us can speak when sober' – a comment of B.L. the other day when Squiff shuffled through an intricate problem with skill and éclat notwithstanding the obvious effects of copious libations. He grows more popular on our side as time goes on. However much we charge him with unscrupulous conduct in supporting measures he disapproves of, and in postponing bills to which he is solemnly pledged, there is a mellow bonhomie, the nonchalance of Charles James Fox, and withal his many human frailties which all tend to conciliate an opposition. Bonar Law he dislikes because of the merciless castigations periodically inflicted. Asquith is all for a quiet life – he wishes to be calm and imperturbable, and is seriously hurt when B.L. descends upon him with lacerating attacks. Otherwise he is happy – full of good cheer, enjoying his position, and ever anxious to avoid whatever is disagreeable or shattering to the nerves.

18 DECEMBER 1912

Curzon's comment on Bonar Law's speech at Ashton-under-Lyne, represents much of the feeling in our party, but none the less was couched in a tone of asperity towards our leaders which arouses regret. We are in difficulties ... We are now on the defensive. A month ago we were anxious for a dissolution – today we would enter upon an election with anxiety, perhaps with dismay.[15]

Surprise is felt in all quarters at the criticism of our abandonment of the referendum. This was decided at a Shadow Cabinet held last February, but the announcement was constantly put off. In the first place B.L. wished to postpone it from motives of delicacy towards A.J.B., then the announcement was not to be unduly hastened forward, then it was to come at a meeting where both Lord Lansdowne and Bonar Law were speaking. We have accordingly waited for nine months: perhaps too long, and as many argue during this period of abounding trade, a great error has been made. I wonder if this is so. B.L.'s speech was a magnificent demonstration of honesty, courage, and straightforwardness, but none the less we are on the verge of a serious crisis.

... The Christmas recess may afford some emollient, but it is too lamentably short either for oblivion or repose. In January our troubles will re-emerge, and I much fear that the demand for a party meeting will prove irresistible. B.L. will not retain the leadership if his policy is abandoned. Lord Lansdowne will also retire. Austen C. is *ex hypothesi* impossible as a successor. Walter Long I fear is ill. There remain George Wyndham, Alfred Lyttelton, F. E. Smith, Carson: each and all impossible from one potent cause or another.

---

[15] No by-elections took place between 26 November 1912 (a Unionist gain at Bow and Bromley) and 30 January 1913, after the crisis had blown over.

December 1912–January 1913

Went to Manchester where I met Sir Francis Bridgeman – what I expected has come to pass. His interview with the King on Saturday has impelled him to withdraw his demand that the Bridgeman–Churchill correspondence should be published. I can well understand the King's anxiety to hush up a grave scandal, but I doubt if he fully appreciates what a conspiracy is to be concealed. He is saving Churchill's political life. I gave Bridgeman the draft of a letter to Churchill withdrawing the demand for publication of the correspondence–probably the admiral will maul and mess it prior to despatch.

27 DECEMBER 1912
We had an immense cracker five foot long or more which was triumphantly carried into the drawing room by Elizabeth disguised as Father Christmas. On investigation this monster (which cost twenty-five or thirty shillings) was found to contain a mass of toys and I really think that this giant cracker gave more amusement than the Christmas tree itself.

28 DECEMBER 1912
I went over to Knowsley to talk to Eddie Stanley about Tariff Reform. The whole family there, and after lunch they all went off to Liverpool to see the pantomime – twenty-six, of whom a goodly number infants. My conversation most disquieting – recorded elsewhere.

What a place Knowsley is – within a stone's throw of Liverpool, cheek by jowl with Prescot, squeezed by St Helens – and yet standing within a park of 3,500 acres. The park is dreary – vast expanses of smoke-laden grass, pastured by sooty red deer, but all the same its scale is so fine as to redeem many shortcomings. The house mercifully was only half rebuilt by a reforming grandfather, and a considerable portion of the handsome old structure was saved. The modern part is like a really first class hotel. Everything is done Top Hole! I saw some good pictures, portraits, and there are a few good books: no archives – all burned!

29 DECEMBER 1912
To London by the early train. Unquestionably we are in a parlous state,[16] and I have not been able to free my mind from this preoccupation during the slender Christmas holiday.

31 DECEMBER 1912
This year I have been occupied throughout with politics – a year of interviews. Day by day I have seen people and collated their opinions, and I am now much more busily engaged on this job than ever! The accessibility of the whips to all members

---

[16] Likewise Balfour, who wrote to Balcarres from Whittingehame on 2 January 1913: 'All the communications that I get about Food Taxes are most pessimistic...'

of the party – that has been the innovation of my control, and the results have been obvious and gratifying, for discipline has merged into cooperation, and all alike now recognise a collective responsibility.

A revulsion of feeling in favour of the full T.R. policy is the ambition of a small proportion of members: how small it is difficult to determine, but my own impression is that not more than forty at the maximum oppose what one calls the *Daily Telegraph* policy.

So far as I can see the motive power of this group rests upon the Point of Honour – upon the belief that surrender so-called must involve immediate defeat. These men also argue that the panic is momentary and will pass away. Amery said that if Joe died tomorrow there would be a tremendous revival of the Preferential ideal. This I doubt, believing that the contrary would result, and that while shedding a dutiful tear the average Tory would feel that the millstone was removed from the neck of our benighted party.

The attitude of the press is our worst enemy. A week ago Garvin made a bitter personal attack on Lord Northcliffe. Today Gwynne has a similar leading article in the *Morning Post*. The *Daily Mail* has hitherto refrained from such personalities, but may perhaps reply with comments on Lady Bathurst's politics or the extraction of Astor. All this tends to make compromise difficult and reflection impossible. The movement to revise our policy is not based on the halfpenny press, but journalism is more than capable of preventing reconciliation.

This infraction of journalistic solidarity and etiquette is novel, and deplorable as well.

Bonar Law, with whom I have had few opportunities of conversation today, actually suggested a party meeting. This I deprecate – all whips do, for apart from the inevitable publicity, the meeting is generally monopolised by the crank and the bore: but I don't see what good object such a gathering would serve.

The sentiment of affection and regard for B.L. continues undiminished. He can readily secure a unanimous vote of confidence, but acquiescence in our present policy, no! The vast bulk of our MPs and candidates heartily desire a change.

I think B.L. overrates the gravity of changing front. The Radicals would of course laugh, but only for a few days, and their smile would at best be somewhat sickly. Discredit of our honesty and conviction amongst our own friends influences B.L. a good deal: but he does not appreciate that persistence in our present course means driving an unwilling army rather than leading a willing host.

It is generally said that George Curzon is 'Tory' who writes disagreeable anonymities in *The Times*. The second of these letters was quite turgid enough to emanate from his pen.

Conference of Lancashire members with B.L.: 5.15 till 6.15, 16 or 17 of us present.

B.L. said our conference was in view of the Lancashire meeting of the 11th: he recapitulated his position – said he could not be bustled, and that a hostile vote might lead to his resignation and Lord Lansdowne's. He suggested that after discussion a vote of confidence should be passed. General acquiescence.

The meeting was unanimous in favour of some change. Dick Chaloner (who is the only Lancs. member, with the possible exception of Wolmer, who is now a food taxer) was absent – playing chess and forgetful. F. E. Smith made a long speech – indicated that he had been utterly misled as to the feeling about the referendum: he pointed out our hopeless dilemma if B.L. goes, and showed that Carson, Walter, Austen are all impossible as leaders – he did not mention himself in this connexion.

6.45 to 7.15. Conversation with Austen. He begins to see the gravity of the situation, the danger of a split for which he will be held responsible.

I told him of the personal aspect as regards himself, and he has been talking to Milner. (What are Milner's views?) He said that if we recede he won't chuck parliament, he can't give up a career, but that were we to come into office and were he offered the Ch. of the Exchequer he would have to refuse. He seemed to think this his natural post, and he seemed rather surprised when I said that it might well be that the Admiralty would be equally important (pleased too!).

He said that twelve months ago B.L. had said to him that under no circumstances would he, B.L., change his policy unless with Austen's assent. Quite recently Austen reminded B.L. of this, and assured him that so far as the promise could be looked upon as permanently binding, there was an unconditional release. I know that B.L. apart from any formal pledge has considered himself much behoven to Austen and has always been anxious to act in the fullest cooperation.

Austen says that if we give way – if we compromise, there will be a serious reaction the moment we have changed: this is true enough. Moreover he interested me by insisting on this aspect of the problem: that if we do change our attitude, the compromise suggested by the *Daily Telegraph* is inadequate. We had better be whole-hearted and surrender the food taxes altogether. If we can't pass them now we never shall, and therefore let us get all possible help by their emphatic abandonment. Perhaps an alternative form of preference may be found, as today's leader in *The Times* tries to indicate.

Gossip about an early dissolution. I doubt if the govt has the nerve to do it; but would the King grant one in view of the contingency contemplated under the Parliament Act?

The right of rejection of bills by the Lords was distinctly conferred to act as a moratorium and there seems no adequate cause for a general election.

It is now said that Oliver is 'Tory' of *The Times*. This may be so, except that Oliver is not a Tory.

On 3 January, Balcarres summed up the situation for Chaplin, who was ill. He saw 'an extraordinary and unbroken loyalty towards Bonar Law, more widespread than

The food taxes crisis

anything I could have thought possible towards any leader ... Certainly no leader on either side of the House has ever succeeded in killing rivalries or animosity as he has done ...' The party as a whole, including many ardent tariff reformers, was ready to unite against food taxes, even if the number of MPs disagreeing was larger than the twenty mentioned by The Times *lobby man, Nicholson. Left to MPs, the matter might have solved itself, but the violent war within the Unionist press on the question artificially stimulated the crisis. Never before had leading editors and proprietors been moved to revile each other by name and on a personal level in print; the lobby correspondents, who had no hand in it, were as shocked as MPs. Garvin in particular was completely losing self-control, with the* Express *in hot pursuit. In contrast, Bonar Law kept perfectly cool and unimpassioned, while Austen was scrupulously refraining from leading a clique or section within the party.*

3 JANUARY 1913

Friday. Thin House. Advanced T.R. party beginning to organise and they are carrying out an active propaganda, mainly on the ground that reversal of policy involves personal discredit to B.L.

It is difficult to estimate numbers. Nobody claims more than forty, most people say twenty, and others say that fifteen or so is their strength.

Garvin they say is going to spend a week at the seaside. This is the best news I have heard – yet more ozone will make him more polemical than ever.

I left London at night. Bonar Law throughout this crisis, which may well bring about his resignation, maintains an attitude of calm which is altogether admirable. He would of course regret to be driven into retirement, but at the same time in spite of his continued success, he would welcome relief from the strain of leadership – and moreover he feels that he has done the right thing, that his policy to which objection is taken, was accepted by his colleagues, and that even if he has to bid farewell to the leadership, there is nothing for which he must blame himself. Then again being human, he cannot regret the frank avowal, poured into his ears from every source that if he goes no substitute can be found ... His serenity therefore is encouraging to our members and gives them a measure of confidence which would not exist were B.L. fussy or thinking of his own future.

The worst of it is that the cause of our trouble is a question of procedure rather than of conscience or principle. B.L. admits this, and yet we are in the throes of an internal catastrophe which should be settled without all the outward signs of strife. Of bitterness there is none, except among the newspaper men, who have shown a fatuous lack of judgement, not to mention the elementary requirements of English gentlemen ... It does not lie in Garvin's mouth to charge us with inconsistency – eighteen months ago he was a Home Ruler.

4 JANUARY 1913

The Duke of Abercorn[17] who died yesterday was a droll little man, void of intellect,

---

[17] James Hamilton, second Duke of Abercorn (1838–1913); succeeded to dukedom, 1885.

but endowed with an address and dignity which more than compensated for other shortcomings. He was a power in Ireland, and this was owing to a friendly stateliness of gesture which won hearts – in some ways Lord Wemyss possesses this same quality. James Hamilton lacks these things, but I fancy will make a good outdoor Duke. And now that the fatigues of parliament are removed from his shoulders, will be a much happier man.

6 JANUARY 1913 ((MONDAY)

4.30 p.m. Lord Derby came to see me: says he has seen Lord Lansdowne and that Lord L.'s lip is very stiff: talks of a party meeting on Thursday at which resignation of both leaders will be announced.

Victor Cavendish came later: same story, but is specially anxious about the H. of Lords position where the duel between Curzon and Selborne will revive all the old and half-forgotten diehard controversies and animus.

5.15 to 6.50 with B.L. – Lord L. there, also Carson and for some time Steel-Maitland. Carson confronted with sudden demand for party meeting and resignation. In course of talk Lord Lansdowne admitted that adoption of the *Daily Telegraph* policy was not a matter of conscience to him, and that if the party authoritatively desired an alteration of procedure he might reconsider his position.

B.L. stiffer. Said reputation for consistency carried credit for honesty of purpose. That climbing down was impracticable, a party meeting essential.

His idea is to announce resignation, giving history of the case from the shadow cabinet onwards. He would state that Lord L. agrees – and having stated the business he would retire from the room after recommending us to meet again shortly to choose a successor. His idea is for this to take place on Thursday.

Meanwhile what would happen? said Carson. Intrigue, lobbying, counting supporters, canvassing merits, jealousies, press campaign and all the rest of it; and after five days' distemper, for we could scarcely reassemble before Tuesday 14th, we should find ourselves begging B.L. to resume leadership, and the more effective his speech on the Thursday the greater his difficulty of accepting renomination a few days later.

The press would praise him as a hero – or one section would, the other section would call him a puppet. In short concentration on the *Daily Telegraph* policy would become hourly more difficult although the party as a whole wants this course.

The fact is that no possible successor emerges. Carson to whom the reversion was suggested by B.L. this afternoon refused point blank: his own health and the fact that Lady Carson is critically ill make such a course impossible. F.E. not universally trusted, Austen ex hypothesi impossible, George Wyndham too fussy, Alfred Lyttelton too weak, Chaplin too senile, Walter Long writes today that he is still too ill to return for another week. A.J.B. is in Scotland and I rather think means to keep away from the storm centre, and he does not wish to reassume responsibilities which were forcibly taken from him fifteen months ago.

Of backbenchers, there is no W. H. Smith: Robert Cecil is mentioned, likewise

George Cave. Neither has ever been in office, and indeed has ever served behind a govt.

Accordingly where are we to turn? B.L. much more inexorable than Lord L. who was quite philosophic about tergiversation ... The Referendum was foisted on us without consultation with the party, and withdrawn without their consent.

I greatly fear that personal considerations weigh too heavily with B.L. It is true the Radicals would laugh for a week, Garvin would have hysterics, but the govt would regret our action, and those who are apt to charge us with deserting the Church and the Union for T.R. would be furious. We risk everything including tariff reform itself.

Conversation was long, indeterminate. Tomorrow I am to receive instructions about a party meeting.

B. Law said that a week ago Garvin was privately expressing himself in favour of postponing corn taxes.

I dined with Carson and Steel-Maitland at the Travellers. Great resentment felt against George Curzon. Austen C. will get the blame for this, as people think that but for his influence B. Law would be able to withdraw. This is a pity. Already nasty things are being said about Austen.

There is a dinner at the Constitutional Club tonight – a ramp, got up by Max Aitken – I will note what passes.

7 JANUARY 1913

Very busy in H. of C. A real crisis – for we are not only in danger of losing our leaders, but equally of losing the Union, the Welsh Church, and Tariff Reform into the bargain.

11.0 a.m. Conversation with Lord Derby. He said he would postpone Lancs. meeting if needed, but most reluctant: all know they are expected and some 300 or 400 will come. Says if a party meeting is called for after Saturday he would postpone it so as not to anticipate our decision.

He says Lancs. retains its opinions, and if anything hardens: he does not anticipate any serious counter-reaction.

2 p.m., Carlton. Conversation with Carson. This morning Capt. Craig told him that late last night he went to Max Aitken's house, found B.L. there – and it was suggested (by Craig?) that a memorial should be sent by MPs to B.L. recapitulating crisis of Church, Union, and Constitution, begging him to harmonise the party, and to accept the tariff compromise.

Carson has drafted a sketch of the memorial. I gather that B.L. knows about it and does not offer serious objection. I think he is influenced by the fact that if he goes he carries Lansdowne's resignation on a matter which Lord L. does not think a question of conscience.

5.30 p.m. B.L. came to my room: said he had heard of Carson's proposal, that he had not seen the draft, but that if the number of signatures was considerable he would treat the memorial as the 'new fact' – otherwise would have to retire.

He has seen Lord L. – and presumably this view is shared by both leaders. This I trust will extricate us from our dilemma. It all depends on our true blue whole-hearted tariff reformers – if they dissent (and still more if they contrived a counter-memorial) the crisis would be more acute than ever – but I do not think that Austen could possibly countenance such action.

B.L. is tired, bored with the House, and has gone out to order a new overcoat – which he says is long overdue.

Carson says that R. Cecil as a free trader will sign the memorial – this is valuable. I doubt if front benchers ought to memorialise a colleague.

6.10 p.m. Derby came to see me. Victor Cavendish present. We agreed to postpone the Manchester meeting called for the 11th, until the 18th, i.e. after our crisis is settled one way or the other, and before B.L. speaks in Edinburgh.

Derby says that Max Aitken has called a meeting of Lancs. candidates for Thursday next at Manchester. Derby is angry – Max Aitken has only been in parliament two years and has small status in parliamentary circles.

Derby also said that H. A. Gwynne told him today that when visiting Joe Chamberlain about Xmas time, Joe admitted that food taxes could not be carried, but thought that no such announcement could be made until say next June! This is rather significant – much as Garvin's assurance quite recently to B.L. that the food taxes are an impossible burden. By the way, Arthur Lee at the Carlton told me that Garvin's attitude is largely based on personal rancour against Northcliffe. Garvin wanted to be editor of *The Times*. He wrote imploring letters to Lord N.: one letter was forty pages long! is such diarrhoea conceivable, yet A. Lee assures me he knows this amazing thing to be true and a fact.

6.30 p.m. Austen C. (Carson has been with him): showed him the proposed memorial. Austen says he could not sign a memorial to have himself decapitated – but that he undertook he would place no hindrance in the way of his friends signing it. He is greatly distressed, has a splitting headache, could not sleep last night, dreamt about Nelson 'yes, I will fight them.'

I said that his friends will demand guidance, and would not be content with a generality: he repeated what he said before, but indicated that while he had promised a minimum, he was not precluded from going a little further for the sake of unity.

I added that if as I believe the whole centre will concur and that Robert Cecil and the free trade group will acquiesce, the responsibility on the small true blue section would be increased immensely, and that a refusal to cooperate would place the whole blame on their shoulders.

Who are they? Hewins, Page Croft, Amery, Astor, George Lloyd, Col. Yate, Peto, Bigland, Archer Shee, R. Gwynne – not one of these men has been in the H. of C. more than a couple of years! and their influence seems greater than either their ability or experience would justify.[18]

---

[18] But cf. Balcarres to Lord St Audries, 9 January 1913: 'The extreme true blue tariff reformers – Hewins, Page Croft, Astor, and men like that, have actively assisted ...'

10.45 p.m. Carson will lunch with some of them tomorrow: try to adjust the draft to meet their susceptibilities which after all must be considered. I have issued a strong whip for 5 p.m. in hopes that by that hour we may have a biggish muster of men who would sign the memorial.

I saw B.L. just before we rose: he is more cheerful and is prepared to run the risk of being charged with inconsistency. His present idea is that to a written request a written reply should be sent. I hate party meetings, all whips do: and he would feel such a situation particularly difficult.

I did not trouble him with a further problem, namely whether he should accept the *Daily Telegraph* policy of a double election or else the clean sweep of corn or meat taxes for ever. Steel-Maitland thinks the latter, and the least equivocal and misrepresentable course is preferable.

8 JANUARY 1913

1.0 p.m. at Carlton, long talk with Londonderry. He has been in Ireland at Duke of Abercorn's funeral, and knows nothing, but his eloquence is undiminished. He says Ulster is not only aggrieved, but angry, and that unless care be taken the clubs and lodges will begin to pass hostile resolutions, thinking their cause has been sacrificed. Andrews specially mentioned as being distressed, but he will try to keep people in hand.

I gather that Lord Iveagh has taken the matter so much to heart that he has withdrawn his subscription from the Union Defence League – I believe it amounts to £1000 a month.

1.15 p.m. Victor Cavendish says he considers the crisis has passed and means to go to Ireland this evening. I protested. Lismore is a long way off, and it is unwise to assume that our difficulties are over. I hope they are, but much remains to be done.

Lunched with bucolic members: at the round table opposite Carson surrounded by the advanced tariff reformers and flanked by the brothers Cecil. The draft is being adjusted to meet every gradation of opinion, no easy task.

At 4.0 or soon after copies of the memorial were in committee room no. 8: Goulding, Ronald McNeill and others in charge.

George Faber says he won't sign because the prose is detestable: think I pacified him.

Fred Hall says it is insulting to B.L. – another man says it is cringing to him. Houston says that he will not swear unconditional loyalty to B.L. and that he has never yet signed a blank cheque. This I can well believe. George Lloyd has strong scruples, and will salve by refusing to sign, but sending a private letter to B.L. instead. That is no good – for a quantity of signatures is wanted rather than personal reservations.

6.10 p.m. Gibson Bowles came to say that unless he can have a seat the govt will outlive its fixed period. He alone can secure their defeat. This is speculative – perhaps also his statement that unless we give way a huge rival organisation with plenty of cash, will be established in Lancashire.

Walter Long, in answer to my letter last night, telegraphs 'suggestion is admirable. I heartily support and put myself unreservedly in your hands. Will of course come up if you want me, have already written you to the same effect.'

7.15 p.m. Carson says that if Austen C. presses for B.L. to give his reply to a party meeting, rather than in writing, that wish should be respected in order to give Austen a chance of stating his views. This requires consideration.

7.30 p.m. Capt. Craig and R. McNeill bring in the first batch of signatures, 150 in number. 180 men have been marked in today – of these some may not have heard of the memorial, and a number being colleagues on the front bench cannot sign.

Attempts to devise a communicative communiqué to the press failed after much perseverance. A bald statement of half a dozen lines was given the pressmen instead.

Saw B.L. at 10.45. He is rather more cheerful. Says that Northcliffe came to Pembroke Lodge at 9.0 this morning having motored up from Sutton Manor on purpose. This showed zeal – I gather he did little more than profess personal affection.

Rumoured in the lobbies that a copy of the memorial is missing and that the newspapers will print it verbatim tomorrow.[19] This would be unfortunate, as it is a real potpourri of compromises.

Two elements in the situation needed careful watching: Lancashire, where Derby was at Knowsley acting as a sort of regional whip, and the press. On 8 February, Derby postponed the imminent meeting of Lancashire Conservatives until the 18th, commenting 'I am in great disgrace... They think I am weakening on food taxes – if they only knew!' Derby warned, however, that whatever happened it would be absolutely necessary to allow his local Conservatives to condemn food taxes at the next meeting. The sudden death of Max Aitken's father-in-law, which had taken Aitken to Canada, was greeted with relief.

As well as managing Lancashire through Derby, Balcarres was managing the Unionist press through Alick Hood, his predecessor as Chief Whip, now Lord St Audries, whom he wanted to pour oil on troubled waters. 'The Press has been our great difficulty... What I therefore beg you to do is to see the right people... By Friday morning, if the matter goes well, the press will probably have got hold of the actual sequence of events; but it is the editorial and leading articles which should now be preparing the way for our change of view.'

9 JANUARY 1913 (THURSDAY)
The press this morning varies greatly in headlines, but (excepting of course the Radical papers) there is no hostile leading article. The *Daily Mail* is reasonable, *The Times* fairly so, *Daily Telegraph* likewise. The *Morning Post* has rather muddled a good idea which Gwynne put before me last night – otherwise we have no cause for criticism.

---

[19] The memorial was not published at the time, but the full text appeared a year later in *The Times*, 10 February 1914. A copy, with signatures, is in the Crawford papers.

The food taxes crisis

A more peaceful and hopeful atmosphere reigns in the H. of C. People are confident that the immediate crisis has ended. The Radicals are by no means elated, and in fact ought to be glad at the prospect of removing what they consider to be an injurious policy.

Some 216 men have signed by 11.0 p.m. and the memorial should be presented tomorrow. Houston has signed and wrote me a fantastic rhodomontade. Archer Shee, Bathurst, and Winterton still refuse, Gwynne has consented. Burdett Coutts rather too grand to sign.

George Lloyd asked B.L. if he minded his not signing it – rather a small question I thought. A.J.B. who arrived this evening and to whom I related the sequence of events said he would see all the reluctant members and beg them to concur.

B.L. in better spirits. It is said that Asquith means to follow B.L. at Edinburgh soon after his speech on the 24th. Yesterday B.L. tells me that Northcliffe made an odd complaint, namely that B.L. was too much under the influence of the 'great families' – silly jealous little nobleman!

10 JANUARY 1913 (FRIDAY)
The memorial was presented to B. Law this evening by Ronald McNeill – informal and no ceremony. A statement is being issued to the press giving the general results and analysis.

Total party strength	280
Signatures to memorial	231
Front bench (not asked to sign)	27
Speaker	1
Vacant seat (Lord Hamilton)	1
Ill or abroad	7
Absent from London	5
Not otherwise accounted for	8

Thus 98 per cent of those who have seen the memorial and are entitled to sign have done so. Those who have abstained are Amery, Archer Shee, A. Bathurst, C. Bathurst, Burdett Coutts, Touche, Winterton, G. Lloyd.

The proposal is that B.L. shall reply in writing, his letter to be published on Tuesday or Wednesday of next week. The alternative of a party meeting does not find much favour. His speech would have to be reported and published verbatim . . .

Market gardening and smallholders who are interested in intensive cultivation will be a difficulty. My inclination is to use the formula about the staple foodstuffs of the working classes – beef, mutton, pork, bacon, cheese, butter and bread – and thus leave open the possibility of taxing asparagus, early peas, potatoes, and so forth. These articles are worth taxing from the development point of view, and to refuse to do so will cause vexation.

B.L. is inclined to make the clean cut, and to exclude all new duties on food of whatever description.

The essential thing is that during the next week or two we should close our ranks and come to the attack with greater vigour than ever ... to divert attention from the counter-reaction which is inevitable.

A long talk with A.J.B. – yesterday also. He told me that during his absence in Scotland he has felt crisis through every pore of his skin, and that on the whole he felt himself better absent during the most critical stage of our troubles. He was interested in the account of our malady and surprised at the suddenness of its development: but had very little counsel to offer. The idea that he would return to the leadership at the present juncture is absurd.

11 JANUARY 1913 (SATURDAY)

Harry Chaplin telegraphs, in answer to a general gossipy letter sent by me, 'Thanks letter. Don't quite understand about memorial and by whom suggested, but please get and send me copy: am much afraid of troubles ahead and that any Tariff Reform is doomed.'

I can't very well send him a copy of the memorial, for the risk of doing so is considerable; we don't want it published, and hitherto the descriptions in the press have been so vague and general, that no real disclosure has taken place.

A preternatural calm reigns at the Carlton Club where it is assumed that we have surmounted our troubles. Let us hope so, But I am thinking of the counter-reaction and of the measure of vexation and annoyance which can be aroused among the disappointed groups.

13 JANUARY 1913

Much discussion about the drafting of B. Law's reply. I found that Lord Lansdowne considers the memorial 'quite good' and insisted upon its being published. I vainly urged that such a course would complicate the situation, and also enlarge the target for attack. It was left however at that.

After Lord L. had gone I reinforced my view, and explained to B. Law what I had not made quite clear, namely that many members would object to publication. F. E. Smith supported this view, which impressed B.L. who drafted a few words to insert into his reply – words which would effectively summarise the memorial itself.

B.L. then went to Lord L. who authorised the change. This caused delay and the letter cannot be issued tomorrow...[20]

14 JANUARY 1913

B.L. looks more worried today than for some time past.

15 JANUARY 1913

The reception of B.L.'s letter has been favourable. There is no disposition either to

---

[20] James Craig, the Ulster leader, wrote delightedly (13 January) that 'the differences in the party are permanently and satisfactorily cleared away! ... My small share was nothing with such a Leader to work under. Long may he reign over us and may the chief whip live for ever!!'

exaggerate its merits or to ignore the difficulties by which we are still faced. The Radical press, notably the *Westminster Gazette*, does not know which way to turn.

Here are comments made to me by various men – just the catchword of their criticisms: their disparity and contradictions do not involve doubts as to the wisdom of the course adopted.

'All right.' 'Lack of cordiality.' 'Prepared to retain leadership, but not to modify programme.' 'Very good.' 'Very good.' 'Very dignified letter.' 'Very nice. I think B.L. wrote it all himself.' 'Awfully good.' 'Grammar faulty.' 'A little stiff-necked.' 'Splendid.' 'Quite clear.' 'Excellent.' 'A very good letter, I call it.' 'Will do us a lot of good.' 'Not so stiff as I was told.' 'Not nearly cordial enough.' 'I call it a damned sight too cordial!' 'Very ambiguous: country won't know what he means.' 'Frigid.' 'Yes, but he is not old enough as a leader to be patronising.' 'Absolutely right.' 'A good business-like letter.' 'Frigid and quite rightly so.' 'A splendid bit of wording.' 'A perfect Godsend.' 'A very good get-out.' 'Extraordinarily good.'

16 JANUARY 1913

Sargent also had a try at Nijinsky, and actually got him to the studio, but the man refused to sit and spent forty minutes blubbing like a child. Sargent was much puzzled at the cause for this demonstration and ultimately discovered that Nijinsky was bewailing the loss of his pearl necklace!

17 JANUARY 1913

Jack Gilmour becomes my new whip in place of Wilfrid Ashley: a ginger-headed soldier who will be useful, and whose appointment will be popular. B.L. wanted me to have George Stanley, but he would be open to the serious objection (indeed the only one) I felt about Wilfrid, namely that he and I represent contiguous seats. B.L. finds that two secretaries are more than he can find work for – a great mistake for he doesn't use them nearly enough. Castlereagh tells me that he is going to desert Maidstone and has an understanding that he shall succeed Claude Hamilton in Kensington. I quite sympathise with his wish to be quit of a tiresome and corrupt seat – though on the other hand I told him that the safe and fashionable London borough is a deadening influence. The high and dry Toryism of Kensington had an ill-effect on Percy and estranged him from the living issues of English politics.

COMMENTS ON THE RECENT CRISIS, 19 JANUARY 1913

I. Our lack of sound information. We had no idea that the Albert Hall speech would be followed by such a panic. If on the other hand we had predicted the tumult, and the tenor of the speech had been different, if in other words B.L. had *then* abandoned the food taxes, there would have been an immediate secession, which B.L. himself thinks would have numbered fully 100 members – with Austen C. at their head.

II. What then is the explanation of the volte-face? I fancy it is that the power of the machine which has been inexorable, was broken from without rather than from within. The excuse for revolt was afforded by dropping the referendum. This was seized upon by members, candidates, chairmen, newspapers, as a method of shaking off the thraldom of the food taxes, imposed upon us by the machine (or as others say 'by Birmingham.') Some overt act was necessary to justify and to explain the revolt. Needless stress was therefore laid on the value of the referendum though its concrete merits were never held unduly high. The food taxes have always been a crippling burden – men have hated them in consequence and this is illustrated by the agility with which they rallied round the first opportunity of eliminating them from the party programme. Members say they are amazed that we should have tolerated them so long, and the the machine should have so successfully maintained the imposture of their popularity and demand. There is much truth in this.

III. The discipline in the H. of C. has been notable. Throughout this crisis there has been a marked contrast with two others I remember – the diehard business in the summer of 1911, followed by the resignation of A.J.B. during the autumn sittings. On those occasions there was much acrimony, and personal feelings ran high. During the last month nothing of the kind has occurred – indeed its total absence has been significant and most encouraging. This is of course due to the personal loyalty and affection felt towards B.L., and it is also owing to the improved organisation of the whips' room. Access to the whips is a commonplace nowadays – formerly they held aloof from the bulk of members, and allowed themselves to be surrounded by small cliques; but now that the youngest backbencher is welcomed in expressing his views, there is an exit for their sentiments, and they begin to feel mutual responsibility in the fortunes of the party.

IV. The press has not helped us. While we have maintained amicable relations among ourselves, the newspapers have engaged in vulgar and personal slanging matches. Garvin is the worst offender. The *Morning Post* has been indiscreet. *The Times* has been badly written, but with the exception of Garvin all the editors are now anxious to give us hearty support. The *Liverpool Courier* has made a remarkable coup.

V. Of our men Capt. Craig, R. McNeill, Hewins, Page Croft, Goulding, and Max Aitken have all worked hard to bring about mutual cooperation. Those who declined to sign the memorial carry little weight. While we may respect their conscience, we must feel doubts about their judgment. Amery for instance is a mountain of courage, but has shown himself so opinionated and intractable that I think he would be a source of danger to a govt.

VI. As we have been so good-humoured about it, there has been no necessity for me to use the weapons with which I worked twelve months ago. It has been needless to play upon vanity – I have flattered none, and not wheedled more than a handful of men. Neither has there been need for severity.

VII. I think the caucus has received a heavy blow.

VIII. The counter-reaction will now begin. B.L. may be able to check it at Edinburgh, but the agricultural difficulty will remain, and must intensify Irish hostility towards our party.

Insurance is not going to help us much – nor them either. Whatever may be the outcome of the future it is well that we should have had our crisis now, and not during the throes of a general election.

23 JANUARY 1913
Conversation in the H. of C. is all about female suffrage. . . . A.J.B. seems to become less zealous every year – he told me that when he was first elected (I think in 1874) the only pledge he gave was in favour of votes for women, and he scarcely remembers being pledged on any important subject ever since. Like so many others he is disgusted by the hysteria and antics of the militant group but he is aghast at the condonation which the latter received from the non-militant section.

After his father's death on 31 January 1913 terminated Balcarres's career in the Commons, his sole remaining duty was to advise on the choice of a successor. His views give a tour d'horizon *of Unionists of second rank which is worth quoting at length.*

BALCARRES TO BONAR LAW, 2 FEBRUARY 1913
The position worries me so much and it is in a sense so personal to myself that I feel unable to offer any advice...

But I shall be glad to see you tomorrow, though I fear this is a problem on which I am obsessed with hesitation and doubt.

This very fact brings home to me the necessity of having a man who can make up his mind – right or wrong. I have been through a hundred affairs of infinite greater moment, but never can I recall a parliamentary difficulty about which I was unable to offer any opinion whatever.

Let me however lay certain alternatives before you: it is of course essential that the chief whip should lead a life of abnegation since all his ideas must be freely placed at the disposal of others, and his aim must be to watch other harvests fructify – hence the man with individual not collective ambition will not succeed. This eliminates various people, for a whip must not desire to 'get on'.

Now you can promote one of my colleagues, bring in an outsider, or replace one of the retired whips.

I. My colleagues. *Edmund Talbot*[21] in many ways would be as good as could be desired, but his health is an impassable barrier. *Pike Pease* next in seniority is keen,

---

[21] Unionist Chief Whip 1913–21; but cf. below, 28 July 1913.

wholly lacks ideas of self-advancement, but is a visionary, too easily persuaded, too readily depressed. *Sanders*: calm, thoughtful, and also a man without an axe to grind, and as astute as any man who ever hunted the fox, but not imbued, at any rate as yet, with the power of drive. *Willie Bridgeman*: he is the last I need mention. He has good qualities, among them that in which I have never once failed. He is like King David in 'hating the thing that is evil.' This gives him momentum. But I fear that Willie is not a very good listener. His patience is not inexhaustible.

II. An ex-whip. *Harry Forster* you will remember retired when Alick Hood became a peer. He was fatigued – things had been going badly, and he was anxious to take a larger part in public as opposed to domestic affairs. He is cool and far-seeing but almost too imperturbable in manner, giving off an atmosphere of nonchalance: but he has great experience, analysing a parliamentary situation with justice and decision. His appointment would cause no jealousy and would place the party under an obligation towards him. It would resemble that of Herbert Gladstone who became chief whip after being first commissioner of works.

III. An outsider. This of course would become necessary in the event of the other alternatives failing. On the whole the difficulties seem hard to overcome. *Frank Mildmay* was once suggested to me, but after twenty-five years of parliamentary life he would never dream of accepting such a post: and his nature has a pleasant lymphatic strain which is agreeable in private life but a disqualification in the whips' room. *Mitchell Thomson* has zeal, great resource, impact and a good knowledge of parliament, but is an Irish member, an Orangeman, ergo a transient phantom which would embarrass us (or him) later on. I doubt if he can tolerate the Bore, and the Bore, rest assured, taken in detail, is the item which can most easily make itself intolerable in gross. *George Younger* – his name had crossed my mind but he won't do. He is doing admirable work from which he should not be divorced; and he is a man of abounding ambition and therefore not receptive enough as the medium of communication between the leader and his followers. *Johnnie Baird*. Here are great merits, but serious shortcomings, still the name should be considered though it will probably be discarded. He lacks knowledge and status and the diplomatic training is not quite what we want, for he always imagines the other man to be much cleverer than he really is. In any case I fancy that Johnnie would not yet command the needful prestige in the party, though he will attain a good position later on. *Jessel* and *Sir William Bull* both have aspirations. Neither name could be profitably entertained. Another man is *Hayes Fisher*, immensely experienced, great knowledge of London, full acquaintance with procedure, and unfailing courage. But, but, but – not equally deferential to all and sundry. He is the source of gossip about his financial ventures, and he is bitterly disliked by ministerialists. *Staveley Hill* is worth thinking of: shy, retiring and a capital speaker, intensely devoted to the cause, but I should say rather deficient in initiative, and might lose his nerve during a crisis: but such a good fellow. *James Hope*: here you would find enthusiasm.

ingenuity, and the faculty of observation. He knows all the tricks of the trade, and on certain occasions has been quite invaluable. He has much courage and a light touch, but I fear would never inspire the obscure and struggling member: that after all is one of the chief things to aim at with the party as a whole.

IV. At the end of my letter, a fourth class must be inserted as a postscript. *Steel-Maitland* was suggested to me from a source whence shrewd ideas have often sprung. I had never contemplated him myself, but at least the thought should be present to your mind. He has good qualities and his training was subtle. He will always hear a case stated. He enjoys a good deal of popularity, but I doubt if he ought to leave the Central Office, and on the other hand the reorganisation is not sufficiently complete for him to combine the two spheres. This I fancy will prove a fatal objection. In any case his promotion would be almost a shadow cabinet question as it involves a serious problem of policy. If you get a chance of talking to A.J.B. he would tell you about this particular situation with which he is familiar.

Forgive me, my dear Bonar Law, for this long tiresome letter ... How I wish I could stay with you for I feel there is still much I could have done. One word more – let me thank you for all your kindnesses and for your unwearied patience.

X

Out of Politics, 1913-16

Death of diarist's father – death duties – his father's philately – Lady Curzon's tomb – death of George Wyndham – plans for his political future – some Scottish families – F. E. Smith – Spencer Lyttelton – the shadow cabinet – the Unionists in the House of Lords – a servants' ball – the Unionists and home rule – the Mintos – Lord Londonderry on Ulster – the Curragh mutiny – Haldane's 'pregnancy' – Lord Carrington's audacity – Churchill and a central party – Lord De Mauley's penury – misgivings about the war – 'Lord K of Chaos' – Herbert Samuel on invasion – Asquith gives naval secrets to aliens – Bonar Law watched by the home office – Bonar Law's wish for coalition – Curzon as a leader – 'body-snatching' by great ladies.

It is a matter of speculation whether Balcarres' political career would in the ordinary course of things have survived his father's death. Interruption there had to be, for the intricacies of meeting death duties on an estate whose assets consisted largely of a capital-hungry, wildly cyclical, rather ailing heavy industry combined with a unique collection of works of art, books, stamps and autographs admitted of no ready answers. There was also a need for rest, pure and simple, for a decade as a Whip had excluded other interests for too long. Even so, had a peacetime election brought the Conservatives to power in 1915, Balcarres must have been a strong contender for cabinet office in a party weakened by deaths and containing few men with experience of office. What the diary shows is that despite this latent ministerial status, he was allowed to drop out of politics in a way that says something about the abilities of his party in managing men. Bonar Law in particular, who might have appreciated Balcarres' reticent professionalism as well as remembering all he owed to him, figures as curiously neglectful.

Otherwise, the diary is useful on two themes. It shows the extent to which the rich worried about death duties even before the war. Secondly, on the main political issue, home rule, which came before parliament in the successive sessions of 1912, 1913 and 1914, the diary shows that the most important thing to note about senior Conservative opinion was that it was deeply confused and uncertain, policies of reckless defiance having little to do with average party opinion. The Irish question of 1912 became the Ulster question of 1913–14; and by 1914 the Ulster question for Conservatives like Balcarres, was one of how much to settle for.

Out of politics

9 MARCH 1913

I pick up a pen again after a long blank, marking also a long and irremediable blank in my life. Father died on 31 January – a peaceful end which gave me a great and unspeakable crumb of comfort amidst distress and gloom. Since then many things have crowded into my life. I have surrendered my work and my seat in parliament. I have had audience of the King, and I am now immersed in a hundred and one things connected with succession to the patrimony and the consequent problems of death duties and so forth.

I shall not try to write in this diary any of the ideas which crowd into my mind about Father's life and the circumstances of his last few hours. These things I must try to record elsewhere with zeal and affection. But I will just note the chorus of esteem and love which his death evoked, and I can never forget the poignant grief shown by humble people in his entourage – valet, commissionaire, housekeeper, doctor and so forth. The funeral was at Balcarres, one of the most stately and solemn ceremonies I ever witnessed.

We have let our London house from the middle of April for the season, and the family will migrate to Haigh. Economy is necessary and the moral value of closing our London house is even more useful than the 600 guineas of rent which Sir Berkeley Sheffield[1] will pay us. For some time to come we shall have to exercise careful control over our expenditure and our residence in Lancashire will give me many opportunities of going into our Company business with closer scrutiny than I have devoted to this all-important subject. What with political avocations I have never devoted sufficient care to the subject, and now that Father's long experience is removed the responsibility falls directly upon myself. Upon the next few years much depends. If the dividend is good my situation will readily respond – if however the Company does badly I shall be faced by financial peril involving severe sacrifices in the way of sales – books, pictures, who knows what! We have already had three sales of the Library, but so much remains that although some of the most precious things have been dispersed, the Bibliotheca Lindesiana is still in its own way a noble and unique possession. To sell it outright would remove from Haigh (which has few natural attractions) an asset which makes adequate compensation for many a shortcoming: and apart from personal enjoyment it is well for our family to grow up amidst the visible respect for learning.

Some things must go to meet death duties and family charges: for instance the incomparable collection of postage stamps. Last year Father sold what he called the odds and ends – that is the stamps of countries other than Great Britain and the U.S.A.: for these trifles he got £25,000, and if the remaining collections sell with proportionate success we shall obtain a cash nucleus for the Inland Revenue. The French historical collections must I fear be realised as well. This gives me a greater pang for I never pretended to be acquainted with philately, and although I was not

---

[1] Sir Berkeley Sheffield (1876–1946), MP (Cons.) Brigg 1907–10, director of Great Central Railway, 1909; owned 40,000 acres.

well up in the Revolution and Napoleonic documents, the subject appeals to me in a general way, and their loss would be a source of real sorrow. It is the most comprehensive collection ever formed by a private individual.

... The financial situation gives cause for anxiety. Father never realised how greatly death duties were increased three years ago, nor how serious is the potential increase of land tax and supertax. Moreover the charges on the estate established by the 1869 settlement have descended to my shoulders. Great caution is therefore imperative and also courage in parting from treasured possessions. I can never look forward to becoming a collector, but I must strive to free the estates from debt and to preserve the pictures and books.

The immediate future will I hope be peaceful although busy in Lancashire and Scotland. Connie will be able to look upon Haigh as her home and surrounded by the children and mistress of the household, will I trust find pleasures and avocations which will really make the place a home for her. This applies in a less degree to Balcarres where the inherent charm and domesticity of the place have made her happier there as a visitor than at Haigh. The attractions of Lancashire must be repellent to all except those brought up within its ambit – and as our interests commercial, literary, political, are so much concentrated at Haigh I greatly hope she may get to like the place. Lovable it can scarcely become to the stranger but its merits are solid, its cultivation remunerative, and to the student and scholar it presents opportunities attainable nowhere else. In short we have got to be at Haigh – it is quite unsaleable, and we must try to develop a family life there to make good many shortcomings.

One thing is necessary, namely a dispersal of the Library staff. I confess my decision has caused no regrets in the family, because bibliography was carried to a point so close to the professional that sometimes it appeared as though Haigh existed for the Librarians and that nurses, children, perambulators etc. were interlopers... The administrative cost apart from purchases and binding has amounted to something like £1,500 a year and the very fact of having from four to six men in the house is an infallible incentive to buying – I can't afford to buy: perhaps indeed were I affluent enough to do so I ought to refrain for the books having filled four big rooms have overrun the passages and have recently invaded the stables. One ought perhaps to sit still for fifty years and study the literature we already possess – but all the same I should greatly like to develop certain branches of the Library – it would be a good thing to get rid of much superfluous material, and above all to concentrate all the valuable things in the Long Library downstairs – removing bookcases from the floor and having all in proper glazed shelves along the walls.

One section of the Library passes by Father's will to the British Museum – the philatelic literature which is massed in Cavendish Square and will therefore cause no ugly blank at Haigh. This is as good a collection of books on any single subject as could be found – and contains masses of pamphlets and periodicals printed in obscure corners of the world and now quite *introuvables*. I am always glad when the

Out of politics

B.M. to which Father was much attached makes itself *facile princeps* in any branch of learning – and as far as this subject is concerned, having already a superb collection of stamps, the B.M. stands unapproachable in the world.

20 MARCH 1913

A long harangue from Steel-Maitland[2] who asked me to choose a political sphere of activity – to arrange the newspaper concerns of the Central Office – or to act as chairman of a land purchase investigation, or to devise a trade union policy – he says he is determined not to let me drop out and hinted that twelve months of lethargy would make my name forgotten and dim my prospects. That leaves me unmoved. I told him that for the moment I am preoccupied by half a million of debts, and that most of the summer must be devoted to this pursuit – I did not tell him that I mean to slip away in September and get a wider vision of the world which may be useful later on. My power of resistance to these entreaties will be much increased when I am settled at Haigh and beyond the normal telephone radius.

21 MARCH 1913

For the first time in my life I made an effort to look at Father's philatelic collection. Hitherto I have never been interested in it as a subject, and as much of the collection and arrangement was conducted on board the yacht, I have not been *au courant* with its progress and development. One reason why Father was so fond of it was that within a small compass it gave him endless opportunities for research and disposition during his long cruises. Moreover given adequate means the collection was one which could be quickly matured – and in the course of ten years he not only acquired, but he arranged with astonishing skill and diligence, three great groups – the foreign, the USA., and the series of Great Britain. The foreign lot, odds and ends as he called it, was sold fifteen or eighteen months ago. I have now skimmed through the remaining collections and I confess I am amazed at the patience and research shown on the one hand, and at the courage in buying displayed on the other. To most people philately represents the hobby of the schoolboy. To myself it was always looked upon – looked down upon perhaps – as a byway in collecting, something not very creditable to those who are raised in the higher pursuits of science, literature, and art: in fact I never thought it quite worthy of Father's attainments.

This opinion I now revise. I do not think I could ever become an enthusiast, but an hour or two has revealed to me the charm of philately . . . But it is not only the stamps themselves which are remarkable, it is their arrangement – for the collection is annotated throughout in Father's neat manuscript, and in looking at a stamp the notes tell one its history and its peculiarities . . . The collection is itself unique, containing hundreds and thousands of specimens to be found nowhere else – but the historical analysis – the display of evolution shown page by page – this is what

[2] Chairman of the Unionist Party organisation.

made Father the greatest philatelist of all time, and his system of arrangement has produced a revolution in the methods of collecting . . . In short this is a great, almost a noble achievement, and in any case the best of its kind, for nothing exists which can remotely compare with it. It is a monument to Father's patience and industry – and I can only hope that circumstances which oblige me to surrender it will also allow it to be preserved intact.

30 APRIL 1913

By the way one result of these high death duties is that the mind is diverted from its ordinary channels and avocations – politics and art in my case – and is driven to concentrate upon money . . . Money in all its variety of sordid and repulsive aspects, this absorbs the innocent and unworldly mind, and becomes a dominating obsession . . . On an estate of a million sterling in value, like ours, one sixth part of the whole has to be surrendered to the state. I calculate that I owe between £500,000 and £600,000, that is taking all family portions and mortgages into account, as indeed I cannot omit to do.

1 MAY 1913

A visit from M. Charles Roux, secretary of the French embassy – he came expecting to see a handful of autographs – and his amazement can be imagined when I confronted him with a thousand signatures of Napoleon alone! It is indeed a wonderful achievement, this French historical collection, but alas must go the way of other things – I can't afford to keep them. I suppose that outside the National Archives of France there is nothing to approach this collection.

30 MAY 1913

I met George Curzon who took me into his fine house in the Terrace to see a sample of Aventurine marble, the scarce and costly material which he is using for the floor of his memorial chapel to Lady Curzon.[3] 'No such thing has ever been done before and no such thing will ever be accomplished again. It took me no less than six years to acquire sufficient of this rare and beautiful substance to cover the small floor space of the Chapel – and the surface of the polished marble is so much like ice that visitors will not be able to walk upon it unless they wear felt slippers – these I shall provide.'

7 JUNE 1913

Money has got to be raised, as the Inland Revenue people tell me with politeness that they want another £40,000 by the end of July. Except by overdrawing I fail to see whence it is to come.

[3] Mary Victoria, daughter of Levi Zeigler Leiter of Washington, USA, married George Curzon in 1895 and died in 1906.

Out of politics

10 JUNE 1913

I am shocked to read of the wholly unexpected death of George Wyndham: poor fellow his end must have been very sudden, and his death will I fear kill his dear mother. George – he was the most accomplished failure of my acquaintance, and twenty years hence when we may hope that Ireland will have lapsed into mellow prosperity, George will be recalled as the statesman who contributed most – or at any rate shared with A.J.B. in the establishment of remedial measures. He must have died a disappointed man, conscious that the suspicions aroused in 1904–5 were not allayed. For he had coquetted with Home Rule... No group of politicians require more cautious handling than Irish Unionists and Loyalists. Somehow George let them become convinced that the maintenance of the Union was not a bedrock foundation of his policy: hence the crisis which ultimately drove him from the Chief Secretaryship. Politically he was ruined. Courage and industry could well have rehabilitated him during the subsequent years of opposition – alas both were lacking. He was indolent and capricious: unwilling to take his share in the dull tedious and unremunerative spadework of the House of Commons. He had many interests outside politics – soldiering, belles lettres, Society, sport – and he missed the opportunities which I so often urged him to grasp of reasserting his claims on the party by employing his brilliant parliamentary gifts. After these exhortations he would make a spasmodic effort, but speedily relapsed – and but seldom would consent to speak except on great occasions and at the best hours. His death eliminates a problem from the next Conservative called upon to form a government. At the present juncture he would not have been offered a post. A charming fellow – nearly a great man...

16 JUNE 1913

Lunched at Carlton Gardens. Jeanie has been staying with Wilfrid Ward[4] who showed her a letter received from George Wyndham... In this letter George W seems to indicate a decision to devote the remainder of his life to the problems of rural England. I had heard of this sudden preference for bucolic life,[5] though he would soon have missed the excitements and excitations of London.. I hope this letter will not be published yet awhile, likewise a letter which A.J.B. showed me yesterday, dated November 1903 and addressed to Moreton Frewen[6] who wishes to print it in one of the reviews. This letter (well composed, and throbbing with life) talks about opening negotiations with John Redmond with a view to composing outstanding problems.

[4] Wilfrid Ward (1856–1916), Catholic writer.

[5] After his father's death in 1911, George Wyndham threw himself into running his estate at Clouds. 'Some people', he wrote, 'inherit an estate and go on as if nothing had happened. I can't do that. I must use all my energy and whatever imagination I may have to get something done that shall last and remain.' A year after his own death, his only son was killed, and Clouds was sold – Lady Cynthia Asquith, *Haply I May Remember* (1950), p. 56.

[6] Moreton Frewen (1853–1924), MP (Irish Nat.) 1910–11; Churchill's brother-in-law.

7 JULY 1913

I gather that Alfred Lyttelton's death was caused by an accident at cricket, not as one supposed by a mere strain or fatigue.

It is a sad loss – what a good fellow he was! Indolent at times, and I frequently had passages at arms with him when trying to rally our scattered and dispirited forces. Moreover he never seemed to appreciate the virtue of parliamentary example – the palpable duty owed by the ex-cabinet minister to his backbench friends.

These things however, though they brought us into friendly conflict during the last few years sink to insignificance when I reflect on his charming personality, the buoyancy of youth which like George Wyndham he preserved long after most men of his age are bald and blasé. And he had a high-spirited nature together with a broad and exalted outlook upon life, which when occasion demanded, invested him with a power and dignity lacking in men of greater gifts. I am sorry, very sorry at his death.

Retirement from public life gave Lord Crawford less pleasure than he had expected. Money was an anxiety, for the stamps, the collection of French historical material and his father's London house all failed to produce buyers.[7] More deeply felt, perhaps, was the receipt of 'the thanks of the House of Habsburg' (that is, no thanks at all) from the party leaders after ten years of arduous service. He had expected to drop politics: he was unprepared for the extent to which politics dropped him.

26 JULY 1913

The Haigh Horse Show. It cost me two and a half hours this afternoon but on the whole was entertaining and I learned a good deal of equine science. This animal institution was founded some years ago in order to 'bring our tenants together', and to improve the breed of horses by encouraging (by means of a money subvention) a good breed of horses. I believe it to have achieved considerable success.

28 JULY 1913

One result is already obvious, namely that in these few months I have completely dropped out of politics, and that I am not missed – indeed my old friend Ned Talbot[8] seems to be carrying out his duties with faultless and unwearied skill. I

[7] His aunt Lady Wantage helped by cancelling £50,000 of the £110,000 mortgage on the Balcarres estate. This had been originally lent by her husband in 1886 to enable the diarist's father to purchase the estate, which had previously been in the hands of the cadet branch of the Lindsays for most of the nineteenth century.

[8] Unionist Chief Whip 1913–21. Cf. Lord Crawford to Lady Wantage, 16 February 1913, saying that Talbot was physically unfit for his post because of an enlarged vein behind the knee which continual standing made worse. 'He accepted the post much against his will. He is a soldier at heart rather than a politician, and I doubt if he possessed the flair and intuition necessary for a swift analysis of a political situation. None the less it would have been difficult to make a better choice. He is very quiet and old-

Out of politics

quietly take comfort to myself that I am responsible for the method he follows.

Shall I drop out of politics permanently? When I was pushed into the office of chief whip, I acquiesced and performed the duties as best I could: but I shall never push myself into a position of my own choice, and being now in the background, nobody else is ever likely to try to do it for me. Moreover I feel that no minister will be able to hold office and at the same time to retain the directorate of a public company. I question if I should be justified in joining a government if it involved abandonment of the Wigan Coal and Iron Company. What folly to make it impossible for businessmen to take an active part in public affairs – this is what we are tending to.

4 AUGUST 1913

I met Alick Hood in the post office: he told me he was in town for a shadow cabinet to be held at Lansdowne House tomorrow. I have not been bidden to the feast, neither indeed have I been invited to a seat on the front bench of the H. of Lords. At Lockinge Jeanie[9] was pressing me to take an active part in organising and directing the younger peers, who at the present moment waste their time because no one helps them to use it . . .

To this I replied that although I was convinced that all hereditary privilege must be abandoned if we are to have a second house, equipped with effective powers, yet it was not my function still less my desire to lead a movement against the wishes of Lansdowne and our recognised leaders. There could be no question of the impropriety of such an attitude were I looked upon as one of their colleagues. If on the other hand, I now regain my freedom and independence I might feel inclined, when the pressure of family business is somewhat mitigated, to take a strong line on various matters of public concern.

6–10 AUGUST 1913

Drove over to Drumour – shooting . . . The equipment, the paraphernalia and above all the cost of grouse driving increases every year. There is a growing standard of comfort for instance in the grouse butts, which are now constructed with great care and accuracy in order the better to circumvent the birds: and the wages of the drivers, mostly boys from the surrounding villages, have largely increased. One now pays five shillings a day to these youths, and into the bargain they have to be driven to the moor from Birnam . . . *Per contra* when the last increase in wages was conceded, their free lunch was knocked off, which is considered a real

---

fashioned, quite free from all personal ambition, an excellent listener, popular on both sides of the house, and respected by all who know him – but alas as I said just now, not a politician. Herein lies the crucial difficulty. B. Law likes him which is a good thing – in fact essential, but somehow or other Edmund Talbot has done ten years' service as my colleague without ever realising the fundamental laws of political strategy.'

[9] Lady Jane Evelyn Lindsay (1862–1948), fourth daughter of the twenty-fifth Earl of Crawford, and the diarist's aunt. Crawford's maiden speech in the House of Lords was not until February 1914.

advantage, as the boys now bring their own frugal bread and cheese with them whereas previously they gorged themselves at their employers' expense, so freely as to find post-prandial walking a hard and uninviting task.

Though the grouse season is short, lasting seldom more than five weeks, a great deal of money is earned – sufficient to keep the local smallholders in cash, which were they solely dependent upon agriculture would fall far short of their requirements. In fact it is the extra and very lucrative work connected with the shooting which enables them to eke out a livelihood: agriculture alone in these exposed parts would reduce them to an oatmeal standard of comfort.

LORD CRAWFORD TO LADY WANTAGE, 29 AUGUST 1913

Haigh has worked coal since the fourteenth century. Every portion and jointure and allowance is settled upon it, the Wigan Coal and Iron company controls every yard of our land, and our entities are inextricably intertwined.

The affection which exists between the company and myself, the fact that there are scores, almost hundreds of *employés* and officials who were working for my great-grandfather before the company was formed, and finally what I look upon as the serious obligation of maintaining the prestige of the concern, which as you know is called 'the Barometer of the Lancashire Coal and Iron Trade', and which has to caution and control other businesses less scrupulous in their dealings – all these things combine to increase my responsibility even if they limit my freedom, so much so that rather than decrease my own holding, which prudent finance would unquestionably dictate, I can well imagine circumstances which might make me take the opposite direction.

18–19 SEPTEMBER 1913

To Pollok – staying with Johnnie Stirling-Maxwell[10] ... I was much interested in Johnnie's disposition of his park. Pollok House is about four miles from the centre of Glasgow, and surrounded by industrial quarters. The park has been regularly opened to the public, but was little used. Johnnie has accordingly made a ten year agreement with the City Corporation, under which they superintend that portion of the ground which is now practically handed over to the use of the citizens. Glasgow finds the police, regulates the admission of the public, places seats and benches, and generally treats the grounds as though they were one of their own parks, though the planting and so forth is done by Johnnie's own staff. The experiment has been a marked success, for the visitors are now constant and numerous. Very little damage is done – indeed the behaviour of the public is said to be generally most praiseworthy ...

---

[10] Sir John Maxwell Stirling-Maxwell, tenth Baronet (1866–1956), succeeded father 1878; owned 10,000 acres; MP College Division, Glasgow 1895–1906; chairman, Forestry Comission 1929–32; chairman, Royal Fine Art Commission for Scotland; chairman, Ancient Monuments Board (Scotland).

Out of politics

I grow more and more convinced that a dissolution must take place before a third reading of the home rule bill.

13 OCTOBER 1913
Went into Edinburgh where I lunched with Edmund Talbot. He is apparently in as great a confusion as I am about the issue of present controversies, and much alarmed lest some sporadic outbreak by Orangemen should precipitate the Belfast crisis and alienate English sympathies.

I made the acquaintance of Balfour of Balbirnie,[11] in these days of motor-cars a close neighbour . . . I hear that Mrs Balfour, an American, has just inherited a fortune running well into the million . . .

18 OCTOBER 1913
Cubhunting in the morning . . . Afternoon, entertained to tea the children of the estate employés, forty-five in number, with their parents as chaperones.

22 OCTOBER 1913
Travelled into Edinburgh with Carlow,[12] the chairman of the Fife Coal Company, vice-chairman of the North British Railway, and responsible also for other large commercial enterprises. Rather an interesting man . . . portly, pompous, prosperous. Later on in the day I asked Dalkeith about Carlow's history, and was entertained to hear that his grandfather was Admiral Wemyss' sailor servant, one Carlos or Carlo, obviously a Spaniard . . .

23 OCTOBER 1913
Lunched with Lonsdale[13] and Charles Craig[14] at the Junior Carlton, rapidly losing its reputation of being a better club than our own pothouse the other side of Pall Mall. I was interested to observe that both these Ulster members seem quite prepared to consider without prejudice any proposal to exclude Ulster from the H.R. Bill.

25 OCTOBER 1913
To Lockinge – travelled down with Marjorie Manners, now Lady Anglesey, the

[11] Edward Balfour of Balbirnie, co. Fife (1849–1927), m. 1879 Isabella Weyman Hooper of Boston, USA. Arthur Balfour's grandfather, founder of the Whittingehame Balfours, was a younger son of this family. Edward Balfour's son married Lady Ruth, daughter of Gerald, second Earl Balfour, of the Whittingehame line.

[12] Probably Charles Carlow, chairman, Fife Coal Co. His son Charles Augustus Carlow, born 1878, was also prominent in heavy industry.

[13] Sir John Brownlee Lonsdale, first Baron Armaghdale (1850–1924), MP (Unionist) Mid-Armagh 1900–18, hon. sec. and Chief Whip of Irish Unionist Party 1901–16, and its chairman, *vice* Carson, until 1918.

[14] Capt. Charles Curtis Craig (1869–1960), MP (Unionist) Antrim S. 1903–22, Antrim 1922–9.

most witty and fascinating little creature. I wonder if he is worthy of this bundle of vivacity and genius. . . . The Prince of Wales and his brother Prince Albert[15] were shooting, and I talked to them – liked them both, particularly the younger one . . . The Prince of Wales seems overburdened with his duties which he performs with meticulous precision – poor boy, somehow he made me feel very sorry for him, as he is allowed but little freedom and I am sure would rejoice in being himself rather more: and then he has a hard life before him. If only he would bolt with a ballet-girl, say for twenty-four hours!

27 NOVEMBER 1913

I see that a biography – and an authorised one! – of F. E. Smith is announced . . . The announcement of this volume seems to cause a good deal of acrid comment in the Carlton. There can be no doubt that he is distrusted by many men who feel that notwithstanding his uncompromising attacks on the government, circumstances might drive him into the enemy's camp, just as the Radicals fancy – wrongly enough – that Churchill is ready to enter the Conservative fold. For my own part I have known F.E. so long, and from his earliest days, that I have always felt strong enough to combat these criticisms. It is true that he has the spirit and sometimes the ethics of a freebooter, and moreover that his egoism is highly cultivated. None the less the whole tenor of his mind is anti-Radical, almost as much so as Churchill's.

9 DECEMBER 1913

Lunched with F. E. Smith at the Carlton and afterwards gave him a good lecture about his extravagance. He is earning a magnificent income, but were he offered a post in the government other than a law officership, he would find his income greatly reduced and would fret accordingly. He tells me he is saving a fair amount, and that he has insured his life for a large sum – but even so he should have put by more, for during the last five years his success has been such that he has earned almost up to his maximum capacity.

10 DECEMBER 1913

I see I have not referred to Spencer Lyttelton's death.[16] I wonder if his diary will ever be published: there is some entertainment in it, and his information on Society gossip and the trend of movement in the musical world, was good. In politics he was not so well versed, as he had the confidence of neither side – he was never quite trusted by the Radicals since Alfred joined a Unionist cabinet, and he was distrusted by ours because he would never express a good word for us. And, moreover, his

---

[15] Later George VI

[16] George William Spencer Lyttelton, CB, FRGS (1847–5 December 1913), fourth son of the fourth Lord Lyttelton; ass. priv. sec. to Gladstone, 1873–4, 1882–5, to Granville, 1880–02; priv. sec. to Gladstone, 1892–4; edited, with others, *Memorials of Brooks's* (1907); described in diary 25 July 1909 as 'nothing but a diarist, just a busy *flâneur* through society.' The late Lord Cobham had no information about 'Uncle Spencer's' papers.

early training as Gladstone's secretary laid him under suspicion: but apart from his politics which will be misleading or based upon imperfect knowledge, the diary will provide some capital reading. He was a pleasant agreeable lovable fellow, with a nice sense of humour, and many acquaintances, though few friends.

LORD CRAWFORD TO LADY WANTAGE, 12 DECEMBER 1913

Our party is distrustful of the negotiating capacity of our leaders – that is really the basis of our nervousness – and I am not surprised. The cabinet approaches these matters in a wholly professional spirit. There have been more cabinet meetings this autumn than at any time since the war. Ministers discuss the situation – quarrel about it, then compromise, assent, reject – but at least they discuss them, whereas our mandarins from one cause or another do not appreciate the immense value of the perspective obtained by an informed and unfettered conference of allies... The fact is certain people have to be invited, whose claims are obsolete – others take an undue share in the debate – Curzon is particularly open to criticism in this respect: some are stone deaf like Harry Chaplin, others obtuse like Halsbury, others lazy as Lansdowne, few alas as modest or as capable as Bonar Law.

31 DECEMBER 1913

Here ends the saddest and at the same time perhaps the happiest year I recall – sad in that it began with the loss of my oldest and closest friend, but happy from circumstances having thrown me more with my own family than ever... I have spent more time at home than any year since my marriage.

... For my own part, after nineteen years in the H. of C., during the last nine or ten of which I have occupied a post of responsibility, I now find myself stranded, with no duties, and apparently none in the immediate prospect. It is extraordinary how quickly one drops into oblivion, how readily one acquiesces in extinction. I have never pushed myself, my aim in political life having been to push others: and I am glad to think that since I became chief whip I trained my successors so well that they are following out my principle with marked success.

Next year will try my political metal to the utmost. I cannot but regret that I must stand beside the central point of the battle. The atmosphere of the Lords (of which my experience only extends to half a dozen sittings) is so soporific, spreading its atrophy with so potent an influence, that it is hopeless to arouse vital interests in its component members. They feel that in consequence of the Parliament Act their duties are abrogated (so they are) and that all life has passed from an emasculated institution. I fancy that fifteen or twenty of the younger men might cooperate and revitalise the old machine – but it is hard to do this, and in some ways undesirable, in the face of apathy or even hostility on the part of the mandarins: and it is not my function unless I were invited by Lord Lansdowne, to take any steps in reorganising our forces.

But with a compact body of twenty younger peers, men of H. of C. experience, I can well foresee the grave dilemmas into which we could force government spokesmen during the ensuing months of crisis. But Lord Lansdowne is oldish and fatigued. Since I retired from politics neither he (nor nobody else) has invited me to help and it is not for me to force myself into their counsels – though I well know that with my intimate knowledge of the parliamentary position my services would not be negligible. I hope there is no note of disappointment or bitterness in these remarks. None is felt or intended. Yet I look upon my being dropped out as symptomatic of a prevalent danger in our party, the neglect of potential help. I used to make a practice in the H. of C. of encouraging the shy, obscure, and ill-informed M.P., and nothing was more appreciated or more valuable: it is rather a pity to jettison cargo merely because it is to be transferred from one ship to another.

However my family finances will give me quite enough scope for energy during 1914. These first few months have shown me the intricacy and the dangers of the situation. Much will depend upon the state of trade during the next two or three years, and having become chairman of the Wigan Coal and Iron Company, it falls to my lot to take a special and personal interest in the conduct of that important concern.

1 JANUARY 1914

Servants' Ball last night in the old photo studio. It appears to have given much pleasure. We were there for an hour and David, Margaret, and Anne danced vigorously. There were vocal interludes. I gathered that the first footman sang a song in his cockney accent which Fife did not appreciate and he was extinguished in loud laughter. On the other hand Ellis, the inarticulate English groom, sang a comic song, which being quite unintelligible was mistaken for a drama, and reduced many Fifers to tears.

8 JANUARY 1914

To Chorley again, for a presentation from my old constituents. They have bought me a genuine and handsome piece of plate . . . A great reception from 200 or 300 mill girls who crowded into the town hall.

In parliamentary terms, 1913 had been a singularly placid year. That 1914 would be very different was obvious from the start. The Home Rule Bill would, under the provisions of the Parliament Act of 1911, become law during the year, on its third passage through the House of Commons. The prospect produced a sudden interest in compromise, combined with occasional flashes of extremism. The latter, however, had been there since 1912; it was the interest in compromise that was new.

Before parliament met, Asquith had, very secretly, sounded both Carson and Bonar Law on a possible compromise, and as a result knew that the Unionists no longer opposed home rule on traditional lines, but would if necessary settle for a free Protestant north-east. The Unionists' terms varied little in the successive phases of bargaining during 1914. Some, especially Bonar Law and Carson, wanted a small, Protestant Ulster permanently excluded from the rule of the new Dublin parliament, in fact partition, probably on terms geographically more favourable to the nationalists than the Northern

Ireland boundaries of today. Asquith's soundings in the winter of 1913–14 were premature, in that he had nothing to give away, and that it was too early in the day for the respective leaders to impose an unpopular settlement. Others, especially Lansdowne and the peers, wanted to make larger demands in order to damage the government and force an election.

In February and March, therefore, worried by their leaders' apparent pliability, by Asquith's unresponsiveness, and moved by good by-election results, the Unionists addressed themselves to a display of extremism, either for its own sake, or to induce Asquith to compromise. Milner and Amery and their English Covenant represented the most militant, if not the most typical, form of Unionist opinion, which was generally waiting for Asquith to put his cards on the table, as Law had already done. On 9 March 1914, on the second reading, Asquith proposed county option for Ulster, allowing a county to be temporarily excluded for six years (i.e. two British general elections). Important though this was as Asquith's first concession to Ulster Protestantism, it was vigorously rejected.

Asquith's first olive branch had failed. Before another was available, there was a succession of shocks; a government attempt to use force against Ulster (or so Unionists thought), a Unionist attempt to destroy army discipline by withholding the annual Army Act (or so Liberals thought), the 'mutiny' at the Curragh (20 March) and the Larne gun-running (24 April), when 30,000 rifles reached the Protestants.

After the Curragh and Larne, the government was tempted to procrastinate rather than again consider using force. On 26 May the unamended Home Rule Bill passed, and only awaited the royal assent to become law. Its formal passage through parliament had done little to alter the need to strike a bargain. On 23 June Asquith, making haste very slowly, introduced an Amending Bill to give effect to his suggestions of March. In the negotiations on this bill, the Unionists stood out as before for permanent freedom for the Protestant parts of Ulster. Redmond had to refuse, and the enterprise broke down, despite its apparent promise. On 18 July the King summoned a conference of English and Irish leaders, chaired by the Speaker, which broke down on its fourth day, upon which the cabinet decided to procrastinate further, an attitude they maintained until it was overtaken by the outbreak of war.

Apart from the political melodrama which was largely confined to the three months of February, March and April, the events of 1914 showed that the British parties were far closer in Irish matters than either had cared to admit for a generation past, that the Unionists were prepared to accept home rule for those who wanted it in exchange for freedom for the north-east, and that the Unionists were far from grasping in what they sought territorially. The melodramas of the spring can indeed be seen as fruitful, in that they led Asquith to make his first and last serious pre-war attempt at settlement in the form of the Amending Bill negotiations of June 1914. At the outbreak of war, both partition and home rule were a fait accompli so far as Britain was concerned, and the three years of party struggle had produced the essential materials for a settlement by consent.

Crawford's attitude to the schemes of Milner and Amery was unenthusiastic. 'I don't quite know what the Covenanters are to do,' he wrote on first hearing from Milner, 'for it cannot be supposed that any pledge is possibly analogous in its severity to that taken by the Irish Loyalists. However I will investigate the proposal which prima facie does not appeal strongly to me.' Discussion with Amery increased his doubts. 'Amery has great courage, but I remember during our recent fiscal crisis that I came to distrust his judgement. Milner too is inexperienced in the interpretation of the average Englishman's ideas.' Hence, after careful analysis of Amery's plan, Crawford concluded that its dangers outweighed possible advantages. Details of the plans appear in Crawford's papers. Their most striking feature is the Unionist belief in Ulster's extreme weakness and in the strength of Asquith's position.

Milner wrote on 16 January 1914 as he was about to depart on a business trip of ten to fourteen days in Spain. Writing before the Curragh and Larne incidents had tipped the scales in favour of Ulster, he argued that if the army was used, 'resistance will very soon be beaten down. There may be considerable bloodshed, but it will be a matter of a few days.' He did not even think the unpopularity of crushing Ulster would overthrow the government. The only hope, therefore, lay in making sure that at the last moment the government 'funked' it, or that the stick would break in their hands. He therefore sought signatures for an English Covenant pledging supporters of Ulster 'to do whatever lay in their power', and referred Crawford for details to Amery, 'who knows my whole mind on the subject'. He concluded, 'I may say that Bonar Law, whom I have consulted, quite approves the idea and is prepared, without actually taking part in the movement, to help it, if we can show him a respectable list of names. He approved my approaching you.'

Amery, on 19 January, gave Crawford an unsigned, undated eight-page typescript which argued that Bonar Law's Bristol speech of 15 January was a 'direct invitation' to the whole body of Unionist opinion to find new ways of preventing coercion of Ulster. 'At the present moment the government does not treat Unionist opposition seriously – and with good reason. Even the Ulster opposition it believes to be partly bluff...' If Ulster made a false step, it would be 'promptly and forcibly suppressed by the troops, or equally effectively, though more slowly, by naval and military blockade, with the general support of the British public'. Nor would the government collapse. On the other hand, Ulster would certainly take action, and civil war once begun could not be confined to Ulster alone. 'To avert such a disaster it is essential to take action', either to frighten Asquith into compromise, or to impress the King with the need to refuse his assent. 'At present only Lord Willoughby de Broke's League for the Support of Ulster and the Union, with four hundred agents and ten thousand men prepared to go to fight with a rifle in Ulster itself', was the only body available, and it was unsuitable. Mass demonstrations were the immediate object of the plan, but 'the organisation created for the purposes of demonstration would be available for such action as the curcumstances require'.

Crawford had a long conversation with Milner about Ireland on 4 February, of which no record survives, but evidently he declined to help launch the new departure, for when the English Covenant appeared, he wrote (3 March) that he was glad he declined to be one of the original signatories, 'though I shall have to append my name; but for the life of

Out of politics

me I can't see what concrete advantage will be gained by this demonstration'. There is no further discussion of extreme measures of this kind reported by Crawford.

29 JANUARY 1914
Leverton Harris is really the most enterprising and resourceful of collectors. He has spent a sum of £15 in buying the contents of two or three rubbish heaps from old palaces in Siena. He has thus acquired several thousand scraps of broken pottery which he is laboriously reconstructing, and after a few weeks' work has already put together vases, plates, and tiles enough to repay him a hundredfold!

Paid a long visit to Bonar Law – I haven't seen him for months – and I recall that a year ago I was in hourly consultation with him: now I am merely an ex-mandarin so little in the secret counsels that I misjudge my power of analysing any political situation.

CONVERSATION WITH BONAR LAW, 29 JANUARY 1914
Walter Long present 12 to 1.20.

Says session must be abnormal – impossible to treat it as normal. Suggests that on first day when called upon to speak shall immediately move amendment to the address asking for dissolution.

I said Speaker would refuse to accept amendment, as it would not have appeared on the order paper, and such an amendment would exclude all private members from debating general topics.

B.L. said that under those conditions, he would content himself with a speech of two or three minutes in which he would announce amendment he would move next day.

As to Birrell's statement that Asquith would in course of time announce 'what had been refused by Ulster', B.L. has written a strong letter to Asquith, complaining that this statement is a distinct breach of the conditions under which the conversations took place... Bonar Law then showed me his letter to Asquith which practically precludes him from referring to the negotiations, even in general terms.

I said that Asquith will disclose his scheme at the moment best suiting himself, and that to discredit the scheme in advance should be our aim. B.L. thinks however that on this point delay may do us no harm (very doubtful).

B.L. said no 'proposals' were made – the term was expressly ruled out as a description of the conversations.

Yet it is clear that Asquith is now ready to grant so much, that had his scheme of autonomy been in the original bill, the measure would by now be law of the land!

5 FEBRUARY 1914
Attended a meeting of the shadow cabinet at Lansdowne House. I suspect Ned Talbot insisted on my being asked. B.L. gave an account of his conversations with Asquith about Home Rule. Carson also described his interviews. Although I am

invited to a meeting of the shadow cabinet, I hope to retain as much freedom as is conferred by sitting on a back bench.

Dined with Ned Talbot. Jack Sandars read to us the reports sent to A.J.B. by B.L. of the conversations. The impression I got was that B.L. was too confiding, perhaps too softhearted towards the traitors on the Treasury Bench. The meetings by the way took place at Leatherhead, [17] at the country seat of – Sir Max Aitken![18] I confess this strikes me as funny: but the *démarche* is justified by the secrecy which has been observed.

7 FEBRUARY 1914

At the Carlton club one hears on all hands the determination of members not to pair during the ensuing session – to treat ministerialists as revolutionaries, and generally to fight a more strenuous battle than our party has ever waged before.

9 FEBRUARY 1914

Dinner at Lansdowne House . . . The King's speech . . . is only significant relative to Ireland. Opinion was unanimous that the paragraph must be the King's own composition, but divergent views were expressed as to which of the two great parties he intended to rebuke most severely.

11 FEBRUARY 1914

I made my maiden speech in the Lords immediately after the dinner hour – audience of about twenty: a very depressing affair, but at least this may be said of the peers, that they sit in solemn concentrated silence whereas in the Commons chattering and movement are continuous.

12 FEBRUARY 1914

This compliment to the peers must be modified. Lord Suffield[19] has today been convulsing everybody with his stentorian comments. He has recently married a young person of forty who is alleged to have been a hospital nurse. They were in the lobby at the back of the Throne, and he bawled at her that she was to go to the peeresses' gallery. They went along the passage together, and in the presence of half a dozen of us he shouted 'Now, my Lady, I am going to introduce you to the peeresses' seats', and by mistake showed her the wrong door and pushed her into the peers' lavatory. The old boy didn't mind a bit. She didn't turn a hair either.

[17] Asquith and Bonar Law met on three occasions, 14 October, 6 November and 9 December 1913, in strict secrecy at Cherkley near Leatherhead. Bonar Law half-offered to accept home rule in exchange for partition on a four or six county basis. Asquith half-accepted but did nothing, leaving Bonar Law with the impression that he was more interested in splitting the Conservatives than in compromise. Bonar Law therefore publicly broke off negotiations in a speech of 15 January 1914.

[18] Sir Max Aitken, first Lord Beaverbrook (1879–1964), MP (Cons.) Ashton-under-Lyne 1910–16, created peer 1917.

[19] Charles, fifth Baron Suffield (1830–April 1914), courtier.

Out of politics

Masterman has lost his seat for Bethnal Green. This caused me great satisfaction, but mitigated by the annoyance of newspaper hawkers who bawled the good news all round Audley Square for at least forty minutes last night... But the affair politically speaking is no trifle. Poplar also, with an increase of 1,100 in the Unionist vote, is significant and the government must feel depressed and humiliated. I opened a Conservative bazaar in Wigan and found our friends in excellent spirits. I have no sympathy for Masterman, he is a sneak and a bit of a humbug into the bargain – quite a nauseous and oleaginous type compared with the frank and honest hypocrisy of Lloyd George.

22 FEBRUARY 1914

... There is a growing feeling in our ranks that compromise on the Home Rule question is impossible – that if we are demanding a general election on the plea that ministers have no mandate, *a fortiori* it is impossible for us to agree to a modified nationalist parliament without sanction of the electors. There is a fear that our leaders will go too far...

25 FEBRUARY 1914

Asquith seems to have withdrawn all the pacific and conciliatory sentiments mentioned in the King's Speech.

27 FEBRUARY 1914

Perceval Landon[20] said that Sir John French[21] is responsible for the ministerial belief that a few thousand men will be able to overcome the resistance of Ulster. If this be so French as an observer of events must be blind, whatever his skill as a soldier may be. Gleichen[22] and Paget,[23] the two men on the spot, are under no such illusions. The situation is hardening. Neither side is so open to compromise as was the case a month ago. Asquith certainly has been intimidated by the hostility of various groups within the coalition. The drain of by-elections is also a restraining motive. Meanwhile a singular story is in circulation to the effect that at Nuneham[24] the other day, Harcourt, Runciman and one other minister seriously discussed the blockade of Ulster – a non-combative strategy, which on the one hand would starve Belfast into submission and on the other give the minimum opportunity to aggressive tactics by the Provisional Government – moreover that in case of need the government should enlist the help of the Ulster *Volunteers* to maintain order in the north! That these fantastic schemes are seriously canvassed is a measure of the profound flux of ministerial opinion. They are in a desperate mess – some panic-

---

[20] Perceval Landon (1869–1927), journalist.
[21] Sir John French, first Earl of Ypres (1852–1925), Chief of Imperial General Staff 1912–14.
[22] Maj.-gen. Lord Edward Gleichen (1863–1937), commanding officer at Belfast 1911–14.
[23] Gen. Sir Arthur Paget (1851–1928), C.-in-c. Ireland 1911–17.
[24] Harcourt's house in Oxfordshire.

stricken like Churchill and Seely who have seen bloodshed: others callous and intriguing like Harcourt and Samuel – a third section merely stupid like McKenna and Grey, but all at variance internally but striving to make a brave show of unanimity in public.

28 FEBRUARY 1914

Lord Wemyss[25] (aged ninety-six) spent the afternoon at Hendon watching the flying machines, and giving his views on the prospects of aeroplaning with much emphasis.

1 MARCH 1914

Lord Minto's[26] death throws many into mourning. He was a notable example of the excellent public service which can be achieved by a second class intellect: but judgment and *savoir-faire* supplied compensation, and he would be regarded as a valued and trustworthy viceroy. Much was owing to Lady Minto who like Lady Hilda Brodrick was able to ease delicate situations – but Lady M. returned from India somewhat elated by her great position, and consequently shook off many old friends and forgot others. She is *femme menagère*, and for a fortnight past has had all the copies of the memorial service for her husband, lying ready stacked at the printers.

2 MARCH 1914

I dined at the weekly dinner of opposition M.P.s in the H. of C. . . . I heard an old friend of mine lamenting that F. E. Smith shows a growing penchant for good liquor. He has always been fond of good cheer, and has never economised on wine bills. It would be a sad pity if he goes the way of so many prominent speakers – George Wyndham was ruined by it, Asquith is fuddled three or four evenings in the week, Churchill is a glutton, and lots of others, especially those who are most successful on the public platform, are addicted to this form of excess. Fred won't retain his mastery if he goes on in this way. Though extremely tough he leads a nervous and fatiguing life – hunts vigorously, travels without respite, and works at the maximum of intensity. But he hasn't got a tooth in his head and he must beware lest he overtaxes his digestion.

9 MARCH 1914

Conference with Lord Lansdowne at 3.30 . . . Lord L has been persuaded by Salisbury that a referendum bill should be hurried through the Lords and sent down (for refusal) to the Commons.[27] I see the case but we mustn't spring too many

---

[25] A page at Queen Victoria's coronation; died June 1914.

[26] Gilbert Elliot, fourth Earl of Minto (1845–1914), Viceroy of India 1905–10.

[27] The idea was taken up by Bonar Law, who in a censure motion on 19 March made a formal offer, on behalf of Lansdowne and himself, to accept the result of a referendum on Asquith's Ulster proposals of 9 March (exclusion of a four-county Ulster for six years). Asquith rejected the idea at once.

Out of politics

fresh dilemmas upon a fatigued public. Curzon complained about the suddenness of this scheme – which was placed before us without the smallest warning. He says that Jim Salisbury has daily access to Lord L, and pumps all kinds of ill-considered notions into his mind.

11 MARCH 1914

Had a long talk about the Irish situation with Londonderry[28] It appears that he is much less confident about the actual majorities of Loyalists in Ulster counties than the average Unionist. He says that the plebiscite would be jobbed by the Nationalists who control the returning officers, and especially the revising barristers – and he is even sceptical as to the result of a general poll of Ulster as a province. Certainly in common with others notably J. L. Garvin,[29] I had always assumed that a joint poll of Ulster counties would give a majority for the Union: even this now seems doubtful. Carson, whom I saw yesterday, said that Asquith's proposal would infallibly be rejected by the Ulster convention on the ground that the four counties to whom exclusion is offered would refuse to desert the border counties of Fermanagh and Tyrone where there is a strong Loyalist minority. Tyrone in particular is organised with exceptional skill and vitality.

The suffragettes acting through a maniac called Richardson have slashed the Velasquez Venus – seven great gashes. What protection have we against such outrages? Not the enfranchisement of women, for they would continue militancy as soon as they realised that the magic vote cannot remove all their grievances. Lord Cromer[30] says that forcible feeding through the mouth is vexatious and dangerous, and that *alimentatio per anum* should be substituted. Donald Stuart[31] did this to certain mutinous soldiers, natives, during the Afghan war, and broke the spirit of rebellion. Lord Wemyss on the other hand says that it is a pity to close the galleries... and the public must accordingly strip to nudity as a condition of entrance.

12 MARCH 1914

It was recently thought necessary to overhaul the Nelson statue in Trafalgar Square. It is estimated that over ten tons of pigeon guano was removed from the figure and the actual top of the monument: no less than four hundredweight from Lord Nelson's hat! – and St James's Park is to be enriched by this precious deposit.

CONFERENCE AT LANSDOWNE HOUSE, 12 MARCH 1914

Absent Austen Chamberlain, F. E. Smith.

Lansdowne and B.L. began by stating their decision, reluctantly reached, to amend army annual bill.

[28] Charles, sixth Marquess of Londonderry (1852–1915), Lord-Lieutenant of Ireland 1886–9.
[29] James Louis Garvin (1868–1947), editor of *The Observer* 1908–42.
[30] Sir Evelyn Baring, first Lord Cromer (1841–1917), Consul-general in Egypt 1883–1907.
[31] Probably Brig.-gen. Donald MacKenzie Stuart (b. 1864), served NW frontier 1897–8.

Curzon, Selborne, Derby indicated dissent.

Carson said Ulster expected something of the kind, though he had never indicated such a course to the Unionist Council.

W. Long said he would support it, but deprecated precipitate action or announcement, as he considers the govt position untenable, and their proposals impossible: accordingly issue should not be diverted.

Acland Hood, Devonshire (?) and Midleton (?) seemed to dislike the scheme. Chaplin raised certain objections. Londonderry, Akers–Douglas, did not speak, nor Halsbury.

Carson said Asquith had a conversation with him prior to the announcement of govt amendments – Asquith seems to think there will be grave disorder in South and West, if H.R. is defeated. Carson was impressed by Asquith's anxiety on the subject and likewise by his desire to avoid anything like civil war.

Decision: provisionally to agree to amendment of army act, but to leave details and decision as to moment of acting to Lansdowne and B.L. (This I fancy was against the general desire of those present.)

Referendum. Discussion about Salisbury's bill. B.L. said it was a point of strategy – he attached little importance to it, though the peers might settle for themselves. Decision apparently that Lord Lansdowne should write a letter signifying his agreement with B. Law's pronouncement in favour of a referendum.

19 MARCH 1914

Bonar Law moved his vote of censure against the government. I spent a long time in the H. of Commons and found some of our men fearful that he had gone too far in particularising the method of referendum he would accept. Anyhow the government refused, and showed how provocative they intend to be by letting Devlin speak instead of Redmond – a natural sequence to letting Churchill make his violent and uncompromising attack at Bradford.

Carson spoke early in the evening. It was rumoured that warrants had been issued for his arrest and that of his chief colleagues; he accordingly hastened to Ireland where his presence is desirable for the exasperation of the Loyalists cannot indefinitely be held in check. Peter Sanders accompanied him to Euston. No hands were laid on him there – indeed the government cannot be so mad as to precipitate a crisis at this juncture. The H. of C. was in great excitement this evening. Likewise the Ladies' Gallery – Lady Londonderry and Mrs Asquith nearly came to blows last week.

20 MARCH 1914

It appears that Mrs Asquith complained to the Speaker who replied that he was so fully occupied with controlling the Devils below, that he could not intervene in the quarrels of the angels above[32] ... It is said that the other day Mrs McKenna and

[32] Cf. Viscount Ullswater, *A Speaker's Commentaries*, II, 155.

Mrs Churchill were chattering to the annoyance of Lady Londonderry – who magnificent in superb furs and pearls, and puffing herself out to her maximum, said, 'Silence, badly-dressed children!'

Throughout the winter of 1913–14 the government was perturbed by an impression that the army would refuse to act in Ulster, and the army was alarmed by the belief that it might be called upon to crush the Ulster movement. On 20 March 1914 these fears came to a head in the so-called 'Curragh Mutiny', which so far as the forces at the Curragh went was not a mutiny at all. At no point did any officer refuse to obey an order. However, the government had only itself to blame for an atmosphere in which misunderstandings were likely to occur. Following the decisive Unionist rejection of Asquith's half-hearted offer to Ulster of 9 March, and Unionist threats to destroy army discipline by 30 April by a refusal to pass the Army Act, the ministerial line hardened, as if to frighten Ulster into accepting Asquith's terms as quickly as possible. Churchill, speaking at Bradford on 14 March, was particularly aggressive. Seely, the War Minister, ordered troops to move into Ulster, allegedly to defend munitions, in what looked an attempt to overawe or crush, or even provoke, the Ulstermen.

General Paget, before sending troops north, invited officers not prepared to act against Ulster to resign. The result was a telegram, 'Regret to report Brigadier and 57 officers, 3rd Cavalry Brigade, prefer to accept dismissal if ordered North'. Their attitude was caused by the impression that the government intended a coup to crush Ulster, and muddled presentation by General Paget. It was the aftermath in London which was the politically serious part of the affair. Brigadier Gough, the leading recalcitrant, was summoned to the War Office, where agreement was reached that the incident was a misunderstanding. This view of the matter was embodied in a memorandum of three paragraphs approved by the cabinet. To this, however, Seely added two further paragraphs, stating that the army would not be used to crush opposition to home rule. This was leaked to the press, and gave the impression of 'a private bargain with a few rebellious officers'. The cabinet then repudiated the agreement reached between the officers and Seely and French, and the two latter resigned, amid clamour for an election. Asquith replaced Seely as War Minister. On Sunday, 22 March, Edmund Talbot, the Unionist Chief Whip, gave Crawford an account of events which he had received from French:

Paget was instructed (? orally) to tell officers that if they were personally connected with Ulster they could leave: otherwise not – that beyond protecting barracks and magazines no troops were to be moved to Ulster: that no shots were to be fired in Ulster but that if Ulster invaded Dublin (!!) troops were to oppose the Volunteers, but not to fire until attacked.

Balfour and Lansdowne met on Sunday at Bonar Law's to plan parliamentary strategy. By Tuesday, Crawford concluded there was 'clear evidence of an elaborate conspiracy, hatched I doubt not by Churchill, and probably not communicated to Asquith and the respectable members of the cabinet'.

25 MARCH 1914

There was a debate in the Lords. Lansdowne was so civil and his criticism so measured as to make my blood run cold. Curzon was adroit but here and there flippant as though he did not realise the depravity of the situation, and he made my blood boil.

A curious episode occured this afternoon. Morley[33] was speaking in a low tone, and gave Curzon the impression that he, Morley, shared responsibility for the two repudiated paragraphs. Curzon asked St John Brodrick who was sitting by him if he gathered the same impression. St. John is deaf, had gleaned little or nothing from Morley's mumbling, and wrote a note which he threw across the table to Morley, asking for the typewritten statement which Morley had read to the House. Then I saw Morley pass the document across. On perusal they found a sentence which Morley had *not* read, admitting that after the cabinet meeting he had *visé* the two sentences which were added. Had Morley deliberately refrained from reading his confession – was it an oversight, or a conspiracy? Anyhow in the H. of C. it seems to have been asserted that Seely is alone to blame. More lying, in short.

26 MARCH 1914

Meanwhile the H. of C. has got on to a new scent. Some of the Labour members and advanced Radicals have made violent attacks on the army and veiled attacks on the Crown: and are in process of persuading the government that a dissolution at this juncture would return them to power on this new cry. I had a talk with Bonar Law on the subject who thinks that the danger feared by our men is overestimated.

28 MARCH 1914

A long talk with Edmund Talbot – two in fact – about French. They are old friends. French hitherto is adamant and means to stick to his resignation. That is Grenfell's[34] advice. Tomorrow (Sunday) French is to see Seely again, also Haldane (Pussy as he calls him) and in short French is not to be left alone and they will bully and cajole him until he gives way. Haldane has drawn up a memorandum, initialled by French and himself – some sort of concordat: but the cabinet refused it and French by the way keeps the original just as Gough[35] has stuck to the original document of the repudiated guarantees.

---

[33] John Morley, first Viscount Morley of Blackburn (1838–1923), Secretary of State for India 1905–10, Lord President of the Council 1910–14; created viscount, 1908. Morley was either aware of, or helped Seely to draft, the paragraph saying the army would not be used against Ulster. The opposition naturally thought that if Seely resigned, as he eventually did, Morley should do so too. Morley's defence was that he had not sent a letter to Gough, as indeed he had not.

[34] Field-Marshal Francis Wallace Grenfell, first Baron Grenfell (1841–1925), created baron 1902, Field-Marshal 1908.

[35] Brig.-gen. J. E. Gough (1871–1915). French and the other officer who had signed the guarantees to Gough which the cabinet had repudiated, persisted in their resignations, and were joined in consequence on Monday 30 March by their co-signatory Seely.

French says 1) that Arthur Paget exceeded his instructions 2) that there was no plot to subjugate Ulster.

29 MARCH 1914

I had a talk with Fred Smith at the Carlton. He is to lead off our debate tomorrow and means to speak with decision, especially to prove the collective complicity of the cabinet. I hope he may succeed. There is a fear no doubt that our men view him with marked suspicion and throughout this session he has kept much in the background. Tomorrow he will have a chance of recovering lost prestige, and I think he means to do this best, and not to spare Churchill.

Let me relieve several pages of gloom by a story about this conspirator. He was at Windsor with Haldane. The latter was lying back in an armchair with his belly protruding. I believe you are going to have a baby, said Churchill. I think you are right, said Haldane. 'And what is its name to be?' 'Well' said the Lord Chancellor, 'If it is a boy I shall call it George after the King: if it is a girl, Mary, after the Queen: if as I daresay it proves to be nothing but *wind*, I shall call it Winston and you shall be godfather.'

31 MARCH 1914

Lord Morley yesterday said that the cancellation of the two paragraphs in the army order (on the strength of which the officers returned to duty) does not mean that they failed to represent the meaning and policy of the cabinet! . . . Last night he told George Curzon among others that he was going to resign. Today he publicly stated that he means to stick to office. I have never heard so painful an apologia. This poor old man with all the reputation of a vigorous intellect and masterful spirit – to hear (and watch) him writhing as he tried to explain away the disparity of his action and Seely's – it was pitiable in the extreme.

Interspersed with these excitements, Crawford was emerging as one of the 'great and the good' who work on committees without reward. He had already taken on, or rather inherited from his father, the chairmanship of a London hospital, where awkward medical rows had to be adjusted: now he became, for a year, chairman of the Mining Association, the coalowners' organisation, while also presiding over the annual conference of the Miners' Permanent Relief Societies. He was also appointed to the advisory board set up under the Ancient Monuments Act of 1913, and became the Honorary Secretary for Foreign Correspondence of the Royal Academy, while his earlier commitments to the National Portrait Gallery, the Society of Antiquaries, and the Society for the Preservation of Ancient Buildings, remained an important part of his life. Within only a year or so of leaving the Commons, he was emerging, though still only in his early forties, as an ideal chairman and as an elder statesman of cultural institutions.

23 APRIL 1914

I spent a short time at H. of L. and had a word with Lord Lansdowne about

Carrington's[36] exhibition. Carrington seems to have made a real buffoon of himself, and received a pretty severe criticism. 'But what can one expect of poor Charlie?' said Lansdowne. 'Years ago it was notorious that his terms of intimacy with Hortense Schneider, the most seductive of the seductive, were of the closest nature. Yet a short time ago he had the humour or the audacity to quote one of her bon mots in the House of Lords – to quote her remark as though it emanated from Seneca or Montaigne. Poor Charlie – but after all are we quite sure there is no genius in his buffoonery?'

2 MAY 1914

To Lockinge – a big party . . . We were talking about the Indo-Mexican strains in Churchill's blood which explains the unaccountable fits of madness which recur from time to time, and Sir James Dunlop Smith[37] told me what I never knew before that Sir William Tyrrell's[38] mother was half Hindoo. Admiral Fisher is also half Malay.

3 MAY 1914

Austen Chamberlain said that if we were offered the services of Lloyd George or of Churchill he would choose the latter.[39] This I strongly contested, though the bulk of opinion round the luncheon table took Austen's view. For my part I hope we shall never enlist the help of either: but there can be no doubt that there is a strong undercurrent of feeling that Churchill wants to form and lead a central party. Our estimate of his character can be measured by this general belief that he is prepared to rat a second time.

5 MAY 1914

A new budget – the offspring of the 'People's Budget' of 1909 – and its complement: for where that earlier taxation has egregiously failed to produce revenue from the land taxes, this new venture will succeed through death duties and income taxes, in raising much money from one small and limited class of taxpayers.

It is no use squealing about increased taxation of the well-to-do: yet in my own case income tax, supertax, mineral duties, and commuted death duties, amount to about six shillings in the pound of my income – and that is not taking local rates into account! No doubt the government thinks rich people are inherently vicious and

[36] Charles Robert Wynn-Carrington, first Marquess of Lincolnshire (1843–1928), president of Board of Agriculture 1905–11, Lord Privy Seal 1911–12; succeeded father as third baron Carrington, 1868, created earl 1895 and marquess 1912.

[37] Lt.-Col. Sir James Robert Dunlop Smith (1858–1921), private secretary to Lord Minto when Viceroy, 1905–10.

[38] Sir William George Tyrrell, first Baron Tyrrell (1866–1947), principal private secretary to Sir Edward Grey, 1907–15; permanent under-secretary, FO, 1925–8; created baron 1929; son of an Indian judge by the daughter of a colonel.

[39] Cf. below, 26 May 1921.

should be taxed out of existence: but it is a pity that in the process the invaluable class of squires should be reduced – in many cases I fear crushed: moreover it will prove a difficult task to raise large sums in the event of some national emergency.

I look forward to the future with apprehension. I well know how difficult it is for me to pay sixteen per cent in death duties. David will have to pay twenty-one per cent – to surrender more than a fifth of his succession!

8 MAY 1914

On a private bill committee . . . De Mauley[40] is one of the members. He interests me as being probably the most penniless member of the peerage. In old days he used to be fond of Society, but was unable to go to a dance on rainy nights as he could not afford a cab fare. Even now he brings his lunch to the House of Lords – a bun or biscuit in a paper bag.

17 MAY 1914

Long talk with Edmund Talbot. He is puzzled. This should not be the case. I can quite understand doubts and hesitations – but his difficulty arises from the fact that neither Bonar Law nor Carson are quite clear as to what their action should be, and do not seem anxious to thresh the matter out. How well I remember this reluctance to seek solutions by the only fitting device, namely that of free and friendly discussion. It has long been the bane of our party that our leaders won't discuss. If they had leisure to think matters out to their logical issues, well and good – debate would be needless: but when they are too busy to give unfettered thought to prospective developments, they should talk – nothing develops possibilities more than the conversation of half a dozen well-informed people: but Ned says they somehow don't prepare themselves, and one of these days we shall be caught napping. It is wonderful how well we have got on hitherto considering how inefficient our forecasts have been.

31 MAY 1914

I do nothing in particular – can't settle down to work . . . It is now sixteen months since Father died, and looking back I can scarcely recall having done anything. My working life was so thoroughly *déraciné*, and politics in the House of Lords are so small and irksome compared with the large responsibilities I had acquired in the House of Commons, that I don't know whether frankly to abandon politics in favour of art and bibliography – or else to continue this nonchalant attitude until the turn of the political tide when fresh interests may present themselves. But I have long held, and used seriously to press upon Bonar Law, the necessity of making all

---

[40] William Ashley Webb Ponsonby, third Baron De Mauley (1843–1918); succeeded father, 1896. His penury was caused by a harsh family trust which applied nearly all the income from his estate to repay debts incurred by a much earlier generation. Despite his blameless character, and the frugality imposed by his trustees, these debts outlived him.

members of a future Conservative ministry resign directorships of public companies. I question whether in the embarrassed condition of family finance, with fresh taxes actually being imposed, I am entitled to retire from the control of the Wigan Coal and Iron Co.... I should not like to retire from the Board – I should not like to be left out of a Conservative government. What is to be done?

4 JUNE 1914

I dined with the Institution of Mining Engineers: sat next to Sir Henry Cunynghame,[41] late of the Home Office. He made no effort to conceal the disgust he feels for the unwise coalmining regulations introduced in Masterman's regime – byelaws which are so ill thought out that they cannot be put into practical effect. The fussiness of amateurs in government offices is a source of endless trouble to masters and men in the practical control of industries.

Cunynghame's reminiscences of the early gatherings of these commercial and technical societies were curious. This evening we dined at the Cecil Hotel, a company of 200 or more, a big dinner, plentiful wine list, orchestra, toastmaster, ceremonials of all descriptions: and cost accordingly. This is the modern fashion. In old days, thirty or forty years ago, the dinner was short, three or four courses at the outside, ale was imbibed, the expense all told was three and sixpence or to the extravagant perhaps five shillings: and Cunynghame (with his 'cute old eye sparkling) indicated that these primitive festivities did not suffer in consequence of their simplicity. In the early days the chief toast of the mining engineers was 'the Devil and the Coal Trade.'

6 JUNE 1914

Anson's[42] death saddens me. He was a man of distinction, a minister of note, an ideal host, and a Warden of All Souls where we used sometimes to stay with him, one of the magnates of Oxford University. We suffer another loss on the front opposition bench, cumulative to the many gaps caused by death since 1906. He was so well recognised an authority on constitutional law and custom that even the most ignorant of ministers had to pay heed to his opinions.

8 JUNE 1914

Attended a long conference at George Curzon's house (apparently at the instigation of Salisbury who presided). Lansdowne seems to have approved our consultation, but there were only five of us (the other two being Victor Cavendish[43] and Milner). That so small a group should offer advice on so tremendous a problem as Home Rule seemed irregular: but Salisbury, as George Curzon eloquently complains, has

---

[41] Sir Henry Hardinge Samuel Cunynghame, KCB (1848–1935), assistant under-secretary Home Office, 1894–1913; chairman, Royal Commission on Mines, 1910.
[42] Sir William Reynell Anson (1843–4 June 1914), Warden of All Souls from 1881.
[43] The Duke of Devonshire

the ear of Lord Lansdowne and seems to secure whatever he wants. Our talk was inconclusive. I was impressed by the readiness with which Curzon seizes and diagnoses an argument.

11 JUNE 1914

Presided at formal meeting of the Primrose League of which I have become Chancellor.

A long conference at Lansdowne House – Lord Lansdowne present and also A.J.B. The latter advanced an elaborate argument (which he said was St John Brodrick's) to the effect that the House of Lords should not try to amend the amending Bill, except by inserting a referendum or general election clause. There is much to be said for such a course which would absolve us from offering terms or an alternative policy. Curzon however was very hostile to the plan and made an admirable little speech against it. Lord Lansdowne offered no definite opinion on this or any other aspect of the problem throughout our conversation.

15 JUNE 1914

After the House rose, I attended a conference in Lansdowne's room (present Curzon, Selborne, St John Brodrick, Salisbury, Victor Cavendish, Milner, and Derby). I strongly pressed Lord Lansdowne to resume the debate tomorrow and he agreed. It had not occurred to him how essential attack has become at the present juncture.

20 JUNE 1914

Long conversation with Ned Talbot. Carson has evidently not made up his mind what course should be adopted in relation to the Amending Bill.[44] His position is delicate. A Southerner himself, he is closely associated with the Northern dissidents, and fears that his own inclinations may have to be waived in favour of the Ulstermen. That he desires a settlement is unquestioned: likewise Captain Craig: but both are prepared and determined to go *à outrance* unless adequate concessions are made.

24 JUNE 1914

Two hours conference at Lansdowne House. There must have been twenty at the shadow cabinet. F. E. Smith arrived an hour late: A.J.B. in flannels: Lord Lansdowne rather testy: Victor Cavendish *essoufflé*:[45] Walter Long quite purple.

---

[44] After the Home Rule Bill passed the House of Commons on 26 May, a lull of nearly a month took place in Irish legislation, pending the introduction of an Amending Bill based on the compromise suggested by Asquith on 9 March. On 15 June it was announced that the new bill would be introduced the following week, and on the 23rd the bill was read a first time. It provided for a four-county Ulster with temporary exclusion for six years – the terms proposed by Asquith and refused by the Unionists in March. The bill passed its second reading by 273–10 (1–6 July) but only so that the opposition could turn it upside down in committee.

[45] Out of breath

We agreed to read the Amending Bill a second time. Finlay[46] dissented, and I fancy Halsbury also, but he wasn't very clear. When we came to discuss amendments our difficulties were manifest, and Carson admitted that the real crisis would come when the government in the Commons puts forward counter-amendments to the alterations made in the House of Lords. It wasn't an inspiring talk, but we all behaved with great decorum.

25 JUNE 1914

Three p.m. – meeting of opposition peers. Several spoke very strongly against giving the Amending Bill a second reading. St John Brodrick by the way is hotly opposed to the exclusion of Ulster – he thinks solely of the Unionists under the Nationalist Parliament, and apparently feels that the greater the Ulster grievance the safer the Connaught and Munster loyalists will be. He is wrong. If we can exclude a substantial part of Ulster, the blow to Redmond's prestige will be great – there will be a split – an opposition will spring up – there will ensue internecine strife among the Home Rulers, and our friends will profit by inattention. It is in a Nationalist split that these Unionists can best look for help.

26 JUNE 1914

Lunched at the club with Gwynne[47] of the *Morning Post*. I think that from his intimate friendship with Sir John French, he is probably the best informed person outside the cabinet about the Curragh crisis, and some odd incidents it afforded. Gwynne says that Asquith was really surprised on going to the War Office, to discover that the army could not be counted upon to coerce Ulster.

1 JULY 1914

I dined at Hampden House – Carson, Lord Lansdowne, George Curzon ... Carson seemed in fairly good spirits, but his position becomes more distasteful every day as he receives very little sympathy from the southern and western Unionists. Some of them are in fact openly hostile. This is stupid – for they would long since have been cast to the wolves were it not for the resistance of Ulster under Carson's guidance. But Carson is a south of Ireland man, and has always been looked upon as their champion. They feel themselves neglected, almost abandoned by his concentration on the northern problem.

3 JULY 1914

Poor old Joe![48] How many people will learn about his death with a feeling of compassion! He died at a moment when the Tariff Reform movement is weaker

---

[46] Sir Robert Bannatyne Finlay, Kt., first Viscount Finlay of Nairn (1842–1929), Solicitor-general 1895–1900. Attorney-general 1900–05, Lord Chancellor 1916–18; created baron, 1916, viscount, 1919.

[47] H. A. Gwynne (1865–1950), editor of *Standard* 1904–11, *Morning Post* 1911–37.

[48] Joseph Chamberlain (1836–2 July 1914).

than at any time since its inception – and he lived long enough to see Home Rule become an impending reality. The two great ideals of his life are thus shattered before his deathbed.

Yet up to the end he retained his indomitable pluck never wavering in his belief that straight and consistent resistance would defeat all our enemies and consummate our political hopes. These last few years must have been a cruel burden to so active a mind, for he has been well enough to follow the trend of politics, but much too weak to take any share in their direction.

I always liked Joe. I came into politics after the first bitterness of accepting him as an ally was abated: but even during the late nineties there were still many men to whom he was *persona ingratissima*. All that he ultimately lived down, and last week there were scarcely half a dozen men on our side who looked upon him with anything but benevolence, and gratitude also. There were few Unionists whom he had not helped on one occasion or another.

4 JULY 1914

A.J.B. and I had a short talk about politics. He wasn't very clear in his assessment of the situation. For the moment his mind is running strongly on lawn tennis.

10 JULY 1914

Dined with A.J.B., and sat next to Lady Northcliffe. A.J.B. is absorbed in lawn tennis, and turns for a change of thought to Irish politics. Northcliffe is very proud of having just discovered the Ulster problem. He is just returned from a grand tour of inspection, having taken *en suite* half the staff of *The Times* and apparently everybody connected with the *Daily Mail*.

LORD CRAWFORD TO LADY WANTAGE, 11 JULY 1914

Northcliffe says that the number of rifles is large, the amount of ammunition enormous. Stores of food are accumulated at all strategic points. Practically every motor in eastern Ulster is at the disposal of Carson. Meanwhile Capt. Craig (so like him) has effected a capture of all the petrol in Ulster. There is a strong desire to precipitate matters, not to await further shilly-shally on the part of the government. I am anxious that the Ulstermen shall be kept closely in hand but every day that passes exacerbates them more and more.

Northcliffe stated categorically, though he could not quote his authority, that Asquith has at last begun to realise that words form an ineffective reply to rifles. Northcliffe said that this was only brought home to him yesterday morning for the first time!

... Here is an episode of last week. Lang of York told me. The Nationalists heard that arms were stored in a farmhouse two or three miles from Londonderry. They called out a battalion of Volunteers to raid the place and late at night they started on their expedition. Capt. White heard of it, rushed off in his motor to intercept them, and only managed to do so with difficulty, and about a quarter of a mile from the farm. He headed the men off with his motor and drove them back into Derry.

He did not know, neither did the Nationalist Volunteers (all armed with revolvers), that at that very moment there were lying entrenched all round the farmhouse, 800 Ulster Volunteers armed with rifles, and with fifty rounds of ammunition apiece. Fancy if the Nationalists had reached their objective – if Capt. White had had a puncture in his tyre. There were about ten minutes between this forced retreat and a pitched battle.

Redmond's position is becoming impossible, and if home rule is passed and any substantial part of Ireland excluded, Redmond will be deposed, or else his life will not be worth six months' purchase.

17 JULY 1914

At the Grafton Gallery, a long whispered conversation with Edmund Talbot and Johnnie Baird.[49] Both are depressed, fearing that Asquith has dodged Bonar Law into a conference before the latter had fully grasped all its ramifications.

Last thing last night a conference had been settled, and the King was to have told Asquith to announce that it would meet by his desire. But apparently Asquith had decided to get the King to intervene in this manner before the King had actually consented! and the announcement which was to have been made this morning with some flourish of trumpets, has accordingly been postponed: presumably till Monday.

But even so, whatever be the initiative of the King, Bonar Law seems to assume that the position of Tyrone is the only outstanding problem. And moreover it would appear that Carson takes the same view. Is this conceivable? What about our Unionists in Fermanagh, and the Covenanters in Donegal and Cavan? What becomes of Carson's bellicose speeches a week old, and of the strong attitude taken up by the whole party and the press in support of the Lords' decision to exclude the whole of Ulster?[50] I can already hear the cry of those who say they are betrayed, who will break out into violent invective against Carson, against England, and perhaps against the King too. I am quite puzzled. Has Carson lost his nerve or is he thinking too much of matrimony? I cannot guess, I am at a loss to account for this decision to enter a conference having decided in advance to vote against the conviction of the whole party.

There may be another side to it all, there must be: yet Edmund was so clear and

---

[49] Unionist Chief Whip, and Bonar Law's private secretary, respectively. The cabinet met twice on Friday 17 July, and the King delayed his visit to review the fleet until Saturday afternoon. On Monday, the day the Amending Bill (as transformed by the Lords on 8 July) was to come before the Commons, *The Times* revealed the plan for a conference, which began the following morning and lasted four days (21–4 July). On its failure, Asquith announced (24 July) that the Amending Bill would be taken on 28 July, but the European crisis prevented this.

[50] The Amending Bill, as introduced by the government, provided for the exclusion of four counties for six years. The opposition had amended this on 8 July to exclude nine counties permanently. Crawford spoke in favour of the exclusion of the whole of Ulster.

Out of politics

specific as to Bonar Law's meaning that I fear the worst: another terrible split, a fresh change of leaders, a dissolution while we are in the throes of internal dispute, another long period under the harrow. The outlook is hateful. Our friends will be dumb with amazement. Redmond too will be in a bad mess, but his difficulties will be of small comfort and even less assistance to ourselves.

TO LADY CRAWFORD, 22 JULY 1914
I leave early tomorrow for Bayreuth. I look forward to Rheingold; but I confess I shall not be surprised if I get a telegram recalling me for politics are uncertain, and a dissolution is by no means impossible. This would cause me sincere disgust, but I imagine it would be beneficial to the State if we could have an election; but to spend most of August spouting in Lancashire would be distasteful and vexatious also.

TO LADY CRAWFORD, 27 JULY 1914, FROM BAYREUTH
The Austro–Servian crisis is wrecking Bayreuth! Ferdinand of Bulgaria was to have come yesterday, but has had to abandon his visit.

1 AUGUST 1914
Reached London: I left on 23 July to go to Bayreuth, heard the *Nibelungenlied*, and then hurried away owing to the Dublin disturbances, but before I got halfway to London mobilisation had begun and my journey was adventurous.

3 AUGUST 1914
To London. Bank holiday. I was some time in the H. of C. listening to the debate about the war. The whole attitude of the Radical rank and file is intensely hostile to the government. It seems to be believed that we can maintain a neutrality, and that we have no concern in the future of Antwerp, Paris, and Rotterdam: moreover that our obligations to France are purely sentimental. Had there been a vote by ballot tonight I do not believe the government would have been supported by fifty of its adherents. The Radical press also bitterly criticises the government: and anxiously argues that we are entering upon a 'Tory war'.

4 AUGUST 1914
Grey's long explanation in the House has greatly changed the situation and has convinced the Radical party that no efforts were spared to maintain peace by our government. Moreover the Radical newspapers are coming into line – what discipline they show!
   The chief points discussed in the Carlton are Kitchener's position, and the probability of the despatch of the Expeditionary Force. Much fear is expressed lest Haldane may return to the War Office. In point of fact there is no real danger of this: all Haldane is working for is to prevent Kitchener going there, for the Lord Chancellor fears the inevitable exposure of his follies which would ensue.
   As regards the Expeditionary Force, it is believed by most that the government is

determined not to send it abroad unless positively forced to do so . . . Haldane again is said to be fighting any course so anti-German as the despatch of troops to France. Eddy Stanley says the French are satisfied with the stage to which our mobilisation has proceeded.

There are talks of a coalition government, but we could never come to satisfactory terms on domestic politics: neither side could surrender its position, and for all practical purposes our support of the war policy is quite adequate to show Europe that we are united.

We are ringing our bells today, tomorrow we shall be wringing our hands. The insouciance and lack of foresight in the patriotic crowds fills me with consternation.

5 AUGUST 1914

London on the whole behaves well. I stood for an hour outside Buckingham Palace between 10 and 11 last night.

Twenty thousand people, calm, respectable, anxious: all there to see the King, and very hearty in the welcome they offered when he appeared (for the third time that night) at his windows.

Later in the evening I watched the vulgar and ostentatious patriotism of a crowd which surged round Piccadilly Circus – waving flags – men sitting on the top of taxis, women too, all so excited as to be quite ridiculous, but I fear worse than that. They made themselves contemptible cheering for a war in which they will take no part, and make no personal sacrifice except the taxation which they will pay with an ill grace later on.

7 AUGUST 1914

Kitchener is on the whole the best war minister, though in some ways I should have preferred Asquith to remain at the W.O., and that Crewe should become prime minister on the understanding that Asquith should preside. The work of organisation is now in competent hands.

8 AUGUST 1914

Connie very busy adapting the Haigh laundry as a hospital for wounded men: it will make an excellent one, well adapted for this object.

11 AUGUST 1914

Primrose League meeting: our work is arrested, likewise our income and we are faced by the disagreeable necessity of reducing our staff or cutting down their salaries.

LORD CRAWFORD TO LADY WANTAGE, 11 AUGUST 1914

I was greatly surprised, and pleased indeed also, to hear from Burns that his reason for resigning was not that the country engaged in war, but that the government would not make up its mind . . . as to the attitude it would adopt. He said he was quite prepared to fight either for Belgium or against Germany, but he could not stand the shilly-shally and dilatory attitude of Asquith, who refused, as you are aware, to say 'yes' or 'no' to every question addressed him by the War Office in regard to military preparations. Walter Long is serving on the Central Distress Committee, which is in effect a committee of the cabinet, and he expresses something little short of amazement at the incompetence which is shown by the ministers with whom he is acting in concert. Austen Chamberlain is practically acting as chancellor of the exchequer. Lloyd George, who knows very little about finance, has completely lost his head.

20 AUGUST 1914

Edinburgh seems to act up to the motto of 'business as usual'. Except for some restriction of vehicular traffic together with the unusual number of khaki-clad men, there is no external sign that Edinburgh is conscious of the war still less of the profound dangers we run. Will they wake up when the Germans take Brussels a week hence? One could recruit a brigade of able-bodied unattached young men in Edinburgh without making any apparent reduction in the crowds of unoccupied or half-occupied youth parading Princes Street.

25 AUGUST 1914

We have about 110,000 fighting men at the front – more will go soon; but Haldane reduced the regular army by 45,000 men on the understanding that the Field Force would amount to 160,000 – which we have failed to send.

28 AUGUST 1914

I had a talk yesterday with Lord Lansdowne who was very fearful of Turkey's intervention against us.[51] He thinks that to reopen the Balkan War will injure us seriously, especially if there is a German crew to navigate the *Goeben* which could be a serious danger to transports bringing Indian troops.

29 AUGUST 1914

On other matters too criticism is brewing. The lack of preparation, the defective stores and equipment, the failure to mobilise as fast as was expected, the absence of ammunition for range practice of territorials – all these shortcomings and a dozen others are begining to cast a ray of light upon Haldane's smug optimism . . . Haldane reduced our regular army by 45,000 men on the solemn assurance that in case of need the expeditionary force would be able to leave the country on immediate mobilisation. That pledge failed – could not be carried into effect. If we had the whole field force at Mons last Sunday, namely a further 40,000 men or so, we should have driven the Germans back, reoccupied Brussels, destroyed the German base, effected a junction with Antwerp – cut the enemy's western communications. Here

[51] Russia declared war on Turkey on 2 November. Britain and France followed three days later.

is a case where armies of a million men were engaged, in which an extra 50,000 might have won the day. How crushing is Haldane's responsibility for this negligence.

12 SEPTEMBER 1914

Yesterday I had a talk with Bonar Law and Ned Talbot, tonight with Londonderry, Carson, etc. The government is going to betray us. Notwithstanding a solemn pledge to postpone controversial legislation, Home Rule and Disestablishment are to be passed into law with some small concession in the nature of delay. What will the result be upon the war?

I am apprehensive. Already Austen Chamberlain has refused to address Churchill's meeting next week. Bonar Law won't appear on the same platform as Asquith at Edinburgh. All this will denationalise the war, cannot fail to weaken the morale and determination of the country as a whole. Every effort will be made by Carson and Bonar Law to limit the area of domestic controversy.

16 SEPTEMBER 1914

Asquith has behaved like a cardsharper and should never be received into a gentleman's house again. Had I been in the Lords yesterday, I might have said so with some bluntness.

23 SEPTEMBER 1914

The shindy about Home Rule has been calmed down to the great credit of our leaders: but intense soreness remains though for the time it is thrust into the background.

11 OCTOBER 1914

Kitchener isn't well – he gets no exercise, his old headaches are returning. He is worried and overwrought. He has not the faculty of delegating work. Is it that he overtrusts himself, or that he distrusts mankind? Anyhow, work is not being done because he won't devolve responsibilities. The other day there were 2,000 unopened letters at the W.O., so Cecil Smith[52] told me. The work of the Education Department has fallen off, and Smith very properly offered some of his staff to carry out the ordinary departmental work of the W.O., such as opening, sorting, registering, and acknowledging correspondence, keeping accounts and so forth, all of it work for which his men are quite well qualified – not a bit! The W.O. doesn't want any extra help: yet they admitted to him that at that moment there were these 2,000 envelopes.

Kitchener has done much. Nobody living could have done more in these two months: but he was amazed at the criminal neglect of his predecessors. His fault is

[52] Probably Sir Cecil Harcourt-Smith (1859–1944), director and secretary, Victoria and Albert Museum, 1909–24.

that he won't enlist the voluntary help which is longing to give competent assistance. Hence the state of confusion in Whitehall. He is called Lord K of Chaos . . .

And Haldane? The apostle of clear thinking is shown to be a miracle of muddle-headedness: if indeed he be not something worse. He should be impeached for high treason.

11 NOVEMBER 1914

Parliament met. I spoke to an empty house and to an untenanted reporters' gallery about the German spy peril in Fife. A speech with serious stuff in it, but treated as of no consequence by Haldane. My record of facts, none of which can be denied, is really noteworthy – but what can be expected of Haldane, he is becoming looked upon as a German agent – indeed one of their newspapers or pamphleteers said he was more useful to Germany in the cabinet than out of it. What a humiliating tribute! and yet the man is still received in decent and patriotic society.

12 NOVEMBER 1914

Conference at the Carlton Club: A.J.B., George Curzon, Bonar Law, St John Brodrick, Selborne, Victor Cavendish, Finlay, Austen C., Cave,[53] and others. A.J.B. told us about his discussions at the Defence Committee on the subject of invasion.

Herbert Samuel it appears was chairman of the invasion subcommittee: is it conceivable? Anyhow he considered the problem of the invasion of our shores by Germany, and reported that the civil population was to – do nothing, except destroy farm carts and motor cars! His solution at least was easy, logical, and simple. The cabinet however threw over the scheme, but have been unable to provide an alternative. Here we are, three months after the outbreak of war, and the government has no idea what advice to offer if a German raid lands: and for the last five years, have they never dreamed of the subject?

13 NOVEMBER 1914

Robin Benson begged me to see him early this morning. I found him full of indignation. Soveral,[54] his informant, says that at a recent dinner party in Downing St at which Mr and Mrs Asquith entertained him, Mr and Mrs Churchill, and *Sir Edgar and Lady Speyer,*[55] the actual position and disposition of the Fleet was the subject of conversation. Soveral was horror-struck at this act of folly. Speyer is not trusted, his wife makes no secret of anti-British sentiments – Speyer himself has actually been watched, so suspicious are the authorities. The man can't speak

[53] George Cave, first Viscount Cave (1856–1928), MP (Cons.) 1906–18; Home Secretary 1916–19, Lord Chancellor, 1922–4, 1924–8.

[54] Portuguese ambassador, society figure, and intimate of Edward VII.

[55] Rt. Hon. Sir Edgar Speyer, Bart. (1862–1932), created baronet 1906; born of German parents and educated Frankfurt; m. 1902 Leonora, d. of Count von Stosch; banker and philanthropist.

English, his brother is one of our most violent enemies in the United States – and yet Asquith permits such a conversation at his table. Was he drunk, is he mad, or does he also care little for our Empire? No sane man and no patriot would dream of talking on such a matter to a German-born and German-speaking financier, even if under obligations to him. One's blood boils at these things – while we know that communications are being made to the enemy.

Moreover the situation of the Fleet is precisely the one thing on which conversation should be guarded. The Fleet is not on the North Sea as the public fondly imagines: it has been off the north coast of Ireland ... The Fleet is out of the way in the event of a descent on the east coast. This is the momentous subject Asquith is prepared to discuss with an alien.

24 NOVEMBER 1914

Very interesting talk with Ned Talbot who has been with Kitchener. Bonar Law was to have gone too but at the last moment asked Ned to come alone. 'You see I am surrounded with spies. I expect McKenna's spies are watching the window now. There's not a member of the cabinet I would trust, unless it is Asquith, whom I trust – a little.'

I should have liked to hear K with the humorous glitter in his bloodshot eyes discussing his cabinet colleagues. He certainly treats them with marked contempt.[56] He even has the war telegrams censored before circulating them.

25 NOVEMBER 1914

Spoke again in the Lords on the spy question. I have succeeded in waking up the government. Haldane made an evasive and oleaginous reply – Curzon vigorous. I get many letters showing how widespread is the public anxiety.

In conversation with Jack Sandars about naval matters I was told a) Battenberg did not really resign owing to his alien extraction, though the bitter anti-British sentiments of his wife made such a course advisable. He resigned on account of really bad health. He has been quite incapacitated for work – in fact could no longer hold a responsible post ... b) the recent raid scare when I believe 80,000 men or more to have been moved to the east coast, was based on the interception of a German wireless message in code and undecipherable, but identical with the combination effected just prior to the German visit to Yarmouth.

2 DECEMBER 1914

To London ... A good deal of talk about Sir Roger Casement,[57] against whom

---

[56] Cf. below, 15 February 1940.

[57] Casement reached Berlin on 31 October and his presence there was announced by the Germans on 20 November. Casement's Norwegian servant told the British legation in Oslo about Casement's homosexuality on 29 October. The British authorities claim to have discovered the Black Diaries only after Casement's arrest in 1916 (Basil Thomson, *Queer People*, 90). Crawford's remark is the earliest known reference to inspired gossip about Casement's homosexuality. Most accounts assume that the smear campaign only started in 1916. See Brian Inglis, *Roger Casement* (1973), 277, 281.

allegations in addition to those of treachery are freely made. In any case his interview with the German Foreign Office makes him deserve hanging.

3 DECEMBER 1914

Selborne joins one of Mond's companies – a good deal of acrid comment.

Crawford was sworn in as a special constable, and spent half the night in soaking rain in Buckingham Palace grounds patrolling for intruders: otherwise he restlessly scanned the news, spoke frequently at recruiting meetings, drilled as a private in the Inns of Court Reserve Corps, and generally felt out of things. Christmas at Haigh was festive, with wounded Belgian officers to entertain, turkey, plum pudding and a Christmas tree for all, including a household still numbering twenty-two: thus closing 'in many ways the quietest year I have spent for a very long time – and by no means the least happy notwithstanding public and private sorrows'.

4 JANUARY 1915

I am sorry about Illingworth,[58] the chief government whip, with whom I had friendly relations in old House of Commons days. He was a good fellow, though by no means so skilful a whip as the ordinary notices suggest. His parliamentary experience was very short, and he had never sat in opposition: but he had two great assets, the freedom with which he could distribute honours, and the potency of parliamentary wages – both of which he used to the fullest advantage of his party.

I find that the feeling against Haldane is more widespread and angry than I had expected. Blumenfeld,[59] the editor of the *Daily Express*, which has been attacking Haldane with severity, is anxious to provoke a libel action at which he says he would produce documents calculated to blow Haldane to Potsdam: hence Haldane's reluctance to take umbrage.

6 JANUARY 1915

Spoke in House of Lords about aliens. Haldane is incorrigible. Every suggestion to strengthen the hands of the Home Office is brushed aside with his turgid sophistications.

Spent four of the dark hours of this morning on the beat in Buckingham Palace Gardens: is it true that the King doesn't sleep there? The rumour is widespread and has been long current.

15 JANUARY 1915

Trading with the enemy is much more common among the newly ennobled aristocracy than the *Daily News* could believe. A ship of the Runciman line is about to sail from the USA on German account!

[58] Percy Holden, Illingworth (1869–3 January 1915), MP (Lib.) Shipley 1906–15; Chief Liberal Whip from 1912.

[59] R. D. Blumenfeld (1864–1948), editor of *Daily Express* 1904–32.

19 JANUARY 1915

Spoke at Lancaster. Lord Ashton[60] has evidently settled to check recruiting as much as he can, for the shortage of labour interferes with his income.

22 JANUARY 1915

Dined with Jack Sandars. He told me that the cabinet has discussed the possibility of withdrawing our army from Flanders and landing it on the Austrian coast. There must be a raving lunatic in the highest counsel of the realm, *or is it a traitor*?

There is much anxiety about recruiting. The authorities are confident that the Germans can't break through our lines, but they are equally clear that we can't pierce the Germans. Nothing but a great accession of well-equipped men can perform that feat for us. Are we getting the men now who in late summer will be able to bring to bear an irresistible pressure? That is the point about which we are all quite ignorant, and because ignorant so nervous, since we fear that the silence, persistent and immoveable, of the authorities means that their prospect is gloomy.

25 JANUARY 1915

Gulland[61] succeeds Illingworth as patronage secretary to the Treasury. He is competent, zealous, knows all the parliamentary rules and is without scruple. He will be much more fitted to the job than Seely[62] whose airy and patronising nonchalance would not have conciliated the shy or bilious Radical. On the whole Asquith has made the best choice, but Gulland's escapade at the Wick election, followed by some pretty brave romance in the House of Commons, will be remembered by old-fashioned Liberals if any such survive.

2 FEBRUARY 1915

Jack Sandars tells me that there is a certain hankering after a coalition. Bonar Law is favouring the idea, Carson of all people in the world takes the same view.[63] I don't like the idea. Whatever was unpopular (e.g. a strong line on recruiting) would be ascribed to our agency and would cause a split among the Radicals, who might well accept conscription if passed by their own government. I see no benefit to the country from a coalition at this juncture, and I much question if Asquith or Churchill or Lloyd George would desire it.

Talked with George Curzon – he is disturbed at the anaemic calm of the House of Lords. Lansdowne is back – arrived late last night and invited his confidential

---

[60] James Williamson, first Baron Ashton of Ashton (1842–1930), MP (Lib.) Lancaster 1886–95, created baron 1895; linoleum magnate.

[61] J. W. Gulland (1864–1920), MP (Lib.) 1906–18, Liberal Whip 1915–17.

[62] Secretary of State for War, 1912–14.

[63] Cf. Sandars to Crawford, 31 January 1915: '*Entre nous*, you know, B.L. has been hankering of late after Coalition, I believe prompted by Curzon. It is very stupid and short-sighted, and, *me judice*, quite impracticable. However, I hear the cold douche has been well administered and I think we shall hear no more of it.'

friends to meet him at 9.30 p.m. Carson, Walter Long, and Austen Chamberlain accordingly left Lady Charles Beresford's house while dinner was going on yesterday – surely Lord Lansdowne might come to town early enough to allow a conference at a reasonable hour, and to permit an adjournment if desirable. No – the parliamentary work was only to begin at the very latest moment possible. As to what was settled at the meeting, Lord Lansdowne seems to have poured cold water on to every proposal – sedition in Ireland, the treatment of British prisoners in Germany, aliens finance, and one or two other things. No, it was a case of 'let the backbenchers do it'. Well, the backbencher is a very humble and retiring person, and he wants the assent if not the support of his leaders.

So there was a perfunctory meeting this afternoon of the House of Lords. Nothing was done, no preparation has been made for future debates, we relapse into the coma from which George Curzon rescued us during Lord Lansdowne's absence from the short sittings of January. I confess it is despairing. Lord Lansdowne has long been a tired man, but it is a sad pity that he should sit upon the efforts of others.

I suppose there is still apprehension in certain quarters that Lord Curzon would not be a success as a leader. He has never been in a cabinet (neither has Bonar Law). His manner is not very conciliatory though he is much less viceregal than a year or two ago: moreover he was one of the most vigorous opponents of the Diehard movement on the Parliament Act. But he is wise and experienced–his energies despite poor health are indefatigable: he loves hard work and he likes others to emulate his own zeal. As a leader he would lose all the little jealousies which are often noticeable in the candidate. Achievement would soften asperities and mellow his temperament. I believe he would be a good leader.

And the time is approaching when we shall have to face the problem. Lord Lansdowne cannot continue indefinitely to stifle all the initiative of his followers and I dare say he would like to retire to the groves of Bowood.

There are two alternatives to George Curzon – Selborne and Victor Cavendish.[64] At one time the former was a serious competitor, but surely can no longer be considered such.[65] In South Africa he lost all the perceptions of home politics. His manner tends to become more brusque with advancing years: his wits become more dull.

Victor Cavendish is the safe man. He would be admirable were there acute and well-balanced rivalry between two rather dangerous men: but his chances, or rather the need for his intervention, diminish as Selborne's claims are depressed.

3 FEBRUARY 1915
I had two talks with Lord Lansdowne today and thought he seemed extremely well, though thinner. His caution and scepticism become an obsession. To every

[64] Then Duke of Devonshire
[65] Unionist eyebrows had been raised over Selborne's chairmanship (1913) of Natal Ammonium Ltd, which was part of the (Liberal and Jewish) Mond family empire.

proposal he sees objections and evidently advocates a quiet and unemotional session. At a meeting of opposition peers when the dates of meeting for the House of Lords were being discussed, he asked if we would wish the House to meet from time to time or 'to put up the shutters' – rather an odd phrase but illuminating.

Arthur Stanley[66] dined with us, he was most amusing in his description of the grand ladies who are running hospitals in France. On the whole Millicent, Duchess of Sutherland,[67] seems to have given most trouble. She got into debt and seemed to expect the Red Cross to extricate her. Her chief crime is body-snatching. All these ladies are known as 'body-snatchers', for they seize an invalid wherever they can catch him, and carry him off willy nilly to their private hospital. So-and-so is envied as having an 'admirable' motor ambulance driver who will squeeze on to a railway siding and whip a wounded man out of a wagon while the orderlies are looking the other way. The worst case was where a consignment of eight men were being escorted to some hospital beyond Boulogne in order to be treated by some surgeon famous for his handling of abdominal wounds. These eight men were all specially selected cases, and all very seriously in need of expert care. She got hold of them all – snatched them out of the train while the RAMC was absent, and took them all to her hospital!

It is really cruel. Duchess of Westminster[68] is herself most tiresome, but has an excellent staff. Lady Sarah Wilson[69] has been giving a good deal of trouble. Lady Diana Manners is trying to get permission to have a hospital of her own; let us hope the Red Cross which can now control the permissions granted to these adventuresses, will be sufficiently proof against the influences of society, to veto any more expeditions of this character.

5 FEBRUARY 1915
Board meeting ... three per cent for the year, as against seven for 1913. It is a big decline and at an inconvenient moment, meaning a diminution of my income by £32,000 in twelve months – with taxation doubled.

In March 1915 the failure at Neuve Chapelle indicated 'the inevitable prolongation of the war' (something forecast by Crawford in a letter to The Times *just after the outbreak of war, protesting against the catchword 'business as usual'.) 'I shall never forget the horror of that week', Crawford recalled. 'Up to then we had all based hopes on our spring offensive which seven months of preparation was to mature.' Crawford was unable to remain at home, with no public work to do. In a state of intense depression, he joined the Royal Army Medical Corps as a private at the age of 43, and by June 1915 he*

---

[66] Hon. Sir Arthur Stanley (1869–1947), fourth son of sixteenth Earl of Derby; MP (Cons.) Ormskirk 1898–1918.
[67] Lady Millicent Fanny St Clair-Erskine (b. 1867) m. 1884 the fourth Duke of Sutherland.
[68] Constance Edwina Cornwallis-West m. 1901 the second Duke of Westminster.
[69] Lady Sarah Isabella Augusta Spencer-Churchill, sixth daughter of the seventh Duke of Marlborough; sister of Lord Randolph Churchill.

was in charge of the operating theatre in a makeshift casualty clearing station at Hazebrouck, near the front, where he spent the next twelve months.

He only just got away in time. Two months later, the first coalition was formed, and Crawford was summoned back from France by Balfour, who pressed him very hard to become Civil Lord of the Admiralty. Talbot, the Unionist Chief Whip, also wanted 'an experienced hand to watch A.J.B. lest he fell a victim to Macnamara's guile', the latter being the liberal junior minister under Balfour. Crawford refused and returned to France. 'I feel sure that after a fortnight in England I should feel as suicidal as after Neuve Chapelle.'[70] In any case, he disliked, and would have liked the opportunity to oppose, the coalition on ordinary political grounds. 'Blunder: it will silence much criticism which is essential; and cloaks the collapse' of the 'malefactors and traitors with whom they have entered into alliance'.

As a private, Crawford was instinctively anti-officer, and all the more so when so many officers were men who had never had servants or cars before and let it go to their head. This was the first war in which officers had appeared in chauffeur-driven cars, rather than on horseback, and Crawford reacted strongly against this middle-class opulence. No less than fourteen per cent of Crawford's unit were officers' servants. 'The amateur officer is our cardinal danger', was his military assessment. As for the staff officers, 'for vanity, ignorance, and self-indulgence, some of them can safely defy competition'. Officers' letters home always caused the censor most trouble; their kitbags were overloaded with fineries; and they caused havoc in hospital, with gambling, liquor and nocturnal parties, even, in the case of one general receiving treatment, bringing their own gramophone.

In time, however, Crawford came to understand that the true enemy of the RAMC, the true tyranny to be overthrown, was that of the lady nurses, employed at the front more because it pleased sentiment at home than for any practical reason. The wounded themselves preferred to be nursed by RAMC orderlies, and at the clearing stations near the front the formal regime imposed by the nurses, 'chattering like magpies and buzzing like bluebottles', was bitterly resented by the men in a way it never was in base hospitals. The nurses, knowing themselves disliked, took it out on the RAMC orderlies. Even men stationed in the reserve trenches, which took the heaviest shelling, 'keep telling us they prefer this danger to the safety of our hospital with the bullying it involves'. From the orderlies' point of view, the nurses 'gave ten times the work they perform and put everybody by the ears into the bargain', as for instance when orderlies were told not to touch the banisters. The nurses' attempt to create a boarding-house atmosphere was resented, as when they used the operating theatre as their common room. 'They ate

---

[70] Crawford wrote to Talbot, 'Ned I have tried, but I can't face it – I should hate the job and do it badly, for my heart is elsewhere. Forgive me ... I have done my best to say yes, but can't bring myself to do so.' Balfour saw his decision as 'not defensible on any of the ordinary rules of conduct; but I recognise that there are inward intuitions and impulses which cannot be argued out on paper, but which, nevertheless, carry with them an authority which cannot be, and ought not to be, ignored.' Crawford replied that some day 'I may be able to tell you how bitterly I regretted what was an impelling and irresistible force'.

chocolate all over the operating table; after lunch they dropped cherry stones on the floor.' Fresh milk, in scarce supply for patients, was used to clean the leaves of potted palms, or in an eternal making of cakes. Their most serious offence, however, was intoxicating their officer patients on champagne and whisky, which in a front-line station was far from the mild abuse it would have been in an English convalescent home.

'Each woman seems authorised to give as many orders as she pleases to any man she selects.' The nurses, who did little medical or cleaning work, came to regard the hospital as their own domain. 'The domination of the nurses becomes unbearable. The place is fast becoming a nurses' home. They eat here and expect us all to act as their parlourmaids; orders are issued every minute sometimes contradictory, often impossible, and always peremptory.' Fortunately, scandal, in the form of nocturnal improprieties, led to a hospital revolution and a clearance of the worst offenders. By comparison the average soldier seemed an ideal human being, and even the local French, 'happy making more profit during a month of wartime than during a year of peace' seemed quite innocuous.

Malingering, even as early as spring 1915, was rife. The first sign was the huge camp for VD cases at Le Havre, containing 1,200 men, including sixty officers. (The RAMC had the highest apparent VD rate because its men recognised the symptoms.) It seemed well established that men deliberately sought infection in order to get to these camps. Self-inflicted wounds were common, though severely punished; Crawford visited one unit for such cases near the front which had fifty cases. Crime was also committed as a way of escaping the trenches. Certain 'illnesses' – trench fever, gastro-enteritis, neurasthenia, debility – were almost connived at by the RAMC as temporary forms of escape. Another form of humane corruption was the granting of leave in return for cash, about which stories were rife. One of the greatest incentives, even in early 1915, for the performance of duty was the pervasive fear of being executed by one's officers, a topic of endless discussion.

Crawford, as a politician, was sensitive to the political aspects of the gulf between officers and men. 'The French said, "English soldiers bons, English officiers no bons." As regards our own soldiers it is lamentable how seldom one hears friendly or favourable criticism.' What would happen, he wondered, if the criticism applied to officers as individuals were to be transferred, in the light of setbacks, to officers as a class?

TO LADY CRAWFORD, EASTER 1915, FROM ALDERSHOT

You can't guess how adaptable I am or how easily four or five days will work a revolution in essentials. I eat cheese, onions, parsnips, carrots, turnips, I can drink tea strong and without sugar, and in a hundred other ways I have turned in my orbit – and not because of obligation, but because I find that what I have neglected in the past from being fastidious, is good for man and for me. I miss nothing except my family. Books, pictures, all the beautiful things of my homes, all the comforts with which I have been surrounded, all the ease and amenity of life, in short precisely those advantages for which the 'idle rich' are envied, have now till Peace or the penalties of war release me, become as dust in the balance.

Out of politics

I APRIL 1916

It is twelve months today since I went to Aldershot and was attested. What reflexions does this past year evoke? Occupation of a specific character calmed my conscience which was distraught by Neuve Chapelle and much which preceded it. I could not have remained at home old as I am. But all the time my heart aches for wife and children, homes pictures books papers flowers trees.

The fundamental fact borne home to me is the ennobling influence of Discipline and Uniform. How splendid the army is – notwithstanding its seamy side and its plague spots, the courage character and good will of the average soldier fill me with boundless admiration – and my opportunities of seeing and assessing soldiers of the line are constant – innumerable.

In retrospect, Crawford regarded these months in France as 'a grim experience upon which I look back with infinite tenderness'.

XI

The fall of Asquith, 1916

The Unionist leadership in the House of Lords – Crawford becomes Agriculture Minister – the home rule crisis of July 1916 – Asquith not at his best before lunch – the cabinet debate on Casement – Bonar Law against an election – Conservative acceptance of railway nationalisation – the food problem – Lloyd George inert and obstructive – Asquith looks to a 'generous providence' for food – Asquith comes to life to prevent conscription of Jewish immigrants – the crisis of December 1916 – series of Unionist conclaves described – Asquith falls.

For a body of its size and collective prominence, the Unionist peerage contained singularly few candidates for a place in high politics. That the Liberals in the House of Lords should operate with a skeleton staff, well handled by Crewe, needs no explanation, but the similar position on the Unionist benches had deeper roots. The Unionist front bench was under-manned, but it was oddly at a tangent to the main stream of Unionist opinion in the Commons and in the country. The Unionists were short of peers, and the peers they had were, in various ways, not the right kind of peer.

Lansdowne was an unquestioned leader. No one wanted to get rid of Lansdowne in order to have Curzon instead. This impasse preserved Lansdowne until 1916 although it did not find him a working post. If Curzon had not existed, the reversion to Lansdowne might have gone to Selborne. Indeed, the events of 1911, which depressed the standing of Lansdowne and Curzon, might have wafted Selborne into top place, were it not that he had returned from South Africa too recently to have established himself. Curzon needed the freedom from party, and the heavy load of war work that coalition brought, to establish the House of Lords as his seminar. Selborne, an administrator but a resigner, needed a coalition to criticise in order to turn his dull righteousness into a political force. Selborne's main achievement was to make it morally respectable for peers to refuse war work and to concentrate on forming an anti-Lloyd George cave instead. The main beneficiary of Selborne's zeal was Salisbury.

Three magnates survived whose credentials included ministerial office in the Commons before 1905: Salisbury, Devonshire and Derby. All were free traders by political instinct. Devonshire had moral solidity but not, apparently, ambition. He was shipped off to Canada in 1916–21; in 1922 he came back as a Colonial Secretary with progressive views on Africa. In 1923 he, like Salisbury, was horrified by Baldwin's protection election. He was the sort of person peers respect and do not argue with, much more so than Curzon or Birkenhead. But what he offered, Lansdowne already provided.

Salisbury and Derby were, or wished to be, professional politicians. As junior ministers they had not shone. Salisbury bore some of the blame for 1906. Derby, a faux bonhomme *and compulsive politician, was supposed to have a rapport with democracy, but his genuine regional and social credentials were counter-balanced by his opposition to tariff reform. Derby, therefore, needed coalition to rescue him from his corner. Salisbury needed a threat to the right-wing identity of the Unionists. With Bonar Law at the helm, this was unlikely to emerge.*

Between 1911 and 1915 the Unionist Party had not got work for their peers to do. There were two reasons for this. One was the wound inflicted in 1911. The Parliament Act hurt not because it passed, but because of the way it passed. The Lords had died not in battle but by their own hand, and with division in their ranks. Curzon, in particular, and Lansdowne lost caste, but Selborne and Salisbury did not gain it, or offer an alternative leadership once the crisis was over. The other reason was that leading peers found it hard to place the same value on tariff reform as did ordinary Unionist opinion. In so far as matters came into the open, the old, pre-1903 attitudes of the peers would be seen to diverge from the new Unionism of Bonar Law. Lansdowne made it his business to see that matters were not brought into the open, a policy strengthened at first by the advent of war. In any case, Lansdowne's wish to make things happen was non-existent (at least until he faced unemployment late in 1916).

When coalition came in 1915, the situation was suddenly reversed. The Unionists had to face the need to produce effective Unionist peers if they were to fill their quota of posts and also if they were to make the upper house a serviceable part of the legislature. They also – Bonar Law particularly – had to find peers who would remain party men in a non-party situation. Derby, for instance, when offered war work, became in all but name a liberal peer; Curzon's position was equivocal. The first coalition gave Selborne a departmental post at agriculture, and Lansdowne and Curzon were brought in without portfolio. Given the assumption that Lansdowne could not take on much work, and that Curzon, who could, was unreliable from Bonar Law's point of view, it only needed the resignation of Selborne in 1916 over Lloyd George's Irish settlement to leave an awkward gap. Someone was needed whose appointment would steady the nerves of a party anxious over the surrender of unionist principles. Who better than Bonar Law's own ex-Chief Whip – even if his acquaintance with agriculture was not obvious and even if Bonar Law had virtually dropped him for over three years? So Lance-corporal Crawford 58740 became Minister of Agriculture,[1] unpaid (at his own request), and resigning his directorship of the family company in order to give his undivided energies.

While Crawford was in Hazebrouck, he was not so entirely outside political discussion

---

[1] Even after the disasters of the Dublin rising and the surrender of Kut, Crawford was loyal enough to the principle of coalition under Asquith to conclude an anti-government tirade: 'Yet the more I look at the problem the more certain I am that Asquith must remain head of the government – indeed that the cabinet cannot be substantially changed' (Diary, 1 May 1916).

as might have been thought. He was in fact considered at one point as Viceroy of India. Hardinge had retired following the Mesopotamian disaster. Curzon wrote, 'I made a strong push to get you sent to India as Viceroy ... Your claims were seriously considered and at one moment seemed more than likely to prevail'; Austen Chamberlain, as Secretary for India, 'hoped that I might have got you for India.'² Chelmsford was chosen, and the pleasure of seeing an RAMC lance-corporal summoned to rule an empire was not to be. But the incident indicated a Unionist need to find new and capable administrators if they were to fill their quota of posts credibly. By July 1916, Crawford's name was on an imaginary list of those whom the party could call on in need. Loyal, obedient, close to Bonar Law and the party in the Commons, capable of managing a ministry without fuss and also of playing second fiddle in the Lords, Crawford was to become for the duration of the war a necessary if minor part of the Unionist contribution to the machine.

The Irish question had receded into the background during the early part of the war. The Home Rule Act had passed into law shortly after the war started, but its operation was suspended for the duration. The Easter rising of 1916 in Dublin reopened attempts to reach a lasting compromise. Lloyd George's plan offered immediate home rule to the south and permanent exclusion to Ulster (defined as at present, with favourable boundaries). Though these proposals had Bonar Law's sincere support, they caused much soul-searching among Unionists connected with southern Ireland such as Lansdowne and Walter Long, and a party split threatened, while in France the battle of the Somme gradually removed any lingering hopes of an orthodox military victory.

Crawford was in France, about to start liaison work with the French press, when he received an unexpected telegram from Bonar Law:

8 JULY 1916

'The party is very much divided and I am certain that in view of the Irish difficulties you should render a greater service to the nation by joining the government than is possible to you in your present position. If you agree I shall propose you as Minister of Agriculture and I earnestly hope you will accept'.

The prose comes from B.L.'s heart; but imagine my bewilderment at the message. The moment I had come out to France A.J.B. made a similar gesture – now that I have transferred from the RAMC and am about to enter upon a sphere of work which promises to be exceptionally valuable and long overdue, comes a fresh invitation ... Moreover I am asked to join a bankrupt concern during a crisis which threatens the very existence of our own party – we having been bamboozled into a hopeless commitment on the Irish question.

How can one be of real service in such conditions? ... The task is repelling.

11 JULY 1916

The more I think of it, the more odious becomes the prospect. Our party is sore,

---

² Curzon to Crawford, 23 January 1916; Chamberlain to Crawford, 16 March 1916, both in Crawford MSS, Box 4.

The fall of Asquith

querulous, and divided – our leaders blamed – not so much for the actual proposals now being put forward, but for having allowed themselves to be jockeyed by the Radicals. Everybody says that Bonar Law is hypnotised by Asquith, that our men acquiesce in all Squiff proposes. Well, I shall have an opportunity of testing that later on – but so far as I can judge now we have been bamboozled throughout over this Irish business. Our first mistake lay in permitting the unqualified statement that the machinery of Irish government had broken down – a fatal admission for us to allow uncontradicted. Once *posé* the proposition carried disaster in its train.

12 JULY 1916
Sworn to H.M. Privy Council and also a President of the Board of Agriculture . . . Went to Downing St for my first cabinet.

It is a huge gathering, so big that it is hopeless for more than one or two to express opinions on each detail – great danger of side conversation and localised discussions. Asquith somnolent – hands shaky and cheeks pendulous. He exercised little control over debate, seemed rather bored, but good-humoured throughout. After a complicated discussion on Franchise he exclaimed 'Well, this is the worst mess I've ever been in' – 'and you have been in a good many, haven't you', said Bonar Law and we all laughed (outwardly).

15 JULY 1916
Today and yesterday spent almost uninterruptedly at the Board making myself acquainted with officials and their work. Much energy has been diverted to special war work which seems to be carried out with zeal and discretion. But I clearly see the lack of central control and guidance of effort – not by Selborne, but by the government as a whole. There is overlapping, duplication of duties, scope for friction and waste of energy. Had there been some clear-sighted person to discriminate between departments and to organise their duties, time, money, and power would have been economised. At present half a dozen departments are concerned in the provision of agricultural labour so much needed and so difficult to secure.

. . . The draft Home Rule Bill was circulated to the cabinet yesterday. The Ulster counties to be excluded under Lloyd George's concordat until they desire a coalition with the rest of Ireland, will be surprised on seeing the text of the measure which excludes them only for the period of the war and twelve months later. This is so palpable a breach of Asquith's public and unequivocal pledge that I suppose the forthcoming cabinet will revise the terms – but it is a fresh source of 'misunderstanding'.

19 JULY 1916
Cabinet . . . Ireland. Longish statement by Asquith – friendly, conciliatory, dull. Ll.G. after B.L. had stated our first difficulty about Ulster, said if Bill was wrongly drafted it must be changed. There was no conceivable misunderstanding with

Nationalists. Pledge was given by himself in writing to Carson, was repeatedly explained to Redmond, was publicly announced by Asquith: accordingly bill must be redrafted to make exclusion of Ulster definitive and final. – A v. frank and disarming statement.

Nobody indeed contested our view except Samuel who said that the bill did all that was required.

(2). Representation of Irish at Westminster.

It appears that after our first general election we shall still have the whole Irish vote in London. This was agreed on careful consideration of the 'heads of settlement'.

B.L. said he (and Carson) had overlooked this. McKenna doesn't want all the Nationalists here owing to their pressure on questions of finance. Asquith rather agreed.

Ll. G. said point had not occurred to him. Put him in a difficult personal dilemma as he accepted our contention, but it involved an amendment to wh. Redmond and Co. would strongly object. However it must be done – and Redmond must have the responsibility of refusing the settlement if he thinks fit.

Ll. G. pressed strongly for early production of the bill. W. Long said it would take a long time to prepare. George said orders in council would do most of it. Chamberlain demurred, whereat Ll. G. said that he had agreed with Carson to have them drawn up with help of an Ulster and Nationalist member.

Finally agreed to promise bill for next week.

21 JULY 1916

I attended the international wheat buying committee. This is one of the offshoots from the Board of Agriculture, and under the chairmanship of Sir Henry Rew, one of our assistant secretaries, a daily conference takes place. It controls the purchases for France, Italy and ourselves: it has prevented famine prices, by controlling freights and checking speculation, and has always kept a reserve of wheat for our own consumption. Thus at the present moment apart from the incoming harvest at home, we have ten and a half weeks consumption in reserve.

24 JULY 1916

Late last night I got a telephone message calling me to cabinet... The meeting I suppose was historic, for we settled to drop the Home Rule Bill on the ground that we cannot detect agreement among the parties. I need not enter into explanations: the basis however of this break rests upon Redmond's inability to carry his friends and enemies on the Ulster question. As to our proceedings, they were as calm and friendly as possible, though I see dangers ahead when we come to apportion blame and responsibility.

Much the most important and novel subject was broached in a typewritten document of which each of us had a copy on entering – a request by Mrs Asquith that we should be cinematographed, the proceeds to be devoted to war charity. This was much too solemn and personal a matter to discuss in public: but we were all a good deal perturbed. Lloyd George opened his letter in the middle of a difficult debate about Asquith's statement on Ireland. As he read it one saw him unconsciously preparing for the photographer – smoothing his hair (now very grey). Bonar Law had discovered his envelope a few minutes before – read the document with curiosity, was utterly bamboozled by the signature, and put the tiresome thing away with a wan and distant smile. What are we to do? Mackinnon Wood who has a very ugly figure wants to refuse. Tennant, with magnificent moustaches, means to be there: Bob Cecil says he doesn't mind so long as he isn't asked to put on his best clothes.

2 AUGUST 1916

Two and a half hours at the cabinet. Asquith's hand very shaky, yet he warms up always when he has to speak in H. of C. – of course the two hours before lunch are those in which his spirits and his stock of spirit are at their lowest measurement.

Casement. Discussion on reprieve[3] lasted two hours. Asquith began by reading many letters from various women and friends of Casement, including Mrs Green![4] Evidently he meant to incline to reprieve[5] – a long disquisition on lunacy. Reference to American opinion. Curzon made a grave and effective protest. Lansdowne expressed himself convinced against reprieve.

Grey much influenced by Spring-Rice's serious warnings from the USA. Crewe said impossible to pronounce the man a lunatic – said he wd. be released in twelve months. Buckmaster read long letter for reprieve from Archbp. of Canterbury – Samuel v. firm and decided.[6]

Asquith boxed the compass, read a most damaging document[7] against

[3] The execution was fixed for the following day.

[4] Mrs Alice Green (1847–1929), widow of the historian J. R. Green; daughter of a Church of Ireland archdeacon, she eventually became a Senator of the Free State. She met Casement in 1904 and influenced him politically.

[5] See Asquith to Miss Bannister, Casement's cousin, 2 August 1916, expressing 'sincere pain' with suitable qualifications (René MacColl, *Roger Casement*, 232); but cf. Asquith's remarks to the US ambassador the previous night, suggesting Casement had no chance, and urging circulation of the diaries (Brian Inglis, *Roger Casement*, 365).

[6] See Samuel's arguments in his letter to his wife, 2 August 1916, stating 'I have had no doubt all through that, as the man is certainly not insane, there is no ground on which he could be reprieved... Had Casement not been a man of atrocious moral character, the situation would have been even more difficult.' (Cited in Brian Inglis, *Roger Casement*, 366). Samuel gave the length of discussion of Casement as an hour and a half.

[7] There are two possibilities about the identity of this document. It may have been one of the two memoranda prepared for the cabinet by Sir Ernley Blackwell, legal adviser to the Home Office. One of these dealt with the issue of the Black Diaries in a most damaging manner. Alternatively, Asquith may have produced evidence, which the government claimed to have obtained only after the trial, that Casement was willing to employ Irish recruits to fight for Turkey on the Egyptian front. For Blackwell's memoranda, see Inglis, 359–60.

reprieve – suddenly Grey produced a draft telegram[8] for Spring-Rice, putting the whole case against Casement in the most damning fashion.

This was amplified and amended by F. E. Smith,[9] and discussion soon ended.

4 AUGUST 1916

Conference with General Taggart about the release of soldiers for harvest work. I have secured 27,000 men – but the matter should have been taken in hand a couple of months ago. Unfortunately no strong steps were taken until I had grasped the situation a fortnight ago – result haste and a great difficulty in providing an organisation which will not prove perilous in practice.

7 AUGUST 1916

Bonar Law dined. He is low and melancholy. He has a speech impending on Wednesday which isn't inspiriting, and he is painfully conscious of the ever-growing unpopularity of the government in the country and the H. of C. He doesn't want an election which he thinks won't improve matters. It would no doubt eliminate cranks and pro-Germans, but he says truly enough that equally dangerous people (the old Little England and No-Navy men) who are lying low or loyal now, would again be returned, and would assert themselves the moment peace negotiations were afoot. This is true – and the danger before us is that Wilson may make peace proposals to influence the Presidential elections, and that our pacifists may be strong enough to exercise dangerous influence. Meanwhile Asquith is tired – not very well either, and Lloyd George trying hard to supplant him. Bonar Law doesn't mean to lend him aid in this ambition. Is it possible that Ll. G. has already found a master in Robertson and is ready to evacuate the War Office?

The whole situation is most difficult. Our army authorities are confident that six weeks more of offensive, costly as they must be, will gravely disorganise the whole foundation of German defence, and that we should be successful by the spring. What then? the post-war problems will become terrific and in many ways will test our statesmanship far more deeply than the war itself.

[8] Grey's statement blamed Casement, most dubiously, for the death through maltreatment of Irish prisoners. Grey also denied that Casement wanted to stop the rising, and claimed that this version had been made up after the trial. However, Basil Thomson's *Queer People*, 89–90, shows that Casement told this story from the beginning, and moreover that Special Branch accepted it. Moreover, the Foreign Office on 1 August had received fresh evidence from the Vatican confirming Casement's anti-rising attitude. It is doubtful whether, on Crawford's account, this fresh evidence in Casement's favour was ever presented to the cabinet. Grey either wished to mislead others, or was himself misled.

[9] Attorney-general, and prosecuting counsel in the Casement case. *Frederick Edwin, Earl of Birkenhead: the Last Phase*, by his son, The Earl of Birkenhead (1935), 93, refers to a slanted interview in the Irish-American press published during Smith's US tour of 1917–18, in which he was alleged to have said 'You will remember that a tremendous effort was made to save Casement, and for a time the Government was wobbling. I gave them the choice of Casement or myself.' While Crawford does not record this kind of pressure from Smith, it is interesting that it was Smith who gave the last twist to the discussion.

The fall of Asquith

I was surprised to find that the War Committee has not only never discussed the demands to be made at a peace conference (that I can understand): but it has never considered upon what terms we should consent to discuss the matter at all. Suppose tomorrow some intermediary were to be authorised to open negotiations. What should we say? We haven't even contemplated such a possibility, we should have no adequate time to convass it with our allies: we should refuse to treat, and thereby might create grievous prejudice among neutrals.

9 AUGUST 1916

Cabinet. Arthur Henderson is reported to have resigned, but he attended this morning and made his points with vigour. I gather that he stays on to devote his whole energies to labour questions. Much more serious is the impending resignation of Lord Lansdowne. It is said that he long ago told Asquith that he would not stay on after the middle of August. He recently underwent an operation on his hand – a trifling thing for a young man, but unwise I thought for one so delicate and frail as Lord L. He is a man of great caution and will be missed in the cabinet. And Asquith? Is he going? Rumour says that his doctor has issued peremptory orders for his retirement. I am bound to say he doesn't look ill – but one never knows.

18 AUGUST 1916

Talk with McKenna at the Treasury... I am bound to say that these radical wretches improve on acquaintance. The common allegation brought against Bonar Law is that he is hypnotised by Asquith. I can't say that I see much evidence of this at cabinets, where the most obvious thing is that individually or collectively there is some influence which has a decidedly soporific effect upon Asquith himself. In cabinets he tries to impress his wishes on nobody – in private perhaps he is more robust.

...I often wonder if the cabinet is as unpopular in the country as in the Commons – I should rather doubt it: but there is no illusion in the Commons as to the impossibility of replacing the present gang. The fact is that too many of our critics are themselves open to rebuke – Carson for instance or Milner being 'unsound' on the Home Rule question, Hugh Cecil being rotten on tariffs and so on.

23 AUGUST 1916

Cabinet... Bonar Law said that he saw no issue from railway nationalisation after the war. Walter Long didn't seem to object.

9 SEPTEMBER 1916

My general scheme for a wheat guarantee and a standard wage for agricultural labour is now pretty clear in my mind – but no drafting of clauses has yet been done – and no consent obtained from the cabinet – in fact I haven't brought the matter to their notice. Will they consent to a scheme which is ambitious and costly, besides sinning against every canon of free trade and conservatism? I can picture to myself the horror of Lord Lansdowne, McKenna, and Walter Long.

1916

23 SEPTEMBER 1916

Some days ago, after long negotiation, the War Office, the Local Government Board, and the Board of Agriculture agreed to terms about recruiting agricultural labourers. It was a provisional agreement and to be revised in January. The War Office authorities who concurred in the scheme, indeed it emanated from them, were Derby, Gen. Geddes, and Sir Nevil Macready. No – Lloyd George on coming back lost his temper, stamped about the room, swore it was a landlord's dodge and said he would not give the matter another thought until next Monday. That is to say he suspended an urgent question at its most critical stage for five days.

It is really intolerable this display of bad temper and worse judgment. Something must have upset him, perhaps being summoned by an NCO in Wales whose bicycle he had broken, perhaps some domestic row at the War Office is answerable. Whatever the cause, the result is to be deplored. But it is Lloyd George all over. He is curiously different as a departmental administrator and as a parliamentary strategist. In the latter capacity he can and does take decisions quickly. In the former he is always too idle to read papers and thus has no confidence to make up his mind. Hence long delays. At length some official has to take action, and when Ll. G. discovers this, he is furious and tries if possible to reopen the matter. All his officials at the Treasury, Board of Trade, and Munitions say the same thing, that as a departmental chief he is intolerable.

In this particular case I fancy jealousy of Derby may be in part the root of these troubles. It is a pity, for Lloyd George spends most of his time in France or at his country seat, and during these frequent absences somebody in Whitehall should be given responsibility.

8 OCTOBER 1916

I sat eight hours today at a conference, after a week's hard work, about the Royal Commission to control wheat supplies. I am to be chairman and a most gigantic and delicate task it will be – the state control of the whole of our bread stuffs. There are some good men on the Commission but the jealousies of various branches of the corn trade are our greatest obstacle.

We are short of food and going to be still shorter. I have persuaded the cabinet to adopt standard bread, which may be an unpopular expedient, but justified by its economy of consumption.

13 OCTOBER 1916

Reconstruction Committee – big and rather vacuous. Asquith in the chair and much more alert than he usually is at cabinet meetings. We discussed demobilisation at some length. Everybody agreed with my view that it is preposterous for the War Office to estimate that they will require 401 days (how exact they are!) to get the troops home from France. I was explicit on the dangers of such a delay and everybody supported me. The W.O. will have to expedite matters. Of course it is not yet decided what army must be permanently retained, nor do we know the numbers which will be needed as an army of occupation.

The fall of Asquith

There is every indication that the amount of wheat necessary for our sustenance is lamentably short . . .

MEMORANDUM ON FOOD COMMITTEE, 26 OCTOBER 1916
McKenna, Runciman, Acland, Harcourt. Long absent. Conferences to be held with millers etc.

I said matter was urgent and that in May we may find ourselves in straits. Runciman said the same thing was said about May '15 and May '16. He had no fear at all.

I pointed out that next May is much more dangerous than the two previous Mays – world shortage of wheat, and growing submarine activity. We consider ourselves lucky when we don't lose more than 10,000 tons in a day.

Runciman said he wd. rather resign than acquiesce in bread tickets.

27 OCTOBER 1916
Went to see A.J.B. at the Admiralty about a difficult transport question. He has a good room overlooking the Horse Guards Parade. I remember going there in May of last year when I was brought over from Havre to discuss my entering the coalition government. There is a writing table, two or three other tables, all very orderly, a number of maps and a few pictures on the walls, some old Admiralty furniture and some high class armchairs – but no sign or symbol of its being an office: no files or papers lying about, none of the ordinary paraphernalia or equipment of the government workroom. Yet he gets through much business, and has the genius for never being concerned with anything except the essentials.

3 NOVEMBER 1916
I went to see Lloyd George at the War Office about the food supply. He is getting nervous and thinks that now, when we are in November, some heroic remedy can be applied. I first wrote to him on 24 August asking for an interview to discuss this and other questions, but got no answer from that day to this. Now at the eleventh hour he is waking up and would like to put into force Selborne's scheme which the cabinet turned down last March! Alas.

CONVERSATION WITH LLOYD GEORGE, 3 NOVEMBER 1916
He has had bad reports of Roumania . . . Also at conference this morning Robertson gave his opinion that war could not end during 1917.

He is accordingly anxious about the food position – and wants to provide for 1918–19.

I told him my immediate anxiety was the pre-harvest months of 1917. He said he wanted a gigantic effort made – industrial conscription, and a treatment and cultivation of land almost communal in principle.

I told them that this was proposed in March 1916 by Selborne in memo. to the

War Committee – he said Selborne did not press his proposal and nothing was
done. I said it would just have been possible to act this winter on those principles,
had the decision been taken in March, but that nothing of the kind is now possible.
The season is late, the weather bad, land dirty, and labour deficient.

4 NOVEMBER 1916

I went to see Asquith to urge him to help us with the labour question. He wasn't
very helpful. His eyes were watery and his features kept moving about in nervous
twitching fashion. I thought he looked ill and frail – also weak and undecided. He is
one of those men whose reputation reposes entirely upon intellectual power and
fertility of language – but to expect firmness or initiative from him would be
quixotic. I have been nearly four months in the cabinet and except for a handshake
on my introduction early in July, this is the first time I have exchanged a word with
him. In politics he ranks as a Field-Marshal and I as a Brigadier – and in
commonsense one would suppose that his business would be to supervise and
control his subordinates, or at least to see and hear them from time to time. At
cabinets he is calm and urbane – but as for ruling his colleagues or abridging idle or
wasteful discussions he is hopeless: I have never heard him say a wise or strong thing
at the Council table, though in the House his mastery of language indicates a
decision which I believe to be non-existent.

And everybody who knows him will concur in this estimate and yet admit that his
departure would be embarrassing and perhaps dangerous. I don't think anybody
can be jealous of him: but his admirers must be very scarce.

CONVERSATION WITH MR ASQUITH, 4 NOVEMBER 1916

Told him of gravity of situation – submarine danger – neutral ships may be
withdrawn – distance of Australian crop, land going out of cultivation, urgency of
labour question.

He said he was quite conscious of it – had a certain hope that in a couple of
months time we might be able to check submarine activity, mentioned a 'generous
providence' – said he hoped matter cd. be discussed at War Committee next week.

I said question was urgent as every day lost meant a decreased yield, that Strutt's
figures are most disquieting,[10] and that strong steps must be taken as regards
labour. He said that the military service act was only passed on the pledge that there
should be no industrial conscription.

I then urged the formation of a central food commission – he thought the idea
good (I had suggested it in memo. to War Committee). He said he greatly disliked
the idea of Rationing. He asked me to write a memo. about it.

[10] In June Strutt estimated the yield of 80 acres on heavy Essex clay at 4 qtrs. In September he reduced
the estimate to 3. He has just threshed and the actual yield is only $1\frac{1}{2}$. This if general is disastrous.
(Diarist's note.)

The fall of Asquith

Memo. from the Whips read – Cabinet ministers invited to make one or two speeches apiece during next three months, to counteract pacifist propaganda wh. is spreading. Meetings are held about food prices, pensions etc. and when the interest of the audience has been aroused, the pro-German gets in his advice.

Army Voting. Army Council, Robertson and Macready in particular, say that from the point of view of discipline, voting by the army is undesirable (except perhaps during an armistice). Ll. G. upheld this view tho' not v. strongly. Great confusion as to the proper course to follow.

Russian Jews. Samuel presented a scheme for their compulsory enlistment. There are 25–30,000 of whom perhaps 8–10,000 are fit for active service. Asquith quite strong against scheme – not worth while, liable to misunderstanding, create prejudice, unprecedented etc. This is the only subject during a cabinet on wh. he has expressed any opinion with decision, since beginning of July.

Ll. G. supported Samuel. W. Long said feeling against Russians was violent in E. London. English Jews support this conscription. My view is that the bill won't pass (because of our refusal to act in the same way towards Ireland).

7 NOVEMBER 1916

Cabinet Food Committee. I have the disagreeable impression that I am always dealing with tired men. Most of the Radicals have been in office six or eight years before these two years of war – is it surprising that they should be fagged to death, and that people should advocate a clean sweep of the whole cabinet.

... Runciman and McKenna said I should send out a Cabinet memo. I mentioned the Central Food Committee. Neither of them knew I had already written a memo. on the subject – indeed Asquith, A.J.B. and Lloyd George were equally ignorant of my effort when I saw them last week. (All have received copies). So it is now suggested I should send out a further note on the labour question.

Central Food Commission I briefly explained my view of the necessity of this, and said that a central control is inevitable. Board of Agriculture cannot possibly do it. We ought never to have been made responsible for wheat, but it came to us as we had happened to become the dept. concerned with buying for allies.

We can't do more: all our authority with farmers will disappear if *we* have to fix prices. Our object is to stimulate production.

McKenna did not see what use the Committee would serve. I said it will be the ultimate authority on all questions of rationing, diet, requisition. Runciman said German rationing system had been a hopeless failure and he would resign rather than introduce such a system here.

MEMORANDUM ON CABINET OF 13 NOVEMBER 1916
Food Control Asquith announced decision of War Committee to accept principle of central control. He said he cd. make no recommendation about personnel or indeed

about functions, or whether the Director should be a minister or not.

Curzon said he was absent from War Committee – knew nothing about it – had had no notice. Runciman said notice was at least given in my memo. Curzon then said he wasn't necessarily hostile, but was not prepared to give a decision. McKenna agreed – said rationing was inevitable – was it contemplated in Board of Trade order about fixing prices etc. Runciman said yes.

Grey strongly supported scheme, AJB friendly, Buckmaster very friendly. Duke said that he doubted if the Board of Trade regulation was legal. F. E. Smith gave no definite opinion on this point. Grey said we were all agreed – should we not settle on the man? (No decision as to his power over other departments was invited).

Asquith said that great energy was required and prime facie he only knew of one man who cd. do the work and who wd. accept the responsibility – namely Churchill. (Ll.G. had previously indicated that D'Abernon might do – especially as he wasn't a minister or in H/C.) I said I thought James Lowther the best man – cool, steady, trusted, strong. Ll. G. said he was much too judicially minded, and that we don't want. Asquith said his health would not stand it. I thought that departure from H. of C. wd. make a new man of him.

On the whole the principle was v. well received but much still remains to be done. P.M. leaves tomorrow – so perhaps another delay of at least a week.

CONSERVATION WITH LORD LANSDOWNE, 14 NOVEMBER 1916
Said he had read my two memoranda with anxiety. They are influencing him in preparation of a cabinet note on a most delicate subject – namely whether the country is strong enough to stand out for all we have threatened and guaranteed. The submarine danger menaces our whole position. Russia is still unprepared, France exhausted, Italy fatigued – Germany increasing her strength internally to compensate for military failures.

How long can we last? He agrees strongly with my view about an armistice, that it wd. be folly to impose terms so impossible of achievement that no discussion cd. ensue. In any case the likelihood of its proposal may now have reached the vanishing point.

18 NOVEMBER 1916
There is a wave of anxiety spreading through the inner circles at home, which will soon he reflected in the public mind. Food shortage is the most grave aspect of our problem, arising from culpable neglect in the past, the last eighteen months I mean, and now made infinitely more serious by the growing power of German submarines. I wear myself out in getting my colleagues to realise the danger, and when they have conceded the main principle I fail to get them to face the details with resolution and despatch. Asquith's somnolence is heart-rending.

19 NOVEMBER 1916
Willie Selborne says that he too used to groan at the poverty of direction shown by Asquith at cabinet councils.

The fall of Asquith

Cabinet – some talk about agriculture, but I can't get my colleagues to face the vital point. I told the cabinet that we are now a besieged country and must act accordingly. This evening I had a conference with Lloyd George and Derby. In point of fact Lloyd George really agrees with me although standing in the way of progress – but he has a big ambitious scheme of his own for cashiering the Board of Agriculture, and he can't make up his mind to begin on a modest scale.

MEMORANDUM ON CABINET OF 22 NOVEMBER 1916

All present I think – Chamberlain Henderson and Montagu came in together rather late.

Can't remember quite how we began a desultory but most important discussion – we got on to conservation of food supply and the question of further restriction of liquor was raised – less importation and consumption of barley etc. This said to be a v. important economy.

Ll. G. said parenthetically that there were no doubt overtures for peace in the air, certainly from Germany via President Wilson, but oddly enough no sign from Austria wh. probably arose from their confidence of striking Roumania. Somebody said that the Austrian Emperor was dead – Grey expressed great surprise – hadn't heard about it.

Buckmaster said it was no use discussing these things until we had faced our own situation and capacities. He thought the capital importance of Lord Lansdowne's memo. cd. not be ignored.

Ll. G. said the memo. was a state document of the greatest importance – he differed from it, as he thought a knock-out blow is possible. If permitted to say so he begged to record his admiration of Ld. L's courage in putting his thoughts to paper. Anyhow we must make up our minds. Can we strike a knockout blow – if we don't settle our policy there will be hesitating counsels, divergence of aim – increased nervousness of neutrals. But subject so great and far-reaching that he wanted a special Cabinet called. General agreement to this, but discussion continued on broad lines.

Grey said the submarine was the real menace. McKenna said there were certainly others – e.g. finance. To conduct war for six months on our present financial powers will be difficult, for 12 months almost impossible. Quite apart from our willingness USA will be able to call a halt next summer or autumn.

Robert Cecil asked what Runciman meant by a 'shipping breakdown' in or before June. Reply that tonnage is short and labour also. Expedition of ships improving but still slow. Three months ago W.O. was told to increase Docker Battalions but it isn't done yet. Likewise in April last W.O. and Admiralty were directed by War Committee to release 200 ships. Actually 69 have been released, but 89 others have been taken on. Curzon said that it was no good for one War Committee to order release and for the next War Committee to order an increase of forces say at Salonika or Egypt. Fact is there is too little tonnage and manpower to go round.

I then said that in considering this question home food supplies must not be overlooked. I made a general statement . . .

I invited the Cabinet to face the fact that we are a besieged country and to take steps accordingly.

W. Long said it all pointed to drastic reduction of consumption. In Bradford and such like places people were eating 50 per cent too much. Severe rationing necessary – Runciman said we must ration beer also. W.L. referred to feeding stuff value from breweries.

Ll. G. then intervened. Said all this concerned the Food Director – said he hadn't had notice etc., was unprepared. I gave him a copy of his scheme which he read out. Longish discussion. Runciman and McKenna said that the scheme superseded the Board of Agriculture. I said if the Director understood farming, my department wd. work most loyally with him – I wd. gladly act as an undersecretary – but it is no good for an inexperienced man to run British agriculture.

I pointed out that I wanted a decision about labour now. Wd. Ll. G. agree to my proposals – I read them out from memo. of November 9th? Even if the food dictator were appointed tomorrow he wd. come back to the basic question of home labour for home supplies? This argument was enforced by several members – Austen C. said if W.O. and B.A. wd. agree M.P.D.B. wd. concur – but Ll. G. tho' ready to concede everything for his own ambitious scheme wd. not consent to concede small demands made in mine. Finally decided that he and I shd. confer to see if agreement is possible.

23 NOVEMBER 1916

At the War Committee Haig gave quite an optimistic estimate of the military position, but assuming that all other aspects of the subject – finance, enlistment, munitions, food, etc., were satisfactory. It is not in France that our danger really lies.

Food Director Ll. G. then turned to this question and said I was pressing for too much and that a reduction of consumption was more necessary than an increase of supplies: and that the Food Director shd. take action. I pointed out that I was far from oblivious – I was the first to suggest wheat economy, and also the first to suggest central food control. But we must have new supplies as well or we shall starve.

Ll. G. quoted Walter Long as saying that the country cd. live on 40 per cent of its present consumption. I said this view was much exaggerated. McKenna said we shd. have to come to rationing – Montagu said the sooner we settled to begin our organisation the better. ?Runciman said the LGB and the Board of Agriculture shd. make a scheme. – I said the department was concerned with production not distribution, and that tho' my department wd. help, this was a whole time job for a permanent body under the Food Director.

The fall of Asquith

Another meeting of the War Committee – much discussion about freight, the most crucial and far-reaching of our difficulties. I thought A.J.B. looked ominously depressed – as a rule he has been quite light-hearted, but now he seems almost bent double by anxiety . . .

25 NOVEMBER 1916

The situation is indeed terrifying . . . The public at home begins to fret about our inactivity. A Food Director was announced ten days ago, but nobody has been chosen for the post – why not? . . . I fear that our empire may be lost by the fatal habit of weekending – Saturdays and Sundays have ceased to count for political business, for three out of five cabinet ministers are in the country, and don't get back to their offices till midday on Monday. This means that any topic in process of solution on Friday has to be held over, and the weary work is begun again next week. How often have I seen this in my own efforts to preserve labour on farms.

28 NOVEMBER 1916

It is well over a fortnight since the Cabinet decided to appoint a Controller of food supplies. Since then the H. of C. and the public, after a friendly reception of the scheme, have heard no more – have wasted their time in speculating about names, while the govt. has wasted public time in failing to secure the man.

29 NOVEMBER 1916

Cabinet . . . R. Cecil referred to his memo. and Army Council circular, wh. shd. be faced at once. He wants a small executive council to deal with non-military matters – e.g. rationing, agriculture, man distribution. Samuel rather agreed, but said a regular office with secretariat was required – three is too small a body. Ll. G. said let's consider the Lansdowne memo. first. L. said whatever we do hereafter let's get our machinery organised if the present system is inefficient.

Asquith strongly of opinion that machinery must be set up. There are many things outside purview of War Committee – and the latter body must be reconstructed or reformed. Moreover steps must be taken to get its orders carried out by Depts. concerned. These orders have been evaded or ignored. Domestic questions, e.g. labour, food, coal, require constant examination and control.

F.E. said the imputation in Army Council's memo. were injurious – the charge that vital claims had been neglected. Austen C. said the charges were v. ill-founded.

12.25 p.m. Crewe in the middle of some remarks Tennant was opening on the general subject, interrupted and said there was an urgent Welsh question (Welsh coal position) wh. he thought shd. be settled by 12.45 so that a Council could deal with it forthwith.

. . . Finance. 12.45 McKenna returning after a conversation with the Governor of the Bank of England announced that the action of the Federal Reserve Board was so serious that a financial crisis of the greatest magnitude seemed imminent. The

1916

expenditure involved in keeping up our exchange is gigantic – and as Wall Street must have instructions in two hours' time he proposed an immediate adjournment for a consultation with the bankers (Chamberlain, Asquith, Lloyd George, McKenna, chancellors past and present). The crisis was so serious that it might involve abandonment of the gold standard...

Lloyd George said the same fears were expressed on the outbreak of war.

The cabinet adjourned at 1 p.m.

Lowther refused Food Controllership after four days cogitation. At cabinet this morning Asquith said four other men had refused – he mentioned no names. Milner is now being asked... This delay creates a grievous impression...

2 DECEMBER 1916

The week has been rather *mouvementé*, and tonight Edmund Talbot told me on the telephone that a first class crisis is about to explode.[11]

MEMORANDUM OF SATURDAY, 2 DECEMBER 1916

Edmund Talbot came to see me after dinner this evening and for the first time I learned that a serious cabinet crisis must shortly lead to its dénouement. A meeting in B.L.'s room on Wednesday the 29th[12] discussed the problem – I was absent having to speak in the House of Lords – Lord Lansdowne told me vaguely of the difference of opinion between our colleagues, arising from the function and powers of the reconstituted War Committee, the corresponding Domestic Affairs committee, and above all the delicate question of personnel involved. Carson now much *lié* with Ll. G. is apparently to be one of the Triumvirate.[13]

3 DECEMBER 1916

Crisis all day long.

MEMORANDUM OF SUNDAY, 3 DECEMBER 1916

At 11.0 I attended a meeting of cabinet colleagues in B.L.'s house, Present Austen C., self, W. Long, B.L., G. Curzon, F. E. Smith, Duke.[14] A.J.B. is in bed and Lord Lansdowne at Bowood.

B.L. explained the situation, his conferences with Ll. G., his discussions with

---

[11] Asquith had rejected Lloyd George's proposals, to which Bonar Law was committed, and had made counter-proposals. Leaks appeared in both the Saturday and Sunday papers, and Lloyd George's resignation was widely predicted.

[12] This is incorrect. The meeting, in Law's room in the House of Commons, took place on Thursday 30 November. It was the first occasion on which Unionist ministers were consulted by Law about a Lloyd George regime. Their views were decidedly hostile and they made a counter-proposal involving division of labour between a War Committee and a Home Committee, as mooted the previous day in cabinet by Asquith. See R. Blake, *The Unknown Prime Minister*, 308.

[13] Lloyd George (chairman), Carson, Bonar Law. By Sunday Arthur Henderson had been added.

[14] Lord R. Cecil was also present (Blake, *op. cit.*, 314).

The fall of Asquith

Asquith, and his personal position, saying that he had pressed for reform a fortnight ago, Asquith had dallied, and he now thought he must resign.[15]

He read a memo. sent by Ll. G. to the P.M. It was a little obscure, but it evidently contemplated the establishment of a small body with supreme power – and the implication of Asquith's exclusion (except in an honorary capacity) was clear.

He also read us Asquith's reply – a considered and not unfriendly letter, in wh. he comments with vigour on the manner in wh. depts. have evaded or avoided obedience to the War Committee. He makes various criticisms, many sensible and the general impression I received was that he was quite ready to negotiate. This letter must have been written on or soon after last Wednesday.[16] Meanwhile Ll. G. was not pacified. The idea of having Asquith as chairman of the new War Committee must reduce the promptitude of its work; and Ll. G. has been openly talking about his resignation. This morning *Reynolds News*,[17] with which Ll. G. is intimately connected, gives the fullest exposition of his mind, his grievances and his decision to resign, this afternoon.

After an hour's conversation we came to the conclusion that it would be dangerous to let Ll. G. force Asquith's hand by resigning this afternoon. Asquith's government would end tomorrow and the best chance of forming a stable administration would be for Asquith himself to resign and ask the King to consider the matter. Presumably Ll. G. would be invited to make a government and the new proposals would then be subject to consideration by those of his old and new colleagues whose opinion he would ask. The point at issue is whether Ll. G. can stand without Asquith. The latter is discredited and unpopular through his invincible indecision – but he has managed to hold Labour and Nationalists, he has immense prestige in Europe even if little here, and he has a parliamentary capacity which somehow impresses the H. of Commons, notwithstanding their hostility and scorn.

We decided that we should tender our eight resignations in the event of Asquith declining to do so for the government en bloc, and we settled also to say that we had failed to get our proposals about a more businesslike system passed, and that internal reconstruction in view of the announcements about Ll. G. was no longer possible.[18]

---

[15] What Bonar Law sought was the assent of his Unionist colleagues to his resignation from the government in an individual capacity. He had made it clear to Lloyd George on Friday night that he regarded himself as bound to do this if Lloyd George was not put in charge of the war. What he was not trying to achieve, and what he can hardly have expected, was collective action by the general body of Unionist ministers.

[16] Typescript copies of both documents are in the Crawford papers. Lloyd George's memorandum to Asquith was written on Friday 1 December; Asquith's reply, insisting on retaining chairmanship of the War Committee, was dated the same day.

[17] Owned by Sir Henry Dalziel, a Liberal MP.

[18] A typescript copy of the letter from the Unionist ministers to Asquith is in the Crawford Papers. It is identical with the text printed in Sir A. Chamberlain, *Down The Years* (1935), 119.

Bonar Law was to see Asquith this afternoon and tell him. He was due back from Deal or Walmer at 2 p.m.

4 p.m. Second conference at Bonar Law's house. Present Duke, self, Bonar Law, Bob Cecil, F. E. Smith, Austen. Curzon and Walter Long[19] had meanwhile gone to the country expecting no further negotiation.

Bonar Law reported his conversation with Asquith, who seemed surprised and rather shocked by our communication. He positively refused to serve with Ll. G. unless his own position of control was assured. He would not dream of being Chancellor of the Exchequer or Lord Chancellor. He said no government could stand which did not contain both himself and Lloyd George. He almost indicated that he would fight, call a meeting of his party for a vote of confidence – and let Ll. G. do his best or worst in isolation. B.L. was impressed by Asquith's total ignorance that things had not been going well – indeed he said that every stage and action he was prepared to justify!

B.L. said Asquith was to see Ll. G. about 3.45 and has therefore asked us to come and wait for consultation after that conference, should Asquith ask for further conversation.

At 5.30 after much talk we settled to move eastward to be nearer Downing St and our own homes; at 5.50 a message came asking Bonar Law to go there, and we went to await developments at F. E. Smith's house. 7 p.m.[20] Bonar Law returned. He had a few minutes alone with Asquith and then Ll. G. joined them. Asquith said he had come to an understanding with Ll. G. – the scheme was to be put on paper; meanwhile – (I forgot to say that Bonar Law reported that at his afternoon interview with Asquith the latter begged him not to hand in the resignations technically – to tender but not deliver them).[21]

Meanwhile Asquith had decided to reconstruct the government, and tomorrow will ask each of his colleagues to offer his resignation! I observed that this being so it was advisable for a statement to that effect to appear in the papers tomorrow.

The net result of today's proceedings appear to be:

(1) We offered our resignations. Asquith refuses to accept them, but proposes to instruct all his colleagues, including ourselves, to do so tomorrow.

(2) We said reconstruction is no longer possible – Asquith proposes to reconstruct.

(3) Asquith means to do the reconstruction, to remain P.M., and presumably to

---

[19] The departure of Curzon and Long from London is recorded by Sir Austen Chamberlain, *Down The Years* (1935), 121, though the implication there is perhaps that they left town rather later. Chamberlain, though present, failed to record this second conference at Bonar Law's house. Blake, *op. cit.*, 326, also makes no mention of Bonar Law returning home to Kensington from the Colonial Office after seeing Asquith.

[20] 'A little before eight' in Chamberlain, *op. cit.*, 121. Crawford's chronology, which differs from that of others, was perhaps noted down soonest after the event; it is not therefore necessarily the most reliable.

[21] Bonar Law gave the same reason for not delivering his colleagues' letter on another occasion (H. A. Taylor, *Robert Donald*, 131, cited A. J. P. Taylor, *English History 1914–1945*, 68). But the question of the non-delivery of the letter is peripheral to the issue of whether Bonar Law gave Asquith the wrong impression.

redistribute a few posts but to make no radical or fundamental change. The country and press don't want a reshuffling of the cards, they want a new pack!

(4) Should Ll. G. fail to agree with Asquith (they have only come to a v. general understanding)[22] the former will probably find that though he can easily form a government it will be difficult to get the assent of Labour and Nationalists. It is also said that our men have only backed him because they distrust Asquith still more – also said that his influence among nonconformists is much on the wane. I wonder! My impression is that he has a big support among our friends in the provinces, in the army too, and that his energy would enable him to carry out policy which the present government as constituted would fail in, even if they were united.

a) Bonar Law expected this morning to have to fight with his colleagues to permit his own isolated resignation – to his surprise he found they would not assent to this unless in company with themselves.

b) W. Long says these Ll. G. intrigues have been largely conducted by Max Aitken – at luncheon rooms in hotels! – where there have been eavesdroppers.

c) George Curzon says he could not serve under Ll. G. as dictator![23]

MEMORANDUM OF 4 DECEMBER 1916

Meeting[24] at India Office, 1 p.m. Austen C., Robert Cecil, W. Long, self, G. Curzon, Lansdowne.

Talked over the matter. We all agreed that our decision of yesterday was wise – no regrets or *arrière-pensées*. This is surprising, and really shows we were right. Lord Lansdowne concurred.

R. Cecil reported conversation with Grey – latter returned to town last night from Bowood, and has heard *nothing*, either from Asquith or Ll. G. None of us has had a letter asking for our resignations.

Grey says he wd. like to leave govt., but if asked to stay on *qua* Foreign Secretary would not refuse, but is v. doubtful if he wd. care to stay on as President of the Council: in other words he wd. stay to continue his present work, but doesn't want a transfer. Grey has only seen Runciman among his colleagues, who was in the same position as himself.

Walter Long says Bonar Law did wrong in not communicating the text of our

[22] At dinner that evening, with Arthur Lee, Lloyd George gave the impression that nothing was settled yet (Alan Clark, *A Good Innings: the Private Papers of Viscount Lee of Fareham*, 161), despite Asquith's general acceptance of Lloyd George's terms.

[23] Cf. Curzon to Lansdowne, 3 December 1916: 'For instance, no one of us would accept a dictatorship of Carson and himself [Lloyd George]', cited by Newton, *Lansdowne*, 453. Curzon wanted Lloyd George brought to heel; he did not want to retain Asquith.

[24] This meeting is not referred to in Sir A. Chamberlain, *op. cit.*, 121, where the narrative jumps from Sunday to Tuesday morning. Crewe and Beaverbrook both alleged that the 'three Cs' present had already seen Asquith that morning; if so, their silence at this meeting served no obvious purpose, and Crawford's account of the talk casts doubt on the story. See Blake, *op. cit.*, 329 n.

memo. to Asquith. We were all in much doubt as to what had actually occurred, and we sent out for an evening paper to see if there was any news! Curzon had previously asked Lord Lansdowne if he had seen Reynolds' newspaper – Lord L. winced!

Curzon says he would not serve if neither in War Committee nor in an effective Cabinet. This applies *a fortiori* to Lansdowne who is not on the War Committee nor does he hold a portfolio.

General opinion that Cabinet might well be reduced in size but if so, all the more important that the War Committee shd. command full confidence. A good deal of distrust expressed in a War Committee of four with two men like Carson and Lloyd George on it. It is quite evident that Ll. G. means to get rid of A.J.B., and McKenna: Runciman and Montagu, both quite excellent men, are supposed to be on bad terms with Ll. G.

*　　*　　*

Conference in Bonar Law's room, Colonial Office, 5.30 p.m., 4 December. Lansdowne, F. E. Smith, W. Long, Austen C., Bonar Law, R. Cecil, G. Curzon, self.

Very little fresh news emerged. Asquith made a perfunctory statement in H. of C. – and incidentally was warmly cheered in repudiating a 'Dictatorship' in respect of Food. Lord L. had seen Asquith at 5.0 p.m.,[25] and rather gathered that he would come to terms with Ll. G. Prime Minister says that the new War Committee must submit to him the agenda and the minutes, that he will attend it.

(N.B. In the letter of 1 December he says the P.M. must be chairman – he cannot be relegated to the position of an arbiter in the background etc.)

McKenna Harcourt Runciman and another Liberal minister saw Asquith this afternoon and it is believed begged him to be firm: but apparently Ll. G. has practically won the day.

B.L. said that now we are 'out of office' Carson should be invited to our gatherings. He pointed out that this would limit our freedom of discussion, and if Carson were invited, Selborne Cave Finlay and others must be invited too. B.L. abandoned the idea.

TUESDAY, 5 DECEMBER 1916

Conference at Colonial Office 4.30 p.m. All Unionist members of Cabinet present except A.J.B.

Robt. Cecil, Austen C. and Lord Curzon reported a conversation of $1\frac{1}{4}$ hours with Asquith, concluded just before our conference.

[25] See Blake, *ibid*. The visit previously only known through an allusion in a letter from Curzon to Asquith written on Monday. Now that the time of Lansdowne's visit to Asquith is known, the question can be posed as to whether it was responsible for Asquith's break with Lloyd George on Monday evening – a dramatic *volte-face*, usually ascribed to a disturbing leader in *The Times* on Monday morning, or to pressure from Liberal ministers during the day. The Asquith who saw Lansdowne at 5 pm was evidently still far from being the man who wrote to Lloyd George later on that evening completely repudiating the compromise reached on Sunday.

The fall of Asquith

Undoubtedly Asquith had misunderstood tenor and intention of our decision on Sunday. He said he was 'flabbergasted by it' – thought it unfriendly, indeed almost looked upon it as desertion by colleagues with whom he had worked in sympathy and for whom he had contracted affection.

(How can this have arisen? B.L. we know did not give him the text of our written message, and I suppose he did not explain that we proposed his resignation on Sunday because we foresaw that to withhold it then would inevitably result in his resignation a day or two later – "48 hours" was my estimate of his survival after a breach with Ll. G.).

The three ministers not only explained to Asquith but convinced him that our advice tendered on Sunday was in the interests of all concerned – of Unionists of govt. as a whole and of Asquith himself.

It appears that messages of distress have come today from allied capitals expressing concern at the possible loss of Asquith's collaboration. The three reported that after verbal agreement with Ll. G. on Sunday evening Asquith had written a letter on Monday (yesterday) morning, not unfriendly – but that this morning he had written again, apparently withdrawing from the concordat.

Lloyd George had replied. The earlier portions of this letter were not read to the three, but the latter part was couched in tones almost violent, laying serious blame on the War Committee (of wh. Ll. G. has been member for many months past) adding that he dissented in particular from the Roumanian policy. Ll. G. threatens to publish this letter and also to ask permission to publish a memo. about the Roumanian situation – a memo. not circulated to the cabinet and I fancy quite recent. Whether this threat was verbal or in the letter I am not clear.

Asquith in conversation with our three colleagues was firm and vigorous, quite different from his own comatose and indolent self: he says he won't be a cypher, thinks Carson unfitted for supreme control, has little confidence in Henderson's judgement on international politics: – and he swept aside all suggestions of concession or compromise with a gesture of finality and scorn.

At 5 p.m. he was to see his Liberal colleagues. Meanwhile we discussed the general situation, and then transpired from B. Law that A.J.B. had already sent in his resignation. Two letters to B.L. and Asquith were read to us – in the first A.J.B. said it was evident Ll. G. was to have his way and he therefore thought the new regime shd. start uncommitted by himself. – To this Asquith had apparently sent a friendly but dilatory remonstrance, and A.J.B.'s second letter (to B.L.) repeated his view that to give Ll. G. a good start it was desirable that the Admiralty should be vacated.

Asquith had discussed the position and possible resignation of the Unionists with three Unionist members of the Cabinet, and never revealed the fact that all the time he had A.J.B.'s resignation in his pocket! This was uncandid.

After further discussion we agreed to send a written memo. to Asquith saying that we adhered to our advice of Sunday – indicating that our view was justified by events (reconstruction being quite hopeless). We hoped he wd. resign for the govt.

374

as a whole, if not we must ask him to act upon our resignations. George Curzon was deputed to take this message to Downing St and if necessary to interview the P.M. He departed about 5.50 p.m. or so. We waited.

It is believed – or at least freely alleged that Ll. G. has made a bargain with those whom he wishes to conciliate, e.g. that a Labour ministry shall be established forthwith, that Ireland shall have Home Rule (this via Devlin) and that Ireland shall accept conscription (this via Carson). I am afraid that the latter might break down in practice – wd. the Nationalists in Dublin be able to carry military service in Ireland? I doubt it. I fancy also that there may be renewed danger of pacifist propaganda at home. Trepoff's hostile reception in the Duma, the blow to Briand likely to follow the fall of Bucharest, the growing difficulties of food supplies in Italy, our rebuff at Athens – all these things combine to weaken the govts of the entente powers.

What is to be our attitude to Ll. G.? Austen C. inclined to refuse to join him in any capacity. George Curzon rather anxious to do so as a public duty if required. Robt. Cecil much the same view. I said if I were asked I shd. in turn ask for terms about agriculture. Wd. Ll. G. grant them? 'Yes, he'll give you Buckingham Palace, or at least promise it, if he wants your help', – this from Walter, 'Well, I hope you'll get it'.

6.20. Curzon returned from Downing St. Asquith was with his Liberal colleagues, so G.C. sent in the paper (wh. was written by B.L.) and said he wd. wait to see if P.M. desired to talk about it. After a short interval he went into the council chamber. He thinks all ministers were there except Ll. G. (? Henderson). Asquith stated that after consultation with his colleagues and bearing our memo. in mind he had decided to place his resignation in hands of the King, and to advise H.M. to call upon Ll. G. to form an administration.

Curzon said on our behalf that he thought the decision was right, and then added an explanation in justice to the Unionist members of the cabinet, to the effect that our message of Sunday had been wrongly construed as an attack on Asquith. Nothing was further from our minds. We held the view that a change of the War Committee was necessary and we had told him so – but our recommendation to resign was based on the belief that reconstruction had then become impossible. 48 hours have elapsed and our view is stronger than ever.

Asquith seemed gratified: and it is clear that apart from our representatives his Liberal colleagues were likewise in favour of resignation – some of them very angry with Ll. G. A question arose by some incidental remark as to whether Asquith shd. ask the King to send for B.L. – not Ll. George. Curzon said quite frankly that clearly it was Ll. G. who had promoted the crisis, and to whom the public turned for consolation. Asquith agreed, and B.L. when this was reported fully concurred.

B. L. also sent (at my suggestion) a message to Ll. G. to say that as Asquith had resigned the publication of his letter wd. be a great mistake – and if Ll. G. wished to talk about it he wd. go to the W.O. I think it would be a great pity if Ll. G. started the new administration with such an error of taste judgment and temper. Later on he can publish his letter, but to do so now wd. alienate support here, and still more on the Continent. Curzon expressed this view to Asquith and gathered that the latter would also try to keep him quiet. If he *does* publish the letter Asquith will have to send a damaging reply – not a difficult task.

Everything that has transpired since our meeting on Sunday morning has explained the justice of our view. We are where we were that afternoon, but with 48 hours of scandal and bitterness added: all might have been avoided had Asquith taken our advice, but he is unable to discern that the respect felt towards him by the H. of C. is not the same thing as the vexation he arouses in the country. He harps on one, is blind to the other. He thinks that he has a great following – so he has but it is insufficient, and though there will be a reaction in his favour before long, many thousands of loyal and patriotic men no longer associated with party politics, will rejoice when they learn tomorrow that he has at length resigned.

WEDNESDAY, 6 DECEMBER 1916

The morning newspapers announce that the King has sent for B. Law. My surprise is unmeasured, for I quite understood that last night the idea was as remote from B.L.'s wishes as from our own. There are four explanations – the King, Asquith, Ll. G., and B.L. himself.

a) The King is entitled to send for whom he pleases. When Mr. Gladstone retired he advised Queen Victoria to send for Lord Spencer.[26] She however preferred Lord Rosebery, and made a bon mot in the process.

b) Asquith. He may have recommended B.L. from distrust of Ll. G. – and in this may have received encouragement from his colleagues.

c) B.L. himself may have suggested it to Asquith, or secured his consent on the ground that Asquith wd. or might serve under B.L. as Ch. of the Exch. – and this might apply to others like Runciman or McKenna who cordially hate Ll. G.

d) Lloyd George. He may have got B.L. to consent to have his name put forward so that B.L. whom he can influence shd. have the task of giving the démission to Grey, McKenna, etc.

It seems to me that this compromise will fail – for B.L. has no majority in Parlt., lacks the drive and enthusiasms of Ll. G. on the platform – and does not carry the weight in press or public opinion.

7 DECEMBER 1916

B.L. soon withdrew from the task of forming a govt. – even if he ever seriously thought of doing so.

8 DECEMBER 1916

The Reform Club meeting was a great success, so Acland tells me, though there was some asperity in Asquith's tone. At one point when denouncing *The Times*, he glared with marked emphasis at Mond and Dalziel who were sitting opposite him. Asquith made it quite clear that he remains Leader of the Liberal party – and keeps hold on its machine!

[26] Untrue. Gladstone preferred Spencer, but his advice was not sought.

XII

The Lloyd George coalition, 1916-22

The Bibliotheca Lindesiana – Sir Joseph Maclay – the King's wartime diet – grain crisis – the Lansdowne letter – its effects in Paris – verses on Chequers – British withdrawal from the war? – Lloyd George on Hensley Henson – the premier's musings at his Unionist breakfasts – death of Redmond – the King explodes in Council – democratic reception for US delegates – Lloyd George on the Maurice letter – adverse effects of war cabinet upon departments – the worst blank verse line ever spoken – Lord Rhondda – Clynes's efforts to absorb Crawford's Wheat Commission – Balfour's memory – Gen. Macready's method with strikers – Milner at work – Lloyd George gives poor account of US army – Kipling at Charing Cross – Lloyd George on T. E. Lawrence – the Unionists and the coalition – impressions of Clynes – of Curzon – of Lansdowne – Austen Chamberlain bitter about the US – Lord R. Cecil on malignity of Welsh bishops – shrill opposition to ministers in the House of Lords – Hoover on the Jews – Keynes's book – the King's indigence – Grey's eyesight – F. E. Smith's early career – Lord Derby's intrigues – jobbery in the royal household – thefts by Australian premier – origins of the 'unknown soldier' – King Charles I's chin – the Office of Works – Craig on Irish reunion – Collins and Craig compared.

Crawford served in the cabinet for two brief, but particularly interesting periods, that preceding the downfall of Asquith in 1916, and that preceding the downfall of Lloyd George in 1922. In the intervening period, when he held a succession of ministerial posts of second rank, his diaries are fertile in impressions rather than in facts, for the obvious reasons that he knew little of high politics, and that his work looking after the nation's scanty bread supplies engrossed his whole energies. The chief exception was his record of what Lloyd George said in a series of breakfasts for the Unionist ministers in 1917-18.

When Asquith's ministry fell in December 1916, Crawford ceased to be Minister of Agriculture and was succeeded by Prothero, later Lord Ernle. Under strong pressure from the Chief Whip, Talbot, he agreed reluctantly to serve as Lord Privy Seal, and had written to Bonar Law accepting this post, when Curzon called to ask him to surrender it in favour of Salisbury. The latter however refused office, and Crawford was Lord Privy Seal, outside the cabinet, from 15 December 1916 to 10 January 1919. His main responsibility during that period, and indeed in the years following the war, was to

377

continue his work as chairman of the Wheat Commission. This was a heavy administrative task, nominally subordinate to successive Food Controllers (Devonport, Rhondda, Clynes, Roberts), but in daily practice autonomous, inconspicuous and vital.

Crawford's most awkward moment came when Clynes, the Labour Minister of Food, unwisely let himself be pushed by an ambitious official into trying to merge the Wheat Commission in the Ministry of Food. Personal and political antipathy were not involved: Crawford saw Clynes as a 'staunch little man' and a 'serious solemn little man, well-informed, persistent, and equable in temper', who never crossed the threshold of the Wheat Commission. However, when Clynes proposed in August 1918 to abolish the commission, the emotional temperature rose. 'Clynes writes to me that he means to dissolve the Wheat Commission, and he doesn't even care to discuss the matter with me!' If Clynes succeeded 'in destroying the magnificent organisation I have so laboriously constructed, I shall retire with dignity and with the consciousness that I have saved the bread situation in Europe, and that I leave our position far stronger than it has been at any previous moment of the war.' Clynes, under pressure from Lloyd George, soon backed down, denied that he entertained designs upon Crawford's commission, and got rid of his ambitious official to another department. After this, Crawford not surprisingly saw Clynes as 'amiable and inconclusive – the most feeble spectacle of a man I have ever witnessed occupying a very responsible post at a moment of anxiety'.

From January 1919 to April 1921 Crawford was chancellor of the Duchy of Lancaster, partly so he could bring bread supplies back to normal, partly to act as a government spokesman in the House of Lords, where the coalition faced a growing opposition from independent Unionist peers. Had Crawford remained another six months at the duchy, he would have given that comatose department a spring-clean, but became First Commissioner of Works instead (April 1921–October 1922), a department at which he made a strong personal mark. Promotion to the cabinet however was delayed until April 1922, at which point this chapter ends.

5 MAY 1917

I had a long talk with the Archbishop of Canterbury who bewailed Lloyd George's preoccupation which is throwing the state patronage into serious arrears. This branch of the prime minister's work is run by a Presbyterian called Stevenson (sex uncertain but I should guess female and Calvinist). Ll. G. is very friendly, says the Archbishop, but quite unable to give a moment's attention to any matter not directly relating to the war. Then why not delegate powers to some trustworthy authority, e.g. the Lord Chancellor who has a well-trained secretariat which deals with these subjects? Lloyd George the other day nearly appointed a man to the Deanery of Carlisle owing to his activist views – he discovered just in time that the 'brilliant churchman' was nearly 90!

19 MAY 1917

I had an audience of the King... He told me that he had visited Liverpool half a dozen times but that never had his reception been so vigorous and so sincere... He was very much annoyed at the strike[1] leaders having been arrested – and just after he had left the district. He says the strikers are split, they are disliked by the public and discredited by their official leaders – if left alone the whole thing would collapse in another 48 hours – and 'I mean to tell the prime minister what I think about it.'

Really the way he devotes himself to his duty is an example to us all. He has been away nearly all the week walking mile after mile through factories and workshops with amiable greetings for all and sundry – really the most fatiguing and backbreaking of all burdens in the world – and on getting to his railway train at night, he would find eight or ten boxes of official papers. However I am sure that this tour in the north has given him real encouragement, and I hope it has dispelled some of the gloomy forebodings which haunted him so much a month ago.

I see Sotheby's have sold Ellesmere's books, the Bridgwater Library... The Haigh Library therefore becomes the greatest private library in the British Empire. Other specialised collections are more notable in some particular group, such as Fairfax-Murray's incomparable collection of illustrated books, or Yates Thompson's tiny assemblage of perfect manuscripts. Aldenham has a good library, and George Holford too – the latter contains a few things of supreme scarcity and value. But all alike are the libraries of collectors alone, without regard to the claims of scholarship and learning: and it is in respect of the scholarship side of books that my grandfather achieved this Bibliotheca Lindesiana. My father developed the aspect devoted to scarce books as such. It is true that we have bowed the head to two sales of printed books, to a clean sweep of the manuscripts, and I look forward with regret to parting from the astonishing collection illustrating French history between 1789 and 1815, the labour of love and money to which my father devoted many years. But even so, the Bibliotheca Lindesiana now stands out as the most important thing of its kind. My ancestor whose 'grate bibliothak' was the ornament of Scotland in the seventeenth century is today represented by a handful of the original volumes. They form the Bibliotheca antiquissima Lindesiana to which a hundred thousand volumes have been added; and it must now become our duty to maintain and if circumstances permit, still further to develop this noble heritage of our race.

21 MAY 1917

I had a conference with Sir Joseph Maclay,[2] the Controller of Shipping... Bonar Law once told me that no papers were ever to be seen in Maclay's business room at Glasgow – and surely enough the pleasant room he occupies in London was a singular contrast to what is usually found in a busy minister's room. Not a paper or file was visible: the blotting paper was white in its virgin candour. There was a diagram on one of the walls, and a very common picture postcard stuck on to it. He himself had what is called a commercial diary, a small folio book with each page ruled off for the entries of a day – and here he jotted down a few notes – he seems a

---

[1] The engineering strike, which collapsed as the King predicted.
[2] Sir J. P. Maclay, first Lord Maclay (1857–1951), Minister of Shipping, 1916–21.

shrewd man, and from a casual appearance might be anything between forty and seventy. I don't think he looks a very strong or determined character, though his successful career points in that direction. He has the soft diffident style of talk which reminds one of Bonar Law.

18 AUGUST 1917

I went to the council at Windsor, and felt a great fool while being driven up to the Castle in an open barouche with postilions. King George was in a very jumpy condition about the projected railway strike. I fancy that the strike will prove abortive – all leave for our soldiers abroad would have to be stopped. This fact alone should mobilise public opinion against the engine drivers – and as the Railway union is split on the subject one hopes matters will not reach a serious stage. Yet the affair is disquieting and one may be sure is being worked and stimulated by the Pacifists. Meat is also causing the King great annoyance. He has been talking to his Sandringham agent, and hearing about the difficulties of carrying fat stock till the early spring. Sandringham is a cattle country and the King though not personally affected by so much loss on so many head of cattle, is none the less keenly alive to the impression of uncertainty which the new meat prices order will leave on the farmers' mind. He was very voluble and quite eloquent. I had a long and friendly audience, listening to a most vigorous denunciation of Rhondda and I am bound to say I see no answer to the charge that he is discouraging production. Let us hope the political advantages may outweigh the economic danger.

I lunched with the Household, Lady Shaftesbury now becoming very comfortable in figure, acting as hostess. The mutton so tough as to be almost unpalatable – vegetables sparse, quantities of butter but bread infinitesimal – fruit fair, no alcohol of any description.

6 NOVEMBER 1917

During the whole of October, London has only imported one week of its consumption – ditto Hull, ditto Liverpool: in other words we are importing a fourth of our requirements or thereabouts. All the rest is being diverted to France and Italy whose claims have been conceded with scarcely an effort at verification. Our own consumption goes ahead as though we were in the spacious days of peace, and as though tonnage and foreign grain were available in plenty. Hoarding is beginning in England. In Ireland it has long been a scandal.

8 NOVEMBER 1917

America comes in twelve months too late, and the problem is one of shipping. Either the European allies must dispense with food, or American troops must be sparsely represented in the field. There is not enough tonnage to perform both functions completely: and so one wonders if the Allies can hold out until the output of new tonnage suffices for the double need.

A bad month ended with Lansdowne's letter, made worse by the fact that it followed hard on the news that 'the German Jews who masquerade under Russian names are opening negotiations with the Boche'.

1 DECEMBER 1917

Though it is well-known that Lansdowne has long been a nerve-wrecked wobbler, I believe the explanation must to some extent be sought in the vexation and annoyance he feels at being out of office. He has held high or responsible positions for thirty years on end, and now he finds himself a private member, sitting in isolation below the gangway, without access to official documents, and no longer in the confidence of either opposition or government. He feels this exclusion from confidential information, he longs to be back in power or at any rate in effective opposition. I have often noticed his desire to make speeches in the House of Lords on matters in which he isn't much interested or concerned – but it is the speech rather than its content which attracts him. He doesn't want to be forgotten. He now stands a good chance of being adored by our enemies and execrated by the British people.

6 DECEMBER 1917

Lloyd George told Jack Poynder that Lansdowne's letter very nearly broke up the Paris conference. Nobody among the allied representatives could or would believe that such a document, coming from so cautious and so experienced a man, could have been made public without the tacit consent of his old colleagues. Fortunately Lloyd George was not alone. Had he been by himself he says publication would have defeated him: but he had four or five colleagues all of whom spent the whole day in visiting people, and giving assurances, strengthened by their obvious innocence and candour, that this démarche was not only unofficial, but repudiated by the cabinet. No more ill-chosen moment could have been selected.

7 DECEMBER 1917

Hoover now demands ten million bushels more of our Canadian wheat to keep the Buffalo mills going till the spring. Where do the interests of the Allies come in? We are now feeding America as well as France and Italy – and nobody exploits and blackmails us with greater zest than Hoover. He could not act in a more unfriendly way towards us. Is the man straight? I feel that he is doing us more injury than some of our avowed enemies.

On a lighter note, there were verses celebrating the irrepressible Arthur Lee, who had just presented Chequers to the nation:

> When climbers were told,
> Honours weren't to be sold,
> They were greatly cast down for a while;

The Lloyd George coalition

Till one of the mob
Who was good at the job,
Implored them to cheer up and smile.

'Though they've barred £. s. d.,
(Said this cute K.C.B.),
'Let all of us keep up our peckers,
As it's perfectly clear,
That I can't be a Peer
By giving a cheque – I'll give Chequers!

11 DECEMBER 1917
I look upon the [*franchise*] bill as the strongest if not the sole bulwark between this country and revolution.

13 DECEMBER 1917
I sent in a strong memorandum the other day to Curzon, Bonar Law, and Carson, urging prompt and effective steps to improve our [*food*] situation, but one is very powerless. Lord Rhondda has made the Wheat Commission a department of the Food Ministry – we now have their name on our notepaper, and we have thus lost direct and personal access to the cabinet. Rhondda's time is absorbed in wrangles about the price of cutlets, and momentous problems of supply go unheeded.

Not only about food supplies, on which the public is profoundly ignorant, as Rhondda insists on directing their attention to prices, but on the general outlook of the war situation, people are downcast. During the last week or two there has been a marked increase in nervousness, in asperity of criticism and judgment... The pacifists are rallying round the Lansdowne standard, gaining courage and confidence, and conducting a propaganda more strenuous than ever, and all the more dangerous because of our rattled morale. It is all most sinister, and nothing short of a victory will rehearten us. People are now talking rather glibly about our ability to continue the war by sea if circumstances compel our withdrawal from the land campaign. The idea is quite attractive, conforming as it does to our military precedent, relieving the strain upon us, and bringing soldiers back for agriculture, for shipbuilding, and for many other trades where they are badly needed. But the advocates of a sea war fail to appreciate the result of our abandonment of the land war in Salonika, Palestine, and Mesopotamia: and were we at war with Germany alone we should soon find ourselves embroiled with our old allies as well as neutral powers on trading matters, and the war would virtually begin again. Moreover I don't believe the country would tolerate a continuance of the war if France and Italy were knocked out. That this argument is put forward illustrates the sense of hopelessness and despair which is gradually invading public sentiment among loyal and patriotic men.

I sat next to Lloyd George at a breakfast in Derby's fine house. The company consisted entirely of Unionist members of the government. It was entertaining, and I did not lose my opportunity of impressing my views on the prime minister and urging him to despatch Reading to America...

Griffith-Boscawen was sitting opposite us, and Lloyd George asked him if he disapproved of the appointment of Henson to the Bishopric of Hereford. Yes – Boscawen thoroughly disapproved, as Henson is a litigious person who offends most people and who is himself disrespectful of ecclesiastical authority. Lloyd George said in defence that in making his selection he had the support of Dr Burge the Bishop of Southwark (a very sane and sensible prelate). With the Church an established body it is essential that all aspects should be reflected in its government: were the Church merely a sect, or a private and unofficial corporation, it would be possible and it might even be right that aspects such as those which Henson reflects should be excluded or suppressed. The little man stated his case with incomparable lucidity and humour, carrying the sympathy of those who heard him, notably of Prothero: but I fancy there is trouble ahead – Wolmer for instance has written an intemperate and vulgar letter on the subject. Halifax is on the warpath and others too I doubt not will take up the hunt.

Breakfast over, to which Ll. G. did full justice, cigars were handed round and the prime minister mused aloud about manpower; how Russia had failed, how Italy had weakened us, how tardy has been American intervention and how slow its fruition. How difficult and obstructive Labour has been, notably the highest grades of skilled labour such as the engineers – 'The House of Lords of Labour' as he slyly called them, but how insolent is the aristocrat of the labour market! Lloyd George still smarts under the cool and off hand manner with which they have threatened national necessities – and their attitude on the new bill will probably determine its success. And Ireland? What is to be done about conscription? Lloyd George seemed to make no concealment of his own belief that Ireland ought to be conscripted, but he fears the immediate result. It would inevitably smash up the Convention which still gives a ray of hope. Probably conscription would be followed by a defeat of the government in the H. of C. – in any case the normal conduct of business would become impossible. There would be scenes of violence – Dillon would be carried screaming out of the Chamber – Labour would support the Nationalists through thick and thin. Though no Irishman occupies a post of supreme responsibility in trade unions, they hold the subordinate places. Murphy's, Conlan's, Cassidy's run the underground intrigue, pulling the strings in the interests of Nationalism, and they would mobilise organised labour against the government.

Whatever would be the effect upon allied opinion abroad? Lloyd George says that throughout these years of distress, the solidity of Britain has been a great asset of the Allies – the knowledge and confidence that England sticks to her guns with unchanging constancy has often been the pivot upon which the war has turned. Were England to be convulsed in some crisis, which would be all the more severe owing to our war reputation, the Allies would lose heart, their pacifists would gain power, and in a week or two the whole aspect of the war might undergo a radical change. The argument is not unimpressive. If organised labour, in despair for a case against Geddes' unanswerable claim for more men, were to suggest recourse to Irish conscription, were themselves to advocate this policy, it might be possible to fight our domestic battle with success. Otherwise to make the proposal without the assent and support of Labour as a whole would involve the gravest consequences.

Col. Craig says that if the Convention fails, the only course to pursue is to exclude Ulster from the Home Rule scheme, and to put her into the area of conscription. A tolerable quota of men would thus be secured, and within three or four weeks a reaction would take place in the rest of Ireland. This scheme made us all laugh – but somehow there is something in it!

4 JANUARY 1918

I fear my commission is as obstructive as the Dean of Westminster. We are on the border of a grave crisis about breadstuffs, and yet everything I proposed this afternoon to the conference of my chairman proved unacceptable. They won't stimulate early threshing, or take a strong line about luxury baking. They won't agree to intercepting a fraction of the miller's output to government reserve. There are difficulties in the way of commandeering the brewers' barley and on all sorts of other things they are more afraid of departmental difficulties than of a national crisis. I confess I left the meeting in despair: for all things are continuing to make a dangerous situation. The meat shortage is really great. Whole towns are without supplies. So long as bread is available a meat famine can't starve us: but it lays greater stress upon the bread position, increases the demand and pro tanto makes that problem more acute than ever. Potatoes remain a great reserve force, but the tuber is bulky, can't be brought to London in abnormal quantities: few facilities for storage exist, and rather complicated machinery is needed for peeling and mashing them for admixture into bread. What makes me most anxious is the unconsciousness of the public as to impending danger. Everyone knows that sugar, butter and tea are deficient. People are now finding their meat is scarce. But when in addition they are conscious of a shortage of bread there will be a panic. Rhondda is difficult of access – he seems to take a long weekend in the remote country with the regularity of a Devonport. When he gets back to London he is overwhelmed with a variety of troubles which he has largely made for himself – and he finds but little time to devote to constructive reform.

10 JANUARY 1918

I had an interview with Reading who shortly leaves to take up his post at Washington. I explained the difficulty: my suspicion of Hoover's reliability, the consequent dangers to the Allies, to civilisation itself: for if Hoover is playing a double game, he occupies a position which enables him to do us untold injury. I may be mistaken. I probably am: but I can't forget that in old days our authorities were so suspicious that they used to watch him, and wherever possible his correspondence. It may be that they were prejudiced by his shifty hangdog manner, by his refusal to look one in the face, and by a general craftiness of manner and phrase which are most discourteous and extremely unsavoury. Reading says he knows him, has himself been puzzled once or twice, but they have been acquainted professionally for years, and at one time I gathered that in his capacity as legal adviser, Reading (then Isaacs) had rendered Hoover good service. Let us hope the latter may prove grateful to our new Ambassador.

...Female suffrage was carried in the Lords by a majority of 2–1. I shared the inglorious decision of George Curzon not to vote – I think on the whole it is a good thing that women are to be enfranchised, for the larger the new electorate the more likely are we to emerge from the dangerous years of Reconstruction with credit and prudence. Nothing but the widest suffrage can ensure a constitutional treatment of these problems. But it is singular how others have been converted to female suffrage, Derby for instance or Harcourt, not on political grounds but on the abstract merits of the case. We are assured that their war work has been so wonderful that they are entitled to the vote. In point of fact the war has demonstrated the inability of women to perform the essential tasks. They cannot dig ironstone or win coal, or make steel, build ships, erect machinery, navigate the oceans – still less can they fight by land water or air. They perform the subordinate functions fairly well – no more can be said.

22 JANUARY 1918

Breakfasted at Derby House, 25 of us, all Unionist ministers to meet Lloyd George. This morning's papers announce the resignation of Carson, and the prime minister's causerie was on the Irish question: and a gloomy tale too! As he went on, describing how the future of the Empire is threatened by a purely provincial crisis, I saw the faces of our colleagues grow old – Hayes Fisher's whiskers drooped till he looked seventy – Cave got wan, others grew grey – our host alone seemed to retain his freshness and the buoyancy of youth.

The prime minister told us of very serious representations which Barclay has sent from Washington, saying that the Irish are hard at work, that Wilson is nervous, and that there may be repercussions elsewhere if as now seems inevitable, the Convention collapses. Carson has resigned in order to devote himself to conciliation, to work for a settlement among the Ulstermen. Lloyd George paid a heartfelt tribute to Carson's loyalty and single-minded spirit – but Carson is not the only actor in this drama. The Southern Unionists have come to terms with the Nationalists: but there has been a pretty serious breach between the latter. Redmond is no longer supreme amongst them, and it is now quite clear that the R. C. Church is determined to destroy any chance of agreement. The R. C. Bishop of Raphoe appears to have coalesced with Devlin – pressing for some claim which it is impossible to concede (customs and excise and police, I fancy) and by his insistence he means to break a settlement while casting the blame on others. How bitterly Lloyd George referred to these wreckers – how unfeignedly have his affections turned against the Nationalists with all their narrowness and malignity. To be defeated by Maynooth is indeed an added humiliation.

5 FEBRUARY 1918
Before long there will be few smiles on the food problem. This morning the Derby House symposium had a statement about it from Rhondda. Lloyd George kept cutting Rhondda's rhetoric short, imploring him to get to the facts. It was clear that the P.M. knew very little about the subject, and it was painful how Rhondda shambled and trembled, leaving the impression of a hopeless and even dangerous confusion. Prothero gave his observations from time to time, amiable and unconvincing.

28 FEBRUARY 1918
Lloyd George discussed the government connection (and partnership) with the Press. I sat next to him, and therefore did not enjoy the pleasure of watching his mobile face – this at Eddy Stanley's breakfast party. I am bound to say he quite failed to persuade us that Rothermere, Northcliffe and Beaverbrook should have been associated with the government en masse. As regards Rothermere, nobody takes any objection, for his predecessor was a newspaper proprietor, and he himself has done and is doing excellent work though Johnnie Baird his under-Secretary says he doesn't behave like a Secretary of State. As to Northcliffe, Lloyd George denied point blank that he was a minister. Beaverbrook sticks in our gizzard. With an inimitable gesture, Lloyd George intimated to us, for he never phrased his sentiment, that for certain jobs certain people were needed, and that for this particular post Beaverbrook!... The Prime Minister was adroit, laid down various propositions we all accepted, absolved Bonar Law from all responsibility for the appointment, treated the whole business with engaging frankness and candour – but at the end of it all we felt our sentiments were well summarised by Edward Talbot who said 'But what do you mean to say to the House of Commons if a hostile motion is put on the order paper?' The fact is that Ll.G.'s defence, much of it such that it could not be publicly repeated, failed to dispel the feeling underlying the whole distrust of Beaverbrook, based on the universal belief that he is a dishonest man. For my part I have quite come round to the view that in these times we must not be squeamish. For dirty work give me the dirty man.

5 MARCH 1918
At Derby House we discussed the settlement of old soldiers on the land. We are deliberately going to make an experiment which has already been unsuccessfully attempted a score of times – yet the feeling of moral obligation towards ex-soldiers is such that we mean to embark on what will in all probability prove to be an economic failure. Whatever the ex-soldier may wish as to a 'back to the land' movement, his wife will probably prefer to stay in the town: and it is only if

transport can be so far improved as to proximate country to the town that the scheme can hope for even a modicum of success.

9 MARCH 1918

John Redmond died a few days ago. Papers are full of panegyrics which I confess seem a little insincere... He was a good sound and solid leader of the Nationalist party, and kept them within moderate bounds – but he was not the great statesman our newspapers allege. He was wholly and entirely deficient in constructive power. Neither was he a great orator. There was a certain rotundity of phrase which may have deceived people, and his speeches were never too long: but they were so carefully prepared and his notes were so scrupulously exact that he relied too much upon forethought. His speeches, when debating caused them to be spontaneous, were indifferent, and more than once when making set speeches I have seen him utterly nonplussed by finding his notes out of order. On one occasion ten or twelve years ago he dropped a sheaf of notes by accident, and proved quite unable to resume his remarks. One liked him – he was a gentleman and cool-headed: very different from the typical Nationalist, and from his successor in the leadership of his party whether it be the aged traitor Dillon or the youthful cornerboy Devlin.

19 MARCH 1918

Addison joined the breakfast symposium at Derby House this morning arriving half an hour late which as Ll.G. says is a triumph for punctuality in Addison. Hitherto Derby's parties, except for the P.M., have been wholly drawn from Unionist colleagues, and Addison felt a bit shy in advancing certain proposals, – and was then surprised to find how fully and frankly his views had been accepted by us long ago. But both he and Lloyd George are getting to learn that husbandry is a mistress who resents novelties and innovation... Then again Lloyd George now sees that if increased production is really the ideal to be attained, great farms with powerful capital and equipment will secure better yields than smallholdings with tenants who will find it difficult to survive a couple of bad seasons.

13 APRIL 1918

At Buckingham Palace this morning I gave the King a list of orders to be approved at the Council meeting. His eye fell upon the first item – a proclamation forbidding the importation of boots and other articles. 'Why may we not import boots?' he asked 'Don't we want boots, aren't other countries short of boots and oughtn't we to have as many boots as we can get?' His voice grew louder and louder, shriller and more strident. Then he paused and said to me quietly 'Why not import these boots?' I told him I was as much puzzled as himself. 'Well,' he said, 'these Council meetings are in many respects a formality but I want to know about the boots. Send for Fitzroy.' So I brought in Fitzroy – giving him one word of warning about the conundrum. Poor man, he was very nervous, mumbled out some explanation about economy of shipping, and indiscreetly revealed that the 'other articles' were – herrings! 'And don't we want herrings?' shouted the King in disgust, 'Surely we want all the herrings we can get!' But recalling a recent visit to Grimsby he told us that half a dozen ships had landed £900 worth of fish apiece – he became mollified all at once, and we then fell to business.

17 APRIL 1918

A group of American labour leaders has arrived, and they have fallen into the excellent hands of Harry Brittain. Every effort has been made by our pacifists to nobble them, but Brittain is a determined fellow and so arranged matters that he never let them out of his sight and influence during the first few susceptible days – and he now says they are sound enough to need no further tutelage. Among other episodes was a night spent at Warwick Castle. Here he gave them a ghost – and a huge burly labour man (whose name I can't remember) was so much alarmed that he fled downstairs and very nearly killed himself. Among the delegations are two or three women one of whom is called Ethel something or other. She had never seen an English 'Lord' and expressed herself most anxious to do so – one wonders what she expected, and also what she thought when Lord Leigh was presented to her – for he is a most singular looking person with a decidedly Turanian cast of countenance. Anyhow Harry B. had warned Lord Leigh to play up, and Lord Leigh did so to the full. Ethel had asked Brittain if peers were democratic – the most democratic people in the world, so H.B. assured her. 'You watch Lord Leigh and see if he isn't democratic in his heartiness and good fellowship.' Lord Leigh was warned, played up to her splendidly, talked with earnestness and also made her laugh, and finally, said, 'Miss—, I want to ask you a favour. If you will consent to call me Francis, may I have the great pleasure of calling you Ethel?' and the poor silly woman nearly cried with emotion!

18 APRIL 1918

Lloyd George however made us a long statement about the military outlook and on the whole his verdict was favourable. If we can maintain our unity for another month, the German exhaustion will assert itself and our star will be in the ascendant... Then the prime minister said that the German losses though severe are by no means so great as our enthusiastic soldiers and journalists have led us to believe. He also said that the German officers and above all their N.C.O.'s are better trained in open warfare than our men whose education has been limited to trench tactics. This is the opinion of responsible soldiers and gives cause for alarm. His general forecast was however favourable – and as for his courage, that is invincible.

25 APRIL 1918

Our Derby House breakfasts are transferred to St Stephen's Club where Edmund Talbot is our host. Lloyd George talked about the military situation, and evidently thinks the loss of Amiens would no longer prove the disaster it would have been a month ago. We have lines prepared west of the town. Dunkirk also he says could be lost without ending the war. I don't think he contemplates the loss of either place, but the new attack now being opened will be severe. The United States as usual is failing to fulfil engagements, or rather is blundering... The fact is that Roosevelt was right in saying that until the United States has an efficient central government, its conduct of the war must be vague and indecisive. Wilson issues orders, right in themselves, but there is no organisation to see these orders are carried out – in fact the machinery of government is quite absent.

9 MAY 1918

At breakfast this morning Lloyd George reviewed the whole situation disclosed by the Maurice letter. He said that its appearance was perhaps the greatest surprise in his life – and until he looked into the allegations he was afraid that through haste or carelessness he had actually misquoted figures. But when he made enquiries he found that not only were the challenged statements correct, but that there is a mass of corroborative evidence of which he was quite unaware.

The most interesting thing he told us – a fact which he will not be able to make public – is that the extension of our line was agreed to by Haig without the knowledge of the cabinet. Clemenceau went to Haig, threatened and importuned him, told him that unless he could tell the Chamber next day that we had consented, that Clemenceau and his government would fall. Haig was in a most difficult position. Clemenceau with all his incomparable skill and decision, insisted on a prompt reply. At last Haig agreed. Clemenceau was satisfied, and staved off a first-class political crisis. Haig reported the facts to the cabinet at home, which fully endorsed his action.

Lloyd George was in excellent spirits – talked so much and with such animation that he let his cigar out a dozen times. He is very firm that as Asquith (Arsquith as he always calls him) had refused the offer of a judicial enquiry, that the H. of C. should settle the matter in the division lobby. I am sure he is right... Anyhow the prime minister's reply is complete and will be crushing. 'This time I have been caught out telling the truth' he said laughingly to George Younger as we walked back to Downing Street.

6 JUNE 1918

Lloyd George talked lengthily to us this morning. He is just back from France. Paris is nervous. The French army is rattled. They feel their defeat much more keenly than our disaster further North. Paris has almost fallen within the zone of operations and is under constant bombardment by day and night. Clemenceau maintains his high and indomitable courage – If Paris falls? – Mais il y a toujours Marseilles!

19 JUNE 1918

Ministers never meet to confer, never exchange notes about their departments, never seek mutual advice. The result is that there is no sense of mutual or collective responsibility. No general papers are circulated, so familiarity with the development of current political questions is lacking. Everything is centralised in the War Cabinet, which is not supported by ministers beneath it, because apart from departmental matters these ministers know practically nothing, and take no interest in the doings of their neighbours. Sometimes they break into open conflict; Hodge versus the Treasury about pensions, Prothero versus the Food Controller about meat, Newton versus the War Office about prisoners. Mr Gladstone or Lord Salisbury would not have tolerated such lack of discipline for an hour.

Dined at Grillions . . . Edmund Gosse talking about parodies told us the origin of the famous caricature of Wordsworth ascribed to Edward Fitzgerald:

'A Mr Wilkinson, a Clergyman,'

It appears the credit for this inimitable line should be ascribed to Tennyson. He was walking with Fitzgerald along the Backs at Cambridge – they had been discussing bad poetry, and conversation drifted on to other topics. A girl of their acquaintance was mentioned; she had recently married. 'To whom, by the way?' asked Tennyson. Then slipped out the line, 'A Mr Wilkinson, a clergyman.' 'Ah' thundered Lord Tennyson, 'that is the line we want, that is the worst blank verse ever spoken, and nobody but Wordsworth could have achieved it.'

20 JUNE 1918

Lloyd George told us that Haig and Foch are completely puzzled as to the direction of the impending German attack, but still more puzzled to explain why the offensive is delayed.

27 JUNE 1918

The P.M. told us that on the western front there is no change in the situation . . . It is lamentable how complete is the Germans' mastery of the initiative.

1 JULY 1918

All kinds of theory prevail to explain the German inactivity . . . One thing however is clear, namely that the renewal of the German offensive is unaccountably delayed.

5 JULY 1918

Rhondda was a success, there can be no doubt of it. He established the sense of equality. Though he helped to bring the food queue into existence, he managed to destroy them; and though he discouraged production by threatening the producer, he did much to eliminate the profiteer. He stabilised bread prices. I was not consulted though the Wheat Commission had the responsibility of distribution and supply; at the time I thought he made a great mistake and it became my business to make good the increased consumption consequent upon the cheapened loaf, by making bread unattractive and by a stricter control of distribution. We raised our milling extraction to 92, enforced admixture, curtailed the cake and pastry, and thus we gradually built up a reserve which is now a source of tremendous strength to us. I now see that from political reasons Rhondda was right to enforce the 9d. loaf. He did this because he was really frightened at bread remaining at its economic price. Happily we were able to prevent his having bread tickets, and we avoided a very disagreeable controversy with him. The *Daily Mail* was screaming for bread rationing and Rhondda was nearly swept away on that tide. In this matter however he took us into consultation and avoided a tremendous blunder.

7 JULY 1918

We have had a week of local successes all along the western front ... But we await the great attack with all the more anxiety that it should be so long overdue. Meanwhile America is doing well, making up for her futilities and muddles of six months ago.

11 JULY 1918

At breakfast this morning Ll.G. told us that we are still bewildered by the German intentions in France ...

Most of our conversation was about aliens. The government has settled that something must be done, but doesn't know what to do or how to act. Cave seems satisfied that the existing system gives ample control, but the Northcliffe Trust is on the warpath and is fomenting a demand which is already widespread for drastic action. The public is certainly annoyed and perhaps alarmed, but the fundamental objection of allowing aliens to remain at large is less a fear of espionage, than indignation at the apparent prosperity of aliens while our own elderly men are seeing their businesses destroyed by the advanced age of recruiting ... But our chief difficulty is that the bulk of the aliens are Russian, Polish, and Jews – few are of real enemy extraction.

Something however is to be done and quickly.

16 JULY 1918

I fear that the government is in evil odour with the peers as a whole. Salisbury and St John Brodrick are never tired of saying that the government is disrespectful to the House. Curzon is perforce absent very often. Milner in these times can hardly be expected to listen to debates about midwives or smallholdings. French is in Ireland, Lord Weir at the Air Board, and so on. The result is that two or three of us have to answer for a dozen departments, and as there is no ordinary cabinet, and no circulation of papers, we are obliged to read to the House jejune and evasive replies prepared in the departments. When debate arises we know no more than our audience, and are powerless to reply. It is unfortunate. The House of Lords stands well with the public as a whole, but the critics of the government are doing much to undermine the authority of the peers, by persistently belittling those peers who form the government. The tedious and reckless speeches of Beresford, Salisbury, Chaplin and Co. are also tending to impair the general view that our debates, though brief, are always businesslike.

The Lloyd George coalition

18 JULY 1918

At breakfast this morning Lloyd George told us that on the whole it would seem that the German attack with Rheims as the pivot, is not the main German offensive... Our G.H.Q. seems in good spirits and provided our men are not too widely dispersed feel that they should resist all attacks. Of course the mass of the German army hasn't yet been in action, and owing to their incomparable position at the axle of the wheel can divert their reserves to any point they choose.

1 AUGUST 1918

Lloyd George told us that the European telephone is ringing hard and often. There are strange 'are you there's' from Switzerland, suggestions from Holland, calls from Spain, and above all a fresh overture from Lord Lansdowne, who is looked upon as the leader of our pacifists. It is all to the good, this cry of distress, provided that we disregard it!

... Lloyd George is now pretty confident that with the good arrival of Americans, and their military capacity having been proven, our future is assured if only we desist from premature parleyings with the enemy.

3 AUGUST 1918

Lunched with Arthur Balfour, Linkie and Ian Malcolm. A.J.B. made us laugh, in describing his failing memory. What constantly happens is that some difficult foreign problem arises for settlement – his officials come in to discuss the matter, place the problem before him from every point of view, put their advice clearly in favour of some particular solution, and then leave him to prepare notes for a speech, or to write a minute. 'What I always forget is the decision come to: I can remember every argument, repeat all the pros and cons – can make quite a good speech on the subject – but the conclusion, the decision is a perfect blank in my mind.'

15 AUGUST 1918

Interview about American breadstuffs with Reading. He quite confirmed my fears that the USA is frankly out for plunder, Hoover aiding and abetting. We were fleeced last year, this year we shall be stripped naked, and Hoover all the time is chattering about altruism.

30 AUGUST 1918

Clynes will gradually drop back into complete obscurity. He will make speeches, and remain the mouthpiece of official announcements, and let us hope he will continue to have a strong and mollifying effect upon trade unions; but so far as policy or office control are concerned he will be negligible. He has not the mental capacity to grasp elementary problems, still less to offer any considered judgements: but he will perform a useful function if wise enough to recognise his own shortcomings.

392

1 SEPTEMBER 1918

Macready knows something of the police. He was in South Wales four or five years ago during a serious railway or colliery strike. He handled a delicate situation with adroitness and decision. The way he bamboozled the strike leaders was cunning and very successful. He is something of a diplomatist, and inherits a good deal of his histrionic ancestry – he looks an actor, or perhaps would disguise well as a bishop were it not for a certain *malizia* in his observant eyes. One night during the Welsh trouble, when the strikers were trying to intimidate him, he got a threatening message from – I forget the name Macready told me – to the effect that the strikers were arming – in fact were already armed. 'Thank goodness for that' he bawled down the telephone. 'What do you say?' enquired the baffled labour leader. 'Thank goodness, was what I said' repeated Neville Macready. The striker said he didn't understand – indeed there must be some misunderstanding. No – Macready was quite clear what he meant but he disliked talking down telephones – would Mr so-and-so care to step round to the general's lodgings and talk the matter over? So the man came, and brought several friends with him who took their toll of Macready's whisky. The interview was not short, but it was quite decisive. All Macready had to explain was that his troops had been and would be reluctant to fire upon unarmed men. Now the strikers were armed all such scruples would disappear on the part of officers and men alike – the industrial dispute had been going on for a long time, much too long and everybody concerned would be glad to have it settled one way or the other, and evidently the dispute had now reached a head – before long the trouble will be over and he would be able to get back to his proper work, and he was thoroughly tired of these civilian squabbles.

The men went on drinking whisky and smoking cigars – the general kept talking in a very offhand way, and treating the whole business as a tiresome bit of police work which the soldiers didn't care about, and were heartily desirous of ending. The men said that it would be difficult to disarm the men of the revolvers they had collected – 'that won't matter a bit', said Macready and got them out of the room as he was very sleepy and wanted to go to bed. The strike collapsed within a day or two.

7 SEPTEMBER 1918

I went to see Milner this morning at the War Office. Our conversation was brief and to the point. I have constantly talked to him, but never before in his office and by his writing-table. I was surprised at what I saw – a large piece of blotting paper, without blemish or trace of ink: beside it a tray containing two or three new pens, and two or three pencils – long, cut for the first time and still unused. The inkpot was shut, scarcely any notepaper visible. No documents or files or letters were on the table except a few papers neatly placed in an open despatch box. 'Do you ever write?' I asked him. 'Scarcely ever,' he replied, and we parted.

12 SEPTEMBER 1918

I lunched with George Cave at the Athenaeum, and he seems hopeful that the threatened recrudescence of the police strike may be averted. I found him smarting under the hostile criticism which had been lavished on the Home Office. Some weeks ago he got severely blamed for his alleged tenderness towards aliens. Then came the police strike which was generally ascribed to Home Office obstruction and heartlessness. Cave says this charge is quite unfounded. In point of fact at the moment when the strike broke out there was no demand before the authorities for increased pay. Cave wanted to make this fact public, but apparently Lloyd George prevented him. 'My treatment has been damnable,' said Cave, and never before have I heard him use so strong an expression – in fact for the first time in my life I saw him, the most mild and equable person in the world, glowing with indignation.

16 SEPTEMBER 1918

The Austrians now open a formal and official peace campaign. Are we ready with our reply? Two years ago I forecasted this démarche (how prematurely) but the cabinet paid no attention. Early last August I again approached George Curzon on the subject, but he said the cabinet was much too busy thinking about the fighting to devote any time to considering an armistice.

27 SEPTEMBER 1918

Hoover promises much, and in return for his engagements exacts crushing terms. I remember his saying that pork is just as good for us as beef – that we should live on pork – and he had so much pork and products thereof that all our needs could be met from his inexhaustible stocks. We agreed to take pork in masses, but we are not getting it. Pigs in America are so numerous as to be vermin, but pork is unobtainable in the moderate quantities we require. Why? Because Hoover scoffed at our advice tendered many months ago when we consented to his ambitious scheme, that he should promptly get possession of the pork. He knew better – yet we were right for the speculator has collared the pork and Hoover can't deliver a fraction of his commitment. It is exactly the same thing with butter. He has failed to give up the mountains of butter which he said we must take, and finds difficulty in delivering the moderate supplies we originally asked. It is the same thing everywhere. We can't get the wheat we want, and he is trying to force unwelcome things like rye flour on us. And all the time the public is being assured, and innocently believes, that America is suffering agonies to keep the Allies fed: moreover that America is the source of all supplies of men, energy, stores, and perhaps of genius too.

17 OCTOBER 1918

We resumed our breakfast parties with Lloyd George this morning, parliament having reassembled. He was in good spirits, never having predicted that since our last meeting such amazing progress would be recorded. He ascribes much of it to the unifying power of Marshal Foch, with whom Haig works admirably. Foch himself has repeatedly impressed on Lloyd George the admiration felt by the French staff for Haig's skill and loyalty, and not less for the automatic success with which Haig does everything asked of him.

Lloyd George however – the parent of the single command – does not forget that he has always been a consistent supporter of the sideshow – and he attributes great things to the belated though brilliant results of the Salonika campaign. The surrender of Bulgaria, involving the excision of Turkey and the final abandonment of the Berlin-Bagdad dream, has terrified Germany...

Somebody asked the prime minister about Italy. What is the condition of Italy? The P.M. drew himself back, and with admirable aplomb – for he is a great actor – exclaimed 'Vigilant ... self-restrained ...' and then went on to say that Italy is immovable: says that she had done her bit. She withdraws no demands, she makes no effort – and notwithstanding entreaties has allowed six weeks of precious fine weather to pass without striking a blow which might have knocked Austria out...

And the American forces? Lloyd George confirmed all the sinister rumours which are spreading over London. Their troops are splendid but they are hopelessly jammed. Transport breaks down. The men don't always get their rations: but Pershing insists on having an American army, refusing to let his men be brigaded with the French and ourselves.

22 OCTOBER 1918

Is it true that USA transport has broken down so hopelessly that on one occasion the troops have had to eat their horses?

23 OCTOBER 1918

Col. Amery says that America is quite ignorant of the tragic condition of her Argonne armies... Pershing is conscious of the terrible chaos in his staff, and actually took steps to prevent the recent deputation of American journalists from visiting the front lines.

24 OCTOBER 1918

At breakfast this morning, Lloyd George confirmed this. He said that one American journalist seems to have broken through the cordon, was profoundly distressed by what he saw, and talked a good deal about the sensational cable he was going to send home. An opportunity presented itself of seeing this telegram after it had passed through the hands of the American censor – and it had been transformed into a warm panegyric of Pershing and all his ways!

The odd thing is that Wilson himself is, or at any rate quite recently was, in sublime ignorance of the truth. Foch and Haig are in despair, especially the former who is in relation with much the bigger part of the American army. Why is no action taken? It is really a most singular thing, but Lloyd George who is much the most courageous man of my acquaintance, gave me the clear and unmistakable impression that he is afraid to tell the American authorities himself. He is a politician as he says: it is not his business to complain of allied generals. They would rightly resent his interference, especially as he can have no firsthand knowledge. This all seems to me weak, and so unlike the little man, but there it is. Col. House is to be in Paris in a day or two, and Milner has been dispatched to see Foch upon whom the duty of making the revelation is to be imposed . . . All that is wanted, is to secure French cooperation in the staff work. That is where the fatal weakness lies. Pershing with 2,000,000 men in France puts a much lower percentage of his men into the line than any other combatant . . . It is with the utmost difficulty that American troops can be moved at night. Recently there was the narrowest escape of a pitched battle between the Americans themselves, each of two large bodies of men having mistaken the other for the enemy. And the whole thing could be remedied by entrusting the staff work to competent Frenchmen: that alone is needed, for the troops themselves are magnificent.

It is a terrible story – and not only has Foch's great envelopment broken down in consequence – but immense casualties are being inflicted on the American troops – 80,000 in the last three weeks or so – and all because of the vanity of General Pershing and his entourage.

As regards the German army, Haig who has been over here . . . says that the Boche is not demoralised, far from it. Though patchy in places the German troops are fighting with great skill and determination, and have succeeded in evacuating all their essential stores.

As to the negotiations, Lloyd George could tell us nothing – he and Clemenceau are not asked their opinion as to the form of reply to Germany. The European allies in short are ignored, and momentous documents are issued from Washington by a potentate who is remote from the real controversy and who hasn't visited Europe for years. I don't imagine he is acquainted with any allied prime minister, general, or admiral.

6 NOVEMBER 1918
Lunched with Rudyard Kipling who is ruminating over two great subjects: one the American débâcle, the other Col. Lawrence who has fought upon Allenby's desert flank from Aden to Aleppo.

Kipling goes to sit quietly in No. 2 Buffet, Charing Cross Station, and listens to the soldiers talking[3] – quick oblique elliptical references to the war, to its facts and fictions, its tragedies and comedies – to all the amazing facts of prowess artlessly told by the actors. Here he has learned much during the last week or two about the American troops operating under Haig – such stories as would make the flesh of America creep with horror and indignation. But how can he use it? Can he tell it as fiction like the *Matter of Fact*, or as a legend, like *The Lost Legion*, or can he write a serious and epoch-making indictment of General Pershing? He says he means to take the last alternative – honest and straightforward – but the record will be unfit for publication.

And his other great theme is Lawrence . . . And how is R.K. to write *this* biography – as fiction or as fact? Here again the subject is too good for anything but

[3] Cf. below, 17 February 1925

an accurate and authoritative treatment, and so the thing must be written 'in prose' – and be placed aside for publication who knows when?

7 NOVEMBER 1918

The war is won! So Lloyd George told us this morning at our *déjeuner intime*. Thank God.

The prime minister too is enamoured of Col. Lawrence – but tremendously puzzled, though greatly impressed. He has been asking Lawrence's advice about Palestine. There is an idea that Allenby should be brought home to attack Bavaria and Saxony – Lawrence says no. Allenby's influence over the Arab and the Jew is so supreme that his removal would be a disaster. He has established a reputation which is partly based upon his name being identical with that of the prophesied Liberator of Jerusalem, partly also from his sturdy common sense and impartiality, and of course from his military successes, such that no conceivable successor could wield his influence, or do so much to rehabilitate the land which has been devastated by the Turk for so many centuries. Moreover during the difficult times ahead when French and Italian intrigues will make our position difficult, Allenby's assured and preeminent status will go far to remove these difficulties. Lawrence was asked by Lloyd George what the Arabs would really like as to the future government of their country. Their views were quite clearly defined. If annexation let it be by the British – if protectorate let it be by the French. They don't like what they have seen of the French – why then prefer them as protectors of Palestine? The answer goes to one's heart! Because the French would allow baksheesh and the honest earning of commissions!

. . . The most interesting thing the prime minister told us was the staunch and determined support he received from Clemenceau about Wilson's Fourteen Points. On two we made express reservations. It appears that Col. House showed no special enthusiasm to meet our views – principally about clause two which relates to Freedom of the Seas. Lloyd George said he could not assent to the proposition as laid down, and explained the conclusive reasons for our view. Slapping his breast Clemenceau exclaimed 'And I agree.' Again the phrase about trade control after the war – Lloyd George explained that our liberty must not be curtailed – and Clemenceau slapping his chest again, shouted out 'And I agree.' We thus extricate ourselves from a dilemma which might have led to disputes later on. I look forward with some apprehension to a very uncomfortable frame of mind between ourselves and the USA next year. We shall find ourselves at issue on a variety of points especially where the Americans are now laying plans to displace us commercially – and the more we can sift and eliminate these differences before the Peace Conference the better.

8 NOVEMBER 1918

I had an audience with the King – his voice rather more shrill, his gestures more syncopated than when I last saw him, two or three months ago, I dare say. He is clearly asking himself what the future has in store for the royal family: and on the whole he is fairly confident. 'Why should our people have a revolution? We are the victors, we are the Top Dog,'(this on a top note) and there is of course much to be said for his forecast.

... Conference at the Treasury about the position of our party vis-à-vis the Coalition. Bonar Law in the chair, A.J.B., Austen, Prothero, Bob Cecil, Walter Long, the two Geddes (I had no idea they called themselves Conservatives) and others.

Bonar Law made a long statement about the general situation and outlook. He concluded by reading a lengthy letter from Lloyd George, dealing with Home Rule, Tariff Reform, and the Church in Wales. The letter was clear and seemed to me satisfactory. Some obscurity caused somebody to ask for an explanation – what did such and such a phrase mean? Some said one thing, some another: then B.L. gave his interpretation which several of us thought a misreading. 'Well I can tell you a secret,' said B.L. with his unique naiveté, 'it means so-and-so, and I ought to know, as I drafted the letter myself.' You can imagine our surprise – Bonar Law framing an apologia which the prime minister adopts as the foundation of the plan to maintain our Coalition Government.

Neither the armistice, nor the landslide victory of Lloyd George's coalition in December 1918, nor his removal from one nominal post to another, much affected Crawford's preoccupations in 1919. His work at the Wheat Commission continued; as before, 'for myself, I can think of little but Bread'. It was really another year of wartime, with his administrative duties keeping Crawford far from general politics. Like other traditional Conservatives, including his friend Lord Newton, he deplored the prospect of a punitive peace in Europe. He also feared unrest at home. 'Labour, or rather those who now control it, don't want conciliation. They want Revolution. They are terrorists and Bolsheviks determined to have riot and if possible Revolution', he wrote in January 1919.

He also feared American designs on Britain. 'It is against us and us alone that a gigantic national conspiracy is being hatched to capture trade hitherto controlled by British commerce.' Crawford's pride and joy, his reserves of wheat 'accumulated by eighteen months of incessant frugality', had been intended by him for post-war emergencies such as the revictualling of a starving Europe. Instead, Clynes and the Ministry of Food let the reserve vanish, throwing this immense power into the hands of the Americans, and enabling President Wilson to pose as universal benefactor while Hoover sought 'above all to establish the USA in the markets of central Europe to the exclusion of the Allies in general and GB in particular'. As Hoover's opposite number, Crawford saw him as wishing to be 'director-general of the world's food supplies – the Foch of revictualling' so as 'to get control of us and our future. He means to use our indebtedness and our continued need of American money to force us into a position of servility.'

Crawford foresaw the myth of the German stab in the back, and blamed it on US military incompetence in 1918. 'Thanks to Pershing's incompetence Foch was unable to bring off a great and conclusive coup. This war did not end with a Sedan as it might and should have done. To that extent Germany can argue that her armies though pressed back were never broken still less annihilated...'

Lloyd George appointed Crawford to the Duchy of Lancaster in January 1919, characteristically without asking him whether he would be willing to serve, so that Bonar Law could take the Privy Seal. Crawford's initial reaction was that the duchy needed radical reform. *'If I felt sure of retaining this office for twelve months I would turn the whole place upside down and inside out – and sack all the officials I saw today.'* These latter he considered *'a group of senile and somnolent officials who know little or nothing of the duties of supervising landed estates'.* However, the rapid succession of chancellors meant that *'none of my last dozen predecessors ever seems to have given a thought to practical reforms'.*

28 DECEMBER 1918

Lloyd George came in with the first news of electoral successes. What pleased him most was the news that a Bolshevik called McLean who has been let out of prison to fight Barnes, has almost certainly been defeated, and has this morning retired to private life – not indeed back into prison, but to a lunatic asylum.

... The electoral process has been significant. Lloyd George's original campaign fell rather flat. He pulled himself together on realising that he was being left high and dry on the shore. He revised his programme, or rather enlarged it by adding items about indemnities, aliens, punishment of the Kaiser, and pledges to end conscription. Then he got on to the wave again and with an advancing tide has been borne to victory. But can these expectations, these pledges be fulfilled? and how long will the electorate allow him before venting its inevitable disappointment?

2 JANUARY 1919

I attended the complimentary dinner to Clynes who is retiring from the Ministry of Food. He was ready and I believe anxious to continue, but the pacifists forced the Labour minister to retire from the government. It is a pity. Clynes is intellectually quite incapable of running a big department, since he does not grasp big political problems: but he has been content to do what he is told, and his sober and quiet judgment have given him a well-earned reputation in Labour circles. This reputation has been based upon his practice of never speaking until pressed to do so. He has always kept silent as long as possible, and being a good listener his speech when delivered, summarised all the good points and dismissed the bad arguments. His manner is deliberate and cool: his temper is equable, and this judicious method has gained for him the reputation of a shrewd and profound thinker, which he isn't. This evening I had to pronounce a panegyric, and I did so with good will for I am fond of the little man: but I was conscious all through my remarks that there were lots of people in the audience who knew that Clynes had tried to smash my Commission, and had come an ignominious cropper in the process.

The Lloyd George coalition

16 FEBRUARY 1919

I hear a poor account of A.J.B.'s health – my informant is his niece. She says he plays too much tennis and too strenuously. Though a chicken of 71, she thinks he ought to begin to be thoughtful of his health: but his only source of vanity is his own buoyant youthfulness – and he is now beginning to feel the strain.

17 FEBRUARY 1919

Dined with George Curzon and his wife, 'Grace abounding' as Connie calls her. As time goes on her charms grow more opulent and her simper demands greater effort: but she is a good-hearted creature, admirably groomed and an excellent foil to George Curzon who wears the petticoat of the regime as well as the trousers. He orders the dinner, engages the servants, writes the invitations in his own hand, and even the cards put on the tables to show one where to sit. Never was there a man of such indefatigable energy. It is a pity, for he is distracted from much more important work by this insistence on domestic detail. But he does it well. His table is well-furnished and his staff well-drilled. I need not add that the quality of his victuals surpasses anything to be encountered elsewhere except of course in the smart set to which neither he nor I ever penetrate.

The more I see of George Curzon the more am I amazed at his versatility and his self-confidence. As a brain I put him as high as any living politician of my acquaintance – above Balfour, Ll.G., Asquith – but somehow he doesn't 'cut ice' as the Americans say. His influence is far smaller than his profound knowledge and experience would justify. It is partly a question of manner – somewhat professorial and challenging, partly also because of his assurance which seems to provoke opposition. Why it should do so I can't surmise for his decision and resource are quite palpable in whatever clothing they may be clad. Perhaps he presses his view too far, for as he is always convinced he is right, he seldom if ever is prepared to concede a point. Whoever differs from him must be wrong and must therefore be vigorously opposed. And he is quite merciless in pressing his views, and untiring as well. He told us this evening that when he first came to Carlton House Terrace he found that the chiming of Big Ben kept him awake at night – so he canvassed every resident in the terrace trying to persuade them to help him get the nuisance abated. He got no sympathy and by now he is accustomed to the striking but he still thinks he was right. How many are there who would have had the cheek and the perseverance to take up so hopeless a quest and to pursue it with such vigour?

18 FEBRUARY 1919

Fred Smith's somnolence on the Woolsack is much *commenté* among the elder and more strait-laced peers.

23 FEBRUARY 1919

Lord Lansdowne and I made a pilgrimage to Captain Beaumont's house near Ascot to see the big portrait group by Romney. We got there in fair time, lunched by the roadside on our return journey, walked a mile or two along Virginia Water, and

400

talked for forty minutes on Staines railway platform. Lord L. seems very well – still infected with the ideas of the Lansdowne letter, and still as Whiggish as ever. With him the ideal and duty of the Whig is to investigate everything, to leave nothing and nobody alone – and all day long he has been fussing about in his charming and courtly manner, but always giving the impression that somebody has got to be corrected or something put right. I suppose that frame of mind is typical of the old Whig who had a passion for governing – at any rate for pushing a finger into every pie.

9 APRIL 1919

The British mission in Paris does not show much enthusiasm towards the Prime Minister. They slave away, produce admirable dates, statistics, résumés, argumentations – but they well know that he won't read them ... I often wonder how we have got so wrong about indemnities. Hewins says Germany can pay our debts, and being a professor in status and pompousness, was taken at his word with lamentable results. Keynes too I fancy, the Cambridge economist, should have restrained the extravagance of ministerial promises. Keynes is the Treasury man in Paris – clearheaded, self-confident, with an unerring memory and unsurpassable digestion. But while he is one of the most influential of men behind the scenes, I cannot help thinking that he looks at large political problems too much from the aspect of currency and exchange; and that in large affairs his advice is often based upon premises which may be correct in technique but utterly misleading in practice. This is an impression which emanates from Keynes's schemes, though his word is all too often taken for gospel. He is a wonderful fellow, but has passed his life in a cloister and has had no experience in handling men or assessing their temperaments.

27 JUNE 1919

Board meeting [*of Wigan Coal and Iron Co.*]. Discussion about the nationalisation of mines. One's feeling is that bad as nationalisation would be for the country, expropriation on just terms would be a relief to the industry, for the conduct of business is made intolerable by the constant strife and bickering which prevails.

29 JULY 1919

Quite recently it appears that royal approval was given to the proposal to establish a University at Leicester, a town without industrial hinterland of its own and well within reach of well-established Universities. The Board of Education is anxious to check these new foundations which will be weaklings from their birth – and now the King solemnly blesses a really bad scheme. I told Fisher that he ought to protest. He said he would do so especially as he had just been paraded by the King for a stentorian scolding about a recent episode. It appears that the King was in a London Board School – pointed to a Union Jack, and asked an intelligent boy what it was – to which the disconcerting reply promptly came, 'The Red Flag'. The King impressed on Fisher that this appalling ignorance came from teaching the pianoforte or drawing etc. etc. One does sometimes wonder what the net results are of our half century of compulsory education. In France I was appalled by the abysmal ignorance of our men, many of whom bordered on illiteracy. Still our army fought well – even those regulars who in the early days of the war left the country chanting 'we're going to fight the Bloody Belgians.'

31 JULY 1919

The government has provoked the implacable enmity of Salisbury in the House of Lords. He attacks us on every possible occasion with the help of St John Brodrick and to a lesser extent Selborne. Nothing we do is ever right, and he scolds us as though we were naughty children. Curzon once told him so publicly and quieted him down for a bit. The time has come for another protest. I doubt not that the government commits many sins, but it is unwise for those who should prima facie give it support to make the public believe ministers are dishonest as well as incompetent. This merely plays into the hands of extremists who certainly will not put Jim Salisbury in our place. Neither do I like being attacked by those who have done nothing but criticise throughout the war. Salisbury's contribution to war work was a brief and inglorious interlude with his county unit. Since then he has done odd jobs, and none with much success. In December 1916 he was asked to join the government – refused to take his share of duty and responsibility and I look upon him now as out of court. It is not by such that I care to be censured.

6 AUGUST 1919

With Austen Chamberlain at the Treasury. Speaks with some bitterness about the American attitude, their boastfulness and the pound of flesh theory on which they act – not indeed to us alone but impartially towards all the Allies. Their temperament precludes them from parting with their money ... I fancy Austen Chamberlain thinks that the plight of Europe will become such as to force intervention by the USA.

8 AUGUST 1919

Walked to the House with Bob Cecil who is furious about the Welsh Church Bill ... So Bob is vexed with us, but still more with the Bishops – the Welsh ones – who he says are bigger liars than the least truthful of our allies.

14 AUGUST 1919

Words with Jim Salisbury in the H. of L. I must say he is a most vexing person, always scolding us in shrill – not to say piercing – tones, shouting at us as if we were naughty schoolboys and he a testy pedagogue. I don't mind criticism in the least, but I rather resent this kind of thing from one who at a moment of stress was asked to give the government the benefit of his advice – but refused to take his share of responsibility. The House of Lords is a pretty dull place just now. Everybody attacks the government, often most unfairly, and with lamentably defective knowledge of the facts. Personally I get out of patience with these professional critics, few of whom have put in a ten hours day of serious work since the war began. Lytton on the other hand and Willie Peel, both of whom have done quite admirably, remain placid under the most malevolent attack, never showing a sign of impatience or annoyance. I envy their calm and philosophic tempers.

6 SEPTEMBER 1919

[*Over dinner Hoover*] talked about his experiences in Poland and Austria – revealed himself as a most uncompromising anti-semite! I was much surprised. He is a cosmopolitan person, Liberal in his politics, American in Race – the last person from whom one would have expected such a strong feeling – yet there it is, unmistakable and indeed quite unconcealed. 'If the Jews in USA had committed half the economic outrages which I have seen in Poland, there would be a pogrom in every single town inhabited by a Jew from the Pacific Coast to the Atlantic.' All this is forced upon him by what he has seen. He came across a small squire in Tarnopol who proved that he had surrendered 1,000 acres of his property in return for sufficient food to keep him and his family alive for twelve months – and the Jews alone could sell the food and take his title deeds. Hoover says that certainly ninety-five and probably ninety-eight per cent of most of the governing groups of assassins are Jews. Hoover was the means of getting that horrible picture of Bela Kun circulated a few weeks ago. We were amazed at this photograph of this cut-throat, so unbelievably vile and ghoulish in appearance. Hoover got hold of the portrait and gave it to every picture paper in the world – 'I wish I had possessed it six months earlier.'

He talked and talked, with much more humour and animation than I have observed before. He is glad to be escaping from Europe, which has worn him out and depressed him too – and the prospect of release gladdens his heart. I should end by being devoted to Hoover – I who started with such prejudice – yet I become more conciliatory every time I see this fascinating man, whose appearance, voice, manner, and countenance are all devoid of charm: but a most remarkable and alluring fellow all the same. I wonder upon what allegations he used to be so suspected by our F.O. Espionage chanced into our talk, and he turned to Harmsworth and said rather merrily, 'I wonder why the Foreign Office always chooses the wrong men to shadow. There are several men I know whom I should like to see secretly buried – but you only try to catch the innocent ones.'

LORD CRAWFORD TO LLOYD GEORGE, 27 OCTOBER 1919[4]

But, but – may I know what goes on? I now only receive one government paper namely Churchill's weekly report on army matters. Otherwise I only know what I pick up from the press or what private secretaries tell me! I am therefore unable to

[4] In reply to Lloyd George's letter of 25 October, announcing the end of the war cabinet system, and regretting that on grounds of number he could not include Crawford in the new cabinet.

influence opinion or to argue the government case, and I have practically had to give up public speaking ...

29 OCTOBER 1919

Bonar Law told me that though he had received much preferment in his time the only appointment which ever gave him real pleasure, real lasting pleasure, was when he was made book-keeper in William Kitson and Co. of Glasgow! All his subsequent posts and honours gave him little or no satisfaction.

3 DECEMBER 1919

At Grillions I sat by the Archbishop of Canterbury who told me about his financial straits. Notwithstanding his official income of £10,000 a year, his accounts showed a deficit of £3,000 last year. This is guaranteed by a private and anonymous person who has undertaken to meet the deficit for three years. All the Archbishop's private income goes towards the maintenance of his see.

10 DECEMBER 1919

How unpopular we[5] are. All our successes are ignored – suppressed by the newspapers – every failure, for many of which the critics were themselves originally responsible, is magnified into a stunt. Never has a government been faced by so well mobilised a press of critics. There is scarcely a newspaper which attempts to give its readers the government case, and as our papers are gradually falling into a few hands – the Northcliffe trust, for instance – the concentration of attack is very formidable. Northcliffe conducts a daily vendetta against Lloyd George. North-cliffe is vindictive, very conscious of the damaging nature of the attack made on him by the prime minister, and smarting also under the consciousness of his failure in the two little jobs given him of public work – he is determined to be avenged. I think he is overdoing it. The *Times* for instance seems to exist to boost Yugoslavia and to burst Lloyd George. Its loyalty to these ideals becomes fatiguing, and I fancy that its influence is decidedly on the wane, though commercially speaking it is magnificent property.

22 DECEMBER 1919

Keynes' book on the economic results of the peace treaty will attract attention. I don't like it – I mean I find it distasteful that a man (apparently of military age) should enjoy a safe and cushy job and then write a book criticising his official superiors and his government's policy ... Lord Reading was deploring it this evening. He told me that Keynes had accomplished a result which it would be almost impossible to achieve – he had given to both Republicans and Democrats of the United States a powerful weapon against Britain. The Republicans will bitterly resent Keynes's outspoken attack on President Wilson, whose obstinacy and

[5] The coalition

ignorance he describes with gusto (comparing Wilson's temperament to that of a bigoted Presbyterian minister). The Democrats on the other hand are told that Lloyd George outmanoeuvred Wilson at every turn, and they will argue from Keynes's lips that we helped to persuade the Americans to join the war – that we professed adherence to their high ideals, but that when it came to drafting a peace treaty, we cajoled and intrigued Wilson into making a hopeless exhibition of himself.

So Keynes has sharpened a double-edged sword which will be wielded against us. His book will provide capital election literature for the warring factions in America. How is it that these clever men, and Keynes is among the cleverest I know, are often so tactless – say such unwise things?

23 DECEMBER 1919

Lunched with Walter Long. Talked about the secret police in Ireland. Walter says that when he left the Chief Secretary's Lodge at the end of our last government, King Edward begged him to see Bryce, then nominated to the chief secretaryship, and to implore Bryce not to destroy the admirable organisation built up by the secret service. Bryce however had his own ideas and let this wonderful service be disbanded, with deplorable results; for when Birrell came on the scene, or rather when he tried to govern Ireland from Cromer, the whole machine became rusty – crime went undetected and now when we are faced with a really grave situation we are unable to grapple with the malefactors.

5 JANUARY 1920

I went to Christie's hoping to buy a hearthrug . . . One Englishman I saw, excluding the auctioneer, namely Keynes. I told him he was wrong in stating in his book that Orlando can't understand English. In point of fact I quite satisfied myself on the point a few months ago when I dined with him at the Travellers Club. He understands English very well though he speaks it hopelessly – his French likewise is pretty poor. Keynes was surprised – and to surprise so dogmatic a prig is quite an achievement. 'But why should Orlando have pretended he didn't understand English?' 'Why,' I replied, 'does Cambon pretend he doesn't understand English?' The unsophisticated Keynes dimly perceived that these astute Latins were playing with him, and that he had been deceived by a very palpable device. 'I must put that right in the new edition of my book.' 'Yes,' I murmured, 'but it would have been still better not to have had to make corrections on this – and other points.'

15 JANUARY 1920

With Roberts the Food Controller. I look on him as a fortunate man as his ministry is to come to an end in August or thereabouts: but I don't think he is an enthusiast for decontrol. He is happy as a minister. He enjoys the influence and the affluence. He loves public speaking and ministerial rank provides many opportunities. He also likes being entertained and most thoroughly enjoys his periodical trips to the Continent.

The Lloyd George coalition

10 MARCH 1920
Lunched with Lady Charles Beresford, to discuss a biography of the gallant Admiral. She showed me the index of his correspondence – breezy and volatile like himself – but so outspoken and so uncompromising as to make publication impossible for many years to come. She seemed to think that elegant extracts could be printed – but I tried to persuade her that a much more modest biography is all that can be expected just now. . . . Lady Charles told us that during her recent visit to Paris she discovered that she is descended on the wrong side of the blanket from the French Royal House. The Princess whom she had always understood to be her godmother was in fact her mother – all this screeched out at the top of her piercing voice with a butler and two footmen in the dining room.

11 MARCH 1920
The King begins to feel pinched, for he has to maintain great state upon a much reduced income. I told him that his net receipts from the Duchy of Lancaster have fallen by forty per cent since 1914 – this reduction being wholly attributable to new taxation. For the ceremony of opening parliament fifty-two horses are required ('and I could do it much easier in two motor cars') and there is one state function which requires eighty horses . . . He told me that quite apart from wages, board, and lodging, the livery of each uniformed servant average £100 a year! This is really an intolerable strain on his purse, and he is fully entitled to economise in a drastic manner.

15 MARCH 1920
Fusion is the order of the day. We are to fuse Lloyd George or Ll. G. is to fuse us – I am not sure which and my mind is confused between the two schemes. Everybody talks of it, nobody understands it and the *bon mot* in the lobbies is that the prime minister has resigned and Lord Northcliffe has sent for – the King.

19 MARCH 1920
Fusion seems off, and a closer cooperation between the two wings of the coalition now seems our ideal.

19 JUNE 1920
Muir Mackenzie and I, as vice-presidents of the Civil Service Athletic Club, received the Duke of York[6] who attended to distribute the prizes. I thought the whole thing very fatiguing. The Duke thought so too but showed admirable endurance and was delightful to everybody and got an excellent reception when making a little speech at the end of the proceedings. He is an amusing youth – more so I think than his brother, though much less of a personality. He has a really bad stammer but by dint of careful training he has almost mastered this infirmity – and

[6] George VI

406

apart from halting pauses between his words, he gets along much better than the average of his contemporaries.

26 AUGUST 1920

Interview with Sir William Lewis – an interesting man, now head of Furness Withy and Co. I think he began life as shorthand clerk to the late Lord Furness – on whose death it was discovered that the wisdom of the firm had for years past rested with the stenographer. So like sensible people the shareholders promptly put him into the place of the deceased magnate.

17 OCTOBER 1920

Spent much of the day at the Wheat Commission nominally preparing for the coal strike which is now upon us. For the moment we can do little ... There is a strong and well-organised Bolshevik element which is doing its utmost to promote a ferocious revolution – accompanied by as much bloodshed as is necessary to eliminate what are called the capitalist classes. These violent people realise that their opportunity has come, and I fancy we now have got to have a real uncompromising fight against the forces of disorder.

2 NOVEMBER 1920

Two hours cabinet committee about home rule – most of the discussion turning on whether second chambers should be set up in Ireland. Walter Long seems to consider it a question of expediency not a principle – at least that is the tenor of a letter written to us following a specific pledge in the H. of C. to devise a second chamber for each parliament. I tried to explain that it would be difficult to persuade the H. of L. to agree that second chambers are needless – especially in Ireland, and not least in Ulster which once attributed its salvation to the H. of L. I got very little support from the Conservatives present though Kellaway (Radical of Radicals) stood up for me manfully as did Greenwood in a lesser degree.

3 NOVEMBER 1920

The question had to go to a cabinet meeting. Lloyd George came in in excellent spirits, cheered by the end of the coal strike. 'I congratulate you about your whisky', he cheerfully remarked to Bonar Law. B.L. didn't understand, so Ll. G. repeated his remark, but B.L. looked as if he thought the P.M. had gone mad. 'Can't you understand,' said Lloyd George, 'Glasgow has just voted in favour of whisky. Pussyfoot is defeated, in all but two or three wards, and I have a very poor opinion if the inhabitants of those wards can't manage to find a drink elsewhere. National honour and the national beverage are saved, and I would never have spoken to you again if Glasgow had voted dry.'

B.L. smiled grimly and we proceeded to discuss the Irish second chambers. Tonight again very little support came from A.J.B., B.L. or my own political friends. Lloyd George on the other hand seems to favour second chambers, especially in Ulster and Kellaway also took a sensible view. I don't think the peers will relish a single chamber government for the savages of Ireland.

10 NOVEMBER 1920

A big gathering at Grillions. Edward Grey was voted to the chair after an absence of five years . . . I am bound to say Grey looks very well, his hair still unrelieved by grey except at the temples, and he is plump and youthful in appearance. But when he came to study the menu one realised how defective his eyesight is – the left glass of his spectacles completely obscured by a black patch of silk – the right eye so weak that the paper has to be put a couple of inches away . . . He seemed in good spirits and though never a good talker his conversation was vigorous and direct.

St John Brodrick is just back from France . . . In execrable French he told us Foch's remark about Pershing after some deplorable fiasco of the American Army. 'If Pershing had been a French General,' said Foch, 'I would have dismissed him. Had he been English, I would have asked Haig to transfer him to England: but as Pershing was an American I offered him the Legion of Honour.'

19 NOVEMBER 1920

My Commission is being vigorously attacked by Beaverbrook . . . He bears an old grudge against me as I thwarted his desire in 1916 to go to Canada and buy up the wheat crop . . . But he wasn't a man of sufficient character to be entrusted with such an enterprise, and he has long awaited an opportunity to riposte.

7 DECEMBER 1920

Fred Smith, Sandhurst and I dined with Donoughmore, an old Oxford friend and contemporary. Excellent victuals and wine so well chosen as to excite enthusiasm from the fastidious Lord Chamberlain, and likewise from the hospitable Lord Chancellor. We discussed our wine merchants, and F.E. to our surprise said he still dealt with the Oxford Wine Company, an obscure firm with whom he had relations in our undergraduate days. At Oxford F.E. lived upon his scholarships and credit, spending in all about £450 a year, with the result that on being announced a first class prizeman, he found himself leaving Oxford owing about £700. He called his creditors together (in itself an act of bankruptcy), made them an eloquent speech in which he recalled his brilliant career (scholastic, as President of the Union, athletics of some distinction), told them that he was certain to get a fellowship, would do well at the Bar, and in the meantime would offer them five per cent on their money (not a bad return in those days). He placed himself in their hands : his career and reputation in fact were at their mercy, and in point of fact he felt sure they would not live to regret making his situation as easy as possible . . .

Whereupon up rose the manager of the Oxford Wine Co. (to whom F.E. owed £150), made a strong speech in favour of the proposal, and finally moved a resolution to that effect which was accepted by the tradesmen – and F.E. has bought his wine from them ever since.

... What a strange person he is – I suppose I know him better than most. His brain power is astonishing – his grasp of a subject is not only powerful, but it is instantaneous in its operation – and yet to certain branches of life his mind is blank – in certain forms of litigation such as those involving science or mechanics, he has always felt hopelessly inadequate. He can't understand machinery – he can never learn to drive a motor car – he cannot even keep his watch regulated. How I sympathise with him.

How extravagant too! He says he has never yet been in an omnibus, on a tram, or even in an underground railway. He must always have a cab in old days, in these times a taxi!

30 JANUARY 1921

A good deal of journalistic hints and mutterings about a crisis in the coalition ranks . . . We shall see. Meanwhile Eddy Stanley is alleged to be a prime mover in the intrigue against Lloyd George. He made a speech a few nights ago in Lancashire which woefully belied expectations. We were told that he was going to 'come out' to make a statement which would rally the malcontents to his standard and that we might soon expect to see him as prime minister, with Churchill as leader of the H. of C., Bonar Law in retirement, and Lloyd George who knows where? In point of fact we had a typical cautious Derby speech: without a glimmer of policy or inspiration. He said he had declined the War Office for private reasons, as he had his own affairs to think about and that he could not take office for some time to come. A few compliments to the prime minister, a few trite and commonplace remarks about economy and that was all.

He is represented as the bluff and honest nobleman with no axe to grind, with an assured position and with an inbred disgust of political logrolling and machinations. In point of fact, good fellow as he is, Derby is a born intriguer. That was patent at the election of 1906 and again in March 1918. But he is as shrewd as possible and far too wise to try a fall with Lloyd George who is still the one great and commanding figure in the country, and who would roll over Eddy as easily as he would crush a fly . . . .

I shall then hope to devote some little time to my own pleasures, and if still in the government to reforming the Duchy of Lancaster administration. It is a hardship on the King that the Chancellor has always to devote so much attention to other matters, to the manifest disadvantage of his Duchy estate, while the constant change of ministers makes continuity of reform almost impossible.

9 MARCH 1921

Attended the Council at Buckingham Palace to prick the sheriffs – had two audiences of the King. During the first he talked with great emphasis about reforming the House of Lords, feeling that we ought to devote an autumn session to the subject, and fearing that our desire for a long recess will cause the problem to be deferred. If we don't reconstitute the H. of L. in 1921, the task may be transferred to a Labour government who would solve the problem by abolition.

The Lloyd George coalition

Bonar Law resigned this afternoon. The prime minister with deep emotion communicated a letter in which B.L. said that he was worn out and that his doctor ordered immediate rest. It appears that last week in the middle of a speech at Glasgow B.L.'s memory broke – there was a painful pause of two minutes, and this warning alarmed the doctors. He resigns his position in the government, his leadership of the H. of C., and is to go abroad the moment he is fit to travel.

It is a great blow to us. His departure weakens the Coalition as a parliamentary force. His debating power, his conciliatory attitude, his candour and disinterestedness, all combined to make him an invaluable asset at any time, most particularly during these years of danger. Moreover he exercised great influence on the prime minister, and was a useful link between the two wings of the Coalition.

19 MARCH 1921

The cool critical standoffish attitude of the Unionist press towards B.L. strikes me as very small and mean. Here is a man of tremendous intellect – witty and convincing as a speaker, calm in times of stress, courageous, self-sacrificing, honest, whose devotion to duty has brought him to death's door. One would have expected warm and heartfelt acknowledgement for such services to the state – gratitude as well. Not a bit of it. The thin-lipped scribes of Fleet Street . . . treat Bonar Law as a good fellow who has done his best, but that his limitations – his acknowledged shortcomings – his lack of inherent statesmanship – and so forth. It is all very ignoble . . .

31 MARCH 1921

Received a letter from the P.M. asking to take the Office of Works *vice* Mond. As I fear this will involve giving up the Wheat Commission, I decided to say no.

LORD CRAWFORD TO LLOYD GEORGE, 1 APRIL 1921

It would involve my resignation from the Wheat Commission. The mills enter upon decontrol today. We have next to decontrol the corn trade, to handle the very delicate question of home-grown wheat, to liquidate our stocks, to adjust finance (our turnover has been £1,000,000 a day) and into the bargain we are this morning being transferred to the board of trade, who know us not.

Pray remember that my Executive colleagues are all volunteers. I have no departmental machine, only 2% of my staff being civil servants. I must stay with them to maintain their morale and courage during a tedious period.

1 APRIL 1921

Conversation with Ned Talbot, on behalf of the P.M. who is disturbed by my letter as it upsets consequential appointments. So I am very strongly pressed to accept. Ned got into communication with Lionel Earle who reassured him as to the call upon my time at the Office of Works, and said that he could get along all right during the next few months with a very modest attendance on my part.[7] On these terms I consented to take over that Department although I regret my severance from the Duchy of Lancaster. If all had been well I should this autumn have cleansed that Augean stable.[8]

22 APRIL 1921

The Office of Works is much concerned with the Civil List troubles, as we have to look after the Royal Palaces ... When King Edward succeeded, he found the whole Household honeycombed with jobbery and corruption. The old Queen resented criticism of Brown and of his successor, the Munshi. When once something was ordered it was never again counter-ordered. On one occasion thirty years before her death she was driving along a country lane and came across a carter who had had an accident and seemed in a fainting fit. The Queen called for brandy. None was to be had. She said that when driving one should always be ready for an emergency, so until the day of her death one bottle of brandy was charged every time she took a drive and it was not consumed by the swooning carter.

In the same way when Princess Beatrice was young, anyhow before her marriage, the doctor ordered her very strong chicken broth during a convalescence. Till the dying day of the Queen two chickens were charged every day for the said service – say 21,000 chickens in all – which likewise were not consumed by the invalid. The late King was furious when he discovered how the money had been poured away. The Windsor tradesmen behaved like vultures (twelve and six pence for instance was the invariable price of a quail). He took strong action both by dismissing superfluous parasites and by changing his tradesmen, and he made himself pretty unpopular especially at Windsor. But during his short reign abuses again crept in, and now when money is so stringent all these matters must be re-opened.

26 MAY 1921

Presided over Austen Chamberlain's meeting at the Conservative Club, who entertained the 1900 Club for the evening. He made them laugh by telling a story against me. He was talking of coalitions. Years ago when I was chief whip we were dining together and Austen said that the time would come when we would want help from those who were radical leaders of that day, 1912 or 1913. Austen hazarded the view that he would choose Churchill or Lloyd George. 'Shut up, Austen,' I said, 'or at any rate don't talk so loud. I never heard so indecent a remark in all my life.'[9]

Well, Austen's view has proved correct; and though I don't lay much store by Churchill's co-operation, Lloyd George has been a pillar of strength to the country.

[7] Modest indeed: Talbot was told by the permanent Under-Secretary that if the minister 'could attend most days about 12.30 to give necessary instructions and be there occasionally for an afternoon, he thought all would be right for the next few months'.
[8] Crawford had intended to make a comprehensive tour of the duchy estates.
[9] Cf. above, 3 May 1914

The Lloyd George coalition

It is little short of marvellous what an influence he exercises on Europe. During the last fortnight he has extricated us from two terrific dangers – Ruhr and Silesia – and although the little man is surrounded by sycophants who discount all his great personality, yet he remains our really big asset.

16 JUNE 1921

I had a long talk with Conway Davies, the Secretary of the Government Hospitality Fund of which I have to take charge . . . Looking through the accounts I notice what different scales of luxury prevail among our foreign guests. Briand and his colleagues habitually drink lager beer, and mineral water – it is quite the exception that they should order wine . . . Hughes[10] is the worst offender, or rather his wife and secretary. He refuses to stay in a hotel which makes it difficult to check accounts. Last year his secretary charged the Hospitality Fund with five bottles of whisky a day. Mrs Hughes sent us in the bills for the medicine for her children, and for framing pictures. That was pretty cool, but into the bargain she carried off a quantity of domestic linen with which we had furnished the bedrooms! Happily this degree of abuse is rare, but it shows how careful we ought to be.

7 JULY 1921

Talked to James Craig about buildings for the N. Ireland parliament. He doesn't seem hopeful about the De Valera negotiations. 'We haven't punished them quite enough yet.'

17 OCTOBER 1921

Henry Wilson told me that the idea of burying the unknown warrior in Westminster Abbey originated with the Dean, and was first communicated to him – to Wilson – who received the idea with enthusiasm. The cabinet however was very sceptical and after a long harangue by George Curzon rather hostile, the scheme being pronounced unEnglish – Lloyd George however, a very unEnglish person himself, liked the proposal which was ultimately accepted here, and is being copied all over the world.

20 OCTOBER 1921

I had the terminal meeting of the Wheat Commission. Our report is already signed . . . A fresh commission, small in numbers, restricted in powers, and official in character, will be appointed to liquidate our finance. I shall continue as chairman, and anticipate a relatively easy task.

This afternoon's meeting marks the end of a long and serious responsibility. As I look through our report I see condensed into two or three lines statements of bald fact which represented weeks and perhaps months of unremitting work, the embodiment of decisions of first class importance. Nobody unconnected with the Commission will ever quite realise the scale of its operations, for having been

[10] Australian premier

412

successful we were seldom talked about. We never courted publicity. I remember a serious moment long after our establishment, when I found that several of my colleagues in the government did not know of the existence of the Commission as an executive agency. But I don't suppose any group of men gave such a wholehearted devotion to duty as my colleagues. They were a good team, and I never allowed them to lose their tempers – at any rate to persist in such a folly. I will do myself the justice of saying that they would have found it difficult to continue upon an amicable basis without my mollifications. That is why I so seldom left London during the period of our hard work – and whenever a shindy did take place it began during a momentary absence of mine. But I repeat that I had a fine body of men to work with.

26 OCTOBER 1921

Lunched tête à tête with George Curzon... We talked home politics, notably in relation to Eddie Derby. George Curzon says that Derby's letters from Paris were quite admirable, that he received better information from him than from any other ambassador of his acquaintance. This he attributes to Eddie's passion for gossip, to a much more effective knowledge of French than people believe – judging from his bad conversation, partly from a faculty of jumping to the right conclusion in spite of sparse materials. Anyhow whatever the explanation his information was excellent. And now he is at home wondering what to do – hostile in many ways to the coalition, probably quite prepared to join any alternative combination, but afraid to take the plunge, as he is thoroughly frightened of F. E. Smith whose influence in Liverpool is still very strong. One eye is therefore kept on the Lord Chancellor, while George Curzon doubtless keeps his own eye on both.

3 NOVEMBER 1921

At the Palace this morning I was invested with the Thistle, and the King was extremely gracious about it. I kept off topics of controversy and he told me some very singular things about the exhumation of King Charles I a few years ago at Windsor. It appears that somebody gave King Edward a tiny scrap of bone alleged to have been the tip of King Charles' chin, the story being that the first blow of the executioner's axe failed to sever the neck. The story seemed well authenticated, and an opportunity presented itself of opening the tomb which was accordingly done with the Queen's permission. Sure enough it transpired that there was a fracture across the lower part of the chin – the fragment apparently fitted on, and was actually replaced in the coffin. The corpse was still in a curiously perfect state of preservation. I told the King the story was new to me and I could not recall any publication on the subject. He said that competent witnesses were present and a careful account was drawn up at the time – but it was not considered a topic about which public discussion should be encouraged.

5 NOVEMBER 1921

Lunched with Horace Farquhar. Sat next to Lady Edmund Talbot, Lady

The Lloyd George coalition

FitzAlan[11] as now is. She seemed a little gloomy about the prospect of peace. I was astonished to hear how freely they entertain – an average day they receive thirty-five guests to meals – not counting tea, or those staying in the house with them. How their modest purse can continue at such a scale astonishes me.

11 DECEMBER 1921

... Anyhow if the predominant middle class in Ireland asserts itself there will be no bureaucracy and much parsimony. We may all live to see Cork the most reactionary corner in the Empire.

... The papers are already talking about personnel of a new government ... It is suggested that George Curzon will go – or rather be omitted for he would never resign. His harshness and bad manners, which prevent any feeling of cordiality or desire to meet him halfway, are said to be the source of many of our troubles. The French don't want to conciliate him, Persia, Egypt, Greece, here there and everywhere our diplomacy seems to have been dejected and much is ascribed to the personal failings of the Secretary of State. It is of course true that he becomes more rigid and less human every day, more unpopular in consequence. He is loathed in his department for he is merciless and can never bring himself to say thank you. The other day he was asking why A.J.B. is thought such a success – a man of 'very moderate genius' – the reason is not far to seek. Popularity is the reward of the heart more than of the intellect, and George is greatly endowed with the one, sadly deficient in the other: what a pity. Even a tiny modicum of heart would have made him into a great man and perhaps a noble character.

15 DECEMBER 1921

There is always a certain amount of unseen sparring between the two, and George Curzon is undoubtedly somewhat jealous of the position F.E. has gained in the House of Lords. The peers like the Lord Chancellor's speeches which combine learning with banter, while they dislike George's which are too didactic or expository. Nobody knows this better than F.E. . . . . .

17 DECEMBER 1921

James Craig[12] came to see me this morning to settle the plans for the House of Parliament at Belfast which has to be built by the Office of Works ... I only had a few minutes of private talk with Craig, who told me in no obscure terms that he was greatly embarrassed by Carson's speech. Craig has to govern Ulster – Carson on the other hand lives in the seclusion of Belgravia and carries no responsibility, yet by his violence has set the tone for the extreme Ulstermen, and they are numerous. Londonderry's speech showed that like James Craig, he too wants peace – for he also is faced by the practical problems. Carson's speech[13] therefore was not a mere

[11] Lord FitzAlan was the last Lord-Lieutenant of Ireland.
[12] The first Northern Ireland premier.
[13] Carson had just violently attacked the Irish settlement in a Lords debate.

act of vulgarity and personal malice, but it was a wicked unpardonable breach of loyalty towards his old colleagues from Northern Ireland. He has made their task ten times more difficult. Craig is upset about the proposed boundary commission. But for that he says he would have been quite ready to sign the Treaty.

24 DECEMBER 1921

Xmas tree at Balcarres to 200 schoolchildren, a great success. The Largo Ward group, sixty strong was carried to and from home in three of the Balniel carts.

10 JANUARY 1922

Sites Committee of the Office of Works – the body which advises the First Commissioner about placing statues and monuments in London. Not a very helpful body. Blomfield is the unofficial architect, Frampton the unofficial sculptor. The former is a great scholar, but in my opinion a poor artist. Frampton made the Cavell memorial. I come away from these meetings with the impression that my function has been to keep Blomfield straight rather than vice versa. However such conferences have an educational value for the Office of Works itself. To discuss purely artistic and aesthetic problems, allied with questions of town planning on a modest scale is in itself an excellent thing for us, and I flatter myself that during the last eight or ten months I have directed the minds of my officials into this channel. It is essential that they should think constructively about these things, and by constant discussion on all sorts of artistic subjects, about many of which we have no direct responsibility, I found that they are beginning to take a much wider outlook on their duties. They respond readily to the tonic I administer – the disposition of galleries and museums, the treatment of historic buildings, the amenity of great showplaces like Holyrood and Hampton Court, all these things concern us, all are in one sense or another allied, and gradually my officials are imbibing a sense of concern which certainly did not exist when I took over the department last spring. I wish I could foresee another year or two of my medicinal inoculations. I have still to consolidate the entente I have established between the department and unofficial artists, notably the R.I.B.A., and much personal propaganda in the office itself is still required before I can say that our relations with the art world as a whole are based on satisfactory and durable foundations.

But so far as I can see my tenure of office will not long continue. A furious controversy has been seething in our party about a dissolution. George Younger made a violent speech and wrote a hot letter protesting against the idea of an early dissolution which was generally attributed to Lloyd George. I should think it very probable that the P.M. would like to dissolve. He is not one of those politicians likely to follow Balfour's policy of delay in 1905 ... But George Younger speaking for the whole party organisation is hostile as he insists upon second chamber reform preceding the election. Whatever is settled now must weaken the party and hasten the moment when an election must come – perhaps when the Coalition must split.

The Lloyd George coalition

So I shall work my office all the harder during the next few days, weeks, or months. I don't think they will forget all their lessons.[14]

11 JANUARY 1922

I went to see Gainsborough's Blue Boy at the National Gallery. Together with Mrs Siddons he was recently bought from the Duke of Westminster for a fabulous sum, rumour saying that a syndicate of picture dealers put up the money. £120,000 is said to have been paid for each picture, the object being to give publicity, actual or surmised, to the abiding value of fine paintings, and thus to check the disastrous depreciation of values of the stock held by dealers, who have suffered much by the commercial slump.

17 JANUARY 1922

I attended the Geddes Committee, the formidable famous Geddes Committee which is to show us how to save countless millions of public money. My department has already shown a saving of thirty-three per cent on our votes for 1922–23 compared with 1921–22. I doubt if any other big department has done likewise. We had a long discussion. I saw how easy it would have been for us to obstruct for they are woefully ignorant of the matters at issue. Geddes himself very much on the spot, and conducted our conversation with good humour and good sense; but his colleagues! Inchcape stone deaf, Joseph Maclay piping at us quite inaudibly and also rather deaf, Guy Grant[15] very late in arriving and looking very ill; Henderson, now Lord———, being——— years of age felt justified in abandoning himself to occasional somnolence. There was one live man there in the person of Sir George Beharel whom I believe to have been a railway magnate. Railways in fact supply the majority of the Committee, shipping the balance.

21 JANUARY 1922

We are having a very animated crisis of our own about Egypt. George Curzon has actually talked about his resignation. Hitherto nobody has ever believed that anything whatever would ever induce him to resign; but he may well believe now that with our general situation so much complicated by problems of economy, second chamber, and dissolutions, he would do well to evacuate the sinking ship, and escape before it is overwhelmed. Exit now would facilitate a re-entry later on.

23 JANUARY 1922

A further conference with James Craig about Irish buildings... I asked him if I might assume reconciliation to be so close as to justify me in dropping the

---

[14] Sir Lionel Earle, permanent secretary at the Office of Works from 1912 to 1931, described Crawford as the best First Commissioner he ever served. One of his achievements was to appoint a strong committee of experts on London bird life, for which he established sanctuaries in the main London parks.

[15] Illegible

Parliament House at Belfast. No: he was quite clear and decided; even if the South behaves well, fifteen or twenty years must elapse before old animosities can be extinguished and be replaced by a feeling of complete confidence. Moreover he says that the South must have ocular demonstration that Ulster is ready and capable to maintain her own government, and can exist independently of Dublin. The Parliament House and public offices will prove this to the South and in themselves be an asset towards ultimate reunion.[16] Craig was favourably impressed by Michael Collins...

25 JANUARY 1922

It is evident that politics are beginning to resume their old party complexion. I regret it – but many of our friends are confident that were there a dissolution now the Conservatives would be returned by a fair working majority. Joynson Hicks was arguing this to me, but I questioned his correctness, for the Conservatives, even Diehards like Jix himself, will have to face and overcome criticism directed against the Coalition government which has been placed and maintained in power by Conservative votes. Moreover our economies will be far from popular.

3 FEBRUARY 1922

... James Craig came to see me about Belfast public buildings. We are now troubled by the problem of new law courts, and the purchase of a site is no simple matter. I was amazed by his knowledge of the town and its citizens. He seems to know the ownership of every plot of land and the character of its proprietor – in other words his political complexion.

6 FEBRUARY 1922

A conference of Unionist ministers at Whitehall Gardens. We all feel uncomfortable. The Diehard movement is in itself the assertion of reactionary tendencies – a desire in itself far from objectionable to regain independence for our party, and to shake off the influence of our Liberal allies... There were many speeches this afternoon – I remember little of them for they were tentative and inconsequent.

... In the evening a big gathering at George Curzon's house. I sat next F.E. who says he has the best private library in London, at least he quotes Dring to that effect and he has recently refused £25,000 for it. When F.E. was making £20,000 a year in the days of modest taxation, what he did not spend on hunting and housekeeping went into his collection, and he has certainly made a very creditable library, almost exclusively English.

13 FEBRUARY 1922

A long audience at Buckingham Palace... I amused the King by telling him how in old days when duck shooting in Hyde Park, the Duke of Cambridge peppered a cab

---

[16] When asked by the Office of Works what would become of Stormont in the event of reunion, Craig replied, 'It would be admirable for lunatics'. (Sir Lionel Earle, *Turn Over The Page*, p. 209)

driver who was crossing the Serpentine Bridge. After an explosion of imprecations the cabman was pacified by two five pound notes. 'Much too much,' said the King, 'I have shot a beater and got off with a sovereign.'

19 MARCH 1922

Willie Peel goes to the India Office.[17] I am delighted. He is an excellent man. Derby refused and talked about it. Victor Cavendish didn't want the post either, but has not been chattering. The papers on Friday said the post had been offered to me. Not a word of truth in it – but on questions of fact our press is incorrigible. I am happy at the Office of Works and should not have been any use at the India Office.

23 MARCH 1922

The Irish Bill drags wearily through the House of Lords. Were it not so uncompromisingly condemned by Carson and Co. I should be sceptical – more sceptical – about the whole scheme. But so distrustful am I of Carson's judgment that I instinctively rally to support what he attacks.

31 MARCH 1922

The Irish Bill received royal assent today. Willie Peel who spent all yesterday at the Irish Conference came away with the poorest opinion of the capacity of Griffith and Michael Collins. I had heard good reports of the former from Austen Chamberlain and it was generally said that the latter though testy was a sensible and determined person. I dare say his nerve has been badly shaken since the conference which eventuated in the agreement last Xmas. Anyhow Willie Peel goes so far as to say that he seems quite incompetent to govern a peaceable English county, *a fortiori* a mass of turbulent countrymen of his own. Not only does he contradict himself and show every lack of balance, but he is extremely uncontrolled in language, and constantly breaks at a tangent. Sequence of argument is quite unknown to him – he runs on to irrelevant and minor issues without the smallest provocation: in fact it is almost impossible to conduct a conversation on the ordinary businesslike methods. Every now and then he brought up some grievance about Belfast, emitting the names and dates and streets and family circumstances of the victim of some outrage ascribed to Orangemen. Collins is small – James Craig gigantic. The latter would seem to blow himself out and push his head forward, with its great nose glowing like an angry searchlight towards Collins. 'You leave Belfast alone.' 'You will be so good as to look after your own mutineers and leave Belfast alone.' Collins appeared cowed on these occasions, and even Willie Peel who fears no man said that James looked positively terrifying.

[17] Just resigned by Montagu. Austen Chamberlain, prompted by Birkenhead, wrote to the premier (21 March) saying he had written to Crawford to allay disappointment. 'In fact he behaved like the great gentleman he is. His position in the Lords has been a very difficult one, for he has been deputy-leader and yet he has never been in our inner councils... It would be a fitting recognition of his services and his loyalty if you would make him a Cabinet Minister without changing his office.'

XIII

The fall of Lloyd George, 1922

Return to cabinet – cabinet on Ireland – the Irish constitution – hysteria of Michael Collins – US war debts – House of Lords reform – Birkenhead's tirade infuriates the under-secretaries – impasse in relations with France – beginning of Turkish crisis – Lloyd George envisages a Balkan alliance – scene between Curzon and Poincaré – strong party against war – Curzon thinks of resignation – cabinet abandons Greeks – Boscawen threatens resignation – a snap election prevented – Amery's ultimatum to ministers – Carlton Club meeting overthrows coalition – position of Viscount Peel – of Sir J. Gilmour – Beaverbrook invites Birkenhead to join the 'ministry of faithful husbands' – series of discussions among the ex-coalition ministers – Austen Chamberlain's views.

The events leading up to the fall of Lloyd George in December 1922 have often been told, from many points of view. Here they are seen by a coalition Conservative, a quintessential Tory and former Chief Whip, who nevertheless was quite outside the scheme of Conservative revolt hatched by the under-secretaries. Crawford was a minor member of the group, the coalition Conservatives, who lost more heavily than Lloyd George himself in the débâcle; for while Lloyd George had to go into the wilderness anyway, the coalition Conservative ministers were robbed of a bright future inside a dominant party. For Crawford himself it was the end of a political career which he had never allowed himself greatly to prize.

6 APRIL 1922

Agreeably surprised by a letter from Austen Chamberlain[1] asking me to join the cabinet.[2] Things are more interesting in the cabinet than upon its borders, and though it will mean more work on the whole, I find that I have to spend less and less time in my own office as I get to know the work and routine better. Moreover my staff perhaps knows me better too and altogether progress is much more expeditious than six months ago. But what a moment to join the cabinet. That the government is seriously discredited I entertain no doubt, so much so that apart from the

---

[1] Lord Privy Seal, and leader of the Unionist Party, 1921–2, following Bonar Law's retirement on medical grounds.

[2] As Minister of Transport (unpaid), while continuing to act as First Commissioner of Works. Crawford's diaries are not informative about his duties as Minister of Transport, which were clearly not heavy. Chamberlain had earlier written apologetically (19 March) about Peel becoming Secretary for India, mentioning that Crawford had been considered for the post.

419

The fall of Lloyd George

Quinquennial Act a dissolution must come soon. Well, I will try to help my colleagues avoid some of the dangers into which they have been falling. Had my advice prevailed we should have asked for no reparations, we should not have claimed the Kaiser's head, nor should we have promised all good things to ex-soldiers, nor should we have passed the Corn Production Acts – perhaps also we might have prevented the coal strike. There is a list of potential successes – the next few months or weeks will show in how many failures I become *particeps criminis*. Ireland apart, our handling of domestic affairs is more successful than foreign politics – George Curzon now seems generally looked upon as a failure – a pity: but during these days the government has strengthened itself by two debates in the House – one about the Genoa Conference.

... The Prime Minister writes as Austen did, a friendly letter. I am a little disturbed as it seems to be contemplated that I shall have to assume the duties of the Minister of Transport. Willie Peel[3] was minister till he went to the India Office. I think however that the office is nearly moribund – at least I hope so. But Neal[4] the parliamentary secretary whom I have met at the Home Affairs Committee seems a pushing little person, or else he has some very ambitious officials at his side.

27 APRIL 1922

At the cabinet this morning the budget was discussed. Horne[5] detailed a large, and I think an excessive series of tax concessions. Churchill[6] who limped in after a hunting accident at Eaton wanted much more, got very cross and very ineffective too in pressing his case. The opinion of the cabinet was that the Chancellor had gone as far as circumstances justified and Churchill babbled expletives under his breath.

It appears that some change is to be made in the supertax law to hit family trusts – it transpired that most of us sitting round the table had such trusts in our own families – Austen, Churchill, Willie Peel, Baldwin,[7] myself and others – I am not sure that Horne hasn't got one himself.

2 MAY 1922

Lunched with Robert Horne... Horne attaches great importance to the *Daily Mail* – practically none to the *Times*.... Lloyd George on the other hand says that the extravagance and hysteria of the *Daily Mail* are so well recognised by its readers that they don't trust the paper though they read it religiously.

---

[3] Viscount Peel, Secretary of State for India March–October 1922, retaining the post under Bonar Law and Baldwin, 1922–4. Peel had been Minister of Transport briefly in 1921–2, but outside the cabinet.

[4] Arthur Neal (1862–1933), MP (Lib.) 1918–22, parliamentary secretary to the Ministry of Transport 1919–22.

[5] Sir Robert Horne, Chancellor of the Exchequer 1921–2

[6] Colonial Secretary 1921–2

[7] President of the Board of Trade 1921–2

10 MAY 1922

Cabinet. The prime minister and Worthington-Evans[8] are still at Genoa, George Curzon[9] is still ill, and there were other absentees which made the attendance small. F.E.[10] is back again, and his doctors have now definitely told him that his eye trouble is due to nicotine poisoning. He has to be careful. Our conversation was very departmental, nothing of large interest coming under review.

16 MAY 1922

Cabinet about Ireland – a very distressing report from Churchill. The moral degeneration of Ireland proceeds apace. Ireland has acquired her freedom after a struggle lasting for a century – and now can only use her liberty for the purpose of assassinations, blackmail, burglary, arson – what a god-forsaken race. The whole Liberal tradition that Ireland is capable of self-government has been dispelled during the first few months of trial.

... Churchill means to keep troops in Dublin, and evidently contemplates the possibility of having to hold the place *manu militari* – to extend our posts well into the country, and actually to establish a Pale into which destitute loyalists may take refuge.

17 MAY 1922

Cabinet council to discuss a contretemps in the H. of C. last night – the defeat of the government by three votes on a motion to adjourn a debate on a bill about teachers' pensions. At yesterday's cabinet Austen Chamberlain warned his parliamentary colleagues that the situation was dangerous, and a difficult division was certain. Members were whipped for 9.30 but at 7.0 Bob Cecil with an astute eye for tactics which his lofty morality has never obscured, sprang a dilatory motion and beat the government at a moment when no less than seventeen ministers were absent – quite a clever stroke which I admire though it oughtn't to have come from so censorious a critic of government morals. Austen wired to Genoa to invite the prime minister's advice. The answer had not arrived when we assembled, but a few minutes later the telephone message came in. 'Stand firm, Moses,' – it made us laugh. It was the adjuration made by the crowd to a Jew who was about to be martyred at a Spanish auto da fe, but the victim showed signs of recanting and spectators implored him to stand firm lest they should miss a sporting affair. So the advice on analysis proved ambiguous. The one issue from the dilemma of resignation was never discussed.

30 MAY 1922

V. important cabinet. The new Irish constitution was to embody the terms of the

---

[8] Sir L. Worthington-Evans, Secretary for War 1921–2

[9] Earl Curzon, Foreign Secretary (under Lloyd George) 1919–22, under Bonar Law and Baldwin 1922–4.

[10] Viscount Birkenhead, Lord Chancellor 1919–22

Treaty – to embody the whole agreement. The document, prepared for the Free State government by Kennedy K.C., is a real negation in spirit and in form of the Treaty, and in effect establishes a Republican constitution. Lord Harcourt has been examining this document on our behalf and has pointed out its diametrical conflict with the pledged word of the signatories. Lloyd George saw Griffith and Collins, and pointed all this out with direct and uncompromising earnestness. The latter made a lot of vague and unsatisfactory excuses but did not venture to deny the implication that the draft repudiates their pledged and solemn word. It is a very grave situation. Lloyd George failed to persuade them to acknowledge that the whole thing must be redrafted from the beginning. Collins seemed to be in a half-hysterical condition and several times said 'We will give you Ireland as a present' – that was pretty paradoxical, but he even went so far as to suggest that our troops should reoccupy the South under martial law! The P.M. said he could not help laughing at this proposal and rallied Collins upon such a volte face – no said Collins – the people like the soldiers and would behave better if they were back at Cork and Limerick. Whereupon A.J.B.[11] said, 'But didn't Collins see the ridiculous side of this idea – has he no sense of humour?' to which the prime minister made a reply which is wise and witty and true. 'No,' he said, 'the Irish have no sense of humour, and that is why they make us laugh so much.' It was decided to send a formal letter to force the Free State ministers to define their position, otherwise we shall have to take drastic action, which will entail terrible consequences.

...Ronald[12] came to see me – the relief of the F.O. officials at the absence of George Curzon is indescribable – it seems as though all the stories about George's brutality to his officials are true. Poor Eyre Crowe[13] has to go to the telephone at eleven every morning through which he receives such a series of scoldings that he is exhausted till luncheon time.

2 JUNE 1922
At the cabinet this morning Lloyd George gave us a long account of his interview with Collins and Griffith. The letter reached them about 5.40 – they were asked to reply by 6.0 and protested with some justice that such short notice, without a chance of consulting their friends in Ireland, placed them in an impossible position. The prime minister seized the opportunity of a conversation in order to emphasise his own resolution, and also to influence their reply. It was evident at once that the categorical questions, six of them, to which we demand replies caused them the greatest concern, and were apparently unexpected. Moreover the questionnaire is framed in such a manner that they will find it difficult to evade direct answers. Collins was 'all over the shop', 'jumping and hopping about', evidently in a state bordering upon hysteria; sometimes threatening, sometimes apologetic, and woolly-

[11] Lord President of the Council 1919–22
[12] The diarist's brother, at this time serving as under-secretary at the Foreign Office, 1921–4.
[13] Sir Eyre Crowe (1864–1925), permanent Under-Secretary for Foreign Affairs 1920–25.

headed nearly all the time. It is clear that he is a great disappointment to Lloyd George, who during the earlier negotiations, fancied that he was dealing with a responsible person, whereas it transpires that Collins has the brain of a western peasant, and lacks the courage of a louse. Griffith on the other hand though alarmed, and apparently intimidated by de Valera and the sinister assassins under Rory O'Connor, kept cool and collected, though at one time he was reduced to tears when the prime minister told them with direct and aggressive insistence, that if they defaulted, if they imperilled concessions greater than had ever been asked by the advocates of Irish freedom ('and I quoted the names of Irish heroes from Wolfe Tone and Edward Fitzgerald downwards'), the names of Griffith and Collins would be handed down to the curses and execration of future generations of Irishmen.

... The interview with the Irish ministers ended with their assurance that they do mean to adhere to the Treaty, although Collins kept asking for latitude here and there and implored the P.M. not to play the part of Shylock and demand the full bond ...

What struck me most at the cabinet was the length and wordiness of Churchill's harangues. His prepared speeches are admirable – those which are extemporised are fatiguing in their turgidity.

The coming of age of Crawford's eldest son, Lord Balniel, was celebrated at Haigh, now once again 'a house of scholarship and art' after the wartime turmoil, in the traditional pre-war way. There was a whole sequence of garden parties, of addresses presented, and replies from the recipient. A special meeting of Wigan town council approved an address of congratulation, and all members and officers of the council were invited to Haigh.

6 JUNE 1922

The Festivities have been a triumph. The place looked really beautiful ... The house party was large and intimate, being confined to our immediate relations ... It was a very merry assembly without any ceremony or formalities.

On Saturday evening there was a supper to the employees on the state. On Monday a garden party to the public officials of the neighbourhood. The Mayor of Wigan attended in state and presented in illuminated address from the Corporation. About 500 or 600 people came that afternoon. On Tuesday the third and last garden party took place, a much more crowded affair as the tenants and guests from the Wigan Coal and Iron Co. numbered something like 1,500. Two more addresses, and David's replies on each occasion were admirable. The weather was brilliant, and everybody enjoyed themselves immensely.[14]

10 JUNE 1922

In camp at Salisbury with the Manchester Territorial Battalion, of which I am

---

[14] Later in the summer there were junketings in Fife, including a garden party for three hundred neighbours, another for three hundred tenants, and a dinner for one hundred estate employees.

honorary Colonel. It was lovely weather and a very curious experience. To sleep by myself in a tent – and in a bed – to have a floor, a chair, table, washing stand – to have changes of raiment. What affluence and comfort! Campaigning under such conditions might be almost a pleasure, and I compare this (as it existed for commissioned ranks in France) with the horrors and squalors to which ninety per cent of the British troops were subjected. The disparity was always great, until these days I never realised how excessive.

16 JUNE 1922

Cabinet discussed our war debts. USA means to make us pay: we will do so even if it bleeds us white. Churchill however all for delay – he voiced what the prime minister calls the 'aristocratic view of debts'. But the cabinet was clear that we could not procrastinate. But if we are debtors to USA, we are creditors of other allies and it was decided that we should inform our allies that if we are forced to pay they must make a like effort towards ourselves. They will receive our missive with annoyance and then do nothing: meanwhile the American Shylock will ensure that our rate of taxation is maintained at a killing level.

30 JUNE 1922

Cabinet at 12.0. A.J.B. read us the draft despatch in which our allies are to be told that as the USA is dunning us for payment, we in turn must ask them to pay up ... We also discussed American legislation being prepared to destroy our mercantile marine. Stanley Baldwin wants to threaten retaliation; Lloyd George, Churchill, and A.J.B. very doubtful if we could enforce it successfully.

2 JULY 1922

To London from Haigh.

3 JULY 1922

Attended the prime minister's conference about House of Lords Reform. Selborne, Salisbury, and Lansdowne came to represent the opposition, and Denman and Gainsford represented the Independent Liberals. The prime minister was rather nervous, said nothing amusing as is his wont, and altogether I think he felt himself on weak ground. The Robinson case has been so disastrous a proof that existing methods are inadequate to prevent mistakes, that he feels some substantial concession is necessary ... The conference was informal and I fancy useful. Lloyd George did not – could not – get the best of the encounter and after every occasion when he flew off at a tangent, Lansdowne's cold and clear-cut question was repeated. (That is what Collins said about his conferences on Irish matters. He was confident of being able to bamboozle Lloyd George, and evade the Lord Chancellor, but it was no use trying to escape from Austen Chamberlain. When an awkward question was put Collins became eloquent on something else, but Austen never forgot the question which encouraged irrelevances. The question was repeated until a reply was given. So this evening.) Austen by the way is pretty bad – ten days or more must elapse before he reappears, which is very awkward considering Curzon's illness too.

4 JULY 1922

We discussed House of Lords Reform at the cabinet. It is quite clear that Curzon's scheme which involves repeal of the parliament act would produce a crisis both inside the cabinet and in parliament as well. We should introduce a needless apple of discord, for there is a pretty strong body of Unionist opinion which is quite prepared to muddle on upon the present lines. Any announcement of repeal would cause endless trouble and possibly the gravest consequences. Why provoke dissensions unless victory is desired and certain as well?

That is the view we all took. Anyhow we decided to jettison Curzon's clauses about Free Conference and Joint Sessions which were to replace the parliament act. What will Curzon say when he returns in two or three days? He does not like his schemes to be amended.

6 JULY 1922

Conference at the Mint about coins and medals. They have got to be improved. Our standard must be the lowest in Europe.

F. E., Churchill, Fisher,[15] and I had a conference about House of Lords Reform and we agreed to recommend the cabinet to omit Free Conference and Joint Sessions, and to leave the Parliament Act untouched for the moment.

7 JULY 1922

The full cabinet readily endorsed this plan, but there remains George Curzon in the background. He is enamoured of his own offspring and I should not be in the least surprised if he objects to the truncation of his logical and well thought out scheme. He is to come to London today.

Most of our time was occupied by a discussion of our debts to the USA. Arthur Balfour, who has charge of the F.O. during Curzon's absence, read at a recent meeting his draft of a despatch to our European allies, telling them that if we have to repay the USA, they must try to repay us. Today we had the final draft, amplified in one or two particulars – a wonderful state paper which will make a great impression: there will be howls in Europe and indignation meetings: in America a good deal of quiet self-questioning.

Auckland Geddes came.[16] He didn't like the prose, he thought the sequence of argument should be inverted ... Geddes' arguments were delivered in a v. pompous manner but they puzzled us all and at one time I had the impression he was extemporising. Anyhow we settled to adhere to the main thesis of Balfour's

[15] President of the Board of Education, 1916–22
[16] Ambassador to the US 1920–24

despatch. Mond and Greenwood were very emphatic that not one word should be changed!

8 JULY 1922

The papers are full of the cabinet crisis – about reform of the Lords, about fabric gloves, and about the cattle embargo: in a lesser degree about Ireland and foreign affairs. So far as I can judge, no crisis exists. Nothing at any rate at the cabinet meetings provokes any serious controversy: our proceedings are harmonious and rather dull. So I can only assume that the crisis is a newspaper stunt. I wonder if the public is remotely conscious of the lies told in the newspapers?

10 JULY 1922

Went to see George Curzon passing through London en route for Orleans where he is to undergo a cure for phlebitis. He was robed in a flowing silk dressing gown, almost unable to rise from his armchair, but otherwise looking very robust, and talking with great energy and decision. He hopes that three weeks will suffice for his cure. He says that on the whole he has chosen his moment of absence well – for he dislikes the cabinet's decision to truncate the H. of L. Reform resolutions, still more was he opposed to the Italian conference which is breaking down as he anticipated: A.J.B. however is acting as Secretary of State for Foreign Affairs, and our newspapers consequently make no fuss about the subject. Had George still been in charge there would have been a violent attack on him for his incompetence etc. This is true. Our press is really hopeless.

14 JULY 1922

A crowded dinner in Downing St in honour of the Prince of Wales – a ministerial affair. The P.M. made a formal éloge, all committed to paper and therefore quite ineffective as a speech ... In point of fact Lloyd George's eyesight is so good that wearing his pince-nez he was able to rest his typewritten pages on the table – reading with ease although standing upright ... The King and the late King Edward were also able to read print at a great range of vision, an immense convenience to the speaker, and so far as the audience is concerned, giving the impression that notes rather than manuscript are being used ... The P.M. has been trying to get me, through the Government Hospitality Fund, to pay for this entertainment, but I have resolutely refused.

20 JULY 1922

Cabinet. Discussed reparations and American debt, a subject to be resumed next week. A.J.B. wrote an admirable state despatch, but it had to be amplified a little. Delay ensued, Geddes was timorous, and now after the fresh crisis in German exchange it seems as if we had missed the psychological moment. It is a pity. I notice tremendous delay in carrying out definite instructions. Ten days ago we were all agreed.

...In the afternoon I spoke in the House of Lords about the Reform Resolutions. They are truncated and incomplete, but even so go a good deal further than most peers desire. There is a strong movement objecting to all change of our constitution though many would welcome a further curtailment of the Parliament Act. People are very unreasoning. Salisbury, Selborne and one or two others are pushing the reform, but I am sure nobody is really keen on the subject beyond a relatively small group... Cantuar[17] made a violent speech in dulcet tones. He is playing up to the Diehards – recently he made a speech about the R.I.C. to whom he has never given a thought until he had a good scolding from Carson.

21 JULY 1922

Dined at Lambeth Palace. What a huge place. I wonder how the Archbishop manages to finance it. The first half of his £15,000 a year goes in rates and taxes. The third quarter goes in upkeep, most of the last quarter in subscriptions and expenses of a public nature – he entertains a great deal. What will happen to Lambeth is a difficult problem – it would be a sad pity to sell off such parts as could be used as building land.

22 JULY 1922

And Fulham Palace? I went there this afternoon with Elizabeth, Mary, and Katharine, and soon found myself playing rounders with the Bishop[18] in a purple cassock. Fulham too is a beautiful and historic appanage of the church though hideously restored in many respects, but it remains a remarkable possession. London House in St James' Square has been let to the Caledonian Club, so the strain on Dr Ingram's finances is mitigated: but even so the upkeep of Fulham must be overwhelming – forty-two bedrooms, a huge garden, and chapel... The Bishop of London is a bachelor. He and I are old allies, from my Oxford House days onwards.

25 JULY 1922

Further cabinet discussion about our note to allies on debt payment. At the last cabinet (or was it the last but one) we agreed to its despatch subject to one or two technical amplifications. The document got held up – how or why I know not, and today Churchill pressed for its immediate issue. We have certainly missed the right moment for action. Had we sent off this despatch within a day or two of our decision we should have anticipated the sudden downrush of German exchange. However we discussed the topic again today. Horne evidently in a fright, and Austen Chamberlain nervous. The former seemed to think that if we offend the USA we may find it difficult to secure favourable terms when we discuss the funding operations. This seemed rather to provoke Lloyd George (hitherto silent). He

[17] Dr Randall Davidson, Archbishop 1903–28.
[18] Dr Winnington-Ingram, Bishop of London 1901–39.

The fall of Lloyd George

resented any idea of adopting a cringing or obsequious attitude in order to reduce our interest payments by one eighth of one per cent. The cabinet as a whole in rather a polemical mood, and far from showing anxiety about American annoyance. Then Geddes gave his views. I was poorly impressed by his statement last time we discussed the matter. Today he was clear and emphatic that however shrill might be the American howl of indignation, it will pay us in the long run to be firm and decisive.

26 JULY 1922
Conference in Lord Chamberlain's room: Austen, W. Peel, A.J.B. (as he still signs himself), Worthington-Evans, Horne, to discuss the situation from the Conservative point of view. It appears that some of our whips and under-secretaries are very apprehensive about the future. They dislike Coalition as such, their constituency associations are hostile to its continuance, and in some cases, especially in the South of England, the Liberal coalition candidate will be denied our support. In some cases too a Conservative candidate will be run against him.

What are we to do? So far as our group of Coalition ministers in the cabinet is concerned, we came to the only conceivable conclusion, namely that we must continue to support the prime minister.

28 JULY 1922
Conference with Horne, Worthington-Evans, W. Peel and others about further economies to be made in civil service estimates. I am allotted a group of departments which will demand much attention, and break up my recess.

3 AUGUST 1922
A v. disagreable conference of the Unionist ministers. It appears that Austen Chamberlain communicated to our whips and under-secretaries the decision we reached the other day to maintain the coalition as long as possible. This displeased them, and they asked to meet us. We were Austen Chamberlain in the chair, Baldwin, Boscawen,[19] A.J.B., Worthington-Evans, Lord Chancellor,[20] Peel; Curzon, Horne and Arthur Lee[21] the absentees. There were twenty-eight junior ministers present including the two law officers. R. A. Sanders[22] started off with a very temperate and cogent plea that as the present situation is impossible as it splits our own ranks in the constituencies, we should end the coalition. He was followed by George Gibbs,[23] Pollock,[24] Jack Gilmour,[25] Leslie Scott[26] and one or two

[19] Sir A. Griffith-Boscawen, president of the Board of Agriculture and Fisheries 1921–2; Minister of Health under Bonar Law 1922–3.
[20] Lord Birkenhead
[21] Lord Lee, First Lord of the Admiralty 1921–2.
[22] Under-secretary at the War Office 1921–2; Minister of Agriculture 1922–4.
[23] Treasurer of HM Household 1921–2, retaining the post in 1922–4.
[24] Sir E. Pollock, Attorney-General March–October 1922.
[25] Sir J. Gilmour, junior Lord of the Treasury April–October 1922.
[26] Solicitor-General March–October 1922.

428

others – who though differing on the actual situation in the constituencies, seemed unanimous that the present state of affairs was menacing and should be ended. It was stated that the under-secretaries were unanimous.

Then the Lord Chancellor began what developed into a long and very violent tirade, the burden of which was that he would not raise a finger to depose Lloyd George. I think he is quite right, and moreover I am sure that if we refuse to acquiesce in the attacks made on the P.M. by the diehards and numbers of old-fashioned Tories who occupy the posts of honour in our county associations, we shall produce a strong reaction – not perhaps strong enough to maintain the existing form of coalition, but nonetheless adequate to preserve harmony and cooperation with Liberals who are as nervous about a socialist government as we ourselves. Much can doubtless be said on the other side but alas, F.E. gave no credit and no mercy to the critics. He attacked them with a vigour and virulence which caused desperate umbrage. He gave real offence to a number of sincere and loyal colleagues, and I afterwards learned that some of them considered his speech had gone further towards smashing up the coalition government than any shortcomings of the Prime Minister himself. It was sad pity. I can't think what made him set his speech in so personal a tone, for he attacked some of them individually, and poured ridicule upon their expressions of opinions and their knowledge of electioneering. It was a vainglorious and vulgar bit of rhodomontade. Why? I fear it may be the atmosphere of the House of Lords. He is habitually confronted by thickheads like Salisbury, Walter Long, St John, Crewe, Chaplin. Intellectually he towers over them and by brilliance of argument and analysis he can triumph even where his case is faulty. This afternoon he smothered his opponents with ridicule, hinted not obscurely that they were disloyal and ill-informed as well. But what one can say to a peer cannot be readily repeated, especially by a peer to members of parliament for the latter enjoy the advantage and reputation of speaking with direct and personal knowledge of the constituencies. One therefore kept feeling that our audience was saying that the Lord Chancellor's scolding was detached from the hard realities of the situation, and it was all the more bitterly resented in consequence. I cannot say how sorry I am. His powers are altogether exceptional and his courage remains unshaken in circumstances of disaster, yet for lack of a little charity he throws away his influence and in point of fact has done us a great deal more harm than good.

A.J.B. made a few mollifying remarks – Austen Chamberlain followed with some tactful and calming observations. The meeting which had lasted nearly two hours – nothing settled – and our younger colleagues went away in a thoroughly nasty temper.

During August, Crawford noted approvingly a paper circulated by Churchill saying 'that now we have settled on a reparations policy, we must stick to it'; considered Poincaré's proposed policy of seizing German assets as futile; and spoke with contemptuous pleasure of the way the USA was 'squealing like a pig' about British debt payments. Crawford's view of party affairs was vaguely prophetic:

The fall of Lloyd George

The papers at home paid little attention to the Conservative conference the other day – partly because our men were cautious and still more owing to the prorogation which has scattered our men all over Britain: but there is a vague consciousness that all is not well, that our meeting[27] had an almost sensational character. For the moment however things are quiet. The trouble will begin after the holiday when associations begin to meet to take stock of the situation.

10 AUGUST 1922

Cabinet at 3 p.m. George Curzon turned up after his French cure at Orleans, much improved as he says, but I confess I thought him looking very worn. When he spoke however during our deliberations, he was as clear in argument and as firm in voice as ever. Absentees included A.J.B., Fisher, Churchill, and Arthur Lee.

The Prime Minister told us of the long conference in which Poincaré's schemes had met with universal hostility. The French and Belgians are not agreed as the newspapers would lead one to suppose. On the contrary both the Belgians and the Italians are keenly alive to the danger of trying to smash Germany. Theunis, my old friend and colleague on *ravitaillement*, is now Prime Minister of Belgium, and made an appeal to Poincaré, so pathetic in character, so poignant in its desire for unity, so dexterous in its references to our common sacrifices and our need for future cooperation that nearly everybody in the room was reduced to tears – great must have been the impression left by such a speech delivered by a man I have always looked upon as phlegmatic. But, said Lloyd George, he made no impression on that cold-blooded fish. Poincaré coldly expressed his desire to maintain the entente, but did not feel able to modify his plans.

George Curzon then took up the parable. He said that the F.O. would greatly regret a breach with France. In all corners of the world they can make our position difficult – Anatolia, Constantinople, Palestine, Egypt, Tunis, Tangier – at every hole and corner of the Mediterranean. He went on to say that the French were recovering their prestige in the U.S.A. which they had lost owing to Briand's attitude about disarmament and that in Washington also they could make themselves most objectionable. The broad effect of Curzon's warning was that we should go as far as possible to meet the French owing to the unpleasant consequences they are in a position to inflict. It was rather a timorous pronouncement and stirred the P.M. into replying that from good information reaching him, he was sure that the French have by no means recovered their position in the USA, and moreover that though she can nag us whenever she pleases, we retain our resort to the League of Nations, while the parlous condition of France herself must ultimately exercise a restraining influence. In any case the cabinet was averse to giving way to France in order to save ourselves trouble.

[27] That of 3 August, described above.

Curzon had also said that by a crack of the whip France can bring Italy to heel, while the Little Entente is still subject to pressure from France.

This was not very convincing and the cabinet separated with an injunction to the Prime Minister to insist upon essentials at the next conference.

In conversation with Grigg,[28] Poincaré used the ominous phrase 'England is no longer an island' – it is true that with its gigantic air fleet France has disestablished the English channel. Poincaré himself is in a highly nervous state of mind, and is apparently in fear of assassination.

11 AUGUST 1922

The breakfast party which assembled at no. 10 sat on until luncheon time, but nothing was accomplished.

12 AUGUST 1922

Dined with George Stanley[29] who was very eloquent about Birkenhead's tirade to the Conservative under-secretaries. I knew they were annoyed – how could it have been otherwise – but I hardly realised how furious they were – George says that had it not been for their arrangement that only four or five chosen speakers should address us, and that nobody else should intervene, there might have been a real explosion. George says that at the autumn conferences resolutions hostile to the Coalition are inevitable, and what is then to follow?

We had two cabinets today, at 3.30 and 6.30. At the first of them the P.M. announced the negotiations had broken down. The French are immovable. We on our side insisted that the Poincaré scheme would not only be nugatory from a finance point of view – thoroughly unproductive in reparations or revenue – but that it would so disorganise German industrial life as to inflict grievous harm on Europe as a whole. The Belgians though anxious to travel as far as possible with Poincaré are desperately afraid of the violent proposals of France. Up till the last moment they kept making fresh suggestions, in which Schauzer joined, but Poincaré would concede nothing. He scarcely argued the points as they arose.

Lloyd George a little puzzled to account for his very rigid attitude. Of course Poincaré is a very stiff and rigid person. The P.M. seemed to think that Poincaré cannot escape from the precise and reiterated pledges which he was given in his weekly articles, although Poincaré knows that the substance has long since vanished: but he adheres to formulae which are now quite meaningless. Moreover the French press as a whole insists on drastic action – hit Germany if Germany can't be made to pay – anyhow hit the *sale Boche*.

For years says Ll. G. we have made compromise after compromise, concession on concession, against our better judgment, and the time has probably come when further affirmations of solidarity would be dangerous as well as futile. It is perhaps

[28] Sir Edward Grigg, private secretary to Lloyd George 1921-2.
[29] Financial secretary to the War Office 1921-2.

well for France to be brought face to face with realities – we don't want a break, and we have laboured hard to prevent it – but there is a limit etc. The Prime Minister argued on these lines, in rather a melancholy spirit, but I fancy pretty sure that acceptance of the latest French thesis would in the long run have produced a graver crisis than can arise from its immediate repudiation. France will now act alone – at least she expressly reserves her right to do so. Will she? Poincaré said he would consult his government and it seems possible that the French Chamber may be summoned to hear explanations, and perhaps to endorse a forward policy. It is difficult to see how Poincaré can report the situation and then calmly announce that he will sit with folded hands and await developments. It seems inevitable also that the French Nationalists will pour bitter invective on us, and in particular upon Lloyd George – whom Poincaré will have to defend, though in a perfunctory manner. And then? what isolated action can the French take beyond fresh measures against Germans in Alsace-Lorraine? Occupation of the Ruhr, still more the control of German forests, seems impossible, and the Belgians would be furious at any fresh cordon of custom houses. I am a little anxious about incidents in Cologne should the French use that city as a base for inroads upon Germany.

At 5.0 the final meeting of the allied governments took place, at 6.30 the second cabinet. At my end of the table French, Italian, and Belgian ministers had sat, and I picked up their cards, the last record of this unhappy conference, the thirteenth I believe since the armistice: the most fateful if the least fruitful of all, and one which marks a new stage in the evolution of European relationships.

To Scotland at night.

The holiday task which Crawford had been set was to prune the estimates of a group of departments. Commuting between Fife and Whitehall, Crawford noted how woolly the Colonial Office officials were, and how nervous were the police authorities (Downing Street and King Charles Street were still closed by 'temporary' wooden barriers which the Home Secretary, Edward Shortt, refused to allow Crawford to remove unless he replaced them with massive iron gates).

29 AUGUST 1922

Dined with Willie Peel. He is a good deal perturbed about the uninterrupted criticism of the P.M.'s recent speech about India. Peel had taken great trouble to coach him, and had laid down a cautious line of argument which would at the same time give confidence to the Civil Service, and also make the Councils understand the extent and complexity of their responsibilities. Unhappily two forces seem at work – one the natural eloquence and expansion of the Prime Minister who was unable to stick to his brief, and thus said things which have aroused natural annoyance in India. The other factor appears to be advice on Indian affairs which reaches him from some v. inexperienced source. It is supposed that his son-in-law, a youth now I believe on the N.W. Frontier, suggests policies and promotions which are unacceptable to the India Office. I wonder how far this is true. It is however clear that Lloyd George does not seem to pay enough attention to what the Indian secretary and Council advise – a pity, for Peel is a very good administrator, and there is no doubt that India is less disturbed today than four or five months ago...

7 SEPTEMBER 1922

The cabinet was called to discuss the Greek situation which is reaching its crisis. Kemal Pasha seems to have broken the Greek resistance in Asia Minor – there has been a certain amount of mutiny in the Greek Army, of which the C.-in-C. is generally looked upon as a 'mental case'. Refugees are pouring into Smyrna, massacres seem inevitable. Flushed with victory Kemal Pasha will probably demand the evacuation of Eastern Thrace and Constantinople. France rejoices openly in the defeat of Greece, notwithstanding the old alliance.

The cabinet therefore assembled in a very depressed condition. We began proceedings by a speech of forty minutes from George Curzon – an admirable résumé of the situation, logical, clear, and unconvincing: for one felt that he would have been just as lucid in regard to Egypt and Persia, where his great knowledge of circumstances has not saved us from collapse. He concluded his long (and tiring) exposition by urging us not to take the initiative in promoting an armistice – then took up a telegram which he had not previously read, but which I fancy he had brought into the cabinet with him – a telegram from Constantinople saying that our High Commissioner, acting upon previous instructions from the F.O., had actually opened pourparlers in this direction. We all felt very foolish, or at least that we had wasted half our morning. I often notice that these long harangues to which we are treated at the cabinet are of very little value compared with the rapid elliptical criticism by which they are followed. So it was today. Ten minutes after Curzon had finished we reached the real heart of the situation, which apparently had scarcely received any attention from the F.O. – namely that Asia Minor has ceased to be of immediate interest. The problem of the moment is Athens – will there be a revolution: Thrace, will there be an evacuation or an advance: Constantinople, will there be a peremptory summons to quit!

The Prime Minister had been very silent – in fact scarcely spoke a word until an hour and a quarter had elapsed. He has the reputation of being the most pro-Greek member of the cabinet, partly from his love of small nations, partly because he abominates the persecution of Christian minorities, and I fancy he is still under the shadow of the spell woven round him by Venizelos. Today he took up rather a singular attitude. In passing he expressed resentment at the ceaseless and aggressive treachery of France who has certainly behaved in a manner quite unforgivable. Then he went on to wonder if the whole Greek retreat was not an arranged affair – the assumption being that the King must have known perfectly well that Smyrna had to be abandoned, and that the incompetence of the High Command and perhaps the disinclination to fight, may have been deliberate. In other words is it possible that Tino may think that the defeat in Anatolia, producing reactions in the Balkans, may ultimately create active allies for Greece? If for instance the

French are fools enough to play us false about Constantinople, Roumania, and possibly Bulgaria as well, might join us (and Greece) in a resolute policy towards the Straits, and Constantinople might again become a Greek objective.

It was rather a curious interlude. It is true that odd and inexplicable things have occurred on the Greek side, for instance the withdrawal of troops from Smyrna to the outskirts of Constantinople: but I find it hard to believe that Tino can have risked his dynasty for such speculative reasons.

Lloyd George was featureless in respect of a policy. Churchill said we must resume a friendship with Bulgaria, though it did not occur to him that we can offer them any quid pro quo except some port now in Greek occupation. Finally Hamar Greenwood[30] in his stentorian voice asked, 'When are we going to base our policy on the incontestable fact that France has ceased to be our friend?' So far as Eastern policy is concerned France has clearly become an avowed enemy – supplying Kemal with munitions after she had made a separate peace behind our backs, intriguing against us incessantly, and actually blaming us for the Greek disaster which was caused by her own desertion. Arthur Lee who is this moment back from Constantinople told us a singular thing – the cause of the high reputation we hold in the capital. The Turks learn all our actions and proposals from the French who reveal all our secrets. We on the other hand give away no secret French information to the Turk, and the latter is therefore convinced that we are the more honest of the two! Perhaps they are right, and perhaps we are the more stupid of the two. Anyhow we have little to boast of for the moment, though the French will have a cold fit one of these days. They are not popular in Syria – the northern littoral of Africa is not without its dangers, and Pan-Mahommedanism may produce anxious moments for the French themselves.

Greenwood's question received no answer: but it was good to hear the remark, for what is a suspicion may soon be acknowledged as a platitude. I am always interested in Greenwood, and place some reliance upon his judgment though he is the subject of a violent Press campaign. A few months ago Asquith told me that Greenwood was a Jew – I have often looked at him since, but find it hard to believe – yet the name has a semitic sound, and I fancy his biography appears in the Jewish Who's Who.

After discussing Greece we turned to Poincaré's recent note about debts and reparations. I pressed that the accounting problems mentioned in the despatch should be dealt with in a separate and subsidiary note. I was a little surprised at the apparent anxiety to argue with the French, to refute their allegation that our position as belligerents differed morally (and therefore materially) from that of the USA – a bold and ridiculous proposition hazarded to create bad blood between ourselves and the USA. For my part I should hear this scolding of an angry and spiteful housemaid with contempt – ignore it.

14 SEPTEMBER 1922

At night to London for a cabinet.

[30] Hamar Greenwood, first Viscount Greenwood (1870–1948), Chief Secretary for Ireland 1920–22.

Spent time with George Younger[31] and discussed the disagreeable domestic situation in politics. He says that unless Lloyd George retires from the P. Ministership a breach of the coalition is imminent. This arises largely from personal distrust of Ll. G. – I pressed him for his solution of the difficulty. It is easy to say Lloyd George must go, but there must be some explanation or excuse – the state of his health, his desire to travel, his decision to write a book – but he can't vanish without some tangible and acceptable motive. We can't dismiss him like an incompetent butler.

Here is the difficulty, and it is accentuated by the international position today. The Greek defeat is considered all over Europe and to a large extent at home, as being a personal blow to the Prime Minister's policy: and to some degree this is actually the case: but this makes him all the more reluctant to resign at this particular moment, as he would appear to bow before a censure he does not accept, or to retreat in face of danger which is not his habit.

Yet G.Y. says we must face the situation which threatens disaster, and the P.M. has told him several times that he will retire if and when our party (to whom he feels much indebted) are tired of him. Younger has tried to persuade the Diehards to drop their pinpricking tactics. It is dangerous as well as ungracious to assault Ll. G. with every form of personal abuse. Nothing could be more ungenerous, and, to assess the matter from the meanest standpoint, it is unwise to vex and gall him into reprisals.

15 SEPTEMBER 1922
The cabinet began at four and we had a preliminary forty-five minute discourse from Curzon. It was a narrative, with which we must all be pretty familiar, of the last week's events. Curzon ended up by suggesting that he should go to Paris forthwith to consult Poincaré, to enlist his active help in defending Constantinople from Kemal Pasha, and to arrange if possible preliminary terms for submission to a peace conference – a meeting to revise the Sèvres treaty to which Roumania and Serbia should be invited.

But he wants the conference in Paris, not in Italy, although Venice is nominally the venue for a near Eastern *aboccamento*. Everybody seemed to think this would cause needless offence to the Italians and gain us no credit with the French. Much time wasted on this point.

Of constructive policy Curzon gave practically no hint. Churchill wants two divisions sent out at once, blockade imposed, cooperation with Balkan allies – each to send x no. of men as qualification for their attendance at the coming conference. W. Evans said that this means calling up the reserves or denuding Ireland. The cabinet shuddered at the idea of either course. I don't think anybody quite realised how difficult it will be unless some quid pro quo be afforded. We possess Cyprus and with it we can do much to ease the Greek position, but Cyprus was never

[31] Chairman of the Unionist Party organisation 1916–23.

The fall of Lloyd George

mentioned. We could almost persuade the Greeks to buy off Bulgaria by offering Dedeagatch Port if they got Cyprus as a set-off. Roumania will want a loan. What can we do for Serbia? or for Italy? Perhaps we could bamboozle the latter with Somaliland.

The Prime Minister silent and rather morose, yawning a good deal. He seems to think the Dardanelles so important that we should fight for it single-handed; Peel very loath to contemplate the effects of such action upon Indian opinion. Ll. G. strongly averse from enlisting American help, though keen to get Australia to cooperate on their sentimental interest in the Gallipoli peninsula.

But what can Australia do except send retired soldiers – who would not arrive for three months. Kemal is within three weeks of Marmorada!

We settled to do lots of things but all seemed to me to be improvisations. We appear to have ignored the existence of Serbia and Roumania, both of which would be incensed at Turkish advances – and only at the last minute do we think of securing their help. Much depends on France. For the moment we seem to be in accord, and the French are perhaps getting anxious about Syria and Algiers. It is not believed that Kemal would fight the French troops – Poincaré has promised to send them, but will he do so? He is quite capable of delaying their despatch while the Italians are working hard against us – one of their intercepted messages shows that they are trying to persuade Serbia to remain neutral.

Had a long talk with Willie Peel after dinner. He is exercised about the continuing reactions from the P.M.'s speech about India. The employment of the innocent word 'experiment' in connection with the constitutional reforms gives the text for every sort of allegation that we mean to go back on our promises. There are hopeful aspects in the Indian position, but Kemal's victory over the Greeks will inflame Moslem opinion against us; and there is still deep anxiety. Reading is to come home to discuss the general outlook; but this involves his resignation of the Viceroyalty during the interim period – ancient practice or statute makes it impossible for him to come to Britain though it appears he is at liberty to go to Aden or even as far as Egypt. It was accordingly suggested that the conference should take place in Egypt. This is clearly undesirable from many points of view, while the resignation of the Viceroy in order to come to England and his reappointment after a short interval is likewise open to objection. Any such course would inevitably provoke rumours of disagreement and crisis which one should avoid. The P.M. cannot find time to make an expedition to the Nile, and apparently Reading is not at all clear that he wants to come as far as England with all the tiresome consequences involved.

What did Ll. G. suggest? – why that the meeting should be arranged in Egypt, and that when Reading is halfway up the Red Sea, it should be found impossible for the P.M. to leave England. Reading would be informed, would have to resign temporarily, and hold the conference in London! It is too simple an expedient to call Macchiavellian! Willie Peel on hearing the proposal, which was advanced in a shy and very tentative fashion, raised his eyebrows – said 'I don't think that plan would do' – and the scheme was incontinently dropped. But that it should ever have been conceived, that is the serious thing. One often hears the Prime Minister accused of unscrupulous intrigue. This I confess is the first concrete example I have ever come across, and I am bound to say it leaves a v. painful impression on one's mind.

How simple it would be to pass a special statute authorising the Viceroy to visit England on high imperial business. Somehow the obvious and straight solution of simple problems never occurs to a certain class of mind.

16 SEPTEMBER 1922

Inspected Downing St gardens, now happily relieved of the huts erected during the war – the Kindergarten as they were called, being the offices of the brilliant young people who knew so much that they bungled all our peace negotiations.

19 SEPTEMBER 1922

Great indignation among the young people of Fife because the Prince of Wales has just telegraphed that he cannot attend the St Andrew's Ball owing to Court mourning for the Duchess of Albany. It is felt that he is stretching family etiquette too far. In any case he ought to have sent word long ago. It is a pity that the impression grows prevalent that he shows ill-concealed boredom with his public engagements.

21 SEPTEMBER 1922

George Curzon seems to be making progress in Paris, in his negotiations with Poincaré about the Near East. But what a task! The French announced that they would fly their flag with ours in defence of the neutral zone opposite Constantinople in Asia Minor. That gave us great encouragement. Then they ostentatiously announce the withdrawal of the troops in question. Today we learn that Poincaré has assured the Chamber that under no circumstances shall French troops fight against Kemalists. Thus we not only seem to have been betrayed again but the action is such as to leave us in a position of immediate danger. It is evident that there is some very precise annexe (secret clauses) to the French Treaty of Angora.

25 SEPTEMBER 1922

Monday, cabinet at twelve. George Curzon started with a forty minute statement of his proceedings at Paris. An agreement has been reached – Greeks must surrender Thrace up to Maritza, Turks must withdraw from neutral zone, subsequent conferences must be held to settle outstanding problems.

Curzon's narrative was clear and precise. Nobody remembers the sequence of events better than he does, and he gave a wonderful picture of the proceedings as they developed. He amused us v. much by describing the violent scene with Poincaré – how Hardinge tried to curb George's indignation whispering 'keep quiet' – '*payons attention*' until finally George hobbled out of the room in protest. This brought us to the point on which we were all anxious for information. There is no record in the telegrams as to what George did on the doormat. Well he seems to have found an empty room close by, he went to the end of it, pulled up a chair to repose his troublesome leg, and awaited developments. 'Did you leave Hardinge in the room?' asked the P. Minister. Certainly, replied George. Well, says the P.M., making us all laugh – 'that was an even baser desertion than what the French did at Chanak'.

George sat there he thinks for ten minutes or so. Hardinge then appeared. Poincaré was furious – he had been screaming like a madman. H. said that Lord Curzon's return to England would cause the gravest alarm. Poincaré blustered, finally said he would apologise if Lord Curzon would withdraw the word 'abandonment' in relation to the movement of French troops from Chanak. A further pause, then Poincaré appeared – did apologise and Curzon said he understood P. objected to the word abandon. He, Curzon, attached no importance to the particular word – 'retreat' might be substituted – anyhow he too was willing to make the *amende*. Relations were thereupon renewed. 'Did you go back?' said the P.M. Yes, replied Curzon in his emphatic way: I went back, but not till after a further ten minutes had elapsed – partly to show my displeasure at the occurrence, partly I must acknowledge to regain my composure. I am not accustomed to these scenes of violence.

. . . Curzon scored – undoubtedly. The signal proof lies in the fact that not one word or whisper of the disagreement appeared in the French press. Ten or twelve people, including the Italians, were in the room, but it was considered politic to suppress the outcome of Poincaré's furious ravings. It shows too that the French can keep a secret when they like.[32]

30 SEPTEMBER 1922
Saturday 5 p.m First cabinet.

Yesterday's instructions to Harington[33] at Constantinople, upon which military action against the Turks would be founded, have not been acknowledged by the General. Rumbold's[34] F.O. telegrams have been more regular. So we adjourned after some desultory talk to be summoned as soon as information arrives.

After the cabinet George Curzon spoke very seriously to me – at the Foreign Office door. He says that the P.M., Churchill, and Birkenhead are bellicose – almost demand war – that Austen Chamberlain though less active is in pretty close sympathy with him: that he, Curzon, went to Paris to secure peace, but that all will be prejudiced if the War Lords have their way. I told him that so few ministers speak at the cabinet that he must be quite ignorant of their views – most

[32] Fifteen years later Hardinge gave Crawford his version of the incident (diary, 24 April 1937): 'At Grillions Hardinge told us the whole story of George Curzon's shindy with Poincaré at the Chanak conference in Paris – how George burst into tears, had to withdraw to a neighbouring boudoir where Hardinge left him on a sofa with a bottle of brandy beside him. Hardinge knows the tale from A to Z and tells it with supreme gusto.' Cf. also below, 4 November 1922.

[33] Sir Charles Harington (1872–1940), commander of army of occupation in Turkey 1921–3.

[34] Sir Horace Rumbold (1869–1941), High Commissioner at Constantinople 1920–24.

however must be profoundly anxious to avoid war. He said is that Arthur Lee's view? I said probably; and Worthington-Evans? – probably too I replied. Curzon seemed surprised – and attributes silence to hostility. Were he less long-winded himself he would have a better chance of support from others. I dined with Lord Peel and Worthington-Evans. The latter is far from bellicose, and Willie Peel being responsible for India is likewise reluctant to do anything likely to excite the Moslem world. About ten o'clock we were summoned to the second Cabinet. As we left the Club, Evans said 'You will see that there will be a strong warlike tendency this evening.'

So there was. We didn't actually begin formal discussion until nearly 10.40 p.m. Harington's reply has not arrived – at least the final part has been delivered and is being decoded. Meanwhile Rumbold telegraphed that he had seen and approved Harington's (missing) message. Prime Minister, Churchill and F.E. had dined together. The latter was very much flushed and excited; Churchill in a nervous condition.

Then a curious temperament revealed itself. The Trio began to attack Harington with varying violence. Why had not his telegram come? not even an acknowledgement of ours! Why keep us in the dark – his telegrams are too political, F.E. in an angry tirade said he could not conceal his indignation at the conduct of soldiers who act as statesmen. But why have we no news? repeated Lloyd George for the twentieth time. Cavan gave some explanation about delays in these messages. Sometimes he has had to wait ten hours. But Rumbold's message has come through in an hour said the P.M. – there must be inefficiency somewhere.

Finally Curzon stood up in Harington's defence; Worthington-Evans ought to have done it. Harington at least has telegraphed, Rumbold in Constantinople has seen the message, and the message is good – the situation is improved and a hostile movement against the Turk at Chanak seems inadvisable. Churchill pressed strongly that we should refuse the projected meeting at Mudania for which we and the French have pressed so strongly – on the ground that the Turk is still in the neutral zone. He got small support – at least let's wait until we get Harington's message! Then the P.M. looking flurried inveighed against this constant whittling down of the Paris agreement. We stretch every point in favour of the Turk, we contract every argument in favour of the Greeks, we dismiss Greek ships from the neutral sea, but permit Turkish troops on the neutral land. It is clear to me that somebody is sorry that the guns haven't gone off!

About midnight a scrap of Harington's message was sent in; decoding was bad – the text had been corrupted in transmission and the thing was unintelligible. What were we to do? The P.M. evidently meant us to sit up, all night perhaps and then discuss the subject. It was pointed out that the Combined General Staff would have to give considered advice on the matter, and as Beatty was not present much delay would ensue. So we sensibly settled to meet at ten o'clock tomorrow Sunday morning.

George Curzon drove me home. He says that all the trouble arises from Lloyd

The fall of Lloyd George

George's infatuation for the Greeks, and his hatred of the Turk. Churchill – why does he adopt this attitude – not surely from sharing the P.M.'s ethnical sentiments. Perhaps Churchill wants to recover a strategic prestige already lost at Gallipoli. As for F.E., my own impression is that he acts more from affection for the P.M. than from any other reason. Anyhow poor George is terribly worried: 'they will drive me out'. I told him it was all nonsense for him to think of resigning at such a crisis – ill and suffering as he is, there are invaluable qualities of coolness and analysis shared by few if any of his colleagues and I am bound to say that the environment of contention seems to be improving his health.

Glad to get to bed. Let me add that apart from the tiresome nagging against Harington, there was no single word of offence – I mean as between ministers. The papers seem to think we quarrel violently all the time – there is not a word of truth in it. The amenity of Councils I have attended is unbroken and – astonishing.

I OCTOBER 1922

Sunday. Cabinet at 10 a.m. I got down there in fairly good time – nobody there except Lloyd George on the balcony and Austen C. finishing his toilette upstairs, and talking down to us. He soon descended and we discussed my restoration of the garden. I am replacing gravel by stones. P.M. thought I was the first Commissioner of Works to give a thought to the subject. So I am.

Harington's telegram has at last arrived. Its deciphering was only finished at half past one this morning. It explains that Turks are withdrawing from parts (? or whole) of neutral zone, that the cavalry were not really threatening in view of our strong artillery and that accordingly it had been thought precipitate to attack the Turk at the moment of his withdrawal.

Meanwhile there were good intercepts, showing that Franklin Bouillon[35] is pressing Kemal to hold the Mudania conference, and to keep quiet in the meantime.

Beatty announced the opinion of the Combined Staff that in view of Harington's report it was no longer imperative for us to attack the Turk in order to save our troops from being hemmed in. Beatty, Cavan and Trenchard then withdrew. Mudania conference seems fixed for the day after tomorrow – and Kemal is concentrating in the direction of Ismid. Then our political discussion began. Churchill very soon produced a draft for discussion – they telegrammed to Harington. He said Harington must stop mixing himself up in political problems. Then he read three or four pages from a manuscript – the most extraordinary tirade one ever heard, convicting Harington of inconsistency, and scolding him for misleading us about the military situation, telling him to leave politics to the Ambassador, but discussing all sorts of political questions, even including the views of the USA. It was in effect a parliamentary tirade – a long polemical speech utterly unsuited to the occasion, wholly inappropriate as an address to a soldier. By the time he had finished reading it everybody, perhaps including himself, saw that the thing

[35] The French special representative in Turkey, regarded with deep suspicion by Britain.

440

was impossible. Refutation was needless – the telegram dropped dead, but it is worth recording that it contained no syllable of relief at our escape from warfare yesterday.

He pressed that the cabinet in 'self-defence' and in justice to the Combined Staffs, should make it clear that the instructions to act against the Kemalists, were based upon the alarmist message from Marden[36] and Harington, which were interpreted by the Combined Staffs here as making an attack imperative. In other words the cabinet only gave these instructions because the people on the spot thought their position insecure, if not dangerous. Instead of welcoming the change Churchill (and the P.M. too) wanted to give Harington a good scolding.

Lloyd George said one curious thing – speaking of the Paris agreement, by which he says we must abide in letter and spirit. 'The F.O. has the supreme responsibility – I have done my very best to support them.' We finally settled to reassemble this afternoon to study draft instructions to be sent to Rumbold by Curzon.

After the cabinet, Arthur Lee, Boscawen, Peel and I walked across the Parade Ground and talked over the situation. Lee is certainly not a fire-eater! Peel v. anxious to avoid conflict with Mahommedans. Boscawen frightened. All of us agreed that it would be impolitic as well as ungenerous to rattle Harington whose difficulties must be incalculable.

Second cabinet met at three p.m.

Somehow or other we stumbled back on to the grievance against Harington whose telegraphic ineptitudes cause so much umbrage. I can't remember in what connection it arose, but the P.M. said he was sure that Sir Frederick Maurice (now in Constantinople as *Daily News* correspondent) was helping Harington with his despatches. 'I recognise certain phrases,' said the P.M. He added that he thought the telegram 2486 (?) had been partly drafted by Maurice to discredit the government and to glorify himself and Harington. 'He is trying to arrange and patch up some "Peace with Honour" combination.'

'I wish to God he would succeed,' growled Boscawen.

What can be in the Prime Minister's mind? F.E. I know does not love soldiers. Was it not Nevil Macready who placed him under arrest? Churchill too never forgave those in authority who vetoed his promotion to a Brigade. But why the P.M. should show this hostility I never understand.

One phrase was put into the message to the effect that Harington was solely responsible for the safety of the troops. This arose from an anxiety for the cabinet to protect itself against the charge of hindering the local commander. There is too much of this consideration for how history will view our action, and too little consideration of how today's action will affect the position tomorrow.

During the cabinet Hardinge[37] telephoned that Kemal invites the main

[36] Major-general Sir Thomas Marden, commander of forces at Constantinople 1920–23.
[37] Ambassador in Paris 1920–22.

conference to Smyrna on 15 October. What fun! and how pleased the Italians will be.

Wickham Steed of *The Times* appears to have changed his views since Northcliffe died. Or else has Madame Rose, the lady of his intellectual affections, changed hers? Well, says the P.M., 'I don't bother about the explanation. Anyhow let's nickname him "Sub Rosa."' For those who know Steed and the Rose woman, the soubriquet is extremely witty.

2 OCTOBER 1922

The press is much relieved by the news from Constantinople. After what the P.M. said about Maurice yesterday I read the *Daily News*. There is certainly animus in Maurice's telegrams. He has not forgiven the P.M. for the tremendous castigation inflicted after Maurice had stupidly coached and cooked poor Asquith into making that attack. Maurice has never recovered, or forgotten that affair. The press is v. unfair as a whole. I don't think the cabinet has been altogether wise, but the zest with which the *Daily Mail* for instance tries to play off Harington against the cabinet seems petty and even ridiculous.

But we are not half through our difficulties. If as seems inevitable Kemal makes a condition of conference that we shall suspend the despatch of reinforcements or that he shall be free to cross the Bosphorus? Who is to stop him except ourselves? and we certainly don't want to bear the sole brunt of a war against Islam. Our relations with France are already strained enough. By the way Mond[38] and I and Peel had tea with the P.M. after yesterday's cabinet. Mond has just been brought back from Munich where he had a long interview with Ludendorff. The latter said that he deplored the present row in the Balkans, as he considered that a breach between France and ourselves would be a serious blow to Germany! A paradoxical statement indeed, and one liable to provoke mirth. The explanation is that L. is terrified of Bolshevism, and says that the only true policy is that of an Anglo-French-German combination against Russia. The latter is more dangerous than ever, and the more Western Europe quarrels, the stronger will the revolutionary sentiment grow all over the world. I wonder if L. was pulling Mond's leg. I rather think not, for no object would be gained by that gymnastic feat. Probably Ludendorff is like the Duke of Northumberland[39] who sees Bolshevism everywhere. Whenever he gets an anonymous letter he immediately thinks that Alnwick will be burned down next day.

3 OCTOBER 1922

The Mudania conference begins today. Its functions are limited; but if the Turks try to extend the conversations to wider issues, or if they try to use the meeting in

[38] Alfred Mond, first Baron Melchett (1868–1930), Minister of Health 1921–2.
[39] Alan Ian Percy, eighth Duke of Northumberland (1880–1930), right-wing publicist.

order to prejudice our positions at Gallipoli, the optimism which is so prevalent today may quickly be dispersed. Mustapha Kemal is not going to attend in person.

5 OCTOBER 1922

Cabinet called at 5.0. Began at 5.10 p.m. Curzon expounded the situation for twenty-five minutes.

A telegram from Rumbold had just arrived, and one from Harington. The latter says that Franklin Bouillon is a perfect curse. The Turks, acting doubtless on Bouillon's inspiration, or at any rate with his acquiescence, become more insistent in their demands and now say that they mean to get at the Greeks somehow or other. Whenever a point arises for settlement the Turk promptly telephones to Angora. Finally the Nationalists have threatened to resume operations.

Then Curzon told us of his interview with Venizelos on Monday evening, with Worthington-Evans. It was a longish interview, an hour and a half, Venizelos being emotional and at times very passionate. His eloquence is unbroken and George complained rather plaintively at being unable to get in a word at all. Venizelos admitted that E. Thrace was lost. Then he wrote to *The Times* – then he interviewed the U.S. ambassador, who is alleged to have given a sort of backhanded pledge to the Greeks. Col. Harvey is capable of any folly – his recent escapade at the Cheshire Cheese made him look pretty ridiculous. Anyhow the bon mot of Washington is that 'America expects every Englishman shall do his duty.' But we mustn't complain; America has at least stretched a point by expressing an opinion on the crisis.

This morning Venizelos came to see Eyre Crowe, and told him that Greece has decided or rather that he has advised for immediate evacuation. But what about the interregnum? we can't leave E. Thrace without any government – that would duplicate our error of generosity in Ireland; nor can we hold Thrace ourselves without active help from the French. Here is the dilemma. George said that the attitude of Venizelos was courageous and correct.

Then came an interval pending the arrival of a fresh telegram. Churchill raised the question of rubber export duties, and we smiled at the theories of this old-time Free Trader, who however defended himself by saying that in this matter he was dealing with practical realities.

After repose from tension the Angora reply arrived, quite conciliatory in tone and wholly inconsistent with Rumbold's last despatch, sent off at 4 p.m. showing fresh claims from the Turks which Franklin Bouillon is evidently supporting.

A word or two with P.M. after the cabinet. He seemed very low – said it was a dangerous situation for the Greeks. Venizelos had always said the Turks were untrustworthy in conference – 'Tarks' he calls them – and he, the P.M., was not surprised at these fresh claims. He said he had always been alarmed since Kemal refused to attend the Mudania conference, sending Ishmid in his place, and Ferid and Fluad, and (smiling) Haroun al Rashid. Certainly the P.M. has a droll touch, and we laughed too.

443

The fall of Lloyd George

Second cabinet after dinner. A terribly hashed message arrived from Harington – corrupted in transmission, and I imagine hopelessly confused in the original text. He is quite a good soldier, but has never been taught to read English, and his account of the situation was turgid and obscure. We get no picture of Mudania except that he is surrounded by intrigues, they are trying to lay traps for him and F. Bouillon as usual is behaving with scandalous duplicity. At one point the mutilation of the message amused us. 'Franklin Bouillon,' it said, 'has twisted the Turks into————', (two groups undecipherable). It was a funny and unconscious remark about their tortuous behaviour.

Nothing could be done on such a message. We adjourned soon after midnight, having despatched a message to say that Harington (at this moment conferring with Rumbold at Constantinople) is not to return to Mudania until fresh instructions are received. The only satisfactory feature is that the French and Italian generals are supporting Harington loyally, though how long will F. Bouillon allow his man to do so?

6 OCTOBER 1922

Friday. At ten this morning Peel, Boscawen, Baldwin, Worthington-Evans, and I attended a private conference at George Curzon's house. This informal talk took place at Boscawen's suggestion, he being particularly frightened lest we get rushed into a war to save the Greeks. This would never be tolerated by the country. As it is we are blamed for having gone too far already.

New telegrams despatched at all hours of the night and early morning have arrived. The really serious thing is that Charpy, the French general, has received instructions from Paris that he is authorised to sign an agreement which varies the terms of the Paris agreement of the 23rd. All pretence at a united allied policy disappears. What are we to do – are we to defend the Straits single-handed, defend the Greeks and fight the Turks alone? That is the central issue.

Curzon depressed. A.J.B. just back and attended last night's cabinet. He hasn't read a telegram for weeks, but made rather a confident pro-Greek pronouncement. Curzon thinks that this alliance will stiffen Lloyd George whose case has been weakening, and that we shall be asked to keep the Turks out of Thrace until some civil administration under civilised powers can be established ad interim. I said the only chance of a solution lay in a personal interview between Curzon and Poincaré – rather a brutal thing to suggest – but Poincaré must be brought right up against the realities – a definite and perhaps irremediable breach of the entente. Poincaré at least must be told in precise words that his refusal to cooperate in putting the Paris agreement into effect, means that the Turks will get into Europe. We can't stop them alone. He refuses to help and the immediate result will be the transference of war from Asia to Europe. Where will it end? I urged that we should not abandon Constantinople until the last minute.

After our talk Peel said he hoped no member of the cabinet would resign without warning him, and giving him the chance to do the same if necessary. Otherwise we

444

may hear of resignations, and the Secretary of State for India continuing a member of an anti-Turk cabinet. The results in India might be serious.

11.0 a.m. cabinet. Telegrams read.

I suddenly became conscious of a rather sudden change of temperament. I don't quite know how or when it began, at least I cannot remember whether the Prime Minister's final acknowledgment that we could no longer hope to save the Greeks, came before or after a cross-examination of Mond.

Last night Boscawen had said that we could not fight for the Greeks. P.M. good-humouredly pressed him, and Boscawen *rather* indicated that we should at least try to prevent the Turks crossing into Europe. This morning I heard Mond booming like an anaemic aeroplane – P.M. asked him straight out if he would fight to keep the Turks out of Europe. Mond said, 'Certainly not. We can't keep them out even if we want to.'

Lloyd George put up no fight. Balfour didn't do so either. On the contrary he said that although history would probably condemn us for letting the Turk back into Europe, we are not in a position to prevent it single-handed. In other words Kemal must be allowed to pursue the Greeks into Thrace. In that case, said Lloyd George, the Greeks must be allowed to bring their ships back into the Sea of Marmora. If we show neutrality toward the Turk we must equally do so to the Greeks. Nobody dissented.

It was a curious situation, which I entirely failed to analyse. Churchill who has been a fire-eater contented himself with a few grumbles about humiliation. F.E. who likewise has been bellicose took the opportunity (suggested to him by W. Evans) of saying that Lord Curzon ought to go to Paris. He did this with some *empressement*. I wondered if he thought the compliment (for such in appearance it is, though undoubtedly cruel to George C. who is much too ill for such journeys)[40] might serve as an *amende* for some harsh things he has recently said.

Anyhow it was agreed that Curzon should leave by the two o'clock boat, see Poincaré tonight, and tell him the full import of his treachery. Yes, said Ll. G., and remind him that the Treaty of Versailles may be put into the fire too.

Something has happened to account for this singular turn of the wheel. The telegrams from Constantinople do not explain it. Has the P.M. the idea that the

---

[40] The strain imposed on Curzon by such meetings is shown in a story told by Francis Humphrys, an Indian administrator who became ambassador in Kabul (diary, 20 November 1939). He once got a message from Curzon, asking him to go immediately to Carlton Gardens. This was at one o'clock in the morning. He dressed, went there, was let in by George himself, who said that next morning he had to go to Paris to meet his arch-enemy Poincaré. He was worried at the prospect, was already tired out, but had to do two or three hours more work before he could go to bed for a brief rest before his departure. Would Humphrys very kindly talk to him, say for an hour, to break the chain of his anxieties – a talk about India would be welcome, say about the North-West Provinces. So they talked together, and Curzon took his full share of the discussion. After an hour they parted, Curzon thanking Humphrys very cordially, saying he felt calm, would finish his writing, would sleep well and be more than prepared to argue with the small-minded and pernickety Poincaré.

The fall of Lloyd George

Greeks can really put up a big fight in Thrace, or (I whisper it to myself) are we on the verge of sensational resignations from the cabinet?

From 3 to 5 p.m. I sat upon the Estimates Committee of the cabinet. Horne and W. Evans there. The former has shown himself a close ally of the P.M. but evidently is not seriously disturbed by this morning's decision. Horne is determined to introduce next year's budget; and the results of our economy committee, so far as they go, are v. promising. Of course this Eastern crisis involves serious supplementaries. Horne is a cheery cove, not very efficient as a financier, but none the less a hard-headed Scotsman full of good qualities. Rumour says he would like a judicial appointment, but still more a rich wife. He spends all his leisure in society and dancing. Old Mrs Horne (above eighty years of age I believe) was presented to the Queen at one of the Buckingham Palace garden parties. It was expected that the Queen would make some charming compliment to the old lady on her brilliant son. 'I hear, Mrs Horne, that your son is an excellent dancer.'

7 OCTOBER 1922

The first thing I see in this morning's paper is that Harington is at Mudania, though we told him to remain at Constantinople. Later on his telegram explained that he had pledged himself to return, and was unable to stay behind, though whether he has actually been in the conference chamber is not clear. His telegram is obscure on the point.

Bonar Law writes to *The Times* this morning to say that we cannot act as policemen for the whole world; that if our allies desert us, we must withdraw, but in that case we are justified in following the American example of concentrating on our own affairs. In other words France must be careful. It is a remarkable letter in its effect rather than striking in its form, and will exercise a good deal of influence. Substantially it reflects the broad opinion of the cabinet.

Cabinet summoned at 2.30, actually began at 2.45. A message from Harington said that Ismid Pasha is in a more reasonable frame of mind. Long discussion on Curzon's reports of his talks with Poincaré. The latter seems to have been a little alarmed at Curzon's emphasis, and prospects have accordingly improved. At 3.30 a message from Curzon was read out, pressing for an answer at once, as the telephone message said that Poincaré leaves for the country at 4 p.m.!

Austen Chamberlain rather tactlessly exclaimed, 'Oh, this is tit-for-tat for that Sunday visit to Chequers' – which drew Ll. G. who assured us that there was all the difference in the world. He had secured Poincaré's assent to his drive to Chequers that afternoon, whereas now Poincaré is off to Eastern France, not for an afternoon, but far from any possibility of recall. When was Curzon's message sent? The P.M. said the French play tricks with our messages – jam our wireless, block our telephones, listen in – at Spa and at Genoa their contrivances were notorious. Then he said that he had just received information (from whom not stated) that one of our people went to the F.O. in Paris (? yesterday afternoon or today) and saw upon the under-secretary's table a note headed 'Telephone conversation between Lord and

Lady Curzon.' I cannot imagine George talking high politics on the telephone to Grace Abounding! But as the conversation was probably about his movements, it was presumably thought worth while to tap it! This old trick of confusing our messages adds to our difficulty – but why don't we jam their wires?

Meanwhile there were one or two rather important moments. Boscawen yesterday had said in effect what Bonar Law writes this morning. The P.M. asked questions: today Mond took the same line. The P.M. cross-examined him, and finally reached the point of saying that if we let the Turks into Thrace at once before the Greeks had fully evacuated, and before the Kemalist government had been established, how would order be preserved? 'What does it matter if order is kept by the Turks or not?'

It was said so abruptly as to give one quite a shock. What does Mond care if the Greeks are massacred was the inference, but he says things in such a caricature of a voice that he always provokes mirth at my end of the table. The P.M. could not help laughing, for the sounds that utter from Mond's guttural larynx are always droll: yet one felt instinctively that the P.M. realised for the first time that British interests must take precedence of all others.

At 4.15 we broke off and walked into the garden, an interval which allowed some telegrams to be drafted, and perhaps tempers to cool, for there had been several bellicose outbursts from Churchill and F.E. who resented Boscawen's suggestion that Curzon should be given a freer hand. The P.M. was calm and collected throughout the meeting.

Walked to Carlton Gardens with A.J.B. who was in a very sentimental mood.

Second cabinet 9.30 p.m. Very desultory talk about messages from Paris. Our telegram to him, suggesting three additions to his provisional agreement with Poincaré, was acknowledged. He said that Poincaré having left for the Vosges (disregarding our request to await the cabinet deliberations) he had communicated our message (from which he by no means dissented) to Peretti del Rocca, the under-secretary. He had telephoned it. Peretti replied that it was *'entendu et bien compris.'* What do these words mean, in relation to a telephone message, and spoken by a man without executive authority? Churchill said that *entendu* meant agreement. I said no, in such a connection it must mean 'correctly heard'. Eyre Crowe gave the verdict against my interpretation.

There was a sense of relief that Poincaré has been brought up to scratch. Gradually a feeling of self-congratulation began to arise. The P.M. in rather a provocative sort of way seemed ready to challenge anybody who criticised our policy, confident that our efforts to keep the freedom of the Straits, to prevent a fresh series of massacres, and finally to confine the war to Asia, would make a deep appeal to public sentiment. Worthington-Evans who had addressed a private meeting of his supporters this afternoon said he was convinced that the country would approve our policy, which even though unpopular is right. Then F.E. outlined a speech he would make on any platform to any democratic audience. Churchill followed suit. I was disgusted at this assumption that all our troubles are

The fall of Lloyd George

passed. I wish I had said so – for in hurried a secretary with a new telegram from Harington to say that 3,000 Turkish infantry had invaded the Ismid zone. It brought the spouters back to realities.

After the cabinet, some of us went to Austen Chamberlain's room – Fisher, A.J.B., Boscawen, Maurice Hankey.[41] We gossiped for nearly an hour. A.J.B., backed up by Fisher, was very strong about our defective system of publicity. They seemed to think that the Paris press, indeed the world press as a whole, do us so little justice because they are ill-informed. In point of fact it is because we don't make it worth their while. Our publicity costs I think £14,000 or so. The French spend £400,000 – how can we compete? though I am never sure that these newspaper propagandists don't overreach themselves.

. . . I again walked home with A.J.B. – in a very detached frame of mind – talking about the crisis as though it raised some nice problem of philosophy. It is singular how aloof he stands from the workaday world – he criticised Lloyd George for not reading despatches, though he himself was quite ignorant of Bonar Law's letter which is far more important than most of the despatches we receive. I am nervous about the situation, most of all about Constantinople. If we retire, as we contemplate doing, there may be massacres beside which those of Smyrna will pale into insignificance. Yet we can't allow ourselves to be besieged there, while many of the French troops are worthless levies from Senegal, who can only be guaranteed to fight against Christians.

8 OCTOBER 1922
Sunday. Violent attack in the *Observer* on the Prime Minister.

9 OCTOBER 1922
The *Daily Mail* article amazes me . . . Alone in the *Daily Telegraph* of London papers does one find a balanced stream of facts – and in the *Chronicle*.

Cabinet at 4.0 p.m.

George Curzon expounded the situation for forty-five minutes. He is too long. He told us of the extraordinary claim advanced by Poincaré, e.g. that Charpy should be at liberty to vary decisions agreed by the three allies. Against such procedure George protested vigorously. Poincaré was angry, screamed a good deal, and when George imprudently smiled at some extravagant pretension, Poincaré turned at him and whistled '*vous me riez au nez*'. But there was no doormat crisis on this occasion. Poincaré was described by Clemenceau as '*lâche et violent*' which describes the combination of obstinacy and chicane so typical of him.

Curzon announced that he was prepared to attend the Peace Conference. Kemal suggests Smyrna – Galli suggests Taormina in place of Venice – Curzon himself would prefer Scutari. It is suggested that there may be two synchronous conferences, one to revise the peace treaty, the other to deal with freedom of the Straits.

[41] Secretary to the cabinet 1919–38.

448

10 OCTOBER 1922
11.30 a.m. cabinet.

The P.M. announced his intention of making a speech, and speaking his mind in the process thereof. On Saturday Hamar Greenwood protested against our leaving the case unanswered – for we seem to have vouchsafed no reply to the malignant and confounded allegations which are the central feature of the newspapers. Lloyd George seemed disinclined to defend himself before parliament meets, preferring to let Asquith and Co. lead an attack, then to smash them up hip and thigh. I suspect however that Garvin's onslaught has vexed the little man, and he no longer consents to let things go by default. He will probably dumbfound his critics. By the way I notice that the charge of amateur diplomacy seems to touch him on the raw. He quite brightened up at the prospect of getting back into the fighting line.

Then a discussion over agriculture. Boscawen startled us the other day by talking about a subvention of £14,000,000. That scheme is now abandoned, but there are lots more – all received a hostile reception, and Boscawen told us frankly that if he cannot persuade the cabinet to help him, his position will become so intolerable as to impel him to resign.

The P.M. answered that he too was in a difficulty. Not only the farmers but the miners too demand subsidies. Each group claims a deputation – how can he give to the farmers and refuse the miners. The dilemma is indeed embarrassing.

Then by one of those odd aberrations which come across the cabinet we found ourselves (apropos of finance) discussing education. Ll. G. never takes any trouble to keep the cabinet orderly – he is as indolent as Asquith in this matter, and we had a merry ten minutes during which everybody, led by the P.M., attacked Fisher who was quite abashed by this sudden and unexpected outburst. Everybody laughed a good deal. One thing said by the P.M. remains in my mind: 'You are teaching Somerset boys to become Londoners.' What a lot of truth underlies this paradox – which Fisher contested with tearful sincerity.

'Yes, but what about the farmers and labourers?' came from Boscawen in his nasal accent – he was soon tired of the diversion about schools: what about agriculture? Well, we appointed a committee, and this will at least hold up Boscawen's resignation for a week.

From 3 to 5 p.m. in Austen Chamberlain's room to discuss the party situation. Present Austen, F.E., Horne, W. Evans, Curzon, Leslie Wilson,[42] Boscawen, Peel, Lee, A.J.B. I hate these discussions about leadership and electioneering. A crisis is imminent, and it is unavoidable. The problem of our party is to shed Lloyd George, the problem of ministers, how to keep him. Most of us v. anxious to maintain the alliance and to work under his leadership. Austen, F.E., Lee said they would be no party to inviting him to resign. On the other hand A.J.B. seemed to think an early election essential in order to anticipate the hostile vote expected at the National Union conference on 14 November. George Curzon said that a dissolution now,

[42] Joint Chief Whip (Unionist) in the coalition, 1921–2.

when affairs are so critical, would produce immense complications, and would weaken the country. Stanley Baldwin however took the strong line the other way – said Ll. G. was the albatross round our neck and we ought to get rid of him. Boscawen at first shared this view, but ultimately withdrew. I confined myself to deprecating an election while war trembles in the balance.

A very unsatisfactory though quite good-humoured symposium.

5 p.m. cabinet. Messages from Angora not having arrived, and no news from Mudania either, we quickly adjourned.

11 OCTOBER 1922

5.0 p.m. Committee about agriculture. Boscawen verges on resignation, but I tell him that the moment is inopportune to resign on a departmental question. The press is hot with date of an election and the prospective breach of the Coalition.

I have a great belief in the recuperative power of Lloyd George: and if only he was in the position to blurt out the truth about Poincaré and F. Bouillon, the reaction in favour of our policy would be instantaneous.

12 OCTOBER 1922

The Mudania Pact is signed. I think we owe all the credit to Curzon and Rumbold, assisted by the shrewd common sense of Harington. Rumbold has been invaluable in keeping us warned and informed, Harington not being able to do this.

... Press much intrigued about Austen's speech tomorrow and the P.M.'s on Saturday in Lancashire.

13 OCTOBER 1922

Longish meeting of cabinet sub-committee on agricultural depression. We drew up a report which contains small consolation to the farmers. The P.M. is by way of receiving a deputation on the subject next week – but will he?

... Read a fullish summary of Austen's speech at Birmingham. This is a declaration of loyalty to Lloyd George and the Coalition. It is difficult to see what else he could have said; but it won't pacify our men.

15 OCTOBER 1922

Sunday. Back to London. Read the P.M.'s speech with some care. My first impression was favourable. His reception was enthusiastic, and my eye caught the passages in which he showed the inconsistencies of Grey, the follies of the Northcliffe press, most of all where he trounced that pompous ass Lord Gladstone. On the other hand his criticism of the French, though well-deserved, will arouse resentment.

After dinner George Curzon sent for me urgently. I spent three quarters of an hour with him from 10.15 p.m. onwards. Things have developed. He is v. anxious, and angry too.

Imprimis – he was invited to a dinner party this evening at (?) Churchill's house, to meet the P.M. and his principal colleagues. It had been practically decided that the final decision in favour of an immediate dissolution was to be taken there, and to be announced tomorrow morning. Curzon declined to go. He gathered that he was alone in opposing the idea, and thought it unlikely his objections would prevail. So he asked Austen C. to see him – the interview took place, and he, George C., told Chamberlain that if an election is sprung on us, he will resign – some of his friends will do the same, and in giving up the seals of office he will make a considered protest, showing the dangers of the situation, and the intolerable intrigues of the P.M. who has made the position of the Foreign Secretary well nigh impossible. George C. impressed these views on Austen for two hours this afternoon. I cannot believe they will fail to exercise considerable influence. We are now reaching the stage where personalities and prejudices may play a supreme part in the political drama.

Let me give three examples of the complaints of the F.O. against the P.M. Recently a secret communication passed between the P.M. and Roumania. F.O. knew nothing about it until they received the news from their secret agencies. Meanwhile the F.O. was blissfully discussing similar matters through our ministers at Bucharest. The same kind of thing has happened with Italy when negotiations have been begun behind the back of the F.O.

Finally France. The P.M. settled to send a communication to Poincaré! How was he to do it? He chose Derby as his emissary, and Derby went to Paris. Curzon learned all about it, again through private sources, wrote a vigorous protest to Derby, asked the latter to see him and then learned that it was all true. Derby had gone to Paris, but only consented to doing so on the express understanding that the P.M. gave full information to Curzon. This he failed or forgot to do. Curzon mentioned his grievance – Ll. G. gave a half-hearted and rather casual apology.

I think George C. expected me to promise to resign if he does so. I saw no special reason to make conditional promises, as the situation will vary from hour to hour.

I should add that Curzon's case against dissolution is largely based on the difficulties of the forthcoming Turkish conference. He means to attend in person, and feels sure he is the only living man who can give us a reasonable peace. He expects nothing very grand, at best, and says that our chances of getting out with even a decent success, are gravely prejudiced, by the unfortunate language addressed to France and Turkey by the P.M.

16 OCTOBER 1922

Monday. This morning's papers don't announce an immediate election, so I presume Curzon's message to the P.M. was not without effect. At four a conference at 11 Downing St discussed the problem. Present Austen, Horne, Baldwin, W. Evans, Curzon, Lee, Boscawen, Peel, A.J.B., and Lord Chancellor.

Austen began – rather on the line of his Birmingham speech. Baldwin indicated pretty clearly that as Chamberlain won't abandon Lloyd George, he, Baldwin, must abandon Chamberlain. Boscawen rather in the same direction. Curzon repeating his old objection to dissolution, Austen kept recurring to the fact that a split means an immediate election, that if we drift on for another week without a split, there will be a dissolution because we simply fall into decay. An election is therefore inevitable.

Chamberlain said something to the effect that we should stand as Unionists, not as Coalitionists, and settle a new government after the polling, if indeed we have enough members to control the situation. I seized on this as the most important new fact – something that has quite recently emerged. I pressed that Chamberlain should make this clear to the further gathering of cabinet ministers and under-secretaries.

This meeting was at five at Whitehall Gardens. All ministers present except three – and of the three Ancaster[43] alone was not accounted for. Chamberlain spoke shortly, very gravely. Amery[44] voiced the views of the under-secretaries. Why ever did they entrust this task to him – so clumsy and tactless – one remembers his fearful blundering when he had to speak for the Admiralty in Lord Lee's absence.

Anyhow Amery began with quite a fair statement of his views, and then, to our horror, produced a paper which he read out as the final and considered statement of the views of sixteen of his colleagues. It was an ultimatum. Chamberlain said he profoundly regretted that this statement of policy should have been crystallised before his opinions had been heard. Ernest Pollock threw himself into the breach, explaining that he had certainly never meant to present an ultimatum – his opinion in fact coinciding with Chamberlain on the general issue – and that the formula was only advanced as a basis for discussion. Pollock saved the situation – momentarily. I still think that the undertaking given by Austen that our men shall stand as Conservatives, uncommitted, and that they shall not preclude the idea of a coalition after the polling, ought to satisfy our friends. It is simple and straightforward, does not prejudge the future, and should be welcomed if it prevents a schism on the eve of an election.

Some dissented – wanted in effect a pledge that never again should Lloyd George be our leader. The controversy really pivots around his mercurial personality, and were he out of the way most of our troubles, and the central force both of our strength and weakness would disappear. Quite a good-humoured meeting. Nobody lost his temper or spoke a harsh word.

17 OCTOBER 1922

Quiet day politically, but much *parlementation* going on behind the scenes.

18 OCTOBER 1922

At the Office of Works most of the day, cleaning off a number of routine questions, so as to leave an unembarrassed slate for my successor to write on.

I hear that Lloyd George is in great spirits, tremendously encouraged by his

---

[43] Parliamentary secretary to the Board of Agriculture and Fisheries 1921–2 and 1922–4.
[44] Parliamentary and financial to the Admiralty 1921–2; First Lord of the Admiralty 1922–4.

reception at the Port of London function – a huge assembly of solid business people who cheered him to the echo. He is so often told that he has lost the confidence of businessmen, that commerce condemns him – yet here we find a very different frame of mind.

Peter Sanders[45] resigns – a pity I think, and premature, for he was absent from yesterday's conference at a moment when consoling conditions were offered.

Salisbury addressed a hundred people in his dining room.

19 OCTOBER 1922

Thursday. Thursday is always my lucky day, so I am the less concerned by the fact that together with my colleagues, I was censured by the party meeting at the Carlton this morning. Pretyman moved a resolution, which by general consent was constructed as a motion hostile to Chamberlain, and this was carried by 186 to 87 votes. The figures were decisive.

We assembled at eleven – a thoroughly good-humoured crowd. We were just about to begin when a waitress advanced with two immense brandies and soda, to lubricate Chamberlain and F.E. Much cheering: also a good deal of merriment when word went round that Harry Chaplin, who was furious at peers not being invited, had settled to assert his right to attend, and was bent on invading us, but unluckily had been told that the meeting was at 2.30!

Austen, who spoke from 11.5 to 11.35, began by reading a letter from George Curzon on this very subject, recording his protest against peers being excluded, he of course having been invited as a member of the government and therefore entitled to hear his commendation or commination as the case might be. It was not right to send such a letter without consulting other peer members of the government – eight of us were there, Balfour, Lee, Birkenhead, besides myself, Onslow,[46] Ancaster, and one or two others. It put us in a false position, especially as the letter reached Chamberlain only a few minutes before we began, and he was unable to reply or to tell us. Anyhow it put Curzon into a favourable atmosphere of Diehardism.

Chamberlain's speech was grave, but very rigid and unbending: needlessly so. Had the P.M. been asked to revise it, I feel sure he would have smoothed off some of the harsh and uncompromising angles. As it was the speech left no exit for those who sincerely wished to find some escape from passing a vote of censure.

Stanley Baldwin followed – gulping and hiccoughing a lot of good sense – no hesitation in denouncing the coalition and Lloyd George in particular – a clear declaration of war. Frank Mildmay, Pretyman, George Lane-Fox,[47] dear old Craik, and one or two others spoke – then Bonar Law. He too condemned the coalition. He looked ill, I thought – his knees more groggy than ever, his face more

[45] Sir R. A. Sanders, Under-Secretary for War; usually called 'Peter' by the diarist.
[46] Parliamentary secretary to the Ministry of Health 1921–2 and 1922–3.
[47] Parliamentary secretary to the Mines Department of the Board of Trade, 1922–4 and 1924–8.

worn with distress. His voice so weak that people quite close to him had to strain their ears – but his matter was clear and distinctly put. After his speech the issue was unmistakable and he was hailed as the Leader of the Party. A.J.B. made a delightful speech, so mellow and genial, full of picturesque touches, but too subtle to count. Then we voted. A few more words of dignified adieu from Austen, and the meeting broke up. The last impression I had was Steel-Maitland standing on a chair and bawling compliments at Austen. Everybody thought this a very stupid demonstration from such a quarter.

I stayed to lunch at the Club, and discussed the future with a lot of Diehard friends. I was a little surprised at their vague outlook. James Hope[48] on the other hand, shrewd fellow, is under no illusions, and much regrets that his advice to adjourn the meeting till this afternoon was disregarded.

At seven I went to 11 Downing St and had a long talk with Austen, F.E., Horne, and several others. I learned that the crowd outside the Carlton gave some of our men a most violent and hostile reception. Austen was well hooted. I suppose the 'Clean Government' gang has really persuaded certain sections of the public that we are corrupt as well as dishonest and incompetent. F.E. says he has sent a vigorous protest to George Curzon for that letter to the Carlton meeting. In this he is fully justified. Curzon's attitude was indefensible, and partly a dodge to curry favour with the new ministers.

Dined at Carlton with Jix, J. G. Butcher, Burton Chadwick, Henderson and other Diehards. They seem to have forgotten all about the obligation to pass the Irish Bill early in December – and as fifteen or more byelections will be necessary before the government can be effectively completed, very little time is available – especially as the Irish Bill may arouse criticism in both houses. Meanwhile Lloyd George resigned this afternoon – recommended the King to send for Bonar Law – and the latter asked to consult his doctor! He should have made sure about his intestines before making that speech, and I suppose several days will elapse before we know exactly how we stand. He ought to have formed his government tomorrow.

20 OCTOBER 1922

Friday. Willie Peel was absent from yesterday's meeting and came to consult me. His inclination would have been to sign the manifesto printed this morning. I however tried to persuade him that if he is invited to retain his Indian post he ought to do so. He has done well. He is gradually re-establishing confidence, he has a good understanding with the Viceroy. A change of office must mean, at any rate in the eyes of India, a change of policy and will probably be interpreted as a reassertion of the O'Dwyer attitude. Such a contingency however ill-founded should be avoided. I fancy Bonar Law will be anxious to retain as many of the old gang as possible, so I hope he will ask Peel to continue. On the other hand I recommended him to decline

[48] Deputy Speaker 1921–3

an exchange of office – if for instance he were offered the Admiralty: that more than anything else would suggest a new policy in India; and were the new Secretary of State to differ from Peel, the position of the latter would quickly become impossible.[49]

Willie had been to see George Curzon who thinks and cares about nothing except his own position. He did not even condescend to ask Peel's views, confining himself to a disquisition on the Turkish situation, and the imperative necessity of his returning to office to solve it. Curzon has all the threads in his hands, nobody else can gather them up. I fancy Curzon is himself immersed and immured in those threads, tied up with all his mass of detail, and unable to see the big points as he pays so much attention to the details. I rather fancy that a new man would leave the subordinate problems to his officers and concentrate on the great issues – seize the big ropes and leave the little strings to others: but that isn't George's way.[50]

Jack Gilmour came to see me. He says George Younger is in a fright about Scotland, and furious that Jack supports Chamberlain. George offered Jack the Secretaryship for Scotland – twice! It was loyal of him to refuse it, for the offer must have been very tempting – however he did so – and any good whip should act in that way, for support of the Chief is his first duty. That sentiment survives in my mind. I see indications of quarrelling upon the cash and organisation. The Scottish members are independent of London, and a large majority of the Unionists are anxious to maintain the Coalition understanding.

At 4.30 to Downing St to tea with Austen, F.E., Lee, Robert Horne, Worthington-Evans. A lot of desultory talk and gossip. It emerged that F.E. has no intention whatever of forming a centre policy, in combination with Churchill or anybody else. I imagine that the Co. Libs don't intend to do so either.

B.L. is calling a Unionist meeting on Monday, to confirm him as Leader – at the Hotel Cecil of all ill-omened places! We don't propose to attend and be humiliated as many of our friends would wish us to be. Having got his mandate, B.L. will tell the King he accepts office, and as he will have had ample time to make his combinations, the ministerial lists should be published the same evening. It will be an interesting document, and I see no reason why the names should not be highly attractive – so long indeed as Beaverbrook is left out. By the way the latter is interesting himself in the new ministry. He has twice telephoned to F.E., acting on behalf of B.L., pressing him to keep the Woolsack. F.E. refused. The second time he got the message he replied, 'No, I won't consider the Lord Chancellorship. I positively refuse to hold that office. In fact there is only one office I would agree to hold, and that I fear is no longer available.'

'What is it?' eagerly asked Beaverbrook down the telephone. 'The Archbishopric of Canterbury,' replied F.E. and clapped on the receiver!

Several times during our talk there emerged signs of malicious glee at the

[49] Viscount Peel remained at the India Office under Bonar Law and Baldwin, 1922–4.
[50] Curzon remained Foreign Secretary, 1922–4.

The fall of Lloyd George

difficulties confronting Bonar Law. I can understand on the part of those who think themselves cruelly injured. F.E. in particular is smarting under the sense of personal rebuff. His polemical nature is not mollified by having been hooted outside the Carlton Club and at one moment he made an incidental remark that he did not speak at that meeting because he was afraid that he might have influenced the voting . . . His real meaning was that after what had passed he does not contemplate with any regret any mess B.L. may inherit or create for himself . . .

He and one or two others seemed to think that B.L. will find the task of forming a government more onerous than people imagine. I recollect that we said the same thing when Campbell-Bannerman formed his administration in 1906 . . . We must not forget the number of competent and hungry Conservatives who have no part in the Coalition.

22 OCTOBER 1922

Sunday. Lloyd George has made an extraordinary series of speeches – five or six at railway stations en route for Leeds, and at this town a wholly retrospective speech. Many compliments to our men, a hit or two at the Carlton Club with references to Mayfair and Belgravia thrown in – but no lead to his supporters, except a general affirmation of Liberalism and Free Trade . . . The little man has a long campaign before him. He is right during its early stages to concentrate on the past, and to dispel some of the ridiculous errors which have long thriven uncontradicted. Moreover B.L. hasn't spoken, and it is obvious tactics to await the new ministerial programme . . .

I spent several hours at the Carlton, talking to various M.P.s – Jix[51] says that if he doesn't get a good job his support of B.L. can be discounted. Johnnie Baird[52] the same view in more modest strains. Murray[53] the Lord Advocate is in a quandary. He is a co-signatory of Chamberlain's manifesto or apologia, but B.L. wants him to continue in his present post.

On getting home at eight o'clock, I found a message asking me to dine with Lloyd George. I went (much against Connie's wishes). The first thing I heard was that B.L. had sent a message to Ll. G. to say that if the Leeds speech had been delivered at Manchester the previous Saturday, he, B.L., would not have made the remarks at the Carlton which brought the Coalition to an end. What an amazing message. I said of course there is some mistake in transmission. On the contrary, said the P.M., it was not a telephone conversation, but an official message personally conveyed by one of the cabinet secretariat now attached to B.L.! We rubbed our eyes. Is it an aside, a misapprehension, a joke, or a trap? Nobody offered any intelligible explanation. Even B.L.'s habit of talking aloud and blurting out unwelcome truths

[51] Joynson-Hicks received only junior office from Bonar Law, 1922–3, being promoted to the cabinet by Baldwin in May 1923.

[52] Baird became Minister of Transport, outside the cabinet, 1922–4.

[53] Murray did not join the new ministry.

can't account for an observation which has no foundation in logic or in fact.

It was an odd gathering. P.M. (who gave us a capital dinner), F.E. who came very late, Atholl,[54] Worthington-Evans, McCurdy,[55] George Gibbs, Seely, Arthur Lee, Ernest Pollock, Ian Macpherson, Jack Gilmour, Murray, Horne, A.J.B., Freddie Guest. Austen Chamberlain in the country.

What were we there for? I soon perceived that it was not a mere complimentary dinner offered to old Unionist colleagues. It was a mixed assembly – Jack Seely was right in saying that its composition was unique. So it was, and uncomfortably so, for I found that we were invited to take counsel together on a new situation which has arisen. Bonar Law finds it difficult to form his administration without the help of certain signatories of the Chamberlain memo – the men who were censured last Thursday. It appears that he requires us to furnish:

2 law officers for England (Pollock, Scott)
1 ditto for Scotland (Murray)
1 Secretary for Scotland (Jack Gilmour)

This really is an astonishing situation, and shows that F.E. guessed correctly the other night. Our present English law officers are nothing very remarkable, but there would be a general scandal if they were replaced by men like Marshall Hall or Rawlinson. Douglas Hogg[56] is competent but he is uncertain of election. In Scotland the only available lawyer in parliament is Macquisten[57] who is generally looked upon as a farceur. Likewise there is no Scottish Unionist who could become Secretary for Scotland except Jack Gilmour, unless they appointed a peer, which would overweight the balance of ministers in the House of Lords. Moreover there seems some question of getting a signatory[58] to act as Home Secretary as well. B.L. is clearly afraid of his ministers failing to return or to secure seats at the dissolution. And this was the problem we were called upon to discuss – at the dinner table of the P.M., and each of us buttressed up against a Radical. Surely these domestic matters should have been first discussed among ourselves – they scarcely require the advice of our Radical colleagues!

We ate heartily. F.E. arrived after eating heartily elsewhere. He began to talk. His prolixity was unpardonable. He took a strong line against our men consenting to serve under B.L. unless the latter gave most explicit pledges to safeguard the minority Unionists, and likewise to refrain from fighting Co. Libs. F.E. actually reduced the formula to paper – drawn up like an affidavit, in such curt terms that B.L. would have smiled indulgently and then invited the messenger to leave his

[54] Lord Chamberlain 1921–2
[55] Coalition Liberal Chief Whip 1921–2
[56] Attorney-General 1922–4. Hall and Rawlinson were not given office.
[57] Frederick A. Macquisten (1870–1940), MP (Cons.) Glasgow Springburn 1918–22, Argyll 1922–40.
[58] Of Austen Chamberlain's manifesto. Bridgeman, an anti-coalition rebel, became Home Secretary.

house. After F.E., Pollock – tedious beyond words. Not very decided, but on the whole against co-operation. Then followed Murray the Lord Advocate, tedious and prolix like the other lawyers, but ending his remarks with a short and definite sentence that he did not see his way to continue in office. Then Tullibardine.[59] All I can say is that he was almost as turgid as the legists. His views were enlivened by scraps of recent conversation with the King, and if the Lord Chamberlain is a faithful reporter, all I can say is that his most Gracious Majesty must be as confused in diction as some of his ministers. Jack Gilmour, now a Lord of the Treasury, has been pressed by George Younger to become Secretary for Scotland. Jack seemed very anxious to make a deal to safeguard the Co. Libs. of Scotland, upon whose help we depend in many seats. Derby's speech foreshadowed such co-operation but one can never be quite sure that he isn't saying too much or too little. There was a good deal of desultory conversation, and Atholl had to be pulled down by his coattails to let A.J.B. have a chance of speaking. He, in turn, was terse, scornful, and very amusing.

Finally Ll. G. He made rather a curious little speech – one felt he was feeling his way: anxious at once to avoid all sources of friction with us, grateful for all the support our people have rendered during the last four years, yet at the same time bent on hitting back. He has long borne in silence the vulgar and ill-informed jeers of our gutter press, and feels quite justified in saying what he thinks, though hindered by our close association with the new government. However he made two points very clear. In the first place he will make no approach to the Wee Frees if we will support the Co. Libs. On this he was emphatic; he certainly does not mean to form a centre party either – and on this we agree with him.

Secondly he spoke of the influence of his Unionist friends – those who supported Chamberlain – on the fortunes of the Conservative party. Ll. G. evidently does not anticipate a strong Conservative victory – in other words some fresh combination may be necessary after the polling. 'A month hence your strength will be manifest – much greater, or rather more influential, than it is today. You will find you have saved your party.'

He repeated this in one form or another several times – but what the sequence of his argument was, I failed to gather.

'Am I dreaming?' whispered Jack Seely into my ear. I reminded him of a story of the late Duke of Devonshire who used to be fond of talking about dreams which came true. 'I once dreamed that I was addressing the House of Lords – I woke up, and would you believe it, I found I was actually doing so.'

Finally Worthington-Evans, all smiles, took up the parable. I shall be rude, he said: rude, crude, and brutal. Here is my difficulty: the Manchester speech of the P.M. was all right. At Leeds he dragged in Belgravia and Mayfair: that didn't matter: but two or three weeks hence – will this sort of compliment come dropping out? and what shall we say when challenged if we agree with the P.M.'s sophistries?

---

[59] The junior title of the Duke of Atholl.

The question was fair, and rather amused Lloyd George, who remarked that these impromptus were not quite so spontaneous as they appeared: some of them in fact required a great deal of preparation! and there followed some sort of pledge to be as discreet as possible...

The last item on our agenda was the arrangement of a weekend at Whittingehame – Horne, the P.M., (and F.E. anxious to partake) after Lloyd George's forthcoming meeting at Glasgow. I came away asking myself the question which repeated itself throughout the evening – 'Who organised this convivial gathering?'

23 OCTOBER 1922

Monday... I often pick up Buckmaster[60] walking along Rotten Row to the H. of L., while I am taking my exercise. This morning I tackled him about the election. He says B.L. will get a majority. Of course Buckmaster dislikes Ll. G. so heartily that the wish is to some extent parent of the prediction: yet I was surprised at this opinion. Few of my friends share it, least of all B.L. himself... Meanwhile McKenna is to support our City candidate – here again dislike of the P.M. is not without influence.

24 OCTOBER 1922

I spent several hours at the Office of Works and gave farewell interviews to thirty officials, all and sundry from Lionel Earle to Sergeant Brereton, the senior messenger who in defiance of all departmental rules retains his post at the age of eighty-three. It was really quite a touching procession of good fellows. They have worked well and as time went on with ever-increasing loyalty and enthusiasm. At the outset I found myself at issue with certain branches, and I soon perceived that the matter had to be fought out. I seldom took action except where I was sure of my ground – bit by bit I gained their respect, then their confidence, finally their affection, and today I was rewarded by many expressions of gratitude – some of these men wept as they said goodbye.

Yesterday B.L. was duly elected Leader of the Party, and about 120 adherents of Austen Chamberlain dined together at the Victoria Hotel. I did not attend the former function. I am glad to have been at the latter, for Austen's speech justified his action and that of his co-signatories on high lines. A.J.B. also spoke, perhaps with less of his customary hesitation than I ever remember, and one or two of his remarks cannot fail to bring home to the Diehards – the authors of the disruption of the Coalition – how bitterly he resents the crisis. 'This is not merely a question of how gentlemen should behave in a given set of circumstances...' The gathering was an encouragement to many men who were afraid of being fired out of the party. At one moment there was a danger of proscription, and even now the *Morning Post* would not take it amiss were we all thrust aside. The result however of keeping one

[60] Lord Chancellor 1915–16

little group together, stating boldly that nobody shall drive us from our party, and showing moreover that if provoked we can be dangerous, has brought Malcolm Fraser[61] to heel, and our candidates are not to be persecuted. All to the good.

Tonight I attended a very different kind of symposium, a dinner given by Sir George Younger at the Athenaeum. I talked a good deal to Lord Justice Younger[62] and about the P.M., the retiring one I mean ... In early days when Ll. G. was a small provincial solicitor he was accustomed to consult Younger, then a struggling barrister. The lawsuits were of the most trumpery description – mean little disputes generally between members of one family. The Welsh are very quarrelsome people and enjoy litigation almost as much as the Scots: but whereas the latter go to law on minute questions of 'principle', the Welshman is generally hunting a £10 note. In those days, Ll. G. used to deal in very small affairs. Younger never picked him out as a man of conspicuous ability – in fact he did not make any particular impression, and in those days the scale of business was so meagre that Younger says Lloyd George must have long suffered from real indigence. His professional income was in fact negligible, while as an M.P. he had no salary, and must have had a severe struggle to keep body and soul together. It was then that he acquired a reputation for violence in controversy, a quality he has never discarded, though it is now mellowed by a strong sense of paradoxical humour, absent in those early days of effort and discouragement. Ll. G. has never forgotten the legal ally of his youth and never fails to give a warm greeting to Younger whenever they meet.

25 OCTOBER 1922

Went to Buckingham Palace to take leave of the King ... we had audiences one at a time. On general politics he said, 'We must be friends with everybody' – the kind of sophism one expects from Edward Grey – though he went on to say that we cannot break our word to Faisal and the dusky monarch who has just appeared from Transjordania.

A longish list of ministers is published this morning. I think Victor Cavendish[63] at the Colonial Office admirable, and his dry heavy good sense will be specially useful in relation to Ireland where he is greatly respected though but little known. Edward Wood to Education, Willie Bridgeman to Home Office both seem quite inadequate. Sanders to agriculture good, but his task desperate. Baldwin to Treasury fair, Derby to War Office fair, Salisbury as Lord President a rare contrast to A.J.B., but it was necessary to placate the Diehard element. There are too many peers in the cabinet – that reminds me of another peer – Novar to the Scottish Office – a lifelong Liberal who though reticent on political matters during the last year or two has never declared himself a Conservative. A truly amazing

---

[61] Chief party agent, 1920–23

[62] Robert Younger, first Baron Blanesburgh (1861–1946), holder of leading judicial offices 1915–37; brother of George Younger, the politician.

[63] Ninth Duke of Devonshire (1868–1938), Colonial Secretary 1922–4.

appointment showing our poverty in Scotland. While he joins us, and while Perks[64] and McKenna support our candidates in the City, there are still practical proofs of coalition!

Somehow I don't gather the impression that the new government is making a strong start. There is something drab and uninspiring about B. Law's appeal to our commercial instincts, and though he boasts of being the plain man, our position in the world cannot quite be judged on the principles of a chartered accountant . . . If as is rumoured the cabinet secretariat is abolished, the government will either neglect its work or find itself in a hopeless mess six weeks hence.

I said goodbye to many old friends this morning while waiting for our audiences . . . All of us seem to have an air of profound and unconcealable relief. Fisher says he feels like an undergraduate on the last day of his schools – a sense of impending and well-earned repose giving balm to his soul. For my part I regret the dislocation. My work interested me and I was not particularly fatigued. What I most fear is that what have been my relaxations will now become my occupations. Today I suppose is the first weekday since the summer of 1916 which I have not spent at some government office or other, and I shall not fail to miss and lament the feeling that I am no longer doing something which is necessary, and doing it well. I do not look forward to the easy-going existence which my few non-political avocations impose, though I confess that if I had £10,000, or, I will say, £5,000, to dabble about with among old books, china, furniture, engravings, and whatnots, I could spend very happy days. But at present no such squandermania is possible.

26 OCTOBER 1922

Leslie Wilson is reappointed Whip – but no minor ministerial post has been filled. This is odd . . . It is very unfair to Depts which are left without any minister in charge – Post Office, Pensions, Labour, Works – to mention a few where ministerial decisions are required every day.

At dinner Aston Webb was most interesting about the danger to St. Pauls Cathedral – far greater than I ever guessed. Arthur Balfour was enthralled by his account. What a wonderful man he is – one would never expect it, but he seems to know the exact colour of every great building in London – the exact degree of whiteness pertaining to every degree of Portland stone which he admires more than the most precious marble in the world. Aston Webb seemed astonished at Balfour's observation and memory . . . What a leisured life I am already leading!

27 OCTOBER 1922

Board meeting. Business certainly does show signs of improvement, but things are still v. precarious, and workpeople are suffering great hardships – with unexampled patience, notwithstanding the efforts of Communists to trade upon the industrial depression.

---

[64] Sir. R. W. Perks (1849–1934), MP (Lib.) 1892–1910 and leading Methodist.

The fall of Lloyd George

In Lancashire the impression I gathered was that many prominent men regret the untoward end of the coalition... The cabinet is going to curtail its own reading material – that at least I presume will result from abolishing the cabinet secretariat. B. Law announced this as the first of his reforms – an odd trumpery little prelude to a great campaign of economy. Two points are involved – one the cost, the other the allegation that the secretariat though tolerable in wartime is unconstitutional in peace. The first is at best a small affair, the second much exaggerated.

Curzon was always against Hanky and Co. as they did work that Curzon would have wished to direct through the Foreign Office – but he was apt to ignore the work done by the secretaries for the cabinet as a whole... Hankey so far as I saw never interfered with the cabinet in the least – all the allegations that he ran us are unfounded, though I dare say he had much influence on Ll. G. Hankey always seemed to me a man of exceptional ability, and his memory is prodigious. He knew exactly where to find one sentence in a pile of documents – though why he got a parliamentary vote of £25,000 in conjunction with the fighting soldiers and sailors, I never could make out.

I notice a legend in process of formation about George Curzon, based on a newspaper theory which is acquiring importance of fact, that he and he alone made a stand against the bellicose group of the cabinet. That such a group did exist cannot be denied, though they would claim that they only desired action because of the despairing and alarmist reports sent by Harington. In point of fact however, Curzon's views were those of the majority of the cabinet, though I don't think he knew it until some of us took pains to make it clear to him on 6 October, when I pressed him to pay his second visit to Poincaré. He is so self-centred that it never occurs to him that the opinion of others should be sought, while on the other hand he has always been susceptible to the pressure of others – of those who knew that nothing would induce him to resign office, except to forestall a general débâcle. He had well-founded grievances against Ll. G. who kept butting in and helping to run the F.O. in his own happy-go-lucky way. Curzon took all this persecution lying down. When Milner found Ll. G. trying to boss the Colonial Office, he told the P.M. that one or other must be Secretary of State, but not both, and the P.M. immediately saw reason. Milner would have left office had interference continued, but Ll. G. knowing that Curzon was immovable traded on this weakness, and caused endless trouble and confusion.

Lloyd George's tour in Scotland seems to have been a triumph. His speech at Glasgow was amazingly adroit. He had little to say – no fresh programme to announce. He defended his past action, appealed for unity, and for the rest chaffed B. Law with a cunning bonhomie. Poor B. Law blurted out 'I don't know where I am' – and Ll. G. seized on this miserable confession and with infinite tenderness turned B.L. inside out. F. E. Smith on the other hand has less scruple. He attacked

462

the new administration with scorn and ridicule, saying that they are incompetent – quite unable to face the tasks which confront them. We shall see. They may be a dull lot, but in the long run dullness wins the day, and the country is tired of the 'brilliance' of F.E. and the rest of us! F.E. went too far – both in the virulence of criticism, and in the degree of good taste. Our professed aspirations for unity will all be falsified if these things are said. Meanwhile Ll. G. must be longing to let himself go. He hasn't been attacked by Conservatives during this campaign (expect by the Diehards whom he is inclined to ignore) and his attacks have been confined to his own ex-colleages; Gladstone, McKenna and Crewe having received smashing criticism. About us he has only uttered good-humoured though sarcastic asides, in spite of temptations which must be almost irresistible to him – now at the zenith of his power. I admire his restraint. Can he maintain it? Somebody will go for him, Salisbury I dare say, and Ll. G. will gladly seize the opportunity to demolish the first Tory who shows fight – but up to now our friend shows praiseworthy discretion. It is noticeable how the fighting is internecine... making the next parliament a speculative affair of combinations.

30 OCTOBER 1922

The *Daily Mail* and *Daily Mirror* continue to belabour B. Law because he hasn't promised the moon! The Northcliffe press seems to think that Bonar Law owes everything to these gutter journals. Meanwhile the Northcliffe interest in *The Times* has passed back to the Walter family which is apparently being financed by John Astor. What a comfort.

31 OCTOBER 1922

Something odd is going on behind the scenes – threats that Ll. G. is so angry at Younger tolerating new Cons. candidates against National Liberals, that he, Ll. G., will nominate a number of his own friends in retaliation. Meanwhile A.J.B. cancelled a local meeting near his home presumably on the ground that he did not want to have a speak against a Cons. candidate, though he was quite prepared to support a coalition liberal. I don't know what passed at the Whittingehame conference – this aspect of the problem must however have been discussed.

Hardinge is resigning the Paris Embassy, before his allotted time. I wonder why.

2 NOVEMBER 1922

The municipal elections have proved a catastrophe for Labour. In London they have lost 300 seats, a phenomenal result. Does this foreshadow a similar débâcle at the general election, does it show that the recent byelection in Wales [*a convincing Tory gain at Newport*] was a model...? Anyhow these results must discourage the socialists in the parliamentary polls, and they certainly discount the fears some of us expressed about the grave extension of socialistic doctrines. It was largely on this thesis that Austen Chamberlain was so emphatic in supporting a coalition.

Minor posts in the government have now been largely filled and one can visualise its character as a whole. They are a very solid unemotional lot – sound in judgment, hopeless as speakers, but likely to command a good deal of respect. Some departments however seem v. inefficiently manned, notably the Board of Trade, the Admiralty and the Home Office. The latter with Bridgeman and George Stanley seems to me lamentably weak. The War Office, too, not over-strong.

4 NOVEMBER 1922

I had a curious talk with Lord Newton at the Carlton. He has been touring the Balkans and turned up at Constantinople just in time to witness the Chanak episode... Having throughout been much in the company of Harington and Rumbold, he is pretty well acquainted with the whole situation. Nobody is more anti-Coalition than Newton himself, but he says the whole business was managed with consummate skill, and that the government deserves all credit. For Rumbold he entertains the highest opinion, but thinks Harington who got most of the praise, is a jumpy and nervous person, changing his views constantly and unable to follow a logical policy. This was rather the impression one got from his jerky and inconsequent telegrams. As for the French, he says their behaviour was scandalous... Newton wrote his views to *The Times,* but *The Times* can't allow fair play to the Coalition, and refused to print the letter...

He asked me what was the truth about the famous shindy[1] [*cf. above, 25 Sept. 1922*] between Curzon and Poincaré. I told him I had only seen the official report and telegrams issued by the F.O. Newton indicated pretty clearly that the facts were misstated – that the very opposite had actually occurred – indeed that it was Curzon who had to apologise to Poincaré, and not the version that reached us. I wonder. Newton said his authority was unimpeachable, in fact that his statement could be proved. I wonder again. Curzon was curiously anxious to vindicate himself, Hardinge is resigning – is there any connection? On the other hand, if Curzon had had to eat humble pie to Poincaré we may be sure that the French and Italian press would never have concealed their triumph.

I attended Lloyd George's meeting at a huge cinema in Kingsway. I was much impressed. Though suffering from a cold his voice, which he seldom seemed to raise above a conversational tone, was clear and audible throughout. His gesture was emphatic, his engaging manner irresistible, and time after time the audience was impelled quite unconsciously to prolonged applause. When for instance he took up the absurd dictum of Bonar Law that Lloyd George's role during the war was that of a drummer boy (was anything more grotesque ever suggested?) he indicated on modest terms that though he had done more than that, even a drummer boy was serviceable – and towards the end of the war, Germany, still strong in men and matériel, lacked one thing, namely the agency which could revive her dropping spirits.

This was said in such gentle tones, with an inflexion so appealing, that the audience was moved to its heart – I could almost have wept myself – and my emotions are well controlled.

464

Bad news from Turkey. The Kemalists seem to have made a fresh series of demands upon us, giving us notice to quit Constantinople. Can one be surprised at this outbreak of aggressive nationalism? Kemal and his friends long ago sized up the French and the Italians. With the change of government here there have been unmistakable signs of weakening purpose. The Rothermeres led the Turk to believe we should undergo a pacifist evolution, and Kemal is now acting accordingly.

There has been a sudden and quite unexpected rally in Independent Liberalism – the Asquith or Wee Free party. A month ago it seemed doubtful if they would increase their representation at Westminster – now, they have placed a large number of candidates in the field, many of them v. formidable and well-trained speakers, and it would appear that the sterile formulae of dear old Squiff are being galvanised into fresh and vigorous life... As things stand the Bonar Law position improves. The electros are rather taken by his claim to be one of themselves – a simple honest fellow, without brilliance or rhetoric, but equally without stunts and blunders and tergiversations. It is time that this negative attitude, this rather vapid ideal of Tranquillity which will not mature, lends itself to such crushing retorts as I heard the other day from Ll. G. and Birkenhead; for the moment however the dull-dog argument has the better of the contest. It is a week to the polling – can B. Law's ascendancy be maintained intact until the fateful day? I am inclined to doubt it. His chances of a good working majority would be better if his position today were postponed for about three days, for there is just time for a measure of reaction to supervene.

8 NOVEMBER 1922
Ronald [*Crawford's diplomatist brother*] came to talk, evidently suffering from the All-Highest [*Curzon*], who is now top dog in the government and a hero into the bargain. To his staff at the F.O. he is more intolerable than ever. 'None but the strongest nerves can stand it.' Poor Eyre Crowe who is susceptible to bullying leads a cruel existence.

What a situation we are getting into about Turkey. St Aulaire, the French ambassador, like many of his compatriots has got the wind up! He has had earnest talks with Curzon and was so much impressed by the growing danger of the position owing to Turkish confidence that the 'warmongers' having been put out of office, Britain is squeezable – St Aulaire ran over to Paris to talk to Poincaré. The latter furious! what business has an ambassador to leave his post without permission? Poincaré refused to scc him! and moreover said that St Aulaire was not to be received at all at the Quai d'Orsay. What a stiff wooden-headed ass the man must be, and what a menace to Europe. He inherits Wilson's mantle of pigheaded obstinacy.

9 NOVEMBER 1922
Curzon's speech yesterday does not add much to the public knowledge of the situation; but he was very severe to the Turks and talked about affronts, and I think insults also, to Europe. Ll. G. was blamed for making similar comments. Our best

465

chance is to be firm and to ginger our allies into sending effective reinforcements – but will they, can they? A battleship is little use – we want a division or two of first class troops.

Tryon the new pensions minister announces that service pensions are to be stabilised for the next three years – I dare say an excellent thing – but where are the morals, the high principles of duty, propriety, economy, promised us by Jim Salisbury and Co? This announcement made a week before the polls is a very cynical bid for votes, and will have many reactions. If pensions are to maintain their present level even if there is a big fall in the price of living, many others will justly claim similar concessions. That is as it may be – all I note is the patent fact that the new government is not ashamed to cadge for votes at the taxpayers' expense.

12 NOVEMBER 1922

It looks to me very much as if Kemal means to go to war. They cannot defeat us in the field ... but if they adopt a resolute attitude they can frighten the French so much that an open breach would ensue – followed by the withdrawal of our troops – and that would be a moral defeat of grave import. Three weeks ago our position was tremendous. We were reestablishing our prestige if we had not already done so, and as Lord Newton said to me our influence in the Middle East was about to become supreme. Now it is clear we are being blackmailed by the French. Pertinax is explicit that French cooperation in Turkey is contingent upon our letting the French have a free hand on the Rhine. The reparations commission has failed to produce an agreed working plan; Poincaré hints pretty clearly that he will not abate his demands on Germany and that his alternative to cash payments is the occupation of German territory... France is imitating Kemal – squeezing us because our government has shown weakness.

Crawford had already made some election speeches in Lancashire industrial villages in October. On 10 November he spoke at Blackpool to about four thousand people, and on 11 November at Oldham to 1,200. He then went to Fife, speaking at Anstruther, Cupar and St Andrews, on successive days, before dealing with estate business and returning to London. On the 15th, with the polls still 'nebulous and contradictory', he unveiled the war memorial at the Chemical Society; on the 17th, Bonar Law had 'a fair working majority' of 70 to 85, even if 'much more than half the electorate voted against us'. Crawford's ambiguous position as a Conservative who was in the wilderness did not prevent him from opening the extension to Wigan Conservative Club later in the month.

17 NOVEMBER 1922

Dined in Park Lane with Sir Phillip Sassoon: a Coalition repast. Present Lloyd George, Austen C., Pollock, Freddy Guest, Macnamara, Churchill, F.E., Lee, McCurdy, Leslie Scott, William Bull, Goulding, Worthington-Evans. We had an excellent meal. Afterwards, remaining in our places in the dining room we discussed the outlook – I can't understand why we should have these joint meetings before private conferences among ourselves.

The symposium began by a statement from Austen Chamberlain. The burden of his remarks was that Lloyd George is now free. All his obligations to our party are discharged – he has more than paid his debt to us – his reticence during the contest was in every way noteworthy: he refrained from attacking our party or from advancing a programme of his own, likewise from authorising as many candidatures against Conservatives as the Conservatives launched against National Liberals. Lloyd George fought throughout with his hands bound to his sides – he did not embarrass our men – in short his debt to us is discharged. Austen concluded a very cordial speech by a general hope for recoalescence in the public interest.

Ll. G. then began, rather diffidently at first, but consistent in all his attitudes. Bonar Law has been returned by a minority vote – it will probably be found that 65 out of every 100 electors voted against the Conservative candidates. This fact completely justifies the desire to keep the coalition government alive – it was argued during the crisis that our party did not command a majority of the electorate – and though the luck of the ballot has given us a parliamentary majority, we have been hopelessly outvoted in the constituencies. The ministers rest upon a minority. As for the future he means to pursue a course of conduct outlined in his speeches, supporting the government wherever they are right, in other words he will not form an opposition the duty of which is to criticise a government right or wrong. On the other hand he will attack vigorously if they depart from the main lines of his cabinet – defence of the Straits, protection of minorities in Turkey, the Irish Treaty, Palestine and perhaps Mesopotamia – all matters on which he would himself have resigned had his cabinet declined to support him. In other words he means to pursue a policy of benevolent delay.

Then came Churchill – looking far from robust, though very decided in voice and gesture. He has just been beaten by 10,000 votes in Dundee, and immediately started the plea for proportional representation or alternative vote – for some electoral amendment which would give fuller support to those who are not run by the party caucus. Churchill spoke about this with much bitterness – and incidentally gave us to understand that he would be out of Parliament for several months, whether in order to recuperate his health or owing to the difficulty of getting a seat I know not. It was generally agreed that during the first session of a new Parliament the government could not be expected to change the electoral law – a most controversial issue among ourselves, and so this aspect of the problem was allowed to drop.

F.E. then announced the attitude he had settled to adopt 'inexorably' – namely one of constant and friendly criticism in the House of Lords. He does not set out to embarrass the government *but* having so many Secretaries of State in the Upper House he must make full use of his opportunities of scrutinising policy, and extracting information on all topics of importance. In other words, though he did not go so far as to say so, he means to adopt Salisbury's attitude in the last parliament of making himself as objectionable as possible to the government. This I regret. It won't succeed in the H. of L. which will wish to give the new government every chance – and such an attitude of constant criticism is least of all profitable in the H. of L. as we shall not have the cohorts behind us which enabled Salisbury to put us in a minority whenever he pleased. F.E. means to sit on the front opposition bench as Selborne did when he retired from office in 1916.

Conversation then became general and resolved itself into constant duels between Worthington-Evans and F.E. Each as it happened had a bottle of liqueur brandy in front of him and the progress of the bottle was uninterrupted while these long exchanges took place. W.E. said that a Conservative government is in power and that it is his duty as a loyal Conservative to support them wholeheartedly – not to give them occasional help in order to promote a fresh coalition when they have failed a year or two hence. There is much to be said for this point of view. Then W.E. went on to say that we can't sit on the fence as test questions will speedily arise – trumpery little things for instance such as attending the party entertainments to be given on the eve of the King's speech – still more if our men are offered posts in the government. At this I remarked that the problem could not possibly arise – why indeed should Bonar Law who has many hungry supporters dream of giving office to those he and his friends have recently censured? The party as a whole would be angry if more of the old discredited gang were reintroduced. W.E. kept coming back to this personal question, and Arthur Lee whispered to me that he had no doubt W.E. wants to be Minister of Health (Boscawen having lost his seat and there being no very suitable constituency available).[65] I wondered. Finally F.E. shouted out with a direct question – at which W.E. said he had not been approached but that if such a suggestion were made he would have to give it friendly consideration. We reached this point after talking for an hour or more. F.E. then hinted that there would be no difficulty in making it known that W. Evans wanted to join the government – the latter very angry and becoming more and more confused and obscure as the bottle got emptier.

Finally Ll. G. intervened in a very cool and adroit fashion – calmed down the storm, but not without stating that in his opinion W.E. was utterly wrong in saying that Austen's attitude (or his own) was a 'sham' since one can perfectly well give loyal help without holding office. Joe Chamberlain did it for years. So far as he is concerned, he had shown the utmost loyalty after his divorce from office. (Here came revelations). He had never once approached the Wee Frees for accommodation. He could easily have done so. Or 'he could have made efforts in some other direction'. He did neither. So keen in fact was he to preserve the possibility of future entente that he prejudiced himself. He went to the electorate without a programme – not even an ordinary election address. A programme would have been constructive, and as such polemical. He refrained. Without a programme meant that he denied himself the assets of enthusiasm, prejudice, and passion to each and all of which he could have appealed effectively had he not been so anxious

---

[65] Boscawen was replaced by Neville Chamberlain. Worthington-Evans returned to the fold as Postmaster-General in Baldwin's cabinet, May 1923.

to prevent a breach with those who still desired unity. The result was that he made forty or fifty dull and rapid speeches and that scores of thousands of his audience went away disappointed. His potential power is not measured by the members returned to support him. This was an interesting statement and I well believe that the little man was sincere. That he never placed his full efforts in the field against us, is of course obvious to all. The bottles of liqueur brandy were now empty. We settled to give a complimentary dinner to Austen C. next week and then we slipped away about midnight, W. Evans still rumbling to himself.

It is clear that we are in power by a very marked minority vote. The opposition is enormously strengthened in personnel and debating strength. It looks to me as if the parliamentary attack would be formidable, and that revival of the discredited methods of direct action is certain. If so, we shall have the Middle Class Union doffing black shirts and starting a fascismo at home.

It is said on good authority that Bonar Law has tried to persuade Horne to become Lord Advocate.[66] The Scottish position is certainly difficult, no ministers in the H. of C. and apparently no competent candidates or seats wherewith to furnish them.

19 NOVEMBER 1922

In this morning's *Observer* Garvin is rather subdued... What interests me in Garvin is the paragraph – which I assume is inspired – that posts are to be offered to the censured ministers and that it is their obvious duty to accept.

20 NOVEMBER 1922

A most surprising and interesting announcement that Crewe succeeds Hardinge as our ambassador in Paris[67] – excellent choice in many ways, but presumably George Curzon has an *arrière-pensée* in this selection. Crewe had a stroke two or three years ago and as it is hinted in very exact implications that Crewe isn't expected to stay more than a year or two, one guesses that George is providing a possible scope for his untiring energies when the government is beaten. He cannot conceive life except as a governor of men, and he may well desire a possible opening as Ambassador.

22 NOVEMBER 1922

Tullibardine told me that he fondly imagined he was Lord Chamberlain until a day or two ago when he received instructions to go to Buckingham Palace to surrender his wand of office – at two or three hours notice. He was astonished – looked at the *Daily Mail* where he found confirmation. So B. Law is as clumsy and ill-mannered as Ll.G. was alleged to be in the case of Cowdray; or perhaps it is pure blundering on the part of subordinates. Tullibardine on the other hand says that George Curzon did it, partly through a misapprehension, partly through a passion for

[66] Horne, one of Lloyd George's prodigies, in fact never returned to office.

[67] Crewe (1858–1945) was ambassador in Paris 1922–8. Curzon died in 1925.

interfering; fancy under present conditions trying to settle the Court appointments. Anyhow it is a bad and vexatious start to make enemies like this.

Dined with F.E., a very mixed assembly, Arthur Lee, Marlborough, Farquhar, about the only Unionist peers who were in the last government, the rest of us rather a nondescript body, Dalziell, Muir Mackenzie, Leverhulme, also Colebrooke, Stanmore, and Gorell representing Liberals in the Coalition administration. We had some speeches after dinner – F.E. giving us a good thirty minutes to begin with. He was very mild, reiterated his intention of living and dying a Conservative, and his refusal to form a separate group. Much desultory talk, then Arthur Lee plunged into a pertinent problem as to where we should sit. It is a relevant and important matter, but one which we should emphatically refuse to discuss coram populo. F.E. said he meant to sit on the front opposition bench. Foreseeing a Liberal reunion, and also a growing desire on our part to have a rapprochement with ministerial conservatives, I took the opposite view, though I could not state my reasons in such a company. Then came the humiliation of being appealed to by peer after peer – radicals – that I should grace the front opposition bench. Dalziell to whom I haven't spoken for ten years had the audacity to give me this friendly advice. It is really preposterous that in our [*Conservative*] domestic affairs we should be subjected to such pressure. These matters should be settled without the assistance of those who will be opposing our party twelve months hence.

23 NOVEMBER 1922

Johnnie Baird, the new minister of Works, came to see me. We discussed Office of Works questions. I think he will do the job all right as he has good sense and is keen to succeed. He was offered the undersecretaryship of the F.O. but wisely refused. Harmsworth [*Under-Secretary at the F.O. 1919–22*] was never allowed by the All-Highest to see a paper. Baird is to answer Scotch questions ad interim.

25 NOVEMBER 1922

The new Labour members are obviously suffering from swelled heads. Their orations with all the repetitions, or rather amplifications of phrase and argument are typical street corner stuff... But for businesslike and constructive argument their speeches are hopelessly inept. Much declamation, a rare display of lack of humour and a good deal of querulous temper are their main characteristics, all coloured by the fallacy that the House of Commons can be bullied or intimidated into surrender.

Ronald McNeill, the new under-secretary at the F.O., when speaking on foreign affairs made the naive avowal that he has not yet seen Lord Curzon! Considering that McNeill had an unopposed return, Curzon might have devoted ten minutes to making aquaintance with his colleague before departing for Lausanne.

28 NOVEMBER 1922

Bishop of London [*Dr Winnington-Ingram, Bishop of London 1901–39*] came to tea. Thirty years since he and I became acquainted. In those days I thought him a wonderful man, but I fear that as a bishop he lacks the scholarship and intellectual powers which are essential to leadership and above all for control of clergy. He remains a delightful and very lovable character, but alas no longer inspiring unless to persons of modest years.

Read another volume of indiscretions, Mrs Asquith's second diary ... To those who remember the tedious indolence of Squiff in 1916 – his dilatory slacknesses and indecisions – the book is utterly misleading, in fact a real travesty. Asquith on the outbreak of war never seems to have shaken off his desire for ease and self-indulgence. I used to attend cabinet after cabinet in vain hope of getting important problems discussed – and by Xmas 1916 it was high time that a change of government was made. Ll. G. may have been wrong in a hundred things then and thereafter, but he at least galvanised us into effort – Mrs Asquith's sneers at him come ill from the daughter of a Glasgow soap-boiler.

I rejoice to think that I have not spoken to Mrs Asquith for twelve or perhaps fifteen years.

30 NOVEMBER 1922
In the park this morning Willie Peel, the secretary for India, told me that he had learned of the executions of five Greek ministers [as scapegoats for military defeat], or rather of our action thereon [recalling the UK minister in protest]; evidently the cabinet has not endorsed the recall of our minister – presumably instructions reached Athens direct from Curzon in Lausanne.

The other person I saw in the park was Buckmaster, gnashing his teeth with rage at Ll. G. who apparently summoned a meeting of Liberal peers to discuss Liberal leadership in the H. of L. The situation is piquant. There are no Nat. Lib. peers who count, no ex-cabinet minister, and though Liberals as a whole would apparently have consented to serve under Grey, the positive refusal of the latter throws one back on Buckmaster.

XIV

A season of repose: out of office, 1922–4

*When politicians retire, they usually fill their leisure by turning, within months, to
politics. Not so with Crawford. Though neither old, ill, discredited, nor disheartened, he
disentangled himself from routine when the coalition fell. He had few regular political
contacts, and kept away from the House of Lords, where he regarded Salisbury's
leadership as like that of a bear dancing, a bear moreover who shamelessly did 'all the
wicked things for which he used to shriek obloquy at me'.*

*In some ways he was busier than ever. The 'stage army of the good' who serve without
reward on public bodies, called him for its own. Within a year he acquired 'interlocking
directorships' stretching across the cultural world: chancellor of Manchester University,
president of the London Society, a member of the committee on the Mint, president of the
Society of Antiquaries, trustee of the John Rylands Library, president of the Society of
Master Glass Painters, president of the Royal Commission on Historical Monuments, a
member of the Historical Manuscripts Commission, a trustee of the British Museum,
and chairman of the Royal Literary Fund. He retained his old posts at the National
Gallery and at the National Portrait Gallery, and presided over the conference of
Miners' Relief Societies.*

*Such commitments left little room for politics. When, to his pleasure, Baldwin became
leader, Crawford did not attend the meeting, saying 'I consider myself outside the arena
of party politics'. As a minor Lloyd George minister, Crawford must have realised that*

472

if he had an outside chance of returning from the wilderness, it lay not in exertion but in the quiet practice of an inoffensive rectitude. The two occasions on which his name was apparently canvassed for the Foreign Office suggest that his policy of withdrawal might just have succeeded.

But if Crawford, fifty-two in summer 1923, was reluctant to leave politics, his diaries conceal it well. As presented here, they must understate his work in cultural politics between the wars, for one committee meeting is much like another, and except at the British Museum and the National Gallery the issues do not come to life in the diary.

The new Bonar Law ministry of 1922–3 was seen by Crawford, not as true Conservatism restored and purified, but as a pale semblance of a capable and serious Conservative ministry, and one moreover which betrayed its initial professions, its chief function being to allow Coalition Conservatives to take well-earned rest while waiting for their moment to come. In Ireland, Healy's appointment at Governor-General gave pleasure, recalling talk of the old days.

How much better Tim is than Dillon, somebody remarked; yes, said A.J.B., but for a big row Dillon is the most valuable asset. This was true, for though at times Healy rose to an almost ecstatic eloquence, he seldom escaped the violences of the cornerboy.

Crawford's diary for December and January showed that his leisure was only relative. He opened a Nonconformist bazaar in Lancashire, unthinkable in the old days; settled with the Director how much the National Gallery should bid for an altarpiece; presided over the Royal Literary Fund Committee, the applicants being 'penny-a-liners and poetasters of the most commonplace type'. He chaired a lecture on the effect of light on museum exhibits, and attended a board meeting at the National Portrait Gallery. He tidied up his confidential papers, now largely destroyed, and began to find more time for Wigan, where he spent Christmas with his family, writing a lecture on 'Roscoe and the problems of today' for the Liverpool Royal Institution.

The Lindsay family still had a part to play in Wigan life. The ancient borough had elected its first Labour MP in 1918, a miner called Joe Parkinson who held the seat until his death in 1942, but the Conservative vote remained strong. It must be said that very little feeling of class war emerges from the diaries. Bitterness or resentment at dispossession are entirely absent, and the unsuccessful candidature of David, Crawford's eldest son, in the 1923 election left no mark, though it was the last time a Lindsay was to take part in Wigan politics.

Crawford was still a central figure in Wigan life. It was he who opened the war memorial in the parish church. He went down pits, and round the Wigan Mining College. It was the profits on the coal retailing side of the family company, indeed, which were keeping Wigan employed in 1922–3, for the pits and ironworks were losing money. And, a pleasant symbol of a return to old times, he entertained two hundred local children at Christmas, cramming them with presents and stuffing them with food.

His return to Wigan brought home to Crawford that six years of concentrated work had aged him politically. His memory for names played him false, though his eye for art was more acute than ever. 'It is a question whether I should not tend to drop out. It would be easy to switch my interests to antiquarian or artistic pursuits.'

The state of politics presented few attractions. On the one hand, Bonar Law's 'government of the second XI' blundered along, falling out with France' – and this 'after the trumpeting about reviving the entente which Lloyd George had smashed'. On the other hand, the Lloyd George ex-ministers were foolish enough to claim that an important letter from a Greek minister had never been circulated by Curzon to the cabinet. It had, but they had omitted to read it, and their claims to superior brains and efficiency were sadly dashed.

15 DECEMBER 1922

I talked to Edward Fitzroy, the new deputy chairman of committees in the House of Commons, and found that he takes almost a hopeful view of the new members. In any case he attaches little importance to the rowdiness of the extreme Labour group. This rather surprises me. There has recently been a sequence of noisy and disorderly scenes, in which one section of the socialists has taken a leading part, though discountenanced by the older parliamentarians, including the trade union group. Fitzroy thinks that these disappointments partly arise from sheer disappointment. The spouters have discovered that a repetition of their election speeches makes no impression on serious men. Their lack of constructive value is now realised. They have nothing except denunciation to offer and unexpectedly find themselves bewildered from sense of impotence; so they have taken refuge in noise – easily accomplished, and providing them with the public attention they would otherwise lose. Tubthumping will never intimidate the House of Commons, though it may attract notice outside. Next session these gentlemen will have to learn serious business or else degenerate into mere hooligans.

Meanwhile the members of other sections of the "opposition", as the Labour party has now become, are annoyed; the old gang who contributed the cost to fight the elections are vexed at control having been captured by the advanced section who contributed nothing but wind – and the Intellectuals on the other hand are bewildered – have not yet found their feet, and feel some reluctance at being allied with the clowns and knockabouts.

Ll. George lies low. He made one unfortunate intervention about the Gounaris–Curzon correspondence, and one speech about agriculture which was tame and ineffective. His remarks on reparations were in effect confined to congratulating the government on maintaining his policy. The movement towards Liberal reunion hangs fire. At first the new members thought they could achieve it, but the busibodies were checked by the reluctance of their leaders to show enthusiasm. But reunion must come, and if only the Liberals had a *rusé* whip it would be accomplished within six months.

As for Bonar Law, I cannot forgive that cynical bid for votes when he stabilised pensions for three years – making his announcement three or four days before the poll; and the cry for economy which gained many votes is now relegated to the background. The Office of Works for instance has been given orders to spend money; in my time we tried to save it. Trade however improves.

The weakness of the government is shown in debate, the opposition is strengthened, and safe men who were dismissed from the Coalition, Austen Chamberlain, Worthington Evans, Horne, etc., are inclined to hold aloof. For my part I have done the same – I have not attended a single sitting of the House of Lords, being more pleasantly occupied elsewhere.

22 DECEMBER 1922
The invaluable Mr Breun of Greek St, Soho, has been useful in finding the engravings I require. His knowledge of portraiture is phenomenal. He tells me that once having seen an engraved portrait identified as belonging to a particular person, he *never* forgets it, and with the aid of an ms. catalogue begun by his grandfather and kept up to date, he is able to authenticate almost every recorded portrait of a British subject. He has three or four big portfolios of unidentified portraits – and these he tells me he can remember almost as well as those who have got authenticated names. He is really a wonderful person.

31 DECEMBER 1922
I spend a sheltered and slothful existence. I think the accumulated fatigue of the last eight years is now beginning to assert itself, and I lie abed for long hours in the mornings. I am busied with rearrangement of books... I am also busy in the muniment room on odd memoirs and documents.

I enjoy retirement – but how long shall I be quite happy in maintaining a resolute silence? I confess I look upon the political and diplomatic problems of the day with a sense of detachment I have not felt for years... However perhaps we took things too seriously. When I last saw Willie Peel [India Secretary 1922–4] he told me that cabinets under the new regime were very simple and almost perfunctory affairs. Lucky people! ours were terribly long and serious functions too.

6 JANUARY 1923
A friendly article in *The Times* about progress in the Royal Parks under my regime. It is indeed the case that more was done during those eighteen months than during the previous eighteen years; moreover an excellent tradition has been established. I hear that money is to be voted to reconcrete the bed of St James's Park Lake, a leaky eyesore. This is all to the good, but what a volte-face in policy! I was told to economise money and did so, ruthlessly. My successor is told to spend money, lucky fellow.

17 JANUARY 1923
A cabinet assembled yesterday, at which only seven ministers attended out of sixteen. Even making allowance for the absence of Curzon and Baldwin, the small number present shows a very serious lack of discipline and sense of duty.

A season of repose

The *Observer* indicates that B.L.'s health is on the verge of collapse, and that he is not strong enough to carry all his colleagues on his back. I think it is a serious task, for there are only one or two whom he can trust to wind up a big debate, and he himself has always lacked the resilience of Lloyd George, the enthusiasms of Gladstone, the aloofness of A.J.B., the cynicism of Campbell-Bannerman, or the festiveness of Asquith – all qualities and temperaments which enabled the great people to shake off their anxieties. I think also that B.L. is haunted by his own gaffes – that fatal remark about tranquillity clings round his neck, while it is already apparent that the high affirmation of principle which was to guide this government instead of the opportunism of Ll. G. and Co., has already been dispersed to the winds. I don't remember any such cadging or cringing for votes as now marks the housing policy of the government.

19 FEBRUARY 1923
While the late Lord Minto was Viceroy of India the court was always brisk, manners without morals was said to be its watchword, whereas under the Curzon regime it was morals without manners.

20 FEBRUARY 1923
Ronald [*Crawford's brother*] dined and told me how the All-Highest [*Curzon*] enjoyed every moment of the Lausanne conference. It lasted long, and has not yet reached fruition, but it gave him endless opportunities of writing notes calling for memoranda, circulating documents and generally displaying himself in his true role, that of a busy departmentalist. He revelled in details, he gloried in his most successful exposure of Turkish ignorance and duplicity; but Curzon has no antennae, no faculty for distant vision, and is much too inclined therefore to magnify immediate triumphs or to resent meannesses as they arise. He is to this day conducting a laborious controversy with Poincaré, who always scribbles a deft reply by return of post, to which we pompously reply three days later. Poincaré repercusses by a prompt evasion, and so the ridiculous and undignified quarrel goes on. Why can't they drop it?

Ronald says that the result of the Lausanne conference is that Curzon is immersed in the Turkish problem, thinks of nothing else, and in point of fact has wholly lost touch with western politics. The Ruhr problem bores him though it governs the Turkish issue, but he will take no interest or concern in a business which he was not able to control.

7 MARCH 1923
Dined at Grillions . . . Graham Murray [Lord Dunedin, Lord of Appeal 1913–32] told us that had it not been for a decision given by Lord Eldon in the House of Lords (a ruling wholly wrong in law) the south side of Princes St, Edinburgh, would have been built along. The Scottish judges had pronounced the proposal to be quite legal.

At the Carlton I talk with F.E. and Horne.[1] I am rather ashamed to confess that I don't feel profoundly sympathetic about the defeat of Boscawen and George Stanley.[2] Both are good friends of mine, but they are victims of the hedging and trimming of the government which seems to change its mind every day. F.E. seems to think that B.L. is getting more and more overwrought and that unless there is a real improvement in the prestige of the government his health will break down in six or eight weeks. This I doubt, for B.L. is a toughish person: yet he warned the party that he would depart whenever he chose, and not being a very brave man, he may take his flight at a most awkward moment. And what then? Is Baldwin to become P.M. – or the All-Highest? In point of fact a P.M. in the Lords is out of the question in present circs. Meanwhile Derby who is none too courageous has wisely made up the detente with F.E. There were certain passages of arms between them during the election, and Derby is the last person in the world to welcome the prospect of having his Liverpool influence sabred by F.E. So a reconciliation has taken place, publicly announced too, and in order to make Derby still more contented with his lot, F.E. has had the impertinence to convey to him through the mutual friend, that the whole party would like to see Curzon replaced at the Foreign Office by – Derby himself! and Eddy swallowed the whole story too. It's really much too grave a matter for such practical jokes, and I gave F.E. a scolding about it.

14 MARCH 1923

Dined at Grillions with Baldwin who told me about his negotiations at Washington in funding our debt to the USA. He certainly impressed me with the difficulties he had to encounter, not merely there, but here as well; and he convinced me that he handled the matter well, much better anyhow than I had been led to believe. B.L. seems to have been very obtuse not realising that, had settlement been postponed from that particular juncture, it would have been far from easy to re-open negotiations in so favourable an atmosphere. It is alleged (though not by Stanley B.) that the sinister influences of Beaverbrook over B.L. had been pretty strong. If Lloyd George was surrounded by bad advisers, B.L.'s trusted counsellor is far more dangerous – not the common scheming parasites who clung to Ll. G. but a much more efficient and cunning intriguer... Rothermere I fancy must be approaching the lunacy which overtook Northcliffe... He is alleged to have tried to blackmail B.L. – an earldom for himself, and a good post in the government for his son. On receiving a politic refusal he determined to be avenged; if this be true, the scoundrel ought to be exposed – and smashed in the process.

[1] Robert Stevenson Horne, first Viscount Horne of Slamannan (1871–1940), MP (Cons.) 1918–37; Minister of Labour 1919–20, president of Board of Trade 1920–1, Chancellor of the Exchequer 1921–2; pursued a business career after the fall of the Lloyd George coalition in 1922, never returning to political office; chairman, GWR, 1934–40.

[2] In by-elections on 3 March 1923 the Conservatives lost Willesden E. to the Liberals, and Mitcham to Labour.

A season of repose

Dined at Grillions – sat by Austen Chamberlain, Victor Cavendish, Dunedin and Salisbury (with whom I am on quite friendly terms though one of these days we shall have a passage at arms if he and his friends continue to let down the Conservative party.) Austen C. talked about Harcourt's life[3] which he finds interesting. A. G. Gardiner tho' a very clever fellow has achieved a really dull book; but I really can't blame him. Harcourt was an amusing, downright person. Harcourt was likewise commonplace and without a vestige of scruple. His friends can never have fully trusted him, but he was excellent company. You should be grateful to providence, said a visitor to Malwood, grateful for your lovely garden! 'Providence?' said Harcourt, 'why it is entirely owing to pig manure.' That is typical of his direct and challenging repartee. I remember at the fancy dress ball at Devonshire House years ago Harcourt was wearing the robes of Lord Chancellor Harcourt. He met Halsbury who was guised as George III – an impersonation by the way which offended the Queen who said 'it is much too close to the Reigning House.' Halsbury who looked exactly like a Hanoverian monarch glanced at Harcourt whom he disliked and said, 'Are you my Lord Chancellor?' – 'No,' thundered Harcourt, 'not unless you are Queen Anne' – and somehow or other poor squat little Lord Halsbury seemed quite crushed. Personally I retain very pleasant recollections of Harcourt, who was always extremely kind to me. He liked young Conservatives 'of quality' although we used to tease and bait him during his later years when his lack of principle, and his almost ostentatious opportunism gave us plenty of opportunity to attack. My grandmother late in life made his acquaintance as one of his county neighbours at Nuneham, and he was always most painstaking and agreeable to her. He had succeeded quite unexpectedly to the property and quickly realized that the family heritage of which he was very proud would have been dispersed if his son had not married a foreign heiress. There are two things I regret in my parliamentary career, he told my grandmother: two acts of parliament, the ground game act and that which increased the death duties.[4]

27 MARCH 1923
Dined at The Club. This Club, *The* Club par excellence was founded by Johnson, Burke, Goldsmith, and their circle... Tonight I presented myself for my first banquet. Nobody to keep me company except Kenyon,[5] so we solemnly ate together – an indifferent meal in the attic of a vulgar pothouse called the Café Royale – a very dull and inauspicious opening of my career!

[3] A. G. Gardiner, *The Life of Sir William Harcourt* (2 vols, 1923).

[4] Harcourt inherited the family estates from a nephew in March 1904 and died in October of that year, thus incurring a double dose of his own death duties within a year.

[5] Sir Frederick George Kenyon (1863–1952), Director and Principal Librarian of the British Museum 1909–30.

F.E. Smith continued to embarrass the coalition Conservatives by his temperamental inability to play the waiting game that tactics dictated. One day he broke loose and dilated in the Lords on the danger of French air power. 'We all know that London is at the mercy of French aeroplanes' agreed Crawford, adding that the French 'might quite readily succumb to a real outburst of hysteria', but finding this no reason to welcome Smith's public hostility to the government. Being out of town, he missed the dinner of ex-ministers given by F.E. to meet Balfour, but found his name in the papers as having been present all the same.

18 APRIL 1923

Dined at Grillions – a most amusing evening – sat with Haldane, Selborne, Asquith, Archbishop of C., and Baldwin. We talked about Einstein, at least Haldane did. Asquith who is a fellow of the Royal Society knows far more about astronomy and so on than I ever imagined, and he was very forcible in denouncing heresies he dislikes. He rejoices that now in his old age two of his ideas are finally realized – firstly the disestablishment and disendowment of the ether theorem, secondly the complete dethronement of Darwinism, or at any rate of the extreme form of the doctrine of natural selection propounded by Darwin's admirers. All his life Asquith has been living under the thraldom of these two outstanding fallacies – and now feels an incubus has been removed. But as Baldwin drily observed many of us have lived happy and blameless lives notwithstanding the errors of nineteenth century science – nor can we be sure that we are not being dominated by new fallacies which will be exposed fifty years hence.

... Then our talk turned on the betting tax which threatens to revive the somnolent nonconformist conscience. Asquith doesn't like the idea though not opposed to it on any very clear ground of principle; but he says that he was made conscious of the prevalence of the habit by an odd circumstance [in 1920] when he happened to pay his first visit to the Derby. He was staying with Crewe. To prepare himself for the event of the day he read two or three forecasts of the race – and came to the conclusion that a horse called Spion Kop possessed notable qualities of pedigree. He announced his preference. The pundits smiled; he argued his case and they laughed. 'Fancy Mr Asquith who has never seen a race laying down the law about pedigrees.'

Well, Spion Kop won the race.[6] Asquith had not backed his fancy or today might have been an ex-millionaire; but by the irony of events the Asquith governess had asked him to place £2 on her behalf. Feeling that he ought not to take liberties with somebody else's money he asked advice – and of course lost the wager. But here is the moral. Asquith's intuition became fabulous. For weeks and months afterwards, people asked him for 'tips' – wrote to him, even sent him reply paid telegrams, people he had never heard of; and this impressed his mind with the prevalence of betting, and also with something of its professional character.

[6] At odds of 100 to 6, moreover.

A season of repose

19 APRIL 1923

Baldwin's position has greatly improved during the last few days owing to his honest straightforward speeches about the budget. He lacks airs and graces. His humour is dry and spontaneous. His manner, if slow, is conciliatory. He has character and strength, and these virtues excel all others, and above all the asset of brilliance.

25 APRIL 1923

At Grillions sat with Asquith, Baldwin, Eustace Percy,[7] and Evan Charteris[8] ... Asquith was junior counsel for Parnell during the famous *Times* litigation. One day he asked Parnell why he had not employed Irish lawyers, Healy for instance. 'Because Healy has left too much wool on the hedge' replied Parnell solemnly. Parnell was at Cambridge – this surprised me – and still more to learn that he was a cricketer of some skill. 'Did Parnell trust you as his lawyer? did he give you his confidence?' 'I doubt it,' said Asquith: 'in any case I never trusted him'.

28 APRIL 1923

So Bonar Law is to go abroad ... Baldwin will lead the H of C with aplomb and good humour, nor is he likely to make any serious mistake: but like his other colleagues he has hitherto made no impression on the country – the platform side of it, and in B.L.'s absence, there is no minister who can make a great popular appeal to our unwieldy electorate. The uncertainties of the H of C situation keep our men pretty closely confined to Westminster.

Some of the papers indicate that Younger's[9] appointment at the Carlton Club in succession to Kintore, is a triumph for the Diehards and a definite blow against the Unionist ex-ministers. I really doubt if there was any *arrière-pensée* in his selection – he was probably chosen as an impeccable authority on wines and cigars. But there are lots of people who approve of his election, even if these reasons be unassignable. This means that there is a strong element in our party which is definitely committed to proscription. It is a pity; but F.E. is largely to blame for he never fails to castigate certain members of the Diehard group. He should be more conciliatory. I believe the underlying cause of his bitterness is resentment which he is now in a position to embody, at the ceaseless pinpricks of Salisbury and Co during the past few years. He did indeed pass through a galling time from these people – every action condemned and every motive misrepresented.

... Derby however has made his peace with F.E., and it is understood that Victor Cavendish[10] won't come into collision with Birkenhead; but Salisbury, Selborne,

---

[7] Lord Eustace Percy, first Baron Percy of Newcastle (1887–1958), president of Board of Education 1924–9, minister without portfolio 1935–6.

[8] (Sir) Evan Charteris K.C., barrister, historian and trustee of the Tate, National and National Portrait Galleries, and of the Wallace Collection.

[9] George Younger, first Viscount Younger of Leckie (1851–1929), chairman of the Unionist Party organisation 1916–23.

[10] Victor, ninth Duke of Devonshire, Colonial Secretary 1922–4.

the All-Highest[11] – F.E. looks on them as fair game. Ronald tells me that the All-Highest appeared at the F.O. at 9.30 the other night, got into his room with difficulty, could not find the electric light switches, barked his shin badly on a coalscuttle, and finally had a furious row with a messenger. The bell system of the F.O. has been revolutionised in consequence.

1 MAY 1923

Met Buckmaster[12] in the Park. He was very acid about Lloyd George's recent speech at Manchester. How he hates the little man! He denounced Ll. G.'s latest pronouncement as a 'return to Limehouse', and evidently thinks we are going to be subjected to a wild Land Campaign. Buckmaster disapproves. He thinks it immoral to arouse passions ('nothing easier' he says) without giving a concrete demonstration of the method of allaying the grievance . . . Buckmaster himself moves steadily towards the right wing of politics. He becomes less radical and more mellow. Ten years hence when the remaining asperities have been rubbed off he will be a very sound and somewhat crusty Conservative.

Considering himself out of politics for good, Crawford now turned his attention to his inheritance and to the making of a second career in the world of art. The library built up at Haigh by his father and grandfather was quickly reduced in quantity, about fifty tons of books being despatched to Quaritch's. Crawford became chancellor of Manchester University, a position which he regarded as involving questions of policy and senior appointments as well as ceremonial, and a trustee of the British Museum, 'the only position I have ever desired to hold'.

19 MAY 1923

My only regret of course is that the clearance has ruined the catalogue to which my father gave so much time and care; but he would have been the first to recognise that the Library as he left it demanded a little army of curators, and under present conditions of finance, not to mention the 'numbers in family', such a course is in every way undesirable. In mutilating the Library however I have only excised the uninteresting books; all the volumes of historic or artistic interest are now gathered into a noble apartment, where they are displayed with a dignity and care they have never received before. The Library in fact as now re-arranged is far more noteworthy than even in the great days before 1900 when our precious manuscripts were still in our possession. The arrangement then was chaotic. Books were in dark corners, unclassified, inaccessible – apparently almost neglected. Neither my father nor my grandfather cultivated the fine art of *étalage*, and I flatter myself that now for the first time our possessions are worthily displayed – pictures, china, furniture, as well as the Library itself.

[11] Curzon

[12] Stanley Buckmaster, first Viscount Buckmaster (1861–1934), the last Liberal to be Lord Chancellor, 1915–16.

A season of repose

21 MAY 1923

B. Law has resigned. For days past the *Morning Post* has been assuring us he is perfectly well, but it is evident that his illness is far more stubborn than it appeared . . . It is a bad business. He was a very useful leader to our party and always anxious for reconciliation with old colleagues who were fired out last winter. Recently he has been making great efforts to get A.J.B. back into the government.

. . . The government however (apart from this personal crisis) has improved its position since their defeat – whips are more careful – attendance better organised, and Baldwin who has led the H. of C. since Bonar Law's departure, has steadily improved his reputation. He is no orator, scarcely even a debater: he has no presence, a rather thick and husky voice with a most tiresome gulp in his throat – a sort of recurrent hiccough, and what is called a stocky stubby figure – altogether a very uninspiring person. Yet there is character, firm, staunch, honourable, – all the virtues which endeared W. H. Smith to the country, and which may serve Baldwin in equally good stead. And it is character that tells in the long run far more than brilliance; though he will never strike the imagination of the electorate and can never be a popular figure at election time, he will gradually acquire the fame which attaches to single and disinterested regard for the nation's welfare – and as such should make an effective leader.

22 MAY 1923

Reading through the lines it is clear that George Curzon would like to succeed B. Law. His ambitions are unbounded, but one thing is lacking, namely the power to attract, and another obstacle exists, namely his peerage. It is on the latter feature that his desire will be thwarted. There are already too many peers in the government . . . So Baldwin will infallibly be summoned by the King, and George will swallow his pride and take credit for patriotic ardour in continuing as Foreign Secretary. I have been amused at several papers talking of Victor Cavendish and Eddy Derby as possible premiers. I never heard so nonsensical an idea.

23 MAY 1923

Baldwin went to the Palace yesterday . . .

24 MAY 1923

This morning's papers announce that George Curzon will remain at the Foreign Office, and they talk loudly of his magnanimity. It is indeed a concession to his pride.

Ronald however tells me that the All-Highest is perfectly furious. It never occurred to him, especially after being chosen to act as P.M. in B. Law's absence, that any alternative could exist; Stamfordham's communication that the King would send for Baldwin produced explosions of wrath. George drafted a letter resigning office – made no secret of the fact to the F.O. officials who were really full of glee – and moreover he spent some time in preparing a letter to *The Times* which was to explain how it had become impossible for him to remain in office after the inference that no peer could be Prime Minister. He was to point out how grave was the blow struck against the privilege and prestige of one House of Parliament – and after a few pious hopes for Baldwin's success and an oblique reference to health and avocations ruined in the public service, he would have bidden us a courteous and at the same time a surly farewell.

But Curzon isn't the man to cut himself adrift. Lloyd George knew it, and knew that he could inflict any humiliation upon him with impunity... Robert Cecil becomes Lord Privy Seal. This will add to the debating strength of the government: Baldwin has done well here – but Bob Cecil is now such a fanatic, and so self-centred, that he is capable of wrecking any government. Great efforts are being made to persuade Robert Horne to re-enlist[13]... Anyhow it is a good thing to see that Baldwin is under no illusions as to the futility of some of his colleagues, and as to the urgent need of strengthening the government sufficiently to make a decent show in debate.

Amery,[14] Derby,[15] and Edward Wood[16] refused to serve under G.C. as Prime Minister: others too were influenced in a similar direction as the All-Highest has made himself unbearable as chairman of the cabinet during these last few weeks. Ronald[17] also tells me that in the Foreign Office his brutality is beyond belief. Crowe[18] for instance cannot long survive the incessant scoldings and violence.

26 MAY 1923

McKenna[19] becomes Chancellor of the Exchequer... It is true that McK. is only just recovering from a pretty serious illness, and Baldwin therefore retains the Chancellorship for the rest of this session.

... My surprise at this appointment was increased this afternoon when I learned from Jack Gilmour,[20] who saw Chamberlain this morning, that he, Chamberlain, had not been approached by Baldwin. No offer to join the government has reached him – not only so – his advice has not even been sought. This seems curiously tactless on Baldwin's part – and now that every post in the government is filled up (except the postmaster-generalship or some such office), Austen has been given indirectly to understand that the Washington Embassy is at his disposal. Auckland Geddes cannot go on much longer owing to grave trouble with his eyes.[21] Jack

---

[13] Horne never re-enlisted.

[14] First Lord of the Admiralty 1922–4.

[15] Secretary of State for War 1922–4.

[16] President of the Board of Education, 1922–4; later Lord Halifax.

[17] Sir Ronald Lindsay, diplomatist.

[18] Sir Eyre Crowe (1864–1925), permanent Under-Secretary for Foreign Affairs 1920–25.

[19] Reginald McKenna (1863–1943), Liberal politician; held important posts, 1905–16.

[20] Sir John Gilmour (1876–1940), Unionist MP 1910–40; Secretary for Scotland 1924–9, Minister of Agriculture 1931–2, Home Secretary 1932–5, Minister of Shipping 1939–40.

[21] Ambassador to the USA 1920–24.

A season of repose

Gilmour describes Austen as 'white with fury'; he has written a letter to his Birmingham chairman explaining the position, for there is a tendency to blame Chamberlain for boycotting the government whereas the facts are in the other direction altogether.

... What amuses one in a grim fashion is the continued hostility of the Diehards (Admiral Hall[22] protagonist) against Austen, and their tolerance towards Bob Cecil who a few months ago formally abandoned Conservatism and flirted in a shameless manner with the Liberal party. Similarly McKenna is accepted after he has only once addressed a Conservative meeting – McKenna who was the bitterest opponent of Ulster, and who carried through Welsh disendowment. It looks as if the vendetta were wholly personal ... Peel tried to ship me off to India for a twelve month job ... and now he has persuaded Arthur Lee to take the post.[23]

2 JUNE 1923

Not without amusement I received from Waterhouse[24] an invitation from the Prime Minister that I should act as chairman of the committee which scrutinises titles and honours ... Baldwin certainly has a sense of humour. I think he must know that I have always ridiculed this vetting body, and on one, if not two, occasions I attacked the scheme gleefully when it was advanced by Selborne. I well remember smashing the notion in such a way that S. withdrew his scheme. Now I am asked to act as its sponsor and spokesman – I refused.

7 JUNE 1923

Received letter from Baldwin offering me trusteeship of the British Museum. This gives me pleasure – but I thought the invitation emanated from the three Principal Trustees.

At Office of Works for meeting of the Sites Committee which I have now joined ... Afterwards Earle told me that Johnnie Baird makes quite a good First Commissioner but thinks too much about his pleasures. How delightful to be young! Earle hinted that Curzon is anxious before long to go to the Embassy at Paris, and that I should succeed him as Foreign Secretary – that the idea was favourably considered in certain high quarters. This rather intrigued me. Personally I am inclined to think such an appointment would be good. I would anyhow undertake to re-establish the morale of the Foreign Office in six weeks.

There was, indeed, no reason why Baldwin or his circle should not have discussed, casually or otherwise, the possibility of putting Crawford in at the FO in the not unlikely

[22] Admiral Sir William Reginald Hall (1870–1943), director of naval intelligence 1914–18; MP (Cons.) 1918–23, 1925–9.

[23] Lord Lee, also a former coalition minister, was chairman of the Royal Commission on the public services in India, 1923–4.

[24] Lt.-col. Sir Ronald Waterhouse, principal private secretary to the Prime Minister, 1922–8.

event of Curzon walking out in huff. The idea remains, however, pure rumour. What is certain is that Crawford changed abruptly at this time from being an opponent of Baldwin to being an admirer. He took Bonar Law's 'honesty' to be a political style, but Baldwin's cultivation of the same quality he accepted as 'character'. He saw Baldwin as sharing his views on the weakness of the ministry, and the need for Conservative reunion and reconciliation. Crawford's initial reaction to the fall of the coalition, that the Conservative ex-coalitionists should hold quietly aloof until the 'second eleven' collapsed, had now been substantially undermined by F. E. Smith's determination to practise spirited opposition. Each time F.E. opened his mouth, it drove Crawford nearer to Baldwin.

13 JUNE 1923

At Grillions, sat between Haldane and FitzAlan, opposite Hugh Cecil and Austen Chamberlain. Haldane started the proceedings by ordering ten dozen of champagne from George Murray, who is a skilled entrepreneur. Haldane then told us that he was as fond as ever of eating and drinking (achievement accordingly), and then announced for the fiftieth time his attachment to the Labour party. That didn't surprise me a bit, but I was a little shocked at his attack, good-humoured enough, upon Asquith's ideals and bona fides. Squiff of course is a bit of a reactionary and shows small sympathy for artisan aspirations for a 'good life' – but why should Haldane of all people pronounce judgment. Austen argued his case well if perhaps with some turgidity of phrase and gesture. Afterwards he told me that Haldane excites in him the most violent, almost uncontrollable, annoyance – he hates the smug inconsistencies and apparent play to the gallery. I am bound to say that Austen's manner showed no sign whatever of vexation – he controls himself well.

2 JULY 1923

Crisis with the French brewing... Baldwin succeeded to a pretty tough situation from B. Law – created largely by George Curzon who Ll. G. had always restrained and embarrassed. I should imagine that George C. is now pretty supreme on foreign affairs, dominating his colleagues though subjected to fitful protests from Derby. Baldwin himself is now the centre of a growing legend or myth – the solid unemotional hard-headed man of business. I should love to see him presiding over his cabinet and grunting at his colleagues, and I suspect we should see a very frail and fluctuating opinion upon foreign affairs unless he has greatly changed during the last six or eight months. However, as I say, he is being invested with a useful tradition of substantial virtues, aided by the homely briar pipe which is always available to console photographers and cartoonists – I suppose this is fortuitious – but it is infinitely better that his pipe rather than his person should be the hallmark of caricature.

2 JULY 1923

Grillions. Sat next to Asquith and Amery, Baldwin, Lord Grenfell, and Roger Keyes. Squiff talked with much erudition about cricket...

A season of repose

23 JULY 1923

House of Lords. St. John[25] raised a debate about compensation for Irish Loyalists... Finally Victor Cavendish.[26] He had been making grimaces all afternoon – less aggressively than usual, for his jaw is beginning to adapt itself to the new *râtelier*. But what a solid person he is – uncouth in gesture, ponderous in appearance, slow in style – yet giving the impression of saying all that requires statement and doing so without any effort to score a success. There is a massive imperturbability about him which gives confidence. He will never let one down, never play for his own advantage, never do anything brilliant, let us hope never do anything wrong. It is upon this sense of solidity, shared to a large extent by the Prime Minister, that the chief strength of the government reposes.

25 JULY 1923

Dined at Grillions... Ed. Gosse[27] amused us about the late Professor Blackie – a real charlatan, and the charlatan always provokes Gosse's best stories. Once it came about that Blackie had to be entertained at Oxford – there was no way of avoiding it. He found himself at Balliol, felt very much in the centre of the picture, and rather boastfully threw out a general question to the assembled guests in response to something in the nature of a compliment: 'But I wonder what you say behind my back?' There was a guilty pause broken by Jowett's silvery voice, 'We never mention you!'

26 OCTOBER 1923

Last night Baldwin spoke at Plymouth... Baldwin seems to have plumped for Protection *pur et simple*; I wonder what the cabinet thinks of it.

27 OCTOBER 1923

British Museum Trustees meeting... I rather fancy the B.M. wants tuning up – there are many aspects where the reforming eye would be serviceable. The Speaker[28] feels this strongly, but vaguely also, because he is quite unversed in Museum problems, and does not know how to begin. Hitherto his efforts seem to have been very fumbling and ill-directed. The Archbishop[29] is perfectly complacent, and believes that the great machine is rolling away to perfect satisfaction of the public. Our agenda paper is really an object lesson: it is congested with every kind of trumpery report about messengers and window-cleaning, and no time is left for considering fundamental problems. Sub-committees are apparently called once or twice a year. It was this kind of easy-going

[25] Lord Midleton (1856–1942)
[26] The Duke of Devonshire, Colonial Secretary 1922–4.
[27] Sir Edmund Gosse (1849–1928), man of letters; librarian of the House of Lords 1904–14.
[28] John Henry Whitley (1866–1935), Speaker 1921–8.
[29] Dr Davidson (1848–1930), Archbishop of Canterbury 1903–28 and, like the Speaker, *ex-officio* a principal trustee of the British Museum.

nonchalance which produced the crisis at the old South Kensington Museum soon after I entered parliament.

10–12 NOVEMBER 1923

To Manchester. I was installed Chancellor ... The Manchester ceremonial all passed off admirably. People from Oxford and elsewhere were impressed by the dignity of our proceedings and by the really magnificent organisation. I certainly have never seen an academic function managed with so much skill and precision. The great occasions at Oxford and Cambridge are drab, dowdy affairs compared with our grand solemnity in the Free Trade Hall where nearly 3500 people were assembled. But these modern universities in great industrial centres cannot afford to give a shabby display.

13 NOVEMBER 1923

Parliament is to be dissolved at once. George Curzon drove me down to the H. of L. from a Board meeting at the National Gallery and makes no secret of his vexation about it. The idea of resignation or losing his job is repugnant to him. There is plenty of scope for his untiring energies, and he has an uncomfortable feeling that three weeks hence his tenure may become precarious, possibly he might be replaced. That would be a disaster in his opinion, though others feel that he is getting so stale that any change of atmosphere in foreign affairs would be welcome.

But this election is a great gamble ... I hear many people predicting that on balance we shall lose 20 or 25 seats which would return the government to power with a small majority, probably too small to carry out a great scheme of tariffs.

14 NOVEMBER 1923

Great anxiety about Scotland. Jack Gilmour told me last week that the party organisers at Edinburgh had never been consulted, and this evening George Younger said that Novar[30] had never heard of a comprehensive scheme of tariff reform until he read the report of Baldwin's Plymouth speech. Some weeks ago Montague-Barlow[31] made a curious and unexpected speech about inflation of currency to which he paid an oblique compliment. This naturally produces a storm of protest from honest finance, and M. Barlow repudiated the inferences of his argument, saying he had been misreported. It now seems to me that what looked uncommonly like a bad gaffe may have been a deliberate attempt to sound public opinion – that strong hostility having been manifest in all quarters against tampering with the currency, the only other remedy for unemployment, namely tariff reform, was promptly announced – so promptly indeed that some members of

[30] Ronald Munro-Ferguson, Viscount Novar (1860–1934), Liberal MP until 1914; Governor-General of Australia 1914–20; Secretary for Scotland in the Conservative ministry of 1922–4.
[31] Sir Clement Anderson Montague-Barlow (1868–1951), Minister of Labour 1922–4; MP (Cons.) Salford S. 1910–23.

the cabinet were blissfully ignorant of government policy. Talk of Lloyd George being an autocrat – he is nothing compared with the mild-mannered Stanley Baldwin!

15 NOVEMBER 1923

To Sandringham for the dissolution and prorogation Councils . . . I had an audience before the Council. The King made no concealment of his opinion that a general election is inadvisable; he vainly tried to dissuade Stanley Baldwin and appears to have actually gone so far as to tell B. that he would refuse a dissolution, and allow Baldwin to say so. In this I think H.M. would have acted imprudently; but it is evident that the King is really afraid of a Labour government, probably more so than circumstances justify.

. . . Johnnie Baird[32] however assures me that good reports are arriving from the constituencies. He is nervous – says it is all a gamble, and that the phraseology of the Plymouth speech went further than was intended by the cabinet. I dare say. Meanwhile, F.E. is asking for too much. It is foolish for him to exact onerous terms at this juncture – indeed he should have made no demands. If the election goes all right his activity on the platform will have re-established his position in the party, and his cooperation will then be gladly invited.

The visit to the King at York Cottage (not Sandringham, still inhabited by Queen Alexandra) was uneventful. While the King shot, Crawford looked round Sandringham gardens – 'weary places'. 'Can one imagine', he exclaimed, 'anything more middle class than a very long greenhouse with small pink begonias, and with a looking glass at the far end to create the illusion of greater length?' After dinner, during the King's absence, the Duke of York[33] amused himself by kicking footstools about the parlour.

The result of the December 1923 election was Conservatives 258, Liberals 159, and Labour 191. There was much doubt as to the next development, but none that the Conservatives had suffered a serious defeat. Baldwin did not resign at once, but waited to be defeated when parliament reassembled late in January. The turn of the year was therefore devoted to speculation and dismay.

8 DECEMBER 1923

Much excitement at the Carlton, where I talked to F.E. who was very scornful about 'the Dud'[34] who has landed us in this impasse . . . Nobody outside the cabinet seems to know what really happened, how the election was precipitated; but it is generally assumed that the pace was forced by Amery, Lloyd Greame,[35] and perhaps Neville Chamberlain . . . Willie Bridgeman[36] to whom I talked seemed quite dazed.

[32] See above, 24 November 1911, n.

[33] Later George VI.

[34] Baldwin

[35] Sir Philip Lloyd-Greame, first Viscount Swinton, president of the Board of Trade under Bonar Law and Baldwin, 1922–4; changed name to Cunliffe-Lister, 1924.

[36] Home Secretary 1922–4

9 DECEMBER 1923

London opinion seems united in thinking that Lloyd George's campaign made very little impression on the voting . . . The fact is that he made too many speeches; and as he did not indulge in much abuse one of his chief weapons was blunted. Southborough[37] told me the other day that when Ll. G. was at the Board of Trade there was some intricate problem on the tapis, trade marks it may have been or patent law, which bored Ll. G. very much. He hated the dull departmental work, and once said rather plaintively to Sir Francis Hopwood as he then was, 'Can't you give me something to denounce?' Well, during this election he has been hard at it, but to his credit there has been very little vulgarity, and less venom.

11 DECEMBER 1923

Long talks at the Carlton. Worthington – Evans[38] explained to a large audience why the cabinet had decided to retain office and meet parliament in January. The reason is simple; because if we don't the Labour party will take office! and W.-E. made our blood curdle by reading his draft of the King's Speech as R. MacDonald would prepare it. No doubt this document had already made the cabinet blanch with terror; it was what one would expect – but W.-Evans had not thought of estimating the cost of the proposed reforms.

13 DECEMBER 1923

I am curious to see how some of these great spouters will succeed departmentally. Hitherto they have been no more than critics, except in so far as they have managed trade unions; but the chief men in the Labour party are doctrinaires, intellectuals and cranks who are bereft of even that experience. The Labour men with whom I came in contact in Coalition days, Barnes, Clynes, and Hodge, were among the slowest-witted folk I ever encountered. Clynes in particular was quite incapable of running a department, Hodge much too lazy to do so. As for Barnes, he had the brain as well as the appearance of a lizard.

20 DECEMBER 1923

Paid a visit to the Office of Works to discuss the Art Commission[39] with Johnnie Baird. He has been First Commissioner for twelve months, and yet it is only three or four days ago when he managed to get a cabinet decision on this subject which was ripe for settlement when I left office. I am to be chairman of the new body, which will give me a lot of very tiresome work; but it can't be helped and something of the kind is needed.

[37] Sir Francis Hopwood, first Baron Southborough (1860–1947), permanent secretary at the Board of Trade 1901–7.
[38] Postmaster-general in Baldwin's cabinet, 1923–4.
[39] The Royal Fine Art Commission, founded in 1924, with the diarist as chairman, to advise the government on questions of taste. The RFAC could only give advice when requested by departments or public bodies. See below, 5 June 1924, 1 October 1934.

A season of repose

We talked about the political situation – still rather obscure and made more so by a curious speech made by Squiff to his reunited party ... what was most interesting was his plain hint that after we are beaten, and then the Labour party in its turn, he, Squiff, will be very happy to form a government! It is a very droll and entertaining conclusion, based on a belief that the King would not allow Ramsay M. to dissolve. The real fact is that Asquith is determined to become Prime Minister once again, for one absorbing and overmastering reason, namely his passionate desire to dish Lloyd George. Asquith has always distrusted him, and now that Ll. G. has lost most of his party, including Churchill, Mond, Greenwood, and McCurdy, Asquith scorns him into the bargain, and intends to put the little man in his place.

24 DECEMBER 1923
Christmas Tree. All the servants file in on these occasions in strict order of precedence, but the masculine section follows the women, so that the Butler is next to the junior scullery maid.

8 JANUARY 1924
Parliament met. Took the oath in the Lords – talked to lots of people there and at the Carlton. Victor Cavendish specially depressed – seems to think himself responsible for the débâcle ... Certain people want to displace Baldwin. He has advised the party badly as things turn out – but who shall replace him – not Austen for he endorsed the appeal to the country insofar that he wished to receive a ministerial post. I advise all I meet not to precipitate matters.

... But people scold Baldwin. Ned Talbot in January 1923 wrote to Baldwin about recognition of somebody's services; no acknowledgement – wrote again and got an evasive reply from a private secretary – and for twelve months the matter has been shirked or sidetracked, until Ned saw him recently and told him what he thought. Frank Coller[40] who of course saw much of Baldwin when at the Board of Trade says that he was always indolent, and moreover showed lack of courage and decision. I wonder who was the real parent and begetter of the recent dissolution – Amery and Neville Chamberlain are credited with the praise or blame; but to me it is incredible that anybody could have his hands forced by such a couple of bores. Well well – they say these issues must be settled by a party meeting – which I should regret.

Rumours: a) that Ramsay MacDonald will pass a bill making it possible for Commons ministers to attend and state their case in the Lords ... b) that Parmoor is to be Lord Chancellor c) that the King is very angry with Asquith's speech now that its full implication is realized d) that before making the speech in question P.J. had had his full share of P.J.[41]

[40] Frank Herbert Coller (1866–1938), secretary to Food Department of Board of Trade 1921–5. Baldwin was president of the Board of Trade 1921–2.

[41] Asquith's nickname, derived from a brand of champagne. In a speech at the National Liberal Club on 18 December 1923, Asquith had interpreted the election result as requiring a Labour government.

16 JANUARY 1924

Haldane apparently is to join the ministry though in what capacity I know not.[42] At Grillions this evening while discussing the champagne (128/-per dozen) he told us he had been entertaining the 'horny-handed sons of toil' and that they were well pleased with the brand. And what was their taste in cigars asked Sir George Murray – 'the biggest' replied Haldane – 'the very biggest' and it would seem that in order to be smoking at the moment of departure and as long afterwards as possible they were in the habit of lighting a new cigar from one which had still twenty minutes of smoke in it.

17 JANUARY 1924

Ned Talbot and I had an appointment with the Prime Minister to discuss the desirability of a party meeting, always the most contentious proposition whips have to handle. My advice was to express complete readiness to have it but not to precipitate it; in other words not to summon it for a week after the new regime has met Parliament.

... Baldwin vacillating rather thinks he ought to resign, then that he should hold a meeting and ask for a fresh mandate; but I think he would like to continue leader although a lethargic person. At the conference was Edward Wood as weak as water, then came Sam Hoare[43] who formulated precise arguments in a very precise manner (public school accent I expect) – finally Willie Bridgeman who rambled. I hope Baldwin's other counsellors are less ineffective than this trio.

21 JANUARY 1924

Dined with Mr Crawford at Ritz. He told me an odd thing. He asked to have an interview with Ramsay MacDonald who to his surprise invited him to spend a few days at his home in Aberdeenshire. Nothing loth Crawford proceeded there and was much interested, though frozen to death! One night he observed that one of the new government's great difficulties would be foreign affairs, which R.M. admitted readily enough, adding however that he would call for the services of men who did not share his political views – and mentioned my name.[44] What can he have meant?

22 JANUARY 1924

A socialist government is installed in office. What will happen? ... I walked across the Park with Gerald Balfour and McCormick,[45] the man who runs the University Commission. I found the latter depressed. He had expected a reign of opulence, but

[42] Haldane became Lord Chancellor, Parmoor Lord President of the Council. Their joint leadership of the House of Lords struck Crawford as an uneasy affair with much mutual jealousy.

[43] Secretary of State for Air 1923-4, 1924-9.

[44] MacDonald's official biographer, David Marquand, kindly informs me that he is unable to trace any evidence supporting this tantalising piece of gossip.

[45] Sir William McCormick (1859-1930), chairman of UGC from 1919.

was much discouraged by a talk with Haldane who says that Snowden[46] is out for economy! I was a little surprised – but in the evening Montague-Barlow told me that he had talked to one of the new ministers this morning (I think he said actually to Snowden) who told him that there was going to be a big surplus on the 1923–4 budget. This doesn't sound very probable – but the belief gives one an idea of the new government's policy – namely to intercept this forty or fifty millions (the figure mentioned) from the sinking fund; to devote it to pensions, sugar and tea tax etc. – to impose no new taxation next financial year – to govern with strict moderation – then to dissolve before next year's budget with a great reputation and manifold promises – and to return with a majority independent of all parties! It is a very pretty programme!

23 JANUARY 1924

The cabinet is announced... Thomas to the Colonial Office. A few days ago when talking to Victor Churchill[47] about the railway strike, he said he was going to 'take the Colonies; I am determined that the Colonies shan't be messed about'. He has good qualities, but is a great talker.

26 JANUARY 1924

Ramsay MacDonald apparently had a 'midnight vigil' at the F.O. All the other ministers seemed to be working wonders, and we hear of an epoch-making innovation of cabinet committees – as it there had not been scores and even hundreds during the last five years. The funny thing is that all these commonplaces of government are puffed and heralded as if they were notable departures from the accepted routine of ministerial life – but nonetheless I doubt not that millions of people are led to believe that for the first time in their lives an active and energetic ministry exists. In point of fact Labour men and in particular trade union leaders have acquired a great taste for indolence and junketing – and a very keen appreciation of... champagne. Anyhow the transfer of seals is now complete. Baldwin has evacuated Downing St – I saw him the other day in the Park tremendously exercised about the waywardness of his puppy – what a mongrel. His outlook on life perhaps a little jaunty and offhand – we exchanged a few words – somehow he doesn't realize the possible repercussions of the mess into which he has landed us.

7 FEBRUARY 1924

Conference at Baldwin's house, twenty or more present including those of us who were fired out in 1922. Baldwin began by announcing that he proposes to drop the General Tariff as a constructive item in our programme. Austen Chamberlain and

---

[46] Philip Snowden, first Viscount Snowden (1864–1937), Chancellor of the Exchequer 1924, 1929–31.

[47] Victor, second Viscount Churchill (1864–1934), chairman of Great Western Railway from 1908.

Lloyd-Greame supported him, to my surprise. Amery didn't like it, nor did I. Willie Bridgeman spluttered but said nothing. George Curzon approved, and among other things said 'I have never been a Tariff Reformer.' I suppose that is why he is always too busy to speak in the constituencies. We talked for a long time. Baldwin's policy received general support, but I thought the general attitude weak and flabby and there are many of our friends whose convictions have not been changed by our defeat.

26 FEBRUARY 1924

Olivier made his statement about India in the H of L. Poor man, he was suffering from a really bad cold and there were stretches of oratory which sank into a husky whisper. But I heard quite enough to realise that Olivier is not going to play mad pranks about Indian autonomy[48] ... Altogether I was well pleased. I remember Olivier as my permanent secretary at the Board of Agriculture, where he had the reputation of being an amiable chatterbox of extreme doctrinaire views, hopeless as an administrator – I mean an ordinary muddlehead – a poor disciplinarian, and the exponent of an illegible handwriting – but all the time an agreeable and quite inoffensive person.

27 FEBRUARY 1924

Dined at Grillions – beside me were Asquith, St John Brodrick and the Archbishop of York. A very amusing evening. Asquith told me that the speech made by Wheatley,[49] the Minister of Health, in the recent debate about the Poplar Board of Guardians, was a masterly performance – in fact one of the best debating speeches delivered for some years past. Not indeed that Asquith professed himself to be converted; but the skill with which Wheatley transferred the blame from himself to his predecessors in office, the good humour and quiet wit he showed and the general construction of the speech were all noteworthy and continued to make a great impression upon everybody.

... Suddenly while talking in a desultory sort of way about the government, Asquith said 'it's a difficult job keeping Humpty Dumpty on the Wall'. St John, deafer than ever, insisted on Squiff repeating the aphorism, and then asked who Humpty Dumpty might be. Why, the Labour party, said Asquith. St John didn't comprehend, pressed Asquith for explanation, and then it transpired that Asquith meant it took him all his time to prevent the Labour party being beaten. He evidently thinks that would be a disaster – certainly if a dissolution were forced at the present juncture the Liberal party would lose from 50 to 80 seats.

[48] Olivier at this time saw the various Indian elites as playing for their own hand under a thin disguise of nationalism, and so was able to support a conservative line by praising the Indian communist analysis of bourgeois revolution. In later life Olivier considered Indian self-government impossible (see Margaret Olivier ed., *Sydney Olivier: Letters and Selected Writings*, p. 157). For Olivier, see above, 29 September 1916, n.

[49] John Wheatley (1869–1930), Minister of Health, 1924.

A season of repose

I went on to Londonderry House where dancing was in progress. George Younger came on too – he had been dining at Grillions, though he was at the other end of the table. As he left he talked to Squiff who had been telling another group of diners about the Humpty Dumpty dilemma. 'Then why the devil did you ever put them in office?' asked George, quite unperturbed and imperturbable, to which Asquith could only reply by a grimace.

29 FEBRUARY 1924

I gave the *Manchester Guardian* the typed text of my lecture[50] last night; they printed a report extending to nearly a column, and managed to achieve forty misprints... It is singular how badly this excellent paper is printed.

15 MARCH 1924

The wife of a Labour member at a recent Buckingham Palace party soliloquised, 'My boots is tight, my corsets is tight, my 'usbands tight. I'm for 'ome.'

20 MARCH 1924

Walked with Atholl[51] who has been interviewing Adamson,[52] the Secretary for Scotland, and Mr. James Brown,[53] a Labour member, who has been appointed High Commissioner of the General Assembly. They have discovered that it is not so simple a function as they imagined, and Adamson has enlisted Atholl's cooperation as they must have the guidance of a member of the 'auld aristocracy'. Atholl is quite ready to play up, and said so. Brown much relieved, but there was something else on his mind, though he would not talk plainly, but kept making vague hints about the great difficulties before him. At last Atholl boldly said, 'Are you nervous about Mrs. Brown?' and then the truth came out. Not only is Mr. Brown very nervous about his wife, but apparently he is in deadly fear of her! Judging from her picture in the newspapers she looks a very sensible buxom person of 55 or so, who will look admirable in black or purple silk – a tentative understanding was reached that the Duchess of Atholl should advise on problems of toilette.

Churchill was beaten in the Westminster election by 43 votes. The aunts voted for him, I believe, and I would have done the same ...Our leaders in fact have been divided. Baldwin wanted Churchill to be chosen, but as the local association preferred the nonentity, Baldwin quite rightly supported their choice. A.J.B. wrote a strong letter in favour of Churchill, whose candidature was helped by thirty

[50] On John Lyly, the Elizabethan author.

[51] John, eighth Duke of Atholl (1871–1942), Lord High Commissioner to the Church of Scotland 1918–20.

[52] William Adamson (1863–1936), chairman of the parliamentary Labour Party 1917–21, Secretary for Scotland 1924 and 1929–31.

[53] James Brown (1862–1939), Scottish miner and MP (Lab.) 1918–31, 1935–9; Lord High Commissioner 1924, 1930, 1931.

Conservative MPs. What will his future be? I feel no hesitation in saying that our party ought to try to find him a good place at any early byelection.

22 MARCH 1924

Trustees meeting at S. Kensington ... Sir Sidney Harmer,[54] the Director, is a very shrewd person, much less obstructive than Kenyon, and the meetings at the National History Museum, where the light is good and the room bright and airy, are much more businesslike than in the dull atmosphere of Bloomsbury. But how drab our meetings usually are! I had always expected them to be of entrancing interest, and my desire to be a Trustee of the British Museum was one of the few ambitions I ever possessed; yet now I am a Trustee I confess the disillusion has supervened. It is a dull function. We are told about porters and messengers, about lost keys or missing books, about the leave granted to some clerk who wants to get married, about this that or the other detail; but on great problems of museum progress or development, seldom a word. No official beyond the two directors ever attends our meetings. Their case has to be stated by Kenyon at Bloomsbury; and when he is not interested, e.g. in the Prints and Drawings Department, his advocacy is a poor and perfunctory version. I am disappointed – for so much could be done to quicken that dead alive institution. The Speaker is a keen partisan of reform, but the Department loyally backed up by the Archbishop has been too much for him. Ullswater[55] also tried to bring the Trustees into closer relation with the different branches which make purchases. I suspect he proceeded in rather an abrupt manner, but that experiment failed as well.

3 APRIL 1924

Willie Bridgeman had tea with me in the H. of L. We discussed the political situation, and he agreed with me that the time has come when we ought to begin to rally the socialist government. It is desirable to make the country smile at these earnest and arrogant folk. They have coined nicknames for themselves – Rabbits for Thomas Shaw, Jellyfish for poor little Clynes, Cuckoo for Wheatley, and Sidney Webb is already known as Nanny. We should further explore the Zoo, and make the country familiar with the soubriquets. It is high time that ministers should be chaffed.

17 APRIL 1924

Snowden seems to lose his temper every time he speaks, Clynes is a monument of amiable futility, Thomas a mere roisterer, Olivier a charlatan, Henderson a good-natured booby! But nonetheless they are all plausible, and a formidable team both in parliament and still more so in the country which takes them at their own word and believes they are performing miracles.

[54] Director of the natural history departments of the British Museum, 1919–27.

[55] James Lowther, first Viscount Ullswater, Speaker (and *ex-officio* trustee of the British Museum), 1905–21.

A season of repose

24 APRIL 1924

To Lathom . . . What can I say about this distressing visit?

In old days Lathom, the fine stately house built by Leoni, was the centre of dignified country life, the home and resort of great personalities. I used to stay there as a boy and was always impressed by the solemnity of 'Cousin Skelmy'[56] – the Lord Chamberlain with that massive white beard – the husband of the charming and hospitable Cousin Alice. He was in turn succeeded by the last Lord L., an ineffective person, whose son now about thirty is disintegrating, indeed dispersing, this fine property and sending the fine traditions of his family scattering down the winds.

We entered the park by the western gate, and were confronted by armies of woodmen cutting down the noble elm trees. Thence passing the little chapel where my grandparents are buried, a murky desolate little spot, we came to the fine facade of the house – dismantled and windowless. We went in. Floors are falling – great masses of stone are dislodged, but here and there one sees relics of the fine cornices and plasterwork, occasionally the deserted symbols of habitation, or the bust of a forlorn Roman emperor frowning down upon the *dégringolade*. What gay parties used to assemble in these gracious reception rooms – what distinguished visitors – how generous was the hospitality of old days, all now gone, all forgotten, and the house perishing, not merely from neglect, but because it has been used as a stone quarry whence to build the fatuous extravagance of Blythe.

Blythe was the dower house, a charming old-fashioned residence about a mile from Lathom, homely and comfortable, unpretentious yet adequate in scale. It has been remodelled, or rather rebuilt by this young booby, who not only spent £60,000 in the process, but ruined the old home to do so. That is what he spent on the structure and I daresay the furnishing cost him half as much again. In return for this monstrous waste he has constructed a big rambling place enclosed in a tiny plot of land and abutting on a high road – the sort of place a Balkan prince might erect for a *bonne amie*. I never saw so wanton a waste of money – so absurd and so incongruous a confection dumped into the cold climate of West Lancashire. There is a swimming bath which must have cost £10,000. The amount spent on glorifying the water closets represents a little fortune, stair balustrades are made of bevelled glass. I felt quite indignant at the abject folly of this youth, at the discredit heaped upon his name and his class, for the place is derelict – empty. An auctioneer's clerk lives there and receives potential buyers – he will be lucky to get a quarter of its cost, for the average Lancashire man however opulent will be shy of purchasing this combination of a manor house with a Turkish bath establishment.

I spent a melancholy hour there. I reflected on the swiftness with which an honourable family can be smashed.

[56] Edward Bootle-Wilbraham, second Baron Skelmersdale, first Earl of Lathom (1837–98), Lord Chamberlain 1885–6, 1887–92, 1895–8, was the diarist's maternal cousin. His son, the second Earl (1864–1910) was succeeded by Edward, third and last Earl (1895–1930), the 'young booby' mentioned below.

1 MAY 1924

Party conference in the morning – all morning I should say. We discussed drafting points interminably, Baldwin retaining a benevolent smile plus resolute silence. A very fatiguing and ineffective affair. Suddenly in walks James Craig[57] – burly, rubicund – he gave that stony glare about the room with eyes which look like steel, and unrelieved because he never seems to blink his eyelids. He started off unceremoniously by blaming Birkenhead for having last night offered gratuitous advice which will embarrass the Ulster case – 'unfriendly', he characterised such a pronouncement made without the smallest consultation with himself. Craig told us about the recent negotiations with J. H. Thomas who tried to cajole him with a money grant if Craig would support the Boundary Commission. 'I will give you your million' he said. 'Yes, and a little more too!' But he little knows the firmness of Craig in making such a proposition, nor how dangerous a weapon he puts into Ulster's hands. Craig told us how ready he was to discuss rectifications of frontier, and various points of mutual accommodation; but also how violently Ulster will react against any attempt to coerce her. The conversation was interesting. To the outsider there could be no failure to notice the contrast between the clear-cut emphasis and decision of Craig's attitude on the subject he understands, with the rambling and flabby talk of the Saxon!

5 JUNE 1924

Fine Art Commission. I must say I have a very difficult team to lead; we keep finding ourselves confronted by questions of professional etiquette – Gotch[58] in particular thinking more about the interest of the architect than about the aesthetics, than about our work; Lutyens[59] on the other hand takes no interest in this, but never stops chattering irrelevancies, often humorous enough, but tiresome when one wants to get to business. I long for the practical hard-headed business minds who surrounded me at the old Wheat Commission.

In a world which had shrunk, in daily routine, to squabbling committees, Museum staff obstructiveness, and the giving and receiving of honorary degrees, one true delight came to pass when Crawford, like his father before him, became an honorary Fellow of the Royal Society – thus making him a member of all three of the great learned societies of Burlington House.

5 JULY 1924

I attended the degree ceremony[60] in St. George's Hall which interested me. The students are turbulent on these occasions, and the programme has often been disconcerted and sometimes completely wrecked by their ebullitions. Adams

[57] Premier of Northern Ireland 1921–40.
[58] John Alfred Gotch (1852–1942), architect and art historian.
[59] Sir Edwin Lutyens (1869–1944), architect.
[60] At Liverpool University

A season of repose

therefore arranged to confine their rowdiness within stated limits, authorising them to sing their doggerel songs at fixed points in the proceedings. The organ plays for them, they have their official conductor and their ridiculous songs and parodies are printed and circulated with the University document. The idea is good, for although these songs are very trite and unoriginal (badly sung into the bargain) at least the conferring of degrees is conducted without constant and senseless interruption.

13 JULY 1924

Board meeting at British Museum. What perfunctory affairs they are, with an agenda (not circulated in advance) sometimes containing sixty items, many of which are trivial or superfluous. Important topics are presented to us at a moment's notice, and our minutes, admirably printed on *papier de choix*, have to be returned to the Director after perusal by the Trustees. Nothing in the way of reform will be feasible until Kenyon's departure; he is a stickler for etiquette and will defeat all our efforts to modernise the Museum and to revise our customs.

27 JULY 1924

All the French autograph letters are packed up, and prints too – a dozen huge cases weighing three tons and covering the floor of the billiard room. They are to go to Sotheby's to auction. The proclamations remain, and they are even bulkier than the manuscripts.

29 JULY 1924

Very small dinner at The Club – Haldane, Oman,[61] Bishop Gore, and Henry Newbolt. Haldane cheered us up as the evening went on, and told us stories of the Rothschilds for whom he used to act as legal adviser – perhaps he does so still in an informal fashion. Years ago, thirty-five or more, he rearranged the Rothschild partnerships which had got into a very vague relation, placing the whole family at the mercy of one dishonest partner. This was handled with so much discretion that Lord R. asked Haldane to draw his will. Haldane refused – that kind of task being outside his professional sphere – but he suggested a name and supervised the document – refusing a fee. One day Garrard the jeweller sent him a magnificent and most costly solitaire stud – not a word accompanied the gift, except a line from the firm to say that they were directed to forward the jewel. Haldane asked no questions, wore it at the Rothschilds' house, but no comment was made. The other night he was dining with old Lady R. – put the thing on and after this long interval of years discussed its origin – yes, Lady R. remembered all about it – she and her husband had chosen it together.

[61] Sir Charles Oman (1860–1947), Professor of Modern History at Oxford 1905–46; MP (Cons.) Oxford University 1919–35.

498

30 JULY 1924

Leaders' conference in Baldwin's room in the Commons. Ireland suddenly emerges into the forefront of politics. A new crisis seems imminent about the Ulster boundary – Thomas is truculent, MacDonald too. Our decisions were vague for nothing can be settled until the government has taken our party into consultation. The general feeling was that if amendment of the Treaty Act is suggested, that the changes should be bilateral; in other words if Ulster is forced to appoint a boundary commissioner Ulster in turn should be guaranteed that the boundary revision shall be confined to a rectification of frontier and not the means of annexation of whole counties by the South

3 AUGUST 1924

Had tea at Carlton where Novar told me that after I left the Unionist conference on Wednesday, a report about progress in the west of England was made by Jackson.[62] Austen C. asked his authority for a v. satisfactory forecast – was told that Peter Sanders[63] was Jackson's informant, whereupon Austen in a sudden access of fury made a violent onslaught on poor Peter (absent – no longer in parliament) and incidentally on Jackson as well. Austen afterwards apologised; but everybody was aghast and could only assume that the outburst was caused by the recollection of Sanders' strong attitude against the coalition. Lloyd George evidently means to attack us about the Ulster boundary. This at any rate is calculated to make a breach with Austen.

Novar has been lunching with Rosebery – and has just solved a mystery which has long puzzled him, namely the cause of Rosebery's quarrel with Loreburn.[64] It appears that the latter stated (? in Canada) that the reason why R. retired was because he had given way to drink! This certainly was a cruel accusation. R. like others in the habit of making long and important speeches, imbibed copiously; but this kind of person holds his liquor well and I never heard anybody say they had ever seen Rosebery the worse for drink.

19 SEPTEMBER 1924

I had tea at the Travellers with Stanley Baldwin and discussed the Irish crisis. It is obvious that Craig would like to be more forthcoming than his colleagues will permit; but that under present circumstances he can give nothing away. It is said that the socialists don't like the idea of an election on the Ulster question – I dare say not...

The 1924 election finally erased the Liberals as a major party, reducing them to forty seats. The Conservatives, with 419, returned to power under Baldwin (1924–9), who

[62] Sir Stanley Jackson (1870–1947), chairman of Conservative Party organisation 1923–7.

[63] Presumably Sir Robert Sanders, Minister of Agriculture 1922–4, who lost his seat at Bridgwater in 1923.

[64] Robert Reid, Earl Loreburn (1846–1923), Lord Chancellor 1905–12.

*by forming a broadly based government ended the civil war within the party which
existed in 1922–3. The diarist's son Lord Balniel[65] was returned for the previously
radical Lancashire seat of Lonsdale, a seat which he held without interlude until he
succeeded in 1940; and it brought a last offer of office from Baldwin, anxious to heal all
possible rifts in the Conservative ranks.*

2 OCTOBER 1924

I am sorry Asquith has lost his seat. The other night at the Carlton, when 300–400
people were assembled to hear the election results, the news that Paisley had been
captured by the Socialists was received with a universal groan of regret! One might
almost have thought Asquith a Tory. Lady Astor's success was greeted with stony
silence... the Duchess of Atholl seems the only popular woman of the lot.

5 OCTOBER 1924

Baldwin asked to see me this evening and offered me my old department, though
with no seat in the cabinet. I told him I would reply tomorrow. The post doesn't
appeal to me much, for were I to become first Commissioner[66] again I should spend
most of my time in saying that the instructions in my old minutes must be followed.
I see no prospect of any new development. Moreover it is tiresome being head of a
department and yet without collective responsibility or indeed access to cabinet
information. It is paralysing when one addresses a public meeting.

I spent five or six minutes with Baldwin who is extremely uncomfortable in
having to omit old friends and colleagues from his ministry – but that is inevitable
as the number is so huge. He had an interview of an hour with George Curzon. I
asked if the All-Highest was very angry at being relegated to an honorary post[67] –
no, he said – but 'painfully lachrymose.' I suppose George blew his trumpet and
heralded his claims with insistence and persistence; but it was an error of taste and
judgement to do so for an hour!

6 OCTOBER 1924

I pondered over my situation all yesterday evening and all this morning; so many
considerations are relevant. Once or twice I felt overwhelmed with the boredom of
having to control the Hyde Park flower beds and to criticise bad designs for new post
offices... Apart from all this I have added to commitments elsewhere –
Antiquaries, Fine Art Commission, Royal Literary Fund, etc. to which I don't want
to be disloyal.

So I ended by saying no; and as I daresay I shall regret my decision, settled not to
give the matter another thought.

[65] David, twenty-eighth Earl of Crawford and Balcarres (1900–75); p.p.s. to the Minister of
Agriculture and Fisheries, 1924–9.

[66] Of Works

[67] As Lord President of the Council, 1924–5; the Foreign Office went to Austen Chamberlain,
1924–9.

11 OCTOBER 1924

Willie Peel[68] goes to my old department for which he is wholly unfitted, and the cabinet is now 21 – I suppose about the biggest in history. I suppose if I had accepted office the cabinet would have been reduced to what Baldwin told me was his final decision – namely one consisting of 19. Nobody knows I was offered office except Connie and David – and those whom Baldwin may have told. ... The newspapers as usual quite at sea; several of them notably the radical press seem to have fancied me for the Foreign Office.

19 OCTOBER 1924

... I sat by Lady Curzon [*at a dinner*] who is a queer mixture of naivete and malizia. She was most amusing about George's new office. Evidently there were poignant domestic scenes. He refused to be Lord President – I mean swore to her he would never accept so subordinate a post; but she pressed him – said it was his duty to the state, but also his duty to her, as he would be intolerable at home if he was at the same time out of office, and no longer Leader of the Opposition. So, like a sensible fellow, he allowed himself to be overborne; and here we are! He will be soon quite happy again. He will be unruffled when any hitch occurs in foreign affairs; but he is galled by having 'all the small men in the cabinet' airing their views on foreign policy. In his day only two or three of the Elect were permitted to make an observation.

10 NOVEMBER 1924

At Grillions I sat with H. A. L. Fisher, Ned Talbot, and Sumner ... Everybody was talking about Ramsay MacDonald's speech on Tuesday ... Fisher was saying this evening that he never met a man more self-conscious and self-centred. Fisher knows him well for they spent months together in personal intimacy doing some enquiry in India. When the post arrived MacDonald's immediate desire was to study the bundle of press cuttings about himself, often enough consisting of acrid criticism from the Leicester papers. Two or three such snippets from these local organs would 'put him off' for a whole day – he would complain bitterly to Fisher who told him to pay no attention to such trumpery attacks; but MacDonald was not easily consoled and brooded over his grievances. Since then MacDonald has become Prime Minister, his vanity has become megalomania, and I shall not be surprised if he dies of it.

12 JANUARY 1925

Dined with Willie Bridgeman, Jack Gilmour,[69] and Lord Peel. If politics are indeed as dull as these three cabinet ministers, the peaceful outlook of these realms is indeed assured.

[68] First Commissioner of Works, 1924–8, with membership of the cabinet.
[69] Sir John Gilmour (1876–1940), Unionist MP 1910–40; Secretary for Scotland 1924–9, Minister of Agriculture 1931–2, Home Secretary 1932–5, Minister of Shipping 1939–40.

A season of repose

Very amusing dinner at The Club, which is now installed in new and most ornate apartments at the Café Royal ... I sat between Rudyard Kipling and Stanley Baldwin. Kipling was telling us war stories, or rather describing to us the nature of his collection.[70] During the war itself he used to go to Victoria station where he sat in the waiting rooms with men who were waiting for their trains to take them back to France after their leave, and from many other sources he acquires direct records of curious and often fantastic events. These he carefully wrote out, throwing them into narrative form no doubt with his own incomparable skill, but always trying to preserve the character and personality of the man himself. He told us the outlines of some of these stories – or perhaps one should say the headlines – often enough disconnected from the main episodes of warfare, those curious sidelights one used to encounter showing odd things which happened incidentally to the main struggle. There was the submarine on the Murmansk coast which was invaded by a dense drove of some subarctic rat – the crew got rid of the pest but each man kept one specimen apiece as a pet, and one by one they all died. There was an archaeologist in Transjordania who when digging trenches came across a statue – refused to budge and had to be courtmartialled; a man who ran his ship ashore at the Falkland Islands because he found there were two Falklands whereas he had only expected one! Another man who got stranded on Easter Island and died from horror of the ghosts sculptured on those colossal images. There was an artillery man who got cut off by the Germans during the advance of 1918. He had two horses. He survived for a month, well within the German lines, kept his horses fed too, and then managed to escape – and so on. An endless mass of unbelievable truth, all carefully transcribed, documented and authenticated. What is to be done with them? They cannot be published for they read like romance at the expense of tragedy. I said he had already handled the problem for instance in *The Conference of the Powers* – and the sea-serpent story is also analogous. Then one saw that Kipling had thought of destroying them from anxiety as to their destination if he died. Some adventurer might get hold of them, and Kipling who is one of those who will never forget the horrors of the war even if he survived Methusaleh shrinks from appearing even to have smiled at any one of its myriad countenances.

Hand them all over to me said Frederic Kenyon. I will deposit them in the British Museum and guarantee that the box shall not be unsealed until the date you specify – 50, 80, 100 years hence, whenever you will; and Kipling seemed to think the idea worth considering.

George Stanley told me that not only did Horace Farquhar[71] die penniless – we had always looked upon him as rich – but that actually some of the fine works of art

---

[70] See above, 6 November 1918.

[71] Horace Brand Farquhar (1844–1923), first and only Baronet (1892), Baron (1898), Viscount (1917), and Earl (1922); master of the household 1901–10; lord steward 1915–22; treasurer of the Unionist Party.

in his house were hired! He left handsome bequests to sundry minor lights of the Royal Family (he was always a perfect snob) and when the estates were valued, it transpired that there was nothing to divide.[72]

7 MARCH 1925

I wasn't conscious yesterday evening that Baldwin had made a very remarkable speech in the House of Commons, about a bill introduced by our men to prevent Conservative trade unionists being coerced by the political levy into financing socialist candidates. Generally speaking, our party supports the bill; the cabinet however showed signs of reluctance three weeks ago, and Baldwin had to oppose the measure which I fancy he has supported on previous occasions. The task was exceptionally delicate, but he seems to have performed his function in a manner which created not only surprise but astonishment. A new Baldwin was revealed. Hitherto he has been regarded as a very solid unemotional man of business, but this speech taken in conjunction with two or three others recently delivered, show that he possesses and at times is prepared to employ, a vein of emotion which one associates with a very different type of parliamentarian, and certainly he brought his new forces into play with notable effect. He had an ovation in the House of Commons whereas most speakers under similar circumstances might have provoked laughter and jeers.

[72] But cf. below, 2 February 1926.

XV

'The Uncrowned King of British Art', 1925-9

*The Crawford Committee on the BBC – Oxford Chancellorship – Curzon's
papers and biography – Epstein attacks modern art – Baldwin on
Beaverbrook – Haldane worshipped by the London restaurants – Crawford
declines chairmanship of BBC – involvement in general strike – intrigues by
ministers against coalowners – rancour at the National Gallery – Sassoon's lavish
hospitality – Grey's disapproval of progress – Balfour's ideal dinner
party – Duveen offers to house the Elgin Marbles – Balfour's eightieth birthday
party – Hartington's enthusiasm for cockfighting – Sir Oswald Mosley.*

*Of all Crawford's activities between the wars, the one which was of greatest visible
importance was his chairmanship of the Crawford committee on broadcasting. In July
1925 the Postmaster-general announced the setting-up of a committee to review the
future of broadcasting, then in the hands of the British Broadcasting Company,
nominally owned by the radio manufacturers, though in practice already a public service.
The committee held its opening meeting, with Crawford presiding, on 19 November
1925, concluded its hearings around the end of January, and presented its report, 'a neat
and modest document', on 7 March. On 14 July 1926 the government announced its
acceptance of the main points of the report, and on 1 January 1927 the British
Broadcasting Corporation came into being by royal charter for a period of ten years.
Crawford was asked by Baldwin to be its first chairman, but declined.*

*In fact, as Asa Briggs has shown in his official history of broadcasting, the Crawford
committee's main task was to give a constitutional form to principles already generally
accepted. 'Monopoly' and 'unified control' were an accomplished fact, as was a dislike of
the American system of broadcasting. Politicians were anxious not to see broadcasting go
the way of the popular press. The creation of the BBC as a public monopoly in 1926–7
therefore involved no great battles.*

*The Crawford committee has usually been seen through the eyes of Reith, who was not
a member. Crawford's own comments say nothing about the evidence given, and little
about the members of the committee, but throw some light on the composition of the
report, and much on the motives which he brought to his work. The English members,
Lord Rayleigh, Sir Henry Hadow, Sir Thomas Royden, Dame Meriel Talbot and
Kipling, are not mentioned, nor is the Scottish politician Ian Macpherson. The chief
division was between Crawford and the Labour ex-minister William Graham on the one*

hand, and Captain Ian Fraser and Lord Blanesburgh on the other, on the issue of whether the Treasury should benefit from licence fees.

Crawford had strong views on this point, but surrendered them in order to secure unanimity. 'I have no clear idea what my colleagues think, though my own mind is quite emphatic on the proper policy to pursue', he wrote when, the evidence having been heard, he was preparing his draft report. This – 'short, sensible, and in certain places weak' – he finished on 11 February, noting

My colleagues dare not go so far as I would wish in acknowledging the right of the treasury to share the proceeds: however I am anxious to get a unanimous report. Blanesburgh is difficult – he always changes his mind, and repudiates at night what he accepted in the afternoon.

His consolation in the discussions on the report was that

Graham who was a socialist minister, and they say one of the ablest of the lot, is staunch on my side ... This man talks like a first-class reactionary in opinions. He argues his case with calm persistence, knows his facts from unerring memory, and in his quiet way is most convincing. The more so he becomes, the purpler and more restive Blanesburgh becomes, while I sit by trying to bring the two factions together.

By 25 February, Crawford had compromised some of his own opinions to secure unanimity, but was pleased with the outcome. 'The report is good: clear, short, decisive, and good sense. The leading propositions are unassailable; but I suspect it will have a bad press.' In fact it was well received. The Daily Telegraph was the most hostile, but Lord Burnham, its owner, was apologetic about its criticisms over dinner. 'I asked him what alternative he proposed, and he was quite unable to suggest any.' As Crawford said, 'Respectable papers won't suffer, and probably know it'.

What was unexpected was Reith's attitude. Sir Arthur Stanley, chairman of the Wireless League, warmly approved of the report, but mentioned that Reith was very angry, and was saying that the BBC staff were very disappointed. Stanley pointed to the handsome compliments paid to the staff in the report. No, said Reith, the report has caused much umbrage. A few minutes later Stanley saw the second-in-command, who seemed quite satisfied, and revealed that the cause of Reith's vexation was that his name was not mentioned in the report. 'Reith has a swelled head,' Crawford commented, 'and is also annoyed because he fears that the commissioners won't be content to act as nonentities and figureheads: and I hope they won't!'

Crawford had one very definite axe to grind: dislike of the popular press, which he regarded as a corrupting factor in British life. The Express was a 'vile newspaper', the News of the World 'infamous'. The proprietor of the latter, Lord Riddell, was prominent among the press lords trying to restrict broadcasting, which made Crawford see his duty with particular clarity. 'There is quite a strong body of opinion which would view the obliteration of the popular press with equanimity.' Crawford overestimated the *harm which broadcasting might do, thinking that 'the low class papers which depend on sporting and betting news' might be seriously affected.*

Such prints as the *Star* and *Evening News* fear that their racing news will be anticipated by the broadcaster, and tremble for their future.

When press criticism centred on the growth of bureaucracy, 'the last thing we desired', Crawford saw this as a transparent camouflage for their threatened monopoly, and did not think there would be much difficulty in getting parliament to accept his proposals. These latter may have been only a reflection of an existing consensus, but Crawford's willingness to damage the irresponsible press lent force to his advocacy. 'I for one shall shed no tears', he wrote about the impending fate of papers 'which batten and fatten upon all the most unsavoury episodes of the law courts.'

The world would be all the better for a violent purging of these vile sheets, and though we are all by way of being afraid of the press, we shall all rejoice more or less openly in its suppression.

To Crawford, and probably to Baldwin also, the foundation of the BBC was an episode in the running battle between conservative decency and the sensational press.

12 MARCH 1925
Hewart,[1] the Lord Chief Justice, dined, and was curiously scathing about Asquith – his pompous platitudes, his perfect English, and his complete lack of initiative and imagination.

27 MARCH 1925
To the Athenaeum ... Baldwin came in – said he proposes to reappoint me to the Nat. Gallery Board; he is rather pleased with having survived another difficult parliamentary week 'without discredit' ... Trade goes from bad to worse ... So Baldwin takes an afternoon's repose in the Athenaeum to read a novel – one in which the first chapter begins with a murder and the last chapter concludes with the happy reunion of separated lovers.
    After dinner to the Italian Embassy where the Prime Minister told me that the novel was exactly what he wanted, something at once exciting and soporific.

28 MARCH 1925
This week is interesting, for we have watched the gradual and effective growth of a gigantic myth, namely that George Curzon[2] was a great man ... And so the world is

[1] Gordon Hewart, first Viscount Hewart (1870–1943), Lord Chief Justice 1922–40; Law Officer under Lloyd George, 1916–22.
[2] Curzon had died on 20 March.

never going to be told the truth about him. I never knew a man less loved by his colleagues and more hated by his subordinates, never a man so bereft of conscience, of charity, or of gratitude. On the other hand the combination of power, of industry, and of ambition with a mean personality is almost without parallel. Personally I liked him well for his great qualities, and seldom found occasion to criticise his smallnesses of character; we got on excellently together, he was first class company, and always stimulated people to work their hardest ... but assuredly I have never attended a funeral ceremony at which the congregation was so dry-eyed!

21 APRIL 1925
Dined at the Club; a small party with Baldwin in the chair, pleasant and very intimate. Talk about Semitism.

27 APRIL 1925
Willie Peel just back from a continental tour. What impressed him most? Why, the unpleasantly low quality of new recruits to the Diplomatic Service! He says they may be extremely clever and no doubt are – they may speak foreign languages well though they show small mastery of our own. They are virtuous but dull, painstaking but wholly unattractive – never invited out to Society ... I think it was Edward Grey who threw open the F.O. exams to all and sundry. It was called a democratic reform, and like many such efforts enshrines an admirable principle which collapses in practice. Grey was always a doctrinaire.

9 JUNE 1925
Dined at The Club. Bishop Gore said that in answer to a recent question as to which is the best hymn of recent times, he selected the 'Hymn to Mithras' in *Puck of Pook's Hill*, a choice which greatly amused Kipling.

2 JULY 1925
Signed the Royal Commission on Wheat Supplies report, and so ends one long chapter in my life. It was on my birthday nine years ago that the Wheat Commission was set up at Runciman's initiative. Little did I then realise either the scale or the importance of the work, which gradually increased until by the end of the war, we were controlling almost the whole exportable grain of the world, and feeding half the populations! Then with the Armistice began a new phase quite as difficult, though less anxious than our duties during the actual warfare. Finally the old Commission was wound up, and the work of liquidation was handed over to a new and reduced personnel of which I retained the chairmanship. Today we signed our final report. It will attract no attention – doesn't deserve to – for so efficient has our work been that we have always eluded public attention.

Curzon had been chancellor of Oxford University since 1907. On his death, the Conservative nomination went to Milner, to Birkenhead's fury. The latter, indeed, said that he had written to Asquith to say that many Conservatives would support his candidature. ('They might indeed do so against F.E.' commented Crawford.) Horne also was virulent about Milner, on the grounds that his Egyptian report had been disastrous. In the event neither Asquith nor Birkenhead stood, and Milner died twelve hours after his unopposed return. The Oxford authorities, fearful lest Milner die on the eve of polling, thus allowing Birkenhead to slip in by default, had prepared a nomination for Lord Cave for use at short notice. In the second election of 1925, Cave, who was a worthy but unimportant Conservative, easily defeated Asquith, but voting turned on personality and desire for moral decorum (i.e. aversion to Birkenhead) as much as on party.[3]

3 JULY 1925

I am delighted at Cave's success. It is a well-deserved rebuff to Sir John Simon and Birkenhead. Each of them worked Asquith's candidature for ulterior motives: Simon to exclude Grey whom the Oxford Liberals preferred, F.E. to strengthen his own claim to the post when Asquith dies. Poor F.E. – he has suffered a series of setbacks – failing to be nominated for Oxford on Curzon's death, now the rejection of his nominee, the veto on his journalistic enterprises, and at least two refusals of his ill-concealed desire for a vacant Garter; and of all blows the last is the most wounding.

Another disappointment, too, was that Birkenhead had pressed his claims to write Curzon's biography (not being indifferent, Crawford thought, to the £3,000 offered by the executors for the job to John Buchan and Whibley, who both refused).

13 JULY 1925

F.E. attacked Lady Curzon on the subject, and in effect claimed that he had the right to write the book. He was in a highly excitable condition – angry at being passed over, and told her, almost with violence, that whether officially or unofficially, he proposed to write the book. She observed that she could not prevent his writing a life of her husband, but that the literary executors proposed to entrust the family documents to someone else. F.E. repeated something in the nature of a threat... But one difficulty presents itself, which F.E. in his impetuous way may not have foreseen. Ian Malcolm[4] has made a deal with Downing St about these documents. He has undertaken that the originals (each of which is headed 'the property of H.M.G.') shall be used with discretion; shall be kept under lock and key at the bank, and shall only be quoted with approval of the departments concerned.

[3] When Cave fell seriously ill in 1928, a panic again arose among the forces of decency at Oxford that Birkenhead might inflict himself upon them by being first in the field. Aghast at this prospect they turned first to Crawford (who refused outright), then to Salisbury (who was initially interested, but withdrew on Edward Grey coming forward, in order not to split the 'high-minded' vote). Viscount Grey, who had been sent down for idleness forty years earlier, was chancellor 1928–33.

[4] Sir Ian Malcolm of Poltalloch (1868–1944), diplomatist and author; MP (Cons.) 1895–1906, 1910–19.

This being so it will be extremely difficult for F.E. to anticipate the official biography by publishing extracts from the identical documents in his possession ... F.E., who is desperately hard up now that his journalism is stopped, may well rush matters; publish his book and risk the consequences.

28 AUGUST 1925

Dined with Edmund Gosse – a party to bid farewell to Nicolson on his appointment to Teheran. Gosse tells me that Nicolson[5] is the first among our younger historians and critics for sound well-balanced judgment; and his reputation at the F.O. stands high. He is an odd person, affected in appearance, *précieux* (and somewhat sloppy) in pronunciation, witty and withal modest. As he loses the Oxford manner and the F.O. diction, he will become more attractive, and I imagine pretty forcible as well.

22 NOVEMBER 1925

Hugh Cecil described in a very loud voice how easily he bursts into tears. He considers himself one of the most emotional people of his acquaintance, which rather interests me as his intellectual outlook is so largely governed by a logical and argumentative mind ... He is quite cold-blooded in discussing any ordinary problem of the day, yet is quite unable to check his tears if he hears of some generous sentiment or courageous action.

25 NOVEMBER 1925

Earle, of the Office of Works amused me by a story of Epstein, who visited the memorial in Hyde Park during the summer. He was quite well known to the park keeper, who heard Epstein say 'Well, I have never seen such a monstrous thing in my life', whereupon a man emerged from the crowd, perfectly furious, and shaking his fist in Epstein's face said, 'How dare you say such a thing? This is one of the greatest works of art of our time', and continued with such a display of passion that Epstein lost his courage and disappeared amidst the apparent contempt felt by onlookers towards this philistine.

22 DECEMBER 1925

I went to see Baldwin about broadcasting parliamentary proceedings. It is part of the wider problem of broadcasting controversial matter generally. We settled the point of procedure in two minutes, and conversation fell on to Beaverbrook. Baldwin has read some of it – says that it gave him the impression of memoirs written by an elderly courtesan who recites with glee the spacious days and sensational conquests of her youth, and cannot altogether conceal her spleen as she realises that never again will these triumphs occur ... Baldwin says that the influence of the *Daily Mail*, etc., is steadily diminishing. The stunt is impressive for a short time but quickly evaporates. Why don't we recognise this, acclaim it

[5] (Sir) Harold Nicolson (1886–1968), man of letters.

publicly, and snuff out these vulgar and ostentatious press lords?... Stanley I thought in excellent spirits. He may well be so having improved his standing in parliament and still more in the country.

14 JANUARY 1926
Baldwin asked to see me, about Waterloo Bridge... He is most anxious to save the famous structure, but he won't find the task easy. We talked about his address to the Classical Association. It was a fine, indeed an inspiring speech, and he says that appreciative letters he has received from unexpected quarters, have given him more pleasure than he has experienced for many a long day.

Dring at Quaritch's told me that he has not got £1,000 of *incunabula* in his stock. It is really astonishing, but the supply seems suddenly to have run out. For years past public libraries have been buying them up in both continents, and scarcely any are available. Dring will buy back at double the price paid by his customers for the last twenty years.

2 FEBRUARY 1926
Dined at The Club... Stamfordham[6] surprised me by saying that he actually received the legacy left him by Horace Farquhar. I always thought that the old boy's bequests proved chimerical, in other words that the estate he so lavishly distributed was swallowed up by debts. Not so. If Stamfordham got his hundred guineas, the others presumably received their share. It was to have been five hundred but Horace was furious with Stamfordham who he alleged had dissuaded the King from giving Horace the G.C.B. Stamfordham certainly discouraged such an idea and quite rightly as such a decoration should be confined to those who have given signal service to the state. But I fancy Farquhar got it after all. He claimed audience after audience, and wore down all resistance by his obstinacy and cheek.[7]

9 FEBRUARY 1926
Board meeting.[8] £157,000 loss on the year, and £300,000 overdrawn at the bank; and I dare say the Miners' Federation will say we have made and concealed enormous profits!

10 FEBRUARY 1926
Ballot at Grillions. A big gathering, and Baldwin who came in late with Eustace Percy had to sit at a little table by themselves where I joined them. Baldwin is appointing Arthur Lee[9] to the vacant place on the National Gallery Board – says it

---

[6] Arthur John Bigge, Baron Stamfordham (1849–1931), private secretary to George V 1901–31.
[7] Cf. above, 25 February 1925.
[8] Wigan Coal and Iron Co.
[9] Arthur Lee, first Viscount Lee of Fareham (1868–1947), trustee of the National Gallery 1926–33.

is the only way to keep him quiet. Also at the dinner Asquith, two Archbishops, Austen Chamberlain, Ned Talbot[10]...

19 FEBRUARY 1926
Annual meeting at Kirklees. 1925 is the first year in our history during which we have paid no dividend. It is not merely that our profits disappeared, but that we have ended the year with a terrific overdraft. This must be extinguished before we can hope to resume dividends... How many such years can we stand?

24 FEBRUARY 1926
Dined at Grillions – Austen Chamberlain, Sir James Barrie,[11] Haldane, Eustace Percy... Haldane talking about his relations with the restaurant keepers of London. Odenino's hold him in such esteem that they send him, gratis, a daily supply of the finest rolls to be had in the world. Monico, Café Royale, Jules, Blue Posts – all fall down in worshipping Haldane, who is equally at home and petted by the masters of the continent. In old days H. was a good customer, but he was also a successful advocate when they got into court, and to this day when he is old and toothless, and much too ill to dine out in public places, they recall his past prowess, in wig and gown, equally with knife and fork, and complimented him accordingly.

15 MARCH 1926
Went to see Amery[12] who wants to persuade the National Gallery to surrender the Lane Bequest to Dublin; being Colonial Secretary... he is anxious to make a friendly gesture at our expense... What a funny heavy-handed little person Amery is – an enthusiast almost a fanatic, yet what an odd frame of mind, to take up this question and to give himself the trouble of seeing me, and yet not to have read the files on the subject. He was quite unfamiliar with the facts of the case.

Ronald[13] home from Constantinople. He dined tonight, and I got Ramsay MacDonald to come – I left them closeted for a couple of hours after dinner and I doubt not that Ronald told him a lot of home truths about democracy amongst eastern nations.

31 MARCH 1926
Dined at the Carlton with Steel-Maitland.[14] We discussed the coal situation, which the government has deputed him to manage as Cunliffe's[15] wife is concerned in coal

---

[10] Edmund FitzAlan-Howard, first Viscount FitzAlan of Derwent (1855–1947), chief Unionist Whip 1913–21; last Lord-Lieutenant of Ireland 1921–2.
[11] Sir James Barrie (1860–1937), playwright.
[12] Leopold Stennett Amery (1873–1955), First Lord of the Admiralty 1922–4, Colonial Secretary 1924–9, secretary of State for India and Burma 1940–45. Cf. below, 19 October 1927.
[13] Ambassador at Constantinople, 1925.
[14] Sir Arthur Steel-Maitland (1876–1935), Minister of Labour 1924–9.
[15] Philip Cunliffe-Lister (changed name from Lloyd-Greame 1924), 1st Viscount Swinton; president of the Board of Trade 1924–9.

mines, and he had readily seized the excuse to be quit of a thankless task. Maitland asked me to meet him, talked round and round the subject, and for the life of me I could not make out what he was driving at. It occurred to me that he wanted to eliminate Evan Williams,[16] Nimmo,[17] and Co., and get the negotiations transferred to Londonderry,[18] myself, and other outsiders. Then I came to the conclusion that he did not intend this and we parted after I had vaguely promised to stand by if required. My impression is that he is thoroughly rattled, has no idea what will emerge in the next fortnight, and is beating about for some happy idea which will provide an exit. He said nothing to indicate comprehension of the central fact that the owners cannot go on paying out unremunerative wages. The Banks will not permit us to overdraw much longer.

21 APRIL 1926
Also declined Baldwin's invitation sent through Mitchell-Thomson[19] to become chairman of the new British Broadcasting body. I was rather amused at the suggestion; I consider myself quite unsuited for such a post, for which by the way the government is prepared to sanction a big salary. I had always thought D'Abernon[20] might be interested, but Baldwin has decided views on the subject.

Saw Steel-Maitland for a moment and discussed the coal situation. He is frightened as well he may be.

I talked to de Seyfried.[21] He tells me that some of the wage reductions are really alarming, if in the bad districts, Northumberland for instance or South Wales, sufficient economies are to be made to cut the existing loss. Lancashire wages do not require so drastic a drop, but even so he says he cannot see how with the best will in the world the miners could acquiesce in the owners' proposals.

31 APRIL 1926
I left Euston at 5.20 last night for Haigh. At Stafford I was intercepted by a message to return to Downing St. They flagged a train back to London and I got to the House of Commons by 11.0. I was with Betterton,[22] Weir, that ass Davidson,[23] and

[16] Sir Evan Williams (1871–1959), president, Mining Association of Great Britain 1919–44.

[17] Sir Adam Nimmo (d. 1939), chairman of Fife Coal Co. and sometime president, Mining Association of Great Britain.

[18] Charles, seventh Marquess of Londonderry (1852–1915), Minister of Education in Northern Ireland 1921–6, Secretary for Air 1931–5; a large coalowner in Durham.

[19] William Mitchell-Thomson, first Baron Selsdon (1877–1938), Postmaster-general 1924–9. The report of the Crawford Committee recommending the creation of a British Broadcasting Corporation came out in March 1926, but Mitchell-Thomson did not announce acceptance by the government until July.

[20] Sir Edgar Vincent, first Viscount D'Abernon (1857–1941), ambassador to Berlin 1920–26; sometime trustee of the National Gallery.

[21] Manager with the Wigan Coal and Iron Co.

[22] Henry Betterton, first Baron Rushcliffe (1872–1949), parliamentary secretary to the Ministry of Labour 1924–9.

[23] John Davidson, first Viscount Davidson (1889–1970), parliamentary secretary to the Admiralty 1924–7; intimate of Baldwin.

Steel-Maitland. I discovered that Baldwin thought that at some moment or other the coalowners might wish to see or consult with friendly outsiders; he had tried unsuccessfully to get hold of Londonderry. At 11.45 Steel-Maitland came out to tell me that the coalowners said they did not want to consult with anybody else, and of course they were quite right. They have been duly appointed by their constituents, and would have been tactless to seek advice of other coalowners. So I returned to Euston, caught the 12.30 am train . . . In evening working through the incunabula with a revised handlist in prospect. It seems strange to be doing so at such a moment but the subject is enthralling enough to give the mind repose from the cruel problem of the moment.

1 MAY 1926
Returned to town . . . At the Academy dinner tonight ministers looked very gloomy, and Joynson Hicks[24] made a speech which happily was without bounce.

2 MAY 1926
Sunday. Willie Peel[25] left the Dilettanti dinner at 9.30 tonight to go to a cabinet.

5 MAY 1926
This afternoon I heard a curious explanation in the Commons. Hugh Cecil asked Thomas why no effort was made to devise a formula to bring the parties together. Thomas replied that such an effort was made, that it was written out by Baldwin, accepted in principle by the T.U.C., who undertook to press it on the miners. During the conference with the miners, the T.U.C. were annoyed to receive a letter from Baldwin breaking off negotiations, on the ground that some employees of the *Daily Mail* had refused to print a leading article.

Meanwhile Baldwin who was out of the House had been sent for to hear Thomas' narrative. He came in, Thomas repeated it in a few words. Baldwin rose in dead silence; quite cool and collected. He said that the formula was not actually his, being prepared by a Ministry of Labour man, but substantially agreed with Thomas' statement, adding that as the first stroke in a general strike had been wielded, and against so important a thing as the press, he had no alternative. I gazed down on David and other Conservatives who looked aghast at this revelation. So it really was the sporadic and unauthorised disorder of a hundred printers and packers at Carmelite House which broke off negotiations . . . All this created a grievous impression on my mind. I can well believe it will exacerbate public opinion when known.

6 MAY 1926
Thursday. To Commons where I sat in the Peers' Gallery with Archbp. of Canterbury.[26] He is much rattled, would not stop talking. Says Lambeth Palace is a

---

[24] William Joynson-Hicks, first Viscount Brentford (1865–1932), Home Secretary 1924–9.
[25] First Commissioner of Works 1924–8.
[26] Dr Randall Davidson (1848–1930), Archbishop 1903–28.

scene of horror! Deputations all day – clergy, laity, nonconformists pressing him to do something or other and he hasn't a notion what to say. He evidently agrees with the government that economic problems cannot be discussed during a political revolution.

7 MAY 1926

I attended a meeting of coalowners at Mond's house to discuss future organisation of the coal trade. We did not progress beyond the preliminary point of the committee which should investigate and report on various schemes – the constitution, personnel, and terms of reference... Mond said one thing in a casual way which struck me, and others too. 'The coal trade should think less about a large production of coal than about making profits.'

8 MAY 1926

Saturday. Late at night talked with Cunliffe-Lister at the Carlton. We had heard Baldwin's broadcast message, which struck me rather as an appeal than a direct and downright reply to the Revolutionaries. Somehow the same impression was left in Lister's mind, but he said that when the PM read the message at the cabinet meeting, it sounded much firmer... Anyhow, Lister says that Baldwin has dug his heels in – George Younger says the same thing. The PM has some of the obstinacy of his cousin Rudyard Kipling, happily for this is not the time for compromise. And I was glad to gather from Stamfordham that the Court is not bringing pressure on the government to weaken. S. himself who is apt to be timorous is quite bellicose.

9 MAY 1926

I listened to the broadcast of the Archbishop's sermon at St Martin's. It appeared to be delivered in a strong and vigorous voice, but the matter seemed weak sloppy stuff – not a note of statesmanship. Willoughby de Broke once said of the Archbishop that he had a season ticket on the line of least resistance... Poor man, he is elderly, he has been ill, he is terribly upset, as I noticed at the British Museum meeting on Saturday – shaky with disordered hair and drooping features.

10 MAY 1926

F.E. asked to see me – went to his house about 2.30 where I found Steel-Maitland with whom I had already made an appointment for later in the afternoon. F.E. had cold feet. I was surprised. I had thought the general situation was in hand; all evidence points in that direction... F.E. however was in a fright, so was Steel-Maitland. I did not ask for explanations.

They want the coalowners to express their readiness to negotiate with the miners. On the strength of such a pronouncement the T.U.C. would be able to call off the general strike. Henderson, Thomas, and Co. would save their faces, and of course labour would say that the government had surrendered in a panic – had forced the coalowners to take this initiative. This all sounds too simple, for the hard fact remains that until Cook's [27] last official pronouncement is withdrawn – namely that no negotiations can proceed on the basis of district settlements, reduced wages or lengthened hours; until that the coalowners have nothing to negotiate upon. No, says F.E., begin to talk about inessentials such as pithead baths, grouping, transfer prices, anything except the fundamentals, as Cook and Co. now realise that a wage reduction is unavoidable.

The other thing, F.E. and S.M. indicated, was that Londonderry, I, Fitzherbert Wright,[28] and others should take over the conduct of affairs. But on what authority? How could we supersede the elected members of the central committee? Well, they say, if we get rid of Evan Williams, Adam Nimmo and the other diehards, we shall also manage to evict Cook, Herbert Smith,[29] etc., and the whole atmosphere will become more peaceful and businesslike. That would be an act of disloyalty towards those who actually elected the Coalowners' Committee, and the Miners' Federation would equally react against the dismissal of their chosen men.

I went on to Mond's house believing that a further committee was to meet – postponed. Talked to Mond whom I found preparing a speech for his company. Mond's committee tried to establish a tribunal to come into being the moment the general strike is over; F.E. suggests in effect that something of the kind should be announced in order to end the strike. Mond immediately saw the weakness of the position, though he would like to be one of the negotiators, as he dislikes Williams and holds Nimmo in contempt – but he was clear that nobody has any power to chuck them except the coal trade as a whole.

Talked to Londonderry at H. of L., dead against any intrigue, and he thinks Williams has done his work as well as could possibly be expected. I saw Mond later at House of Lords – situation rather complicated by a curious message about a meeting between Herbert Samuel and the Miners' Federation, giving the idea that the latter are prepared to accept a reduction in wages; but there seems to have been a *démenti* and everybody is puzzled. Steel-Maitland is to call on me early tomorrow morning.

11 MAY 1926
The conversation did not lead very far. The more I think of F.E.'s scheme the more dangerous it seems. Even if the approach was made by the coalowners, the Revolutionaries would treat it as an appeal for terms by the government. Later in morning Steel-Maitland asked if I would talk to Herbert Samuel; I said yes – went to discuss situation with Londonderry, who was in bed after a night with the Specials at Blackfriars.

[27] Arthur James Cook (1883–1931), secretary, Miners' Federation of Great Britain 1924–31.
[28] Probably Henry Fitzherbert Wright (1870–1947), chairman of the Butterley Co. 1938–44 and a public figure in Derbyshire; MP (Cons.) 1912–18.
[29] Herbert Smith (1862–1938), Yorkshire miners' leader; president, Miners' Federation of Great Britain 1922–9.

At House of Commons about 3.45 Sir A. Cope[30] told me that the coalowners won't accept any government committee. They said it would be a new arbitration – that they have already submitted to four or five government inquiries and each has made the situation worse...

At H. of L., Londonderry told me that many members of the government have cold feet. Asked Victor Churchill about it – he didn't think so, but went to H. of C. to see Stanley Baldwin, and came back saying that at any rate the P.M. is not trying to compromise.

12 MAY 1926

Wednesday. To our general surprise the strike has collapsed... Went to the Commons. The P.M. made a statement in which he did not say that the strike was unconditionally cancelled. This caused great anxiety among our friends. They feared that there had been a discussion of terms, and this was exemplified by Ammon,[31] a Labour member, rushing down to the cloakroom shouting out that there had been a great Labour victory! Salisbury in the Lords was quite as soft-hearted as Baldwin; I asked Bobby Monsell[32] what it really meant. He said that the surrender was quite unconditional, and that in view of the misrepresentations being made, he would broadcast the verbatim report... Baldwin allowed himself to be inveigled by Thomas and Bevin into a general and rambling discussion about the future, about victimisation, and never once did he pin this shifty gang to the fact that the general strike was smashed and that their admission of defeat really was unconditional. I hear deep disappointment and some bitterness, and not only among the diehards on our side.

13 MAY 1926

Thursday... Late at night however I saw F.E., who I was glad to find less nervous than when I last saw him. He had been with the P.M. in conference with the miners after dinner... This is another score, and face-saving advantage for the T.U.C. However F.E. says that for the first time Herbert Smith seems inclined to listen to reason – talked with some sense of the economic situation of coal, while Cook sat 'like a tired third class tart'.

Crawford's position during the general strike was clear enough, but does not lend itself to quotation. He was sympathetic to the miners, clear that they could not reduce wages except under force majeure, *and only choleric about the 'revolutionaries' who exploited the economic impasse, and 'the hordes of well-dressed idle young men' whom he saw in*

[30] Sir Alfred Cope, senior civil servant 1919–22; general secretary, National Liberal organisation, 1922–4; managing director, Amalgamated Anthracite Collieries 1925–35.

[31] Charles George Ammon, first Baron Ammon (1875–1960), parliamentary secretary to the Admiralty 1924, 1929–31.

[32] (Sir) Bolton Meredith Eyres-Monsell, first Viscount Monsell (1881–1969), Conservative Chief Whip 1923–31, First Lord of the Admiralty 1931–5; cr. Viscount, 1935.

London, not pulling their weight as volunteers in support of law and order. He knew that the 'right' answer for the coal trade was for a third of the mines (including probably his own) to have gone bankrupt; he thought that the coalowners' leaders, though not harsh men and justifiably mistrustful of government intervention, were maladroit and unpleasing. He was extremely anxious about whether the 'safety men' would continue to be allowed to go down the pits. But there was nothing he could do, and he did not propose to waste energies in vain in attempting to be a creative coalowner.

He therefore gave his energies to saving Waterloo Bridge from the LCC, who wanted it replaced. He saw Baldwin many times during the coal crisis on this issue. The rest of the art world required governance; and December 1926 saw the foundation of the Council for the Preservation of Rural England, with Crawford as president, and Neville Chamberlain as the speaker at its inaugural meeting.

1 JUNE 1926

H. of Lords War Memorial. Tweed[33] produced a tiny model – a youth offering his dead father's sword to Britannia. I liked it – the style is very stiff and classical; but poor Tweed was embarrassed by our naive questions, such as Lord Lansdowne's.[34] 'Mr Tweed, what I want to be clear about is why the youth hasn't got his clothes on?'

26 NOVEMBER 1926

The coal strike is over. I don't think an agreement has been signed yet, but the men are hastening back to sign on and presumably recognise the disaster they have met. They could have got better terms three or four months ago, but the incredible vanity of Cook, and the abysmal ignorance of Herbert Smith have proved too strong a combination. Of the two I look upon Smith as the greater danger for his stupidity was clothed in a kind of bluff Yorkshire hypocrisy – and many people really believed him to be a man of judgement. By degrees the sorrow and distress inflicted on the country by these two men will be recognised by the colliers – but the dupes will be duped again, if not by Smith, by somebody else. There is no limit to the susceptibility of the collier to blandishments and threats.

10 DECEMBER 1926

A small dinner party, the only one this year, for finance has not encouraged such enterprises. We were Trustees of the National Gallery – Witt,[35] D'Abernon, Sassoon,[36] Daniel,[37] Arthur Lee and myself – and we talked N.G. matters

[33] John Tweed (1869–1933), sculptor of memorials to Wellington, Chamberlain and Kitchener. His peers' war memorial was completed in 1932.
[34] The fifth Marquess of Lansdowne (1845–1927), Unionist statesman.
[35] Sir Robert Witt (d. 1952), solicitor and art historian; trustee of the National Gallery 1916–23, 1924–31, and from 1933 (chairman 1930).
[36] Sir Philip Sassoon (1888–1939), trustee of the National Gallery 1921–8.
[37] Sir A. M. Daniel (1866–1950), trustee of the National Gallery 1925–9 and its director 1929–33; see below, 22 March 1928.

assiduously from beginning to end of the evening. As the conversation progressed I think we all realised what great reforms are necessary – in procedure, in policy, and in our educational and publishing work. But Holmes[38] is most difficult – so jealous and peppery that one has to proceed with the greatest circumspection lest he should have a fit. However during the last year or two some real progress has been made and with patience I hope to accomplish a good deal more.

The era of bad feeling at the National Gallery had deep roots, and was not readily amended. The director all but refused to inform the trustees of prospective acquisitions; 'the Trustees never ask for unreasonable things, but every suggestion is turned down offhand', noted Crawford after one confrontation.

7 JANUARY 1927

Long and painful conversation with Holmes at the National Gallery. There must be very few government officials who look upon me as a tyrant, or who have felt that I was jealous of them; and yet Holmes displays all the meanness and evasion, all the rancour and vexations one would expect to encounter in some departmental row in the Foreign Affairs Department in Paris. Anyhow, Holmes' attitude is inexplicable in all directions – not merely as against myself; but as I am chairman of the Trustees I am perhaps most affronted by this extraordinary behaviour. How does it come about that the N.G. has such a bad reputation for rows between the Director and his Trustees? I can only suppose because the Director is brought into the public service late in life, whereas the men at the British Museum have had years of training before reaching the high administrative posts.

Most unhopeful Board meeting.[39] We made a lot of money during November, the first month following the strike; December profit so moderate as to suggest that during May we shall make little or nothing. This is the most serious monthly sheet I have seen for a long time as it indicates that we have not even now reached an economic basis.

26 JANUARY 1927

I attended a conference at the Society of Arts where the P.M. made a good speech about the preservation of old country cottages.

5 FEBRUARY 1927

Herbert Fisher[40] told me about the effort being made at Oxford to prevent the place being hemmed in by industrial quarters and suburbs. He is trying to raise a big sum, but is reluctant to make any public appeal which would of course put up prices

[38] Sir Charles Holmes (1868–1936), director of the National Gallery 1916–28.
[39] Wigan Coal and Iron Co.
[40] H. A. L. Fisher (1865–1940), historian; president of Board of Education, 1916–22; Warden of New College 1925–40.

against the colleges . . . The cheap motor car and the passion for bungalows have got a tremendous start on the highroad to vulgarity, and one is at issue with half the community. I fear that in many areas we are too late.

17 FEBRUARY 1927
Lunched with Sassoon; Lord Lansdowne there and Arthur Lee . . . What a lunch Sassoon gives! I have always had a pardonable ambition to make the acquaintance of a *Grande Cocotte*. Sassoon's lunch is precisely the style and manner of lunch I should expect from the G.C. Table napkins are yellow satin. Fruit for the four of us would have fed twenty people. Salad for four filled a large bowl as big as a large washing basin. The waste, the robbery of it all – and yet I derive great pleasure from a combination which makes me extremely greedy; and Sassoon himself, despite an Asiatic outlook, remains quite simple and unaffected in the midst of all this opulence.

26 JUNE 1927
I went to luncheon at Trent Park, Sassoon's country mansion close to Barnet. The place has been transformed . . . The house has been refaced with fresh well-tinted red brick and much of the stonework of old Devonshire House has been applied as window settings. The cornice comes from Devonshire House and very well it looks. The inside of the house has been completely renewed and also is a becoming interior. How does this extraordinary young man manage to attract people to his side? Partly finance no doubt. The quality of our luncheon, the luxury of the housekeeping, the gardens, cars, tennis court (covered in, and with a professional in attendance) – everything points to a most lavish and unchecked expenditure – but even these comforts would in themselves be inadequate to draw so many – there were at luncheon A.J.B., the Salisburies, Pembrokes, Churchills, Lovats, D'Abernons and I don't know how many more; we were quite twenty-five at lunch, and not merely people who are drawn to good living. Personally I try to keep aloof from the rich Jew or American and I don't much want to be mixed up with Asiatics – but Sassoon is a keen and loyal colleague on the National Gallery Board, and I wish to see him often; and I acknowledge a peculiar charm in his cool friendliness, or is it a friendly coolness? What fantastic sums that young man must spend on his entertainments. I hope the firm is secure.

28 JUNE 1927
Dined at The Club, Edward Grey in the chair. His troubles have now been diagnosed as colitis, involving periodical inoculations, which cause him discomfort, but which are apparently doing him good for I never saw him looking better during the last two or three years. I fancy also that his eyesight is not so weak as previously. We were a small party and had some pretty general talk partly about natural history (the new salmon at the Zoo), partly about the burdensome gifts of modern science

and ingenuity. Grey sees little advantage in our progresses, medicine apart; but he considers the push bicycle as a great help to mankind. The motor car is useful but corrupting, so too with many inventions which do little more than accelerate. The bicycle did that but not to the extent of making us ignore the things we should have appreciated on foot. There was something else he approved of but I can't remember what.

....I think we were eight in number, which conforms to what A.J.B. laid down the other day at Trent for the ideal dinner party – not too large for general talk, not too small to prevent surprises and vicissitudes. He told us that were he a young host he would begin again on that basis. The table however must not be round. The wine must be good, much more carefully considered than is usual nowadays; the fruit also must be plentiful and choice.

'And would you have a hostess?' we asked Lord Balfour. No, he said pensively. 'I do not think I should have a hostess.'

19 OCTOBER 1927

I tackled F.E. at the Carlton about ministers being so much abroad ... He said it was an excellent thing on general grounds that a tiresome bore like Amery should spend a long time abroad. When Churchill (who feels small affection for Amery) was asked about the travelling allowances, he said that for every week Amery was absent from the country, the weekly rate of allowance was to rise, and to do so handsomely.

In the diaries for 1928–9 one sees rather a new pattern of life, not that of an ex-politician turned observer of politics, as in the mid-1920s, but that of a man who had decided to leave politics, and even political consciousness, to others. There is a deliberate shortening of sail, even, in his own words, of indolence – reflected by increasingly irregular diary entries. As an established figure in the world of cultural administration, Crawford had found a load which he knew suited him, and he did not sigh for new worlds to conquer. Even if his private affairs had been in good order, he would have found ways of repelling calls on his time.

His only overt political activity was making eight speeches for his son in the 1929 election (where the paucity of posters struck him as a great change from the old days). The Labour government of 1929 produced no frisson, though he was happy to report the Whitehall description of a Labour leader, Susan Lawrence,[41] as virago intacta; and he did complain, as in 1924, of the extremely good press that Labour got when in office. Even before the June 1929 election, he understood that Rothermere was keeping in close touch with MacDonald (14 April 1929). His only surprise about the Conservative defeat was that anybody should be surprised by it; he had early taken it as read. He saw gloom abroad, partly because he believed Germany to be still militarist at heart, partly because

[41] Susan Lawrence (1871–1941), MP (Lab.) 1923–4, 1926–31; parliamentary secretary to the Ministry of Health, 1929–31; chairman of Labour Party 1929–30; a mathematics graduate.

of the way the Foreign Office officials (rather than Henderson, in Lloyd's view) forced the British Proconsul in Egypt, George Lloyd, to resign. His conversations with Baldwin and MacDonald arose because of their interest in art; of the lesser lights he saw little.

Refusals of office and honours included an Oxford DCL (but he already had five honorary degrees), high university offices at St Andrews and Leicester vacated by Haldane's death, and the chairmanship of the Egyptian Exploration Society. On the other hand, he sat on BBC committees, 'permeated with a fragrance of earnest endeavour', and on the soirées committee of the Royal Society, where he persuaded his colleagues to draw up a new invitation list which excluded those long dead. He presided, as often before, at the Miners' Permanent Relief Societies Conference, and, again not for the first time, showed a conference of two hundred librarians over the collections at Haigh. Perhaps his favourite commitment was the Royal Literary Fund, a good-humoured body which never found any difficulty in its task of giving away money to impecunious writers of notably modest attainments. Less fortunate was the newly-founded Council for the Preservation of Rural England. Not only did Crawford think that it had come on the scene too late in the day, but he found himself not acting as a figurehead, as he had intended, but taking part in helping it to raise funds, and making his first broadcast on its behalf. After many disappointments, including refusals from peers like Fitzwilliam and Portland, the CPRE was finally set on its feet by an unexpected gift of £10,000 from an American called Penrose who had an estate in Somerset. The cause of conservation advanced by minute particulars, rather than by a broad advance in public support such as occurred after the second war; thus one of the happier events of 1929, the purchase of Stonehenge for the nation, was achieved through the slightly amateurish enthusiasm of the poet Sir J. C. Squire. If Crawford noted that none of these things really engaged his whole energies, this reflected deeper changes than his increasing sense of being a grandfather and belonging to a generation which was now loosing its grip on public affairs. Money was the root of the problem.

In February 1928 the Wigan Coal and Iron Company announced its third successive year of losses, and this even in a year of relative prosperity. Business continued poor throughout 1928. The situation was desperate, and behind Crawford's apparent uncertainty about engaging deeply in public affairs, lay a gloomy feeling that he should be saving the firm. 'I can't accept new responsibilities ... I must be as free as possible in respect of the Company affairs' (30 October 1928). Whether the firm could have been saved under free trade, is doubtful; but what precipitated reorganisation was not action by the owners, but an unwelcome letter from the Westminster Bank indicating that their patience was exhausted, and that the company should call up its unpaid capital. This was seen by Crawford not as a mere unpleasant financial exercise, but as involving the threat of dispersal for the books and pictures. Baldwin had indicated that there could be no hope of 'safeguarding' against cheap imports before 1930 at earliest; upon which the bankers moved in. In November 1928, Montagu Norman 'suggested' amalgamation with the other great Lancashire firm of Pearson and Knowles, a project often considered and as often deferred, but now brought forward under continuing pressure from the banks. The diaries do not tell the story of the negotiations that led (with help from

'The Uncrowned King of British Art'

tariffs) to the formation of the new and strikingly successful Lancashire Steel Corporation of the thirties; all that need be noted here is that the Wigan Coal and Iron Company was a dying concern well before the great slump of 1929 hit England.

Crawford's occasional comments on politicians of his own persuasion were usually unflattering. For instance, Austen Chamberlain, once very much Crawford's leader, had fallen from grace since he returned from Locarno with a Franco-Italian habit of speaking by gesticulation. Frequent disparagement of him occurs, reflecting Foreign Office views, especially those of Crawford's brother Ronald, now a permanent under-secretary (1928–30). In July 1928 the Foreign Secretary was 'tired and only comes two days a week'; in December he was constantly absent, 'Leaguing in Switzerland'.

3 JANUARY 1929

I had some talk with Austen Chamberlain who seemed a very wan and woe-begone figure, lacking all that animation for which he was so notable: Ronald had told me that the life and energy seem to have gone out of him, though he has not relaxed his control of affairs or his confidence in himself. Today I found him very *piano* – inclined to ask questions rather than pronounce judgements.

13 APRIL 1929

Ronald dined; not very happy about foreign affairs. The cabinet is tired and inefficient while Chamberlain is seldom at his desk more than a few weeks at a time. I wish I were chief whip again for six months; by the end of that time I would ensure at least that the Empire is governed from Whitehall.

3 JULY 1929

Ronald observed *sotto voce* that the Foreign Office feels as if it is being run by six Secretaries of State. I gather on all sides that ministers are looking after one another's business – particularly the ubiquitous Prime Minister, a sort of miniature Mussolini.

The strange world of museums and academies was much less dull than that of parliament. Here, a trifling dispute could ignite a conflagration, there were forgeries to detect, and promising new performers like Munnings[42] taking the stage.

25 FEBRUARY 1928

At the Natural History Museum a shindy is brewing because the Trustees moved Darwin's statue from its position on the staircase to a place nearer the door, Owen's[43] statue taking its place. The Darwinians are up in arms ... It is opined that Darwin has been dethroned and that Professor Owen (a nobody according to some of these biologists) has been given the post of honour.

[42] Sir Alfred J. Munnings (1878–1959), president of the Royal Academy 1944–9.
[43] Sir Richard Owen (1804–92), naturalist, and first superintendent of the natural history collections at S. Kensington; attacked Darwin's *Origin of Species*, 1860.

522

18 APRIL 1928

An entertaining evening at the Garrick Club ... The most astonishing feat was the recitals by A. J. Munnings the painter – one a long ballad about a hunting squire called Anthony who defied a ghost – really a masterly thing, composed by Munnings himself, and recited with gusto and bravura – witty, sometimes quite tragic, altogether something approaching genius in its tout ensemble.

23 FEBRUARY 1929

At the B.M. this morning Kenyon reported a first class gaffe by Campbell Dodgson[44] who much against the wish of the Trustees, persuaded the Board to pay 300 guineas for a soi-disant portrait of Marie Antoinette by David. When the thing was shown us a fortnight ago I told Dodgson so far as politeness allowed, that the thing was doubtful. Now it is admitted to be a very commonplace sophistication which should not have deceived the department for a moment. We buy badly at the B.M. We fritter away our money on trifling objects instead of concentrating on important things; the fact is that the Trustees don't exercise adequate control – partly because they are appointed for reasons other than experience in museum affairs, partly because the tradition is to attach sacrosanctity to the Keeper's advice. Fancy if we had applied this principle to the recommendations made by the egregious Holmes of the National Gallery.

But the main issues consisted of three long drawn-out episodes; Duveen's[45] successful attempt to 'buy' himself a trusteeship of the National Gallery while still a dealer, the attempts to keep the sculptor Alfred Gilbert off beer long enough for him to complete a great statue of Queen Alexandra, and the continuing fracas over the Chantrey bequest. MacDonald, a British Museum trustee, and Baldwin, a sympathetic if indecisive listener, flit across the scene, finding in art a grateful change of employment.

Alfred Gilbert[46] (1854–1934), the sculptor of Eros in Piccadilly Circus, engaged Crawford's anxious surveillance. It seemed to lie in the balance whether his memorial to Queen Alexandra would ever be accomplished. He was given a studio in Kensington Palace; this did not prove enough. A great lady, herself no mean artist, Violet Granby, Duchess of Rutland, exerted herself on his behalf. Those in charge of the memorial had to weigh such imponderables as whether comfort in Kensington would produce more exertion than the sculptor's customary routine of beer quaffed in the company of commercial travellers in the Strand. As with Rodin a generation before, Crawford was surprised to find that a sculptor might, in his person, not greatly suggest the idea of beauty. In the end, everybody got what they wanted, Gilbert moved into Kensington Palace, and the memorial was duly placed at Marlborough Gate.

At the British Museum, Ramsay MacDonald was a good colleague, and tried so far as rather limited powers permitted to be a good trustee:

[44] Keeper of prints and drawings, British Museum, 1912–32.
[45] Joseph Duveen, first Baron Duveen (1869–1939), the leading dealer of his time; trustee of the National Gallery 1929–36.
[46] Cf. below, 11 November 1934.

'The Uncrowned King of British Art'

10 FEBRUARY 1928

Building committee at B.M. Afterwards a longish talk and a walk through the streets with Ramsay MacDonald. I can't make him out. His conversation (on Museum matters) is reasonable, his outlook calm, his appreciation of difficulties acute. He attempts no short cut, and has no formula for success; no violence either. And yet when discussing affairs of state his temper is uncontrollable, and he insults everybody within reach. Every opponent is incompetent or actuated by base motives, and generally speaking he seems to be an intolerant and unscrupulous person. Wherein lies the true Ramsay MacDonald? This evening I had a little dinner party of National Gallery trustees ... They would like to have MacDonald on the Board to replace Sassoon[47] ... I am quite ready to agree, though I am reluctant to give the impression that politicians are necessary to us; were it not for his parliamentary status we should scarcely suggest him.

13 FEBRUARY 1928

Two of our trustees now come to National Gallery meetings attended by nurses.

Baldwin was in surprisingly close touch with artistic affairs:

20 MARCH 1928

Went to see Baldwin who wanted to talk about the Chantrey Trust ... I wasn't in a position to tell much to the Prime Minister but I promised to adjust the difficulties if possible. I also recommended Daniel[48] to succeed Holmes, and MacDonald to succeed Sassoon on the Board. Baldwin seemed well and glad enough to see someone he hadn't recently talked to ...

22 MARCH 1928

Daniel came to see me, hot-footed from the Prime Minister whom he interviewed at ten this morning. I asked Baldwin, by the way, why he appointed Daniel a trustee of the National Gallery. Baldwin seems to have remembered some conversations at Cambridge,[49] and also that Daniel had been a fine football player. Anyhow he is now one of the most astute members of the Board and I greatly hope he will become our Director. Daniel's impulse was to refuse – change of home, environment, leisure, and so forth – but he consented to think over the proposal by which he is evidently tremendously flattered.

Sir Joseph Duveen, the great art dealer, was not easily to be brushed aside. In July 1928 he settled with Crawford to increase the sum he had offered for additions to the National Gallery. At the same time Crawford learned from Arthur Lee (Viscount Lee of

---

[47] Trustee 1921–8
[48] Daniel (1929–33) succeeded Holmes (1916–28) as director.
[49] Baldwin and Daniel had both been at Trinity.

Fareham) that Duveen's one ambition was to become a trustee while still an active dealer. Crawford at first thought it out of the question, at least until Duveen had retired from business. Then in December 1928 Crawford found himself presiding over a British Museum conference on Duveen's offer of a new room for the Elgin marbles, a far from simple matter for every addition at the museum, unlike at the National Gallery, was at the expense of some other department – in this case Egyptian antiquities were threatened. After discussion with Baldwin, the matter came to a head:

6 FEBRUARY 1929

N.G. Board meeting – important. Discussed two paramount pictures – also discussed Sir Joseph Duveen. The Prime Minister is quite prepared to appoint him to the vacant trusteeship. Lee, Ormsby-Gore,[50] Witt, agree. We know that D'Abernon does; to my surprise Ramsay MacDonald took the same view. Daniel consents too. Heseltine[51] and I feel old-fashioned scruples at a man buying a seat on the Board, especially as Duveen has been canvassing hard and has now reached the stage of telling us how tired he gets of making big contributions without adequate returns; threatening us in fact with the loss of his largesse. It is a lamentable situation. Duveen has established a terrorism over buyers in the USA, and apparently his generosity to us has forced our hand. The dealers will feel that Duveen hasn't paid too much for the tremendous advertisement in America of getting a trusteeship – and also for the advance information he will get through membership of our Board, say about export taxes for instance. Duveen's competitors will be angry but they have never done much for the Gallery.

14 FEBRUARY 1929

To see the Prime Minister, to whom I communicated the view of the N.G. trustees that Duveen should be appointed to the vacant trusteeship. D'Abernon, Lee, Witt, MacDonald, to some extent Daniel, and Sassoon also (who has a strong claim on the vacant post) all want Duveen as a colleague. I have my doubts and told both my co-trustees and Baldwin, that even if the press may be amiable in view of Duveen's generosity, the precedent is awkward, and the professional dealer will have a real grievance. Baldwin said we have placed ourselves in Duveen's hands by accepting his largesse; pray at what point of his payments were we to decide that Duveen was buying a seat on the Board? – it would have been difficult to refuse his gifts just because he is the protagonist in the export of British possessions. Courtauld[52] has

---

[50] William Ormsby-Gore, fourth Lord Harlech (1885–1964), MP (Cons.) 1910–38; First Commissioner of Works 1931–6, Colonial Secretary 1936–8; succeeded to title 1938; trustee of the National Gallery 1927–34; published *Florentine Sculptors of the Fifteenth Century*, 1930.

[51] J. P. Heseltine (1843–1929), a trustee since 1893; 'a picturesque and stately figure in a Chinese silk gown with gold buttons' (diary, 18 December 1926).

[52] Samuel Courtauld (1876–1947), chairman of Courtaulds 1921–46; endowed Courtauld Institute; trustee of the National Gallery 1931–8 and from 1939.

promised us £50,000; must we decline it, or tell him that he must not look upon it as establishing any claim on the government?[53].

Miscellaneous comments on men and matters in 1928–9 include:

15 FEBRUARY 1928

At Grillions Club I sat with Lord Dawson,[54] and Londonderry; two Archbishops present, and Baldwin in the chair. A good deal of talk about our deceased member, Lord Oxford and Asquith[55] ... He was a genial agreeable companion, with a host of excellent stories, a marvellous memory for quotations, a fine knowledge of English literature – a real scholar who loved scholarship for its own sake and always turned it to its best uses. Gosse says Asquith was the perfect orator; that the sequence of his argument never flagged and that his sentences never came out wrong. This is true – but Gosse's experience is based upon the last fifteen years, since he, Gosse, became Librarian of the House of Lords. Gosse used to go to the Gallery on great occasions to hear Asquith's important speeches. Being as blind as a bat Gosse never realised that every word of these orations was read from typewritten documents. Campbell-Bannerman did the same. Churchill, the most fluent of speakers, occasionally does likewise, and I am told that recently Baldwin has read his discourses.

Arthur Balfour's enjoyment of life was unabated, though he had characteristically allowed someone, perhaps Israel Gollancz, to perpetrate an opulent redecoration of the British Academy[56] which Crawford found painfully vulgar.

4 JULY 1928

At Grillions sat with Hartington,[57] Dawson of Penn, A.J.B. and H. A. L. Fisher ... A.J.B. was in very good form; ate and drank sufficient to call for congratulation from Dawson who was recently called in to see him, for Balfour has been very ill. He had a mass extraction of teeth and the shock nearly proved too great – weeks have elapsed since I saw him and I was overjoyed to see how well he looks, how exuberant his spirits, and how pointed his conversation.

---

[53] Duveen, while remaining a dealer, was trustee of the Wallace Collection 1925–39, of the National Gallery 1929–36, and of the National Portrait Gallery 1933–9. He was created a baronet in 1927 and a baron in 1933.

[54] Bertrand Edward Dawson, first Viscount Dawson of Penn (1864–1945), physician to George V 1914–36; president, Royal College of Physicians, 1931–8.

[55] Asquith had died on 15 February.

[56] The refurbished British Academy was described by Crawford as 'a sad combination of the Office of Works and the late Sir Israel Gollancz – could worse taste in arranging a suite of apartments be produced? and the place is dark, draughty, and grimy into the bargain.'

[57] Edward William Spencer Cavendish, tenth Duke of Devonshire (1895–1950), MP (Cons.) W. Derbyshire 1923–38.

25 JULY 1928

Balfour's eightieth birthday. Derby organised a birthday present for him, a Rolls Royce car, and this was duly presented in the Speaker's Court this afternoon – a fine strong businesslike machine which will give him great pleasure. Baldwin, Lloyd George, and Clynes[58] made the gift on behalf of various groups of parliamentary colleagues and admirers – all these three speeches, delightfully short and appropriate. Then A.J.B. settled down – back to the car, one hand on the spare wheel, and we were treated to eighteen minutes on parliamentary life, together with a panegyric of Lloyd George which seemed both too lengthy and too cordial. At one time Balfour described certain aspects of ministerial cooperation 'when I was at the Home Office.' 'Foreign Office' whispered somebody close by. Ah yes, went on Balfour – Foreign Office – I should have said Foreign Office – and went serenely on to another serious blunder – but how like him it all was, and how disappointed we should all have been if he had given us a precise, accurate, and documented analysis of his sentiments.

1 AUGUST 1928

Grillions at night, a very small party in which Hartington took the lead as conversation turned by chance on to cock-fighting. To our astonishment we discovered him to be an enthusiast, even an apologist, looking upon it as a clean and kindly sport – for no cock fights unless it wants to! There is nothing in it to compare with bull or badger baiting, and the silver or steel spurs are actually less dangerous than a blow from the spur *au naturel* which is inclined to produce septicaemia. It was all most entertaining and surprising too. I took occasion to remind him that if he happened to be caught by the police he would certainly lose his seat at the next election.

5 OCTOBER 1928

We were taken a trip to Rivington ... What a place! The late Leverhulme[59] bought it years ago, kept extending it – only a year or two before his death he added a huge ballroom – and now this preposterous accumulation of rooms and verandahs is perched in the middle of Rivington Moore; large gardens surround the house itself, and the week after he died a hundred gardeners were sacked. What a queer old fellow he was. Here he was uncontrolled and one sees the odd potpourri of rubbish and good things he collected – a few really nice bits of tapestry hung between monstrous forgeries, and a number of wretched canvases by R.A.s of the eighties and nineties.

1 FEBRUARY 1929

I had to see Baldwin about National Gallery trusteeships, and took occasion to

[58] J. R. Clynes (1869–1949), Labour politician; leader of party, 1921–2, cabinet minister 1924, 1929–31.
[59] William Hesketh Lever, first Viscount Leverhulme (1851–1925), soap magnate and philanthropist.

congratulate him on his recent speeches – a good speech at Newcastle, followed by Dundee (where he was astonished by his reception) – finally an address to 400 Baptists. Funny, he said, fancy a Tory Prime Minister being cheered by the most representative Baptists in the country; yes, I replied, and fancy that personage making a panegyric of Dr Clifford[60] whom we remember as the author of the most malignant attacks launched against ourselves... He was a passive resister of the most sour type. And now to be praised by our party! Well, the whirligig of time would appear to find justification for Dr Clifford; and if in the process we snaffle the Baptist vote, so much the better. We shall want all the votes we can get... I thought Baldwin in pretty good spirits, though weary.

2 JUNE 1929

Ronald drove me to Burcote – horrified by Garvin's suggestion (which may result from a hint) that Sir Oswald Mosley may be Foreign Secretary. It is almost incredible that a sane journalist could make such a suggestion – it is all the more sinister in consequence; the idea that this cad should be at the F.O.! For the last year or two he has been a parasite on R. MacDonald; they have gone about together, and Mosley perhaps gives MacDonald just those things which MacDonald may fancy he lacks – a companion with a certain smartness in costume, conversation, and address – a showy talkative woman versed in the society side of diplomatic life – and somehow or other I really feel that Garvin may be right in suggesting that this toady is destined for high office; but if this be true, Ramsay MacD. stands condemned as a judge of men, and his party would be justly incensed at such an appointment.

5 JUNE 1929

To Londonderry House – the Derby Ball; a somewhat gloomy affair as the place was full of Conservative ministers who are just out of office... Mrs Baldwin I thought a little tearful, poor woman; the Socialists are in a tremendous hurry to get into Chequers and Downing St, and she was at a loss to find a suitable house – however the Duke of Westminster seems to have come to the rescue. I saw many other old friends and colleagues who in accepting Londonderry's invitation thought they would attend a jollification after a Conservative victory. I can't make out why such miscalculation should have existed – probably because so many of our prominent men sit for safe seats in the midlands and south.

12 JUNE 1929

I went on to Lady Rothschild's ball. They say that at this function one should stay on till 3.0 a.m. when many gentiles have departed. One then sees the *haute juiverie* undiluted; but it is always remarkable to see which Jews are excluded by Lady R. from *la haute juiverie*. The number is not inconsiderable.

[60] Dr John Clifford (1836–1923), Baptist preacher who led the militant Nonconformists against the Conservatives' Education Act of 1902.

11 JULY 1929

To Lady Witt's party, where I saw the owners of the Warren Gallery, whence a dozen paintings by a nasty wretch called Lawrence[61] have just been seized by the police. I never saw a more degenerate looking couple than the two owners of this gallery. I felt inclined to box the young man's ears.

23 OCTOBER 1929

A long talk with John Burns who is horrified at Lansbury's schemes to make playgrounds[62] of the central parks. I share this apprehension. Burns doesn't change much. I still see him walking all over London without a stick, umbrella, or overcoat. I often wonder what he does when it rains – I have asked but he never quite seems to know. I dare say he has friends in every other street of the metropolis. His passion is still London – he is a great Londoner. A keen bibliophile too. I fancy Burns was one of those to whom Carnegie left an annuity, anyhow J.B. is now quite independent and can gratify his tastes which are rather expensive...

Lansdowne House is about to fall into the hands of the housebreakers. Dorchester House is now level with the ground – indeed the big cranes are already moving masses of earth being grubbed from the site – preparing the foundations of a super hotel, the most luxurious hotel in Europe, in London, in Park Lane, beside which the Grosvenor will be a pothouse. I remember so many London palaces disappearing, in fact one can count on one hand those which survive, and soon they must be doomed before long. I particularly regret Lansdowne House, a building of great scale and dignity, well furnished, and decorated by the original architect... The late Lord Lansdowne himself whom one associated with the spaciousness and magnificence of his house told me when he had left the place and was installed in the small comfortable house in Brook St, that then for the first time in his life he realised what real comfort was – the ease of always being within reach of a bell, of a table, of a book, and not being obliged to take a walk if he wanted to reach anything.

[61] D. H. Lawrence

[62] Lansbury, as Minister of Works, had shown his golden heart (and the dullness of his colleagues) by making his new Serpentine Lido the main talking-point in Labour policy. Cf. diary, 27 July 1931, for Burns's grievances: 'Burns it appears had a collision with Lansbury in the H. of C. lobby, and Lansbury scenting advertisement began to shout and bluster. "Don't bully me" said Burns, "and above all don't shout..." One phrase of his addressed to Lansbury is worth quoting, "You corrupted the East End and now you are vulgarising the West End – can't you leave London alone?"'

XVI

The slump,
1929-35

*Montagu Norman in action – British Museum affairs – the Royal Fine Art
Commission – shindies at the National Gallery – Duveen and the Elgin
marbles – the Prince of Wales as a National Gallery trustee – Alfred Noyes blows
his own trumpet – a Lancaster tyrant – Lutyens and Liverpool cathedral – Lord
Parmoor in age – devious conduct of Master of Peterhouse – G. F.
Watts – Churchill on tariffs – Labour leaders unable to concentrate – Lord Derby
and Knowsley – Dr Gore – the King enjoys his tea – the premier's telephone
tapped – a visit from Berenson – a water closet blocks the new Elgin
room – Skittles and Lord Hartington – Trenchard on police corruption – St Paul's
and Dean Inge – the Duke of Kent – the Prince of Wales and his food – Alfred
Gilbert – Churchill on India – horrors of Apsley House.*

*The slump brought about great changes for Crawford. His family firm, the Wigan Coal
and Iron Co., was forcibly 'rationalised' by Montagu Norman, the governor of the Bank
of England. Its last board meeting as an operating company was on 31 July 1930. Much
of Wigan's heavy industry closed down, the rest becoming part of the new and ultimately
successful Lancashire Steel combine. At first Crawford served as caretaker chairman;
then, at Norman's behest, he resigned on 31 March 1931. Norman's choice as his
successor, John James, proved, as Crawford later acknowledged, a brilliant success.
Crawford, and later his eldest son, continued to play an important part in the new firm,
but the unique position of the family in Wigan was ended more by the sweeping changes of
1930–31 than by the war or by nationalisation.*

7 JANUARY 1930

The argument Norman employed [*for rationalisation*] was occasionally weak and
sometimes contradictory. He seemed to rely overmuch on the opinion of his
doctrinaire colleague, Sir Andrew Duncan,[1] who was present throughout our
interview. At the luncheon table it occurred to me that the Board of the Bank of
England is largely composed of statisticians, retired civil servants and war
phenomena – Blackett, Stamp, Niemeyer, Andrew Duncan, and he himself,

---

[1] Sir Andrew Rae Duncan (1884–1952), director of Bank of England 1929–40, chairman of executive,
British Iron and Steel Federation 1935–40, minister 1940–45.

530

Norman; in their own affairs they have never given more employment than that vouchsafed to gardener, chauffeur, and valet. They are too much detached from the realities of production with its tremendous problems; they are usurers and nothing else... The banks sail serenely above the tempests of industrial trouble.

31 JULY 1930

We shall never again have that friendly and intimate feeling of the family business which has always prevailed... but amalgamation is essential however much one may lament its necessity.

13 JANUARY 1931

At Warrington, an executive meeting of the Lancashire Steel Corporation; I find it all very interesting, and as time goes on they become reconciled to my chairmanship, about which many of them must have been doubtful at first. The expert is naturally timorous about the non-expert chairman: on the other hand my experience of such posts is wide, and people especially businessmen are all alike; and I long ago laid down broad principles for guiding committees or boards or commissions. Never have these principles failed me; great patience, an occasional laugh, consultation of all and sundry, collective responsibility under my guidance – not easily attained or maintained, but none the less within our grasp if enough trouble be taken. So I am gradually consolidating my position in the big new Steel Co. and I am flattered by certain expressions, certain hopes that I will not treat that post as purely transitional, which of course has always been my avowed intention...

17 FEBRUARY 1931

Montagu Norman came to see me, the Governor of the Bank of England, about Lancashire Steel. I have only seen him once before – then in his Threadneedle St parlour, now in my own house. He told me that all our troubles are owing to my chairmanship of the concern, and all will vanish if he appoints somebody else, if necessary from Chicago. Bravo I said, but not from Chicago please – preferably from Czechoslovakia or the Ruhr, we shan't understand Chicago ways in Lancashire or perhaps we understand them too well.

During the 1930s, Crawford considered changing his way of life and becoming a full-time Lancashire businessman. The District Bank beckoned; so did the Manchester Ship Canal. 'They want a chairman, not a hydrographer.' He thought of dropping his commitments in the world of art. In the end, he preferred to live off capital and sell some pictures rather than give up public service in order to enrich himself. Some jobs, however, he refused; the chairmanship of the National Trust, of the revived Wheat Commission, of an inquiry into the House of Lords. What remained was the British Museum and the National Gallery, the chancellorship of the University of Manchester and the chairmanship of the Royal Fine Art Commission, and talk at the clubs with other men of his generation, now in their fifties and sixties. This provides some of the most interesting pages of the diaries, but it should not be forgotten that his life included much else that hardly figures in the selected passages that follow. Crawford had almost no interest in being rich for its own sake, but was deeply melancholy about the impossibility of maintaining the inherited achievement of his family as private collectors.

31 DECEMBER 1931

The fact is that the situation, my own I mean, worries me so much that I feel *désoeuvré* and quite disinclined to settle down. Who knows how long our precious possessions will remain with us – possessions which give us the only position worth having, the status of thoughtful and cultivated people.

10 JANUARY 1932

Yesterday I wrote to Dr Beets of Amsterdam telling him that I have it in mind to sell one or more of my Dutch pictures.[2] Alas! but I see no alternative, and I feel that this may be the beginning of a terrible dispersion. Were our fine pictures assembled they would make one of the greatest collections in England – scattered their comprehensiveness and their quality are ill-appreciated. They form the appanage of our family and their loss will cause us profound distress. Books and pictures combine to make Haigh one of the great and famous houses of England – stripped of those treasures the place would be uninhabitable.

At the British Museum, Kenyon's directorship was drawing to a close, but the trustees deferred the problem by asking Kenyon to stay on until the ripe age of sixty-seven, no obvious internal successor being in sight.

4 NOVEMBER 1929

Kenyon told me of his projected resignation . . . He has been a valuable Director though apt to resent suggestions of reform. He wants Hill to succeed him. I did not commit myself, though my first impression would be to concur. Some of the Keepers, such as Walters, Dodgson, Barnett, are quite impossible; but Hill, good scholar as he is, and man of wide tastes, scarcely has the personality or physique for so onerous a post. Kenyon's difficulty is obvious; he has to talk to his principal Trustees – Lang, Fitzroy, and Sankey. Lang has been to the Museum half a dozen times, Fitzroy twice, Sankey never – and these three men have all the patronage in their hands.[3]

[2] In 1932 Crawford's *Titus* by Rembrandt went to the National Gallery for appraisal, but the trustees considered it too costly to buy.

[3] The three principal trustees were the Archbishop of Canterbury (Lang), the Speaker (Fitzroy), and the Lord Chancellor (Sankey). The diaries frequently refer to Cantuar's poor health and weariness at this period; a holiday on Pierpont Morgan's yacht in the Mediterranean did not help, despite a special train home from Venice provided by his host (spring 1931).

The Royal Fine Art Commission, which had been set up under Crawford to review public policy from a standpoint of Olympian impersonality, fell short of the ideal. The proposal by the South African government to appoint their own leading architect, Herbert Baker,[4] to build South Africa House in Trafalgar Square, provoked violent denunciation from Lutyens and Blomfield,[5] two architect members of the commission who were otherwise not on speaking terms after a particularly painful contretemps *on professional ethics. South Africa House achieved the impossible and united the two great British architects in a common ebullition of rancour. 'Their personal antagonism is so intense that they generally attack one another exclusively and so conceal their spleen.' The discussion showed Crawford that a man of Baker's high standing could not count on fair play from the RFAC.*

Lutyens of course can say nothing too violent about Baker and his 'South African style', and the frank and almost openly avowed hostility towards a rival architect produces an awkward situation. Professional jealousy I have encountered from time to time, but never anything quite so cynical or uncompromising.

Even without South Africa House, the RFAC remained one of the most vexatious of Crawford's commitments.

The personal animus of Lutyens and Blomfield is a source of endless difficulty to me, and I wonder at times if it is worth going on with the Commission, to which I have devoted such care.[6]

One of Crawford's main headaches in 1929–32 was the increasingly unsatisfactory collection of trustees inflicted upon the National Gallery where Baldwin and MacDonald had each made the other a trustee.

14 DECEMBER 1929

Baldwin by the way has been appointed to our vacancy at Trafalgar Square. That makes four members of parliament, and as they always get restless at 3.30 p.m. they are unsatisfactory colleagues. They are overworked at Westminster and in their constituencies and seem to think their duty is fulfilled if they attend Board meetings pretty regularly, whereas they should of course visit the Gallery constantly, and get to know and feel its inner and outer life.

11 FEBRUARY 1930

Board meeting at N.G. Baldwin attended for the first time, I should fancy having already missed two or three of our monthly meetings. When Prime Minister he

---

[4] Sir Herbert Baker (1862–1946), architect of many public buildings in South Africa and England.
[5] Sir Reginald Blomfield (1856–1942), architect and historian of architecture.
[6] Cf. below, 1 October 1934.

The slump

appointed R. MacDonald, who could scarcely do less when a vacancy occurred than repay the compliment. R.M. himself hasn't attended for several months, and Baldwin was in one of his tiresome moods of silence – never uttered a word the whole afternoon . . . Duveen also absent in USA, and as there are two other M.P.s on the Board our attendance is bad and there is always an unwholesome tendency to hurry our deliberations.

Duveen's character did not improve on closer acquaintance. It was known that he was drawing in his horns with regard to donations, following the collapse of the US market; and it was suspected that he was looking for an exit, via a quarrel, from his offer to re-house the Elgin marbles. The issue was whether to employ an American artist whom Duveen named as the only possible architect for the Elgin rooms. The British Museum, when first accepting Duveen's offer, had done nothing to encourage this, but on the other hand it had not expressly stipulated against it, and so was in a rather weak position. Duveen's terms then hardened further.

17 JUNE 1930
Had words with Duveen. After long talk about the new Elgin room he said in effect that if the wonderful scheme prepared by Russell Pope[7] were modified, he would chuck the whole thing. I said I regretted that menaces should enter into the problem and left the room. He then telephoned to Kenyon in a fright and annoyed as well, and K. pacified him, or at least hopes he did so. Duveen's ignorance is tiresome, but his obstinacy and his impotence to understand an argument, are really galling.

24 JULY 1930
N.G. Board, discussed values of paramount pictures. The more we see and hear of Duveen the more futile does his opinion on ordinary gallery problems become.

26 JULY 1930
Some days ago it was rumoured that the Prince of Wales was to be appointed to the vacancy caused by the retirement of Herbert Cook.[8] I refused to credit the rumour, but today the appointment is gazetted. I fail to understand the motive of so extraordinary a gaffe. It is precisely the kind of snobbery a man like MacDonald would commit, but I strongly suspect that the initiative came from Sassoon, abetted perhaps by D'Abernon. For the last few years appointments have been made on merits and not as rewards for social or political services. Now we have MacDonald and Baldwin, followed by the Prince, with Duveen as no. 4 who has avowedly bought his Trusteeship. I look upon it as most unfortunate, and if the Board is to be changed in its essential outlook it will be necessary to review the position of the Director. It may be necessary for him to revert to the dictatorship of Barton's day.

[7] John Russell Pope (1874–1937), US architect.
[8] Sir Herbert Frederick Cook (1868–1939), connoisseur; one of the founders of the National Art Collections Fund and the *Burlington Magazine*; trustee of the National Gallery 1923–30.

11 NOVEMBER 1930

The Prince of Wales turned up at the National Gallery board meeting today. He fairly amazed us. About halfway through our proceedings, which happened to be extremely important, he got bored and began to smoke... The cigarette however enlivened the Prince and he began to talk to his neighbours, Sassoon and D'Abernon. The latter grows slow and deaf, but his voice is still resonant. Sassoon on the other hand with his raucous Syrian voice and his acute desire to 'honour the King' chattered away – and between them the two made business practically impossible. We were quite bewildered by the time our meeting ended. So far as I could make out, the chatter was chiefly about racing and society.

12 DECEMBER 1930

Dined with Prince of Wales at St. James's palace; all men, obviously a duty dinner... The Prince talked to me about our N.G. discussion – said laughingly that he was one of its causes, which is true enough. But he said, 'I want to attend – I like pictures. I don't go to the B.M. because I don't like Egyptian antiquities and that sort of thing.' The King was v. scornful when the appointment to the N.G. was announced – vexed in fact, and said he was sure the Prince would not attend.

In point of fact the latter was told to shoot at Windsor last Tuesday. 'I don't much care about shooting,' he said, 'but it was a splendid excuse to say that there was an important Trustees' meeting at Trafalgar Square. So I told the King that public business prevented my attendance. Rather a good score, wasn't it?'

19 MAY 1931

Board meeting N.G. – the Prince of Wales scarcely stopped chattering from beginning to end, and as both his neighbours, who happen to be Sassoon and Duveen, have got penetrating and raucous voices, it is almost impossible to conduct our business.[9] Poor Arthur Lee is in despair.

9 NOVEMBER 1931

N.G. board meeting; attenuated – for Duveen is in America, P. of Wales doesn't habitually turn up, and we have now four ministers of whom three are in the cabinet (MacDonald, Baldwin, and Ormsby-Gore, together with Sassoon). It is preposterous to have such an assembly of duds, and we had important, v. important business on which the fullest consultation was desirable. Ormsby-Gore did do us the favour of looking in for a few minutes, and gave opinions upon problems which he had not heard discussed. I retire from the board next spring, and on the whole I shall not regret a sojourn in retirement, though I should no doubt wish to reoccupy an official post on the board again. But the future does not seem to be very rosy. Somehow we seem to be getting back into the atmosphere of contention which used to prevail in Holmes's day, and which gave me so much anxiety. I had hoped great things of

[9] To be fair, Crawford also records several meetings at which the Prince did behave.

The slump

Daniel, but he has not maintained a fresh and whole-hearted interest in the gallery or in the welfare of its staff. He is unable to delegate work or responsibility with the result that we are losing Constable[10] who should have succeeded Daniel in the Directorship. Constable accepted the appointment at the Courtauld Institute because his position at Trafalgar Square had become intolerable.

9 FEBRUARY 1932

Lunched with Sassoon... From Sassoon's to N.G. board. He tells me that Ormsby-Gore says he won't attend so long as Lee is chairman. This is like the sulkiness of a spiteful schoolgirl, especially as he, Ormsby-Gore, was an unsuccessful candidate for the chairmanship. How a cabinet minister could also fulfil the heavy duties of such a post I don't understand, but he has great confidence in himself. It is tiresome that the N.G. is again getting into a state of paralysis. I attribute this to our political appointments.[11]

26 NOVEMBER 1932

N.G. board... The Prince of Wales present, I thought rather amused at our vivacities. While we were discussing a picture by Jerome Bosch he said, 'Is this by one of the painters they call a Primitive?'

If trustees were touchy or erratic, their directors could be just as maladroit. The diary records a joint approach by the directors of the three great London galleries, who, conscious of their disinterestedness, put in a claim to sit ex officio *on the National Art-Collections Fund. They considered that their opinions might be of use in deciding which galleries to benefit; but Crawford thought otherwise, and there the matter ended.*

1 APRIL 1931

Committee about the Elgin Room. Pope has made revised drawings but his disposition of the Marbles remains very bad and it seems more than probable that 'Joe' Duveen will say all or nothing – in which case I hope we will be firm. Duveen of course would bless us in his heart of hearts.

5 MAY 1931

At B.M. conference with Duveen and Russell Pope about the new Elgin Room. Duveen ridiculous and impossible; his ignorance is so dense as to make argument unserviceable. Pope understands the situation, but as we left it today we have practically reached an impasse, and Duveen may settle to withdraw his offer. Kenyon's letter of acceptance in the first instance was very ill-guarded.

---

[10] W. G. Constable, Assistant Director, National Gallery, 1929–31; Director of the Courtauld Institute; Slade Professor, Cambridge University, 1935–37; curator, Boston Museum of Fine Arts, from 1918.

[11] Cf. below, 30 March 1935.

8 MAY 1931

We resumed our conversation at the B.M., Duveen in a much chastened mood. I think D'Abernon has given him a talking to; Pope also less inclined to pontificate. Anyhow the main principles of the Trustees' contentions were accepted and Pope is to try again ... Duveen lectured and harangued us, and talked the most hopeless nonsense about cleaning old works of art. I suppose he has destroyed more old masters by overcleaning than anybody else in the world, and now he told us that all old marbles should be thoroughly cleaned – so thoroughly that he would dip them into acid. Fancy – we listened patiently to these boastful follies as Duveen owed himself some revenge for having to capitulate.

8 DECEMBER 1931

N.G. meeting. Discussed Hermitage pictures and the Duveen room, which is now generally acknowledged to be a complete failure. They talk about remodelling its lighting, but as the thing is fundamentally wrong little can be done. I have the satisfaction of having warned them that both in design and method Duveen's scheme was ill-considered, but I was overborne, and now we have a gallery which is not only tiresome in itself, but which also throws neighbouring galleries out of harmony. Duveen is generous, but obstinate and without taste.

17 NOVEMBER 1932

Elgin Room Committee at British Museum. I think our long controversy is now ended and that Russell Pope will now proceed to inflict a very grandiose affair upon us – a great palace for which the Elgin Marbles will form the chief decorative feature. We have whittled down his extravagances; I dare say we have exscinded £20,000 worth of superfluous ornament – but the place still remains a painful contrast to the strength and simplicity of the New Pergamon Room at Berlin.

2 MAY 1930

I wonder what may be the etiquette among poets in dealing with public appointments, say for the vacant Laureateship. May they canvass, should they pay ceremonial visits as is obligatory on postulants to the French Academy? I wondered when this morning Alfred Noyes[12] came to see me, and discoursed for just about an hour on his unique claim to succeed Dr Bridges. I was a little nonplussed, but I frankly admitted after hearing Noyes' merits and the demerits of other candidates, that the Noyes claim is considerable. He showed how he had always upheld the sanctity of his art, how his tremendous series of American lectures had been good propaganda for Britain – how numerous are the reprints of his poems, how Mrs

---

[12] Alfred Noyes, poet (1880–1958) but never Poet Laureate. The appointment on this occasion went to Masefield.

The slump

Noyes is likely to subscribe to the Bedford House fund, – as I say, I ended by being quite convinced that if W. Watson is too old for the job, Masefield too Republican, Kipling too much of a prose writer, Housman too retiring, Newbolt too much of a historian, Seaman too closely associated with *Punch*, de la Mare with novels, etc. etc., then nobody's claims can vie with those of Alfred Noyes.

Our conversation was very cordial. Once or twice he apologised for blowing his own trombone, but I put him at his ease, and I must say I never saw anybody less embarrassed by so very personal a task. My politician friends are poor advocates compared with Noyes – and I got much pleasure at watching his smooth broad smug face grow animated as he enlarged upon his own virtues and touched lightly – ever so lightly – on the shortcomings of his rivals.

7 MAY 1930

Dined at Grillions. We have moved to Grosvenor House as the Cecil Hotel is now the headquarters of some international oil ring. We have a pleasant room and a good dinner. Cantuar in the chair. Talked to Austen Chamberlain, or rather he talked to us, at us, over us, on to us, through us over and above us; in fact he did all the talking.[13]

Crawford declined the sinecure of Constable of Lancaster Castle, an office recently vacated by the death of the linoleum millionaire who practically owned Lancaster, Lord Ashton.[14]

15 JUNE 1930

The old curmudgeon died a few weeks ago, intestate, but as he must have left many millions his heirs won't have much to complain of. He was a tyrant. I remember Sir Norval Helme[15] who was Liberal member for Lancaster, and Williamson's nominee, telling me that Williamson once threatened him with dire penalties should any independence in politics appear. I asked Helme what would have happened. It appeared that Helme was modestly engaged in linoleum, the same business as his patron's, and that the latter would have dropped prices in Helme's line of business, low enough to involve bankruptcy to the little firm. Williamson, or Lord Ashton as he became, was always a vindictive man.

3 OCTOBER 1930

Lutyens in good form ... He is thrilled by the prospects of building the new R.C. cathedral for Liverpool – a church bigger than Scott's, better sited, more dramatic, more beautiful. He has a hundred fantasies about it – how to arrange the holy water

---

[13] Cf. below, 28 February 1935.

[14] James Williamson, first Lord Ashton (1842–1930); father-in-law, surprisingly, of the Conservative minister Willie Peel.

[15] Sir N. Helme (1849–1932), MP (Lib.) Lancaster 1900–18.

stoops, how to design liveries for the sacristan (he asked to borrow our papal guard uniform) – how to do this that and the other in some fashion which will be new as well as canonical, picturesque as well as conventional. He certainly is full of witty fantasies and must amuse even if he doesn't sometimes alarm the portly Archbishop . . .

7 NOVEMBER 1930

I again saw Parmoor[16] at his house. It was rather a pathetic interview. He is now seventy-nine and failing. I remember him as a brisk and successful Tory M.P. – today he is a Socialist minister, ostensibly so on the plea of Free Trade and humanitarianism, but thoroughly out of it, probably disliking his colleagues, and unable to exercise any effective check on their follies. He greeted me with effusion, wished to revive the cordial relations of old days, and seemed happy to talk on the terms of equality and persiflage which were habitual to us in old days. None of his colleagues can or would chaff him now! or he them, and there was something almost touching in his effort to revive memories and relations which he severed in a moment of pique.

9 MARCH 1931

I paid a visit to Neville Chamberlain who asked me to take the chairmanship of a committee he is to set up to investigate H. of Lords problems – reconstitution, powers and so forth. I naturally had to say no, though ready enough to serve on the enquiry. He told me that Astor[17] is very keen on it and offered £1,000 towards the expenses, rather indicating that he would like to be on the committee, if not to take charge of it. That would never do. He is not persona grata to our House – lectures us too much, and his wife annoys us by coming to the bar and disturbing us by her loud talk.

14 MARCH 1931

To Cambridge, to stay at Trinity College where my grandfather studied and where my father took life easily as it came. I stayed with J.J. Thomson[18] who invented the electron . . .

The visit was marked by a glimpse of Housman,[19] an unlikely appearance by Jimmy Thomas in Trinity Master's Lodge, and stories of devious behaviour by Lord Chalmers,[20] the Master of Peterhouse. Chalmers had a fatherly feeling for his house-

---

[16] Charles Alfred Cripps, first Baron Parmoor (1852–1941), MP (Cons.) before 1914; Labour minister 1924 and 1929–31; father of Stafford Cripps.

[17] Waldorf Astor, second Viscount (1879–1952), MP (Cons.) 1910–19, and husband of Lady Astor, the first woman to sit in the Commons.

[18] Sir Joseph John Thomson (1856–1940), physicist; Master of Trinity 1918–40.

[19] A. E. Housman (1859–1936), poet and classical scholar.

[20] Robert Chalmers, first Baron Chalmers (1858–1938), civil servant; Master of Peterhouse 1924–31.

The slump

maid, to whom he taught Greek. He provided both for her and for his own old age by marrying her to a young clergyman, getting him presented with a college living which had a fine parsonage, and then going off to live with the young couple in the rural retreat thus provided. Cambridge buzzed with the story, the details of which were long and most entertaining, especially 'as Chalmers who escapes with all the swag is an Oxford man'.

15 MARCH 1931

A very busy day. Thomas at breakfast in boisterous form. His son is an undergraduate. Last night after our dinner and a reception in the Master's Lodge, Thomas retired to the common room where some concert or other took place. He made them a witty and apposite speech containing much persiflage but a few sentences at the end, of great fervour and patriotic emotion. After that he played bridge and smoked and drank till 2 a.m. At breakfast he discovered to his dismay that the 10 a.m. train to London doesn't run on Sundays; he was due in town for a conference at 11.30. So he was hustled into a charabanc – what a comedown for this railway boss – I dare say he kept his fellow passengers in fits of laughter all the way.

...Housman interested me more, much more, than anybody else I saw at Cambridge... I asked J. J. Thomson about him – I learned that Housman is tremendously interested in astrology, that he takes no part in college affairs, that he is concerned in Jacobite lore, and that he has a 'sensitive palate' – in other words that he is quite an epicure,[21] a shrewd critic of victuals, and that a famous Paris restaurant has named a dish furnished according to his recipe.

11 APRIL 1931

The Sargent portrait of A.J.B. at the Carlton Club is insured for £25,000 – what an illustration of the fictitious fame attaching to the painter. I told them that £1,250 – the sum needed to buy two good copies of other portraits of A.J.B. – would amply suffice in the event of the big picture being burned.

23 APRIL 1931

I went to Guildford for a meeting of the Watts Trustees at the Limnerslease Gallery. The old lady there is in good spirits but feeling the burden of advancing years. We discussed the future, not without some questionings amongst ourselves as to the verdict of posterity, for old G. F. Watts. Signore, as we called him, no longer commands the respect and affection which gave him such a position during his lifetime. I was never an enthusiast, for the best of his paintings after the period of early portraiture, seemed to partake of the amateur – but now – now that one looks upon them critically as one admires old masters, one sees their formlessness, their indifferent knowledge of technique, their sentimentalities, their faulty anatomy; and as time goes on we shall more and more realise their defective painting. Pictures which I recollect thirty or forty years ago as glowing with colour are now gloomy murky affairs with the pigment resolutely sinking into the canvas.

[21] Cf. below, 19 April 1937.

11 MAY 1931

Royal Literary Fund dinner – sat with the Duke of York, chairman. He made quite a good little speech, though I thought perhaps rather more hesitating than usual. He stammers, but silently; that is to say though the throat appears to be gulping, and making an effort, no sound emerges; so there is nothing audible, nothing painful – just occasional pauses during which one might suppose him to be searching for the correct word.

In June 1931, no less than 130 members of that jovial body, the Lancashire Authors' Association, arrived at Haigh for tea – or rather a series of three slap-up teas, some members assisting at each sitting. A thoroughly good time was had by all, and the family vision of Haigh and its treasures as a cultural beacon for the county, especially at teatime, was triumphantly vindicated.

28 JULY 1931

Victor Churchill[22] tells me that Josiah Stamp[23] and Keynes are conducting a vigorous intrigue to displace Norman from the Governorship of the Bank of England. Dangerous as I believe Norman to be, I prefer the neurotic to the spouter; Stamp has reduced the L.M.S. to chaos, spends his time lecturing about statistics to the nonconformist intelligentsia, and appears to do all sorts of things except look after his railway company – the finest commercial proposition in the empire ten years ago, and now under Stamp's tutelage a disastrous failure. Meanwhile Norman is vigorously criticised. He confessed to me – and without the smallest idea of how grave the implications were – that he can only devote an hour a week to the commerce of England – that from the Governor of the Bank of England!

Crawford showed little reaction either to the minority Labour ministry of 1929–31, or to the political and economic crisis of 1932. In the first case, his criticism of ministers was limited to 'their humbug, their sanctimonious outlook, their assumption of good fellowship and amity'.[24] His affinity for Baldwin remained unshaken during the Conservative leadership crisis of 1930, not surprisingly since Crawford's most recent project, the Council for the Preservation of Rural England, was Baldwin's rural nostalgia in action. In 1931 Crawford's personal interest lay in a tariff on steel imports before he had to make a forced sale of his pictures on a depressed art market. But he did not welcome the 1931 election landslide, fearing that it would lead to a revival of 'true Socialism'.

14 OCTOBER 1930

Talked to Baldwin at the Athenaeum. I thought he looked a bit worried, but he said

[22] Victor, second Viscount Churchill (1864–1934), chairman of Great Western Railway from 1908.
[23] Josiah Charles Stamp, first Baron Stamp (1880–1941), president, London Midland and Scottish Railway 1926–41.
[24] Diary, 1 November 1929

The slump

he has had the best holiday he remembers for many years. It is maddening to think that a man of his staunch and loyal personality should be in danger of eclipse...

15 OCTOBER 1930

I talked to Churchill at the Carlton Club where we seldom see him. He too says he has had a good holiday though busy writing a book (juvenile reminiscences). I found him very gloomy about our prospects which he rightly says ought to be rosy – but he argues that we should lay down a cut-and-dried tariff programme before the election, and evidently he would not mind a pledge against food taxes.

29 OCTOBER 1930

At Grillions Londonderry told me that the party at his house was noisier than usual because it was smaller than usual. In other words the crowd was less dense, and people were actually able to talk. When the place is really full the guests are jammed so close together that inclination as well as ease of conversation are impossible. Baldwin stood at the top of the stairs with our hostess helping to receive the guests – pulling faces according to his tiresome habit. He stayed with Ned Talbot[25] for the weekend and Ned found him in excellent spirits notwithstanding our parlous situation.

29 OCTOBER 1931

I don't like the prospects. I wish we had P.R.! That is a queer confession but the diversion of Socialist energy from parliamentary to industrial counter-attacks will be serious as soon as the opposition has settled its own internal quarrels and can begin to fight again.

8 NOVEMBER 1931

Politics have lulled pending the King's Speech early next week. The most striking thing has been MacDonald's insistence on a holiday – and he has gone off to Scotland at a highly inconvenient moment. The real fact is that these Labour people have never been trained to political and departmental work. Ronald[26] has often told me that Henderson was quite incapable of sitting down and reading documents for one hour at a stretch. Thomas's inability to do anything but *converse* on politics is notorious. MacDonald is for ever complaining of having to work and to be so long absent from his Scottish home. There are many people who during all the weary and anxious years of the war didn't get more than a week's holiday. I wish these new national heroes would not squeak so shrilly about their achievements.

[25] Edmund FitzAlan-Howard, first Viscount FitzAlan of Derwent (1855–1947), chief Unionist Whip 1913–21; last Lord-Lieutenant of Ireland (and the first RC one) 1921–2.
[26] Sir Ronald Lindsay, the diarist's brother, was permanent Under-Secretary at the Foreign Office, 1928–30; Arthur Henderson was Foreign Secretary 1929–31.

A visit to Knowsley, Lord Derby's[27] house on the outskirts of Liverpool, revealed the early stages of the process that led to its present use as Lancashire police headquarters.

19 NOVEMBER 1931

This morning I rambled about the house and saw a mass of bad pictures and hideous pretentiousnesses – interspersed with good old English furniture, and a very big library of modern books most admirably kept. There is a queer old workman whose life is devoted to dusting every volume three times a year. The whole house in fact is in apple pie order and shows few signs of the proximity of the Liverpool smoke. The park on the other hand begins to look rather seedy. Roads as at Haigh are going into disrepair and the scale of husbandry falling. Eddie Derby was one of the first to reduce his home farm – he has always been inclined to pessimism, and now he has decided to sell his London house – the big building looking down Stratford Place which he says is very inconvenient as a residence, and to which he has no sentimental attachment.

... Derby grows portly, and apace. He says his rotundity though wearisome to himself, provides an unfailing source of amusement which he is never tired of exploiting, and which his Lancashire audience always relishes.[28] I have often heard such references, and his good humour is inextinguishable: but beneath this bluff and almost Falstaffian exterior, there runs a vein of very marked pessimism – the nervousness born in the intriguing outlook which is always present to him.

21 JANUARY 1932

I am sad about Bishop Gore's death.[29] During the last few years we used to meet often, and on easy terms, as he was a very faithful and regular attender at The Club. I often sat next to him. He was good company, liked a good glass of champagne, liked a good story, and could even approve of a discreet measure of riskiness therein. He was a popular figure at our gatherings ... I first made his acquaintance at Oxford ... He was then Librarian of Pusey House or something of the kind, and my first definite recollection was that he taught me how to bicycle. I was a ready pupil, and within a few minutes of my initiation we were speeding together along the Woodstock road, and we reached Blenheim without mishap. We were alongside of one another when a sudden impulse of Christian affection led Gore to throw an arm round my neck, and I was as nearly as possible pitched off my machine.

He laughed with the intonation peculiar to the advanced Ritualists of that time. They had well-defined mannerisms including a hearty rather guttural laugh, which often emerged at very inappropriate moments or in response to very meagre wit.

---

[27] Edward Stanley, seventeenth Earl of Derby (1865–1948); succeeded his father, 1908.

[28] Derby used to have popular audiences in stitches with his story of a weighing-machine whose novel feature was that it spoke your weight. When he tried it the apparatus merely groaned, 'One at a time please.'

[29] Dr Charles Gore (1853–1932), Bishop of Worcester, Birmingham and Oxford successively, 1902–19.

The slump

Then these High Churchmen had a movement and carriage of their own, with a projected head and if possible an elongated neck. They gazed on the ground a few paces in front of their feet; most of them wore spectacles – all of them I think used to take long walks ... However he had dropped the old mannerisms of his youth – no longer did he pronounce 'God' as if it were spelt 'Gudd' ...

As workhouse fever spread among the serious and solid members of the upper class, the activities of gossip writers like Evelyn Waugh's 'Mr Chatterbox' became harder to bear.

30 JANUARY 1932

People cannot or will not run a risk nowadays even with a guinea, and yet the vile social columns of the *Mail* and *Mirror* and *Express* describe day by day the extravagance and vulgarities of the smart London set – a positive disgrace. And it is all ascribed to fashionable society whereas the heroes and heroines of this tittle-tattle from the cocktail parties and night clubs are all second-rate people ... Yet the blame for these things, the boastful record printed week by week by *déclassés* like Donegall[30] and Castlerosse,[31] is meted out to innocent groups in the community. The Sunday papers describing the doings and witticisms of the smart set provide the Socialists with their most telling arguments when they denounce the idle rich and contrast this pursuit of costly pleasure with the grinding poverty of the unemployed.

2 FEBRUARY 1932

A good report of Ramsay MacDonald's operation. Anything wrong with one's eyes is infinitely alarming, but Sankey says he showed great courage about it – almost nonchalance.

6 MARCH 1932

I went to Sassoon's house to help him entertain the King and the Queen who came to see the Exhibition called 'The Age of Walnut'[32]. The party consisted of the Angleseys, Lady Desboro', Mrs Gully, our host and myself. We went all round the show and as we came to a room the public were discreetly pushed to one side, and seemed to enjoy getting in advance of the Queen and being pushed on or off again. After a longish peregrination we retired to the dining room and sat down to a magnificent tea. I never remember such a tea. The King was offered an egg, a boiled egg, tactfully prepared in anticipation. He refused it and it disappeared. Then Marjorie Anglesey asked if she might have it – Sassoon called for its return – but it

[30] Edward Chichester, sixth Marquess of Donegall (1903–75), hereditary Lord High Admiral of Lough Neagh, and Duc de Chatellerault in France (see parody of these titles in *Vile Bodies*, ch. IV, first paragraph, as 'Marquess of Vanburgh ... Hereditary Grand Falconer to the Kingdom of Connaught').

[31] Valentine Browne, Viscount Castlerosse, sixth Earl of Kenmare (1891–1943); earl 1941–3; crony of Beaverbrook and director of his newspapers.

[32] A loan exhibition in aid of hospitals, held at 25 Park Lane.

didn't arrive and Sassoon got more and more fussy, we all laughed. Marjorie then begged him not to bother about it, but the huge butler bestirred himself and after some minutes – presumably three, the egg or its substitute reappeared, and was put on her plate. We began to laugh again. Some wonderful grouse sandwiches arrived – the King refused them because he could not stop eating haddock sandwiches: more laughter, and then I suddenly realised I was in the noisiest party I could recall. The whole house might have shaken with the shindy which reached its height when the King denounced the new tariffs which cause him to pay an extra ten per cent on any foreign stamps he buys abroad. 'Who is responsible,' he cried out, 'the Treasury, or the B. of Trade or the three Tariff Commissioners?' – He turned to me defiantly as if I were answerable, bawled his questions again right at me, and I said, 'The authority for this is in the Statute your majesty signed a few days ago.' Whereupon the Queen said, 'You see, George, you should not sign papers without reading them', and the King ended the passage by a tremendous guffaw, and the remark 'Oh, that silly thing.' Then we fell to again and a chocolate cake of unique and incomparable distinction was handed round in quarter pound slabs. I could not eat it having partaken so freely of the grouse: but Lady Desboro' was undaunted, and the conversation resumed its lurid tone. We must have sat at that table nearly an hour, and I confess I was immensely amused though nothing witty was said from beginning to end. I am quite sure the King was thoroughly amused (with himself).

24 MAY 1932

The P.R.A.[33] was amusing about Sickert, amusing to me, that is to say, because evidently he has greatly annoyed the academy. He is constantly trying to intrigue them into boosting him and his work, and it actually reached the stage of a suggestion that the Lazarus in Room XI should be auctioned on the sacred spot for the benefit of a hospital! In fact all Sickert does, all his extravaganza, even his apparent insobrieties are designed to advertise himself and to sell his wares. He is a great salesman, and cooperates skilfully with the trade. Several of his relatives are picture dealers. So Llewellyn has a low opinion of him – and by the way of Alfred Gilbert too...

25 MAY 1932

Simon said R. MacDonald had been telephoning to Washington – to Stimson,[34] and that the conversation had been thoroughly tapped. But however important in intention the conversation was at times inaudible owing to atmospheric conditions – or else, as I wondered, to the tapping. I said rather testily that I resented the way in which the P.M. runs the departments of his colleagues, but Simon said that though that idea might prevail, might seem plausible, MacDonald in point of fact was a very loyal chief and always wished and tried to help forward the wishes of his colleagues.

[33] Sir William Llewellyn (1858–1941), president of Royal Academy 1928–38.
[34] Henry Lewis Stimson (1867–1950), US Secretary of State 1929–33.

The slump

2 JUNE 1932

Dined at Gray's Inn... After dinner talked with Churchill and the Lord Chancellor[35], the former talking very freely about international affairs, apparently ended by a declaration in favour of bimetallism. Silver he says represents about ten per cent of our troubles and it may therefore be worthwhile to buy American help with that counter. I wonder. The Lord Chancellor as usual, amiable, indolent and acquiescent.

31 JULY 1932

Lutyens keeps us all laughing[36] with his droll stories and his most amusing illustrations, which he jots down on any bit of paper to be had; but how tiring he is! To have to laugh at every remark he makes (and all are witty) – to have to do so incessantly (for he never stops talking for a moment) is the most fatiguing experience I know! One can't remember anything he says and yet his conversation is brilliant – often wise, always vivacious; none the less his good spirits depress everybody – and one sees people quietly getting out of the way – simply because the effort of sympathetic laughter is overwhelming.

1 OCTOBER 1932

Bernard Berenson[37] came to see me; it is years since we met and I always recall with particular pleasure our meetings at Florence in old days. He has now lost the resilient movement and the auburn touches have deserted him; but he does not become more semitic with advancing years as one would expect. He brought a whole train of admirers and shorthand writers with him... We went carefully over all the Italian primitives and to each Berenson made some observation in which only the names of second and third rate painters emerged – not that he thought our pictures uninteresting, far from it – indeed some of them he admired with enthusiasm, notably Jeptha; but his mind revolves round the periphery of the artist and the central fact or feature ceases to interest him. He wants to reconstruct the entourage whom he knows by document and intuition must have existed and his aesthetic pleasures are now narrowed down to these personal issues; and very productive his inductions are. His new book isolates dozens of painters whose names were unknown in his earlier editions. Some exist – most of them exist: but some don't. Afterwards I took him upstairs, sat him on a sofa in the window and put the Rembrandts before him – one at a time. I really think the little man was speechless with astonishment. He could see the painting, the brushwork, the palette knife, the colour schemes, the great conception and the noble accomplishment and he seemed to be asking himself if even Titian or Tintoretto ever equalled such achievements – if perhaps his own concentration on the small masters of early Italy may not have

---

[35] Lord Sankey (1866–1948), Lord Chancellor 1929–35.
[36] On a tour of war graves in France.
[37] Bernard Berenson (1865–1959), authority on renaissance art in Italy.

deprived him of enjoyments of greater things elsewhere. He would answer himself that there is only a chance of studying one great subject in a single lifetime – and yet to have boycotted Rembrandt for half a century!

21 NOVEMBER 1932

Afternoon party at Londonderry House – political to meet P.M. and Baldwin ... Baldwin greeted me very heartily, I never quite know why we should be on such friendly terms together. Although the assembly was a party gathering the place was full of opposition including all the Samuel group and some Socialists too. These afternoon affairs are pleasant, much more homely and amusing than the old full dress evening entertainments, the reason being that we are more natural in our day costume, especially the women in so mixed an assembly; and indeed some of the males would be self-conscious in their white ties and waistcoats.

27 JANUARY 1933

I had hoped that 1933 might have shown an effective recovery, but I begin to despair of it – and a failure this year means a tragedy to the family – the dispersion at derisory prices of the treasure we have accumulated with so much pride.

11 FEBRUARY 1933

B.M. Board. The owner of a water closet at the bottom of a garden in Bloomsbury Square has rights, means to assert them, and thus threatens to block the new Elgin Room which would abut his property. I was annoyed to find that the Office of Works seem to think that we could build the new galleries leaving a few feet unfinished until we can get possession of the land four or five years hence. If that is a measure of the competence of the new Secretary of the Office of Works that department will very quickly lose all its reputation both for efficiency and good sense. It is bad enough that their Lands department should have allowed us to plan a scheme extending over lands which do not belong to us – but still more alarming that they should think such a thing can be ignored, and that a truncated gallery with the Marbles higgledy-piggledy at one end could satisfy anybody.

20 FEBRUARY 1933

At the Victorian Beauties Exhibition I met the Duchess of Devonshire and we discussed the portrait of Skittles. This is a showy equestrian figure of a personage with no apparent beauty, though Skittles was reputed to be the most fascinating fascinetrix of her day. She could have married the late Duke of Devonshire – he in fact was most anxious to do so but she like an honourable and very sensible woman saw that it would not succeed, and declined, although she was sincerely attached to him. I like her for this, though the reigning Duchess still bridles with wrath at the handsome presents Skittles used to receive. It is believed that this portrait, by a man called Lacretelle, is from Sandringham, so it would appear that the late King must

The slump

also have been an admirer. When the last Duke died Victor[38] wanted to recover the correspondence in Skittles' hands. She declined to give it up saying that he was her closest friend and that she could not bear to part with the papers. The late Lord Coventry[39] (a friend since the Sixties) had approached her on behalf of the Cavendishes and was determined not to be foiled so he immediately went to see the Jesuits in Farm Street (she was an R.C.) and put the case to the blue chapped fellow who directed her spiritual affairs. He was nothing loth to intervene in worldly affairs too, and in due course the correspondence appeared and Victor Cavendish had the satisfaction of burning it himself.[40] He must have snorted tremendously during the conflagration.

10 MAY 1933

Dined at Grillions – talked to Trenchard[41] who was pretty emphatic about police insubordination – they paste up seditious resolutions passed by their society, under the very nose of the Chief Commissioner himself . . . Trenchard in conversation says that many are definitely corrupt or hopelessly incompetent: I wonder if a short service system will remedy that . . . Trenchard seems to be nervous and almost afraid of a strike. He is a great believer in the Specials, and angry at the hostility shown by the regular force.

22 MAY 1933

The Prime Minister[42] was in the chair at the Royal Literary Fund dinner, and as I was between him and Miss Ishbel I learned much about the MacDonald family. He smoked a huge cigar, given him by the Belgian Ambassador and did not stint himself of wines. He told me that he often gives up both. Sometimes he won't smoke for a week or ten days and is always the better for abstention. I suspect his eye troubles are mitigated by this occasional excision of nicotine poisoning. He told me a curious thing, namely that his eye weakness caused an irregularity in his pronunciation – that an occasional word would issue from his lips malformed or truncated. This for a man whose diction is correct, and I think pretty carefully studied too, must be a source of anxiety. I gather this irresponsibility of his tongue has now stopped. Certainly this evening in conversation and during the rather lengthy speech he gave us, no such impediment occurred. His address was cordial and he had been primed with some interesting documents from our archives which

---

[38] Victor Cavendish, ninth Duke of Devonshire (1868–1938). Skittles (Catherine Walters) was the friend of his uncle, Spencer Compton Cavendish, eighth Duke of Devonshire (1833–1908) when he was Lord Hartington; see Henry Blyth, *Skittles* (1970).

[39] George William Coventry, ninth Earl of Coventry (1838–1930).

[40] According to Elizabeth Longford, *A Pilgrimage of Passion: the Life of Wilfred Scawen Blunt* (Weidenfeld, 1979), p. 37, Hartington's letters to Skittles passed, several hundred of them, via Blunt to the Fitzwilliam Museum, where they now are.

[41] Hugh Trenchard, first Viscount Trenchard (1873–1956), Chief of Air Staff 1918–29, Commissioner of Metropolitan Police 1931–5; see also below, 13 July 1933.

[42] James Ramsay MacDonald (1866–1937), premier 1929–35.

added some originality to an effort which was clearly that of the tired man. His speeches are turgid and woolly, his mind distracted; but he arouses himself at the thought of a holiday and he was all animation when describing his projected air trip to Lossiemouth – how he passes by Balcarres, lunches at Leuchars, how a new aeroplane he is to travel in goes fifty miles quicker than the last – his dress – all told with pleasure and vivacity.

He was very much on the spot when explaining a wartime episode which attracted much attention at the time. He tried to sail from Aberdeen to Russia... Anyhow the boat crew refused to take such a passenger – struck work and MacDonald had to stay on land, crestfallen, humiliated, and the target of violent attack for his pacifism. Here is his own version. Lloyd George wished him to go, encouraged him to do so. The hostility of the crew was not only foreseen but was provided against, and if this occurred R.M. was to telephone to Lloyd George from Aberdeen and next day a destroyer was to take him across. He accordingly telephoned to Ll. G. but no response, no destroyer. The P.M. gave no explanation and Ramsay MacDonald may be forgiven for having given me his vindication with a certain measure of gusto.[43]

28 MAY 1933

Newspapers full of biographies of Horatio Bottomley,[44] the ticket-of-leave man who died two or three days ago. I used to see him at Westminster though to the best of my recollection I never spoke to him. I recognised him as a crook, but did not scruple to send him 'tips' through our men, not a few of whom were on friendly terms with 'Bumley' as he was called, and we found him a very useful ally during the strenuous parliament of 1906. He was a thorn in the flesh of Campbell-Bannerman and his unco' guid supporters. Bumley on licensing questions was formidable: at one moment he seems to have made approaches towards our party, but I am glad we kept him at arms' length. He was a consummate speaker – cool, reasonable, good-humoured, one of the most convincing men I ever heard. It is a pity he was a swindler born.

13 JUNE 1933

Pleasant dinner at Grillions. Sat with Salisbury, George Lloyd, Hankey, Vansittart.[45] Hankey told us about his passion for sunbathing[46] on the built-out

---

[43] For MacDonald's unsuccessful attempt of June 1917 to sail from Aberdeen for Petrograd, see D. Marquand, *Ramsay MacDonald* (1977), pp. 213–15. MacDonald had dined with Lloyd George the night before he left for Aberdeen.

[44] Horatio Bottomley (1860–1933), editor of *John Bull*; MP (Lib.) 1906–12, (Ind.) 1918–22.

[45] James, fourth Marquess of Salisbury (1861–1947); George Lloyd, first Baron Lloyd (1879–1941), High Commissioner in Egypt 1925–9; Maurice Hankey, first Baron Hankey (1877–1963), secretary to the cabinet 1920–38; Sir Robert Vansittart, permanent Under-Secretary for Foreign Affairs 1930–8.

[46] Hankey is even remembered as exposing the palms of his hands and the interior of his mouth to the sun. Also, after his daily cold bath, he would go out on to his verandah and slap himself dry, priding himself on never using a towel. More reasonably, he threatened to cut his eldest son off with a shilling for wearing a homburg and thereby resembling Eden, whom Hankey particularly disliked.

verandah of his country cottage. In London this indulgence is impossible, so he walks in the Parks at 7.30 a.m. – and with whom? with Ramsay MacDonald. They talk business – they are fresh – suggestions are made, instructions are given, and sometimes they will breakfast jointly and severally at 8.0.

15 JUNE 1933
This afternoon the annual meeting of the Friends of the National Libraries was held at the British Academy, Bernard Shaw the chief speaker... He walked up to me and made something like a set speech recalling the occasion when we last met (at the Molière celebration in London)... My own recollection of the Molière tercentenary[47] was my amazement at discovering that Bernard Shaw could not talk a word of French – not a syllable – and his horror, his positive horror, on finding that at the government luncheon I had placed him between two Frenchmen.

At the Royal Society Club, Herbert Jackson[48] though not talking antisemitism was very emphatic that we cannot provide berths for the expatriated Germans except where exceptional services can be rendered. There seems to have been an impression that we could give asylum to all the displaced doctors etc. and Jackson's caveat was well received. Beveridge seems inclined to welcome all and sundry.

13 JULY 1933
Police bill in Lords; a good deal of division about the short service proposal. Trenchard did not go into the Chamber during the debate and I talked to him outside... This afternoon I noticed more than ever that he bases his justification upon dishonesty of the force; I begged him not to overdo this argument and so dispel public confidence in the police, but he repeats his case... He actually said to me that one good argument for the short service is that there will be no proper opportunity for these younger men to learn the ways and means of iniquity – in other words that ten years is too short a time to corrupt them[49].

25 JULY 1933
Lunched in Downing St – we gave the P.M. the honorary degree we hoped he would receive at Manchester two or three months ago. How changed he seems to be – such an overpowering lassitude – and now so quiet and gentle compared with the arrogance so habitual to him. I thought it all rather pathetic, and alas I nearly put my foot into it – he was showing me rather proudly some very second rate pictures lent by the National Gallery, and I came across a sort of Turner – looked very much like a fake – I hazarded an opinion that it wasn't by the great man, and then discovered the thing was one of MacDonald's own purchases. I extricated myself and ended by seeing that the canvas is much better than I had thought.

[47] Of Molière's death in 1622.
[48] Sir Herbert Jackson, chemist (1863–1936), director of Scientific Instrument Research Association 1918–33.
[49] Cf. above, 10 May 1933.

9 NOVEMBER 1933

I had an amusing talk with Maurice Hankey, whose views on politics (especially the Alien question in all its bearings) coincide with my own – and we therefore like to compare notes...

Mrs Ronnie Greville[50] showed me her pictures... How entertaining she is, this widow of my old friend and parliamentary colleague, R. Greville. She is daughter of M'Ewan[51] the Edinburgh M.P. whom I remember in my earliest parliamentary days – a very rich man who distilled whisky and I suppose left an immense fortune as his daughter still entertains on an immense scale. Full of stories, and if with a spice of scandal so much the better; very anti-semitic – a real good sort; but I should love to see her in a temper.

30 NOVEMBER 1933

Canon Alexander[52] came to see me. The subject of our conversation was the structural stability of St Pauls, but I very soon discovered that he is absorbed in one problem and one only, namely his chance of succeeding Inge[53] in the Deanery which will be vacated three or four months hence. His hatred of the Dean is frank and avowed. He looks upon him as an unbeliever, dislikes his habit of reading more or less secular books all through divine service, but most of all Canon Alexander is indignant at Inge's refusal, maintained I suppose for fifteen or twenty years, to raise a finger to fight the battle of the Cathedral structure. The whole of this he left to Alexander, who got uncommonly little help from other members of the chapter. Meanwhile Inge pursued his cynical journalism, and cultivates his hobby of eating and drinking. He can attend public dinners five nights in a week, and often enough does so, without apparent ill effects, though for the last year or two somnolence added to deafness has made this untidy ill-kempt churchman a very poor colleague in conference.

11 DECEMBER 1933

I opened an exhibition of documents illustrating the early history of Wigan. The Mayor in the chair, and in his introductory speech the queer old stick announced that the show was meant as a surprise for me, to commemorate my tenure of the chairmanship of the Library Committee for twenty-one years. This bit of news was indeed a surprise – and even now I can hardly explain it. The work is interesting and all the heavy burdens are taken off my shoulders by my excellent vice-chairman Farr, and by the first class Librarian.

---

[50] Leading society hostess, and confidante of Sir John Simon (Foreign Secretary 1931–5); widow of Ronald Greville (1864–1908), MP (Cons.) 1896–1906.

[51] William M'Ewan (1827–1913), chairman of M'Ewan and Co., brewers; MP (Lib.) Edinburgh Central 1886–1900. Mrs Greville was his stepdaughter.

[52] Canon Sidney Alexander (1866–1948), canon and treasurer of St Paul's from 1909; raised £400,000 in appeals for its preservation; author of *The Survival of St Paul's*, 1945.

[53] Dr W. R. Inge (1860–1954), Dean of St Paul's 1911–34.

The slump

21 JANUARY 1934

Attended the Library Committee at Wigan... My task has been made easy as the library service has managed to steer clear of party politics... Wigan is justly proud of its public library, and I have every reason to be proud of my committee. My vice-chairman, a local coachbuilder called Alderman Farr (a good Tory) takes all the routine work off my shoulders, and the clever librarian Hawkes[54] is a real scholar.

23 JANUARY 1934

I went to the memorial service for the late Lord Halifax,[55] the gallant old fellow of ninety-four – a few months ago he was photographed out hunting!... I was frankly shocked that the catafalque was surmounted by an outsize peer's coronet. They ought to have known better, but no peer seems to know the rules of propriety about his coronet unless he is fourth or fifth on the roll of his title.

23 FEBRUARY 1934

I was invited to become chairman of the body known as the Independent Peers; declined. I have no leisure, apart from inclinations: amused. A few years ago the independent peers, guided by St John, Salisbury, and Selborne, fought the coalition government all they knew, and made the great gaffe of defeating the proposals put forward by W. Peel and myself on Lords reform and the parliament act. Now Salisbury is bringing forward his own scheme of Lords reform, no better and no worse than ours, but not affecting the parliament act. Lloyd George had agreed to our projected amendments which I always considered would have given a very grave blow to the efficacy of that iniquity – but Selborne knew better, so after a delay of ten years or so we have this new inchoate scheme which won't do any good, and which in any case won't pass into law. And now they ask me to be their chairman!

It reminds me of my chairmanship of the Oxford University Elections Committee, a position I held for a long time with success. Linkie[56] (one of the Unionist members) did much to break up the coalition government of which I was a member: and thereupon in the ensuing election it fell to my lot to draft his election address for him – such was the practice. I have done it several times, and no easy task, for Hugh Cecil was Free Trade and High Church, Oman[57] his colleague being Low Church and Protectionist; however I got them both elected at least three times.

10 MAY 1934

A very pleasant man's dinner with Frank Mildmay[58]... I found myself *planté* with Hilton Young[59] and Prince George[60], recently home from a South African trip in

[54] Arthur John Hawkes, FSA, scholar (1885–1952), borough librarian of Wigan 1919–50.

[55] Sir Charles Lindley Wood, second Viscount Halifax (1839–1934), Anglo-Catholic leader.

[56] Lord Hugh Gascoyne-Cecil, first Baron Quickswood (1869–1956), MP (Cons.) Greenwich 1895–1906, Oxford University 1910–37: Provost of Eton 1936–44.

[57] Sir Charles Oman (1860–1946), historian.

[58] Francis Mildmay, first Baron Mildmay of Flete (1861–1947).

[59] Sir E. Hilton Young, first Baron Kennet (1879–1960), Minister of Health 1931–5.

[60] George, Duke of Kent (1902–42); cf. below, 20 November 1934.

which his manners and deportment did not excel – so much so that his misbehaviour is said to explain the fact that the Duke of Gloucester is to undertake the Australia tour instead of Prince George. It is a pity that these young men have not been better licked into shape; Prince George is quite intelligent, and I fancy really interested in things. He talked about housing, pressed Hilton Young on the subject and evidently had kept his eyes open when travelling about the countryside. I say he is really interested in these matters, because it appeared that he had settled to leave Berkeley Sq. by 10.30 when his aide-de-camp, one Buller, discreetly reminded him that he had a long day before him. The Prince nodded – continued to ply H. Young with questions on the assumption that the Ministry of Health is a building dept... And so on until 11.15 when Prince George consented to move. They say that he had no sense of the lapse of time.

1 OCTOBER 1934
Royal Fine Arts Commission. How different Lutyens is now that the Commission has shaken off the incubus of Reginald Blomfield. Lutyens pays close and loyal attention to his work, gives the best of himself, and seems quite unselfconscious; whereas with Blomfield in the room always anxious to trip him up Lutyens took refuge in flippancy, was irrelevant in his conversation and spent much of his time drawing caricatures. It is only now that Blomfield has happily departed that I realise what a burden I had to carry in his professional jealousies and touchiness.

6 NOVEMBER 1934
An amusing dinner at the Garden Society – sat next the Prince of Wales who arrived nearly half an hour late after a busy day at Bristol: it is some time since I have been beside him at table and I watched his processes with interest. He began with a tremendous confab with the head waiter. No hors d'oeuvres, no soup, no fish, no champagne – 'No, certainly not any champagne, some Perrier water.' I began to wonder what he would like and then a pair of cutlets turned up and a salad. By now he had thought better of the champagne and he had a glass or two: but uncommonly little victuals of any kind. Then at the very end of the meal he began to talk about salads: that is the ideal of his table pleasures – salads but ingeniously contrived. He has many theories – so I said 'Talk to Sir Daniel Hall,'[61] (whom I had placed on my right) 'he is the greatest living authority on salads.' H.R.H. immediately cheered up. Daniel Hall, always an amusing talker started off on endives and how to splash lettuces, how to spread chives on brown bread, when a taste of tarragon or pennyroyal is desirable – above all how to grow the herb garden, and how the cook must gather her own pot herbs and never trust the gardener, who should limit himself to their cultivation. The P. of W. opened his eyes. Having spent a month in Biarritz he fancied he knew all about salads but here was Dan Hall, with his rolling

[61] Sir Daniel Hall, agricultural scientist (1864–1942), director of Rothamsted experimental station 1902–12, chief scientific adviser to the Ministry of Agriculture 1920–7.

eye and his cavalry moustache, talking away in his best broadcasting manner and laying down the law with an ease and authority quite new to H.R.H. 'Above all not too much vinegar' pronounced Dan – and finally the head waiter was summoned (when the rest of us were finishing dessert) and was given the recipe for a salad, of which the governing feature was camembert cheese in small triangles – fried but just softly enough to be viscous – each piece being the size say of a rose leaf. Hall added a hint or two and the confection duly appeared – I could not be tempted to try it, but Hall had a helping and criticised wisely. The Prince was enthusiastic at having met so keen and so sage a connoisseur.

I found him excellent company, talking with freedom and good humour, but on the whole too visibly engrossed in the menu: why for instance should he keep sending away the toast in order to get a new and very hot supply? He was intelligent about flowers, still more about shrubs...

11 NOVEMBER 1934

Alfred Gilbert[62] died a few days ago. I had a good deal to do with the old boy when the Queen Alexandra Memorial was being made. Earle[63] had the idea of employing him and I managed to get the reluctant and nervous committee to agree. We certainly ran great risks, but I am confident our boldness has been justified: whatever be the faults of the memorial they are preferable to the correctness of the smug kind of affair wanted by Knutsford and Lady Haig. Gilbert was his own worst enemy. His passion for low company and bottled beer nearly produced a renewal of the old catastrophes. He used to spend his evenings in a little smoking room of a Strand hotel, a v. modest place, talking for hours with the clerks and commercial travellers who patronised the little hotel. Then Earle with a stroke of genius, picked him up and packed him off to an old shed by the Orangery at Kensington Palace where a comfortable bedroom was fitted up and a really excellent studio was alongside.

Earle also found one of the foreman carpenters of the O. of Works who made templates and so forth, a really tiptop craftsman who was a great help to Gilbert. Very slowly the statue emerged and Gilbert used to run down to see the bronze caster who had to supply him with beer to avoid a shindy. Then came the moment of unveiling at St James's Palace, and the old boy wearing a top hat of terrifying proportions, with a most rakish rim, was the centre of curiosity. He looked so little like the typical artist. It was a great day for him, and I shall never forget his sweeping bow to the Queen. He was much praised – overpraised. The cunning old fellow always had a good press (bottled beer I suppose) and in spite of the scandals which drove him out of the Academy, and out of the country into the bargain, he was always treated as a sympathetic personage, whereas of course he had no scruples

[62] Sir Alfred Gilbert (1854–1934), sculptor of Eros in Piccadilly Circus and of memorial to Queen Alexandra at Marlborough Gate.
[63] Sir Lionel Earle (1866–1948), permanent secretary, Office of Works, 1912–33.

1929-35

about swindling a client or tradesman. Robert Dunthorne told me damning stories about his subterfuges, and King Edward was quite as eloquent. However, all ended well; a knighthood came along, he was reintegrated in the Royal Academy, and I was never more surprised than when entering the reception gallery, and passing along the row of greeting Academicians, to be met at the end of it by Alfred Gilbert who had taken up a place among the President, Trustees, and officers. A twinkle of his wicked little eye, which gleamed angrily like the orb of an elephant, made me think that he wanted everybody to realise that in his old age he was capable of asserting himself.

A great artist? I wonder – but certainly a master of the little bronze and of course everybody excused his vagaries by talking of the artistic temperament. Once when displeased with some of his work he smashed up the models. Leonardo might have done the same and the world heard about Gilbert's uncompromising rectitude. In point of fact the affair happened one fine day when Gilbert had discovered that brokers were waiting in the passage, and he quickly determined that the philistines should get a minimum of the swag.

14 NOVEMBER 1934
At Grillions Churchill talked rather loud and smothered A. P. Herbert and Rudyard Kipling. I sat between the Bishop of Durham and Harold Macmillan.[64] The latter is a bit pompous for his years and is reputed to be overprone to philander with the Socialists. He is executor of the Waterford estate, with Hartington; neither was aware of this until the unfortunate death of the late man[65] – and Macmillan who is hard worked, is disturbed at the prospect of the long minority, and equally of the vile journey to County Waterford. Hartington says he will gladly leave all responsibility to his brother-in-law.

19 NOVEMBER 1934
Went to Londonderry House for the political squash at the opening of parliament. The P.M. and Baldwin at the head of the stairs received the guests, while Charles stood rather disconsolate in the background, oppressed I imagine by the very risky marriage threatened by his daughter with a young man of semitic caste called Muntz[66] ...

20 NOVEMBER 1934
At The Club sat by George Trevelyan ... On my other side were Clive Wigram[67] and Cantuar, the latter ever so much better ... These neighbours of mine talked

[64] Premier 1957–63
[65] John, seventh Marquess of Waterford (1901–34).
[66] Londonderry's second daughter Margaret married Frederick Muntz in November 1934. They were divorced in 1939.
[67] Clive Wigram, Baron Wigram (1873–1960), assistant private secretary to George V 1910–31, then, on Stamfordham's retirement, private secretary 1931–6, retiring six months after George V's death.

555

The slump

about the royal wedding[68] – Wigram who talks more freely than his predecessor says that he is desperately afraid that the horde of minor royalties now about to descend on London will think themselves entitled to the comforts of Buckingham Palace, which would indeed be consoling after the very mediocre life they have been spending in the lounges of continental hotels, and as the guests of pushing and opulent Americans. One of the Grand Dukes it is feared may be too much attracted by the Palace champagne – another even by the silver spoons. (I told Wigram an excellent story of the Balkan monarch and the Min. of Agriculture man who went out and who had his watch stolen at the royal banquet of welcome). Altogether it is clear that there is not much enthusiasm in exalted quarters for the entourage of the charming little princess. At one time the Duke of Kent was alleged to be anxious to marry Anne Wood[69] and the Prince asked his father's permission. The King thought about it for a very long time, so long in fact that the Prince got tired, and also got mixed up with some pretty young parcel, and the matrimonial project ended, much to the satisfaction of Irwin himself, and I can well understand his relief.

7 DECEMBER 1934

Long panegyrics of Riddell and Buckmaster,[70] two much overrated men: the former based his popularity on a genial mind and a fund of good stories, while Buckmaster's passionate flow of sob stuff was readily mistaken for oratory. His torrent of language was what one expects from the normal eloquence of a Spanish or Italian deputy, but it was too rhetorical for our taste and usage, and depended upon qualities of speed and emotionalism which are alien to our traditions. He was a good fellow and during recent years much less liable to fly into a rage during ordinary conversation, perhaps having learned through his brief but disastrous excursion into high business, that things in this workaday world are not so simple as they seem. Riddell on the other hand showed none of Buckmaster's zeal and enthusiasm. He was the pure cynic, and would really have passed for a success had he not committed the folly of preaching a sermon to youth, expanded I believe into a little book.[71] This was so smug, replete with such mock piety and paternal affection that somebody was provoked into contrasting Riddell, the guide of struggling youth with Riddell, proprietor of the *People* newspaper. To youth Riddell preached all the virtues. To his readers he sold all the vices. His critic analysed the contents of this popular Sunday rag, and showed how the moralist searched the garbage heap for crime and indecency to tempt his weekly readers. The analysis was cool and searching. It was devastating

---

[68] George, Duke of Kent (1902–42) married Princess Marina (1906–68), daughter of Prince Nicolas of Greece, 29 November 1934.

[69] Daughter of Lord Irwin, later Lord Halifax.

[70] George Riddell, first Baron Riddell (1865–1934), chairman, *News of the World*, 1903–34; Stanley Owen Buckmaster, first Viscount Buckmaster (1861–1934), Lord Chancellor 1915–16.

[71] *Things That Matter* (Hodder, 1922)

and I felt that Riddell never quite recovered his nerve after this exposure of cant and hypocrisy.

19 DECEMBER 1934

At Grillions ... Ormsby-Gore told us that our Ambassador in Berlin was invited to dinner in Berlin, found himself unexpectedly in company of Rothermere and his son – not a word of warning – and then questions and cross-examination by Goebbels and co. So unpardonable a breach of taste and manners could only be committed in Germany. The conversation was turned on the German colonies. Rothermere said nothing can be gained by attacking this government who are adamant on the subject, but the Socialists will be in office before long, and Germany will then get whatever she cares to demand. It is difficult to believe that the man can be such a traitor – but there is the message from Berlin.

31 DECEMBER 1934

This year 1934 has brought many anxieties, beginning with the death of my mother. I spent two months in the doctor's hands, Connie six weeks ... The strain on my finances twelve months worse than last New Year's Eve – though prospects are good realisation is remote, and my attempt to sell the precious Rembrandt boy has failed. The situation has become precarious now that no financial reserves are available. All are exhausted.

30 JANUARY 1935

I have an idea that I was once president of the Mining Association, but it is long since I had any relations with them. Today I attended a conference about the recruitment and education of higher officials, Evan Williams[72] in the chair. He lamented how few representatives were present, not a quarter of those summoned and none was asked unless the pit was a million ton affair. So we started off at a disadvantage. A few good speeches, but far too many to the effect that the man who turns up is generally good enough, and that it is hopeless to introduce young fellows from outside the coal trade parentage and ancestry. This is the kind of self-centred isolation which makes a colliery village so dreary and so impervious to the living movements and impulses of ordinary civilisation: and it is perhaps also an explanation of the failure of our industry, that we do not produce leading men of sufficient personality and power to look after the industry properly and to protect us against the attack of Tom, Dick and Harry – of an agitator who short of a subject settles to have a go at the coal trade and above all the coal masters. I watched them for two or three hours – they looked on the whole intelligent, some of them good-humoured and easy-going, but in all the speeches I listened to I could detect no sign of leadership.

[72] Sir Evan Williams (1871–1959), president, Mining Association of Great Britain 1919–44.

The slump

13 FEBRUARY 1935

Dined with Grillions. Sat with Hartington,[73] Trenchard,[74] Ilchester[75] and the Attorney-General.[76] Talk about aliens; Hartington amazed us all by saying that he is secretary of the Jewish Committee in the H. of C. Whatever can have led him into such a milieu, and how little he must know of the race! Conversation turned on forged passports, bogus insurance, incendiarism, smash and grab – the Attorney-General said that the percentage of income tax cases in which he is concerned is abnormally Jewish. Trenchard said that very few of the jewel robberies are genuine, many being ramps to rob the insurance companies: even house burglaries are constantly contrived for the same reason. The Jews are the habitual receivers of stolen goods. They run the cut-price shops. Ilchester knew all about it – so did Inskip – and yet never a word in public about this consuming canker!

19 FEBRUARY 1935

I paid a visit to Baldwin this morning to talk about a C.P.R.E. speech he wants to make. Gave him notes of relevant matter. I found him well, in fairly good spirits, but oppressed by a hundred sources of anxiety. He carries a heavy burden in the person of Ramsay MacDonald: but the moment he talks of the countryside reminiscence wells up and he forgets the cares of office in the happiness of contemplation. He told me that his family originally belongs to Shropshire, but between that county and Worcester, his ancestry has revolved for several hundred years in a circle of some twenty miles diameter. Just over the border are Baldwins who have sat on their estate for 700 years – 600 certainly, though they have needlessly lost their name in the process. In spite of a Scottish mother, Baldwin retains the tawny hair and stocky frame of the Saxon; probably also much of the English power of biding his time which he combines with the Scottish faculty of vision. He remains a powerful man who so far as I know has never yet put out his full strength.

27 FEBRUARY 1935

At Grillions we all heard a good deal about India from Churchill by whom I sat. He arrived as we were sitting down, determined to have a copious meal, to tell us all about India in the intervals between courses, and then to hurry back to the House of Commons to make a violent and tendentious attack.

... Nothing checked Winston's declamation. He harangued us as though we

---

[73] Edward William Spencer Cavendish, tenth Duke of Devonshire (1895–1950), MP (Cons.) W. Derbyshire 1923–38.

[74] Commissioner of Metropolitan Police 1931–5.

[75] Giles Fox-Strangways, sixth Earl of Ilchester (1874–1959); succeeded his father, 1905; trustee of the British Museum and chairman of the National Portrait Gallery.

[76] Thomas Inskip (1876–1947), Solicitor-General 1922–4, 1924–8, 1931–2; Attorney-General 1928–9, 1932–6.

were a public meeting, denounced the government as though his listeners were anti-Conservative; he was amusing, determined, heartless in his insistence, never letting anybody else get a word in – one might say he was in a highly excitable frame of mind.

28 FEBRUARY 1935

There was something indecent in the glee with which Churchill denounced the government last night . . . At Grillions Austen Chamberlain was by me, and Eustace Percy just opposite, but though they were both members of the Select Committee and must know something about Indian affairs, they were never allowed to say a word while Winston was spouting; but afterwards Austen said bitterly that Churchill's attitude reminded him of Dr Clark and Henry Labouchere who were caught giving advice to the enemy during the Boer War. Churchill is certainly using the Princes to play into the hands of Gandhi and Co. who are every bit as much our enemies as were Kruger and de Wet.

But after Churchill had left Grillions last night, Austen had his revenge – pouring out an incessant flow of reminiscence, which might be amusing were it crisp and to the point: but every sentence is expanded and every trifling incident magnified, until dear good Austen begins to rank as a first class bore – he is so insistent as to be a positive fatigue.[77]

The Prince of Wales presided at a huge dinner of the National Trust at the Dorchester – he came to us within a couple of hours of his return to England from a holiday in Austria – there he says he thoroughly enjoyed himself, and was particularly well pleased with the cuisine of Budapest. I am afraid this lithe and supple young featherweight begins to pay too much attention to his victuals. He loves talking food, and at meals he orders his dishes in eccentric order and with meticulous care. He ate nothing tonight from the excellent menu, but was busy all the time, and ended up with an omelette while we were having an ice. He was also most fussy and particular about his drinks. He was very friendly, made us a speech of genuine interest in the cause.

12 MARCH 1935

Lunched at Apsley House. The Duke of Wellington[78] whom I don't know asked me in order to get advice about a project of selling pictures . . . What a queer place Apsley House – surely one of the very dingiest of the London palaces. There is no sign of its ever having been occupied by an intelligent owner. The Duke – I mean the first and great Duke – acquired a certain number of fine pictures by chance or by pillage – stuck them up amidst a welter of trash – furnished his palace with third rate furniture – then died, and from that date to this none of his successors has ever thought of reforming the chaos, or even of giving the place a lick of paint. The

---

[77] Cf. above, 7 May 1930.
[78] Arthur Charles Wellesley, fifth Duke of Wellington (1876–1941); succeeded his father, 1934.

The slump

squalor and ignominy of Apsley House is beyond belief, and I should imagine that the new Duke and his Duchess are perfectly incompetent to get the place into order; to do them justice, I think they feel neither shame nor discomfort in their surroundings.

27 MARCH 1935

I presided at the inauguration of the differential analyser at the University, a calculating machine of human sensibilities and a triumph that the first of its scale in Europe should be at our place, manufactured in Lancashire too. We were all enthusiastic and Hartree[79] the professor of mathematics means to make the most of his new toy, which we owe to the generosity of our second Treasurer, McDougall[80] the flourmaker.

30 MARCH 1935

Eden is at Moscow or thereabouts and becomes a Trustee of the National Gallery. He replaces Ramsay MacDonald who was one of those I described as dud Trustees, to the bitter indignation of Billy Gore who thought I was fitting the cap on to all politician Trustees – and well might I have done so. Sassoon on merits has few claims other than a position acquired through political prowess; Baldwin is a nonentity on a standing committee. Duveen and the Prince of Wales contribute nothing unless it be cash or prestige, and D'Abernon is now completely past all work. I believe in a strong board of Trustees, otherwise the small permanent staff will soon become ossified.... The place is no doubt given to Eden as a kind of genteel retaining fee for the time when he is out of office. Direct qualifications he has few if any.

[79] Douglas Rayner Hartree (1897–1958), mathematician; held chairs at Manchester 1929–45 and Cambridge 1946–58. His machine was a non-electronic forerunner of the computer.
[80] (Sir) Robert McDougall (1871–1938), a Manchester graduate.

560

XVII

The approach of war, 1935-40

Derby's seventieth birthday – British Museum philistinism – Churchill at Grillions – silver jubilee – Lloyd George and the BBC – Kipling's prophecy of 1984 – Abyssinian crisis – Curzon's affairs – genius of Kingsley Wood – Mrs Simpson – Londonderry – a family controversy – History of Parliament fiasco – abdication – Baldwin's nervous breakdown – life at Chequers – Eden's desire to please – the Duke of Bedford – Hensley Henson nonplusses Churchill – George V's stomach – the Duke of Windsor proposes to tour North America – ugliness of Duke of Norfolk's belongings – Mrs Neville Chamberlain – Ramsay MacDonald and squires – Eden resigns – Hankey – Freud's statuettes – Ellerman and rodents – Franco's card-index – Rosebery – Lady Dudley – intellectuals at the Palace? – anti-semitic doggerel – Lord Chancellor Maugham – Eire willing to declare war – police raid The Times – Churchill shows Admiralty secrets to the Duke of Windsor – Churchill's assessment of the war – art in wartime – Belisha resignation – Kitchener as War Minister – Churchill's greatness.

5 APRIL 1935

Derby thought it would be nice to send to the Preston ceremony[1] a number of old Knowsley employees. So he said he would send anybody who had worked on the estate for twenty-five years. There were no less than 125. He then thought it would be nice for each man to be accompanied by his wife or a daughter – that raised the party to 250 – then he settled they ought to have lunch, so all sat down to a square meal at the historic Bull Hotel at Preston – and there drank his health with enthusiasm.

13 APRIL 1935

At B.M. a discussion about my proposal to organise a Bible room – a permanent exhibit of our Bible wealth in all its manifest branches. While pronouncing themselves sympathetic it is clear that the keepers of departments are very hostile to the proposal, and perhaps it was a little tactless of George Hill in summarising

---

[1] To celebrate the seventieth birthday of Edward George Villiers Stanley, seventeenth Earl of Derby (1865–1948), 'Uncrowned King of Lancashire'. 82,000 people signed a testimonial to him on this occasion.

criticism to say that popular as such an exhibition might be, care must be taken not to interfere with the 'serious scholar'. The snobbery of the B.M. was never more nakedly displayed – the assumption that what may be popular is against the interests of serious scholarship. Whenever a trayful of junk is bought by a department, those who protest are told that the B.M. is designed for pure scholarship, that gaps must be filled, that artistic questions don't arise – Trafalgar Square and the V. and A. are looked upon as mere collections of bric-à-brac.

18 APRIL 1935

Vexed at Maypole colliery at the roughness of G – the manager towards an old collier whose inquisitiveness about a bit of timber in process of petrification brought him into my line of vision. I was amused at the old fellow and was passing the time of day with him when G – viciously ordered him out of the way – a very needless display of authority. The collier seemed rather deaf and I fancy did not realise what had passed, but I was annoyed at this officiousness on G – 's part. One is at the mercy of the bad manners of a colliery manager and this kind of behaviour causes bad blood which leads to serious trouble later on.

8 MAY 1935

At Grillions I sat at the end of the table with George Lloyd, Montagu Butler and Winston Churchill. Various people came in late, Austen Chamberlain, Ormsby-Gore and Eustace Percy, all making their way to the other end of the room as Churchill became a formidable personage at the dinner table. In point of fact he became an embarrassment and a veritable nuisance, declaiming at the top of his voice and occupying the conversation without intermission. Besides he is bellicose on just those matters which ministers do not want to discuss in mixed company at the dinner table; but he is most entertaining if you surrender yourself to his domination. He made us laugh because Roger Keyes made some remark about the need of battleships which sent Churchill off at a tangent when he denounced the poor admiral for wanting a big ship to take him off to the West Indies out of range of German aeroplanes. Keyes tried to riposte (his sense of humour is pretty thin) but Churchill shouted him down (and the gallant little admiral's voice is meagre). Towards the end of the evening Austen moved to the seat next my own, offered some rather elaborate persiflage which set Churchill off like a bunch of crackers and he denounced poor Austen who was nonplussed at finding himself speechless in such a welter of chaff. He is really very witty, Churchill I mean, with a daring cut and thrust, a perfect knowledge of public affairs, and so much self-confidence that he pontificates with greater gusto than any member of parliament with the exception of Macmillan.[2] At ten o' clock he called for beer, but the head waiter said there wasn't any, in fact there was no such thing to be had at Grosvenor House . . .[3]

[2] Harold Macmillan, MP, Prime Minister 1957–63; regarded by Crawford at this date as ineffably pompous.

[3] Beer was speedily obtained from outside.

Trenchard told us that on Tuesday morning, the day after the service[4] at St Paul's, there were only three cases of disorderly conduct at Vine St police station . . . On a Boat Race night there might be a hundred cases. In fact everything has run with exceptional smoothness. At Scotland Yard there has been an emergency room, linked up by telephone with all police stations, barracks, etc., and authorised to act if any unforeseen crisis occurred. The special staff sat and sat and sat – never a message did they receive. All the same there have been anxieties. It was obvious that thousands of people had reached central London without houses to go to, and determined to sleep in the Parks in order to secure the best places for the procession – they intended to take up their places at dawn. The King consented to Trenchard's leaving the Royal Parks open. The head of the women police took note of the order, and said to Trenchard, 'I suppose I had better put on double patrols.' 'No' said Trenchard, 'so far from doing that, you will only use half your normal staff, and you will tell them to *see nothing*.' Trenchard says the lady is a very 'sexy person'.

7 JUNE 1935
To BBC to discuss with a Mr Lotbinière[5] a draft report I drew up of a committee to consider the present situation in the light of the new or revised Charter which is to be shortly expected. The committee, appointed in my absence, consists of myself as chairman, Lloyd George, Sir Walter Citrine, Beveridge, Prof. Nicholson, and Miss Hadow. I realised at once I was in a radical milieu, pushed in to give the impression of a non-party committee – such is the virtue of a chairmanship. I did not bother to press my views except when something preposterous or fatuous was proposed. What really interested me was Lloyd George's intervention. He began by saying that there was too much concealed or objective propaganda. He quoted Chesterton, said he is making a practice of preaching what Ll.G. called 'midaevalism'. I could not quite work out why Chesterton should not puff the middle ages if his audience doesn't rebel. No, said Lloyd George, it is all part of a regular system. Belloc does the same thing; and then suddenly he said to Reith, is it true that Graves[6] your new head man is a Roman Catholic? Reith agreed and Lloyd George let the matter drop with an observation that the propaganda of Roman Catholicism is subtle, penetrating, and never abridged.

17 JULY 1935
I dined at Grillions. Somebody asked Kipling why he persistently refused honours, particularly the Order of Merit, and I was amused how curiously embarrassed he was to make an intelligent reply. He mumbled something inaudible – not that he was offended with the question – far from it – but he was simply gravelled for a reply. I doubt not that the real reason is his inveterate dislike of the politician as such, and

[4] For George V's silver jubilee.
[5] S. J. De Lotbinière, subsequently director of outside broadcasts, BBC.
[6] Captain Sir Cecil Graves, BBC controller of programmes 1935–38, deputy Director-general 1938–42, joint Director-general 1942–3.

though the Order of Merit is by way of being an honour controlled and distributed by the King himself, one has a shrewd suspicion that the government may intervene. Kipling is embittered about our vacillations during the war, about our bouts of pacifism ever since, and although he is fond of Stanley Baldwin his own first cousin, his prejudice against the politician is farcical – if only these doctrinaires would sometimes descend from their exalted seats and test their theories in the market-place! He amused us by describing the aristocracy of the future, to emerge after England is nauseated by another fifty years of sloppy paternalism; it will be a quasi-territorial aristocracy in so far as it will live on the land, and in out of the way parts of the country. It may flourish along the slopes of the Black Mountain, on some of the East Anglian plains, or in the vague areas bounding the Roman Wall; anyhow, the people will foregather in remote districts to which their ancestors will have fled from the bunkum and ballyhoo of modern socialism. There the new race of men will grow up, powerful in physique, almost illiterate, and totally ignoring public opinion, they will sally forth and drive out the intellectuals who will have brought the country to disastrous concessions and compromises. The new aristocracy will be wholesome in outlook, simple in diet, frugal in all things, and merciless towards the mushy highbrows inspired by Geneva and Moscow.

25 AUGUST 1935

On Thursday I called at Montrose to see Jack Gilmour just retired from the Home Secretaryship... We talked of the death of Willie Bridgeman, a man of restricted intellect and slow of speech, yet endowed with such a fund of robust common sense, a man of such integrity that I would have willingly entrusted the national fortunes to his care rather than to people like Simon or Birkenhead or Ll. G. who had ten times his capacity. Willie was one of the team I chose and trained in the opposition whip's room in the days of our political afflictions; from 1903 to 1913 all my energies were devoted to the technical machinery of our party – to reorganisations of method and morale with a view to our ultimate control of affairs. Lots of political whips before my day had made their men attend. I did so, but also made them work – choosing some special task for each man suited to his ambitions and capacity. They responded wonderfully. I can only remember a handful who would not help and played their own game for their own benefit – Max Aitken led that selfish little gang...

I remember years ago that Mussolini met Bonar Law: I have a kind of impression that the meeting took place in London. Anyhow B.L. was asked his opinion of the new constellation – said without a moment's hesitation 'Sheer Lunatic'.

24 OCTOBER 1935

At the House of Lords much discussion about the situation in Abyssinia... They say certain ministers are as ignorant as the outsider, e.g. at a recent cabinet, conversation began about Ethiopia, went on for some little time, until a minister impatiently exclaimed, 'It is all very well to discuss Ethiopia, but the really critical subject to which we should give our attention is the war in Abyssinia.'

Beatty on the other hand says we know all about the Italian Fleet movements and that the position of every Italian submarine is charted. Not long ago a couple of them were in our waters outside Gibraltar, so an order was given to practise depth charges, and one or two of the lightest charges were exploded, just giving a pop underwater and no more; then lo and behold, there was a swirl on the surface, up bobbed a couple of Italian submarines, the hatchways burst open and the crew bustled out and actually surrendered, believing that war had been declared. The captain of our nearest ship advised them to 'carry on'...

I found Hailsham a little nonplussed by the strong pro-Italian sentiment in H. of Lords – much more vocal than in the Commons.

29 OCTOBER 1935
I dined with the American Ambassador, Squire Bingham I call him, which tickles him immensely as his passions are his English ancestry and the Dorsetshire home of his forebears. He considers himself cousin of the Binghams, Lucans I mean... Afterwards talked with Pierpont Morgan [*who*] said that Cantuar [*Dr Lang*] acceded to the Archbishopric determined to give a great moral and spiritual uplift to the Church, but he finds himself overwhelmed by an unending mass of administrator's duties. This sounds so true that I feel sure it must be a *cri de coeur* from the Archbishop himself. They are very close friends and I fancy it is Morgan who is responsible for the upkeep of Lambeth garden. At the same time let us acknowledge that Cosmo Gordon Lang is fond of being occupied and that he seems to derive much pleasure from most of the routine duties. All the same devolution is necessary, more so than he realises.

13 NOVEMBER 1935
Spoke for David at Carnforth and Ulverston. At the former meeting David gave an answer to a question about poultry and the price of lard which I thought masterly. I am sorry that at a crisis with such great issues before ourselves and the world, so much should pivot on the price of lard, but at any rate I'm glad David is master of the subject.

5 DECEMBER 1935
I went to see Lady Curzon – 'Grace Abounding' – who wants to live at Montacute, and asks my help with the National Trust who own the place. I gave her some good advice and we talked about George – of what or whom else could we have talked? and she told me that on his death she was faced by a demand of £60,000 for unpaid income tax which had been claimed during his lifetime – but George with a magnificent gesture of indignation had turned the income tax commissioner out of the house. But the Inland Revenue did not forget and descended upon the widow with disastrous results. She had to meet her creditors and make an arrangement.

The approach of war

She has been in Argentina, her finances are improved and she wants a country seat as Hackwood is sold to Lord Camrose. In old days she and George used to stay at Montacute and it was from there that he made the fateful journey to London expecting to become prime minister. He was actually photographed at the door with his wife! . . . And now Grace Abounding wants to return to this beautiful manor in the West Country – she has all the necessary furniture – in fact the equipment of the place itself, much of which she told me with real amusement was chosen by Elinor Glyn with whom dear George had a passage (before his second marriage according to his widow) and she, Lady Curzon, says that the rooms furnished by the Glyn woman were exactly what are described in *Three Weeks* . . .

11 DECEMBER 1935

I went to the Ministry of Health to attend an inaugural meeting of a huge variegated committee set up by Kingsley Wood[7] to advise on housing matters: forty of us there I should think. I was interested in the way he handled us. I have always looked upon this rubicund little solicitor as the most astute man in the party, as the cleverest propagandist and the master mind of political publicity. He sat at the end of the table, addressed us in mellifluous tones, purred compliments at the Socialists, told us what he wanted and got his way without apparent effort surprise or pleasure – it all came so naturally, so inevitably to his conclusion. A very shrewd little person, this rosy persuasive knight bachelor and they say that when he wishes to be acid he can be quite tart.

2 FEBRUARY 1936

The King again spends the weekend at Belvedere and one assumes that Mrs Simpson is there. If the emotions of the past fortnight have not been strong enough to bring that liaison to an end, we must contemplate its continuance until she is supplanted by some younger rival . . . . Criticism may become insistent, bitter; then he may do something fatuous by talking of abdication: he has done so *en famille* before now. People are nervous, rather vexed about it all, and beginning to talk freely: hope is reposed in the influence of the Queen, and not a little in his own fickleness.

3 FEBRUARY 1936

At the Literary Society Ian Hamilton[8] told me how he is worried by British Legion affairs. The Prince of Wales pressed for the Legion to make a rapprochement with the German Legion – England agreed, Scotland was more cautious, and now the committees are bombarded with protests by the Jews who urge with some force that we should not condone persecution by the Germans. That is typical of the fatuous

[7] Sir Kingsley Wood (1881–1943), Postmaster-general 1931–5, Minister of Health 1935–8, Air Minister May 1938–April 1940.

[8] Gen. Sir Ian Hamilton (1853–1947), commander at Gallipoli.

attitude of the Jews. They protest and declaim, but if they would boycott German goods and abstain from trading with the Boche these protests would not be needed – Hitler would be swiftly brought to his knees.

5 FEBRUARY 1936

At Grillions... I sat by Austen Chamberlain who told us *à propos de rien* that he is a Unitarian – Joe was the same, though after the distress of the loss of his second wife Joe's religious faith underwent an eclipse: but all the same I suspect that he was 'married in Church' and no doubt Austen as well. I recall that old Henry Fowler[9] who was the staunchest of nonconformists was rallied by his friends when a daughter of his (or was it a son?) invoked the blessing of the Anglican Church at wedlock.

27 FEBRUARY 1936

Talked to Londonderry[10] about his position. I found him surprisingly bitter against Baldwin, who he says settles all kinds of important matters without consulting the cabinet. He says that the Hoare-Laval affair took the government by surprise. He, Londonderry, protested when in office that he was at a great disadvantage in debate and in conversation from being quite in the dark about broad lines of policy. He pressed that ministers (and cabinet ministers too) should be more fully informed. 'And the next thing I heard about it was that I was outed.'... Poor Londonderry has had many disappointments – but he has been very lucky too, like his father before him, for their natural bent and genius was never towards statesmanship.

4 MARCH 1936

At Grillions... In front Trenchard; beside him Sir Philip Chetwode[11] and then Churchill. Towards the other end of the table Roger Keyes[12]... As dinner progressed Churchill, rather flushed and talking pretty loud, challenged the great people on his left, but could not drag Keyes into the conversation as he was too far off; but Churchill fairly set the Army and the Air service by the ears. We know that discussions about defence have been animated, and that there is no semblance of agreement on broad principles. The Admiralty is too firmly entrenched, too detached from workaday affairs of the land, to acknowledge the right of anybody to criticise. As Trenchard well says, the Admiralty won't argue, they will only consent to resign. So they fire ultimata all the time at the Committee of National Defence, while the War Office and Air Ministry are quite impotent. Trenchard was very bitter about it. Chetwode on the other hand was annoyed when Churchill à propos

[9] Lord Wolverhampton (1830–1911), the first Methodist to sit in the cabinet.
[10] Charles Vane-Tempest-Stewart, seventh Marquess of Londonderry (1878–1949), Secretary of State for Air 1931–June 1935, Lord Privy seal and leader of the House of Lords, June–November 1935.
[11] F.-M. Sir P. Chetwode, first Baron Chetwode (1869–1950), C.-in-c. India 1930–35.
[12] Adm. Sir Roger Keyes, first Baron Keyes (1872–1945), MP (Cons.) 1934–43.

of nothing at all, said that most of the army promotion was done by jobbery. The Field-Marshal began to try to refute this on strictly statistical lines; but that sort of argument doesn't tell in the rapid elliptical cut and thrust of the dinner table – and Churchill had merely to raise his voice and quaff a glass of champagne to suppress the gallant soldier. I am not sure that he really enjoyed his first evening at Grillions Club.

By the way there was one passage (Churchill was at the moment haranguing in the other direction) when Chetwode seemed to show a lamentable lack of understanding. Trenchard is just back from Bremen, and brings a depressing report of German fatalism about the prospect of war. Everybody feels that it is inevitable, and in the near future. Impossible said Chetwode, the Germans can't fight – won't be able to do so for two or perhaps three years because they haven't got any steel, and without steel war is impossible. I said but the Germans won't move a ship or an army corps if they mean to fight us. They will give us an ultimatum, say about colonies, then demand a categoric agreement within twelve hours – and in the event of their not getting it they despatch 2,000 aeroplanes to bomb London... Chetwode – it had never occurred to him that the next war might begin and end in the air. He seemed rather nonplussed, in fact made no reply and Churchill sailed back into the conversation and told Chetwode that the sooner cavalry were converted into tanks the better. Chetwode then proudly announced that the cavalry produced eight Field-Marshals during the war. There is a portrait of each of them in Chetwode's club. This fine soldier doesn't shine in conversation, but he looks as though he would be formidable in the field.

17 MARCH 1936

A pleasant dinner at Grillions... Clive Wigram[13] unburdened himself about Court anxieties – and in connection with the King's broadcast (pronounced 'broadcairst' by the royal lips) Wigram said that H.M. tried to interpolate a sentence about the realisation of Indian aspirations, which would in effect have conceded Dominion Status. Simon who was deputed to assist the King managed to get the phrase excluded, but not without difficulty. All goes to show that we have to deal with a very opinionated man who probably feels much more resentment than anybody knows at the restraints and restrictions which have surrounded him hitherto.

Wigram told us that the late King was a much more methodical and businesslike person than was generally known. They have found all the letters addressed to him by his children, each bundle being folded, docketed and wrapped into little cotton or linen bags. There are also fifty volumes of manuscript diary which Wigram got hold of and immediately deposited in the Round Tower at Windsor. The great collection of archives there is safely housed and as free as things go from risks of fire. H.M. goes ranging about the palaces with his eyes open for suitable things to take to his country seats...

[13] At this time Edward VIII's private secretary; see above, 20 November 1934, n.

Finally Wigram told us that a few weeks after the outbreak of the Great War he pressed the King to don khaki. Wigram says he considers he did a good bit of work in offering this advice. I replied, 'Why, without it we should never have won the war.'

26 MARCH 1936

Read C. J. Holmes' reminiscences,[14] or rather a couple of chapters in which he indicates that the Trustees of the National Gallery treated him infamously. It is regrettable that he was so hostile to all and every project of reform. I well remember his bitter hostility or supercilious disregard of every scheme suggested – e.g. to correct the labels, to improve the frames, to revise the scandalous catalogue, to keep the records accurately, to use the Witt Library – it was his jealousy of Witt which made him buy various wrong 'uns – which a message to Witt would have avoided. He was strongly opposed to making it easy for young scholars to study at the Gallery. He hated having to watch the market at Christies, and discouraged his subordinates from doing so just because the idea emanated from the Trustees. He was in short most difficult to work with owing to his ever-growing contempt of the 'unprofessional' – and yet many of us, journalism apart, knew just as much as he did, about *authenticity* .

8 APRIL 1936

Cromer[15] at Grillions was interesting ... Cromer is just back from two months in the West Indies, so he arrives with a freshness of judgement we feel we are losing, and it is clear that he is nervous about the tendencies of the Court. To his surprise the King asked him to continue as Lord Chamberlain. Cromer did not quite take it as a compliment; for he knows that war was in effect declared against the old gang; but it is possible that H.M. is beginning to realise the paucity and meagreness of his own entourage – perhaps he now sees how small is their fund of experience and *savoir-faire* – hence a reaction in favour of King George's staff. I found the Lord Chancellor frightened – he seems to fear that something must happen sooner or later which may produce an open scandal. For my part I feel certain that a crisis must occur and without much delay as our newspapers will not long forego their claim to discuss what is already the subject matter of articles in France and America, probably in Australia too. And then what is the little man going to do – how can he face that storm?

10 APRIL 1936

At Haigh. I arranged some papers in the muniment room ... I came across a family controversy, 1910 I think, in which my mother was engaged – when my father

[14] *Self and Partners – Mostly Self. Being The Reminiscences of C. J. Holmes* (1936). Cf. above, 10 November 1926, 7 January 1927.
[15] Rowland Thomas Baring, second Earl of Cromer (1877–1953), Lord Chamberlain 1922–38.

discovered through taxation returns, that she was saving money out of the household allowance. I don't know how long this had been going on, but I think the sum amounted to £20,000 or so. Our home was run on exceptionally frugal lines – I never saw wine on the table for instance, except for my father, and everything in the house was managed at the minimum cost and lowest standard of comfort... I sometimes wonder if my father was not encouraged to sail the southern oceans in order to control his own victuals – anyhow he was furious to learn that the meagre household allowance wasn't spent, and ultimately the investments were distributed among my brothers, to whom they were to have been bequeathed. It was an unfortunate controversy arising out of my mother's great wish to see her younger sons provided for – and in spite of the honourable motives she found herself put in the wrong.

6 MAY 1936

I presided at the Grillions dinner... Churchill very noisy and too glib in denouncing the government, Sam Hoare[16] too, but I only heard him talking once or twice – he also expressing the greatest contempt for some of his recent colleagues.

19 MAY 1936

I presided at the Garden society dinner, the Duke of York[17] by me – agreeably surprised at his improvement during the last year or two. The stammer, or rather the impediment in speech which used to be so marked has practically disappeared – in fact it is now little more than an occasional hesitation or drawl. He was quite gay and immensely tickled by somebody saying that some plant or other was 'quite hardy in Cornwall' – he kept repeating 'quite hardy in Cornwall' on all occasions, relevant or the reverse, for the remainder of the evening. Apart from this continued lapse he was sensible and on the spot; like his brothers he takes a very intelligent interest in gardening.

He told me that as the King's coffin was just reaching the far end of the Sandringham drive on the way to the station, an immensely high pheasant flew right across the procession, almost exactly above the dead monarch, to whom the King of game birds paid his last respect...

He also told me that he, his late father, and King Edward shared a superstition about asparagus – if you have an odd number on your plate you must either leave the last, or else supplement it by taking another stick from the dish! King Edward used always to send for the even-numbered stalk; the late King and the Duke of Gloucester leave the odd one on the plate. I like this, have never heard of it before. Whence does it emanate – query the Court of Hanover, or did Mrs George Keppel invent it?

---

[16] Hoare had resigned as Foreign Secretary in December 1935, returning to office as Home Secretary in May 1937.

[17] George VI (1895–1952)

30 MAY – 1 JUNE 1936

To Melbury – the Ilchesters ... Lady Ilchester showed me a volume of *Tess of the D'Urbervilles* given her by Thomas Hardy with the names of the actual places written in upon the margins, a series of geographical notes showing how the great writer had studied the countryside.

16 JUNE 1936

I attended a meeting of the History of parliament committee. I was bullied into joining it by Jim Salisbury who pressed it on rather personal grounds. He did not attend today, Onslow could not, Wedgwood who has been devoting his whole time to the enterprise, too ill to be present. I soon found that the latter is a boss fiend who has been allowed a free hand because nobody cared to question or criticise – most unsatisfactory situation, and I said so – whereupon Winterton, Acland, Pickthorn M.P. and Ullswater who was in the chair, endorsed my view and the secretary was instructed to act with caution about appointments, etc. The whole business is unsatisfactory and I shall soon regret my complaisance in joining the committee.

8 JULY 1936

Talked to Pickthorn M.P. about the History of Parliament now being bossed and run by Wedgwood. It appears that he has secured control, and insists on making all appointments himself, and he has written a long gossipy introduction to the forthcoming volume which makes the professional historians' blood boil. But he is said to be so attractive a person that he always gets his way and has even won over Trevelyan to write a thoroughly unmerited puff. They also say he is ill and that members of the committee feel estopped from criticism. If true this is pretty ridiculous.

14 JULY 1936

A meeting of the Parliamentary History committee ... Jim Salisbury in the chair – Wedgwood who is really responsible for the enterprise took the opportunity of explaining to new members of the committee (like myself, Acland, Ponsonby) how the scheme came into being: all v. interesting, but the pronunciamento lasted nearly forty minutes, and might have continued longer, but Winterton interposed a question which broke the continuity. How well a parliamentary committee behaves – there we had sat for forty minutes listening to a discourse which was both tedious and irrelevant, but never a murmur of resentment. Perhaps we are over-scrupulous in these matters, at any rate Wedgwood seemed encouraged, for he repeatedly threw off other speeches at regular intervals. The man's vanity is colossal – people call him 'Joss' affectionately, but for my part I thought his attacks upon the historians were unjust and malicious beyond words. As for his introduction to the earliest of the volumes of the history, it seemed to be a very amateur sort of affair, and scarcely of the serious type requisite for a large compilation of this character. Jim Salisbury's patience in conducting the meeting filled us with admiration, as he tried to bring a glimmer of reason and conciliation into Wedgwood's obstinacy and conceit; but his efforts were of little avail, Wedgwood being too much consumed with his own importance to appreciate the wishes and apprehensions of others.

22 JULY 1936

Yesterday Evan[18] told me a story of Osbert Sitwell who found himself in conversation with a young rather tough-looking American who asked about popular estimation of the King. Sitwell made some general remarks and observed rather casually that the public is disturbed that H.M. does not seem to go to church. The American was interested and rather surprised, finally said, 'Wall, I'll put that across him next time we meet', and Sitwell then discovered that this smart gangster feller is in the habit of meeting H.M. – at Corrigan's house I suppose.

11 OCTOBER 1936

Looking back over sixty-five years, I consider my youth must have been thoroughly happy. I think my school career was on the whole. Eton I liked without enthusiasm. At Oxford I found myself – enjoyed all my years in parliament. The only interlude of unhappiness in all these years was the second part of the war after I came home from France. Otherwise I look back upon unbroken happiness and felicity from the age of fifteen or twenty, and most of all throughout my thirty-seven years of married life.

25 OCTOBER 1936

The latest gossip about the Court is that H.M. is putting aside very large sums of money, presumably for the Simpson woman. It seems to be contemplated that she should accompany him on a coronation tour.

3 NOVEMBER 1936

Opening of parliament – never saw such a crowd of peeresses and a great number of us had to stand in the gangways ... The King read his speech quite well – without the resonance or sonority of his father's voice, but deliberate and delivered with coolness and here and there a nuance of emphasis. His pronunciation is poor – one might say bad: the inflexion on the letter R in America was noticeable, and Route pronounced Ro-ut as though it were a composite word. There was however nothing so noticeable as during the broadcast after his accession when he said 'Wiles' instead of Wales. I was too far off to see how the little man looked, or whether he paid attention to Mrs Simpson who was said to be in the gallery just to the right of the *corps diplomatique*, escorted by Lady Brownlow.

The King and the Lady – the source of endless talk and speculation. It seems to be the only thing that counts and we are paying small heed to matters of terrible

---

[18] Sir Evan Charteris, barrister and chairman of the Tate Gallery.

moment abroad. At the same time the papers never breathe a word on the subject; this has no doubt been most unfortunate, for it has given the King a false sense of security.

10 NOVEMBER 1936

The King was to have come to the Garden Society dinner, settled to do so months ago, so we circularised our members and told them they were to bring no visitors to what would have been the guest night. Yesterday however he sent to say he could not come... One hears these stories of engagements being chucked, or of outrageous examples of tardiness – he doesn't yet realise how much trouble is taken on his behalf nor what inconvenience is caused by his forgetfulness and vacillation. Somebody in the H. of Lords this afternoon said that the King would be blackballed for any respectable London club – and I see what the man meant – the all-absorbing egocentricity.

3 DECEMBER 1936

Thursday. Sudden outbreak in the press – in the press united. After months, one might almost say years, the torrent is overwhelming – a cascade of articles, pictures, headlines, one would think that the relations of the King and Mrs Simpson must exclude all other topics. Lots of portraits of the lady: posters about her, one says she is ill, another suggests that she has bolted. I went to Lancashire and kept picking up later editions of the evening papers and all alike break loose after the long period of self-suppression. The temptation to magnify the affair is irresistible – to propagate every possible rumour however absurd. In London I heard that the police are anxious as they think it possible some indignant person might fire a revolver at her, still more that the burglar confraternity might have a shot at her jewels.

6 DECEMBER 1936

Sunday. In the press this morning there is a distinct tendency to scold the Church for butting into an affair which does not concern them... They announce that Cantuar was mobbed and that ministers were hooted in Downing St – merely the ebullitions of a score or two of rowdies; but it is evident that the gutter press has been enlisted to support the King in all he does and wishes to do with the object of overthrowing Baldwin. The old vendetta is to be revived... Some papers publish long (and most entertaining) panegyrics of the lady who must assuredly be one of the most alluring people in the world – her tastes, her knowledge of public affairs, her keen interest in English politics, notably in the unemployed problem – all these virtues are so highly developed in her, and so different from the dull and faded outlook of the average English woman of his acquaintance!... Meanwhile Wedgwood and the Harmsworths are organising a King's party. Arnold Wilson[19] whose judgement is always bad is intriguing freely. Winston Churchill ranges

[19] Sir Arnold Wilson (1884–1940), MP (Cons.) 1933–40.

around and will be mischievous the moment he sees his chance. But these people cannot prevail. The more this marriage with Simpson is discussed the more the King will be discredited. Innes[20] the herald told me that from Edinburgh northwards but one per cent of the population will support such a royal marriage. He says that already in Aberdeenshire feeling is intensely bitter.

7 DECEMBER 1936

Back in town. At H. of Lords one topic only of conversation. Opinion is united in deploring the attitude of the King. Stanhope[21] (now in the cabinet) told me that Baldwin's report of the King's actual demeanour is good – he has remained at Belvedere to be out of the way and to avoid the cheering crowd who could be easily whipped up to demonstrate outside Buckingham Palace. He wants no King's party. This is all to his credit, but one remembers how he has been talking to the Harmsworths etc. during the summer. Some of that gang though being discountenanced now must have had something in the nature of encouragement. Stanhope also told me that in all the discussions at the cabinet there has been no question of cash or civil list – this makes it difficult to understand why Edward Peacock, the Duchy financier, and Monckton the Duchy solicitor have been so constantly in conference at Downing St. Bessborough says that Peacock is a really sound man. The King was badly rattled by the sudden burst of newspaper criticism – his first experience of attack was very bitter. 'He hasn't been accustomed to this sort of thing', said Stanley Baldwin to the cabinet; but nothing has shaken the King, though he must be sorely disconcerted.

Meanwhile intervention by the King's Proctor is talked about. I wonder if Baldwin warned the King that Mrs Simpson's divorce is by no means a foregone conclusion.

9 DECEMBER 1936

Rhymes, riddles, and ridicule, not to mention occasional ribaldries about the couple, are now beginning to circulate; public opinion is growing incensed. There cannot be much more delay without a serious outburst of popular anger. Public opinion has changed rapidly and is now openly hostile to making any concession to the King.

10 DECEMBER 1936

Thursday – King Edward abdicates. In the morning, at the Carlton which was very crowded, a strong manifestation of personal hostility to the King – his brothers united in making a final effort to persuade him to release Mrs Simpson, but all argument, all admonition is useless.

[20] Thomas Innes of Learney (b. 1893), lawyer, landowner and (1935) Albany Herald.
[21] James, seventh Earl Stanhope (b. 1880), First Commissioner of Works, with a seat in the cabinet, 1936–7.

...For my part I feel a profound and inexpressible relief, and I rejoice that rumours we heard earlier in the day were falsified – for it had been said that the Duke of York was proposing to decline the succession in favour of his eldest daughter to act under a Council of Regency.

11 DECEMBER 1936

To Leicester to fulfil an old engagement to attend a CPRE[22] meeting... Those to whom I talked all cordially approved the course of events and the manner Baldwin has handled the situation, e.g. the Lord-Lieutenant, the Sheriff, the Bishop, and the Lord Mayor of the City. For my part I am more and more confident that all will go well. We are on an even keel again.

The throne is again founded upon a solid public respect and esteem. The background of domestic unity and happiness will give confidence to all, and affection towards the sovereign will quickly revive. But there is much to do. The American gang has got to be dispersed – the Rogers, Mendl, Corrigan, Lady Astor, Lady Cunard, Lady Furness – all the touts and toadies who revolved around Mrs Simpson, and whose influence upon society was so corrupting. But there were lots of weak and complacent English people who were all too ready to bask in the sunshine of royal favour – what one may call the cabaret set – Dudleys, Marlboroughs, Sutherlands, and others who were glad to entertain the King at the price of entertaining his mistress; and finally the little group of misguided people who for no particular reason were brought into the Court set – the Brownlow, Beaufort, Sefton lot, must likewise have an emphatic reminder of how to behave.

12 DECEMBER 1936

We have already had clear demonstrations how Beaverbrook and the Harmsworths tried to make the Duke of Windsor the focus of their political intrigue. Churchill too notwithstanding his disclaimers was suspiciously close to a party ramp. George Lloyd told me that he, Austen C., and Horne had protested to Winston at the dangerous course he was pursuing, but Churchill was already coining his phrases, and though expressing warm personal friendship for the King and ascribing all his action to these sentiments, he none the less saw the fruits of office temptingly close before his eyes. His judgment is nearly always wrong however resonant his prose – he is an evil counsellor, and I thought him nervous and distracted as he coasted about the Palace this morning.

13 DECEMBER 1936

Sunday... There are many stories about the King's behaviour (the D. of Windsor's) during the last ten days – how he would argue with Baldwin with good sense and then suddenly go off into a paroxysm of rage. All evidence points to the loss of self-control. At the end only one of his servants would consent to go abroad with him* – is not this the most tragic symbol of all?

[22] Council for the Preservation of Rural England
*Lt-Col. Thetton, Sir Piers Legh, 1890–1955; second son of Crawford's friend Lord Newton

The approach of war

16 DECEMBER 1936

How happy-go-lucky the late king was. He borrowed some pictures from the National Gallery for York House. The other day the Duke of York told the N.G. he was having his home redecorated and he thought it safest to return the pictures to the N.G. during that period. The N.G. had no idea the King had passed them on to his brother; and then it was discovered that the N.G. frames, labels, and numbers had been removed. The old frames were found stowed away in a bedroom – meanwhile the N.G. Trustees discover that it is illegal to lend pictures to a residence: public offices are permitted.

17 DECEMBER 1936

A heroic test match is in progress...this monopolises headlines and evening posters. The Duke of W. scarcely mentioned in the papers though there are some paragraphs about his hostess in Austria who has been twice heroine of divorce courts (Yankee too).

20 DECEMBER 1936

Rumour has it that the solicitor who flew to Cannes to see Mrs Simpson ostensibly about the lease of her London house, returned with his pockets full of Queen Alexandra's jewels. Query didn't he travel back by land? But if the tale be true were the things brought back here for restitution or to be put safely into Wally's bank?

29 DECEMBER 1936

It is the 'social set' we want to scarify and for the moment the less we say about the Duke of Windsor the better. He poor man, leads a very dull and obscure life in Austria – all the journalists can report is golf and skittles, a drive to Vienna, purchase of hosiery, of confectionery – the adventures of his dog, the circumstances of his photo being taken – and paramount excitement of all, how he read the second lesson in Church. He disappears from the political sphere – how long will he remain in eclipse? That some people are still watching their opportunity to exploit him is pretty clear from a message wired to him by Lloyd George from the West Indies – based perhaps on very defective information as to the facts.

15 JANUARY 1937

I had a very pleasant time at Chequers – found Baldwin well and in good spirits – looking sturdy and stocky, without the nervous affections of the overwrought man, and hearty in his appetites – decided too as to what he did or did not want to eat at luncheon. Mrs Baldwin told me that when he went into retreat in the summer he was completely done – on the very verge of a collapse in which mental exhaustion would soon have followed physical debility. Lord Dawson told her that three months was the minimum required, and she says his colleagues behaved very well – spared him all papers, and for the first fortnight he seemed to sit still in an armchair as though he were a frozen man being thawed back to life.

Response was satisfactory, and when the dynastic trouble became acute he was in a position to tackle it with firmness – though he told me that one of its most vexatious aspects was the burden of having to drive up and down that infernal vulgarity of the western exit – at all hours of the day and night and at impossible speeds. He is conscious of having handled that tragic affair with success, and he is now confident again of himself and of his health, confident too that whatever be the outcome of these vile Italo-German intrigues this country has behaved in a gentlemanly way.

And now he seemed wavering whether he should take a peerage or not. His instinct is against doing so almost as if he felt such a course disloyal to the House of Commons. I pressed him to join us in the Lords – he will want a *pied à terre* in political life and the convenience of seeing his old friends, but he has to get a new house, doesn't quite see how he can afford it. But I told him that if he stays in the Commons he will have the expense of a constituency – and I ended up by getting the impression that he will become a peer. He is anyhow determined to get out of Neville C.'s way, so as to leave him free and unembarrassed in remodelling the government, or in laying down his line of policy. Baldwin retires on May 27/8/9 – all this conversation at Chequers arose from my request that he should come to Manchester on June 2 for a degree...

I had never visited Chequers till today... The house is full of very doubtful furniture, silver and works of art, not to mention reconstructed heraldry etc. contrived by Arthur Lee in the early days of his passion for bric-à-brac, with the result that the place lacks all feeling of spontaneity and genuineness: in fact the only authentic item in the house is the library which consists of sermons and other trash from 1750 onwards. The Chequers situation is a little awkward, as the conversion of government debt has actually reduced the income by £1,500 a year and makes it difficult to keep the place in decent repair. The drive for instance is very much like a farm road...[23]

20 JANUARY 1937

At Grillions... Churchill perhaps not quite so boisterous as usual on these occasions – I wonder if he has some little nervousness about his behaviour during the Palace crisis – he certainly ought to be a little self-conscious for he narrowly escaped a real cropper... Churchill seems almost to rank among those who vanished at the critical moment, though by the way he did not pay his visits to Belvedere without Baldwin's cognizance. I remember the other day how bitter Baldwin felt towards those who deserted the poor little King, and equally his disgust for those who had tried to exploit him.

10 MARCH 1937

Dined at Grillions... Hardinge told me how unpopular Mrs Simpson is on the Riviera. This is the real explanation of her early flight to the Loire. At one restaurant

[23] See below, 12 February 1938.

she and her party were politely told that they would not be served. The waiters downed serviettes. The explanation is that the staff consider she has behaved badly to the Duke of Windsor who is popular there.

22 MARCH 1937
I dined at the Belgian Embassy to pay my respects to the young Sovereign who is having a semi-incognito visit to talk to ministers and a wholly incognito interlude to play golf...

Baldwin and Eden changed places for nearly half an hour in this dim light and I had a good long talk with the former. I asked him abruptly if his foreign secretary was capable of frowning. I had been watching his amiable countenance with his quick self-conscious smiles – his rabbit teeth, his pretty mouth surmounted by a moustache curled inside out – altogether the very portrait and emblem of confiding sympathy and good nature – just as Edward Wood's radiant goodness credits everybody else – Gandhi, Ribbentrop, Lansbury, Grandi – with possessing all the Christian virtues. The indelible friendliness of Eden's face must discount his strength be it the strength of steel – for strength should not always be concealed. Can your foreign secretary frown? I asked Baldwin, can he rap the table? The Prime Minister went off into a short series of grunts which means he is interested and wants to ruminate for a moment or two. Then he said 'I wonder. I have never asked myself that question. It's a very interesting question. I wonder.' And then pulled a quick series of grimaces in which his nose took its part. He gazed across the table intently, but I did not await a reply which might have been evasive.

6 APRIL 1937
I dined at The Club... Anthony Eden close by. I again watched him and noticed a brow which is tortured in a queer fashion – divides vertically down the middle and the impressions of one side are not repeated on the other – this is perhaps why he can't concentrate on the centre and frown. Tonight he looked far from amiable or genial – he droops his head like a shy schoolgirl, he blushes and registers modesty like a cinema star, he pouts, he tosses his little head and I dare say stamps his little foot into the bargain. If ever I saw a *petit maître* Anthony Eden is the man.

19 APRIL 1937
Tom Legh[24] drove me down to Woburn to pay a visit to Bedford.[25]... We expected to find him alone. We sat down ten to lunch, and there were ten menservants to look after us – I did not know and can still scarcely believe that such survivals remain – and on my way home Tom bitterly complained of the quality and style of the victuals.[26]

[24] Thomas Wodehouse Legh, second Lord Newton (1857–1942).
[25] Herbrand Arthur Russell, eleventh Duke of Bedford (1858–1940), co-founder of Whipsnade, whose wife had just died.
[26] Cold chicken and strawberries

It reminds me of Stephen Gaselee[27] at The Club. We were talking about A. E. Housman, an old friend of Gaselee. Both of them were proud of their learning and enthusiasm in gastronomic affairs. Year by year they had a quiet meal together in which the *pièce de résistance* was a stew of tripe and oysters washed down with Russian stout... One more food item worth noting is the omission from Trevelyan's life of Grey,[28] of all reference to the fact that after fly-fishing and nature study, Grey's most continuing pleasure was drawn from the dinner table.

5 MAY 1937

Sat with Churchill at Grillions – he told us how much the Commons was impressed this afternoon by Baldwin's valedictory speech... Baldwin has established a mystique in public esteem comparable only to that felt for Disraeli, and I think that subject to one contingency, his reputation will continue to grow. Fifty years hence it will be a great thing to have known Baldwin.

Henson[29] of Durham was in the chair this evening, just opposite us, and the conversation kept returning to the poor Duke of Windsor, the lady's divorce now permitting the discussion of an early marriage. Churchill as everybody knows ranked as a 'King's man', and he said that he and Lloyd George would have fought with violence any proposal to omit the Duke of Windsor from the Civil List had there been no assurance that he was already adequately provided. Ah said Henson who is anything but an admirer of our late monarch, this financial affair must not be made the subject of discussion or else the Duke's conduct during the last eighteen months will cause a serious scandal. Churchill rather nonplussed – and throughout the evening especially when the circumstances and technique of the courtship of Mrs Simpson, of her divorce, and of the prospective marriage were discussed, Henson in the quietest and most friendly manner in the world upset Churchill, rolled him over and over and left our argumentative friend without a plausible argument in his armoury. When Henson explained that in the eyes of the Church the Reno divorce of Mrs Simpson (for incompatibility of temper) is not recognised as a divorce by the Church of England, and that a marriage with the Duke of Windsor will therefore be doubly bigamous, Churchill said plaintively 'but why were we not told this before?' Some of us had the same idea in our minds, and assuming Henson to be right, it might still affect history were this view made public with recognised authority. Henson himself is no bigot on these matters, because he supports A. P. Herbert's divorce bill – but he said that if any clergyman of his diocese were to marry the Duke, he, Henson, as Bishop would inhibit the man at the doors of his parish church. We must have talked for a couple of hours, our party was small, and the conversation was very general; and after Henson had left us Churchill ordered whisky and said that he had been greatly struck by the foundation of history

[27] Sir Stephen Gaselee (1882–1943), Foreign Office librarian 1920–43, and classical scholar.
[28] G. M. Trevelyan, *Grey of Fallodon* (1937).
[29] Dr Herbert Hensley Henson (1863–1947), Bishop of Durham 1920–39.

upon which the Bishop had throughout based his opinions – how different, he said, from our ordinary political disputes where we lack this solid stratum of fact and expertise. We all saw the truth of this. Everything Henson said was supported by authority from the New Testament, from the Fathers of the Church, right down to the Royal Marriages Act – and throughout our animated talk he kept interposing wise and witty anecdote or quotation which gave an exceptional lustre to his conversation. Churchill was right in saying that Henson was impressive, and not the least convincing proof of it was the fact that Churchill who is apt to declaim on these occasions was piano and modest from beginning to end.

16 MAY 1937

From all accounts the King and Queen who are taking some well-earned repose at Windsor, survived the ordeal of last week in excellent health and spirits . . . I hope the King has inherited the constitution of the House of Hanover; I hope he has the unrivalled intestines of King Edward VII. The other day Dunmore repeated to me a conversation with King George which embodied a single fact and explained the endurance and fortitude of the Royal Family. He was driving somewhere or other with the King, between tea and dinner – a long drive and the King kept on smoking cigarettes. At last Dunmore[30] protested, and said this was extremely bad for His Majesty's health, especially on an empty stomach. 'Empty stomach' roared the King, 'empty stomach? I never have an empty stomach.'

This I quote as a great historical phrase, an elucidation, a truth no less profound because statistical, and if one recalls the royal occupations, one sees why cigarettes should not operate on the Kingly stomach when void. Breakfast, a bowl of soup about eleven, lunch and a late-ish glass of cognac, a vigorous tea, a full dress dinner, followed by a sustaining supper before midnight – this must be a source of the bustling vitality of our Sovereigns.

Churchill was insisting the other night on the correct attitude adopted by the Duke of Windsor. 'I know him very well,' he said. 'No,' I replied, 'you only know him when on his good behaviour – you only know him in your capacity of elder statesman. In point of fact the Duke of Windsor is only himself, only really wakes up at one o'clock in the morning in a night club.'

12 JULY 1937

I spent some days at Edinburgh for the visit of Their Majesties to the capital. We all agree that everything went off admirably, and the notable crescendo of their popularity gave satisfaction to all. Edinburgh was more forthcoming, more vocal than ever before – attributed in a casual way to the Scottish extraction of the Queen, but actually arising from personal respect for the domestic life and basis of their personalities, with a profound sense of thankfulness to Providence for the

[30] Alexander Edward Murray, eighth Earl of Dunmore (1871–1962), Lord-in-waiting to George V 1930–36.

catastrophe we have escaped. Indeed retrospect over the last twelve months makes me infinitely grateful to those who forced the last King to understand that a revolution might well follow the Palace crisis. We hear very little of the Windsors, though it was said that the unpunctuality of Their Majesties at the Court Ball was owing to the fact that the Duke of Windsor chose that very moment to telephone a tirade that his wife wasn't made a Royal Highness.

At Edinburgh I had several opportunities of a word with the King and Queen, their graciousness is impressive and many of us have noted how their looks have improved with growing confidence. When I remember his glum and dejected demeanour at the Coronation, only a couple of months ago, I am astonished at his sprightliness and vivacity, and what is nice is their modest recognition of the fact that all goes well.

29 JULY 1937

Rather an amusing conference with Sassoon [*Minister of Works*] about the statues of Beatty and Jellicoe. The difficulty has been Lady Jellicoe who has refused to sanction her husband's statue if Beatty is in the neighbourhood. As a pair of statues is clearly intended she has made every possible difficulty. At last in an unguarded moment she agreed to Trafalgar Square on the assumption that Nelson's Column and Landseer's Lions will separate the naval heroes, and now at the last moment a fresh idea is started – namely placing our gallant Jack Tars in the fountains, one each side of General Gordon. Sassoon liked the idea, which emanated in a casual phrase I inserted in the Royal Fine Art Commission report on the subject. William Llewellyn, the P.R.A., was all at sea. He is sometimes so clear and emphatic, and again so often quite off the mark. His amiability has been of service to the Academy but the next man ought to have a little punch.

2 AUGUST 1937

Duff Cooper is at times unaccountable. The other night I was amazed at Grillions at his vivacity – his drolleries which seem set off by the cast in his eye, as was the case with Charlie Beresford – and then he told a short story in French, to my amazement with the woodenness of accent which Austen Chamberlain used to have. I was astonished – I thought the biographer of Talleyrand was a faultless linguist.

28 AUGUST 1937

I have been indexing my book [*not published*] about Scottish lairds and laird-ships – the book itself must have been finished six months ago, and I suppose was begun three years ago. Its actual writing must have taken six or eight months in my leisurely fashion ... It is nearly very good but falls between two stools ... hence a tendency to confusion which will make it impossible to publish the volume. It is a compilation of curious facts interspersed with a couple of score of good stories.

I am now occupied in the centenary address to the Manchester Geological Society of which I am shortly to become President: a very unfamiliar topic to me.

The approach of war

4 OCTOBER 1937

Opened the Public Library in Wigan, now redecorated after accumulating the grime of sixty years – a very pleasant little function. I went over the new nursing home opposite the Front Lodge gates.

11 OCTOBER 1937

At Wigan Oliver Stanley [*1896–1950*] opened our new Grammar School ... He has much more of the professional sense of ministerialism than his brother or his father [*the seventeenth Earl of Derby*] who was always a bit of an amateur. But I hear people say that in spite of his brilliance and great oratorical gifts Oliver Stanley is less reliable in judgment than his less noticeable brother Edward ... Today Stanley made us an excellent speech, well furnished with practical advice and framed with a pleasing and lambent humour. He had a capital reception: all the Stanleys are popular in Wigan.

17 OCTOBER 1937

At Leamington for the annual Conference of the Council for the Preservation of Rural England, a very successful gathering. I recall an excellent paper by Trevelyan about national parks and some very good practical speeches by Abercrombie, Chorley, and others ... We were shown over Compton Wynyates, Lord Northampton's Tudor house, set at the bottom of a saucer – in its way a very wonderful survival but we all agreed that neither for money nor for love would we consent to live in such a dank and dismal cavern: hills towering over it in all directions. We should have thought the place less repellent had it been cared for with greater intelligence – but neglect was very obvious and the smell of dry rot combining with damp and dirt gave a very unwelcoming impression.

18 OCTOBER 1937

Ronald [*Sir Ronald Lindsay, ambassador to Washington 1930–39*] dined in very good form – told us about his embarrassments likely to arise from the Duke of Windsor's visit to Washington*. The King and Queen are in a state of extreme nervousness about it or rather about all the Duke's activities – his theatrical appeals to popularity and these visits of inspection – perfunctory and no doubt pretty insincere, but none the less evidence of his readiness to bid for popularity. Hitherto he has been quiet and has shown no desire to study housing conditions in France and Austria – and now he wants to go to Washington – wrote himself to Ronald with broad hints – a typewritten letter, by the way, executed by himself, as indicated by his apology for bad typing. Ronald was summoned to Balmoral to discuss the subject, met Eden there and it was settled that he should invite them to a dinner but not offer to put them up. That is perfectly correct and follows the precedent of our embassies at Paris and Berlin: all the same the fidgety little man will give Ronald lots of worries, not least from the newspapers which will buzz around his nose more persistently than ever.

*Cf. below, pp. 616–21

21 OCTOBER 1937

At Royal Fine Art Commission. Now that Blomfield is off the Commission, Lutyens works hard and gives us all admirable assistance.

I got a letter from John Buchan [*Governor-general of Canada 1935–40*] who is faced with the same difficulty as my brother Ronald – namely a desire of the Duke of Windsor to visit Ottawa. But it is more serious in so far as Canada is British territory and as Buchan says they took a very serious personal view of his conduct. One might even expect him to be boycotted in the Quebec area. On all sides one hears people speaking angrily about these visits of sympathy with the 'working man' – he issued a communiqué to that effect which almost read like a challenge to our Sovereign. I don't suppose he really means anything hostile, but is trying to escape from the stupefying boredom of his aimless and inconsequent life – in fact that he wants to gad about and dance as he has been doing for the last ten years.

23 OCTOBER 1937

At the Natural History Museum we talked about the Rothschild bequest. The old boy [*Walter Rothschild*] was induced to make a regular codicil to his will, but probate has not yet been granted. I pressed Cantuar to get busy with the Treasury, to whom no word has yet been whispered.

25 OCTOBER 1937

I dined with Sir Edward Wood to hear the King's Speech – assuredly more congested with undertakings than for years past . . . Coal is mentioned ominously early in the speech – I fear another of the disastrous efforts by the State to run the industry.

Swinton told us about the visit of the German airmen to London – he thinks he impressed them, in fact I am sure he must have done so. His account of their reaction to entertainment amused us very much, and later on in the evening at Londonderry House I heard more about the subject from Trenchard. One thing in particular struck my informants, namely the frankness and openness with which they described the perquisites enjoyed by the influential airmen in Germany – not only did one of them express great surprise that we receive no such douceurs in this country, but he boasted about a huge motor car presented to him by an armament manufacturer – not only a car but the wages of two men to look after it!

A great crowd at Lord Londonderry's – how hospitable they are, how they love this friendly but expensive compliment to the party – which is really very civil of them considering that he lost his post in the government in a manner which was almost abrupt; but his parents were just the same. I suppose this is the last great house which can conduct entertaining on this scale – Bridgwater House is now en retraite, but in many ways a finer palace. Alas that Dorchester House, the best of the lot, has vanished – its successor though only a few years old had got very dowdy, so they faked it up for the coronation and it now looks like a pat of fresh butter.

The approach of war

26 OCTOBER 1937
Spent hours at Warrington discussing miners' superannuation.

27 OCTOBER 1937
Opened a Church School bazaar at Wigan – I like our new Rector – a very hearty person and not censorious.

28 OCTOBER 1937
One of our housing conferences at the Ministry of Health. I admire the skill and geniality with which Kingsley Wood conducts these meetings which are largely packed with his opponents who watch every movement in hope of tripping him up – but he knows a great deal more than the socialist critics.

29 OCTOBER 1937
Crawford interviewed candidates at Conservative Central Office for his old seat of Chorley, and was pressed to let his younger son James stand, on the grounds that 'however inexperienced he may be he would score from association with myself'.

Jackson says all the old women of Chorley would support me (and therefore James) – to a man – to a woman I mean, and I think this is true. They used to help me 30 and 40 years ago, and the other day at Wigan I noticed the marked and demonstrative friendliness of my contemporaries.

30 OCTOBER 1937
I am glad I went to Rutherford's funeral in Westminster Abbey. Of Rutherford I think one most vividly recalls the happy boyishness – which he retained until the very day before his death. The freshness of personality corresponded to a joyful friendliness of outlook as he confidently pursued his experiments. A. J. Balfour used to say Rutherford had the most powerful intellectual machine of his day.

1 NOVEMBER 1937
I paid a short visit to Eddy Derby [*the seventeenth Earl*] to discuss the route and routine of the King's visit to Lancashire next summer. Eddy told me that the last visit of the kind, ten years ago or more, lasted over a week – he had forty guests staying at Knowsley, forty to dinner every night as a minimum, and most remarkable of all, he himself travelled 3000 miles to and fro on Lancashire roads when working out the programme and timetable. He in fact organised the whole thing himself. Now he feels himself too old to repeat such an effort... It is not certain that this projected method of visitation will bring Their Majesties to Haigh. I should look forward to such an honour with apprehension for Connie's sake and also owing to the big expenses the visit would entail. But they ought to come to us as did King Edward VII when I was an infant. A royal visit was also to have taken place in 1913 but was cancelled by the death of my Father.

Derby is suffering from his eyes – bloodshot, watery, and protuberant – but he is immensely plucky and loves being busy – that in fact supersedes his passion for racing.

6–7 NOVEMBER 1937

So the Duke of Windsor has cancelled his journey to America. Ronald told me he had put himself hopelessly in the wrong by starting his visit with a preliminary tour in Germany where he was of course photographed fraternising with the Nazi, the Anti-Trade Unionist and the Jewbaiter. Poor little man. He has no sense of his own and no friends with any sense to advise him. I hope this will give him a sharp and salutary lesson. He deserves this rap on the knuckles for the nature of his announcements about the forthcoming trip was not over-loyal towards His Majesty.

The newspapers print masses of extracts from the American press showing how bitterly hostile the Duke's reception would have been. Altogether the Duke is lucky to have escaped before the situation had got out of hand as would undoubtedly have been the case – fancy if he had had to flee from the United States.

10 DECEMBER 1937

Hewart [*Lord Chief Justice*] speaks of Simon with scorn and distrust. I remember Ronald seemed to have the worst opinion of him when he was in charge of the F.O. That was because he made a practice of asking one ambassador what he thought of another, and as all of them thought themselves much more important than a parvenu in foreign affairs like Simon, the Secretary of State was soon stranded and could get nothing out of his chief officials, so suspicious had he made them.[31]

8 JANUARY 1938

I paid a visit to Norfolk's palace[32] ... The great rooms were prepared for the sale of effects by Christie's. What a house! I have never seen so ugly a house, so dirty a house – one so crowded with trash, I mean to say trash which in itself is a scandal. I think there must be very few great English families in which there is no evidence of taste, amenity, refinement – no sign, symbol or scintilla of culture, extending over a couple of centuries. This afternoon people were simply astonished at the meanness of the squalor – and the Norfolks have always been really rich.

9 FEBRUARY 1938

Mrs Neville Chamberlain opened a Conservative bazaar at Chorley. She made a

[31] Cf. diary, 30 December, 1939, for Sir Ronald Lindsay's 'inability to restrain his prose' on the subject. Simon 'gave the impression of wishing every one of our men to talk against their colleagues in the service ... I remember (said Ronald) my dismay when Simon indicated that he would like me to call him Jack – I felt as though I were being subjected to the blandishments of an adder ... All feel the same in the foreign service including Rumbold and Chilston'.

[32] For the exceptional interest aroused by the sale at Norfolk House, which was to be demolished, see *The Times*, 10 February 1938, p. 13 d. The music room was acquired by the Victoria and Albert Museum.

delightful speech.[33] She told them that she is in the habit of giving her guests in London a Lancashire hotpot – that she adds to it pickled cabbage, red cabbage (renewed applause) – and all the housewives from the countryside felt flattered. Then she shook hands with everybody within reach for half an hour and took the name of the person who had made the presentation bouquet in order to write her thanks. How these engaging manners and friendly approaches excel the normal political speech, measured by the successes of popularity and esteem. It is because women are so seldom women on the political platform that their success is so exiguous.

12 FEBRUARY 1938

At the National Portrait Gallery the other day we acquired Epstein's bust of Ramsay MacDonald, which reminded me *à propos de bottes* of his first visit to Chequers. He arrived as Prime Minister, as squire, as host – but he was unaccountably bumped on the stretch of drive between the Lodge and the Mansion: could not understand it, and at first was inclined to think a motor tyre was defective. No – they explained to him that the roadway was in bad order, that the shakeup was caused by potholes. Well, let the thing be mended – that surely is simple enough. And then next day he noticed trees which had fallen, were lying about, and dead branches had not been removed from living trees. Here again he was nonplussed that his country estate should not be as spick and span as the front gardens of the Hampstead Garden Suburb of his choice. Then came conversations with the agent, and it dawned upon him that a country estate is a costly luxury, that the landlord doesn't batten or fatten off the land, in other words that in spite of generous endowments, Chequers can scarcely pay for its upkeep. And then during the next few weeks he was made conscious of expenditure on drains, fences, garden buildings, and what not. It was a revelation and made a great impression on him. I well remember his telling me of the genuine distress he felt about the squire class which he came to realise was threatened – by maintenance of his property during life and by death duties thereafter. But what could be done, how could the alternative taxation be imposed?

23 FEBRUARY 1938

At Grillions I had an entertaining evening next Churchill who ate and drank in moderation which was perhaps the cause of his moderation in tone and argument. As a rule he is boisterous on these occasions and often shouts one down; but tonight he argued with ease and deference. We naturally talked of Eden's resignation. Churchill's speech in the H. of C. on the subject contained one lapse of good sense about which the audience immediately made its sentiment felt. It was disconcerting – just as he made an unexpected faux pas when speaking of the Palace crisis in 1936. So this evening he quietly stated his case for Eden and his views about

[33] Cf. below, 2 May 1939.

the Italian situation, and the disregard of diplomatic custom and propriety... I think Churchill is right in saying that Mussolini must be in a parlous state – longing for a pretext for bringing his troops home from Spain...

Geoffrey Dawson[34] told me that he had just spent an hour looking through the last hundred letters reaching *The Times* about the crisis. The first observation – how many came from the seaside; the second, the apparent youth of his correspondents; thirdly the fact that many came from young women, apparently; he could not be sure but he had that strong impression, largely borne out by the fact that many of them spoke of Eden as if he were a cinema star.

... Beside me was Runciman.[35] He scolded Churchill for being too ready to supplant coal by oil for the navy to which C. pleaded guilty, though he reminded us that he has not been in office for ten years. That surprised me; but he hasn't been inactive and everybody tells me that his historical books are quite first class. He was always a good architect of prose. He says he has lost the faculty of writing by hand, and now dictates everything including his work on Marlborough. I asked if he prepared careful notes in order to maintain his sequence of argument and narrative – no; he has read carefully enough to trust himself to talk the book to the shorthand clerk, but from time to time he finds his argument developing in the wrong direction, sometimes almost reaching a conclusion he would wish to avoid and then he must begin the page afresh... Churchill's memory continues most retentive, with an excellent taste for accurate chronology. He is like Joe [*Chamberlain*] in this; unlike A.J.B. who could not remember facts from day to day. Once when walking across the parade ground after a cabinet he said to———, 'What an interesting cabinet we have had; can you remember anything we decided?

26 FEBRUARY 1938

Eden's resignation speech last night addressed to his constituents of whom sixty per cent in the audience were under thirty, was a very quiet affair, with no revelations or claims for further publication; a correct speech to justify himself and to avoid incriminating others... At the Carlton the general impression of the moment is that Chamberlain was right, that we ought to be 'realist' and that if Eden had stayed at the F.O. the right moment for beginning conversations would never have been reached. We have already shilly-shallied for a year or more and every misdemeanour of Rome was advanced to postpone effort.

... We hear people say that in spite of having prevented a real cabinet split, Chamberlain ought to reconstruct and dispense with three or four of the duds – even that Baldwin should be invited to join – Churchill too. They little know Stanley B. who can believe that at the present moment he would consider such a call to duty. He will remain *perdu* and re-emerge only if some supreme necessity

---

[34] Geoffrey Dawson (1874–1944), editor of *The Times* 1912–19, 1923–41.
[35] Walter Runciman, first Viscount Runciman of Doxford (1870–1949), Liberal cabinet minister 1908–16; president of Board of Trade 1931–7.

should arise. He hates the limelight. A few years ago some journalists protested against his habit of shrinking into the shadow. Yes, he said – 'You want me to get into the limelight. Sometimes I have tried to do so, but each time I noticed a spot I have found Ramsay MacDonald in front of me, and then we have discovered Lloyd George plumb in the middle of it!' One likes his modesty. At Cambridge he recognised a contemporary, was reintroduced to the man he had not seen since they were undergraduates together: they exchanged a word or two and the man said, 'What are you doing now?' To which the Prime Minister answered, 'Oh, for the moment I have got a job in London.'

30 MARCH 1938

Onslow, Pickthorn, and I had a conference with Winterton about the parliamentary history. It appears that Wedgwood is about to sail for the United States in order to beg for money. I am horrified at the idea which has never been sanctioned by the committee but no power on earth will stop his departure – but we are all so frightened of him that we give way all along the line. I have constantly been told that if we criticise him he may have a heart failure and die. This is a strong deterrent to criticism though I notice that when I comment on his blunders he has never shown the smallest inclination to swoon. On the contrary he has perked up and has made a noisy though ineffective defence. It is scandalous that this great enterprise should be at the mercy of this literary adventurer, though to do him justice one must remember that had it not been for his efforts at the outset we should have started with a very meagre financial backing: he has never spared himself in promoting the scheme – considers himself its parent, and accordingly would like to write the whole of the introduction in his amateur jaunty journalese. Winterton says Wedgwood has the lowest opinion of myself – and well he may ask why outsiders like Pickthorn and I should criticise when we did none of the hard work at the start. If only Wedgwood's prose showed a little more cadence and modesty I would concur – but this blatant vulgar stuff disgusts.

31 MARCH 1938

I had a long talk with His Majesty about the forthcoming tour to Lancashire. Suddenly he said he would like to revisit Irlam, the most striking thing he recalls of his previous tour. How far is Irlam from Warrington, from Manchester, and before I had time to collect my thoughts he called up somebody (whom I did not know) and asked what the timetable was that day, and could a halt at Irlam be arranged. The man seemed very much embarrassed and later on thanked me for saying that Derby is actually arranging the timetable that afternoon – to interpolate an hour or more will dislocate the whole programme, and at best provide for a most inadequate inspection of the works. What H.M. wanted most to see again was the men standing against the sky at the top of a blast furnace – no doubt men engaged on repairing an empty cylinder.

20 MAY 1938

My eldest son and I went down to the Town Hall where we were acclaimed by the civic fathers of the Boro' and proceeded to march en masse to the Market Square for the reception of our Sovereign. We had a very friendly reception from the populace en route – I am always surprised when people recognise me so I was glad to be greeted by many old people, chiefly old women in the crowd.

16 JUNE 1938

At the Royal Society Club, Carter[36] told us that the great disappointment of the famous tomb was that the actual mummy although protected by three unbroken and unrifled coffins had completely perished. The body was calcined – a mere shrunken shapeless cylinder. He rewrapped it in the best linen Burroughs and Wellcome could supply, steeped the relict sovereign in a preservative, replaced him in the tomb, surrounding the actual mummy by golden conservative sand – then invited the clergy to read the funeral service. This they declined to do so he performed the ceremony himself, *rite Anglicano*, and the inner coffin was closed again, closed a second time after an interlude of 4,000 years.

28 JULY 1938

Hankey has just retired amidst a shower of panegyria – one would imagine him to be a consummate statesman and diplomatist. Actually he is the most accurate painstaking and methodical clerk who ever served a government. His memory is incredible. He has never forgotten a date, a minute, or a gazette. He can quote precedent and describe procedure to perfection, altogether the most skilful and mechanical mind I ever encountered. There are few ministers during the last twenty years or more who are not indebted to his good offices. He is a man wholly without ideas or initiative, and quite one of the dullest talkers of his day.[37]

19 SEPTEMBER 1938

Horrified that we should actually have proposed the partition of Czechoslovakia.

25–7 SEPTEMBER 1938

To London ... David and I spent two or three hours packing pictures into the Haigh lorry which has come to town to remove things to safety – sent off 25 pictures and I followed them by train.

29 SEPTEMBER 1938

To London. I paid a visit to Hopie,[38] very doubtful about his return to India. Feels

[36] Howard Carter (1874–1939), Egyptologist; discovered tomb of Tutankhamen, 1922.
[37] Cf. below, 17 January 1940.
[38] Victor Alexander John Hope, second Marquess of Linlithgow (1887–1952), Viceroy of India 1936–43.

he ought to go in case of trouble but anxious to curtail his holiday as little as possible. I thought him well, yet rather flushed and worried about himself. He is always accompanied by two or three shelves full of drugs and medicaments – nobody doctors himself with greater assiduity than our Viceroy, and he is seldom the better. Still he tells me he is bearing the strain wonderfully well and that the Indian legislatures notwithstanding blunders and blusters are beginning to grow conscious of their duties. He gives them all the help he can.

20 OCTOBER 1938

There was a very big congregation at Westminster Abbey to the memorial service of Lord Stanley[39] – many must have been there (like myself) from respect for his father. From what I can hear he was a real good fellow, very popular among his colleagues, and a man of good judgment – but deaf, indifferent in health for some years past, and fairly caught in the toils of the smart racing set, to which he was not particularly attached.

2 NOVEMBER 1938

At Grillions Eden was fussing and fidgeting, very self-conscious and blushing with handsomeness – vain as a peacock with all the mannerisms of the petit maître – very studied costume, moustache curled inside out – that always galls me – altogether a most uncomfortable dinner companion. Macmillan M.P. who has just distinguished himself by supporting the Master of Balliol in the Oxford byelection, kept pumping sedition into his ear. This seemed to be agreeable to Eden and every now and then one could see a wicked, vindictive gleam in his eye. I imagine that Eden's *amour propre* is deeply wounded. People no longer pay much attention to what he says now that we realise his continuance in office would have plunged us into war. David however says he is a good fellow.

9 NOVEMBER 1938

Churchill beaming with pleasure when I made him preside at Grillions dinner table, though profoundly disturbed at the fact of his being so violently attacked by the German press and ministers. He says there must be some *arrière-pensée* – as though this were the prelude to some fresh campaign against us. And well it may be. He is not so bitter against the government as he was, but is very emphatic that Chamberlain's policy is incomplete. A vigorous campaign of rearmament is all to the good, but it should be accompanied by a policy of moral courage and determination, something which will place definite personal responsibility on every Tom, Dick and Harry in the land. Here I feel he is right. Chamberlain seems to be drifting lest action on his part should appear to discount his profound desire for peace, and cast doubt on his credentials when resuming negotiations for a

---

[39] Lord Stanley (1894–1938), eldest son of the seventeenth Earl of Derby, and father of the eighteenth Earl; Secretary of State for Dominions, 1938.

settlement. An active policy on his part would return him triumphantly to power. But if in the meantime Hitler is engaged in picking a quarrel with us, the P.M. will scarcely dare to dissolve parliament.

We had some general conversation about the Jewish position – Winston C. was quite unaware of the Anti-Semite Movement – and seemed deeply interested when I told him some of its evidences.

10 NOVEMBER 1938
Introduced to a fugitive Austrian professor, Otto Loewi[40] by name, fired out of his post at Vienna. How vile is the German behaviour. This distinguished man won a Nobel prize for physics, £3,000 or so, and left the money in Norway (or is it Sweden). The Germans got wind of it and made him assign the money to the government at Vienna, and then fired him out. The meanness is incredible, but the pogrom now in progress makes me ill – and so little cause for it whereas if anything of the kind took place here one would know that the Jews contribute much too high a proportion of the criminal classes.

Dr Scott told me about the Elgin marble scandal at the British Museum – cleaning, scraping.

12 NOVEMBER 1938
The Elgin marble affair is much more serious than I had anticipated, much damage having been done by overcleaning in a drastic manner. Forsdyke much disturbed. Cantuar was in the chair, and the keeper and assistant Hincks were called in to give explanations. Lang began life as a lawyer and his cross-examination of the two men was masterly – I can only say that it was better than Cripps at his best! Why did he not stick to the law?

13 NOVEMBER 1938
Henry Dale[41] took me to see old Professor Sigmund Freud – he picked up Loewi on the way, and found the old gentleman busy at work, but almost unintelligible owing to a crisis in dentures...

Freud escaped before the worst outbreaks and managed to bring away his library and his collection of statuettes – of all kinds and types – except renaissance. He showed me a little bronze – a puzzling fragment and asked my opinion. I said offhand Pieter Fischer – the old boy was quite offended and made his daughter hunt up a book – she was ten minutes in finding it – to show me that it was a second century terminal of the Roman Legion's mast – well I didn't feel quite convinced! His spacious workroom is crammed full of his collections – a very mixed lot of Egyptian, Chinese, Cypriot and Roman material, statuettes predominating. One

[40] Otto Loewi (1873–1961), biochemist, Professor at Graz 1909–38; Nobel Prize, 1936; imprisoned, 1938, then worked in Oxford and New York.
[41] Sir Henry Dale (1875–1968), president of the Royal Society 1940–45.

whole table was covered with thirty or forty of them. We had not been in the room two minutes before Loewi and/or Dale bumped against it and knocked half a dozen down – they were re-erected. The daughter came in – said that there had been no mishap in bringing over the collection, whereupon Dale said, 'Well, we have only just escaped breaking some of them.' 'No,' said Freud, 'look one *is* broken.' He had noticed it but had said nothing which was considerate, but thought there should be some rebuke for clumsiness which did not realise its blunders – whereupon he picked up the little Ushubbi which had been broken in two and promptly glued the pieces together with secotine which got all over his fingers. Thank goodness I was nowhere near the table at any time. I am bound to say the old philosopher evidently understood that the figurine was only worth half a crown. Dale will have to be reassured on the subject, as I expect he is in agony for having been so awkward. Freud is eighty-three and quite serene – so are the other Jews I see.

26/30 NOVEMBER 1938

Important meeting at Cromwell Road about Tring. Rothschild will present the park and mansion if we can keep it up, and Sir John Ellerman is prepared to do this, on conditions. He is a keen student of rodents and he wishes to present us with a new rodent gallery, but must be given a free hand. As he is the greatest authority on rodents we can make the concession without risk, and we have also settled to issue as a Museum publication, his monograph on the subject. He is a curious retiring person with a passion for anonymity; they say he has got ten millions and doesn't wish to be harried by the beggars. Anyhow, he is going to look after Tring for seven or fourteen years. As to the gift itself, I was surprised that Tizard and Gardiner were very sceptical if the place would be serviceable to science, and Bragg suggested that the Royal Society should give its views as to the desirability of acceptance. I believe that the scheme may develop into a splendid benefaction to science.

Ellerman is a benefactor of the Natural History Museum and is infatuated by the study of rodents. He is an enthusiast, and moreover really professional in his pursuit of the subject, so much so that we settled to publish his book on these animals. He has the appearance of a rodent himself – of the harmless and amiable type, perhaps of certain members of the hare family. Anyhow if carefully handled this shy and modest young man is going to make an impression on zoological science, and is going to be highly serviceable to the Museum. We must make a Trustee of him before long. He must be fabulously rich. His father was the stingy old German shipowner who acquired millions, lived practically in retirement and was only known by sight in a very limited circle. I used to see him occasionally getting in or out of his car. He lived a few doors off us, and I remember that his chauffeur had the livery of a hallporter in a Berlin hotel. And now the son of this curious elusive creature is qualifying to be the world authority on rats and polecats.

1 DECEMBER 1938

Spent the morning at the Royal Fine Art Commission on the problem of street lamps. This is the kind of responsibility placed on the Commission, as the instrument of the Ministry of Transport. Everybody is struck by the tawdriness and often by the ostentation of the big electric lamps, which change as one changes the lighting authority, and which generally seem to be chosen and often designed by a surveyor or engineer. A number of manufacturers were therefore convoked, harangued, and as a consequence they agreed to make an effort to improve matters. Between them they produced 62 lamp designs, not one of which showed spontaneity or intuition. They were a wicked mechanical combination of tubes embellished with hideous brackets, flutings, cornices, and what not. We had to set to work to extract something, so I turned the problem over to Richardson and Holden, and lo, two designs have emerged one in steel the other in concrete which are most promising. The trouble is that neither of my colleagues will get a fee, still less any credit for their excellent work. I am afraid I drive my five architectural colleagues pretty hard, but they are public-spirited people. It is much easier to find this sort of colleague among architects than in the ranks of the painting fraternity – in fact it is most difficult to find a painter who apart from willingness is capable of taking a personal share in our executive work. A pity – but I have noticed this for years.

10 DECEMBER 1938

At B.M. the Elgin marbles affair reached its climax. They have been dangerously overcleaned by using unauthorised methods and instruments. The matter has been carefully investigated by a committee under the guidance of Macmillan and Wilfrid Greene. The outcome is that the keeper of the department retires with a medical certificate. His second-in-command is severely reprimanded and loses ten years seniority, and one subordinate on a weekly notice is no longer required at Bloomsbury. We discussed the affair for the best part of two hours, and settled (much against my advice) that no public announcement should be made. Baldwin was very emphatic against dismissal of any civil servant – said the man's case would immediately be raised in the House of Commons. The defence would have to be by (or perhaps of) Simon – 'and he would not do it particularly well.' We laughed and concurred. I shall be much surprised if the damage to the marbles isn't the subject of general conversation by Monday noon.

28 JANUARY 1939

I congratulated and I also chaffed Macmillan[42] on the manifesto of men of good will printed in this morning's paper – an appeal to the sentiments of peace-loving Germany . . . Was it [*intended*] to address it to Germany, to broadcast it alone in the German language, twenty-four hours before Hitler makes his important speech? I

---

[42] Lord Macmillan, Minister of Information, September–December 1939. The 'manifesto', an appeal to the German government and people for a supreme effort of co-operation, was broadcast on the BBC German service before its existence was reported in the English news. The signatories included Lutyens, Masefield, Vaughan Williams, Kenneth Clark, Eddington and G. M. Trevelyan.

thought the effort to forestall him seemed a little too palpable, and then to my astonishment Macmillan said the proposal came from Halifax!

28 FEBRUARY 1939

Very pleasant dinner at Grillions, a small party... The conversation was about India. Willingdon[43] was all for a firm resolute and unwobbling policy, in which Chatfield,[44] who is just home from an important investigation of Indian defence, cordially agreed. I think he will make his influence felt in the cabinet, where there must assuredly be many timorous people. Willingdon always impresses me. He talks like the Viceroy, always shows the utmost deference of the great personage, and now he is snow white he becomes very impressive. And *chez lui*? With the masterful Lady Willingdon how does he fare? She must be the real ex-Viceroy! Lutyens is complaining bitterly of her improvements in Delhi, but now we hear curious stories of Sassoon's[45] complacency about her treatment of Walmer Castle. The famous little apartment where Pitt and Nelson met (only once in those great lifetimes) has been converted by this unconscionable woman into a lavatory and it is alleged that she shows her guests the historic apartment with an appropriate giggle...

Willingdon looks back 'to sixteen years of unbroken happiness in India – and I would go back tomorrow if asked to do so.' He says the best thing he ever did was to support the foundation of the Willingdon Club at Bombay (where British and Indians are members on terms of equality). He says that the death of Brabourne[46] has been a great shock to him. Evidently he was confident that B. could occupy the Viceregality with conspicuous success.

8 MARCH 1939

Churchill talked freely and in admirable good humour at Grillions – much less dejected than he was a very few months ago – for though he believes the Germans are increasing their armaments quicker than we are doing, he feels that our power to strike back is in itself a great moral asset, while he is perfectly sure that with all her wiles Italy could make no show against our Mediterranean forces... Churchill says that the anti-submarine defence is so greatly improved that we should soon dominate their fleet, especially as during this war the Italians cannot sit safely in port – they have to keep supplies and reinforcements going to Spain, Libya, Dodecanese, not to mention Abyssinia. This was all comforting.

---

[43] Freeman Freeman-Thomas, first Marquess of Willingdon (1866–1941), Viceroy of India 1931–6.
[44] Alfred Chatfield, first Baron Chatfield (1873–1967), First Sea Lord 1933–8, Minister for Co-ordination of Defence January 1939–May 1940; chairman, India defence committee, 1938–9.
[45] Sir Philip Sassoon (1888–1939), First Commissioner of Works 1937–June 1939.
[46] Michael Knatchbull, fifth Baron Brabourne (1895–February 1939), Governor of Bombay 1933–7, of Bengal 1937–9.

11 MARCH 1939

Everybody has cheered up wonderfully during the last fortnight, and even the Stock Exchange approves... If only we can pull through what a triumph Chamberlain will have – a triumph over external foes, but [*also*] over those of our own family who day after day try to trip him up. Some of these gentry ought to be impeached.

15 MARCH 1939

Dined at Grillions. Churchill confident of the power of our navy but low about the general outlook. The other night Chatfield recently home from India spoke with confidence about the Fleet and seemed to have no anxieties about the Mediterranean. Like all sailors he has a low opinion of the Italian navy based upon our experience during the war... Chatfield was very strong on our duty to support the Princes against the machinations of Gandhi... It is doubtful if native ministers will for any length of time consent to forgo their posts, patronage and emoluments. Willingdon agrees with this view, thinks a good start has been made with parliamentary government, that the Indian is flattered by the loaves and fishes, delighted at the chance of jobbing a nephew into some subordinate post... Willingdon says that considering how new the constitution is and how raw ministers are, their initial success is very striking.

17 MARCH 1939

Halifax in the Lords frightened me with his apparent unconsciousness of a wicked world around us. Public opinion much perturbed, largely a reaction from the preposterous speech made by Sam Hoare a few weeks ago when he scolded us for our anxieties.[47]

18 APRIL 1939

At The Club sat between Salisbury and the Master of the Rolls; the former talked in calm and sedate fashion which contrasts with the staccato and abrupt conversation of old days. I remember him young and impulsive; now he is elderly and calm; at seventy-seven he commands less attention in speechmaking but more in conversation. We only talked of casual topics, but I was entertained that on the whole he was most impressed in Baldwin by the habit and faculty of indolence. When Jim wanted to talk over something serious, with the professional emphasis usual to men of his generation, he used to fail to command Baldwin's undivided attention. From time to time his interest would wane and he would hazard some observation about a cricket match. Jim found this puzzling – indeed he says he was baffled by it.

---

[47] See *The Times*, 11 February 1939, p. 7 c, for Hoare's Plymouth speech, under the headline 'No ground for pessimism'. Hoare argued that 'there was no question in the world today that could not be settled by discussion or negotiation'. Later, speaking at Chelsea (*The Times*, 11 March 1939, p. 7 c), Hoare recalled that Germany and Italy had constantly repudiated any intention to attack the democracies.

The approach of war

2 MAY 1939

At the Club I sat with Hensley Henson and the Prime Minister. This reminds me that yesterday afternoon Mrs Chamberlain entertained the C.P.R.E. at the Downing St house . . . She is a most delightful person and made us a charming little speech . . . Henson remains vivacious, easily amused, and an experienced talker – drew Chamberlain well. The latter talked freely on various things, we got on to Anti-semitism and Henson said he was no Anti-semite, but he thoroughly appreciated the attitude. Chamberlain gave me the impression of being blissfully ignorant of the feeling on the subject, and accordingly of the vital importance of keeping the safety valve of Palestine, indeed of extending it. The Prime Minister said he knew Weizmann of whose capacity he has a high opinion, so much so in fact that he, Chamberlain, was always reluctant to meet him as he was persuaded to acquiesce in views to which he was instinctively opposed.

The return of prosperity enabled Haigh to offer what turned out to be its last garden party to all salaried staff of the Lancashire Coal and Steel combine. On a blazing day in June 1939, Lord Crawford provided 1,758 guests with three thousand ices and much else besides – 'a very pleasant informal gathering, as nearly a family party as such a thing could be'. One party, in three huge vehicles, came from the Nottinghamshire coalfield; in Lancashire each pit came as a unit to the garden party, managers and agents with their subordinate staffs. It was the last flourish of the un-nationalised industry where local loyalties and connections still counted for much.

21 JUNE 1939

In the Lords I had rather a curious talk with the Bishop of Liverpool[48] [*about anti-semitism*] . . . Of course his Christian Principles forbid any such intolerance, and the very idea is distasteful: but then he went on to say that he had recently been shown a copy of the *Protocols of Zion*. – But, I interrupted, these are forgeries, which he admitted. The copy he had seen was thirty-five years old, but it contained the passage about getting control of popular sports in order to influence, indeed to break down the Gentile resistance. This impressed the Bishop, but the naive fellow little realised how far the process had gone; prizefighting, dogracing, ordinary horse betting, football and the disgraceful pools – in all these directions the Jew betting man is supreme. Other amusements and occupations are rapidly falling into their clutches, and the *Protocols* whether Jewish in origin or not, at least provide a definite programme for Jewry of today. Why don't the respectable Jews assert themselves?

23 JUNE 1939

I talked to Hailsham[49] recovering from his long illness. I asked him about Simon as

[48] Dr Albert Augustus David (1867–1950), Bishop of Liverpool 1923–44, author of *Life and the Public Schools* (1932).

[49] Douglas Hogg, first Viscount Hailsham (1872–1950), Lord Chancellor 1928–9, 1935–8, Lord President March–October 1938.

a possible successor to Chamberlain. Hailsham was almost as horrified as Alness[50] to whom I put the same question last night. H. says that Simon is tremendously keen, and that he was ready to forgo the Lord Chancellorship in order to preserve his freedom for the other post, but that the very idea of such a person leading the Tory party is too distasteful to contemplate; and Alness (Robert Munro as was) he too though a lifelong Liberal was even more shocked than Hailsham; as for Simon becoming P.M. he would prefer Inskip or Hoare or even Kingsley Wood – in fact rather pleased with this last hazard, and, although Edward Wood is a peer, he would probably be the best of the lot: but Simon – impossible!

... Katharine and Godfrey[51] lunched at Churt the other day ... and they were tremendously impressed by the scale of the farm and the advanced scientific method employed by Lloyd George, who told them that he has actually got 800 acres under cultivation. He has all the most modern implements, and a complete equipment for irrigating his more valuable crops... I remember an amusing story of H.A.L. Fisher who lunched there, and everything in the place was grown on the estate.

The summer of 1939 saw Crawford conducting business as usual: finding help for an emigré Jewish scholar, securing the support of Ellerman's money for the Natural History Museum at Tring as the original Rothschild benefaction was unexpectedly reduced, attending to the conservation of medieval cottages in Lancashire and the affairs of Wigan public library, and dining at Holland House. Though the foreknowledge of war was there as it had not been in the summer of 1914, the life of innocence outside history continued; this was no country mobilised to vanquish. It was still important to knock together the heads of architects, Giles Scott's not least, over such matters as George V's statue. There had never been an armistice, for Crawford, in the war against mechanical art, and he relished the recollection that 'his' Royal Fine Art Commission had saved Scott's reputation by preventing his putting pylons on Waterloo Bridge. One architect restored to favour was Lutyens, now forgiven his past vanities, whom Crawford wanted to press for an O.M.

28 JUNE 1939
Thomas Inskip talked with tolerable freedom at Grillions. It appears that a few days ago a number of German seaplanes made a long exploratory flight over Scotland, the Midlands and down to the Channel – four or five of them; they were signalled all the way and one of them actually came to grief in the North Sea but outside the three mile limit, and was collected by a German trawler.

7 JULY 1939
London Society dinner ... Herbert Morrison made an excellent speech, in reply to

[50] Robert Munro, first Baron Alness (1868–1955), Secretary for Scotland 1916–22, then a judge.
[51] Godfrey Nicholson, a Conservative MP, had married the diarist's daughter Katharine in 1936.

an extremely handsome panegyric from myself. Morrison must now have completely lost the sight of one eye, without however impairing his good spirits. I often wonder if he is going to develop into a great man. I strongly suspect him of reactionary tendencies...

13 JULY 1939

I talked to Philip Chetwode[52] about Spain where he spent some very uncomfortable months arranging about the repatriation and exchange of our nationals... Committee in the library, then walked round the museum. It is years since I was at sitting at a little table and Chetwode noticed that his legs were dangling down and didn't reach the floor – like Lord Roberts. I think he and Chetwode got on pretty well. Franco told him he had a card index of two million Communists with whom he intended to reckon.

22 JULY 1939

A very interesting day at Tring: meeting of the British Museum Standing Committee in the library, then walked round the museum. It is years since I was at Tring House, now to be devoted to the British Museum and to biological research. There are two trusts, one administered by the Trustees for their own purposes, including the Museum and its great collections, the other is the Park, part of the house and the stables, to be run for research. It is on this trust that I was asked to serve: Macmillan and Cooper are my B.M. colleagues, and the other six trustees will be nominated by Lord Rothschild and the personage we call 'the anonymous benefactor', namely Ellerman. I feel it may be rather a curious body. Ellerman is fabulously rich and is prepared to pay up handsomely to promote the scheme but he has a mania for anonymity being terrified of being pestered for money. He is himself a good biologist, and has made a very specialised study of rodents about which the Trustees are to publish his catalogue. Ellerman and his two nominees will no doubt have a preponderant voice on the Trust; it is believed that the Trustees will be his business advisers. Then Rothschild – he too will name two trustees, probably biologists. It rather seems to me that Macmillan and I, assuming Foster Cooper agrees, will rule that board as neither Ellerman nor Rothschild can have any administrative experience, and their voting power will most likely be thrown into our balance.

Ellerman is an inverse claustrophobe, one might call him a claustrophil. Sir Robert Hutchinson used to know the father well – thought him racially a regular German, but with little if any semitic blood. During the war they used to travel about a great deal inspecting hospitals. Ellerman used to listen carefully to Hutchinson's talk, used to press him to talk, seemed to take possession of what Hutchinson said, but never did he volunteer a remark himself – why give away anything, even a comment or criticism? I used to live a few doors from old

---

[52] See above, 4 March 1936.

Ellerman's house, and Harewood was next door to him, but we agreed that we had never seen this shy and furtive creature going in or out of his front door. What a tragic life to have to take so much trouble to conceal one's fortune.

Lord Rothschild wasn't there – he is doing an obesity cure. In his place Miss [*Miriam*] Rothschild acted as hostess and we had a very grand luncheon. She is rather good looking in a demure sort of way, a remarkable woman who is an authority on the siphonaptera collection which I suppose was formed by her melancholy father, while her own predilection is for parasitic worms. The other night at the Royal Society soirée she had an exhibit which attracted much attention, and over the luncheon table she described her difficulty in keeping the seagull in her London home – this bird provides habitat for the parasite, but requires the most careful diet in order that if necessary she could swear an affidavit that the parasite only got into the gull's intestines by the well documented process of incubation. She is happy in her studies.

Tring House itself interested me immensely. I was horrified by the whole mise en scène. Though many of the pictures have been removed and furniture has been collected in various rooms according to categories, one has a very good idea of what the house was like. In one room was a group of thirty clocks, table clocks which were all modern and would cost up to £50 apiece. Horrors. Another room seemed to have 20-30 sideboards ornamented with modern Sèvres plaques. Awful inlaid chairs and tables were classified, huge costly fitments, vast China vases of the worst period, sophisticated tapestries, mantelpieces which ruined the whole room – I passed from one monstrous apartment to another with ever growing consternation at two aspects – firstly how to cleanse the premises of the terrible fixtures (doors, cornice, ceiling, mantelpiece, shutters) all of them inconsistent with use of the room by nice stuffy bearded men of science – secondly my own problem, my own personal confession, that when I stayed with Lord Rothschild years ago I must have acquiesced in all this overpowering ostentation and vulgarity. How otherwise could I have forgotten it all – was I so insensitive in those days and is the critical judgement on which I now rely of quite modern growth? ... I talked to Connie about this; she consoled me by saying that as we left Tring together after a weekend there, I told her that I was so much shocked by the place that I would never again stay in one of the big Jewish houses. This reminiscence revived my spirits.

23 JULY 1939

Went to Kenwood. Instinctively it made me recall the Rothschilds and their fine collections of English paintings. Yesterday I saw the incomparable *Morning Walk* still hanging in the scatterbrained saloon at Tring; Gainsborough at his best. How Squire Hallett and his wife would triumph in Trafalgar Square. I feel overcome by the fatigue I associate with the opulence I saw yesterday. I went once or twice to Waddesdon where the ostentation was as marked as at Tring, but being a bachelor establishment there was less nonsense and perfumery, but I very well remember how mercilessly Haldane chaffed Ferdie Rothschild about his inflated staff and victuals. Ferdie writhed under such pleasantries – to be laughed at for being over-lavish in entertainment when those who seem most anxious for its enjoyments make fun of it all, must be galling; and he would twist his black moustache nervously while Haldane developed his witty and mordant attack.

Alfred de Rothschild[53] rather prided himself on his foreign blood – poor little fellow, the war broke him up as he lived in unrelieved terror of being blown up by a bomb. He had something which looked like rabbit wire erected over his house in Seamore Place, now demolished.

He used to send a brace of pheasants to every busman in London – he began his largesse when their number was modest, but he stuck to it and towards the end of his life tremendous orders had to be placed in Leadenhall Street. He had a wonderful cook and when hearing of somebody's illness when a special soup or pâté would be welcomed by the invalid he used to send a well-chosen little hamper of good things. Alfred or 'Mr Alfred' as he was called had a good heart, but a mean and miserable little mind – dear me they are all tinged with the tarnish of wealth – Rosebery who married into it was odious, and ungrateful too. One night at Mentmore when Hannah Rothschild had had a house party in which her compatriots were unusually numerous, all the ladies had gathered at the foot of the great staircase and were about to go up with lighted candles. Rosebery standing aloof from the bevy of beauty raised his hand – they looked at him, rather puzzled, and then he said in solemn tones 'To your tents, O Israel.'[54] Laurie Magnus[55] told me that within a week of Hannah's death he began to cut off subscriptions to Jewish charities, and before long all had been cancelled.

Miss Rothschild told me that her brother, Victor Rothschild, hates old pictures and modern books, and that he accordingly collects eighteenth century literature and pictures by Cézanne. 'Queer taste, isn't it?' said Miriam.

28 JULY 1939

Lord Dudley[56] is a busy person in his own line, he runs a private zoo and appears to have prospered. I knew all the older generation of his family including his father[57] who late in life married the enchanting Miss Gertie Millar. Old Lady Hillingdon[58] was fond of Dudley and whereas people criticised him for this second marriage, she collected a big luncheon party in order to give the young couple a friendly start. All went well, the new Lady Dudley looked charming and was charming, and when they had departed Lady Hillingdon said to the last lingering group of her guests, 'I

---

[53] Alfred Charles de Rothschild (1842–1918), second son of Baron de Rothschild, the first Jewish MP.
[54] Cf. G. Leveson Gower, *Mixed Grill* (1947), p. 98.
[55] A Jewish publisher who had been a friend of the diarist at Oxford.
[56] William Ward, third Earl of Dudley (1894–1970).
[57] William Ward, second Earl of Dudley (1867–1932) who married secondly, in 1924, Gertrude, *née* Millar (d. 1952), widow of Lionel Monckton, composer.
[58] Edith, Lady Hillingdon (d. 1969), wife of the third baron.

told you what a good sort the new Lady Dudley is – anybody can see in a minute that she has never lived with anybody but a gentleman.'

29 JULY 1939
A week or two ago I asked Bertie Clarendon[59] to look into the boycott of science and art by the King except in a very restricted semi-official degree. The boycott is so marked as to fill one with amazement. A minister sent to a small republic in South America is received in audience, but the President of the Royal Society, the Director of the British Museum, the chairman of the University Grants Commission, and so on – why never is their name or status whispered in Buckingham Palace. A whole section of British greatness and enterprise is taboo. In my innocence I thought I should be thanked for my suggestion especially as I safeguarded myself by saying that a dozen such interviews in a twelvemonth would suffice. Imagine my consternation to receive a long considered reply in which the Lord Chamberlain says that the King has not time for such a thing.

3 AUGUST 1939
I heard lots of gossip about Wigan Town Council. The Mayor himself is a quack herbalist doctor, ultra-socialist. He got on to the Jewish problem, in which Wigan can be very little involved, and a new jingle[60] was produced, which made me smile and interested me as symptomatic of the way the anti-semitic movement grows in all directions, though still confined to chaff and sarcasm. Before long it will take more destructive and aggressive complexion.

> Onward Christian soldiers
> You have nought to fear
> Israel Hore Belisha
> Will lead you from the rear
> Clothed by Monty Burton
> Fed on Lyons pies
> Die for Jewish freedom
> As a Briton always dies.

A victory by the Axis would have one result which we have never thought about ... we should have to find homes in these islands for a million Jews from the continent of Europe – would not such an infliction preclude for ever the revival of Britain?

24 AUGUST 1939
At the Athenaeum lunched with Moberly.[61] At the request of the Ministry of

---

[59] George Herbert Villiers, sixth Earl of Clarendon (1877–1955), Lord Chamberlain 1938–52.
[60] Later forbidden by the War Office for use as an army marching song (diary, 12 October 1939).
[61] Sir Walter Moberly, Vice-Chancellor of University of Manchester 1926–34, chairman of University Grants Committee from 1935.

The approach of war

Labour he agreed to organise the register of scientific men – a classification of available people who could be called upon to do any particular job, or make any specialised research. The idea sounds excellent and by dint of hard work for several months thousands of names have been collected, analysed, catalogued, and so on. Now the crisis is upon us and it is necessary to distribute the lists. But no adequate copies exist. The Treasury refused the rather complicated and expensive stationery on which the names were to be compiled, and the work has now to be begun at the eleventh hour.

... There was a considerable gathering to hear Halifax in the House of Lords – what a speech! To anybody not understanding English it might have been a lecture on mensuration or botany – a calm equable voice, a wholly cool and unemotional discussion, not one slogan, scarcely a word of encouragement. I never conceived it possible that at a moment of supreme crisis one of the protagonists could so completely detach himself... To listen to Edward Wood one asks oneself if he can say boo to a goose. Can Ribbentrop and Co. bring themselves to believe that this namby pamby person could fight? From beginning to end he did not show one spark of vitality. His substance was no doubt all we expected and the House accepted the government assurances with relief as there is always a certain fear that another appeasement interlude might be repeated.

25 AUGUST 1939

Eddie Winterton told me of a conversation he has just had with Winston Churchill, recently home from a long tour of the Maginot Line with Gen. Gamelin. Churchill was immensely impressed by its physical strength, but still more by the calm and resolute morale of the occupying troops. The most curious thing he saw was a party of Germans working on the Siegfried line which in certain places is only just across the river – no distance. He watched a party of men erecting barbed wire defences. Through his glasses he could see their actual countenances. He was amazed at the leisurely half-hearted way in which they worked. He discarded the hypothesis that they were play acting in order to deceive the observers from the Maginot line; and he came to the conclusion that the men who were working so slowly must either have been dead beat, or half starved; perhaps both.

30 AUGUST 1939

I had a long talk with Charles Londonderry[62] who was a bit harassed by his responsibilities as lord-lieutenant in two countries and chairman of some biggish man's war service affair in London. He says that if he were not an aviator things would be impossible but he is fond of flying and travels from Co. Durham to Co. Down in a couple of hours. He has always been a staunch advocate of a conciliatory attitude to Germany and at one time showed excessive friendliness towards Ribbentrop. Of this I have no doubt he is now wholly contrite, for of all the German gangsters Ribbentrop comes out nearly worst.

[62] Author of *Ourselves and Germany* (1938); see above, 27 February 1936.

3 SEPTEMBER 1939

At the end of our sitting in the House of Lords... Lord Maugham[63] rather unexpectedly broke into reminiscence – said that never had there been a more hardworked lord chancellor than himself – that for eighteen months he had had to take charge of bills which should have been managed by departmental ministers; and generally he seemed to have a grudge against parliament or his own colleagues – his own inclination would be to retire to a country cottage and devote his remaining years to reflection. An hour or two later I talked to Tom Inskip[64] at the Carlton and learned that he has been appointed to the Woolsack. I thought of Maugham, who will be looked upon, and rightly, as the most inefficient Speaker of the House of Lords within living memory. I make no comment on his judicial work of which little is said – but seldom have I heard anybody so hopeless in putting an amendment or conveying a decision – he even blunders over the effort of adjourning a debate and adjourning the House which he seems to think are interchangeable processes. Often enough he forgets to put the question at all, and a very familiar sight is that of the Clerk of the Parliaments hurrying from the Table to the Woolsack in order to coach the indolent Chancellor... Inskip gave me the impression of being thoroughly pleased with his new post. As to the remaining appointments, I was surprised at the amount of critical remarks about Churchill's getting the Admiralty. They wanted him to be minister without portfolio, but he was strong enough to stand out.

6 SEPTEMBER 1939

We had a tiny Wednesday dinner at Grillions and Inskip as new Lord Chancellor presided. He told us that he had been approached informally by Dulanty, the S. Irish Commissioner, to find out if a common deal with James Craig[65] would be possible. If Craig would agree to unifying Ireland (no doubt on terms which Ulster would consider favourable) Eire would then come in and declare war on Germany. I must say the idea is ingenious; many would think it tempting, and we wondered what we thought.... Thomas Inskip himself I fancy was hostile to the idea...

At Grillions tonight Devonshire[66] told us that his grandfather, the old seated gentleman in the Eastbourne statue, was awakened in bed by a servant who noisily entered the room shouting 'The house is on fire.' 'Very well,' said the Duke, 'go and help put it out – it's your business not mine.'

---

[63] Frederic Herbert Maugham, first Viscount Maugham (1866–1958), Lord Chancellor March 1938–September 1939. Maugham, who had no previous political experience, took the post on the understanding that he might soon be asked to resign and return to his judicial career (D.N.B.).

[64] Thomas Inskip, first Viscount Caldecote (1876–1947), Minister for the Co-ordination of Defence 1936–January 1939, Secretary of State for the Dominions January–September 1939, Lord Chancellor September 1939–May 1940.

[65] James Craig, first Viscount Craigavon (1871–1940), first premier of Northern Ireland 1921–40.

[66] Edward William Spencer Cavendish, tenth Duke of Devonshire (1895–1950). The 'old seated gentleman' was his great-grandfather, William, seventh Duke of Devonshire (1808–91).

The approach of war

In our House we debated censorship and the Ministry of Information. We had the maiden speech of Lord Macmillan, the new minister... Macmillan's reply was calm, conciliatory; he expressed himself anxious to remove the difficulties of which the affair of last Monday was an inexcusable blunder. France broadcasted the arrival of British troops. Our censorship passed the news, then cancelled permission after large issues had been printed – finally gave permission again. Geoffrey Dawson told me that the *Times* office was actually invaded by police to see that no copies escaped! It was pretty hard on the Press who wished to be ultra-loyal, and of course Macmillan got all the scolding whereas the fault lay with Hore-Belisha and his clumsy press department.

... The Duke and Duchess of Windsor are back in England – it is announced that he is about to take up a public appointment; but a stray field-marshal is not easily placed, nor a superfluous admiral of the fleet, and he can't do the work allotted to his younger brothers Kent and rolypoly Gloucester. He is too irresponsible as a chatterbox to be entrusted with confidential information which will all be passed on to Wally at the dinner table. That is where the danger lies – namely that after nearly three years of complete obscurity, the temptation to show that he knows, that he is again at the centres of information will prove irresistible, and that he will blab and babble out state secrets without realising the danger. I dined with Howe[67] at The Club. He is working at the Admiralty, and to his consternation saw the door of the Secret Room open – the basement apartment where the position of our fleet and the enemies' is marked hour by hour – and Lo! out came Churchill and the Duke of Windsor. Howe... was horrified – and of course Churchill has been long mixed up in the intrigue woven around the little man... All the same I suspect Churchill knows his man well enough to have withheld all information of a really serious character; but it was a compliment to the Duke which should never have been paid.

19 SEPTEMBER 1939

Ronald[68] and I talked about USA and the war – he anticipates little real help though where American interests are concerned Roosevelt may register annoyance. Germany however must well know that however much the States are provoked they would not be able to ship a man to Europe for twelve or eighteen months.

21 SEPTEMBER 1939

Zetland à propos of nothing suddenly said at lunch, 'The other day Charles Londonderry passed along the Front Bench in the House, and I said "Dear old chap, I'm glad to see you haven't been interned," whereupon he glared down at me in fury and said, "Not one of my old colleagues, and not a single newspaper, has one good word to say for me."' But so it is. There was a very substantial rumour that he

---

[67] Francis Curzon, fifth Earl Howe (1884–1964).
[68] Sir Ronald Lindsay, ambassador to Washington from 1930 to 29 August 1939.

had been interned; today the same story was going round about Brocket[69] who used to visit Germany in Hitler's tame parties.

27 SEPTEMBER 1939

After Chatfield[70] had made a very dull and unconvincing defence of the Ministry of Supply he said to us as we left the House of Lords, that he did not find himself nearly so hard pressed now, as a few months ago when all the preparatory work was in progress. Anyhow he doesn't feel overworked now. I thought it odd – a complacency which popular criticism does not endorse; he has very little political sensibility and no experience in weighing up public sentiment. Anyhow he seems fairly confident: not so Hankey[71] I should imagine. I was shocked at his appearance – wan, hectic, at the same time pallid as a frightened rabbit should be; really a very alarming spectacle, but I hope it is not rising anxiety about the situation, and only the burden of his novel experience of having to take decisions rather than take minutes.

At Grillions all applauded Churchill's spirited speech describing the naval situation – helpful, hopeful, determined; the very tonic the House of Commons wanted and a real foil to Chamberlain's stiff summary without light or shade. Churchill wiped Chamberlain's eye, and I expect he did so with gusto ... And of course we talked about Russia ... The universal feeling is that we scarcely deserved our escape from the Russian ambush. Fancy if we had made the deal and had then been confronted by an Italo-German-Russian entente. We must not forget Churchill joined Lloyd George and the Socialists in advocating the Russian deal. Eden did so – the tale of his follies mounts up. His clumsy tactless handling of Italy, his ridiculous visit to Moscow, his preposterous cinema tour in the United States, all show a defective reading of men and nations including our own, but he remains a source of danger, for his screen star attitude and moustaches, his mannerisms and faultless costume ensure united enthusiasm among the flapper vote. He reminds me of George Wyndham whose career was ruined by impeccable manners and address.

... In these conversations I notice that Charles Londonderry is very reserved. I think he deeply feels the humiliation, not to say the equivocacy, of his situation, brought about partly by thoughtless good humour, and his family tradition of entertaining all and sundry without question asked – partly from his desire after leaving office to keep in the swim. He allowed Ribbentrop to become his familiar and what was worse, used to defend him long after the offensive fellow had made his attitude clear to the rest of us. If Charles L. is penitent we see no such signs in Lord Brocket who was flattered to death by Hitler's compliments, and now spends his time in the Carlton and the Lords whispering that we ought to come to an understanding with the Germans.

[69] Arthur Ronald Nall-Cain, second Baron Brocket (1904–67).
[70] Minister for Co-ordination of Defence January 1939–May 1940.
[71] Maurice Hankey, first Baron Hankey (1877–1963), secretary to the cabinet 1920–38, minister without portfolio in the war cabinet September 1939–May 1940. See below, 17 January 1940.

The approach of war

I presided at Grillions, with Winston Churchill on my right, Bertie Horne on my left and Hartington opposite – a pleasant and informative evening. Churchill throughout sparing of victuals and liquor – dull and restless at first, but he soon cheered up as is his wont, ended by taking charge of the conversation, describing his office, his work, his ambitions louder and louder, with complete disregard for the waiters some of whom must be foreigners. Once or twice I was horrified... It was when we were alone after dinner that he talked most eloquently... He told us about the recent attack by German aircraft upon our ships at sea. Two encouraging facts emerged, firstly that the attack began at 10,000 feet, but that the Boche planes very soon rose to a height of 20,000, to get beyond the range of our guns. Secondly that only once did the German aeroplanes nosedive at our big ships – from these two facts he argued that German courage was far from conspicuous.

Then about submarines; our new apparatus (which the Germans don't possess) is almost foolproof, and does not depend (or wholly so) upon sound. In fact we sometimes sight and destroy innocent hulls lying on the bed of the ocean. Recently the depth charge ship blew up a boat they had located – awaited the appearance of débris, when to their surprise a big flat object was thrown out of the water, and fell flat on its side. It was a big wooden door painted white, and on it painted in big letters 'W.C.' 'My own initials' said Churchill, 'and I took it as a real compliment.'

... Churchill as I say is very confident, but all the time he is acutely conscious of the danger from German bombers, and how we could stand up to the strain of an uninterrupted week of high explosives and incendiary bombs... Trenchard of course said that we have lost our chance of striking while Germany was so busy in Poland; Churchill would not reply...

... However as I say he is confident, and said in tones of pontifical emphasis that the British navy had command of the seas and could ensure that practically all our freight ship convoys could be safely escorted to home ports. Well then cut in Walter Elliot rather abruptly, then you must give us convoys to bring home the shiploads of butter and bacon which the Danes are frightened to send us. Churchill was nonplussed; said that the country would not allow him to risk a capital ship for 10,000 tons of pork and butter – and he had to admit that our command of the seas excludes the Sound, the western littoral of Denmark, and I dare say the southern coasts of Norway.

And then the conversation changed and we got on to the subject of lice and bugs... It began by Hartington loosing off a general attack on bureaucracy... Elliot defended his department skilfully, assisted with the background of medical experience gained in his younger days, in fact I was impressed by Elliot's defence of the good work done by the Ministry of Health in the last ten years... Then Churchill told us that he was concerned in the problem as a short time ago a bug made its appearance in his country house – he said the animal caused a kind of panic in the household, the place had to be fumigated – he had to turn out for three days and meet a bill for £8.

... Horne whispered to me, Churchill is the man, our man, the only possible successor to Neville Chamberlain ... I wish they would get Horne back, but he is wedded to his G.W.R.

19 OCTOBER 1939

I lunched with physicists at the Athenaeum ... Tizard told us about one of the mysterious air raids in Berlin where nothing occurred except an explosion of air raid precautions followed by official denials. In one of our planes, which had been overflying Berlin, two of the men at 18,000 feet got numb with freezing, and the pilot saw he had to decongeal them; so he descended as quickly as was safe, and with improving oxygen he flew up and down Berlin with no rhyme or reason, sometimes as low as 300 feet – never a pursuit plane within reach and the searchlights utterly unable to catch him up. 'I wanted just to warm the boys up,' said the young Canadian officer, 'I thought it a bit of good sport to give Berlin twenty minutes of the best of it.'

Stanhope[72] told me that the destruction of the Royal Oak threw Scapa into a panic – such a feat was inconceivable to them, and he, Stanhope, had satisfied himself long ago that all the defensive works were in good condition and up to date.

24 OCTOBER 1939

James[73] is with his men in some school at Holloway and I was surprised to learn that this territorial battalion is scheduled for civilian duty, that is to say for keeping order in case of riots after an air raid or incendiary attack, when it is expected that there will be an outbreak of looting!

15 NOVEMBER 1939

A queer debate in the Lords. We constantly seem to have little debates promoted by the wealthy brewer Lord Brocket who himself remains in the background, doesn't speak. He is a good golfer and a great *intrigant*. Today his little pacifist group staged a motion for a secret session – Arnold, Buxton, Astor, Ponsonby, Harmsworth, Elton, even Charles Londonderry, Crewe, and fancy Trenchard being flattered into the intrigue, not to mention dear old Rennell Rodd and the ex-Chancellor who committed a tremendous false analogy. Not one word raised against the motion until I hazarded a protest. Stanhope I am glad to say refused the idea ... What interests me however is Brocket – this debate was all arranged in the tea room last week – Samuel told me all about it, and Brocket as is his wont takes a seat at the extreme end of one of our benches, constantly slipping in or out, almost unnoticed,

---

[72] Stanhope had been First Lord of the Admiralty, October 1938–September 1939, being replaced by Churchill on the outbreak of war.
[73] The diarist's second son, b. 1906.

to lobby somebody or other. I wonder what his real game is . . . Is it that Brocket is fundamentally an admirer of Hitler, or is he terrified by the man? Anyhow one hears people talking with great suspicion about Brocket himself.

Ebor[74] presided at Grillions tonight – talked no pacifism and so far as I could hear did not urge forgiveness of Germany and love of our neighbours. On the contrary he was heartiness itself, enjoyed his meal and went into tremendous guffaws of ventral laughter – a process which elivens the whole company, and puts us all into good humour.

Items garnered by Crawford during the 'phoney war' were wide and varied. The financial plight of artists of all kinds seemed insoluble, though Kenneth Clark, 'a very arrogant little chap, but as clever as a monkey,' had a committee on war artists, fancying himself 'well able to distribute the official patronage.' Among the sculptors, Reid Dick[75] was busy on the statue of George V, but had run into difficulties over his scale model. Queen Mary wanted the statue brought more within range of the eyes – 'Why won't Sir Giles agree', she said, tapping her long umbrella on the floor, 'I should like to say D—— the architects'. George VI also thought the pedestal was too high and finding the little model was made of wood, called loudly for a saw.

The news from Italy struck the diarist and his circle of London clubmen favourably. The Italian revival of colonial claims in November seemed to mean that

Italy must have lost all belief in a German victory, hence her desire to peg out the claims in good time, and later on to blackmail us into making concessions because she deserted the Boche.

At home the state of affairs left more to be desired, with a stray German raider producing 'a good deal of panic' in Wigan market place, while at St Helens a mere air raid warning had led to 'young men snatching gas masks from people.' In his own specialist field, Crawford was disappointed by a conversation he had on 17 November with the Food Minister, W. Morrison.[76]

Crawford mentioned two unsolved problems of the first war, the question of combining maize and wheat flour, and the production of a satisfactory potato flour for admixture, and asked Morrison if he had a scientific diet and nutrition committee set up, such as had existed in 1914–18. Morrison had never heard the idea mentioned, and said

a thing which shocked me, as illustrating his lack of knowledge and lack of vision. He did not contemplate that it would ever be necessary to have to add any dilution to the wheaten loaf! Why in the war we had to add barley and rice, even pulses – we

[74] Dr Temple
[75] Sir William Reid Dick (b. 1879), a specialist in statues of George V.
[76] William Shepherd Morrison, first Viscount Dunrossil (1893–1961), Conservative minister; Minister of Food September 1939–April 1940, Speaker 1951–9.

wanted to add maize flour and if the war had continued till February 1919 we should have added potato flour as well.

Morrison had only just set up the equivalent of Crawford's Wheat Executive of the first war: 'I fear he hasn't studied his war books.' His ignorance of the history of the loaf (e.g. 'how we had two millions of tons of wheat at our disposal in Australia, but no tonnage to move it') alarmed Crawford, especially as Morrison was one of the brightest of the younger Conservative ministers.

Crawford's brother, just returned from the Washington embassy, encountered its architect, Lutyens, at the Athenaeum. Lutyens joined his hands in prayer and said, 'Am I forgiven?' The diplomatist forbore to mention that, because of his use of ceiling heating, ceiling after ceiling at the embassy had collapsed. The conduct of the war was more obscure. When Stanhope[77] was asked why the air force had not bombed the Rhine bridges, he said he had himself put the question to the authorities but could get no reply. Only Hore-Belisha[78] made an 'excellent impression' in his address to an unreported conference of 120 peers on 29 November.

'Thank heaven we are not in alliance with those savages', Crawford wrote as Russia advanced westward to attack Finland. 'A new war is upon us, Sweden is immediately menaced, ourselves later on: it is a nightmare to think of Russia facing us on the North Sea.' The moral considerations that made Crawford anti-Soviet made him also unequivocally anti-defeatist at a time when establishment opinion had not found its bearings.

5 DECEMBER 1939

For some time past we have had regular debates on foreign affairs in the Lords in which the defeatists have been most prominent. We have actually had discussions without a single vigorous advocacy of our case being presented. I have complained, and so today Templemore[79] warned Stonehaven and me to speak and we were ultimately reinforced by Maugham. We stated our case against Hitlerism without qualifications or apology, and I am glad we did so, to the manifest surprise of the mugwumps who have had everything their own way hitherto. Johnnie Stonehaven and I received congratulations from several people who have been angry at the pleas for peace and forgiveness – nothing but a smashing defeat of the enemy in the field can give us an abiding peace. I wonder if our influence gingered up Halifax – anyhow he made the most decisive pronouncement since the war began. His voice was firm, and non-apologetic. He even tapped the box no less than three times ... Ebor leads a group of people who say the peace terms must be positive ...

---

[77] At this time Lord President of the Council and leader of the House of Lords.

[78] Lesile Hore-Belisha, first Baron Hore-Belisha (1893–1957), Secretary of State for War 1937–40.

[79] Sir Arthur Chichester, fourth Baron Templemore (1880–1953), Captain of the Yeomen of the Guard 1934–45.

The approach of war

There was some conversation last night at Grillions on the naval situation, and Churchill was far from confident about intercepting the *Deutschland*. He says that the ship has done uncommonly little, measured in the tonnage of captured shipping, but that none the less she 'keeps us on the hop.' In effect she immobilises some of our ships which would be useful nearer home ... I should say that on the whole Churchill is in fairly good spirits – nothing like so optimistic as a month ago, and now without rhetoric or bounce. He remains the person who gives me the maximum sense of power, initiative, and drive. He doesn't look particularly well.

13 DECEMBER 1939
Today we had another debate in the Lords staged by the little group of defeatists who get far more attention than their numbers deserve. Arnold and Noel-Buxton aired their usual grievances, supported by the Bishop of Chichester ... a most pestilent performance, while Bligh[80] emitted a sort of panegyric of Hitler ... I must get an opportunity of telling Cantuar[81] how much harm is being done to the Anglican Church by those divines. Ebor is pretty bad, Birmingham intolerable. Tonight Halifax so far as style and vivacity are concerned made the most forcible speech he has yet delivered – a really strong utterance. I think he has been much moved by accounts of the German massacres of Poles.

We attended a private confabulation with Churchill about the naval situation, a sequel to Belisha's address about army matters. Churchill's speech was very carefully prepared and he showed us some instructive charts about merchant shipping losses, and how the mine is now much more dangerous than the torpedo. I don't think he told us much which was really confidential but it was all very illuminating and certainly gave me a vivid picture of the stupendous and unremitting effort required by our ocean patrols. The attendance wasn't as good as one would have wished ... but Churchill had a very attentive audience and much appreciated our vote of thanks. There was no bounce about him, no boastfulness – he didn't look particularly well – rather flushed – very few of his humorous flashes, but on the whole I would say in pretty good spirits.

14 DECEMBER 1939
A pleasant dinner with the Royal Society Club ... Mellanby[82] somehow or other got on to the subject of Dorman-Smith,[83] the new minister of agriculture – a real diatribe, said that he is a virtual nominee of the National Farmer's Union, is surrounded by people who pride themselves on being 'practical men' – people who look upon science applied to husbandry as a fad: in point of fact the scientific side of

---

[80] Esme Ivo Bligh, ninth Earl of Darnley (1886–1955).

[81] Dr Lang

[82] Sir Edward Mellanby (b. 1884), nutritionist; secretary of Medical Research Council.

[83] Sir Reginald Dorman-Smith, Minister of Agriculture January 1939–May 1940; president, National Farmers Union, 1936–7.

the ministry's work is being sadly neglected at a moment when increased effort should be devoted to its penetration. Consequently there is confusion in the ministry and worse may follow. I did not ask for his authority, or at least for illustrations, but he was very emphatic, indeed really bitter in his jerky casual way.

25 DECEMBER 1939

Eden was in France – there was a theatrical performance which was attended by the French brass-hats and our own. All of them retired . . . and the Duke of Gloucester was left in a box with Anthony Eden. The lights went up, the troops in the theatre recognised the Duke and gave him a vigorous reception, whereupon Eden pushed himself forward, pushed the Duke to one side, and went to the front to take the salutation, to the surprise of the audience . . . Churchill too committed a first class blunder, he had the bad taste to bring Capt. Sandys[84] out in his suite – a man whom the whole army hates for his attempt to magnify himself by dragging the army into a political dispute. It is a pity that Churchill should make such errors of judgment, but at least Sandys is young and active.

8 JANUARY 1940

A most curious letter from Ronald describing an interview with Neville Chamberlain. He was summoned to Downing St on January 3rd (last Wednesday) and to his amazement learned that Belisha was leaving the War Office, that the P.M. thought of sending him to the Ministry of Information, but was doubtful if having a Jew in that office might not offend the USA, and at the same time give a fresh weapon to Goebbels. Ronald was able to reassure him that he need fear no political reactions[85] . . .

17 JANUARY 1940

There is no doubt that the public is thoroughly bamboozled by the Belisha affair . . . but here are three opinions: no. 1, Lord Londonderry. Belisha came to stay with him in Ireland, to review a battalion or something of the kind. Throughout his stay at Mount Stewart he was pleasant in the house, agreeable with the officers he met, easy in manner and natural with NCOs and men – talked good sense and left an excellent impression. Opinion no. 2 – Lord Hailsham. I may say that Hailsham flushes with indignation when Belisha is mentioned – 'a vulgar unreliable man with a passion for self-advertisement' who arouses a bitter personal animus in Douglas Hogg's reasonable temperament. Then no. 3, Somerset Maugham via his brother lately Lord Chancellor. It appears that Belisha invited himself to Maugham's

[84] Duncan Sandys, Baron Duncan-Sandys (cr. 1974), b. 1908; entered parliament and married Churchill's daughter, 1935.

[85] Chamberlain was looking for a replacement to Lord Macmillan, a Scottish lawyer who had not been a success as the first Minister of Information. Reith was appointed to that post on 5 January 1940, while Belisha declined Chamberlain's offer of the Board of Trade and remained out of office, except briefly in 1945, for the rest of life. Belisha resigned the War Office on 4 January.

Riviera villa, stayed a fortnight, made himself quite pleasant, and Maugham got to like him, but thought it would be friendly to offer a word or two of advice. So the day of Belisha's departure, Somerset Maugham delivered a homily – that three things might continue to ruin a career which in many ways is most promising, viz. arrogance, bad manners, and 'the fact that it never occurs to you to raise a finger to help anybody but yourself.' Belisha was not in the least offended, indeed he thanked his host for his attentions. A few days later Maugham had a conversation with a lady to whom Belisha had proposed – and by whom to his sincere chagrin he was refused. Belisha asked her if her refusal was based on his racial extraction. She said no, whereupon he continued, 'could I hope to persuade you to reconsider your attitude, when I give you an assurance that in the ordinary way I stand next in succession to the Prime Ministership.' No, neither would that prognostication induce the damsel to change her mind.

The fact is that the man is completely egocentric, so much so that he has lost all sense of time (very much like the Duke of Windsor) and thinks nothing of breaking engagements... He asked Jack Gilmour to see him... [Gilmour] said he would call on Belisha at his own house next day – did so – drove down to Wimbledon and at half past ten in the morning was shown into Belisha's – bedroom – was harangued by the Secretary of State in purple pyjamas. The insolence of the man!

... In the Lords Hankey spoke about the control of German trade. He stood at the box with hands in his pockets and for ten minutes read us a casual scrappy record of the situation – not one word to illuminate a thrilling subject, to encourage us for what is accomplished or to inspire fresh efforts: altogether one of the most lamentable performances I have heard for many a long day. Why is this second-rate little civil servant in the cabinet? He is no more than an efficient minute clerk.[86]

18 JANUARY 1940
Two papers have just published articles on Belisha which throw a fresh complexion on the whole subject – *Truth* and the *Investors' Review* give detailed biographies of six or eight wildcat companies of which Belisha was promoter or director... all have gone bust... Pickthorn[87] told me that he had sent a letter to Downing St weeks ago warning that some such revelations were possible... But the press won't whisper a word of this scandal. Belisha is one of those who lunches every week with Beaverbrook and considers himself a member of the Fleet St fraternity... The plain facts are however so simple, that one wonders what humorist spotted Belisha for the Board of Trade, which is the department in charge of the bankruptcy laws.

23 JANUARY 1940
Some talk at the Carlton with Kingsley Wood who told Zetland and myself that we

[86] Cf. above, 28 July 1938.
[87] Kenneth Pickthorn, MP (Cons.) Cambridge University 1935–50.

are sending a hundred aeroplanes to Finland. Some are already there, the rest will arrive in three, four, or five weeks. 'Do you think we are doing right,' he asked, almost with eagerness, and we both said we emphatically agreed ... It was evident that Kingsley Wood approved of running the risk – a far less risk than that of allowing the gallant Finns to be overrun by Russian hordes.

26 JANUARY 1940
About Churchill many people feel that he is splendid as a fighting minister, but that his judgment is not of the calibre required for a prime minister: but if Chamberlain broke his leg Churchill would be driven to Downing Street by public opinion.[88]

15 FEBRUARY 1940
Churchill gave an encouraging report about the naval situation. This was at Grillions, and though he told us little of a technical character, he seemed in good spirits, assured us that we have (almost?) mastered the magnetic mine, and that though we have just lost some big and valuable merchantmen we have destroyed four submarines in a week. He thinks that our new procedure may succeed in preventing the Boche from scuttling his ship. We went on to talk of general war questions ... [He talked of] Kitchener's service to the state as minister in 1914. He thought him too rigid and inflexible, perhaps one might say too logical in a military sense. But he made a great contribution to our sense of reality, firstly by imposing on the government something of which they had never dreamed, namely that we should have to produce a huge oversea army, and concurrently that the war was going to be a long drawn out affair. We have all heard of Kitchener's excursions into cabinet debates, and how he used to get bamboozled – contradicting himself, and failing to answer the simplest question. I had never before heard about the discussion in which Lloyd George pleaded earnestly and very convincingly too that some concession to Welsh sentiment would greatly stimulate recruiting. Kitchener was adamant but could not reply to the arguments and this of course occurred long before conscription. He realised that he was failing to make out his case – he glared angrily to one side and the other: his fiery bloodshot eye made no impression on Lloyd George who was really zealous in his cause. Suddenly Kitchener got up, walked behind Asquith's chair towards the door and the cabinet was horrified to realise that he was about to retire – from the room, from the government, and that a terrible crisis was impending. Kitchener stalked the last few paces to the door, slowly, sombrely, until to his surprise and everybody else's, Jack Pease whom nobody had noticed, was in front of him, and stood with the folding doors behind him, with his arms widely extended to either side ('with a sickly grinning grin on his face' as Churchill added.) Kitchener found his exit barred. 'You can't leave the cabinet room,' said Pease two or three times. 'You can't leave the cabinet room,' and

[88] Crawford 'continued optimistic' as to the 'earlyish and successful' outcome of the war (diary, 2 February 1940).

then Kitchener with the slow subconscious movements of the somnambulist moved silently back to his seat and the Welsh problem was tactfully dropped for the moment.

18 FEBRUARY 1940[89]

Churchill's speech to the officers and company of the *Exeter* on her return to Plymouth was splendid . . . People say Churchill is tactless, that his judgment is erratic, that he flies off at a tangent, that he has a burning desire to trespass upon the domain of the naval strategist – all this may be less or more true but he remains the only figure in the cabinet with the virtue of constant uncompromising aggressive quest of victory. He delivers the massive killing blow, encourages the country, inspires the fleet – the more I see and hear of him the more confident I become that he represents the party of complete totalitarian victory!

Lord Crawford's sudden death on 8 March 1940 marked the close of a life of which the keynote was perhaps doing good by stealth, or at least outside the public gaze. He touched history at many points, he moved easily among the great of his time, yet despite his remarkable range of achievement and interest he neither sought nor received much public attention. In this, he is an important example of how aristocratic and territorial traditions have continued to play a part beneath the surface of British public life.

In politics, his tenure of the necessarily silent office of Chief Whip saw a demoralised Conservative Party, shattered by three successive defeats, regain its confidence. By the time Bal left the House of Commons on inheriting his father's title, the worst was over, and the Conservatives went on to take a responsible part in wartime government, followed by a long period as governing party.

As the wartime minister who controlled Europe's wheat supplies, his practically unaided good judgement was vital in the feeding of hungry peoples. Perhaps the least remarked of Lloyd George's new men, he was not the least successful. His postwar berth as Minister of Works was a happy period, for among other things, the building of Britain's war memorials was put in the hands of the author of two books on Italian renaissance sculpture.

Lord Crawford was a museum reformer from first to last. He believed the public should see the best objects displayed in the best manner. Today, his ideas prevail. His campaigning created the Victoria and Albert Museum in its modern form. His chairmanship created the BBC in what is essentially its present shape. As effective founder of the National Art-Collections Fund, he stepped in quickly and effectively to see that the public interest was not buried beneath the commercial spirit of the art market.

Lord Crawford fought for the greatness of the English heritage, whether in the form of art, books, the countryside, responsible broadcasting, the proper use of museums and galleries, or the interests of Manchester University in its most distinctive period. He did all this, moreover, in the intervals of business commitments in coal and steel.

---

[89] The last entry in the diaries.

In such industries it was hardly possible to be successful; instead Lord Crawford was exemplary. He understood and liked the working people of Lancashire and of Wigan. He went through life without social fear, and was free of the enthusiasms which on occasion infect Conservative politics.

But if he had an ambition, it was perhaps as a diarist. A man does not write down his impressions over fifty years without some thought of posterity. To record facets of character, or the inner movements of events, or a good story, was to him both duty and pleasure. Only literary subtlety, only social intimacy, could catch the reality of the men and mood of his times. His most lasting preoccupation was to explain the elusive nature of the remarkable individual. In this he showed himself not just an enlightened patron, connoisseur, or cultural administrator, but a true artist in his own right.

Appendix: The Duke of Windsor's attempted comeback, 1937

When the Duke of Windsor took up residence abroad in 1937, his standing with the British public and his relations with his family were still good compared with what they were to become during the course of the year. Frances Donaldson, in her Edward VIII (Weidenfeld, 1974) has told the sad tale of how, during the summer of 1937, the Windsors fell into the hands of one Charles Bedaux, an international millionaire whose fortune came from a system of time and motion study for making workers work harder. Bedaux offered his French chateau for the Windsors' wedding, and they accepted, though knowing nothing about him and never having met him before. The Windsors naively hoped to make a comeback in British public life and, more naively still, saw Bedaux as the man who could bring this about. Bedaux can only be called a designing person, for his German companies had been confiscated by the Nazis in 1933, and he was using the Windsors, with some success, as bait to get his business returned. After a quiet summer, the Duke of Windsor issued a press statement on 3 September announcing his intention of studying labour conditions in Germany and the United States. His German tour, which followed shortly afterwards, was inevitably stage-managed by the Nazis, and included a genial interview with Hitler. There remained the question of the American tour. Here the central figure was Sir Ronald Lindsay, the unfortunate ambassador at Washington, and his papers on this topic survive among his brother's muniments. They add a little to Lady Donaldson's excellent account, and show that the 'second abdication crisis' of autumn 1937 threatened for a while to be a serious storm in a teacup, and certainly widened the gap beyond the point of no return*.

The Duke wrote from Vienna on 20 September 1937, informing Lindsay of his 'purely private' visit to study working conditions in America, but expressing a wish to see the President. Lindsay wanted to avoid giving any impression that the visit was disapproved of, for fear of making the Duke look a martyr, and therefore wanted to invite him to stay at the embassy, 'give him a Belshazzar, and present him at the White House', but to have nothing to do with subsequent attempts 'to stage a semi-fascist come-back in England' by 'playing up to labour in America'. He was soon to learn that a more rigid view was taken in high quarters.

Lindsay, who was on holiday in Dorset, was first called by Vansittart to see the Foreign Office file about the Duke's visits in Europe.

*Cf. above, pp. 582–3

616

I must say I was staggered by the instructions sent to our Ministers and Ambassadors. They are *forbidden* to put him up in the house, or to give him a dinner, though they may give him a bite of luncheon, or to present him officially to anyone, or to accept invitations from him (except for a bite of luncheon) or to have him met at the station by anyone bigger than a junior secretary.

Lindsay was then summoned to Balmoral:

SIR R. LINDSAY TO LADY LINDSAY, 11 OCTOBER 1937

... I got back yesterday from two extraordinarily interesting days in Scotland ... Arrived at Balmoral I was instantly pushed, unwashed but fortunately shaved, into the King, and instantly we fell to on discussion of the topic for twenty minutes. Then after a bath etc., I had a long talk with Tommy Lascelles. Then a walk with Tommy and the Equerry, and back for luncheon with the Queen, Princess Elizabeth, Tommy, the Lady in Waiting, the Equerry and the two Governesses, the King being on the hill side after the stags. Then a game of golf with Tommy, and after tea an hour with the King. Then all over again with Alex Hardinge. Dinner with the King and Queen, Tommy and me, the Lady and the Equerry, and then after dinner in the drawing room, suddenly the Lady and the Equerry vanished and in the twinkling of an eye we four were at it again, hammer and tongs, till after midnight, and that was my Waterloo!

The King is lithe, brown, and walks like a mountaineer, the very picture of health. He talks a great deal and you would never think he could be tongue tied before a crowd except for an occasional and momentary check noticeable to anyone on the look out for a stammer. He talks quite well and vigorously ... I should say he was an almost exact repeat of his father both in manner and in mind, though not in appearance, and he made a good impression on me, much better than I had expected.

The gist of my argument all through was much what I said in my last letter to you. In America people would naturally expect the Duke and Duchess to be put up at the Embassy. In all the ballyhoo they would notice his going to a hotel – they would infer official coldness to him – a semi-snub – disapproval of the visit – disapproval of his alleged interest in labour – and all this resulting in a bad reaction in America, which would spread to England – just what we want to avoid. And all this I maintained stoutly, Athanasius contra mundum, till midnight. And the men's answer was that the Duke was behaving abominably – it was his duty not to embarrass the King – he had promised not to – and he was dropping bombshell after bombshell, and this was the worst of all. What could come next? He was trying to stage a come-back, and his friends and advisers were semi-Nazis. He was not straight – he hadn't let the King have an inkling of his plans, and the first news of them was a letter from him to the King's own agent. He had not been countenanced by any of the King's people abroad so far, and how could he now be put up in the King's own house in Washington? What if he were to go to a Dominion? or to cross over from the United States into Canada? There was a lot of talk about a scheme by which I should invite him to stay at the Embassy, and then a swift emissary should speed over and persuade him to decline. This absolutely horrified me and it was, thank God, discarded because 'that woman' would never allow him to decline, and because there exists no emissary who would command confidence and at the same time stand the smallest chance of influencing the Duke.

But the Queen was quite different. She is really quite pretty, with a lovely complexion... She will always be altogether charming. While the men spoke in terms of indignation, she spoke in terms of acute pain and distress, ingenuously expressed and deeply felt. She too is not a great intellect but she has any amount of 'intelligence du coeur'. Her reactions come straight from her heart and very strongly and a heart that is in the right place may be a very good guide. In all she said there was far more grief than indignation and it was all tempered by affection for 'David'. 'He's so changed now, and he used to be so kind to us.' She was backing up everything the men said, but protesting against anything that seemed vindictive. All her feelings were lacerated by what she and the King were being made to go through. And with all her charity she had not a word to say for 'that woman'. I found myself being deeply moved by her, and when midnight came though my flag was still flying, it was really but a battered bit of bunting and the only reason why I didn't pull it down then and there was that Anthony Eden was to arrive next morning and the final decision could not be reached without him. The next morning I only saw him for ten minutes alone. From the way he talked I am not at all sure I might not have had my way, but in fact I surrendered at discretion and agreed not to put the Duke and Duchess up at the Embassy, but to leave it at a dinner party of moderate dimensions.

It interested me to notice that really the King does not yet feel safe in his throne, and up to a certain point he is like the medieval monarch who has a hated rival claimant living in exile. The analogy must not be pressed too far because I don't think George wanted the throne any more than Edward, and if he is there it is owing to a sense of duty which Edward lacked, and not owing to a love of power which one sometimes thinks Edward may have after all. But in some ways the situation operates on the King just as it must have done on his medieval ancestors – uneasiness as to what is coming next – sensitiveness – suspicion. I greatly wonder what Edward really wants. They all say he has no will but what is hers, and what does she really want? Is she really ambitious? Perhaps; and opinion at the palace has no doubt of it, but is certainly violently prejudiced... On the other hand, in marrying a man she has pulled him down from a very high place. There are lots of women who have done the same thing and who then, without being ambitious themselves, try hard to stick him up again on as high a stool as can be found. I can't help wondering.

And now this over lengthy chronicle is coming to an end. I hadn't been talking to Eden for ten minutes before we were all whisked off for a walk up an adjoining cliff... Then luncheon. And immediately after another walk was proposed. Eden couldn't come, as he had to stay and await some messages from London, but I, when I had climbed with them into a vast Daimler car, had my full reward when I answered their anxious enquiries as to what Eden had decided, and brought an immense relief to a very harassed couple. So we crossed the moor to the next valley, and then drove up a narrow road, and tumbled out, and with four dogs, walked two miles straight up a mountain side and two miles back – heaven!, what mountain air! I could have walked all night. Then back, just in time for tea, with just time to change clothes and catch the night train to London.

No sooner had Balmoral settled the main question of what the Washington embassy should do, than other and no less painful matters arose. The Duke sent a peculiarly arduous itinerary – Atlanta to Detroit, Seattle to New York – for what amounted to a major royal tour, and asked for the ambassador to arrange a visit to the President. The local visits presented no difficulty, for British consuls had orders not to receive the Duke, but the presidential visit was more of a dilemma. The president would only receive British visitors if they were accompanied by their ambassador; and the British authorities were fearful of giving his visit an official status if they did so. 'The Palace secretaries are extremist, the Foreign Office still more so. All are seeing ghosts and phantasms everywhere and think there are disasters round every corner', wrote Lindsay on 17 October. Certainly this view existed. A senior palace official wrote angrily after this crisis, 'what is really wanted is that the public should cease to take him seriously, and realise the truth – that his mental and moral development just stopped dead when he was about 15, and that though a sad figure, he is no longer a particularly interesting one'. But, as Lindsay himself thought, there was also the difficulty that 'he is being turned into a purely Nazi show, and of course he is known here to have decided Nazi tendencies'. Lindsay, unlike the palace, was in favour of giving the Duke enough rope to hang himself.

In one sense the British authorities were correct in being suspicious of the Duke's tour. In November 1937, Lindsay surreptitiously obtained two letters written by Bedaux about the plans for the tour. Lindsay inferred that the Duke intended to issue a quasi-political manifesto at some stage during his American tour, along these lines:

... A world wide peace movement must have as its task to raise humanity's level of life's enjoyment ... The wide movement referred to must study the practices, laws, and customs affecting the home, the leisure, and the work of labour ... This is the most important way to secure peace, and the Duke of Windsor is deeply interested in it. He has always been concerned with the lot of the working man and he has now become a real expert in sociological questions; but he is not satisfied with this, and plans to widen his knowledge by a personal study of housing and working conditions in many lands. No better leadership for such a movement could be found than in the Duke of Windsor.

Appendix

In fact the tour was called off, for obvious reasons, though in curious circumstances. Bedaux was anathema to American organised labour. The Duchess was hardly popular. The visit to Germany had offended much press opinion. Hostility to the tour developed rapidly. On 4 November, the workers of Baltimore issued a condemnation of the tour; Bedaux, in New York, sought advice from Lindsay as to whether the Duke should leave Paris; the Duke lost his nerve, and after telephoning Lindsay (but receiving no distinct advice from him) issued a statement on 5 November 'postponing' his visit.

There was one curious presidential intervention. Mrs Roosevelt said that it was feared the Duke would arrive on 11 November in time to lay an armistice day wreath on the unknown soldier's tomb. This they were determined to prevent, and they were arranging for his train to be 'delayed' so he would not be able to get to Arlington in time.

The cancellation was as ineptly managed as the proposed tour itself. The Duke met the US ambassador in Paris, Bullitt, and consulted him about the growing clamour in the American press. Bullitt made light of it, and pressed him to go ahead with the tour. The following morning the Duke talked to Lindsay, who was discreetly discouraging. The Duke then recalled Bullitt's optimism, and asked the switchboard for the embassy. By a surprising error, the Duke found himself addressing the British ambassador, Phipps, whom he took to be Bullitt. As Phipps in turn poured cold water on the tour, the Duke's frail morale was shaken by what he took to be a sudden volte-face *by Bullitt, and cancellation followed.*[1]

The storm in a teacup was over so quickly that it might seem to have left no marks. This was not so. The Duke had annoyed his former supporters, Beaverbrook and Rothermere, whose newspapers became hostile; while Labour, in the form of Morrison, Laski, and the Daily Herald *(that 'excellent paper' as Hardinge called it) came out strongly against him.*[2] *In a sense it was a second abdication, in that even his supporters came to agree that he must abdicate from being a public person in any way at all. But, if the palace was pleased and relieved over the American fiasco in the short term, in the longer term the affair made it almost impossible for the abdication to be gradually lived down.*

One relic of the crisis, treasured for its language, and significant as representing what the makers of policy took to be average opinion, was the letter which Lindsay received from the British nannies:

Central Park,
New York City.

Your Excellency:

We are the British Nannies Scotch and English who meet in this park with our charges, we note with pain and dismay the news in the papers that you are to receive and entertain at our Embassy this Mrs. Simpson. We protest vigorously against this, to us the Embassy is our only bit of England. Last year at this time we lived through weeks of shame and despair due to this same woman. We are the people who try to teach our young children how to fear God and live a clean life. You are

---

[1] *New York Times*, 20 February 1938.
[2] *Daily Herald*, 8 November 1937.

now about to condone what our church and bible say is wrong leaving out our own views of right living, at the time you receive these two people the woman will have 3 living husbands on the soil of America. We cannot believe you and Lady Lindsay can feel you are serving England by doing this, nor do we believe knowing your background that you are happy about it. To us the Edward we knew and loved is dead.

Yours truly,
H. Hagues

Index

622

Index

of, 328–9; wishes to film cabinet, 357;
as daughter of Glasgow soapboiler, 471;
memoirs of, 471

Astor, Nancy (1879–1964), wife of 2nd
Viscount and MP (Cons.), 500

Astor, Waldorf, 2nd Viscount Astor
(1879–1952), MP (Cons.), 244, 299,
539, 607

Atholl, Duke of, see Tullibardine, Lord

Avebury, 1st Baron (1834–1913), 61 n.

Baird, John, 1st Viscount Stonehaven
(1874–1941), 247–8, 257, 270, 277, 285,
307, 339, 386, 456, 470, 484, 489, 609

Baker, Sir Herbert (1862–1946), architect,
533

Balcarres, Lord (1871–1940), known as
Bal, see Lindsay, David

Baldwin, Stanley (1867–1947), premier,
on war debts (1922), 424; on Ll.
George, 450–51, 453; Bal on, 460; on
US debt, 477; on Darwinist fallacies,
479; his political standing, 480, 482,
484–5; invites Bal to vet honours, 484;
offers Bal BM trusteeship, 484; calls for
Protection, 486; his indolence, 490;
considers resigning party leadership,
Jan. 1924, 491; his mood in Jan. 1924,
492; drops Protection, 492–3; and Irish
issue (1924), 497, 499; offers Bal non-
cabinet post, 500; a new Baldwin
revealed, 503; offers Bal post of first
BBC chairman, 504, 512; re-appoints
Bal to National Gallery, 506; takes
afternoon off to read a novel, 506; on
Beaverbrook, 509; on popular press,
509; on Waterloo Bridge, 510; his
speech to the Classical Association, 510;
on keeping Lord Lee of Fareham quiet,
510–11; and general strike, 513–14,
516; his speech on rural cottages, 518;
and art, 524; on Duveen, 525; as
speaker, 526; on Baptists, 528; at a loss
for a house (1929), 528; as N. Gallery
trustee, 533–4, 560; in 1930, 541–2;
pulls faces, 542; at Londonderry House,
547; on his ancestry, 558; Londonderry

on, 567; and abdication, 574–7; his
nervous breakdown (1936), 576–7;
retirement of, 577, 579; suggested entry
into reconstructed cabinet, Feb. 1938,
587–8; has 'job in London', 588; as
BM trustee, 593; Salisbury on
Baldwin's indolence, 595

Balfour, Alice (d. 1936), A.J.B.'s sister,
230–32

Balfour, Arthur James, 1st Earl of Balfour
(1848–1930), speaks to Bal, 31; going
too far, 43; on Zola, 47; on Dreyfus,
47–8; with Frau Wagner, 51; on
religion, 52; and Fashoda crisis, 52; and
museum reform, 55–6; health of, 60;
exhausted, 64; illness, 70; aloofness, 74;
on Irish devolution, 77; proposes
imperial referendum, 77; and Dogger
Bank outrage, 77–8; Tory voters hostile
to, 79; defeated on snap vote, 83; in
defeat, 88; challenged by Chamberlain,
88–92; doctor advises rest, 92; rest cure
of, 94; attacked for inactivity, 99; on
procedure, 119; alarmed over defence,
122; unwell in Jan. 1910 election, 147;
as orator, 157; on 1910 conference, 160,
164, 166; at Edinburgh (Oct. 1910),
165; inaccessible, 168; on Riviera
(1911), 173; on Jewish influence on
protestant succession, 183; helps
Liberal ministers, 185; seeks successor,
June 1911, 186; on his colleagues, 207;
leaves for Gastein, Aug. 1911, 210, 215,
219; and his health, 212; inmost views
on party indiscipline, 215; on
Lansdowne, 215; returns, Sept. 1911,
220; and family, 222–3, 230–31; on
resignation, 224–5; on F. E. Smith,
225; expects violent political reaction,
225; preferences as his successors, 225;
on W. Long, 225; his own future role,
225; his estates, 225; on Long's letter,
226; on ambition, 226; resignation,
242–4; refuses to reconsider, 246–7; his
eminence in debate weakens party, 253;
in retirement, 255; returns to England

Index

Index

Index

Charteris, Evan, friend of A.J.B., 226, 480, 572

Chatfield, Alfred, 1st Baron Chatfield (1873–1967), 594–5, 605

Chatsworth Library, 120

Chequers, verses on, 381–2; state of house, 577; an object lesson to R. MacDonald, 586

Chetwode, Sir P., 1st Baron Chetwode (1869–1950), 567–8, 598

Chichester, Bishop of, on war (1939), 610

Chilston, 1st Viscount (1851–1926) *see* Akers-Douglas, Aretas

Chorley, Lancs., electoral politics of, 104, 106, 141–2, 170, 186, 321

Church Discipline Bill (1908), 105

Churchill, Mrs (1885–1977), as pregnant nun, 186

Churchill, Lord Randolph (1849–94), as blackmailer, 93

Churchill, Victor, 1st Viscount Churchill (1864–1934), chairman of GWR and Unionist Whip, 216, 253, 257, 492, 516, 541

Churchill, Sir Winston (1874–1965), as coming man, 54; as prig, 59; as dissident, 70; and Aliens Bill, 75; thought 'born cad' by Edward VII, 83; delicate health prevents Irish post, 99; unpardonable attack on dying man, 101; wishes to leave party politics, 123; and F. E. Smith, 131; as cad in France, 134; petty tricks of, 138; hurries to Paris, 151; not admitted to Palace, 153; disgusts House, 179; Elibank on, 180; as cardinal, 180; nepotism by, 187; hooted at 1911 Coronation, 189; Balfour on, 215; attacks B. Law, 279; sacks Sea Lords, 291; a natural reactionary (1913), 319; gluttony of, 327; and Ulster plot, 330; and Haldane's pregnancy, 332; Churchill and 'centre party', 333; his bad blood, 333; divulges naval secrets to dubious party, 344; rumoured coup against Ll. George by (1921), 409; babbles expletives in cabinet, 420; on Ireland, 421; his turgidity, 423; and war debts, 424; impractical in Chanak crisis, 440; hostile to army, 441; demands PR, 467; supported by A.J.B. at Westminster election, 494; his dislike of Amery, 520; his views in 1930, 542; on bimetallism, 546; conduct at Grillions, 558, 562; and India, 559; on defence (1936), 567–8; denounces government, May 1936, 570; and Abdication, 573–4, 577, 579–80; on Duke of Windsor, 580; his parliamentary gaffes, 586; on coal in Navy, 587; his methods of authorship, 587; suggested entry into cabinet, Feb. 1938, 587; on position after Munich, 590–91; increased optimism, March 1939, 594; on naval outlook, 595; on Maginot Line, Aug. 1939, 602; his return to Admiralty, 603; receives Duke of Windsor in War Room, 604; advocates Russian alliance, 605; on naval position, Oct. 1939, 606; and in Dec. 1939, 610; addresses peers on naval war, 610; and Duncan Sandys, 611; opinion on, Jan. 1940, 613; on Kitchener, 613; his inspiring speech at Plymouth, 614; seen by diarist as future saviour of the country, 614

Clare, O. L. (1841–1912), MP (Cons.), 73

Clarendon, 6th Earl of, *see* Villiers, G. H.

Clark, Sir Kenneth, Baron Clark (1903–1983), 608

Clemenceau, Georges (1841–1929), 47–8

Clynes, J. R. (1869–1949), Labour leader, 378, 392, 398–9, 489, 495, 527

coal strike (1912), 266

cockfighting, 527

Coller, F. H. (1866–1938), civil servant, on Baldwin's indolence, 490

Collins, Michael (1890–1922), Irish leader, James Craig on, 417; Willie Peel on, 418; cowed by Craig, 418; confronts Lloyd George, 422–3; unable to bamboozle A. Chamberlain, 424

Committee of Imperial Defence, 59

Compton Wynyates, Lord Northampton's house, 582

Index

Congo Free State, 61

Connaught, Princess Patricia of, 114

Constable, W. G., art historian (1887–1976), 536

Cooper, (Alfred) Duff, 1st Viscount Norwich (1890–1954), 581

Cooper, Lady Diana, *see* Manners, Lady Diana, 109

Cope, Sir Alfred (d. 1954), coalowner, 516

Corelli, Marie (1855–1924), novelist, 63

Coronation (1911), 188

Cottenham, 4th Earl of (1874–1919), 19–20

Council for the Preservation of Rural England, 3, 521, 541, 558, 582, 596

Coutts, Burdett, *see* Burdett-Coutts

Coventry, George William, 9th Earl of (1838–1930), 548

Craig, Capt. Charles Curtis (1869–1960), MP (Cons.), 298, 301, 303, 305, 318, 338

Craig, James, 1st Viscount Craigavon (1871–1940), N. Ireland premier, 412, 414–17, 497, 499, 603

Craik, Sir Henry (1846–1927), MP (Cons.), 453

Crawford, Countess of, (Connie), *née* Constance Pelly, wife of diarist, 142

Crawford and Balcarres, Earls of, *see* Lindsay

Crewe, 1st Marquess of (1858–1945), 74, 99, 179, 210, 341, 463, 469, 607

Cripps, Charles Alfred, 1st Baron Parmoor (1852–1941), MP (Cons. and Lab.), 539

Croft, Sir Henry Page (1881–1947), MP (Cons.), 299, 305

Cromer, 1st Earl of, *see* Baring, Sir Evelyn

Cromer, 2nd Earl of, *see* Baring, R. T.

Crowe, Sir Eyre (1864–1925), diplomatist, 422, 443, 465

Crump, Sir William (1850–1923), MP (Cons.), 266

Cunliffe-Lister (previously Lloyd-Greame), Sir Philip, 1st Earl of

Swinton (1884–1972), 488, 493, 511, 514, 583

Cunynghame, Sir Henry Hardinge (1848–1935), engineer, 335

Curragh Mutiny, 330–31

Curzon, George Nathaniel, 1st Marquess Curzon of Kedleston (1859–1925), returns to parliament, 58; opposed to Chamberlain, 92; declines LCC chairmanship, 100; takes Hackwood, 130; and 1909 Budget, 138; on Kitchener, 163; on Lords reform, 179, 192; dominates Balfour and Lansdowne, 201; contest with Selborne, 206; threatens disloyalty, 210; and Lansdowne, 213; Balfour's choice as leader, 225; on food taxes, 290, 292; pseudonym of, 294; blamed for 1912 crisis, 298; Lady Curzon's memorial, 313; dominates shadow cabinet, 320; and Curragh 'mutiny', 331; readiness of, 335–6; on spies, 345; and coalition, 347; as leader in Lords, 348, 353; on female suffrage, 385; on peace negotiations (1917), 394; as host, 400; attempts to silence Big Ben, 400; and Lords opposition, 402; on Unknown Warrior, 412; on Derby, 413; on A.J.B., 414; loathed by FO, 414, 422; and F. E. Smith, 414; threatens to leave sinking ship over Egypt, 1922, 416; well-timed illness (July 1922), 426; on need to appease France, 430; shindy with Poincaré, 437–8, 464; on Ll. George, 439–40; his method of relaxing, 445; French eavesdropping on, 446–7; and Carlton Club meeting, 453–4; on his need for office, 455; his role over Chanak, 462; and Paris embassy, 469; neglects his junior minister, 470; meddles in Court appointments (1922), 469; idleness of 1922–3 cabinet, 475; as viceroy, 476; and Lausanne conference, 476; 'out of question' as PM, 477, 482; mishaps at FO, 481; considers resignation on not becoming PM,

628

Index

Index

Index

Index

Index

memo. influenced by Bal, 365; peace overture from (1918), 392; his Whiggery, 400–401; and Lords reform, 424; and nude statue, 517; his first experience of comfort, 529

Lascelles, Tommy, 617

Lathom House, 496

Law, Andrew Bonar (1858–1923), 102, 112–13, 132, 139, 160, 173, 202–3, 226, 234, 237–8, 240, 244, 245–50, 252–4, 256–7, 262–3, 275, 277, 282–5, 289–90, 292, 294–7, 300, 303, 316 n., 320–21, 324, 328–9, 331, 345, 347, 359–60, 398, 404, 446, 453–4, 456, 474, 476–7, 480, 482, 564

Lawrence, D. H. (1885–1930), 529

Lawrence, Sir Joseph (1848–1919), friend of Bonar Law, 252

Lawrence, Susan (1871–1947), MP (Lab.), 520

Lawrence, Col. T. E. (1888–1935), Lloyd George on, 397

Lecky, W. E. H. (1838–1903), on Parnell, 53

Lee, Arthur, 1st Viscount Lee of Fareham (1868–1947), 78, 122, 148, 160, 299, 381–2, 468, 470, 510, 535, 577

Leeds, Unionist conference at (1911), 227, 232, 235–6, 238, 242, 248, 253–4

Legh, Thomas Wodehouse, 2nd Baron Newton (1857–1942), 138, 200, 398, 464, 578

Leicester, University of, 401

Lever, W. H., 1st Viscount Leverhulme (1851–1925), 527

Leverhulme, Lord, see Lever, W. H.

Lewis, Sir William, shipowner, of Furness Withy and Co., 407

Liberal Unionists, fusion with (1912), 266, 267, 272, 275

Lindsay, Alexander, 6th Earl of Balcarres (1752–1825), 4–5, 174

Lindsay, Alexander William, 25th Earl of Crawford and 8th Earl of Balcarres (1812–80), bibliophile, 6, 174, 268

Lindsay, David, 27th Earl of Crawford and 10th Earl of Balcarres (1871–1940),

character and achievement 1–3; habits of life, 7; estates, 7 n.; and East End, 8, 12–17; on Thomas à Kempis, 8; advice to his son, 8; and Oxford Union, 10; on Fife middle class, 18; on Edzell Castle, 18; retrospect at 21, 19; his coming of age, 21–3; marriage, 24, 57; effect of E. End on, 28, 32–3; elected MP, 29; his hopes for Ireland, 43; on royal neglect of Ireland, 45; on the back streets of London, 47; anxiety about Wigan, 53; his reform of the South Kensington Museum, 55–6; cultural achievements 1900–05, 58; as whip, 58–9; on Rosebery, 59; role of Lindsays in Wigan, 60; accepts office, 68; his first opposed election, 68; on tariff reform, 68; on library finances, 69; on Osborne, 71; on Sir E. Grey, 81, 86; non-political interests for the future, 85–6; and Chorley election of 1906, 88; on John Burns, 103; on J. S. Sandars, 104 n.; depressed by work as Whip, 111–12; on old age pensions, 112; on Asquith, 116, 122; on Haigh muniments, 120; on tactlessness of peers, 136; loathing of election (1909), 139; on tariff reform, 141; local electoral programme of, 142; on Irish Party, 144; views on possible promotion to Chief Whip, 150; sends collier on German tour, 159; on Land Tax, 164; death of father, 173; becomes Chief Whip (July 1911), 189; holiday at N. Berwick, 1911, 211; reaches middle age, 230; looks to Austen C. as new leader, 237; arranges leadership, 242–50; on Bonar Law, 245, 258–9, 261–3; on new political atmosphere, 258; on bestowal of honours, 259; self-criticism as Wigan employer, 268; sells car, 277; buys car, 282; prevents turmoil in House, 284; the anonymity of his work, 285; on electoral prospects (1912), 289; and Christmas at home, 293; on food taxes crisis, 304–6; advises on his successor, 306–8; death of father, 310; problems

635

Index

of inheritance, 310–14; excluded from
front bench and shadow cabinet, 316;
on Lansdowne as leader, 320–21; and
Servant's Ball, 321; retrospect and
prospect (1913), 320–21; dislikes
Milner's extremism, 324; joins shadow
cabinet, 324; his finances, 333–4; on
party weaknesses, 334; predicts Irish
split, 337; on entry into war, 340–41;
adapts Haigh as hospital, 341; on
Asquith's trickery, 343; on spy peril in
Fife, 344–5; joins RAMC, 349; pressed
to join 1915 coalition, 350; views on
officers, 350–51; and nurses, 350–51;
and malingering, 351; on loss of
comforts, 351; view of army, 352;
appointed Minister of Agriculture, 354;
on Asquith's war leadership, 354 n.,
356; Curzon urges him as Viceroy, 355;
on state of party, 1916, 355–6; relations
with Asquith, 363; on fall of Asquith,
369–76; as Lord Privy Seal, 377; at
Duchy of Lancaster, 378; and Haigh
Library, 379; and Lansdowne letter,
381; on female suffrage (1918), 385; on
weakness of war cabinet system, 390; as
dogsbody, 391; and continuation of
coalition, 398; fears revolution, 398,
407; on nationalisation, 401;
on House of Lords (1919),
402–3; wish to know
what goes on (1919), 403–4; on
unpopularity of coalition (1919), 404;
and fusion (1920), 406; on future of
Ireland (1921), 414; on Curzon, 414;
entertains Fife schoolchildren
(1921), 415; and Office of
Works, 415; and conference of
Unionist ministers (Feb. 1922), 417; A.
Chamberlain on his loyalty, 418 n.;
considered as India Secretary, 419 n.;
outlook on joining cabinet (1922),
419–20; and Ministry of Transport,
419 n., 420; and coming of age
festivities for his son (1922), 423; and
privileges of officer class, 424;
conference of Unionist ministers, July

1922, 428; further disastrous meeting of
Unionist ministers, Aug. 1922, 428–30,
431; restores Downing St garden, 440;
on B. Law ministry, 460–61, 464–5;
and 1922 elections, 466; final departure
from politics, 472; cultural committees,
472; canvassed as possible Foreign
Secretary, 473, 484, 491, 501; and
Wigan affairs, 473; on B. Law
(1922–3), 474–5; and royal parks, 475;
and Manchester University, 481, 487;
reduces Haigh Library, 481; becomes
BM trustee, 481; on scrutiny of
honours, 484; on Sandringham, 488;
and Royal Fine Art Commission, 489;
and Xmas Tree for servants, 490; on S.
Olivier, 493; becomes FRS, 497; on
Liverpool University, 497–8; disposes
of French collections, 498; offered
Works (outside cabinet) by Baldwin,
500; declines, 500; Crawford Committee
on BBC, 504–6; declines Baldwin's
offer of BBC chairmanship, 504; on
popular press, 505–6; and coal strike
(1926), 511–15; life in 1928–9, 520–21;
and CPRE, 521; on Asquith, 526; as
Lancashire businessman, 530–31;
disposes of Dutch pictures (1932), 532;
declines office of Constable of
Lancaster Castle, 538; refuses chair of
House of Lords reform committee, 539;
visits Cambridge, 539–40; as G. F.
Watts Trustee, 540; and Lancashire
Authors' Association, 541; on politics
1929–31, 541; financial troubles, 547;
and Wigan Library Committee, 551–2;
declines offer of chairmanship of
Independent Peers, 552; as chairman of
Oxford University Elections
Committee, 552; medical and financial
gloom (1934), 557; on failings of coal
industry, 557; vexed by colliery
manager, 562; as chairman of
committee to revise BBC Charter, 563;
his mother's frugality explained, 570;
retrospect at 65, 572; on Eden, 578;
visits Duke of Bedford, 578; on

636

Index

Baldwin's place in history, 579; on Duke of Windsor, 580; his unpublished book on Scottish lairds, 581; reopens Wigan Public Library, 581; on state intervention in coal, 583; involvement in local affairs, 584; on History of Parliament project, 588; and George VI's tour of Lancashire, 588; on Hankey, 589; opposes Czech partition, 589; removes pictures to Haigh during Munich, 589; reforms street lamps, 593; on mood of optimism, March 1939, 595; gives last Haigh garden party, 596; activities in summer 1939, 597; on royal boycott of intellectuals, 601; on food supplies in war, 608–9; on Russia, 609; on defeatism, 609; his confidence that Churchill would lead the country to victory, February 1940, 614; his death, 614; his part in the national life, 614–15; as a literary artist in his own right, 615

Lindsay, David, 28th Earl of Crawford and 11th Earl of Balcarres (1900–75), 58, 500–501, 513, 565, 590

Lindsay, James, 24th Earl of Crawford (1783–1869), 5, 104, 174

Lindsay, James, younger son of diarist, 584, 607

Lindsay, James, Ludovic, 26th Earl of Crawford and 9th Earl of Balcarres (1847–1913), as collector, 6; as MP, 7; entertains Wigan, 22; tires of books, 64; as investor, 174; neglects Wigan, 268; fears for his sofa, 276; death, 306, 310; and philately, 310–13; at Cambridge, 539; and his wife's household allowance, 570

Lindsay, Lady Jane Evelyn (1862–1948), diarist's aunt, 314, 316

Lindsay, Sir Ronald (1877–1945), diplomatist and diarist's brother, 511, 522, 528, 542, 582, 585, 604, 609, 611, 616–21

Lindsay, Thomas, stationmaster, 113–14

Linkie, see Cecil, Lord Hugh

Liverpool University, 497–8

Llewellyn, Sir W. (1858–1941), PRA, 545, 581

Lloyd, Sir George Ambrose, 1st Baron Lloyd (1879–1941), MP (Cons.), 299, 302

Lloyd George, David, 1st Earl Lloyd-George of Dwyfor (1863–1945), premier, 2, 99, 126–8, 133–5, 140, 164, 169, 179–82, 208, 217, 233, 266, 271, 274, 280, 286, 292, 361–3, 366, 383–4, 388–9, 398–9, 407–8, 412, 415, 421–4, 431–49, 458, 460, 462, 464, 467–8, 474, 481, 489, 499, 527, 549, 552, 563, 576, 579, 588, 597, 605, 613

Lloyd-Greame, Sir P., see Cunliffe-Lister

Lockwood, R. M., 1st Baron Lambourne (1847–1928), 134

Loewi, Otto (1873–1961), scientist, 591

Long, Walter, 1st Viscount Long (1854–1924), 43, 79, 80, 90, 113, 122, 133, 137, 140, 157, 175, 182, 186, 190, 208, 210–11, 214, 217, 221, 225, 226, 229–30, 232–4, 238, 239, 242, 244, 245, 249, 254, 258, 260–61, 270, 275, 281, 297, 301, 324, 329, 342, 367, 405, 407

Londonderry House, afternoon party at (1932), 547

Londonderry, Lady, wife of 6th Marquess, 247–8, 273, 330

Londonderry, 6th and 7th Marquesses of, see Vane-Tempest-Stewart

Lonsdale, Sir John Brownlee, 1st Baron Armaghdale (1850–1924), MP (Cons.), 249, 318

Loreburn, 1st Lord (1846–1923), formerly Robert Reid, 208, 270, 499

Lovat, Lord, and 1911 Parliament Bill, 216

Lowther, James, 1st Viscount Ullswater (1855–1949), Speaker, 249, 369, 495, 571

Ludendorff, views of (1922), 442

Lutyens, Sir Edwin (1869–1944), 497, 533, 538–9, 546, 553, 583, 593, 597, 609

Lyttelton, Alfred (1857–1913), 71, 113, 122, 132, 139, 160, 176, 199, 211, 223,

Index

Index

Morgan, John Pierpont (1867–1943), benefactor of Dr Lang, 532, 565

Morley, John, 1st Viscount Morley of Blackburn (1838–1923), 124, 180, 211, 331–2

Moroccan crisis of 1911, 203, 208, 252, 255

Morris, William (1834–96), 29–30, 33–5

Morrison, Herbert Stanley, Baron Morrison of Lambeth (1888–1965), 597–8, 620

Morrison, W. S., 1st Viscount Dunrossil (1893–1961), 608–9

Mosley, Sir O., 6th Bt (1896–1980), as possible Labour Foreign Secretary, 528

Mountbatten, Louis Alexander, 1st Marquess of Milford Haven, *see* Battenberg, Prince Louis of

Munnings, Sir A. J. (1878–1959), artist, 522–3

Munro, Robert, 1st Baron Alness (1868–1955), 597

Munro-Ferguson, Ronald, 1st Viscount Novar (1860–1934), 460–61, 487, 499

Murray, Andrew Graham, 1st Viscount Dunedin (1849–1942), judge, 476, 478

Murray, Sir George Herbert (1849–1936), Treasury official, 135, 485, 491

Mussolini, Bonar Law on, 564

Nall-Cain, Arthur Ronald, 2nd Baron Brocket (1904–67), 605, 607–8

nannies, British, in New York, letter from, 620–21

Napoleon I, letters of, 7, 313

National Art-Collections Fund, 58, 68, 86, 536

National Gallery, 517–18, 523–6, 533–7, 569

National Insurance Bill (1911), 184–5, 187, 204, 220, 233, 251, 256, 260, 270, 306

Natural History Museum, 522, 583, 592, 597

Neal, Arthur (1862–1933), MP (Lib.), 420

Nelson's Column, guano from, 328

Nicholson, A. P. (1869–1940), journalist, 296

Nicholson, Sir Godfrey (b. 1901), husband of diarist's daughter Katharine, and MP (Cons.), 597

Nicolson, Sir Harold (1886–1968), diarist, 509

Nijinsky, necklace lost by, 304

Nimmo, Sir Adam (d. 1939), coalowner, 512, 515

Noel-Buxton, N. E., 1st Baron Noel-Buxton of Aylsham (1869–1948), 607, 610

Norfolk, Duchess of, 109

Norfolk, 15th Duke of (1847–1917) and 1911 Parliament Bill, 211, 213

Norfolk House, sale at (1938), 585

Norman, Montagu C., 1st Baron (1871–1950), governor of Bank of England, 521, 530–31, 541

Northcliffe, 1st Viscount (1865–1922), 177, 219, 294, 299, 301–2, 338, 386, 404, 406, 442, 477

Northumberland, 8th Duke of, *see* Percy, Alan Ian

Novar, Lord, *see* Munro-Ferguson, R.

Noyes, Alfred (1880–1958), poet, 537–8

O'Brien, William (1832–1899), Irish leader, 149, 166

old age pensioner, gives birth, 121

Oldham, by-election at (Nov. 1911), 250

Oliver, F. S. (1864–1934), journalist, 295

Olivier, Sydney, 1st Baron Olivier (1859–1943), Labour minister, 493, 494

Oman, Sir Charles (1860–1946), historian, 552

Orlando, V. E. (1860–1952), Italian premier and head of Italian delegation at Versailles, 405

Ormsby-Gore, W. (1885–1964), MP (Cons.), otherwise Billy Gore, 243, 249, 535–6, 557, 560

O'Shea case, 34

Owen, Dr John, Bishop of St Davids (1854–1926), 274

Oxford University Elections Committee, 552

Index

Index

Index

Index

Index

644

Index